Holyoak and Torremans
Intellectual Prop

Holyoak and Torremans

Intellectual Property Law

Second Edition

By

Paul Torremans, Licentiaat in de Rechten (KU Leuven),
Licentiaat in het Notariaat (Examencommissie van de Staat, Leuven),
Geaggregeerde voor het HSO in de Rechten (KU Leuven),
LLM (Leicester)

Lecturer in Law and Sub-Dean for Graduate Studies
University of Leicester

and

Jon Holyoak, BA(Cantab), Barrister

Senior Lecturer in Law
University of Leicester

Butterworths
London, Edinburgh, Dublin
1998

United Kingdom	Butterworths, a Division of Reed Elsevier (UK) Ltd, Halsbury House, 35 Chancery Lane, LONDON WC2A 1EL and 4 Hill Street, EDINBURGH EH2 3JZ
Australia	Butterworths, a Division of Reed International Books Australia Pty Ltd, CHATSWOOD, New South Wales
Canada	Butterworths Canada Ltd, MARKHAM, Ontario
Hong Kong	Butterworths Asia (Hong Kong), HONG KONG
India	Butterworths Asia, NEW DELHI
Ireland	Butterworth (Ireland) Ltd, DUBLIN
Malaysia	Malayan Law Journal Sdn Bhd, KUALA LUMPUR
New Zealand	Butterworths of New Zealand Ltd, WELLINGTON
Singapore	Butterworths Asia, SINGAPORE
South Africa	Butterworths Publishers (Pty) Ltd, DURBAN
USA	Lexis Law Publishing, CHARLOTTESVILLE, Virginia

© Reed Elsevier (UK) Ltd 1998

A CIP Catalogue record for this book is available from the British Library.

First edition   1995

ISBN 0 406 98133 7

Printed in England by Clays Ltd, St Ives plc

Visit us at our website: http://www.butterworths.co.uk

Preface to the second edition

Intellectual property is an area that is subject to rapid change. Many developments have taken place over the last three years and we felt that it was therefore appropriate to produce the second edition of the book one year earlier than planned, rather than to reprint the first edition.

This second edition is not simply an updated version of the first edition though. We have taken the opportunity to expand many of the chapters and to provide fuller coverage of areas such as remedies and information technology.

Paul Torremans has been responsible for rewriting most of the chapters. Chapters 1, 4 (partim), 6, 8-23 and 25-29 bear his signature. Jon Holyoak has provided the drafts for the new versions of chapters 2, 3, 4 (partim), 5, 7 and 24. He would like to thank Wendy Hurst for her valuable secretarial assistance and Paul Torremans for helping him to bring this project to a successful conclusion.

All references to the EC Treaty in this edition are based upon the pre-Amsterdam situation. The new renumbered Amsterdam version of the various articles is found in the second edition of our Butterworths Student Statutes book. This is a brief summary of the changes:

Original EC Treaty (as amended at Maastricht)	Amsterdam version of the Treaty
Article 6	Article 12
Article 30	Article 28
Article 36	Article 30
Article 59	Article 49
Article 85	Article 81
Article 86	Article 82
Article 222	Article 295

We are grateful for the ease with which the publication of this second edition has been facilitated by Butterworths.

The law is stated as at 1 October 1998.

Paul Torremans
Jon Holyoak

18 October 1998

Preface to the first edition

In proposing the publication of this work to Butterworths, we offered a comprehensive textbook of intellectual property law. Obviously a textbook requires that the substantive law be covered in appropriate detail, but we have aimed to do more than this potentially arid description suggests. We feel that the law must be placed in its context and we seek to do this with an extensive introduction, though one which may be read with benefit during as well as before the study of the substantive law, and through frequent overviews of the law and its potential for development. In particular our aim has been to achieve, firstly, a readable and accessible book that will make what is often seen as a forbiddingly difficult subject one to which the reader can relate. Secondly, we hope that this is a book that will break down the barriers between domestic, European and international law; the book is about the law in the UK but all three of these elements make up that law. The international flavour of the book is, we trust, assisted by the fact that much of it was written in Australia, Greece and Belgium and parts of the manuscript have visited Hong Kong, Tahiti, the USA, Germany, France and Czechoslovakia too. Thirdly, we hope to use the primary materials in such a way as will enable the reader to get the 'feel' for the way arguments are constructed in these fascinating areas. We are well aware that the primary sources are often in specialist, not mainstream, reports and journals. Finally, while describing the law, we do not withhold our view thereof.

The prime target of this book will be typically a final year undergraduate coming to terms with the mysteries of intellectual property law. But we hope that many others will find it of value - teachers and postgraduates of course but also those in practice who also have to get to grips with the issues with which we deal.

In writing this book we have relied heavily on our experience of teaching the subject at Leicester at both undergraduate and postgraduate level. We thank our student victims as our thoughts have evolved and acknowledge our debt to our erstwhile colleague Fiona Patfield who was instrumental in the establishment of our courses. We are grateful for research assistance helpfully provided by Korinna Georghiades. Wendy Chantrell has provided invaluable assistance in the production of script from scrawl and we also wish to record our gratitude to Louise Smith and Samantha Burke for vital secretarial help at the end of the project ....

Jon Holyoak
Paul Torremans

15 March 1995

Contents

Section B

Patents

Chapter 2

Origin and background of the patent system   37

Chapter 3

Patentability   54

Chapter 4

Use and grant in the UK and Europe   92

Chapter 5

Infringement and revocation   131

Chapter 6

Supplementary protection certificates   152

Chapter 7

Section B – an overview   161

■

Chapter 18

Copyright – an overview 291

Chapter 22

Designs – an overview   338

Chapter 23

Trade marks   343

Chapter 24

Tortious protection of intellectual property rights 414

Section F

Issues in intellectual property

Chapter 25

Confidentiality and trade secrets   457

Chapter 26

Computer technology and
intellectual property   493

Chapter 27

Character merchandising   523

Chapter 28

Franchising and intellectual property   535

Chapter 29

Remedies in intellectual property litigation   550

Postscript   569

Index   571

Table of statutes

References in this Table to *Statutes* are to Halsbury's Statutes of England (Fourth Edition) showing the volume and page at which the annotated text of the Act will be found.

Page references printed in **bold** type indicate where the section of an Act is set out in part or in full.

Table of EU legislation

List of cases

W

X

Y

Z

Decisions of the European Court of Justice are listed below numerically.
These decisions are also included in the preceding alphabetical list.

Introduction

Chapter 1

Themes in intellectual property

PRELIMINARY THOUGHTS

This book is not just about ideas. It is about ideas skilfully expressed in writing, in music or in a sculpture. It is about the bright idea for an invention, the details of which have been worked out and which takes the form of a product or a process that can be applied industrially. It is also about a logo or name applied to products in order to distinguish them from other products in the same category and to indicate their origin. And it is also about clothes, and about exhaust pipes for cars made to a new design. Intellectual property is more than a reward for inventors and creators on the basis of a bright idea.

We will investigate this further on all other pages of this book, but let us start with a down to earth overview of the plot of our story. The background is a concert given by a famous opera-singer. His performance consists of songs taken from various operas. The lyrics and music of these songs can attract copyright protection for their authors, he will have a right in his performance of them. A live recording is made and published on CD and the concert is beamed around the world as a satellite broadcast, two further occasions on which copyright interests arise. Satellite technology involves various patented inventions both in relation to the missile technology and in relation to the transmission of broadcasts. The CD will bear the logo of the record company which allows customers to distinguish the CD from that of another record company. It is most likely that the record company secured a trade mark for its logo to guarantee its exclusive right to use it. The CD's accompanying booklet raises copyright issues as it contains a photograph in which the star is pictured standing next to a sculpture his wife made. The photograph, the sculpture and the text of the booklet can all be protected by copyright. T-shirts bearing the star's picture are of a different style, but allow him to merchandise his image and to benefit from his celebrity status.

By the time we will have unravelled all the intellectual property aspects of this concert, or at least the legal provisions underlying them, we will have reached the final page of our book; but we hope that this down to earth example provides a first impression of what intellectual property means in practice and alerts the reader to the intellectual property aspects of many elements of our everyday life.

INTRODUCTION

In recent years intellectual property has attracted a lot of attention. Its importance for international trading relations was emphasised during the negotiations that led to the successful conclusion of the GATT[1] Uruguay Round on the world trading system. The GATT TRIPs initiative that led eventually to the Agreement on Trade Related Aspects of Intellectual Property Rights 1994 that was signed in Marrakesh,[2] was sparked off by a strong desire to eradicate international counterfeiting and piracy, but it became clear at a very early stage that the cure against the fake Gucci or Cartier watches, Lacoste shirts or even counterfeited fire extinguishing systems in jet engines for passenger planes,[3] or against what is often described as a plague threatening (among other things) the worldwide exploitation of intellectual property, required also a harmonisation of national intellectual property laws. It is much easier to eradicate counterfeits at the source with a common set of minimum protection rules than afterwards at a national border once they are in circulation. At European level the realisation of the Single Market gave rise to a series of initiatives in the intellectual property area. Harmonisation Directives, eg the harmonisation of the duration of the term of copyright protection[4] and the Trade Mark Directive,[5] were coupled with moves towards a set of truly European intellectual property rights[6] and Community responses to the

---

1   The General Agreement on Tariffs and Trade, basically the world free trading system which will, as a structure and organisation, be succeeded by the World Trade Organisation (WTO) as a result of the Uruguay Round of trade negotiations.
2   The final text of TRIPs was published in (1994) 33 ILM 1197 and in (1994) 25 IIC 209. The agreement is administered by the World Trade Organisation (WTO), which succeeded to GATT.
3   See Piatti 'Measures to combat international piracy' [1989] 7 EIPR 239 at 239–240.
4   Directive 93/98 harmonising the term of protection of copyright and certain related rights (1993) OJ L 290/9.
5   Directive 89/104 on the approximation of the laws of member states relating to trade marks (1989) OJ L40/1.
6   Eg the Community Trade Mark, see Council Regulation 40/94 on the Community Trade Mark (1994) OJ L11/1.

need for adequate protection felt by the computer industry.[7] Our own legislation was updated as a result of a number of these developments and we have also seen the further development of, for example, the tort of passing-off and the protection offered to the merchandising activities involving real and fictitious characters, to fill the gaps not covered internationally (eg goodwill, characters and information).

Due in part to these developments the various intellectual property rights have become relatively well known:

(a) trade marks;
(b) patents;
(c) copyright;
(d) rights in performances;
(e) registered designs; and
(f) design rights.

Let us add some more examples to our concert example discussed above. Intellectual property addresses problems such as how the Compact Disc system, as a technological invention, is temporarily protected by patents, how the aesthetic appearance of a telephone in the shape of a golf caddy can be protected as a registered design and whether the functional design of kitchen utensils can attract (unregistered) design protection. We could also use intellectual property laws to examine how the registration of the trade mark 'Sprite' by the Coca-Cola Company for its lemon taste soft drink is linked to the fact that it allows consumers to identify the drink and to distinguish it from similar soft drinks and how such a trade mark is protected against imitation, how copyright grants and protects certain rights in literary, artistic and musical creations and which rights exist in performances. Other related areas that we will equally have to consider include the law of confidence and passing-off. These form an essential national addition to the types and level of protection provided on the basis of international conventions.

A BRIEF HISTORICAL OVERVIEW: THE ORIGINS

When we refer to intellectual property rights, we do not wish to make the distinction between the industrial intellectual property rights, such as patents and trade marks, and artistic intellectual property rights, such as copyright. We think this distinction is no longer valid as copyright is now used in such a flexible way, for example to protect computer programs, that

7   See eg Directive 91/250 on the legal protection of computer programs (1991) OJ L122/42 and Directive 96/9 on the legal protection of databases (1996) OJ L77/20.

it can no longer be called an exclusively artistic right. The same concepts underlie each type of intellectual property. A strong form of unity exists between all types of intellectual property and the common law concepts in use in this area. But this dichotomy between 'industrial' patents and 'artistic' copyright has been an essential element in the historical development of the protection of what we call intellectual property. Before we try to define this term and to justify the continuing existence of intellectual property rights, let us have a brief look at the historical roots of our topic.

The origin and the evolution of the patent system

Patents can be traced back as far as the end of the Middle Ages.[8] Inventor privileges, which in England took the form of royal grants under the prerogative, were granted all over Europe. Although not altogether absent, the idea of the promotion of inventive activity through the grant of a market monopoly was strongly overshadowed by the idea that these privileges were the perfect tool to reward political creditors and give them a trading monopoly granted by letters patent.

In England, Parliament reacted against this practice and in 1624 the Statute of Monopolies was issued. It was primarily a reaction against the existing practice and the trading monopolies to which this practice gave rise, but it was also influenced by the idea that in certain circumstances a market monopoly would be necessary as an incentive to innovate. The result of this influence is found in section 6 of the Statute of Monopolies. The 'true and first inventor' was granted a patent monopoly for 14 years upon 'any manner of new manufacture'. As England felt that France and Holland were clearly further advanced in their technical development, any person who imported new technologies with a view to establishing an advanced domestic industry was equally considered to be an inventor. The flexibility on this point emphasises that this new patent system should be seen as a deliberate act of economic policy.[9] By rewarding eventually both devisors and importers of new technologies, the development of industrial activity, growth and employment emerges as the primary aim of the legislation. Gratitude towards the inventor is only of secondary importance. The policy aspect is reinforced by the provision that manufactures that are 'contrary to the law or mischievous to the state, by raising prices of commodities at home, or

---

8   See also D Young, A Watson, S Thorley and R Miller *Terrell on the Law of Patents* Sweet & Maxwell (14th edn, 1994) pp 1-5.
9   See Dölemeyer 'Einführungsprivilegien und Einführungspatente als historische Mittel des Technologietransfers' [1985] GRUR 735. This German article is the best source for this view.

hurt trade, or generally inconvenient'[10] would not be protected. Only those manufactures which fit in with the policy will be protected as the realisation of the aims of the policy is the ultimate reason for the existence of the patents.

These early developments represent only the start of a long development process wherein the industrial revolution in Europe was the key element. The eighteenth century saw the development of the patent specification, first as a tool to define the content of the protected invention against infringers by means of a statement enrolled with the Court of Chancery and later, in the modern sense, as a source of technical information, provided by the patentee as consideration for the monopoly granted to him by the patent. The novelty concept, which corresponded previously to the fact that the invention was not yet practised in the country, was enlarged to incorporate also the question of whether the trading community did already know of the invention through publication.

The Patent Law Amendment Act 1852 removed the inefficiencies and uncertainties in the procedures for securing a patent. The applicant could register his specification with the Commissioners of Patents, with an option to file a provisional application up to one year before the complete specification was worked out and filed. Patents were granted simply upon registration and at a reasonable fee. This lead to an increase in the number of patents, some of them of dubious value due to the absence of any examination of the applications. The problems arising from the inadequacy of the patent litigation procedures were addressed by the Patents, Designs and Trade Marks Act 1883. A single judge replaced the juries and patentees were obliged to delineate the scope of their monopoly in at least one of their claims, but even more important was the replacement of the Commissioners by the Patent Office. This Patent Office was charged with the examination of the patent applications. In a first stage it examined whether the formal requirements and the requirement that the patentee should provide a proper description of the patent had been observed. An examination of the novelty of the application based on a search of previous British specifications, was added to the examination process from 1905 onwards.[11] This change clearly demonstrates how strongly the origins of intellectual property are linked to, and the evolution of them is a response to, commercial necessities.

All over Europe and in North America specific patent legislation was introduced at national level in the course of the nineteenth century. As a similar evolution took place in all these countries and as the technology that was being developed was not only to be used in the country in which it was developed, a need for international co-operation arose. In 1883 the Paris Convention for the Protection of Industrial Property was created as the basic

10   See Statute of Monopolies 1624.
11   See Patents Act 1902.

instrument for international patent protection.[12] It provides minimal rules of protection, which were translated into the national patent legislation. On top of that it contains a rule of national treatment:[13] foreign inventors shall be treated in the same way as their domestic counterparts and their inventions shall be granted the same level of protection.

The development of the first half of the twentieth century can be characterised as a consolidation effort at legal and organisational level. The new phenomenon of the vast number of newly independent states created a crisis in the patent system in the early 1960s. A flood of patent applications had to be dealt with independently by an ever-growing number of national patent offices. International and regional co-operation was seen as the solution. Attempts to arrive at regional patent systems[14] and treaties providing assistance and combating the seemingly endless duplication of the examination procedures, such as the global Patent Co-operation Treaty,[15] were started in this period. Another problem newly independent states faced, especially in the third world, was the inappropriateness for their purposes of the existing patent legislation. The adoption of new patent laws in these countries and the reform of the international patent system to this new environment form processes which have not yet been concluded.

Trade marks

The use of marks which are added to goods to distinguish them from similar goods has a history of at least 2,000 years. Indeed, the Romans embossed their pottery or impressed it with a mark and merchants have used marks ever since to distinguish their goods. Although the courts became involved in the actions against infringers,[16] no proper trade mark legislation was enacted and the system was based purely on common law principles. The main problem traders faced was that each time they brought an infringement action they had to prove their title to the mark. This depended on the existence of an established reputation associated with the mark.

In France this problem had been solved by the introduction of a registration system and a similar registration system was introduced in England in 1875 by the Trade Marks Registration Act.[17] Our trade mark

---

12   See Beier 'The Significance of the Patent System for Technical, Economic and Social Progress' [1980] IIC 563 at 570.

13   Article 2 of the Paris Convention.

14   Eg the Nordic Patent System and the European Patent Convention.

15   See below under International Intellectual Property Conventions.

16   See *Sykes v Sykes* (1824) 3 B & C 541, a case which contains some basic principles (damages at common law – deceit).

17   For a comprehensive overview of the historical development of the law of trade marks (and passing-off) see T A Blanco-White and R Jacob *Kerly's Law of Trade Marks and Trade Names*, Sweet & Maxwell (12th edn, 1986); the latest step, the Trade Marks Act 1994, is obviously not included in this now slightly outdated work.

legislation was consolidated by the Patents, Designs and Trade Marks Act 1883. In the same year the Paris Convention was signed. The principles contained in this Convention apply to trade marks as well as to patents.[18] The next step in the consolidation process was the statutory definition of the term trade mark in the Trade Marks Act 1905. This was followed in the Trade Marks Act 1919 by the division of the register into Part A, where stringent requirements were coupled with better protection in terms of remedies, and Part B. The Trade Marks Act 1938 was based on the same principles but the drafting was more detailed. It was amended by the Trade Marks (Amendment) Act 1984 to include also service marks. The division of the register into two parts was abolished by the Trade Marks Act 1994, but the British system still contains an examination stage before the mark is registered.

We have seen that at international level many of the principles applied to patents are equally applied to trade marks.[19] This is not always the case for copyright, to which we now turn our attention.

The origin and the evolution of the copyright system

Copyright is historically linked to written literary works. As handwritten copies were such a formidable investment of time and effort, the number of copies available was low. Plagiarism was not a problem. All this changed when Gutenberg invented movable type and Caxton developed the printing press in the second half of the fifteenth century. The arrival of this technology made the printing of multiple copies possible. This could be done quickly and at relatively little expense.

Stationers acquired the works from their authors and organised the printing and the sale of these works. These entrepreneurs took the commercial risk to exploit the works of the authors and wanted exclusive rights in the publication of the works to protect them against copiers. They found an ally in the Crown which wanted to control the importation and circulation of books. The stationers organised themselves in a guild and the Crown granted the Stationers' Company a charter in 1556. Lawfully printed books were entered in the Company's register and, as the right to make an entry in the register was reserved for the stationers, this system effectively amounted to a licensing system and secured a printing monopoly for the Company members. On top of that they were granted powers to act against infringing copies. This system remained in place until the end of the seventeenth century.

A brief period of anarchy was followed by the first real copyright statute: the Statute of Anne 1709. It gave the 'sole right and liberty of printing books'

---

18 See supra.
19 Industrial designs are also found in this category.

to authors and their assignees. There was however no shift from an entrepreneurial copyright to an author's right with the emphasis exclusively on literary creation and its creators. The emphasis remained on the commercial exploitation of books. Printers and booksellers were explicitly named among the author's assigns.[20] The right started from first publication and lasted for 14 years, but it was only enforceable by seizure and penalties if the title of the book had been registered with the Stationers' Company before publication.[1] Before publication the author could rely on certain rights of literary property at common law to obtain protection against unauthorised copying[2] and if the author was still alive on expiry of the term of protection of 14 years the right was 'returned' to him for another 14 years.

At the end of the eighteenth and during the nineteenth century the duration of the term of copyright protection was gradually increased. Simultaneously the scope of copyright was widened to include other types of works apart from literary works. Engravings, prints, lithographs, sculptures, dramatic and musical works all received copyright protection during that period. Drama and music did not fit in well with the existing 'copy-right', the right to produce copies of the work and prevent others from doing so, as their exploitation involved much more performances, rather than the sale of printed copies. A 'use' right was sought by authors such as playwrights and composers. A performing right for dramatic works was created in 1833[3] to remedy this problem. It was extended to musical works in 1842.[4]

The British emphasis on the entrepreneurial exploitation aspect of copyright was not shared by those who saw copyright almost exclusively as the expression of reverence for the creating artist and his act of artistic creation. The latter tendency was particularly strong in France and Belgium, as illustrated by the use of the term *droit d'auteur* (author's right and not copy-right). As a major exporter of copyright material, Britain had an important interest in a compromise which secured at least some form of copyright protection abroad. The approach taken bears strong similarities to the contemporary evolution regarding patents. In the copyright area the Berne Convention was signed in 1886.[5] A personal connection between the author and a member state of the Berne Union, or first publication of the work in a member state of the Union, is from that moment onwards sufficient for protection in all member states on a national treatment basis.

---

20   See s 1.
1   See ss 1 and 2.
2   *Donaldson v Beckett* (1774) 2 Bro P C 129, 4 Burr 2408, 17 Hansard Parl Hist 953.
3   Dramatic Copyright Act 1833.
4   Literary Copyright Act 1842, s 20.
5   For a full account of the history of the Berne Convention and the Berne Union see S Ricketson *The Berne Convention for the Protection of Literary and Artistic Works: 1886–1986* Kluwer (1987) Ch 1.

When the convention was revised in 1908 the need to agree on further minimal rules was felt. Copyright protection was no longer to depend upon registration or any other formality, but upon the act of creation of the work and the term of copyright protection would last at least the author's life and 50 years. When these changes were incorporated into the Copyright Act 1911, it signalled the end for the Stationers' Company. The 1911 Act also widened the scope of copyright further. The producers of sound recordings were granted the exclusive right to prevent unauthorised reproductions of their recordings.[6] Significantly, this right was not given to the performing artist, but to the entrepreneur involved. The right was also labelled copyright, but the *droit d'auteur* tradition would instead distinguish it as a neighbouring right, because it does not directly protect the original artistic creation of the author. The work protected is only derived from the author's original artistic creation.

This right in sound recordings was an important precedent. It indicated that copyright would be flexible enough to offer protection to all works in whose creation new technical possibilities for artistic expression had been used. Protection was granted on a similar basis in cinematograph films, broadcasts and the typographical format of published editions by the Copyright Act 1956.

At international level the developing countries advocated major changes to the Berne Convention during the 1960s. The Stockholm 1967 and Paris 1971 Revisions of the Berne Convention granted in the end only minimal concessions with a lot of strings attached to them: they can allow certain translations and publications of foreign works if these are not otherwise made available.[7]

In a separate development, performing artists have been granted certain rights. The Convention on the Protection of Performers, Producers of Phonograms and Broadcasting Organisations was signed in Rome in 1961. Under the provisions of this Convention, performers have the right to prevent the fixation or the broadcasting of their live performances.[8] Record makers can prevent the reproduction of their records[9] and broadcasting organisations can control the re-broadcasting and the public performance for an entrance fee of their broadcasts.[10] The Rome Convention has

6   Section 19(1); The courts later held that the producers could also prevent public performances of their recordings, *Gramophone Co v Cawardine* [1934] Ch 450.
7   For more details, see the appendix to the Berne Convention upon which agreement was reached at the Paris revision conference (1971) reproduced in J Phillips (Consultant ed) *Butterworths Intellectual Property Law Handbook* Butterworths (3rd edn, 1997) pp 1295–1302.
8   See Articles 7–9. The same right does not exist in relation to recorded performances.
9   See Articles 10–12.
10   See Article 13. They cannot control the diffusion by wire or by cable of their broadcasts however.

unfortunately never reached the same level of adherence between nations as the Berne Convention.[11] A second Phonograms Convention which deals with mutual protection against the unauthorised commercial copying of sound recordings was signed in 1971. These international provisions have been translated into the Copyright, Designs and Patents Act 1988 mainly as Part II: Rights in Performances.[12]

This brief historical overview of the development of patent and copyright law clearly demonstrates that the divide between patents, as purely industrial rights, and copyright, as a purely artistic right, was never absolute in nature. Especially in Britain copyright always had an entrepreneurial, almost industrial, orientation. Copyright was never an exclusively artistic right, as opposed to the other industrial property rights. In recent years this tendency was emphasised by the use of copyright to protect computer programs. It is however true that copyright is different from the other rights. Patents protect the invention, but copyright protects not only the creation, but also grants some strong, additional, personal rights to the creator. These moral rights have always been an essential aspect of the French '*droit d'auteur*', and in Britain they were incorporated in their own right for the first time in the Copyright, Designs and Patents Act 1988.[13]

Each right is an intellectual property right, but each right has its own characteristics. Before examining each right in detail, we will try to define the term intellectual property and we will also examine whether the continued existence of intellectual property rights can be justified.

A DEFINITION AND A JUSTIFICATION OF INTELLECTUAL PROPERTY

Intellectual property rights are first of all property rights. Secondly, they are property rights in something intangible. And finally, they protect innovations and creations and reward innovative and creative activity.[14]

11   Hopefully the WIPO Performances and Phonograms Treaty that was signed in Geneva in 1996, but that has yet to come into force, will be more successful. The text of this treaty is reproduced in J Phillips (Consultant ed) *Butterworths Intellectual Property Law Handbook* Butterworths (3rd edn, 1997) pp 1355-1364 and in P Torremans and J Holyoak *Butterworths Students Statutes: Intellectual Property Law* Butterworths (2nd edn, 1998) pp 26-31.

12   Before the Copyright, Designs and Patents Act 1988 came into force the Performers' Protection Acts 1958–1972 offered some protection to performing artists, but the level and the type of that protection were unsatisfactory.

13   Part I, Chapter 4, ss 77–89.

14   US Council for International Business *A New MTN: Priorities for Intellectual Property* (1985) at 3.

Property rights

The essential characteristic of property rights is that they are exclusionary rights through which third parties are prohibited from the use and exploitation of the subject precluded by these rights.[15] Through property rights externalities[16] can be internalised; in other words the subject of the right is brought under the control of the owner of the property right. These rights will only develop when the cost of this internalisation is smaller than the gains of it.[17] If we take a bicycle as an example of an item of tangible property, it becomes clear that the owner of the bicycle has the exclusive right to use the bicycle and such a monopolistic right in real and personal property is conceded almost naturally. Property rights in items such as our bicycle developed because nobody would be prepared to invest time, materials and skills in designing and producing bicycles[18] if he or she would have no right in the result of the process that would enable them to benefit from their work. The most obvious way to do so is to sell the bicycle, but again there would be no interest in the bicycle, this time in acquiring it, should the buyer be unable to get the exclusive right to use the bicycle. The nature of the object gives this right a monopolistic character. If someone uses the bicycle, no one else can use it. The physical nature of the unique embodiment of certain limited resources in the bicycle automatically leads to a particular competitive[19] exclusionary effect.[20]

Intangible property rights

In this respect intellectual property rights are fundamentally different. The nature of the property which is the subject of the right and which is protected does not necessarily lead to competitive exclusionary effects. Concurrent use of inventions by a number of manufacturers, including the patentee, or

---

15 See Lehmann 'The Theory of Property Rights and the Protection of Intellectual and Industrial Property' [1985] IIC 525 at 530.
16 An externality is an economic situation in which an individual's pursuit of his or her self-interest has positive or negative spill-over effects on the utility or welfare of others. It can be seen as a market failure and in this context a property right is a tool used to correct such a market failure. See R Ekelund and R Tollison *Economics* Little, Brown & Company (1986) pp 404–405.
17 Demsetz 'Toward a Theory of Property Rights' 57 (1967) American Economy Review 347 at 350; for an overview of the property rights theory see Cooter and Ulen *Law and Economics* Harper Collins Publishers (1988) especially Ch 4, but also Ch 5.
18 At most they would design and produce one bicycle to get from A to B themselves, but even that cannot be taken for granted in a situation where no property rights exist.
19 The difference is that between *my* bicycle and bicycles as a concept.
20 Lehmann 'The Theory of Property Rights and the Protection of Intellectual and Industrial Property' [1985] IIC 525 at 531.

simultaneous performances of a musical are possible.[1] The invention and the musical will not perish, nor will any use or performance lessen their value. The subject matter of intellectual property rights, eg inventions or creations, has a link with knowledge and ideas. In economic terms this subject matter constitutes a public asset and its use is not by its nature individually appropriable.[2] In many cases imitation is even cheaper than invention or creation.[3] The competitive exclusion only arises artificially with the creation of a legally binding intellectual 'property' right as an intangible property right. This gives the inventor or the creator, owners of the intangible property right, the exclusive use of the invention or the creation.

An economic justification[4]

Why are these intangible property rights created? Economists argue that if everyone would be allowed to use the results of innovative and creative activity freely, the problem of the 'free riders'[5] would arise.[6] No one would invest in innovation or creation, except in a couple of cases where no other solution would be available,[7] as it would give them a competitive disadvantage.[8] All competitors would just wait until someone else made the investment, as they would be able to use the results as well without investing money in innovation and creation and without taking the risks that the investment would not result in the innovative or creative breakthrough it

1   Ibid.
2   Ullrich 'The Importance of Industrial Property Law and Other Legal Measures in the Promotion of Technological Innovation' [1989] Industrial Property 102 at 103.
3   See Mansfield, Schwartz and Wagner 'Imitation Costs and Patents: An Empirical Study' [1981] Ec J 907.
4   We will approach the justification issue from the point of view of the developed countries. The international transfer of technology and the different level of development in developing countries present additional problems: see eg Primo Braga 'The Economics of Intellectual Property Rights and the GATT: A View From the South' [1989] Vanderbilt Journal of Transnational Law 243.
5   See R Benko *Protecting Intellectual Property Rights: Issues and Controversies* American Enterprise Institute for Public Policy Research (AEI Studies 453)(1987) at 17.
6   Inappropriability, the lack of the opportunity to become the proprietor of the results of innovative and creative activity, causes an underallocation of resources to research activity, innovation and creation: see K Arrow 'Economic Welfare and the Allocation of Resources for Invention' in National Bureau for Economic Research *The Rate and Direction of Inventive Activity: Economic and Social Factors* Princeton University Press (1962) at 609–625.
7   Eg a case where the existing technology is completely incapable of providing any form of solution to a new technical problem that has arisen.
8   See Ullrich 'The Importance of Industrial Property Law and Other Legal Measures in the Promotion of Technological Innovation' [1989] Industrial Property 102 at 103.

aimed at.[9] The cost of the distribution of the knowledge is, on top of that, insignificant.[10] As a result the economy would not function adequately because we see innovation and creation as an essential element in a competitive free market economy. In this line of argument innovation and creation are required for economic growth and prosperity.[11] Property rights should be created if goods and services are to be produced and used as efficiently as possible in such an economy. The perspective that they will be able to have a property right in the results of their investment will stimulate individuals and enterprises to invest in research and development.[12] These property rights should be granted to someone who will economically maximise profits.[13] It is assumed that the creator or inventor will have been motivated by the desire to maximise profits, either by exploiting the invention or creation himself or by having it exploited by a third party, so the rights are granted to them.[14] This argument applies as well to intangible property rights, such as patents which determine the value of an item in a direct way, as to rights such as trade marks which do so only indirectly through their use as a means of communication.[15]

But how does such a legally created monopolistic exclusive property right fit in with the free market ideal of perfect competition? At first sight every form of a monopoly might seem incompatible with free competition, but we have already demonstrated that some form of property right is required to enhance economic development as competition can only play its role as market regulator if the products of human labour are protected by property

9   One could advance the counterargument that inventions and creations will give the innovator an amount of lead time and that the fact that it will take imitators some time to catch up would allow the innovator to recuperate his investment during the interim period. In many cases this amount of lead time will, however, only be a short period, too short to recuperate the investment and make a profit. See also Mansfield, Schwartz and Wagner 'Imitation Costs and Patents: An Empirical Study' [1981] Ec J 907 at 915 et seq.

10   See R Benko *Protecting Intellectual Property Rights: Issues and Controversies* American Enterprise Institute for Public Policy Research (AEI Studies 453)(1987) at 17.

11   See R Benko *Protecting Intellectual Property Rights: Issues and Controversies* American Enterprise Institute for Public Policy Research (AEI Studies 453)(1987) Ch 4 at 15, and US Council for International Business *A New MTN: Priorities for Intellectual Property* (1985) at 3.

12   Lunn 'The Roles of Property Rights and Market Power in Appropriating Innovative Output' [1985] Journal of Legal Studies 423 at 425.

13   Lehmann 'Property and Intellectual Property – Property Rights as Restrictions on Competition in Furtherance of Competition' [1989] IIC 1 at 11.

14   For an economic-philosophical approach see also Mackaay 'Economic and Philosophical Aspects of Intellectual Property Rights' in M Van Hoecke (ed) *The Socio-Economic Role of Intellectual Property Rights* Story-Scientia (1991) pp 1-30.

15   See Lehmann 'The Theory of Property Rights and the Protection of Intellectual and Industrial Property' [1985] IIC 525 at 531.

rights.[16] In this respect the exclusive monopolistic character of the property rights is coupled with the fact that these rights are transferable. These rights are marketable; they can, for example, be sold as an individual item. It is also necessary to distinguish between various levels of economic activity as far as economic development and competition are concerned. The market mechanism is more sophisticated than the competition/monopoly dichotomy. Competitive restrictions at one level may be necessary to promote competition at another level. Three levels can be distinguished: production, consumption and innovation. Property rights in goods enhance competition on the production level, but this form of ownership restricts competition on the consumption level. One has to acquire the ownership of the goods before one is allowed to consume them and goods owned by other economic players are not directly available for one's consumption. In turn, intellectual property imposes competitive restrictions on the production level. Only the owner of the patent in an invention may use the invention and only the owner of the copyright in a literary work may produce additional copies of that work. These restrictions benefit competition on the innovative level. The availability of property rights on each level guarantees the development of competition on the next level. Property rights are a prerequisite for the normal functioning of the market mechanism.[17] Or, to take the example of patents: 'patents explicitly prevent the diffusion of new technology to guarantee the existence of technology to diffuse in the future'.[18]

This clearly demonstrates that it is not correct to see intellectual property rights as monopolies which are in permanent conflict with the fundamental rule of free competition. Free competition can only exist and a market economy can only flourish when certain restrictions in furtherance of competition are accepted. Intellectual property rights are necessary to achieve this. The main problem is that this only justifies the existence of exclusive property rights as the result of innovative activity. The particular form intellectual property rights have taken in a particular national intellectual property statute and even more the way in which these rights are used and exercised are not automatically justified by this theory. The restrictions on competition are only justified in so far as they are restrictions in furtherance of competition on the next level, which is either the production level or the innovation level. Any restriction which goes further hinders the optimal functioning of the market economy. It is the task of the provisions on competition law to regulate this system in such a way that

---

16   Lehmann 'Property and Intellectual Property – Property Rights as Restrictions on Competition in Furtherance of Competition' [1989] IIC 1 at 12.

17   Lehmann 'The Theory of Property Rights and the Protection of Intellectual and Industrial Property' [1985] IIC 525 at 539.

18   R Benko *Protecting Intellectual Property Rights: Issues and Controversies* American Enterprise Institute for Public Policy Research (AEI Studies 453)(1987) Ch 4 at 19.

this optimal level of functioning is achieved and maintained. This co-existence of intellectual property and the rules on free competition is a permanent balancing act and one of the most challenging and interesting parts of the study of intellectual property.

Goods perish through use, while intangible property is, at least in theory, perpetual.[19] But the socio-economic value of these rights is not so important that a perpetual restriction on competition is necessary and justifiable to enhance competition on other levels. Innovative activity will be sufficiently enhanced, without too far-reaching restrictions of competition on the production level, when the intellectual property right is restricted in time. For patents, which grant the patentee extensive restrictive powers and whose protection is wide in scope, the term of protection is relatively short (20 years). From now on literary works are to be protected under copyright for a period of the life of the author plus 70 years, but the protection granted is weaker. Only the particular expression of an idea is protected; the idea as such is left unprotected. This attempt to get the balance between restriction on and freedom of competition right through the use of a fixed term can be seen as lacking precision and potentially unjust, but introducing a sliding scale would require the determination of the term of protection on the basis of the merits of each individual invention or creation. This would create massive administrative costs that outweigh the benefits derived from the system and on top of this it would create an undesirable climate of legal uncertainty.[20]

Another way of getting the balance right is the duty to exercise and use which is linked to patent and trade mark rights. Compulsory use and compulsory licences are an integral component of most intellectual property legislations. The idea behind it is first of all that use of the intellectual property right will provide an income to its owner and that this profit will encourage him to continue his innovative work. The only reason why a restriction of competition at the level of production is acceptable is the enhancement of competition on the innovative level through the possibility for the owner of the right to realise a profit. This justification collapses if this right is not used. This defect is remedied by the introduction of the duty to exercise and use.[1] The weaker protection accorded under copyright law renders this restriction superfluous in that area. Such a duty equally does not exist for real and personal property. It can be seen as an important

---

19 It may lose its economic value after a number of years though. Eg an inventive production process protected by a patent can be applied indefinitely, but will after a number of years be overtaken by new technological developments and lose its economic value.

20 For more details see Lehmann 'The Theory of Property Rights and the Protection of Intellectual and Industrial Property' [1985] IIC 525 at 535–536.

1 Lehmann 'The Theory of Property Rights and the Protection of Intellectual and Industrial Property' [1985] IIC 525 at 532–533.

difference between intangible industrial property and (normal) real and personal property.

A second reason for the obligation to use is that it is felt that the grant of an exclusive right should be counterbalanced by the fact that the previously unavailable subject matter of the right is made available to society. The obligation to use is necessary because, due to the exclusive right, the owner of the intellectual property right is the only one who makes it available. More specifically, for patents there is the additional requirement to reveal the technical details and specifications of the invention, to bring them into the public domain. In exchange for the exclusive right, society has the right to share the development of technical knowledge and eventually to use it for further research and further developments. This represents an additional advantage of the patent system, as the alternative is to be found in the use of the secrecy system. Technological developments are, in the absence of a patent system,[2] kept secret. Society is unable to share this new knowledge and the inventor can only use the invention in a way which does not reveal the technical functioning of it, because once in the public domain it can be used freely by all competitors. The inventor is put in a very weak position. It has been demonstrated that a patent system that grants the inventor adequate property rights fulfils the task reserved for such a system in a market economy in a better way. The law of secrecy cannot replace the patent system fully; it can only be a useful addition to it.[3]

Maybe some additional remarks on the type of monopoly granted by intellectual property rights are appropriate. It is in no way an absolute monopoly. It is limited in time. There is also competition with similar products, similar trade marks etc. Inventions compete with substitute technologies so that the profits based on the exclusive use of the invention are rarely monopolistic rents.[4] The latter situation only arises in those rare situations in which an invention is such a radical step forward that there is a (temporary) absolute lack of substitutability.[5] And in copyright only one particular expression of an otherwise unprotected idea is granted copyright protection. Intellectual property rights do not give their owners an automatic profit. They are directly oriented towards demand. The reward they provide for innovative activity depends upon the competitive structure of the market

---

2   This technique can also be used as an alternative in a particular case for a patent application if the costs of revealing the technical detail of the invention and the other costs linked to such an application are perceived to be higher than the benefits of the stronger protection offered by the patent system. Potentially the duration of the secrecy is endless, which is also an advantage over the patent system.

3   See Lunn 'The Roles of Property Rights and Market Power in Appropriating Innovative Output' [1985] Journal of Legal Studies 423.

4   Ullrich 'The Importance of Industrial Property Law and Other Legal Measures in the Promotion of Technical Innovation' [1989] Industrial Property 102 at 105.

5   Lehmann 'The Theory of Property Rights and the Protection of Intellectual and Industrial Property' [1985] IIC 525 at 537.

concerned. Only when the market appreciates the innovation on its merits will the owner be rewarded and make a profit.[6] 'The ownership of intangibles in the sense of abstract property rights (...) is therefore limited to a temporary, ephemeral competitive restriction.'[7] Intellectual property rights confer exclusive rights, but they hardly ever confer a real monopoly in the sense that the monopolist can act in an arbitrary way without being influenced by his competitors.

It has to be added that a number of economists have argued against the existence of intellectual property rights and especially against the existence of patents. In their view patents do not promote technological innovation, or there are more effective ways to promote innovation.[8] They are, however, unable to provide clear evidence that intellectual property rights do not fulfil a useful economical function and none of their alternatives has ever been tested successfully in practice.[9] All they can demonstrate is that some features of the existing patent system cannot be justified economically. They prove that the existing system does not always achieve a perfect balance between the various levels of competition. This is undoubtedly true, but the solution is not the abolition of the whole system. What is required could rather be described as fine-tuning of the system.[10]

There is also a substantial amount of empirical economic evidence in support of the economic justification for the existence of intellectual property rights. Most of these studies deal with patents and the causal relationship between the availability of patent protection and investment in research and development and in innovation.[11]

6   See Ullrich 'The Importance of Industrial Property Law and Other Legal Measures in the Promotion of Technical Innovation' [1989] Industrial Property 102 at 112.
7   Lehmann 'The Theory of Property Rights and the Protection of Intellectual and Industrial Property' [1985] IIC 525 at 537.
8   See eg Fritz Machlup *An Economic Review of the Patent System Study* No 15, US Congress, Senate, Judiciary Committee, Subcommittee on Patents, Trademarks and Copyrights, Washington DC (1957) and Edith Penrose *The Economics of the International Patent System* John Hopkins University Press (1951), see also Machlup and Penrose 'The Patent Controversy in the Nineteenth Century' (1950) 10 J Econ Hist 1.
9   This is admitted by Fritz Machlup at the end of his study.
10 See Beier 'The Significance of the Patent System for Technical, Economic and Social Progress' [1980] IIC 563 at 572.
11 Eg C T Taylor and A Silberston *The Economic Impact of the Patent System* (1973), the 1973–1974 study of the Ifo-Institut für Wirtschaftsforschung in Munich concerning the relationship between the Patent System and Technical Progress which is discussed in Oppenlander 'Patent Policies and Technical Progress in the Federal Republic of Germany' [1977] IIC 97 and A Silberston *The Economic Importance of Patents* Cambridge University Press (1987); an overview of older studies can be found in J Schmookler *Invention and Economic Growth* Harvard University Press (1966); see also Lunn 'The Roles of Property Rights and Market Power in Appropriating Innovative Output' [1985] Journal of Legal Studies 423.

■

This economic theory provides a justification for the existence of intellectual property rights. A related point is the issue of who gets these intellectual property rights. It has been suggested that the economic theory proves that it is valuable to have intellectual property rights, but that it is unable to guarantee that the enforcement of these rights will have valuable results in each individual case. The author and the inventor must obtain these rights to secure the best possible system. This can only be accepted if one uses the labour theory to justify the allocation of the property rights whose existence the economic theory justifies.[12] This theory was formulated by John Locke[13] and is the combination of two concepts. The first concept is that everyone has a property right in the labour of his own body and brain and the second concept adds to that that the application of human labour to an unowned object gives you a property right in it. When applied to intellectual property rights,[14] this could explain why it is the author who gets the copyright in the book and why it is the inventor who gets the patent in the invention. The combination of the economic theory and the labour theory provides a full justification for the system of intellectual property rights.[15] This reference to the labour theory explicitly justifies the fact that it is the author or the inventor who should own the intellectual property right, but it is submitted that this is already implicit in the economic theory. An intellectual property right as a restriction on competition at production level, because not everyone can produce the goods protected by the right, will not stimulate competition on the innovation level if the right is not given to the innovator, be it an author or an inventor. One will only be stimulated to innovate when one gets the intellectual property rights in the innovation. This effect, which is the key element in the economic justification theory for intellectual property, disappears when someone else gets the intellectual property rights in the innovation. The actual exploitation of the right can be done by the rightholder or by a licensee – this does not affect the justification at all.

Other ways to justify intellectual property

This economic analysis justifies the continued existence of intellectual property rights and economic history confirms the correctness of the

---

12   Spector 'An Outline of a Theory Justifying Intellectual and Industrial Property Rights' [1989] 8 EIPR 270 at 272-273.
13   John Locke 'The Second Treatise' Section 27 in *Two Treaties of Government* edited by Peter Laslett, Cambridge University Press (1970).
14   See Robert Nozick *Anarchy, State and Utopia* Basil Blackwell (1974) at 181-182.
15   Spector 'An Outline of a Theory Justifying Intellectual and Industrial Property Rights' [1989] 8 EIPR 270 at 273.

analysis.[16] One also finds a series of other elements of justification in an historical analysis and in a socio-economic analysis.[17]

There seems to be a need for a system protecting innovation once a country starts to develop its industry. This becomes especially clear when one takes the example of patents. There is a correlation between industrialisation and patent protection. Patents are introduced when the process of industrialisation starts and each increase in the level of patent protection corresponds to progress in the industrialisation process. This evolution is present in most European countries from the fifteenth century onwards, but it becomes very prominent in the nineteenth century due to the Industrial Revolution. It has to be added that this link between patents and industrialisation is based on the idea that a country will not be able to benefit from the industrialisation process in Europe if it does not introduce a system of patent protection – a conclusion that was reached as a result of an active debate in which both the advantages and disadvantages of the introduction of a system of patent protection were fully taken into account.[18]

Apart from this historical correlation, we should turn our attention also to the evolution of economic output. The introduction of a system of patent protection in a country's legal system goes together with a clear increase in the industrial production of that country. We can refer here to the English example in the eighteenth century, but all other industrialised countries could equally serve as examples. Another striking feature is the high level of industrialisation in all countries with a high level of patent protection. It could even be demonstrated that their level of industrialisation is higher than the level reached by countries which refuse to grant patent protection or which only grant a weak form of patent protection. The successes of the Spanish and Italian pharmaceutical industries and the Swiss chemical industry at times when patent protection was not available do not prove the contrary. No new product emerged and the success was based purely on imitation. This situation only improved with the introduction of a system of patent protection.[19] It is not, however, possible to establish a causal link between these two facts in a conclusive manner. Other factors than the patent system may be responsible for the higher level of industrialisation.[20]

These historical elements provide additional arguments in favour of the patent system and a system of intellectual property rights in general, but taken in isolation they do not provide a complete and convincing justification for the existence of intellectual property rights.

16   See Lehmann 'Property and Intellectual Property – Property Rights as Restrictions on Competition in Furtherance of Competition' [1989] IIC 1 at 11.
17   Beier 'The Significance of the Patent System for Technical, Economic and Social Progress' [1980] IIC 563.
18   Ibid at 571–572.
19   Ibid at 573–574.
20   Ibid.

Other theses that have been suggested as justification for the existence of patents rely on natural rights, rewards for the inventor, and disclosure.[1] Immediately after the French Revolution a tendency to explain and justify individual property rights as natural rights on the basis of a series of moral and philosophical arguments became fashionable and was extended to intangible property such as patents and other intellectual property rights.[2] This theory never found much support outside France.

Similar arguments are found in the reward theory which sees patents as a reward owed by society to inventors to reward their creativity and their services to society.[3] Society has a moral obligation to compensate and to reward the inventors.[4] This argument cannot justify the existence of the patent system, even if one agrees that the inventor should be rewarded. We demonstrated above that a patent offers only a potential monopoly, a potential reward to the inventor. Not all patents, only those which are commercially attractive and whose commercial exploitation is successful, offer a reward to the inventor. Furthermore, this is an indirect reward. A direct reward, such as a lump sum, a decoration or a title, would be a better idea if the aim of the measure is to reward the inventor.[5] The inventor would be assured of a reward and would be able to assess the nature or amount of the reward in advance. These two theses based on natural rights and rewards are no longer fashionable as justifications for the existence of intellectual property rights,[6] although the possibility to reward the inventor is still rightfully considered as a positive side effect of the patent system.

A last thesis we have to mention emphasises the role the patent system plays in encouraging inventors to disclose their secrets to society. Diffusion of technology, which is considered to be desirable for society, will only take place when they make the technical details of their inventions public. If, as explained above, there is no protection for the invention and everyone can use the technology freely, the inventor will rely on secrecy as imitation of the invention entails only minimal costs when compared to those of the

---

1   R Benko *Protecting Intellectual Property Rights: Issues and Controversies* American Enterprise Institute for Public Policy Research (AEI Studies 453)(1987) Ch 4 at 16.

2   This theory was endorsed by the French National Assembly and became part of the preamble to the patent law of that period, see the quotation in Machlup and Penrose 'The Patent Controversy in the Nineteenth Century' (1950) 10 J Econ Hist 1 at 11.

3   This theory applies also to the other intellectual property rights.

4   Machlup and Penrose 'The Patent Controversy in the Nineteenth Century' (1950) 10 J Econ Hist 1 at 17 quote in this respect J S Mill's statement: 'That he, the inventor, ought to be compensated and rewarded ... will not be denied ... it would be a gross immorality of the law to set everybody free to use a person's work without his consent, and without giving him an equivalent.'

5   See M Blakeney *Legal Aspects of the Transfer of Technology to Developing Countries* ESC Publishing (1989) at 51–53.

6   R Benko *Protecting Intellectual Property Rights: Issues and Controversies* American Enterprise Institute for Public Policy Research (AEI Studies 453)(1987) Ch 4 at 17.

inventor. The technical details of new inventions will not be disclosed in such a system and society will not benefit to the same extent.[7] Although this theory is helpful and the disclosure of technical knowledge is a very positive aspect of the patent system, it has to be said that its value is in part undermined by two important details. The inventor without patent protection would have some lead time during which he enjoys a kind of market monopoly and during which he can collect a reward for his work as it would take the imitator some time before he is ready to produce and to enter the market.[8] This is reinforced by the fact that the exploitation of a patent quite often requires a substantial amount of secret know-how which the imitator will have to acquire if he is to exploit the invention successfully.[9] It has to be added though that in many cases the lead time will not be long enough to recover all costs and make a profit.

The last paragraphs have focused extensively on patents. Many of the arguments can also be used for trade marks, but are there perhaps other additional elements which can justify the existence of copyright? Originally copyright dealt with literary and artistic works. It could be argued that the author was given certain property rights in these works to reward his artistic performance or that the author's claims were based on a natural or moral right. Specifically in the droit d'auteur system a lot of emphasis is placed on the fact that the work involves an expression of the personality of the author. Copyright is then also given certain aspects of a personality right (cf moral rights) and does not remain a pure property right. This was perfectly acceptable for works such as novels, songs and poems, but it becomes increasingly difficult to justify copyright exclusively on this basis. Clearly this theory does not suit computer programs and other highly technological works which are now equally protected by copyright. As copyright has more and more entered the technological field, it becomes clear that the real justification for it is equally to be found in the economic justification theory.[10] Works protected by copyright are knowledge goods, they are concerned with creativity and innovation and present in this respect the same characteristics as inventions. They too need to be protected as economic rights if artistic, creative and innovative activity in this area is to

7   See M Blakeney *Legal Aspects of the Transfer of Technology to Developing Countries* ESC Publishing (1989) at 53 and R Benko *Economic Theory and Intellectual Property Rights* (1987) at 16-17.

8   See Braunstein, Baumol and Mansfield 'The Economics of R & D' in B V Dean and J C Goldhar (eds) *Management of Research and Innovation* John Wiley & Sons (1980) 19–32.

9   See F M Scherer *Industrial Market Structure and Economic Performance* University of Chicago Press (1980) at 447.

10   See Grosheide 'Economic Aspects of Intellectual Property Rights, especially of Copyright' and Strowel 'An Appraisal of the Economic Analysis of Copyright Law' in M Van Hoecke *The Socio-Economic Role of Intelllectual Property Rights* Story-Scientia (1991) pp 65-72 and 103-135.

be promoted. There is however one essential difference with inventions and trade marks. The right involved here is a copyright whose subject matter is the particular expression in a literary work, in a piece of music, in a sculpture etc by the author of an idea. There is no direct link between the copyright and the idea embodied in the work. One can distinguish between a book and the ideas expressed in it, whereas an invention and the novel idea involved are one and the same inseparable concept.[11] The ideas contained in a work protected under copyright are on top of that not necessarily novel. It would not be possible to justify the protection of these ideas under the economic justification theory. Fortunately this is not necessary as copyright only protects the expression by the author of a certain set of ideas. These ideas themselves are not protected by copyright.

CURRENT ECONOMIC IMPORTANCE OF INTELLECTUAL PROPERTY

Our historical overview demonstrated that intellectual property rights were introduced because they were thought to be essential for further industrial and economic development. We will now try to analyse the current economic importance of intellectual property rights. It is suggested on the basis of indirect evidence that this importance is huge.

The recent GATT agreement contained the TRIPs initiative on intellectual property. This initiative was a reaction by the governments that were concerned by the complaints of industry. Figures pointing to multi-million dollar losses in royalties due to the counterfeiting of famous trade marks in countries which offered a low level of protection for intellectual property rights were published by industrial sources. One can understand and accept these figures on the basis that almost every product and almost every service nowadays bears a trade mark. In 1974 WIPO, the world intellectual property organisation, estimated that four million trade marks were in use in the world[12] and there is every reason to believe that there are more trade marks in use now than in 1974. The recent GATT agreement attaches great importance to the strengthening of the protection for trade marks and the other intellectual property rights, which clearly emphasises their tremendous economic value.

---

11   See R Benko *Protecting Intellectual Property Rights: Issues and Controversies* American Enterprise Institute for Public Policy Research (AEI Studies 453)(1987) Ch 4 at 21 and 23.

12   This figure is quoted by M Blakeney *Legal Aspects of the Transfer of Technology to Developing Countries* ESC Publishing (1989) at 113 with a reference to the UNCTAD report *The Role of Trade Marks in the Promotion of Exports from Developing Countries* (1981).

The evolution to an economic system based on high technological developments has resulted in the proliferation of patents. Many of these patents have an enormous commercial value. Just think about the whole evolution in the field of genetic engineering. These disease resistant plants, purified seeds and drugs produced by genetically engineered bacteria, all protected by patents, are the products of the future and the patentholders are cashing in. It is clear that there would be no incentive to invest huge resources in high technology research and developments if there was no prospect of recuperating the investment and obtaining a fair return on the investment on top of that if patent protection was not available, especially when one takes into account that not every research programme will lead to success. One should also not forget the vast number of patents granted for relatively slight improvements upon the existing technology. They may not grab the headlines, but they have a tremendous importance in industry as they allow the improver to appropriate the results of his work and gain a competitive edge over his or her competitors who would otherwise, in a majority of cases, be able to reverse engineer the improvement at a fraction of the original cost.

What about the economic importance of copyright? Just imagine the range of products covered: books, compact discs, movies, television broadcasts, computer programs etc. Copyright has become very wide in scope and a number of the new technological developments protected under copyright are of enormous commercial importance.

Add to that the business generated by the phenomenon of character merchandising which allows real and fictitious characters, such as pop stars and the likes of Popeye and Mickey Mouse, to earn more money by allowing others to market goods more easily because they are linked to these real or fictitious characters through a picture or a name than the amount they earn through their normal activities and you understand that the current economic importance of intellectual property is indeed huge. This is even more so because intellectual property is now involved in almost every aspect of our highly developed economic life with its strong emphasis on technological progress and brand names. Intellectual property is indeed pushed by market forces. One could even argue that the original presumption in favour of free competition and the perception of intellectual property rights as exceptional rights whose grant was only appropriate in cases of exceptional innovative and creative activity no longer exists. This point of view accepts that industry now presumes that intellectual property protection will be available for every new product and every new development and sees full-scale free competition as the exception.[13] It is clear that such a reversal of attitude cannot be encouraged unconditionally.

13 Merges 'The Economic Impact of Intellectual Property Rights: an Overview and Guide' conference paper delivered at the ICARE international conference on The Economics of Intellectual Property Rights, Venice, 6–8 October 1994.

INTERNATIONAL INTELLECTUAL PROPERTY CONVENTIONS

It has become clear in the course of this introduction that intellectual property is not necessarily exploited at a national level,[14] it is in fact exploited at a global level. Video cassettes and CDs which contain materials protected by copyright are marketed in an increasing number of countries. Patents in CD technology are exploited wherever a CD pressing plant is built. And the Coca-Cola trade mark is found on cans and bottles all over the world.

Inventors and creators would under these circumstances lose out if intellectual property regimes were completely different in each country. They would not get adequate protection and they would not be adequately rewarded for their work if intellectual property rights, based on the same principles and equally applicable to inventions and creations made abroad, were not available in each country in which the patent, trade mark or copyright is exploited. The whole economic justification theory would also collapse in such a case. A global economy presupposes a global intellectual property system.

Two types of international co-operation can be distinguished in this respect. First there are the treaties and conventions laying down minimum uniform provisions and standards of protection.[15] They recognise that each country will have its own intellectual property laws, but they harmonise the minimum standards and the basis underneath all these laws and they also secure protection under these laws for works of foreign inventors and creators or for works created abroad. Anti-counterfeiting initiatives are also part of this category, as they link in with global minimum standards of protection and their effective enforcement.

These treaties and conventions still require an inventor or creator to register in each country in which protection is sought. Only copyright, which, as we shall see, does not have a registration requirement, is an exception to this rule. The second category of treaties and conventions operates at this level. Many of them involve a single application and examination procedure or at least a certain level of co-operation between the national intellectual property authorities in this area. The more advanced types of measures provide for uniform provisions in the various national intellectual property laws or at least for a thorough harmonisation of these provisions. Many of these more advanced measures are found in Europe.[16]

---

14   All historical arguments refer to more than one country and the economic justification theory is not restricted to a particular national market.

15   This is of course a second best solution, but the best solution, uniform intellectual property laws, is clearly not available in practice.

16   It is also worth mentioning the initiatives taken by a large group of South-American countries, the Andean Group as they call themselves. It would lead us too far though to discuss these measures in this book, in which we are primarily concerned with UK and European law.

We will now give an overview of the various treaties, conventions and other measures.[17]

Patents

In the patent area the minimum international rules are found in the Paris Convention for the Protection of Industrial Property which was signed in 1883, but which has been updated by later Acts. The Convention has been implemented in the states adhering to the Convention by means of national Patent Acts. Over 100 states adhere to the Paris Convention. The impact of the Paris Convention was enlarged even further by the TRIPs Agreement. Article 2 of that agreement obliges all contracting states to comply with the main substantive provisions of the Paris Convention, even if they are not members of it. This guarantees a coverage that is virtually worldwide in scope, since very few countries will be able to afford staying outside the WTO administered system, of which TRIPs forms part. On top of that the TRIPs Agreement contains further and tighter substantive minimum rules in relation to patents in Articles 27 to 34.

Normally an applicant files a separate patent application in each country where he or she intends to work the invention or desires protection for it. This was felt to be a complicated procedure, because the details are different in each country, and a waste of time and effort. The Patent Co-operation Treaty (Washington 1970, PCT) provides for the filing of a single application and also provides a facility for a preliminary international search for the requirements for patentability. Only 50% of the member states of the Paris Convention adhere to the PCT.

Patents are also an important source of technological information. If the patent system is to fulfil this role adequately at an international level a uniform system of classification is necessary. An invention must also be new if a patent is to be granted for it. This can only be tested by means of a well-structured patent register. This classification system is contained in the Strasbourg Convention on the International Classification of Patents (Strasbourg 1971, IPC).

17   For the text of these instruments see P Torremans and J Holyoak *Butterworths Student Statutes: Intellectual Property Law* Butterworths (2nd edn, 1998) and J Phillips (Consultant ed) *Butterworths Intellcetual Property Law Handbook* Butterworths (3rd edn, 1997).

Trade marks

The minimum rules for trade marks are also contained in the Paris Convention. The TRIPs Agreement has added to that,[18] apart from requiring all its contracting states to comply with the substantive provisions of the Paris Convention.

The international exploitation of a trade mark is facilitated by the Madrid Agreement Concerning the International Registration of Marks (Madrid, 1892). Registration in one state that is a signatory to the Madrid Agreement gives a person the right to file a single application for registration in any other signatory country designated in the application. A separate application in each state is no longer required. Some states, including the UK, could not accept some of the provisions of the Madrid Agreement. They joined the system only through the Protocol to the Madrid Agreement, signed in Madrid in 1989. There are a number of differences on substance between the Agreement and the Protocol.[19] A further attempt to harmonise the procedural aspects of a trade mark application is made in the Trademark Law Treaty (Geneva, 1994).

A uniform classification system for trade marks, based on classes for goods and services and lists of goods and services that fall in each of the classes, is provided by the Nice Agreement Concerning the International Classification of Goods and Services for the Purposes of the Registration of Marks (Nice 1861, last revised in Geneva in 1977) and the Vienna Agreement Establishing an International Classification of the Figurative Elements of Marks (Vienna 1985). The latter deals with device marks.

Design rights

This is the third area covered by the Paris Convention and the TRIPs agreement. An industrial design can be deposited internationally and will attract protection in all member states of the Hague Agreement Concerning the Deposit of Industrial Design (The Hague, 1925). An international uniform classification for industrial designs was established in Locarno, in the Locarno Agreement Establishing an International Classification for Industrial Designs (in force since 1970).

---

18   Articles 15–21.
19   See infra in the Trade Marks chapters, see also Kunze 'The Protocol Relating to the Madrid Agreement Concerning the International Registration of Marks' [1992] 82 The Trademark Reporter No 1 and 'The Madrid System for the International Registration of Marks as Applied under the Protocol' [1994] 6 EIPR 223–226.

Copyright

The most important international convention in the copyright area is the Berne Convention for the Protection of Literary and Artistic Works (Berne 1886, latest Act is the Paris Act). This Convention is to copyright what the Paris Convention is to industrial property rights. A competing Universal Copyright Convention (Geneva 1952, revised at Paris in 1971, UCC) was promoted by UNESCO, but lost most of its importance when its most influential member state, the US, joined the Berne Convention. This effect is now reinforced by the fact that the TRIPs Agreement requires its Contracting States to comply with most of the provisions of the Berne Convention.[20] Further substantive provisions are found in Articles 9-14 of the TRIPs Agreement and yet further measures to take account of the new developments in copyright are found in the WIPO Copyright Treaty (Geneva, 1996),[1] which is closely linked to the Berne Convention as a special treaty under Article 20 of that Convention.

The rights of performers, recorders and broadcasting organisations required supplementary protection. In this respect the most important Convention is the Rome Convention for the Protection of Performers, Producers of Phonograms and Broadcasting Organisations (Rome 1961).[2] When it enters into force, the WIPO Performances and Phonograms Treaty (Geneva, 1996) will provide major improvements in this area.

All conventions, treaties, agreements and protocols described above are administered by the World Intellectual Property Organisation (WIPO) with headquarters in Geneva. International registrations are dealt with by its International Bureau. The UCC forms an exception to this system.

As part of the Uruguay Round of world trade negotiations, the GATT contracting states reached an agreement on the TRIPs initiative. Its aim was to impose worldwide minimum terms for the protection of intellectual property. This system does not replace the existing conventions, but it works in addition to them. It obliges those countries which do not yet protect intellectual property to introduce that protection if they do not want to be excluded from the world free trading system and from membership of the World Trade Organisation (WTO), which runs the system. The old system worked on an entirely voluntary basis. The standards of protection introduced by the TRIPs initiative are also slightly higher than the minimum standards contained in the old conventions, as was seen above.

---

20   Not with those on moral rights though: see Article 9.
1   This treaty is not yet in force.
2   We do not discuss plant variety rights in this book, please refer to the International Convention for the Protection of New Varieties of Plants (the UPOV Convention); in the biotechnology area the Budapest treaty on the International Recognition of the Deposit of Micro-organisms for the Purpose of Patent Procedure, in force since 1980, is also relevant.

■
EUROPEAN INITIATIVES

The creation of a single European market based on the principle of free competition required a further substantial harmonisation of intellectual property provisions. The rather loose international co-operation on a standard basis of minimal rules was not sufficient.

Patents

In Europe co-operation in the patent area was taken further. The European Patent Convention (Munich 1973, EPC) provides a system comprising a single patent application and search. This is carried out by the European Patent Office in Munich, which started working on 1 June 1978. At the end of the procedure the applicant is granted a bundle of national patents, one for each member state indicated in the application. The EPC is not an initiative of the European Union, other European Countries such as Switzerland and Liechtenstein adhere to it as well.

The European Community wanted to go further and replace the bundle of national patents at the end of the granting procedure by a single Community patent. This was the aim of the Community Patent Convention signed at Luxemburg in 1975.[3] The Convention is not yet in force because no agreement could yet be reached on a couple of practical details.[4] The Commission now plans to give the system a new chance. It has already published a Green Paper in order to get the discussion started.[5]

Other initiatives of the Community relate to pharmaceutical inventions and inventions relating to plant protection products where the term of protection was extended by means of the introduction of a Supplementary Protection Certificate for Pharmaceutical Products[6] and a Supplementary Protection Certificate for Plant Protection Products[7] and to biotechnological inventions.[8]

3   See Convention for the European Patent for the Common Market (Community Patent Convention) (1989) OJ L401/10.
4   Latest unsuccessful attempt to reach an agreement was made at an inter-governmental conference at Lisbon in July 1992.
5   COM (97) 314, Community patents and the patent system in Europe, adopted by the Commission on 24 June 1997.
6   EC Council Regulation 1768/92 concerning the creation of a supplementary protection certificate for medicinal products (1992) OJ L182/1.
7   EC Parliament and Council Regulation 1610/96 concerning the creation of a supplementary protection certificate for plant protection products (1996) OJ L198/30.
8   After a first attempt to get a Directive approved failed, the Commission made a second attempt. This lead to a Common Position being adopted on 26 February 1998 (1998) OJ C110. The Parliament gave its final approval to the Directive on 12 May 1998 and the member states will have two years from the date of publication of the Directive to bring their legislation in line with it.

At the lower end of the innovation scale some form of protection is planned for inventions that do not qualify for full patent protection. The utility model that is currently proposed should provide that protection. [9]

Trade marks

The Community acted on two levels. The national Trade Mark laws of the member states have been harmonised[10] and a Community Trade Mark has been created.[11] This latter system is in force since 1996, with far greater success than expected, and provides a single Trade Mark for the Community as a whole. The Community Trade Mark Office, which is officially called Office for Harmonisation in the Internal Market (trade marks and designs), is located in Alicante, Spain.

Industrial designs

The Community plans the same action in this area as the one taken in relation to trade marks: harmonisation of the national design laws and a single Community Design Right.[12] The Council and the Parliament had originally adopted very different positions in relation to the repair clause and the negotiations leading to the final drafts of both instruments had been particularly lengthy and cumbersome. At the time of writing a conciliation procedure had just produced a compromise that could see the Directive through if approved by the Council and the Parliament. It is understood that the compromise is acceptable to all parties and the Directive may be published before this book comes out. All further work on the Regulation seems to have been postponed until a compromise is found in relation to the Directive.

---

9   Draft European Parliament and Council Directive approximating the legal arrangements for the protection of inventions by utility model (1998) OJ C36, COM (97) 691 final; see infra chapter 2.

10   First Council Directive to approximate the laws of the Member States relating to trade marks (1989) OJ L40/1.

11   Council Regulation (EC) 40/94 on the Community Trade Mark (1994) OJ L11/1.

12   See the proposals for a European Parliament and Council Directive and a Regulation on the legal protection of designs (1993) OJ C345/14 and (1994) OJ C29/20, as well as the amended proposal for the Directive (1996) OJ C142/7 and Common Position 28/97 (1997) OJ C 237/1.

■

Copyright

The Community has up to now refrained from making an attempt to harmonise copyright as a whole. Only certain aspects of copyright, such as the term of copyright protection have been harmonised.[13]

A number of areas have received special attention: computer programs,[14] rental rights and lending rights,[15] satellite broadcasting and cable retransmission,[16] and databases[17]. And a new Directive to harmonise certain aspects of copyright and related rights in the Information Society has been proposed[18] as well as a Directive to harmonise the provisions on droit de suite[19]. The EC also plans to accede to the WIPO Copyright Treaty and the WIPO Performances and Phonograms Treaty[1].

Miscellaneous

The Community has also adopted measures in the areas of counterfeiting[2], topographies of semiconductor chips[3] and comparative advertising[4]. A Directive dealing with the legal protection of conditional access services is expected to be adopted in the near future[5].

---

13   EC Council Directive 93/98 harmonising the terms of protection of copyright and certain related rights (1993) OJ L290/9.
14   Council Directive 91/250 on the legal protection of computer programs (1991) OJ L122/42.
15   Council Directive 92/100 on rental rights and lending rights related to copyright in the field of intellectual property (1992) OJ L346/61.
16   Council Directive 93/83 on the co-ordination of certain rules concerning copyright and rights related to copyright applicable to satellite broadcasting and cable retransmission (1993) OJ L248/15.
17   Parliament and Council Directive 96/9 on the legal protection of databases (1996) OJ L77/20.
18   COM (97) 628 final, 10 December 1997.
19   (1996) OJ C178/16
1   See COM (97) 193.
2   Council Regulation 3842/86 laying down measures to prohibit the release for free circulation of counterfeit goods (1986) OJ L357/1, now replaced by Council Regulation 3295/94 laying down measures to prohibit the release for free circulation, export, re-export or entry for a suspensive procedure of counterfeit and pirated goods (1994) OJ L341/8.
3   Parliament and Council Directive 97/55 amending Directive 84/450 on misleading advertising (1997) OJ L290/18.
4   (1997) OJ C314/7; Conditional access services are typically only available through the use of a decoder or upon payment of a fee. The number of these services that is available on the internet is increasing rapidly.
5   Council Directive 87/54 on the legal protection of topographies of semiconductor products (1987) OJ L24/36.

AN OVERVIEW

Intellectual property rights play an important role in economic life in this age of technological innovation. Their existence can be justified on an economic basis, with other factors offering further support. Intellectual property rights are also international in character and in that respect they fit in rather well with the economic reality of the global economy. We now turn to the detailed examination of each of the separate intellectual property rights.

Section B

Patents

Chapter 2

Origin and background of the patent system

The longest standing, best known and, arguably, economically most valuable form of protection of rights by the law of intellectual property comes in the form of the patent. A patent is in essence the grant of a monopoly to an inventor who has used his skill to invent something new. The monopoly is not absolute; patents are only granted for a limited period and are accompanied by public disclosure enabling others in the field to consider and perhaps subsequently improve on it. Each year tens of thousands of patents are granted creating a monopoly right within the UK alone and they may cover a whole range of different types of subject matter, though it is fair to note that the level of patenting activity in the UK seems much greater than in many major industrial nations. They may cover entirely new products or, more often, enhancements to pre-existing products or they may cover a new or an improved process for performing an activity. A legal structure has been created to cover all these variants, elegant in its simplicity but complex in its operation. However, before we explore the detail of its ramifications, we must explore its origins and purpose and the background to and sources of the modern law of patents.

HISTORY

It will be seen shortly that patent law has a very distinct European dimension. So it is only appropriate to begin with the origins of patent law which are found in Europe. The German miners of the Alps seem to have been first to develop the notion of monopoly rights in their new processes as far back as the thirteenth century,[1] but the first more universal patent

1   Wegner *Patent Harmonisation* Sweet & Maxwell (1993) pp 2-3.

scheme evolved in Venice, then at the height of its international power, in a Decree of 1474 which rewarded inventors of new objects with a limited monopoly on condition that the invention was disclosed to the state, a model in its essentials still followed by the patent system five centuries later. It has been argued[2] that the earliest example of a patent being granted to an inventor in England, by Queen Elizabeth I, was to one Acontius, an inventor from Italy who had been granted one of the earliest Venetian patents but had fled to England for religious reasons.

However patents at this period were often not a reward for invention but a reward for royal supporters and patents were granted simply so as to reward loyalty with monopoly. Such abuses of power could not be countenanced by the courts, as was finally shown in *Darcy v Allin*.[3] A patent had been granted conferring a 14-year monopoly in the entire trade in playing cards and was not upheld on the grounds that it conferred an unreasonable monopoly; it was accepted that patents could be granted for new trades and inventions, however, on the grounds that there was a public benefit in the form of whatever advantages the new development conferred;[4] there was no such benefit on the facts of this case.

Against the background of the changing roles of monarch and legislature at this period in history, Parliament also decided to flex its muscles in relation to the grant of monopolies. It passed the Statute of Monopolies 1624 which, while seeking generally to stamp out monopolies, expressly allowed their retention in favour of inventors in respect of inventions of new methods of manufacture who were allowed a 14-year maximum period to exploit their creation, subject to certain protections for the public interest.

It may be that the essence of the modern patent can be traced back to this law, but this cannot be said in respect of the system for gaining a patent. The grant remained an exercise of the Royal Prerogative and only very slowly, as the number of patents sought increased against the background of the developing Industrial Revolution, did clear rules and formalities begin to make their appearance in the eighteenth century, with a requirement of a written specification coming in at this period. From the chaos of informality, the burgeoning bureaucracy and ever greater demand for patents produced a different chaos, the chaos of sclerosis, and it became clear eventually that steps had to be taken to reform and regularise the system lest it threaten the then dominance in world trade enjoyed by the UK. This finally was achieved by the Patent Law Amendment Act 1852, greatly simplifying the system – the existence of the Patent Office dates from the appointment of Patent Commissioners this time – but also greatly liberalising the criteria for patentability. Perhaps this made obtaining a

2   Phillips (1982) 3 J Leg Hist 71.
3   (1602) Noy 173, 74 ER 1131.
4   Ibid at 183 and 1139.

patent too easy. The next landmark was the Patents, Designs and Trade Marks Act 1883 which set up as such the Patent Office and empowered it to investigate applications to weed out those which did not meet the official criteria and (after the Patents Act 1902) investigate whether the subject matter of the patent was truly novel. Of course there was tinkering by Parliament over the years but the basic system then in place continued until the Patents Act 1977 which made significant changes to the system to reflect the growing internationalisation of the world of patents which will be noted later.

PURPOSE

The long history of patents and the remarkable consistency that has lain as a strand through that history from the earliest times to the present day of common ideas and principles suggests that strong forces led to the creation of the law and those forces have remained in place ever since. What then are the factors which have shaped the law of patents? What purposes does it fulfil?

To answer these questions it is best to consider the often competing interests of those involved with the patent system. Looked at first from the standpoint of the actual inventor, the traditional assumption is that what is going on is the grant of a reward to him for all the skill and hard work that has gone into the invention. There is much to be said for this; undoubtedly some inventors carry out their work with the future benefits which it will confer on them very much in mind; large firms can justify their research and development staff to their accountants and thus to their shareholders with reference to the future rewards that will be gained. However, this is too simplistic to be regarded as an acceptable universal solution. Some inventors receive no reward because their invention is not a commercial success or if they do not have the resources to exploit it effectively. Little commercial benefit is likely to have flowed from the invention of jet engines for aeroplanes since years were to pass before aircraft construction technology caught up. Indeed, the number of successful applications for patents which give rise to a fully exploitable commercial product or process is believed to be a small fraction of the total amount though this may be a consequence of the ethos and financial structure of the industrial sector generally rather than a criticism of the patent system as such. Does industry generally want to take what is inevitably a risk when failure might be at the expense of shareholder's dividends (and, cynically, directors' fees)? The relationship between small-scale inventors who cannot afford to exploit an invention themselves and other larger firms who may be rivals in the same trade or companies primarily interested in providing venture capital in the expectation of a return is bound in either case to be a fraught one. Many inventors receive no reward because they lose the race to patent their product; this is often the case in respect of pharmaceutical products where a new problem will be seized upon by all the major firms, all of whom will race to get an answer in the form of a new or improved drug on to the market but where, this being a 'first past the post' race, there will only be one winner. The quest for an effective viable drug to combat the AIDS virus is a classic example. The link between invention and reward has always seemed tenuous. Arkwright's important 'Spinning Jenny' may have been a key ingredient in the Industrial Revolution but was refused a patent[5] while Watt's steam engine needed special legislation before it was regarded as patentable.

Other inventors are not in the game to seek a reward. The public image of the typical inventor as a bumbling pseudo-scientist working away in his potting shed in an attempt to create a perpetual motion machine may be far from the reality of most companies' R & D divisions, but such individuals do exist and are clearly not in the game for the money. Significant inventions such as the 'cats' eyes' that enhance road safety by marking the middle of the road, are from time to time created by enthusiastic individuals rather than businesses. It also appears that the 'post-it' type of gummed message label was devised by a choir member exasperated at the way traditional bookmarks fell out of his hymn book. More significantly much research is carried out by people motivated by a love of the subject, a quest for knowledge and a desire to push back the proverbial frontiers, for example in universities by academics.

Perhaps a more appropriate refinement is to suggest that at the least the patent system offers an incentive to invent. If reward is not guaranteed, at least there is a chance of it and it is there for the lone inventor and university professor too, if they choose to avail themselves of it, as they usually will. It may be best to regard the chance as, relatively, not a great one. If the risk of unexploited or unexploitable inventions is added to the problems created by the limited time in which the reward can be enjoyed and the loss of secrecy when the patent application is made, the grant of a patent is a distinctly double-edged reward.

In looking at the patent system from other standpoints, other possible views emerge. The state, or society, is the other key player as the grantor of the patent. The grant is not a generous act in the sense that the state is not giving up anything of its own; rather it simply sacrifices the interests of other traders. In so doing, however, the state makes major gains. Clearly society benefits from the improvement in transport, industry, health care or whatever that is conferred by the patent and, more intangibly, by the increase in knowledge created by the inventive process. Sometimes the state benefits more directly, for example by its ability to take over an invention

5   *R v Arkwright* (1785) 1 Web Pat Cas 64.

and prevent its use by others.[6] In a capitalist society too the increase in trade and wealth generated by the advances of the patent system are also important justifications for it. It may be queried in the light of all the developments of the Industrial Revolution occurring when patent protection was minimal, as the fates of Arkwright and Watt demonstrate, just how significant a role the patent system plays in the expansion of new industries, but this is perhaps a weaker argument now than then, given the need to provide legal protection for the huge investments many companies make in their R & D activity. All the factors clearly justify the state's involvement in the patent system and go far to explain the presence of a system in all developed and developing countries. However, taken on their own they may tend towards the over-generous grant of many patents, as in the UK after the 1852 legislation, yet this is not the norm in most patent systems today.

The reason for this lies in the interests of other parties, parties who are not directly involved in the grant of a patent but are closely and directly affected by it, and whose interests require a more cautious approach to the patentability question. The two obvious groups concerned here are consumers and trade rivals. The interest of consumers as a class is of course served by the invention of new products and processes but not if their inventor is able to take advantage of his monopoly position by abuse of it, for example by restricting supply or jacking up price. We have already argued that such potential rewards are not always there for the enjoyment of the inventor but the possibility clearly exists. Thus the monopoly is limited only to a set period and, should the inventor refuse to share the benefits thereof with society, there is also the compulsory licensing system.[7] Similar factors arise in relation to rival traders. Clearly a permanent monopoly, granted to an inventor would unduly distort the market; even a time-restricted monopoly distorts the market for that period, but the harm that may be caused thereby is diminished by the disclosure requirement, giving the rival trader the chance to experiment and develop the original concept into a patentable improvement.

Clearly no one interest group can shape the patent system. If there is a single justification or common purpose that underpins the system it must be the attainment of a balance between the different interests involved. The consumer wants new products – so grants patents readily – but not at any price – so restricts the scope of the monopoly. A business wants the advantage of monopoly as a reward – but not at any price – so insists on public disclosure as its price. Society wants increased trade and wealth – but not at any price – hence the various restrictions and limitations. In assessing the detail of the patent system in due course it will be useful to

6   Patents Act 1977, ss 22, 55-59. See Ch 4.
7   Patents Act 1977, s 48. See Ch 4.

reflect on which interests are being harmed or promoted by different aspects of the law and their contemporary interpretation.

UTILITY MODELS

Against this background some felt that the balancing of interests act left valuable smaller inventions unprotected. Maybe a new balance could be struck between on the one hand a weaker system of protection and exclusivity for less important innovations and on the other hand some restrictions on competition which society is prepared to accept in order to get hold of the full benefit of these innovations. So, there is now a further area of patent-related intellectual property activity that needs to be created. The utility model is perhaps best regarded as a 'baby patent'. It is a concept familiar across much of Europe and the EU Commission has proposed[8] that we would all benefit from the introduction (in the UK, Sweden and Luxembourg) and harmonisation (the other 12 have widely differing provisions in relation to basic definitions of their domestic utility models) of laws relating to utility models. It must be emphasised that this proposal, while part of the general drive towards the protection of the principle of free movement of goods by rationalising intellectual property law, is nevertheless at an early stage and it is not obvious whether or when the UK will enjoy the provision of a utility model.

Definition

As its bland name implies, the utility model is not easy to define. It may be most easily described as a form of right similar to a patent in that the usual requirements of novelty, inventive step and industrial applicability need to be present, but the key difference is that the level of inventiveness is lower than in the case of a 'full patent'. The EU Commission propose[9] that the inventor needs to show that the invention offers particular effectiveness in terms, for example, of ease of application or of use, or confers a practical or industrial advantage. Clearly this may well not amount to what seems like the giant leap into the unknown that at times it seems is necessary for the purposes of the patent legislation. So if the invention is a better way of doing something rather than a radically different way or an improvement whereby

---

8   Com (97) 691, 97/0356 (COD). See Suthersanen 'A Brief Tour of Utility Model Law' [1998] EIPR 45. Proposal for a European Parliament and Council Directive approximating (1998) OJ C36 the legal arrangements for the protection of inventions by utility model.

9   Article 6 of the draft Directive.

the same process works in the same general way but with greater efficiency and/or profitability then it is the utility model that offers a way forward in the future, assuming its introduction into UK law.

All inventions must be new, involve such an inventive step and be susceptible of industrial application. But, aesthetic creations, presentations of information, discoveries, scientific theories, mathematical methods, as well as schemes, rules and methods for performing mental games, playing games or doing business, are considered to fall outside the scope of the concept of 'inventions'.[10] An invention that can be made or used in any kind of industry, including agriculture, will be considered as susceptible to industrial application.[11]

Rationale

Let us say by way of analogy that we all enjoy travelling by sea for leisure. What could be better than a cruise around the world on the liner 'Queen Elizabeth II'. Reality soon rears its ugly head. Examinations of bank balance and diary alike rapidly demonstrate that this will only ever be an ambition. However there is still hope of pleasure on the sea if time and money permit a day cruise from Glasgow down the Firth of Clyde instead. Likewise the patent system is not for all. The cost of obtaining a suitable patent and the time it takes to register it from the initial priority date render this 'luxury' intellectual property right inappropriate in many cases, especially for small businesses. Thus there is a clear need to have a lesser right and the Commission's proposal, based on a middle way through the different domestic approaches. If implemented the idea would be that, with an investigation of only the formalities of the application for utility model, the right should be conferred within six months of the initial application. Equally this protection would then only last for six years, though with the possibility of two short extensions.[12] Within this restricted period similar protection would be enjoyed by the rightholder to that given to the patentee. Utility models that cover a product will confer the exclusive right to make, use, sell, offer for sale or import for these purposes the product on the proprietor of the right. Utility models that cover a process will confer on their proprietor the exclusive right to use the process and to use, offer for sale, sell or import for these purposes at least the product directly obtained by that process. However, acts done for private and non-commercial

10 Article 3 of the draft Directive.
11 Article 7 of the draft Directive.
12 Article 19 of the draft Directive.

purposes, as well as acts done for experimental purposes relating to the subject-matter of the protected invention will not infringe.[13]

However it is easy to overestimate the apparent disadvantage of the short term of protection. Whereas the motivation behind the supplementary protection certificate is to extend protection in particular cases, the utility model may have particular value in instances where the present patent term is unnecessarily long and the long wait for registration potentially detrimental. The 'shelf-life' of many inventions is now much less than 20 years, especially perhaps in relation to the kind of relatively minor improvements under consideration here. The Commission refers to the toy industry, watch manufacture, optics and microtechnology as areas where it is felt that there is demand for the utility model. Overall, it claims, the average lifetime of an invention is less than six years.

There may also be an overlap between patents and utility models 'The same invention may form the subject-matter, simultaneously or successively, of a patent application and a utility model application.'[14]

Do we need it?[15]

'Yes' is the simple answer. The arguments above demonstrate a clear niche where utility models provide a cheap and cheerful form of protection where the full patent would be uneconomic. It is also clear from figures in the Commission's report that in some countries utility model applications are as numerous as patent applications, though it must be said that the precise proportion varies from state to state depending on the relative level of protection afforded by the two rights. A final argument in favour of protection of rights via the utility model route in the UK is simply that this route is available almost every where else in Europe and that, therefore, in its absence, UK industry is at a relative disadvantage.

That said, the joys of utility model protection are not unalloyed. The cost argument is perhaps overplayed since the main cost incurred by the rightseeker is professional advice, whether a patent or a utility model right is sought.[16] The definitional problem of what is meant by the lower level of inventiveness required remains at present vague and can in all probability only be resolved in due course by expensive litigation. Finally there is also a risk that this low-level protection of patent-type rights will cut across separate provisions protecting know-how/information rights and,

---

13   Article 20 of the draft Directive.
14   Article 22(1) of the draft Directive.
15   Llewelyn 'Is there a need for a European Utility Model? A view from the UK' (1997) 31 Annales de la Faculté de Droit d'Istanbul 1.
16   Llewelyn (1997) 31 Annales de la Faculté de Droit d'Istanbul 1.

conceivably, even trade marks and other image rights. These are all issues which will need to be considered before utility model protection is taken on board.

Summary

At present there is no domestic utility model protection. But, at some stage, there will be. Market forces or, perhaps more precisely, single market forces, will see to that. The value of the proposed right is self-evident, but so are the serious problems which remain to be resolved.

THE INTERNATIONAL DIMENSION

It is self evident that trade between nations can be affected by the existence in each nation of differing intellectual property regimes. If I develop a new product in the UK and gain patent protection for it at the very least it will be inconvenient if I cannot extend my business into France because someone else has succeeded in gaining a monopoly there. It will be equally awkward for my French counterpart, of course, if he seeks to expand into my market. The more international trade there is, the more of a problem it becomes, especially when that trade is taking place in what purports to be a common market, such as that created between the members of the European Union, with free trade without any national interference as its core.

Inevitably cries have long been heard clamouring for greater levels of harmonisation in domestic patent law (and other aspects of intellectual property too) between trading nations. Such cries long predate the Treaty of Rome, but equally have tended to emanate from Europe. The culmination of the first round of patent harmonisation came with the agreement known as the Paris Industrial Property Convention 1883, the main feature of which was that each signatory state had to offer the same treatment to all within that jurisdiction irrespective of nationality thus, to revert to the earlier example, enabling me to file my patent application in France knowing that the dispute between me and my French counterpart will be dealt with fairly on a footing of equal treatment. A common priority date (ie from when protection runs) also applied as between all signatory states. Slowly the web of co-operation broadened. The USA did not accept the 1883 Convention not least because of different approaches to the priority date but after the Convention was amended in 1890 in Brussels, the USA became a signatory to it.[17] Slowly further conventions extended the scope of co-operation and the numbers of countries involved in it, but it would be wrong to see the

17   *Wegner*, p 22.

Paris Convention as a harmoniser of substantive law; rather it is best seen as a way of facilitating procedural compatibility between the patent systems of signatory nations.

The next level of international agreement saw an attempt to ease the burden placed on a patentee by having to claim patent protection separately in each jurisdiction. This came to fruition in the form of the Washington Patent Co-operation Treaty 1970 which sets up a system of international patent applications, overseen by WIPO, the World Intellectual Property Organisation, an international body. The system allows for a single application to be made which, if successful, will give patent protection in those signatory states where protection is sought by the applicant. There is provision for either or both of an international search of other patents and a preliminary examination of the claim made. What there is not is an international definition of patentability; it remains a domestic matter as to whether the criteria of patentability are reached by an application. This scheme is not without its value with thousands of applications made each year. The main problem with it, and with much else in patent law, is its limited basis of both accessibility and acceptability.

Less than half of the world's countries and territories participate in the scheme (97 at the last count in June 1998). This may sound more damaging than it is, given that most major developed countries active in world trade and in innovation, with a developed patent system, are there amongst them. It raises, however, the problem of whether worldwide patent law is ever likely to be feasible, given the different levels of development, innovatory capacity and legal systems found around the world. What is appropriate for France or Germany may not play well in Burkina Faso or Papua New Guinea or in more significant cases, countries in the Far East such as Thailand which until recently have taken a distinctly relaxed view of their international obligations in respect of intellectual property rights.

This remains an important issue. Extensive discussion has taken place as part of the Uruguay Round of GATT negotiations with a view to creating a broader international level of protection for patents and other intellectual property rights. This is a path paved with difficulty, however, especially for countries such as India who have consciously developed their patent law to reflect local rather than Western conditions and who are faced with the need to return to a more mainstream approach to patent law as a result of the GATT negotiations, this prospect leading to violent demonstrations in the streets, a rare case of public disorder being occasioned by patent law reform. But the alleged effect on India's burgeoning industrial sector justifies such concern.

In the light of all this, it is perhaps unsurprising that the most successful and, in terms of its impact on domestic patent law, the most significant move towards integration of patent law has come amongst the relatively homogenous nations of Europe (though the homogenousness can be exaggerated; for example the Netherlands between 1869 and 1912 had no patent system whatsoever).[18] It is significant to note at the outset that these developments fall outside the ambit of the European Union, although closely associated with it, dating from the time when the UK was a major trading country outside the Treaty of Rome.

The search for a common European concept of the patent led to the signing in Munich in 1973 of the European Patent Convention which established the European Patent Office which has, since 1978, offered to applicants a European Patent in effect. This is achieved by signatory states agreeing to harmonise their own patent law with the definition in the European Patent Convention – hence the 1977 Patents Act in the UK – and the European Patent Office then awarding patents in all member states where the applicant has sought to acquire patent protection.

This system has proved to be a considerable success. Applicants have shown a marked trend to seek the broader protection provided by the EPO to the extent that over 70% of all applications seeking patent protection in Britain are now routed via the EPO in Munich, rather than through the domestic Patent Office, reflecting graphically the international nature of both trade in general and innovation in particular. The system slowly extends its ambit; all the EU states are now within the scheme along with other states such as Switzerland.

Its significance and far reaching impact on the law of the UK is perhaps best shown by section 130(7) of the Patents Act 1977. This declares that most key sections of the legislation are framed so as to have

'the same effect in the UK as the corresponding provisions of the European Patent Convention, the Community Patent Convention and the Patent Co-operation Treaty.'

In the light of this it is clearly appropriate for the courts to consider not only those agreements but also interpretations of them. In practice this means that domestic litigation can and does make use of decisions of the EPO as to interpretation of key phrases common to the Convention and the 1977 legislation.

There is, however, one further level of co-operation. Following the 1973 Convention further discussion took place with a view to setting up a single European Community Patent. This was separate from the EPO's harmonisation work, because differences between member states at that time meant that it was easier to offer a measure of harmonisation of the law between those countries prepared to proceed than to impose a single patent law on all member states. However, as far back as 1975 the Community

---

18   *Wegner*, p 17.

Patent Convention was agreed,[19] although agreement on its implementation has still to be reached. Indeed the Commission is in the process of suggesting that the Convention be both amended and extended so, if this view is taken, we will doubtless have to wait another couple of decades before there will be a Community patent. Now that EU states have harmonized their laws, however, it should be easier to reach a common agreement.

If or when such an agreement is reached there will be one clear benefit in making an application for the Community patent, namely that a single application (made to the EPO who will, it is proposed, administer the scheme) will result in a single patent conferring protection throughout the member states. Whether this is a benefit worth the expenditure of so such time, heat and energy is perhaps more questionable given the two alternative systems already in existence. But, in time, a clear picture will emerge enabling the patentee to select whichever option is appropriate to his resources and trading pattern.

The domestic system will remain, and will provide domestic protection; the EPO's present system will remain if protection is sought either in a limited number of EU states (applicants select which countries they wish to have protection in often choosing all signatories) and/or in relation to those states who are signatories to the Convention but not EU members, while the Community patent will eventually automatically confer protection in all the Union's member states. For the sake of completeness it should also be remembered that the WIPO procedures established under the Washington Patent Co-operation Treaty also remain, allowing an application for patents protection more widely again, beyond the frontiers of geographical or united Europe.

Our discussion henceforth will be focused on the British Patents Act of 1977, but it will be appreciated that due to the EPO's harmonisation requirement which was the raison d'être for the legislation the same principles govern the application for a domestic patent, an EPO patent, or the future Community patent, and the same very broad principles will be significant features in an application made under the provisions of the Washington Treaty.

OBTAINING A PATENT

This is not a book designed to give full instructions on the practicalities of applying for a patent. However the substantive law and in particular some of the problems it poses for applicants are shaped by the way the procedures operate so it is therefore appropriate to begin our survey of the substantive

---

19   (1976) OJ L17/1.

law by providing an outline of the key steps to be taken in pursuit of a domestic patent.

The first vital point to establish is the priority date of the applicant's invention. The essence of a patent is that it is something new which has not existed hitherto, and so it is vital to establish a priority date ahead of anyone else in the field, particularly if in a typical patent race where rival firms are pursuing the same or a similar line of research. The relevant date is the date of filing the application for a patent;[20] the only exception is where an earlier date is claimed, being a previous application within the past year which discloses matter which supports the subsequent application.[1] This priority date is important; not only does it establish priority over any rival applications from the date, it also sets the clock running for the period of validity of the patent itself.

Given that the priority date is the date on which the application is filed, the next issue to consider is what acts amount to a filing. This is defined in section 15(1) of the Patents Act and the vital elements which are needed are the presentation to the Patent Office of documents which indicate that a patent is being sought, which identify the applicant for the patent, which contain a description of the invention and which, naturally, are accompanied by the appropriate fee.

These acts together create the filing date, but beg a vital question. When should an inventor time his filing date? If he files at too early a stage of the development of his invention there is a risk that in subsequent examination by the Patent Office or later revocation proceedings instigated by a rival the invention will be found not to fulfil the precise requirements of the law for patentability. On the other hand, the earlier that a claim is filed, the better placed the inventor is as against his rivals in a patent race, especially since the state of the art against which the novelty of the invention is judged is that pertaining at the date of filing the application.[2]

Some assistance is given by the law which helps to support a decision to apply earlier rather than later. The requirements of section 15 are really very minimal and considerably understate the true amount of documentation which will be required by the Patent Office. Indeed the section hints at this by stating that after a period of twelve months,[3] the application will be deemed to have been withdrawn unless the claims and abstract have been submitted by then.[4] This in effect gives the applicant a year's leeway to get from the minimalist position at the date of filing to finalising the detail of the application before it is formally examined during

---

20   Patents Act 1977, s 5 (1).
1   Patents Act 1977, s 5 (2).
2   Patents Act 1977, s 2 (2). See Ch 3.
3   Patents Rules, SI 1995/2093, r 25.
4   Patents Act 1977, s 15(5).

which period it is protected by having a priority date to use against other subsequent applications.

What then are these all-important claims and abstract which must form part of the application? A starting-point is section 14 of the Act which states that every application shall contain the following elements, namely a request for a patent to be granted, a specification containing a description of the invention, a claim and an abstract of it (though the position of other documents which still comply with section 15(1) is reserved and these may also initiate an application). The vital elements are the specification and claim (the abstract simply being a help to later searchers through the files of the Patent Office) with the claim being supported by the description.

The reason why they are vital is that the specification and claims form the basis of the invention applied for and thus delimit its scope. Precise drafting of them is important since any subsequent litigation, whether on patentability, infringement or revocation is bound to be very closely concerned with what the true basis of the invention is. Statutory guidance is given as to the broad nature of these two crucial components in a patent application. By section 14(3)

> 'the specification of an application shall disclose the invention in a manner which is clear enough and complete enough for the invention to be performed by a person skilled in the art,'

while section 14(5) establishes that the claim shall define the matter for which patent protection is sought, be clear and concise, be supported by the description and relate to either one invention or a related group of inventions.

In practice the level of detail that goes into these documents, particularly the specification, is quite significant. The specification has in effect to contain instructions for someone other than the inventor, though skilled in the art, to reproduce the invention, and so the fullest information should be given for this purpose, since if the specification was found to be unworkable no patent will be granted. Likewise, the claims are so-called because they delimit the extent of the monopoly that is being claimed, so it is essential to include as many different aspects of the new invention as possible. These documents are easier to read than to describe; extensive extracts from them appear in many reports of patent litigation; two examples which have the added advantage of being in relation to ordinary (ie non-scientific) subject matter are *Procter and Gamble Co v Peaudouce (UK) Ltd*[5](nappies) and *AC Edwards Ltd v Acme Signs and Displays Ltd*[6](petrol price indicators).

---

5   [1989] FSR 180.
6   [1992] RPC 131.

Again in this area practical difficulties are quickly placed in the way of the applicant. It is apparent from the foregoing that in terms of gaining and retaining patent protection the fullest information possible should be provided for the specification and claims. For other reasons, however, it is tempting to provide as little information as possible. Remember that a key aspect of the patent system is public disclosure of the patent, so the more information provided to the Patent Office the more information is also provided to trade rivals. Also, the longer the time spent in checking and testing that procedures work or in adding additional claims the greater the likelihood is that a trade rival may jump in first and claim patent protection for himself. In fairness the latter point is somewhat tempered by the fact that amendments may be allowed during the application procedure, though not so as to extend the protection of the patent.[7] Typically an amendment may consist either of a refinement of an aspect of the specification or claim within its terms as research work continues, or may be a withdrawal of some aspect of the protection sought, in the light perhaps of new evidence of the prior state of the art becoming available. It is even possible to seek an amendment of the patent after its grant[8] which may be useful to pre-empt a threat of revocation by another.

Returning to the steps necessary to be taken in order to gain a patent, on receipt of all the information furnished by the applicant the Patent Office will conduct a search amongst other patents – records of all patents are held – with a particular view to a provisional assessment of the application's novelty and obviousness, two vital factors in deciding whether it is patentable. After this takes place, assuming of course that the applicant has not been deterred by the experience, publication of the application then takes place no more than 18 months after the priority date. This is again an important point in the tactics of patent application and opposition. From the time of publication the information in the application is obviously in the public domain; this is good for the applicant in that he will now be able to establish clearly that he has won any race to patent the invention and can claim damages for infringement from this time onwards, but bad news because rivals are now able to find out about his invention and so can, variously, seek to go beyond it by developing it further, consider issues of revocation and/or infringement or, most immediately, decide to register an objection to the grant of a patent; interested parties have a right to submit observations as to patentability during the next stage of the patent procedure.[9]

The Patent Office will now proceed to a full examination of all aspects of the patent application with ample opportunity for the applicant to

7   Patents Act 1977, ss 19 and 76(2)(b).
8   Patents Act 1977, s 27. See also s 75.
9   Patents Act 1977, s 21.

contribute his own observations to the process. Obviously the time that this will take varies enormously from case to case, depending on the problems which arise, including possible section 21 representations by third parties. However, the domestic legislation stipulates a maximum period of four and a half years from the filing date (or any earlier appropriate priority date).[10] It may seem harsh that at that time the application is deemed to have been refused unless of course an appeal is pending,[11] but since one may be made against the deemed refusal,[12] no great hardship is wrought.

So after four and a half years (usually a little less) a patent can be granted by the relevant Patent Office. This has the effect of creating a proprietary right in the patentee,[13] one which exists for 20 years, subject to the payment of a fee for renewal after the first five years have passed.[14] However it is significant to note that the 20 year period is calculated not from the grant of the patent itself but from the date on which the application is filed, which we have just seen will be up to four and a half years earlier. This may seem on the restrictive side representing around a 20% loss of usable exploitation time for the patent.

In fact the trend has been slowly to lengthen the term of patent protection. The 1883 Act only offered 14 years from the date of filing while the 1939 Act stretched this to 16 years, the current period stemming from the EPC and the 1977 legislation. In fairness too during the period between filing and grant much preparatory work can be done to get the patent ready for the market and there is protection against others in this period. That said, there may be some substance to complaints from industries such as the pharmaceutical trade who can point to the fact that even after the grant of a patent more time will be lost not only by the usual final preparations for marketing the launch of a new product common to all industries but also the further delays that result from the need to comply with the rigorous testing requirements that have to be undergone by new products. However, it does not seem likely that the 20-year period is likely to be extended any further for now except in particular areas such as pharmaceuticals; the EPC was amended in 1991 to permit such extensions, subject to the ratification by signatories following the lead already set by the USA and Japan. It may be doubted whether this ratification will occur in the near future.[15] In addition this problem has to an extent been alleviated by the idea of the Supplementary Protection Certificate which can in limited circumstances extend the period of protection for medical products and which is considered

10   Patents Act 1977, s 20; Patents Rules, SI 1995/2093, r 34.
11   Patents Act 1977, s 20(1).
12   Patents Act 1977, s 97.
13   Patents Act 1977, s 30.
14   Patents Act 1977, s 25.
15   Adams 'Supplementary Protection Certificates: The Challenge to EC Regulation 1768/92' [1994] 8 EIPR 323 at 326.

separately in Chapter 6. This point is of course relevant to the previous discussions about the incentive to invent provided by the patent system. Until the argument from the drug firms was accepted it could be argued the battle to gain a monopoly would only bear a result for a little over a decade, which suggests that general profits from sales rather than the extra profits from monopoly sales may be just as much of an inducement.

Whether a valuable asset or not, the volume of litigation arising from the process of awarding a patent suggests that it is seen to be, and the way in which the law has created such a thorough system/ordeal before a patent is granted tends to assist the development of such a perception. The fact that a proprietary right is being created is perhaps some justification for the elaborate procedures involved, but hardly reflects the relative ease whereby trade marks and copyright can be acquired. Perhaps a better justification is that the criteria issued by the law in deciding the issue of patentability are not easy to use, reflecting the difficulty encountered in translating an abstract concept such as an invention into black and white legal principles. However these are issues that need to be considered in the light of the substantive rules that now follow and the whole area can be overviewed in Chapter 7. It is more than time to turn to consider the criteria used in the patentability assessment.

Chapter 3

Patentability

Few things appear simpler in patent law than the basic definition of patentability. According to section 1(1) of the 1977 Act (based on Article 52 of the EPC):

> 'A patent may be granted only for an invention in respect of which the following conditions are satisfied, that is to say:
> (a) the invention is new;
> (b) it involves an inventive step;
> (c) it is capable of industrial application;
> (d) the grant of a patent for it is not excluded by subsections (2) and (3) below;
> and references in this Act to a patentable invention shall be construed accordingly.'

Section 1(2) goes on to make clear that discoveries, scientific theories and mathematical methods cannot be regarded as inventions and are thus not patentable; likewise barred from this status are works properly found within copyright, schemes for performing a mental act, playing a game or doing business and computer programs, and also the presentation of information. Section 1(3) also limits the role of patents by denying their protection to offensive, immoral or anti-social inventions and also for any animal, plant or biological process. So the discovery in a tropical jungle of a new curative drug, or the development of a new relaxant but unlawful drug cannot be patented even if all the section 1(1) requirements are met.

All these different points will require clarification and elucidation; many have been the subject of extensive litigation and resultant case law. Our methodology will be simply to examine each aspect in turn so as to build up an overall picture of what the law will regard as matter appropriate for a successful patent application – what in other words will come within the legal definition of the concept of an invention. As will be seen later the meaning of 'invention' itself has to be given some consideration but initially we will approach the issue of patentability through the elements declared by section 1(1) to make up the overall concept. As a warning it should be said that the key concepts tend to overlap and discussion in many leading cases covers more than one closely related aspect.

NOVELTY

Most laymen would understand that an invention is something new and the law reflects this. The way in which section 2(1) of the 1977 Act expresses this is to say that 'an invention shall be new if it does not form part of the state of the art', so the reward (if such it be) of a patent goes to those who have gone beyond pre-existing knowledge, whether by creating a new product not previously available on the market or by developing a process not hitherto available and either to manufacture or in the provision of service. (The Act for the most part does not distinguish between patents for products and those for processes.)

The basic definition of novelty obviously begs the question as to what matter is regarded as forming part of the state of the art. Section 2(2) helps:

> 'The state of the art in the case of an invention shall be taken to comprise all matter (whether a product, a process, information about either, or anything else) which has at any time before the priority date of that invention been made available to the public (whether in the UK or elsewhere) by written or oral description, by use or in any other way.'

Clearly the state of the art is broadly defined and represents a major hurdle for the patent applicant. Several points need to be emphasised in considering what information forms part of the state of the art and what effect it has on the later patent application. An obvious point is that the key date is the priority date, and applications made after that date cannot form part of the state of the art by definition not anticipating the plaintiff's application. Particular problems arise however in relation to patents which have been applied for on an earlier date, but have not yet been published. It may seem harsh for something which is inherently not available to the public to be nevertheless regarded as part of the state of the art but to allow the later applicant to proceed would lead to a very high risk of 'double patenting', that is two people having exclusive patent rights in respect of the same thing which is of course a complete contradiction in terms. Accordingly section 2(3) establishes that for the purpose of assessing the state of the art for an invention material in subsequently published patent applications is included, so long as the priority date of that application is earlier than the priority date of the invention in question, and this is so even if the actual material in the subsequently published specification was not filed until after the priority date of the invention in question. The EPO in applying this rule will only consider those applications that have been made in respect of the same states.[1] A harsh rule, perhaps, but a clear rule which promotes certainty and in a patent race is an inducement to make an application sooner rather than later. The only potential dent in the rule comes from the *Asahi* case considered later.

The next problem is created by the widening of the relevant prior information that makes up the state of the art to include any material available to the public anywhere. Availability to the public is not too difficult an issue, at least in the sense that a clear line can usually be drawn between public and private circulation of information. An internal company document is clearly private, but publication of a research paper in a learned journal, even one of some obscurity, clearly places its contents into the public domain. This is particularly so in respect of any publication in the UK, copies of which must be sent to the British Library and normally to the other five so-called copyright libraries, in Oxford, Cambridge, Edinburgh, Aberystwyth and Dublin.[2]

Borderline cases on the public/private divide have been the subject of some litigation. It is clear that internal documentation may become public by its subsequent use; this is clear from *Monsanto Co (Brignac's) Application*[3] where a patent was being sought for a process for colouring nylon. This was successfully opposed on the grounds that 30 or 40 copies of a brochure giving information about the process had been given out to salesmen employed by the patentees and these in turn, it was expected, would be passed on to potential customers and so amounted to prior publication. This decision may seem to make advance publicity and prior contact with potential customers a risky business and it is clearly safer to wait until after the priority date. However, this is not essential as shown by *Pall Corp v Commercial Hydraulics (Bedford) Ltd*[4] where a new membrane could be patented in spite of an earlier demonstration to a potential customer and others. It was a private gathering under what all present understood to be circumstances of confidentiality and also the demonstration was such that vital information about the nature of the new product was not disclosed and could not be deduced. Not only was it not a disclosure to the public, it was not an enabling disclosure either; it did not allow any witness to gain enough information to make a similar membrane themselves. Thus it was not

1   EPC Art 54.
2   Copyright Act 1911, s 15; British Library Act 1972, s 4.
3   [1971] RPC 153.
4   [1990] FSR 329. See also *Strix Ltd v Otter Controls Ltd* [1995] RPC 607.

relevant. This concept of the enabling disclosure is important and will be considered later.[5]

Greater problems arise not so much with the 'public' aspect of public availability but in considering what is meant by availability. Copyright libraries may resolve the problem domestically, but on the face of it a literal interpretation of section 2(2) means that anything anywhere in the public domain will form part of the state of the art. Revelations, unknown to anyone in the West, in the press in, say, Mongolia could, when finally unearthed, render an invention unpatentable and liable to revocation. This may seem unlikely but major and growing trading nations pose similar problems of accessibility of information: Japan, China or Thailand are all obvious examples. One argument would be to give the word 'available' a broad interpretation, in the spirit of the European origin of this part of patent law,[6] and exclude matters in the Thai technical press as not being de facto available to the public since in practice the public would have no access to it. Indeed it is a fair point that searches by the Patent Office are also unlikely to discover such obscure items of information, whether at the domestic, EPO or Washington Patent Co-operation Treaty level of search. However this could once again lead to the menace of potential double patenting and it is suggested that the better view is that the existence of material anywhere publicly available, even if only with the greatest difficulty, as a bar to patentability reflects best the interests of the international trading community. This has the support of the *Woven Plastic* decision noted in the section of this chapter on the inventive step.

One type of information that is available to the public is expressly excluded from any consideration when the state of the art is being assessed. This is any information which has been disclosed from six months prior to the filing date onwards which is information that has been obtained either unlawfully or in breach of confidence or alternatively if it has been divulged in breach of confidence; the protection also extends to disclosure resulting from the display of the invention at an international exhibition,[7] this being a limited category of events such as World Fairs and Expos. This subsection will often confer a double benefit on the inventor who in an appropriate case can not only exclude the revealed information from the state of the art but also in appropriate cases bring an action against the confider for breach of confidence. This is a most useful reminder that actions for breach of confidence often arise from situations where patents are being discussed and developed and form a useful supplement to the remedies of the patentee even, or especially, if no patent is awarded, as seen in Chapter 25.

---

5   See p 60 below.
6   See discussion on interpretation after the *Catnic* case in Ch 5.
7   Patents Act 1977, s 2(4).

So far we have concentrated on what information forms part of the state of the art. Now we must investigate more carefully the nature of that information and in particular whether it actually does anticipate the patent that is applied for subsequently. Anticipation is the word commonly used to assess the impact of the prior state of the art on the later invention and the question is whether the operation of the prior product or process forestalls the later patent.[8]

A simple example is provided by *Windsurfing International Inc v Tabur Marine (GB) Ltd.*[9] Here a patent had been granted in 1968 to the plaintiffs for the invention of the windsurfing board and other related forms of propulsion. On finding that the defendants were also selling such equipment they sought to take action for infringement of their patent. The defendants in turn objected to the initial validity of the patent and sought to have it revoked. It should be noted that this is a very common method of raising the patentability question as a counterclaim to an allegation of infringement. The acts that were put forward as evidence of anticipation were those of a boy aged 12 back in 1958 who while on holiday at Hayling Island in Sussex made and used a primitive sailboard for his own amusement. The temporary, personal and little-known character of the user were all regarded as irrelevant[10] and although the patented device had a more sophisticated control mechanism than that of the boy's this apparatus was irrelevant for the purposes of anticipation given that the same basic control principles were used. (Whether the improvements were obvious will be reviewed under that heading.) Likewise the existence of an article featuring the excitement of the new sport of sailboarding which appeared in 1966 also anticipated the patent by demonstrating something similar to the patented boards again adopting the same basic principles of construction.

It is clear from the case law that relatively minor acts are sufficient to anticipate but more may be needed since the anticipation has to be of the invention itself. *Fomento Industrial SA v Mentmore Manufacturing Co*[11] illustrates both points. The plaintiffs had a 1945 patent for the manufacture of a particular type of improved ballpoint pen and its revocation was sought on the basis of prior user, in the form of the limited availability of pilot models of the new pen in the 1944-45 period. There was enough non-private use that these events could and did amount to anticipation but now we must consider if what was revealed by these events was the subsequently patented invention. Mere use of a biro may well not disclose anything about its workings - the patent was specifically for a method of producing the more regular flow of ink - but of greater significance was an earlier patent

8   *General Tire & Rubber Co v Firestone Tyre & Rubber Co* [1972] RPC 457 at 485, per Sachs LJ.
9   [1985] RPC 59.
10   Ibid at 77-78, per Oliver LJ.
11   [1956] RPC 87.

application by a group related to the plaintiffs for a broadly similar pen. This however did not amount to anticipation since the best that could be said for it was that it 'might well' achieve the result of the later patent, whereas the effect of the later patent was effectively to ensure that the desired result was achieved. Thus the prior use but not the earlier patent application was a ground for revocation.

Since 1977 public availability has been the sole test and it would therefore have to be asked whether the use of the pen disclosed the inventive concept. This will be a question of fact – in *Windsurfing* (though also on the pre-1977 law) there was a clear visible relationship between the anticipating user and the later patent, but in a case like *Fomento* it is less obvious that mere user will reveal the inventive concept of the improved operation of the ball point which is almost always firmly encased in plastic, and it may be unlikely that there would be any anticipation on the facts of *Fomento* today.

Here too, though, further refinements are needed before the law can be fully appreciated. One interesting problem is that provided by the facts that underlie the decision in *Merrell Dow Pharmaceuticals Inc v H N Norton & Co Ltd*.[12]

The fundamental issue here is whether the availability of a product to the public necessarily carries with it all the relevant knowledge/information that lies behind that product. In *Merrell Dow*, litigation arose in relation to an anti-histamine drug including the ingredient terfenadine. The problem was that it was 'available to the public' in the sense that it was known to exist under a patent from 1972 onwards. But research, including clinical trials, continued as to how precisely it worked for some years thereafter, until fuller understanding was reached as to its workings. As a result of this research the vital by-product which resulted from its use, the acid metabolite, was identified and itself patented in 1980. So did the use of terfenadine, inevitably producing the acid metabolite, after 1992 infringe Merrill Dow's earlier patent or did their rights survive until 2000?[13] The House of Lords took the view that the earlier patent which, albeit unknowingly, produced the acid metabolite was the relevant patent, so accordingly rivals were free to use this drug from 1992 on. Anticipation had occurred by use and the creation of the acid metabolite had been occurring since 1972; so the specific 1980 patent for it was revocable.

Lest the complexities of anti-histamine drugs are less than clear, Lord Hoffman,[14] in the sole speech in the case, uses an example that is perhaps clearer. For centuries Amazonian Indians have used a powdered tree bark to treat malaria. In 1820 it was discovered by French scientists that the active ingredient within the particular bark in question was quinine and by 1944

12   [1996] RPC 76.
13   In each case 20 years from the original patent's priority date.
14   [1996] RPC 76 at 88.

its precise chemical composition had been worked out, meaning that it could be made synthetically. Lord Hoffman argued cogently that the centuries of past history would anticipate any post-1944 attempt to patent the creation of quinine:

'The Amazonian Indian who treats himself with powdered bark for fever is using quinine, even if he thinks that the reason why the treatment is effective is that the tree is favoured by the Gods. The teachings of his traditional medicine contain enough information to enable him to do exactly what a scientist in the forest would have done if he wanted to treat a fever but had no supplies of quinine sulphate'.[15]

So even ignorant use may anticipate, with the result in the case, which is one with wide implications, that the years of subsequent research into the precise working of terfenadine would be, at least in terms of patentability, pointless,[16] at least for the purposes for which the drug was used.[17] This issue has been further considered in *Chiron Corp v Evans Medical Ltd*.[18] Applying *Merrill Dow*, it was found that for the purposes of anticipation there was no need to know that a product was being created by a process but anticipation would occur where it was a conscious decision to engage in a process rather than where the product was created unintentionally and, perhaps, unexpectedly.

The notion of ignorant use of a product or process begs a further question. We need to know whose use is under consideration. To revert to the *Fomento* example, we all pick up biro pens continually without (until now) considering how they work; but to a biro expert much would be clear very quickly even from mere use, let alone a quick examination. We therefore need to consider the issue of whose eyes should be used in assessing whether the anticipatory event reveals the actual inventive concept or, to put it in the alternative, whether the prior disclosure is an enabling disclosure.

Clear guidance on this issue is provided by *General Tire and Rubber Co v Firestone Tyre and Rubber Co*.[19] The plaintiffs had a patent for making tyres from a mixture of synthetic rubber, oil and carbon black. The defendants attacked it on various grounds, including anticipation of the patent by three earlier specifications for similar products and an article in the journal 'Rubber Age'. The Court of Appeal approached the issue by comparing the patentee's claim and the earlier documents and construing them at the respective relevant dates by a reader skilled in the art to which

15 Ibid at 91.
16 See Karet 'A Question of Epistemology' [1996] 2 EIPR 97.
17 Per Lord Hoffman in *Merrell Dow* [1996] RPC 76 at 91.
18 (1998) Times, 20 January; noted [1998] EIPR 273.
19 [1972] RPC 457.

they relate having regard to the state of knowledge in such art at the relevant date.[20] This creates the idea of the court placing itself in the position of the 'notional skilled reader', an upmarket version of tort law's reasonable man, blessed with reasonable knowledge but not, here, universal knowledge appropriate to the area in which the patent applies. Further, the notional skilled reader should, in an area of high technology, be replaced by a team of readers whose collective skills would be those employed in making the comparison. It was also established that it is the result of the alleged anticipatory process or product that is vital, not the expression or intention of the author thus enabling anticipation to occur by virtue of the inadvertent qualities of the earlier activity.[1] It was found by the Court of Appeal that use of none of the alleged anticipations would have been likely to have achieved the particular benefits of General Tire's new method of manufacture. *Union Carbide Corpn v B P Chemicals*[2] provides a different slant on this by noting, appropriately, that doing something which was in the prior art regarded as something which, though recognised, was something that should not be done, was clearly novel, going, as it would, against the perceptions of the normal skilled man.

A useful application of this approach is to be found in *Quantel Ltd v Spaceward Microsystems Ltd.*[3] This concerned computer based videographic systems, the plaintiffs owning the patents of their 'Paintbox' system for producing graphics; this was a popular system with the BBC and NBC amongst its users. In considering whether four other earlier videographic systems anticipated the plaintiffs' system, it was emphasised by Falconer J,[4] following *General Tire*, that the prior publication had to provide clear and unmistakable directions to its addressee before it would count as an enabling disclosure. The use of stored data in the graphics of the plaintiffs' system was not present in the first rival, Levoy, so that did not anticipate. The second, Paint, had many similarities but again did not go as far as the plaintiff's did in not having processing means, and variants of it also did not anticipate. Two systems devised at NYIT (New York Institute of Technology) were not seen as being properly regarded as video image creation systems. Finally the demonstration by the plaintiffs of a prototype of their system did not anticipate since key features had not at that stage been invented, and a demonstration which allowed use but provided no inspection or explanation of the equipment used was not to be regarded as an enabling disclosure.

---

20   Ibid, per Sachs LJ at 485.
1   Eg *Molins v Industrial Machinery Co Ltd* (1937) 55 RPC 31.
2   [1998] RPC 1.
3   [1990] RPC 83.
4   Ibid at 112.

This area has now been considered at the highest level in *Asahi Kasei Kogyo KK's Application*[5] where a patent was sought for a genetically engineered polypeptide, a product useful for treating tumours. The problem was that an earlier application had claimed the existence of polypeptide, but had not gone so far as to describe how it may be produced. The House of Lords held that this did not count as an anticipation. The indication of the existence of polypeptide did not itself show how it could be produced nor was it so self-evident how it may be produced that it would be regarded as an enabling disclosure.

The problem with the case is that by interpreting section 2(3) of the 1977 Act as only applying to enabling disclosures in earlier applications it dents the force of that subsection by creating cases where there is a risk of double patenting of the same invention. Here different patents could exist for polypeptide and for its use, which seems unproductive. This issue was recognised by the House of Lords but was thought to be something that would only happen rarely,[6] and in any event appeared to accord with the approach of both the 1977 Act and Article 54 of the EPC.

It should be noted that the jurisprudence on the nature of the addressee in patent cases is more extensive and more developed in the context of obviousness, but care must be taken in applying that law here since there are clear differences in the law for example as to the mosaicking (ie combinations) of two separate aspects of the state of the art[7] and in any event a different question is being asked; the novelty of an invention is easier to assess than its obviousness and arguably it is for this reason that the law in the latter areas has had no option but to become more developed.

The areas where the characteristics of the notional addressee of the patent claim and the anticipatory material are particularly important is when the patent claim is, as is quite usual, not a bolt from an otherwise clear blue sky but rather a development of some pre-existing product or process where it is easy for an objector to say that the pre-existing product in its claims or by its working was an anticipation – *Quantel* is perhaps a good example. The problem is heightened where all that is being sought in the subsequent patent is a new method of using pre-existing matter.

Sometimes it is easy to see that there is novelty even in such a case. This problem can particularly arise in selection patents, that is patents which select one particular category from a more general group that is already known. A good example of this is *Beecham Group's (Amoxycillin) Application*[8] where Beechams had been granted a patent for a large class of various penicillins for use as antibiotics and had then in a further patent

5   [1991] RPC 485, approved in *Biogen Inc v Medeva plc* [1997] RPC 1.
6   Ibid at 542.
7   See p 64 below.
8   [1980] RPC 261.

singled out nine of them as being especially effective. At issue was a further application for a patent for one type of one of those nine penicillins which was especially amenable to absorption into the blood, the question being whether naming this sort of penicillin in the earlier patent was an anticipation. The Court of Appeal denied that it was an anticipation. The earlier patent simply showed that this sort of penicillin appeared to be effective in mice whereas the patent in suit was for a developed, tested and workable application of one type of that particular penicillin and was not anticipated by an earlier patent which gave no hint of whether or how its subject matter could be used for human consumption, even to its skilled addressees.

The essence of this type of case is to emphasise the advantage and/or difference that the selection makes so as to create a clear gap between the earlier and later matters. So in *Re Shell Refining and Marketing Co Ltd's Patent*[9] Esso had made a 1940 patent application concerning improved fuel consumption which referred to the use of a particular chemical additive to fuel as being of benefit to combat corrosion in fuel tanks, while Shell subsequently had obtained a patent for the use of several additives, including a small proportion of the one used by Esso, for various purposes including the prevention of engine knock, and of fouling of the spark plugs and exhaust valve corrosion. It was held that Esso's application did not anticipate the final version of Shell's patent, amended to emphasise the small amount of additive and its effectiveness in dealing with the problems. Shell sought to counteract. However a more broadly drafted claim which did not emphasise the precise amount of the additive to be used by Shell was anticipated - it was after all the same additive in the same fuel.

The case is also useful in giving more general guidelines on the correct approach to selection patents. Lord Evershed M R starts[10] with the obvious basic proposition that a man who merely picks out a number of items from an already disclosed group or series has not 'invented' anything, but this would not be the case where later research reveals

'that certain items in the group or series possess qualities or characteristics peculiar to themselves and hitherto unknown'.

He adopts[11] the approach of Maugham J in an earlier case[12] to selection patents, identifying them as being grantable where there is a substantial advantage associated with the selected group, where that advantage is

9   [1960] RPC 35.
10   Ibid at 53.
11   Ibid at 55.
12   *Re I G Farbenindustrie AG's Patent* (1930) 47 RPC 289 at 322–3.

common to all of the selected group, and where that advantage is peculiar to that group.

This approach has the approval of the House of Lords in two more recent cases, *Beecham Group Ltd v Bristol Laboratories International S A*[13] and *E I Du Pont de Nemours & Co (Witsiepe's) Application*.[14] In *Du Pont* Lord Wilberforce points to the need to protect the original inventor while encouraging others to improve and enhance that invention by the discovery of fresh advantages in the selected class. On the facts this was reflected by the finding that a previous disclosure by ICI that the use of nine glycols would produce a particular result in no way anticipated the discovery by Du Pont after extensive research that one of the glycols had particular benefits in a different field; this was clearly the fresh advantage of the selected class.

In a sense these patents are not best served by being described as selection patents; what signifies them and justifies their patentability is not the mere fact of selection but the uniqueness of what is selected and the development or advantage which that selection represents. As such their recognition is entirely justified as a reward for the work that will go into making the selection, as both *Beecham* and *Shell* demonstrate and in recognising them the law reflects the commercial reality of the nature of much of the inventive work that goes on in the pharmaceutical and other chemical industries.

In one respect the 1977 Act makes specific provisions for particular patents of this type. Section 2(6) expressly permits the patenting of a substance used in medical treatment even if the substance itself is already part of the state of the art, so long as the use of the substance in medical treatment is not part thereof. It is clear that this only applies to first use as a medicine and not to second and subsequent medical uses, even if completely distinct. This arises from the interpretation of section 2(6) by the court in *John Wyeth and Brother Ltd's Application; Schering AG's Application*.[15] Two appeals were heard together: Wyeth found that compounds called guanidines used to lower blood pressure also were valuable in combating diarrhoea while Schering sought a patent for their research finding that substances used for the treatment of breast cancer could also be used against prostatic hyperlasia. The Patent Court *in banc* interpreted section 2(6) as described above on the grounds that the precise wording of the legislation is that medical use of a known substance is allowed so long as its use 'in any such method does not form part of the state of the art' and a prior medical use would be 'any such method'. However the matter did not end there; amended claims were also considered which sought a patent for the use of a known subject in the manufacture of a new drug,

13   [1978] RPC 521 at 579.
14   [1982] FSR 303 at 310.
15   [1985] RPC 545.

thus emphasising not the use of, say, the guanidines as a treatment for diarrhoea but their use in a new drug (which of course by coincidence would be used in the treatment of diarrhoea). Claims in this form had been allowed by the EPO on the grounds that the use in manufacture of the new drug could provide the necessary element of novelty.[16] Since, by section 91(1) of the 1977 Act, judicial notice has to be taken of decisions of appellate decisions within the EPO, the court was obliged to follow this lead and allowed the subtly amended claims.

In making this point on a narrow issue, a broader point also becomes relevant and is an appropriate note on which to end this section. The proper approach to issues of patentability and of novelty in particular is a constructive one, and the proper question is not 'Is this patentable?' but rather 'What parts of this are patentable?' Given that the courts are prepared to allow quite fine adjustments as being patentable as in *Quantel*, it will be often possible to find some part of the product or process which is novel, even if other aspects are not. This care in identifying the true novelty must then be matched by equal care in drafting the application for a patent, taking great care to emphasise those elements that have been identified as being novel; *Wyeth and Schering* stands as a monument to careful drafting even in the post-1977 era of broader attitudes to the interpretation of patents.

Overall, with the courts taking a fairly positive attitude both to what information is in the public domain and whether that information as properly understood does amount to an enabling disclosure, this is an area of law that appears to be working with reasonable effectiveness. The obstacle presented by novelty will be resolved, either way, at an early stage of most applications, though our interpretation of section 2(2) would occasionally lead to disruption when a patent's revocation is sought on the grounds of the discovery of a long-standing but unknown article in the trade press in Japan. However a more typical problem – that of prior use – has been resolved by the 1977 Act and that such use now has to be an enabling disclosure revealing its inventive concept should minimise the kind of problem epitomised by the *Fomento* decision. *Merrill Dow*, however, while probably correct in its conclusion, does create an additional doubt where ignorant prior use has taken place and will therefore stop a later patent application in its tracks. At least this might stop the disagreeable habit of some multinationals of acquiring sundry secrets of indigenous peoples and then gaining their own monopoly by patenting them.[17] Overall though the sensible attitude of the law towards selection patents better exemplifies the general workability of this aspect of patent law and shows a reasonable balance is maintained between patentees and their rivals in trade.

16 *Re Eisai Co Ltd*: Decision Gr 05/83 (1985) OJ EPO 64.
17 On this see, inter alia, Blakeney 'Bioprospecting and the Protection of Traditional Medical Knowledge of Indigenous Peoples: An Australian Perspective' [1997] 6 EIPR 298.

INVENTIVE STEP

Not everything that is new is patentable. The next requirement imposed
by the law is that the invention contains an inventive step, a leap forward
by the inventor that puts him ahead of the pack and, it may be said, justifies
rewarding him with a patent. Section 3 of the 1977 Act states:

> 'An invention shall be taken to involve an inventive step if it is not obvious
> to a person skilled in the art, having regard to any matter which forms
> part of the state of the art by virtue only of section 2(2) above (and
> disregarding section 2(3) above).'

So that which is obvious does not gain patent protection, only that which
is inventive. Note also that, by excluding section 2(3) from the definition
of state of the art for the purposes of this section the discussion of
obviousness ignores patent applications which have already been filed but
are yet to be published.

A good example of the concepts of inventiveness and obviousness in
operation is provided once again by *Windsurfing International Inc v Tabur
Marine (Great Britain) Ltd*.[18] We have already seen in the context of the
discussion of novelty that the plaintiffs' 1968 patent for windsurfing
equipment had been anticipated a decade previously by a boy on holiday.
However, the two boards were by no means identical. The boy used a simple
straight boom with which to hold the sail taut and provide a handhold for
the rider, while the patented boom was a more sophisticated arc-shaped
model which helped the sail assume an aerofoil shape and thus attain greater
speed. This difference was held to be insignificant; the use of the boom was
common and the arc-shaped design was an obvious improvement on the
boy's design since when in use even his boom began to assume an arc shape.
Thus the admitted improvement carried out by the patentee was not
sufficient to gain the protection of a patent because there was no inventive
step in making an improvement that was regarded as an obvious one to make.

In discussing what is or is not obvious great care needs to be taken. What
is an obvious improvement to all in an ordinary commonsense situation like
that in the *Windsurfing* case may be much less clear in a high technological
field. In particular in such a case what may seem to be a dazzling miracle of
invention by the ordinary citizen will be routine or commonplace to the
person expert in that particular field. It is thus necessary to take care in
formulating an approach to the obviousness question appropriate to all cases.
It is also important to note from the start the significance of the obviousness
question. Even where, as in the *Windsurfing* case, an advance is said to be
obvious and thus non-patentable, it is still likely that the disappointed

applicant will have put a significant amount of work into the development and perfection of the product. If patents are intended to reward the efforts of inventors or if, more generally, intellectual property rights are expected to match up with activity of value in the commercial sector the failure to protect such activity by the grant of the patent is a significant failing in the system. Obviously the more often that the law depicts an advance as being obvious the greater that this failing will be and also any willingness to expand the notion of obviousness will clearly go against the interests of new inventors and favour the interests of those already in the game and whose activities will already form part of the state of the art.

How then is obviousness approached? The basis test is clearly outlined by Oliver LJ in the *Windsurfing* case[19] as a four-fold approach. Firstly it is necessary to

'identify the inventive concept embodied in the patent in suit.'

This is the problem that fell to be considered in *Biogen Inc v Medeva plc*[20] where it was made clear that the inventive concept was neither the identification of the problem nor the general approach to be taken to it but rather the problem and its precise resolution. To adopt an analogy employed by Lord Hoffman, people for centuries ruminated on the problem of flying machines, so this could not be on its own an inventive concept. Later more precise thought was given to matters such as wing shape and engine type but, again, mere thought is not enough. Only when the Wright brothers succeeded in making a machine which was capable of powered flight can it be said that the 'inventive concept' had come into existence. In *Biogen* itself the House of Lords assumed, without deciding, that the genetic engineering techniques employed to resolve a known problem in a new way were not obvious.

Oliver LJ continues to his second point:

'Thereafter, the court has to assume the mantle of the normally skilled but unimaginative addressee in the art at the priority date and to impute to him what was, at that date, common general knowledge in the art in question'.

This second stage is vital and will be considered in detail shortly. The third stage is to identify the differences which exist between the generally known matter and the subject matter of the patent for which the application is being made and, finally,

---

19   Ibid at 73–4. This approach is confirmed by *Mölnlycke AB v Procter & Gamble Ltd (No 5)* [1994] RPC 49 at 115, per Sir Donald Nicholls VC and, more significantly but not uncritically, by Lord Hoffman in *Biogen inc v Medeva plc* [1997] RPC 1.

20   [1997] RPC 1.

'the court has to ask itself whether, viewed without any knowledge of the alleged invention, those differences constitute steps which would have been obvious to the skilled man or whether they require any degree of invention.'

On the facts of the case, as we have seen, the development was obvious. The essential inventive concept in the patent was the free-sail concept, as opposed to the rigid masts of rigging of conventional yachts. However, the state of the art included the 1966 article describing sailboarding and that revealed the essence of the later invention to an audience who were, given the specialist nature of the publication, almost by definition going to be knowledgeable in the art. The only differences were in the shape of the boom and the shape of sail used, and these differences would be obvious in the view of the Court of Appeal to the informed reader who would use their own knowledge to make the same adjustments themselves, thus depriving the holders of the patent from legitimately claiming that they had made an inventive step.

It is apparent that it is at the second stage of this process that the key feature arises for, in deciding through whose eyes the question of the inventive step should be viewed, the law is able to set the level at which the dividing line between obviousness and inventiveness is to be drawn. The classic formulation of this test is provided by Lord Reid in *Technograph Printed Circuits Ltd v Mills and Rockley (Electronics) Ltd*[1] when, in discussing obviousness, he described the notional addressee in the following terms.[2]

'It is not disputed that the hypothetical addressee is a skilled technician who is well acquainted with workshop technique and has carefully read the relevant literature. He is supposed to have an unlimited capacity to assimilate the contents of, it may be, scores of specifications but to be incapable of a scintilla of invention.'

On the facts, the House of Lords found that the jump from a pre-existing American electrostatic shield to the patentee's printed circuits was an inventive one in the light of expert evidence that the necessary adaptations and the alterations were far from obvious. It is clear that such expert evidence will often be of the utmost value in deciding the obviousness question.

However this particular variant of the reasonable man is not without his critics. His character would seem to be an unrealistic one; like a sponge he soaks up all known facts from, since 1977, all over the world. Yet, although he understands all this, demonstrating a brain of great understanding power,

1   [1972] RPC 346.
2   Ibid at 355.

he has no idea what to do with it and sits, bloated with facts but bereft of ideas, incapable of developing ideas from all that he knows. Leading comedy actors must yearn to play his part. The courts themselves have expressed occasional concern as to whether such characters hinder rather than help the law's development. In the *Windsurfing* case[3] Oliver LJ notes that such figures must not be permitted to obscure the basic statutory terminology in the objective quest as to whether an invention is obvious or not, and the temptation to add various human qualities to this non-existent entity may well lead to confusion in the view of the judge. Hoffmann LJ has also been critical[4] of the way in which this distended version of the reasonable man has come to be utilised, noting that what may be 'a folksy way of explaining the law to a jury' is no substitute for an analysis of the actual statutory language.

In any event it may be that the character used to test for obviousness is due for change. The German equivalent is far from being a mere technician and is found to possess imagination[5] and clearly it is important to harmonise these approaches; doubtless in due course the EPO will have to consider this issue. Meanwhile the courts have in one significant decision already moved away from the traditional approach to one more closely reflecting the German picture.

The case of *Genentech Inc's Patent*[6] is of great significance. It is also of great length – the report extends to 140 pages – and complexity. Nevertheless careful analysis of the case and its implications is needed. The case arose from the area of genetic engineering. A patent had been granted to Genentech in respect of various claims relating to the production of human plasminogen activator by the use of recombinant DNA technology in workable quantities. The relevant technology had been used previously in synthesising a number of other substances, but this was the first time that it had been employed to synthesise a particular activator known as t-PA which was of great value in combating blood clotting and thus of importance in treating thrombosis. The production of quantities of t-PA was clearly of great medical and commercial value. It was also the result of much work. Genentech took over a year to achieve the production of enough t-PA and many skilled scientists were involved. Equally other teams elsewhere were racing towards the same approach but lost out in that particular race to Genentech.

In effect then Genentech were the holders of a patent for a new application of pre-existing technology and the nub of the dispute – others

3   [1985] RPC 59 at 71.
4   *Société Technique de Pulvérisation Step v Emson Europe Ltd* [1993] RPC 513 at 519.
5   Pakuscher [1981] 12 IIC 816. See also Schmidt–Szalewski (1992) IIC 725 for the position in France where the average person skilled in the art is the test. Presumably such a person has an average amount of imagination.
6   [1989] RPC 147.

in the field sought a revocation of the Genentech patent – was whether what had been achieved by Genentech was a breakthrough permitting the synthesis of the valuable t-PA for the first time and thus deserving of patent protection or whether, alternatively, the discovery was just part of the ordinary process of development of the pre-existing recombinant DNA technology, and thus did not amount to an inventive step.

The Court of Appeal found that the patent had been wrongly granted and ordered that it should be revoked. A key issue was how the hypothetical addressee concept could cope with an area of such intellectual complexity as this, and the Court of Appeal recognised that the traditional model was unworkable in these exceptional circumstances. As Purchas LJ recognised[7] in this type of situation,

'the artisan has receded into the role of the laboratory assistant and the others have become segregated into groups of highly qualified specialists in their own spheres of all whom must possess a degree of inventiveness.'

In other words, since there is no one working in the field who is incapable of invention, the 'person skilled in the art' must have inventive capacity. Mustill LJ noted[8] that it was wrong to assume that the person skilled in the art for the purposes of section 3 was the same person as that envisaged in considering the information in the specification and its use by the person skilled in the art envisaged by section 14(3). The latter character could be realistically seen as non-inventive in the context of having merely to read and understand a specification, but for the purposes of section 3,

'where one is looking at the research team one cannot treat them as dull plodders, for such people would not be members of the team at all, except as laboratory assistants.'

Later[9] he comments that in a case of this type

'some substantial measure of ingenuity is an essential qualification for being engaged in the enterprise.'

In the light of these views, not apparently shared by the third member of the Court, Dillon LJ,[10] it became clear that Genentech should not be allowed any patent protection. The problems faced by the firm were the problems to be expected out at the cutting edge of genetic engineering and,

7   Ibid at 214.
8   Ibid at 279.
9   Ibid at 280.
10   Ibid at 241.

as such, were capable of being surmounted by others skilled in the arts, with their inevitable high intellectual and inventive qualities. As Mustill LJ expresses it[11]

> 'it is inventiveness which counts, and I cannot find it here in any degree which exceeds the amount of resource expected of a group mustering the skills, remarkable as they seem to the layman, ordinarily to be expected of persons skilled in this most difficult array of arts.'

Purchas LJ, however, found that some of the steps taken along the way were inventive steps even by the high standards expected in this field, but found against Genentech on other grounds.[12] Dillon LJ found[13] it relevant in the establishing of obviousness that the other participants in the patent race were following the same track as Genentech confirming him in the view that the steps being taken were obvious to those skilled in the art.

There is much more to *Genentech* but this is an appropriate moment to make some comments on this core part of the decision. It is unfortunate that such a range of judicial opinion exists on the obviousness point and this merely adds to the problems of the complex subject matter. However the confusion should not mask the result. Here the company spent substantial amounts of time and money, using their resources and those represented by their highly qualified staff (almost all with a Ph D) in devising a workable method of making a pharmaceutical product of great potential benefit to society. This sounds just the sort of scenario where, on a traditional analysis of the rationale of the patent system, the endeavour and beneficial result to society should be rewarded by the grant of a patent. Yet here the patent was revoked. So no incentive or reward for the patentee exists, other than in the form of short-term market-leading profits. Of course society and consumers benefit in the short term from the freer availability of this type of treatment, as do the rival firms freely able to market their rival treatments. But in the longer term Genentech get no high-yield return on their investment in the absence of a patent, and may as a result not be able to find the next step forward in the (far from cheap) advance in scientific technique. In the absence of reward or incentive too they may simply feel it unwise to devote resources to R & D where the chance of a patentable result being reached has been substantially diminished by this decision. Society and the customers may in the future be less likely to gain any benefit from future advances in genetic engineering technology.

Not, of course, that the *Genentech* decision is confined to that one particular field. It would seem logical to assume that it will apply to any field of scientific activity where the players in the field are all working at a high doctoral or post-doctoral level. This is of course the norm in most major industries, such as electronics or telecommunications for example, and means that *Genentech*'s impact is of great significance in reducing the availability of patents by raising the standard of inventiveness in a potentially significant range of commercially important activities.

On the other hand *Genentech* has not been widely used in the decade since the decision and it may increasingly come to be regarded as a decision decided very much on its own facts which is, of course, the common lawyer's classic method of marginalising or (to be blunter) ignoring unhelpful decisions!

Either way, it should be made clear that the problem raised by *Genentech* exists only in a small minority of patent applications where protection is sought for an advance in an area of high technology. At lower levels, the traditional approach to obviousness still makes sense, for instance in a typical patent application for a relatively routine development or extension of a previous patent, such as a minor, but new improvement in the way the ink flows in the operation of a biro pen. Here invention and obviousness are genuine alternatives, but unfortunately *Genentech* reveals that this cannot always be the case.

Why has this come about? The key problem is alluded to in the judgment of Mustill LJ[14] and is simply that the definition in section 3 of the 1977 Act and in EPC Art 56 does not make universal sense. It makes the assumption that inventiveness and obviousness are but two sides of the same coin, but the facts of a case like *Genentech* blow up that assumption with a violent blast. Simply, in high tech areas such as genetic engineering with its teams of highly qualified and experienced scientists, the process of invention is the norm; invention here is an obvious thing for its skilled proponents to undertake. To deny invention its legal protection and economic reward in the very kinds of activities where inventive activity is most common and where, arguably, society gains some of the greatest rewards from that activity is most regrettable, to say the least. To have standards of inventiveness varying so greatly from industry to industry arguably also runs contrary to the traditional idea that the inquiry into inventiveness was to be an objective one. By changing the nature of the hypothetical addressee to one who in certain cases is possessed with the facility of invention, the decision also changes, for the worse, the availability of patents. If nothing else, the case shows the vital importance of determining the true character of the hypothetical addressee and warns of the immense significance of changes to those characteristics, a lesson that should be borne in mind if the superficially more attractive continental models are ever to be adopted.

This is not necessarily a criticism of the judgments in the case; rather it

14   Ibid at 274.

suggests that the legal definition of inventiveness needs to be fundamentally reconsidered in the light of the hi-tech times in which we live. The fact that Purchas LJ was able to find some inventive steps even on the basis that the hypothetical addressee had some inventive capacity also gives some ground for hope; perhaps we should now be looking for a new category of 'super-inventiveness' in businesses such as genetic engineering, or else still finding that there is inventiveness on quite narrow grounds in such a context.[15]

Equally there are many points raised in the judgments which go some way to resolving arguments from the past. It is clear that the focus of the obviousness question should be asked in the context not of each individual but by looking at the overall team with their varying specialities that would be typical in such cases,[16] and with all appropriate time and equipment at their disposal.

There was particular discussion of some factors which have from time to time been found significant in determining the obviousness question. The fact that Genentech had won a patent race did not help them, but neither did the fact that there was such a race in the first place. Dillon LJ was quite clear[17] that the fact that the competing research teams were all following the same path tended to show that their activities were obvious and that the position may very well have been different if Genentech were out on their own pursuing a novel idea to a successful conclusion and Mustill LJ commented to similar effect[18] and also in the context made the telling remark that 'first to the post is the test of novelty, but novelty is not enough'.[19]

Also canvassed was the idea that an inventive step is one which will often be signified by the heavy expenditure of time, skill, money and energy. Again the words of Mustill LJ summarise the position:

'it may be that (diligent and skilled) labour and the resulting success deserve a prize, but the law, as I read it, calls for something more.'[20]

This must be right; the time and energy may be being expended because of the inefficiency or stupidity of the workers involved, perhaps engaged in no more than honest plodding though Purchas LJ[1] takes a contrary view, suggesting that the time taken on the project suggested that there was something non-obvious present.

One further factor in dealing with inventiveness may conveniently be

15 Eg *Chiron Corporation v Murex Diagnostics Ltd & Organon Teknika Ltd* [1996] RPC 535 per Aldous J at 574 cf Morritt L J at 608.
16 *Genentech Inc's Patent* at 247 (per Dillon LJ) and 278 (per Mustill LJ).
17 Ibid at 243.
18 Ibid at 277.
19 Ibid at 278.
20 Ibid at 280.
1   Ibid at 221.

dealt with here, though not arising from *Genentech*. A further argument that has been said to favour a finding of inventiveness is the subsequent commercial success of the invention. The argument appears to be based on the idea that the popularity and utility of a new device indicates that it fills for the first time a longstanding want, and this commercial success shows that there must have been an inventive step in the process of thinking up something new which users have greeted with such acclaim.[2] This is evident nonsense. All manner of factors go to explain the success of a new product with the marketing effort being often of as much significance as the qualities of the product itself while the award of a patent, unless solely seen as the conferral of a reward by grateful society, can hardly be denied to a product which is only of use in a small number of perhaps highly technical situations. The view of Mummery J expressed in *Mölnlycke A B v Procter and Gamble Ltd (No 3)*[3] that obviousness is a technical question and not a commercial one is to be preferred.

This view was followed by Jacob J in *Beloit Technologies Inc v Valmet Paper Machinery Inc*[4] where commercial success was no more than a matter of some evidential value in considering the issue of obviousness. Laddie J goes further in *Brugger v Medic-Aid Ltd*[5] and suggests that commercial factors may disguise the issue of the obviousness of, for instance, a development, which though obvious, has not occurred for purely commercial rather than technical reasons. This is further confirmed by the judgment of Laddie J in *Raychem Corpn's Patent*.[6] Again, novelty alone is not enough. In *Biogen Inc v Medeva plc*[7] Lord Hoffman also took the view that commercial factors were irrelevant in so far as a commercially motivated decision to research in the area did not stop the research strategy and its consequences from being an inventive step.

Just as is the case with the issue of novelty, problems arise in this area too in the not unusual case where a patent is being sought not for some entirely new product or process, but for something which is only a relatively minor advance on what has gone before. It therefore becomes very important to consider whether the step forward that has been made is an inventive one. This was a problem in the *Genentech* case. At the beginning of their research, DNA technology existed and at least in theory could be adapted to produce t-PA as it already had been to produce growth hormones and insulin and other valuable products of a broadly similar nature. The

---

2   The classic formulation is by Tomlin J in *Samuel Parkes & Co Ltd v Cocker Brothers Ltd* (1929) 46 RPC 241 at 248. A more recent example of this approach is *Fichera v Flogates Ltd* [1983] FSR 198.
3   [1990] RPC 498 at 503.
4   [1995] RPC 705.
5   [1996] RPC 635.
6   [1998] RPC 31 at 66.
7   [1997] RPC 1.

production of t-PA was a natural challenge to take on, in view of the known value of the substance. In the light of these factors, and bearing in mind the high level of the hypothetical addressee's knowledge and inventiveness, it was obvious to try and match the DNA technology to the challenge of t-PA production.[8] Dillon LJ adopted the notion that it was an obvious development where the materials were 'lying in the road' and there for the research worker to pick up.

Where *Genentech* is less clear is as to what type of work is necessary for the steps being taken to be transcended into inventive ones. We have already seen that hard work alone does not confer inventiveness and there is also discussion about the type of work. Mere trial and error experimentation is not sufficient because such work is an obvious way for the uninventive to proceed, according to Mustill LJ.[9] However, in the view of Dillon LJ 'empirical research industriously pursued may lead to a patentable invention',[10] and he cites House of Lords dicta in support of the view.[11] It is suggested that this latter approach is incorrect insofar as it begs the question as to why the industrious work was being carried out and as to whether the decision to embark on the work was obvious or not; it is also necessary to consider the inventiveness/obviousness issue at each stage of the research programme.[12] In doing this the focus should be on the process and materials employed and their obviousness (or not) rather than on their use and its consequence.[13]

The quest for inventiveness at the beginning and at each stage of the development of the product or process is obviously important to the writer of the specification, enabling him to focus on those aspects where inventiveness is most clearly to be found. It is also a helpful way of approaching the question of whether a minor step forward from what has gone before is inventive or obvious. A good example is the idea of 'mosaicking'. This is where an inventor takes two or more pre-existing products or processes and combines them together. Whether this combination is then able to gain patent protection will depend on whether the decision to combine is one which is inventive. The classic example is *Williams v Nye*[14] where a patent was obtained for a combination of the previously separate mincing and filling machines used in the manufacture of sausages into one machine that was able to perform both functions. The Court of Appeal ruled that the patent was invalid because the only step taken by the patentee was an obvious one; it was not inventive to combine two

---

8   [1989] RPC 147 at 243 (per Dillon LJ) and 276 (per Mustill LJ).
9   Ibid at 274.
10   Ibid at 241.
11   Lord Simonds in *May & Baker Ltd v Boots Pure Drug Co* (1950) 67 RPC 23 at 34.
12   See Mustill LJ in *Genentech* at 275–6.
13   Per Laddie J in *Raychem Corp's Patents* [1998] RPC 31 at 41–2.
14   (1890) 7 RPC 62.

machines performing closely related functions into one, with no real alteration to the operation of either of the two machines. However it would be easy to think of slight changes to the facts whereby it would be possible to claim inventiveness, for example if one machine was from a completely unrelated field of activity where the patentee would have made an inventive step in realising that its utility was transferable or if the combined machine offered enormous savings in time or cost which it was not obvious to seek. That said, where the two separate previous objects are, as is likely, in some way related to a common field, it is likely that the courts will expect the hypothetical addressee to make the obvious connection between them.[15]

Similar issues arise where the patent is sought for a new use of a pre-existing product or process. If the pre-existing item is unchanged then the same objection as that in *Williams v Nye* will be appropriate. If, on the other hand, some adaptation of the earlier item is necessary, the patent application should focus on this and the question will be whether inventiveness was present in the decision to make the adaptation and/or during its exercise. It is the combination of the inventive idea and the inventive method of putting it into operation that seems to give the best chance of securing patent protection.[16] This approach is also applicable to selection patents; if the selection and development of one from a larger class is obvious that will be fatal to any patent claim. It must be shown that the decision to make the selection was itself an inventive step.[17]

In all the discussion of the hypothetical addressee one important factor has until now been ignored. That is the question of how much he knows – just how limitless is his limitless capacity for knowledge? The theory is clear that here, just as in relation to novelty, the state of the art encompasses all material available to the public at any time anywhere (the definition from section 2(2) of the 1977 Act appears equally applicable here). A clear illustration of this point is provided in the context of both novelty and obviousness by *Woven Plastic Products Ltd v British Ropes Ltd.*[18] With evident regret, the Court of Appeal found that apparently unworked patent applications made some years earlier in Japan, not unreasonably in Japanese, had to be regarded as part of the state of the art, thus rendering the patent being worked by the plaintiffs as being invalid on the grounds that the use of polyvinyl chloride as the basis of a floor covering was not novel and the difference between the Japanese proposal and the English product was too

---

15   See eg *Allamanna Svenska Elekriska A/B v Burntisland Shipping Co Ltd* (1951) 69 RPC 63.

16   *Burrough's Application* [1974] RPC 147 at 158.

17   *Du Pont's (Witsiepe) Application* [1982] FSR 303. See also *Hallen Co v Brabantia (UK) Ltd* [1991] RPC 195 where a combination of known technologies (self-pulling corkscrew and friction-reducing coating material) was obvious and not patentable even as a selection patent); but cf *Mölnlycke AB v Procter & Gamble Ltd (No 5)* [1994] RPC 49.

18   [1970] FSR 47.

minor to be regarded as anything other than an obvious variation.

A more difficult problem is in identifying the relevant art; the hypothetical addressee in, say, a medical case will be expected to know all there is to know about matters medical and, possibly, after *Genentech*, even have to think about these matters. But what happens if there is a development in a very different field which may in fact be relevant to him but of which in practice he is likely to know nothing? A possible example might be developments in metallurgy which produce a new and lighter alloy. Once our hypothetical medical addressee learns of this it may well be obvious to consider using it in the making of artificial limbs, but it being in a very different art he may never learn of it. Guidance is provided by *Johns-Manville Co's Patent*.[19] The patent had been granted for the use of a flocculating agent (which cause particles of solutions to adhere to one another thus assisting the separation of the solids from the liquids in a solution) in the manufacture of shaped asbestos cement articles which are made from a slurry-like solution. In seeking revocation of the patent it was argued that what the patentee had done was obvious in the light of two previously published documents relating to the use of such flocculating agents in two other industries, mining and paper manufacture. Both these industries, though very different from that of the patentee, can readily be imagined to find flocculating agents to be valuable. The Court of Appeal agreed to revoke the patent; the common factor of flocculation was sufficient for them to say that the patentee's knowledge should extend to what were effectively applications of the same art in different circumstances. This finding was easy to reach in the light of evidence that one of the patentee's employees had investigated (and rejected) the use of the agent in question some time previously on hearing of use in other industries. A similar decision was reached in the recent case of *Buhler A G v Satake Ltd*[20] where the use of a milling machine for milling grain in a case where such a machine had been used in a similar way in the paint and chocolate industries was held to be obvious to the skilled expert in the construction of machines of that type, even though it was accepted that the particular use was novel.

It appears from these cases that the courts will interpret the 'art' in question broadly to include related matters in other areas of activity. It will be regarded as obvious to transplant ideas from those related areas to that of the patentee. However the corollary of this would appear to be that it is not obvious for the patentee to have considered apparently unrelated fields which do not form part of the state of his art, and so to do will represent an inventive step.

It has been held recently that a team member whose expertise was in the field of obtaining regulatory approval for a new drug was not the notional

---

19   [1967] RPC 479.
20   [1997] RPC 232.

■

addressee in question since their expertise lay in regulation of drugs rather than in the drug's creation.[1]

The quest for the inventive step is perhaps the most difficult aspect of the patent application procedure. It involves the Patent Office, on application, or the court, in subsequent revocation proceedings, in forming a qualitative judgment about the work of the patentee. Difficulties abound at every stage as to what was known originally, what the patent's role in relation to the original matter is, and what not the patentee himself but the hypothetical addressee in his place would have known and deduced from that knowledge, with the value judgment then being made as to whether that deduction, often in a field of great technicality, was one which was obvious and thus not worthy of patent protection or one which can be described by the magic word 'inventive' and thus secure the coveted reward. This has always been an onerous burden on the applicant but the *Genentech* decision has made it harder in raising the standard of inventiveness to be expected from the hypothetical addressee in industries employing the highest levels of modern technology so that some developments which are accepted as being an inventive step are nonetheless damned by obviousness. The realisation from *Genentech* that there is such a concept as the obvious invention reveals a fatal flaw in the approach of the law, since section 3 declares obviousness and inventiveness to be incompatible opposites. Until this is resolved, the inventive step cannot be lauded as an effective legislative approach and a resolution of the problem. Either *Genentech* is accepted with its common ground with some European jurisdictions that some inventions may be obvious, with its serious adverse implications for inventors in hi-tech industries and subsequently for the broader interests of society, or inventiveness will have to be redefined in new terms, perhaps by demoting obviousness to being merely a factor to be considered and/or by equating inventiveness with that which the reasonable exponent of the art in question would regard as an inventive step worthy of patent protection. The only alternative is for a court to cast around to find something which is inventive even in the post-*Genentech* era, as in the *Chiron* case at first instance.

Certainly the difficulty of defining, let alone proving the existence of, the inventive step must be the largest single contributor to the time and expense involved in making a patent application, whether successful in the end or, disastrous in economic terms, ultimately unsuccessful. It may be that the whole area needs to be reconsidered[2] but that time has yet to come and the current patchwork is the only picture that we have.

---

1   *Richardson-Vicks Inc's Patent* [1997] RPC 888.
2   See Cole 'Inventive Step-Meaning of the EPO Problem and Solution Approach & Implications for the United Kingdom' [1998] EIPR 214 and 267.

Industrial application

The third key requirement of the 1977 Patents Act is that in order to be patented an invention must be capable of industrial application. This phrase is new to the 1977 Act; hitherto the invention had to represent 'a new manner of manufacture'[3] and this clearly shows that a broader approach, more favourable to patentees, is now being taken and also that previous case law is not now of great assistance. This part of the law casts a useful shaft of light on the aims and purposes of the patent system. Only that which is usable, or, to be precise capable of industrial use, is regarded as deserving of the protection afforded by the grant of a patent. It also poses an important practical barrier to a patentee deciding at what stage of the inventive process an application for a patent should be sought; clearly if the invention is still at a theoretical stage, no matter how advanced, it will be premature to make an application if its potential industrial applicability is yet to be demonstrated.

Section 4(1) of the 1977 Act is of little assistance in explaining the new terminology simply informing the reader that an invention is capable of industrial application if it can be made or used in 'any kind of industry, including agriculture'. This broad approach does seem to signify that it will be no ground for objection to a patent that it is found to work in a different field of industry from that which the inventor originally had in mind.

More significant is the remainder of section 4: subsections (2) and (3) state:

'(2) An invention of a method of treatment of the human or animal body by surgery or therapy or of diagnosis practised on the human or animal body shall not be taken to be capable of industrial application.'

'(3) Subsection (2) above shall not prevent a product consisting of a substance or composition being treated as capable of industrial application merely because it is invented for use in any such method.'

The basic effect of these two subsections is clear. Section 4(2) disallows the creation of a patent monopoly on a method of treatment. This is best explained on policy grounds; it is not in society's interests for one doctor to be able to rely on a monopoly to deny the use of a method of treatment to other doctors and of course their patients too. The benefits of a new treatment should be available to all. Section 4(3) however takes the opposite approach to pharmaceutical products which in many cases will form a vital part of the treatment method, and it is seen as entirely appropriate to permit a monopoly over the supply of drugs for the lifetime of the patent. This might be thought by cynics to be a reflection of the respective lobbying

3   Patents Act 1949, s 101(1).

strengths of the medical profession and the drugs industry but can be justified to an extent. Precise methods of treatment will vary from surgeon to surgeon and would be hard to define accurately for the purposes of a patent specification, and it is also fair to note that doctors have duties towards their profession which have no parallel in the case of a researcher employed by a pharmaceutical company.

This area must also be considered alongside section 2(6) of the 1977 Act which has already been noted. It will be recalled that this allows the patenting of a pre-existing product for the first occasion only on which it is found to have a medical or related use. In extending the definition of novelty this provides further assistance to an applicant for a patent in the area of pharmaceutical products and the circumvention of the ban on patents for a second or subsequent medical use[4] by focussing on the manufacturing process used for that drug with a view to that use only goes to confirm that there is ample scope for patenting the drugs used in treatment and confirms the contrast in the approach to the two aspects of medical care.

Problems are created by this area. The intelligent patent-seeker will make use of this area of the law to seek backdoor protection by patent of the inherently unpatentable. Careful drafting of a patent claim can give a monopoly on the drugs used in a method of treatment and thus confer a de facto monopoly on the treatment itself. An extreme example of this arose recently under the admittedly different provisions of US law where a child was born with leukemia and its placenta preserved for use in future medical treatment. When the time for treatment arose, it could not occur without payment of a substantial royalty to the owner of the patent in respect of that kind of treatment.[5] This sad tale explains why section 4(2) is so important but equally demonstrates the potentially alarming consequences when it can be circumvented.

The main area of concern in this part of the law has traditionally been with the establishment of the boundaries of the medical treatment exception. The proper approach to be taken is spelt out in *Unilever Ltd (Davis's) Application*.[6] Here a patent was sought for a method of immunising poultry against the disease coccidiosis by using certain micro-organisms as food additives. Such immunisation has the effect not of curing the animals of disease but rather preventing them from catching the disease in the first place. The question arose whether this was a therapy for the purposes of section 4(2). After extensive consideration of both general and medical dictionaries Falconer J found that therapy had a broader meaning than just the curing of diseases and covered any form of medical treatment of disease; this broad interpretation, albeit the result of classic common lawyers'

---

4   *John Wyeth & Brother Ltd's Application; Schering AG's Application* [1985] RPC 545.
5   BBC 2 *Newsnight* 22 July 1998.
6   [1983] RPC 219.

pedantry, appears to fit well with the new era of purposive construction of the patent legislation.

Still, however, the frontiers of the section 4(2) exception have to be delimited. The connection with disease seems an important feature of the exception in the *Unilever* case and this is reflected in *Stafford-Miller's Applications*[7] where patents were sought for a method of chemical treatment of headlice. Whitford J refused to throw out the application on section 4(2) grounds. Regarding the case as 'on the absolute frontier',[8] he held that it was arguable that an infestation of headlice while an undoubted irritant may very well not be regarded as disease and thus its treatment is potentially patentable. Likewise the view has been taken by the EPO that medical tests which may be carried out in order to see whether a disease is present do not fall within this exception and thus in an appropriate case may secure patent protection.[9]

Particular problems have been generated by contraception which in the form of birth control pills involve the use of chemicals on the body. However, in a decision on the then common law based exception which appears to be equally applicable in the current statutory regime it was held in *Schering A G's Application*[10] that it was acceptable to patent contraceptives; again this is consistent with the need for there to be some connection with a disease for the section 4(2) exception to be applicable and represents a significant advance on the previous refusal to grant patents for contraception.[11] An alternative method of securing patent protection for contraception without getting entangled with the medical treatment exception is illustrated by *Organon Laboratories Ltd's Application*[12] where a patent was permitted for a pack containing two different types of contraceptive pill with clear indications as to the dates when each should be taken and the pills presented in an appropriate order. Taken together, these elements amounted to what was then a new and more effective method of contraception. However it seems that the novelty of the combination of the pills was of the essence in this case; merely making an improvement in the packaging or presentation of a product to improve its use is not sufficient to gain a patent, according to *Ciba-Geigy AB (Durr's) Application*.[13]

In general, the requirement that patents must be capable of industrial application adds little to the general picture, though it represents bad news for the ever-optimistic designers of perpetual motion machines. Its only significance lies in the associated refusal to allow medical treatment but not

7   [1984] FSR 258.
8   Ibid at 261.
9   *Bruker's Application* [1988] OJ EPO 308.
10   [1971] RPC 337.
11   *Riddlesbarger's Application* (1936) 53 RPC 57.
12   [1970] RPC 574.
13   [1977] RPC 83.

the drugs used therein to become the subject of a successful patent application.

NON-PATENTABLE MATTER

Even if the requirements of novelty, inventive step and industrial application are satisfied by an applicant for a patent there is one further group of hurdles placed in his way, namely the deliberate exclusion of various matters from the ambit of patentability by section 1(2) and (3) of the 1977 Act.

It will be recalled that the excluded matter under section 1(2) is:

'(a) a discovery, scientific theory or mathematical model;
 (b) a literary, dramatic, musical or artistic work or any other aesthetic creation whatsoever;
 (c) a scheme, rule or method for performing any mental act, playing a game or doing business, or a program for a computer;
 (d) the presentation of information'.

It is vital at the outset to establish one important restriction on the ban in section 1(2); it is only applicable to the prohibited matter 'as such' and the effect of these two vital words is that while it is not possible to patent, say, a discovery on its own, it is quite appropriate to patent some process embodying the discovery or a product in which the discovery has been transformed into a product of practical value. This means that in this area too the drafting of the specification and the claims is of vital significance. A scientist may discover a new source of energy but it is highly likely that much work will need to be done to harness and control the new energy source and to create the necessary technology which will embody it, and it is all this kind of work that should be the focus of the application for the grant of a patent.

The classic example of this is provided by *Otto v Linford*[14] where patent protection was sought for an internal combustion engine at the very early stage in the development of the motor car, the engine for the first time introducing air into the combustion process to enhance its effectiveness. The claim was found to be valid not as a discovery of the role of air which as a discovery would not be patentable, but as a machine which embodied and gave practical effect to that discovery. A more recent example is provided by *Rhodes' Application*[15] where a patent was successfully sought for a new speedometer that informed the driver both of his road speed and the square of that figure this representing the kinetic energy and thus, as it

14   (1882) 46 LT 35.
15   [1973] RPC 243.

was termed, the impact speed of the car. The application did not founder on the rock of being merely a presentation of information, since there was in the then statutory phrase 'a manner of new manufacture' in the form of a working machine which combined the idea of providing a driver with an indication of his impact speed with a workable method of so doing: today too this is more than just a presentation of information as such.

However the precise relationship between non-patentable matter such as a discovery and an attempt to gain patent protection for a product or process closely connected with it has been subject to a further review in *Genentech Inc's Patent*.[16] It will be recalled that this case concerned the use of known DNA technology to produce quantities of a potentially valuable activator, t-PA, for use against blood clots. Purchas LJ expressed the view that 'a claim to a method embracing a discovery which may well be an invention … is patentable',[17] rejecting the view previously expressed in *Merrill Lynch Inc's Application*[18] that the method of using the discovery must be novel, over and beyond the novelty of the discovery. In *Genentech*,[19] Dillon LJ made clear his view that a patent could be sought even though, once the discovery is made the way forward to the application of it is an obvious one. The additional albeit obvious work to harness the discovery provides the additional element which means that the patent is not just for a discovery 'as such'. It was clear that Mustill LJ[20] was unhappy with the reasoning at this point, though not with the ultimate conclusion reached. However this did not avail Genentech since the court found that some of their claims were for pure discoveries and non-patentable and, as we have seen, the steps they had taken to isolate the t-PA were obvious to people of their expertise.

To an extent it is appropriate to share the doubts expressed by Mustill LJ. A combination of a non-patentable discovery with an obvious application of it does not seem to provide the strongest of bases for the grant of a patent. However the wording of section 2 appears to lead inexorably to that result, with a very fine line emerging between the non-patentable discovery of something without more, which is not patentable even if inventive, and the inventive discovery of something which is then obvious in its application, which is. The user of the discovery is protected, where the discoverer is not. Again this could be said to show that the function of patent law is the conferral of a reward on the inventor of something useful which benefits society. Also, given earlier criticisms of other aspects of *Genentech*, it may seem churlish to object to what appears to be one of its more generous aspects. The approach has been confirmed by the Court of

16   [1989] RPC 147.
17   Ibid at 208.
18   [1988] RPC 1 (but see [1989] RPC 561 on appeal, and p 86 below).
19   [1989] RPC 147 at 240.
20   Ibid at 269-270.

Appeal in *Chiron Corpn v Murex Diagnostics Ltd & Organon Teknika Ltd*[1] where it was held that the patent claim was for the polypeptide that resulted from the genetic sequence that had been discovered.

There is also a broader aspect to this part of *Genentech*. Mustill LJ points out[2] the importance of identifying that there be an invention in the first place before proceeding to consider the three legal elements that make it patentable. He is fortified in this view by EPO Guidelines which make clear that this is a question which is separate and distinct from the other elements.[3] Actions which may fall foul of section 1(2) as being non-patentable are, he argues, in some cases in any event not going to pass the first test of there being an invention.

Purchas LJ took the same view. However this argument has been somewhat dented by the approach adopted by Lord Hoffman in *Biogen Inc v Medeva plc*.[4] He doubts whether the question of whether there is an invention or not is one of any practical importance because the requirements in the legislation for patentability have the effect of restricting claims within the general category of 'inventions'. Lord Hoffman claims that the drafters of the EPC and the Patents Act 1977 and even learned counsel in *Biogen* where unable to think of any examples of something which would be unpatentable purely because it was not an invention. So it is to an extent useful to check that there is an invention, but the check is unlikely to add anything to the consideration of patentability.

From these matters relevant to the whole of section 1(2), we can now move on to consider the specific exclusions. The first exclusions in paragraph (a) are self evident in their character but what may be less clear is the rationale for their exclusion especially since, for example, the development of scientific theory is much more likely to be as a result of years of effort than the product of a 'Eureka' shriek whilst idling in the bathtub. However, the explanation is that what these exclusions have in common is that they do not advance progress in the sense of creating something new, but merely reveal the existence of something that has always been there although only now is revealed. The application of science is thus much better rewarded than its pure form; research is not enough - there must be development too.[5]

The second group of exclusions – that of matter more at home in the field of copyright – is easier to explain in so far as it is clearly convenient to have a clear dividing line between the law of patents and that relating to copyright. Paragraph (b) appears to achieve this; a new method of painting may be the subject of patent but the painting itself will only qualify for

1   [1996] RPC 535 at 605–6 per Morritt LJ.
2   Ibid at 263–264.
3   Guidelines for Examination in the EPO Ch 4 paras 1.1 and 2.2.
4   [1997] RPC 1,
5   Ibid at 228.

copyright; it may be however that the electronic creation of music or the making of technical and similar drawings may push the intended division closer to the limit, as would a novel work of art capable of an industrial application; in the latter example the approach of section 1(2) in allowing patents for excluded matter not used 'as such' would seem to give rise to a potential clash with both patent and copyright protection being secured, contrary to the assumed intention that lies behind paragraph (b).

The next category – those in paragraphs (c) and (d) – gives rise to the usual need for care to be taken to read the patent application to see whether it covers the excluded material 'as such'; if it goes beyond the excluded material it will be able to get a patent but it would be prudent to emphasise the matter over and beyond, say, the presentation of information at the drafting stage. A useful set of facts to illustrate this simply is that of *ITS Rubber Ltd's Application*[6] where a patent application was made for a squash ball coloured blue in order that its location could be detected more readily by players. At the time it was found by Whitford J to be potentially patentable as a manner of new manufacture but now it would appear likely to fall within paragraphs (c) or (d) as being the presentation of information as to the location of the ball and since this would make no change to the method of playing squash it would seem to be claimed 'as such' and thus non-patentable whereas the dual speedometer noted above in the *Rhodes* case was incorporated into something new and would still be awarded a patent, if drafted appropriately.

A recent case which illustrates this well is *Lux Traffic Controls Ltd v Pike Signals and Faronwise Ltd.*[7] The patents here were for traffic light control systems one of which extended the green period by an additional period if it detected a vehicle crossing, thus ensuring opposing traffic was held by a red light, and the other of which gave a pause on each change of lights where no one had a green light for a time. Aldous J found that a method of regulating traffic as such would not be patentable as not being an invention, but rather merely an abstract plan, which at best presented information, following the EPO's decision in the *Christian Franceries*[8] case. However the patent claimed was for the device which by detecting both the movement and non-movement of traffic in a novel way created a new form of technological contribution to traffic management; it is the technical character of the improvement made that is vital[9] and that was found to be present in the first patent. Likewise in the second patent a known type of traffic regulation was in consideration, so on the face of it both non-patentability and anticipation applied. Again, however, what was in fact

6   [1979] RPC 318.
7   [1993] RPC 107.
8   T16/83 [1988] EPOR 65.
9   Guidelines for Examination in the EPO Ch 4 para 1.2(ii).

being created was a new device to control centrally with the maximum ease this type of traffic regulation and that was sufficient to justify the grant of a patent in that instance too.

The decision in *Raytheon Co's Application*[10] provides a contrast with this. It was concerned with a system for improving ship recognition by creating a digital record of known ships which could then be compared with the digital silhouette of an unknown ship. This was seen as non-patentable; its two sole features were that it was a system for performing a mental act and non-patentable as such and its other feature was a computer program and also non-patentable; there was nothing that amounted to a technical advantage here. It was the obvious mosaicking of two non-patentable items.

In mentioning the computer element in *Raytheon*, it should be noted that detail on this area is to be found in Chapter 26. However it is appropriate to note briefly a particular point that arises in relation to computer programs but also casts light on the preceding area. In *Merrill Lynch's Application*[11] the Court of Appeal was faced with the issue of patentability of a program drawn up by the applicants for a data processing system for making a trading market in securities. In the post-*Genentech* world it was clear that the applicants were under an obligation to prove that what they had done was to create something more than a computer program 'as such' so they pointed to the programming of the computer by the program as being the necessary extra element. This was rejected by Fox LJ:

> 'it cannot be permissible to patent an item excluded under section 1(2) under the guise of an article which contains that item – that is to say in the case of a computer program, the patenting of a conventional computer containing that program'.[12]

There must once again be technical advance in the form of a new result, and this was a requirement that had not been satisfied in *Merrill Lynch*.

This was a standard computer program and thus non-patentable and its application was to do no more than create a method of doing business which is also non-patentable. A similar decision was also reached in *Gale's Application*[13] where an inventor created a program on a disc which gave an easier method of calculating the square roots of numbers. No patent was allowed; all that the computer did was to generate a program; placing it on the disc was, as in *Merrill Lynch*, not a technical advance; in any event it was only a discovery of a mathematical method and thus fell foul of section 1(2)(a) as well. The fact that the retired plaintiff appeared in person probably

10   [1993] RPC 427.
11   [1989] RPC 561.
12   Ibid at 569.
13   [1991] RPC 305.

explains why this matter had to go up as far as the Court of Appeal for its ultimate, and obvious, disposition.

BIOTECHNOLOGY[14]

Two distinct types of matter which are of fundamental importance as biotechnology develops apace are excluded by section 1(3) of the 1977 Act which states:

'A patent shall not be granted –
(a) for an invention the publication or exploitation of which would be generally expected to encourage offensive, immoral or anti-social behaviour;
(b) for any variety of animal or plant or any essentially biological process for the production of animals or plants, not being a micro-biological process or the product of such a process.'

These matters are not exclusive to issues of biotechnology but impact more in this area than any other. Likewise in considering this topic regard should of course be had to important cases considered elsewhere such as *Biogen* and *Chiron* and, earlier, *Genentech*.[15]

The first group of exclusions is the UK's response to the EPC's[16] requirement that no patent should be granted where so to do would be contrary to '*ordre public* or morality'.[17] There is little jurisprudence on this section, but the key issue would appear to be whether the Patent Office and the courts are prepared to recognise personal views, genuinely held but controversial, as a reason for invoking section 1(3)(a). A patent which in some way made abortion easier would be deeply repugnant to many people but greatly welcomed by many others; but given that, as has been seen, patents are granted for methods of contraception to which significant minority groups in society are opposed, it would seem unlikely that the section would be invoked in such a case.

The legislation refers to matters 'generally' regarded as objectionable and this, it is suggested, appropriately reflects the universal rather than personal ideals which make up the notion of *ordre public*. So a patent which is designed to assist in some action universally regarded as wrong, such as safe-blowing,

---

14   See generally Llewelyn 'The Legal Protection of Biotechnical Inventions: An Alternative Approach' [1997] 3 EIPR 115.
15   See Jones and Britton 'Biotech Patents – The Trend Reversed Again' [1996] 3 EIPR 171.
16   EPC Art 53(a).
17   See Ford 'The Morality of Biotech Patents: Differing Legal Obligations in Europe?' [1997] 6 EIPR 315.

would be unlikely to secure patent protection; this is so, it is suggested, notwithstanding section 1(4) which ordains that the mere fact that an act is contrary to the law does not of itself translate that act into one within the ban on patent protection within section 1(3). Thus a patent for something which enables cars to travel at speeds above the current statutory limits may be patentable if it is felt that the attainment of such speeds is not contrary to the *ordre public*. A harder case which could fall either side of the boundary would be weapons or explosives, the existence of which may benefit a state's military power but the use of which in wrong hands would be against the public interest: an undetectable explosive such as Semtex is a case in point. A real life example of a finely balanced decision would be the objections to the patenting of the genetically engineered 'Onco-mouse' which, however, offered potential benefits to cancer victims. These were made under Article 53(a) of the EPC and were ultimately rejected on the basis that the suffering of the animal, which was intended to develop cancers, nonetheless conferred benefits on humanity and were unavoidable at this stage of our scientific development.

The other exclusion in section 1(3)(b) means that a patent cannot be granted for an animal or a plant or for a biological process for the production of animals or plants; microbiological processes are however patentable. The reasons for excluding animals and plants are in many ways very different.

Plants are appropriate to be excluded from the realm of patent law since there is a separate intellectual property regime in respect of them. This is now provided in the form of the Plant Varieties Act 1997[18] which develops the pre-existing law[19] by incorporating into domestic law an implementation of the 1991 revisions of the International Convention for the Protection of New Varieties of Plants (the UPOV Convention), and also fulfils the obligations created by European regulations.[20] However the basic principles remain, namely that in order to gain protection the plant variety must be distinct, uniform, stable[1] and new[2] in order to secure patent-style protection.[3] Unlike patents, though, the protection extends not only to the plant breeder but also to anyone who discovers the new variety. It should be noted that entirely new plants appear to fall within the traditional patent sector.[4]

---

18   See also The Plant Breeders' Rights Regulations 1998, SI 1998/1027. The Act came into force on 8 May 1998 (SI 1998/1028).
19   Plant Varieties and Seeds Act 1964.
20   Regulation (EC) 2100/94.
1   Plant Varieties Act 1997, Sch 2, Pt 1.
2   Ibid at paras 4–7.
3   Plant Varieties Act 1997, s 6 expands the scope of protection.
4   See Roberts 'Patenting Plants Around the World' [1996] 10 EIPR 531.

The period of protection varies; for example new types of roses acquire a 15-year term of right[5] while developments in rhubarb gain a 20-year period[6] and potatoes enjoy a 30-year period of protection.[7]

The ban on patents for animals creates more problems since there is no separate system for granting intellectual property rights in respect of them. The basis for the exclusion of animals seems to be based on moral grounds, the law viewing with disfavour Frankenstein-like experiments on living things. The problem is that such a model is quite inappropriate in modern times. The law clearly allows patents to be granted in respect of living matter through its recognition of microbiological processes and the distinction between a biological and thus non-patentable process and one which is patentable as a microbiological process is a very fine one and rather artificial too. The circumstances where a new animal may be created are in reality likely to be in highly controlled laboratory conditions with the purpose being an advance in medical science and thus a benefit to society. Whether patents are seen as a reward for the conferring of benefits on society or whether they are seen as a recompense for hard work and energy is immaterial here; both factors separately suggest the refusal of the law to give patent protection to animals is now anomalous.

This might be thought to be an entirely academic issue. Now, though, it is not. Experimentation has created the famous 'Dolly', a cloned sheep, and a substantial number of mice have also been created in the same way. Meanwhile Europe has been struggling to find an acceptable answer to the problem of legal control of biotechnology, as will be seen.

There are several ways in which rights in new or cloned animals may be considered. The issue could be considered as an issue of *ordre public* or it might be argued that a separate sui generis right should be created,[8] by analogy with plants.

The law has already had to consider the moral issues involved in the famous 'Onco-mouse' litigation. Following the lead from the US, the EPO has granted a patent for the so-called 'Onco-mouse.' This is a live mouse genetically adapted to develop cancers as part of a new approach to the treatment of cancer, and as such clearly is deserving of some form of legal protection. However, such a conclusion can only be reached via a very narrow interpretation of EPO Article 53 (the counterpart of the domestic section 1(3)(b)). The decision distinguishes new animals which are not patentable from new animal varieties which, not being expressly mentioned in the relevant article, can be granted patent protection. The 'Onco-mouse'

5   SI 1965/725.
6   SI 1966/644.
7   SI 1992/454.
8   See Peace and Christie 'Intellectual Property Protection for the Products of Animal Breeding' [1996] 4 EIPR 213.

was merely a variation on a pre-existing species and could be the subject-matter of a patent. It is an area that now calls for reform to allow the patentability of animals without recourse to artificially and atypically narrow interpretations of the law and the EPO is in the process of reviewing its policy in this regard. After all, the more general ban on the patenting of that which is generally offensive remains, and would be appropriate to control undesirable animal experimentation. Whether it is more appropriate to allow patent protection for the creation of new animals or whether it is better to create a new animal variety right by analogy with the law relating to plant patents is debatable; certainly an independent right would need an *ordre public* provision to protect society from undesirable or dangerous attempts at genetic manipulation.

Moves are being taken but inevitably in this legal, moral and scientific minefield they are being taken slowly and cautiously.

Years of discussion have finally led to advance on the European front in the form of a draft Directive on the legal protection of biotechnological inventions.[9] After much discussion this was approved by the European Parliament in May 1998. This provides for the protection of such inventions through the patent law of member states but does not extend to plant or animal varieties or essentially biological processes for their creation. There is also a specific exclusion within a general *ordre public* exception that prevents the registration of processes for human cloning and related activities including the use of human embryos for industrial or commercial purposes. Likewise excluded is the genetic modification of animals which cause suffering and are not conferring any substantial medical benefit. Thus the 'Onco-mouse' would still be patentable but more experimental variation would not be.

It is clear that the Euro-art of compromise was instrumental in securing the safe passage of the draft Directive but the consequence of this is that it fails to address the most pressing concerns in this controversial area. Science presses ahead while the law lags behind. The creation of new animals and the cloning of pre-existing animals, including in theory humans, is taking place and the law must, therefore, have a response. The draft Directive is not the full answer to the problems that remain in this ethical minefield.

PATENTABILITY – OVERVIEW

It is appropriate to step back at this juncture and assess the way in which the law has approached the overall question of patentability. The obstacles placed in the way of an applicant are quite considerable, particularly when viewed in the light of the result achieved, a monopoly right only over the

9   (1998) OJ C110/17.

matters directly claimed for a de jure 20-year period which in actual fact will only be capable of commercial exploitation for a lesser period, while all the time rivals are, as will be seen, free to experiment on producing a better product at any time or a rival imitator as soon as the 20 years are over.

In order to win this somewhat less than glittering prize novelty is a reasonable requirement for the applicant to have to satisfy but this cannot be said in relation to inventive steps where the convolutions of the judges in the Court of Appeal in the *Genentech* saga stand as a pointer to the fact that it is not sensible to define an inventive step as one which is not obvious to take. The case makes it harder to gain protection in economically important areas of high technology but more generally indicates the difficulties which will inevitably attend any tribunal seeking to place itself in the face of a non-existent profoundly stupid but highly knowledgeable reasonable man and then asking the qualitative judgment to be made as to whether a step made was, at that time, an obvious one to make or not. It is a question asked by the ill-equipped which is close to unanswerable.

Reviewing what a court will regard as non-patentable matter also shows that this area is not without its problems. Section 1(2) excludes much which may be the subject of prolonged research work though careful drafting and the generosity of the courts in allowing inventive non-patentable matter to provide the element of inventiveness in a broader patent both go some way to limiting the difficulty for patentees, while the law seems reluctant to invoke section 1(3) to stop patents being granted even where, as in the 'Onco-mouse' case, so to do would on the face of it be contrary to the words of the legislation.

If a patent is a reward it is one not readily gained. The need for the applicant to satisfy the various requirements coupled with the years that the process will take both suggest that the law regards the grant of a monopoly as a matter of the utmost seriousness and gravity. Whether the consequences of being granted a patent are so wondrous as to justify the application of so much seriousness and gravity is more questionable, especially when evidence indicates that many patents are granted for inventions which do not lead to commercially successful exploitation and when the 'cutting edge' of biotechnology is not well protected by the patent system. It may be that a lifetime obligation of confidentiality *inter partes* may increasingly be seen to be a better answer.

Chapter 4

Use and grant in the UK and Europe

WHOSE PATENT IS IT ANYWAY?[1]

We have so far referred generally to applicants for patents without examining who is in fact entitled to be granted a patent. Section 7 of the 1977 Act is the starting-point for this enquiry. By section 7(1) any person may make an application either alone or jointly. However under section 13(2) the applicant must include in his application a statement as to who the inventor is, in case the inventor himself is not applying, and, if others are involved, an indication of what right the applicant has to be granted the patent. So there is no danger of a patent being granted to a usurper. This is borne out by section 7(2) of the 1977 Act, which states that a patent may be granted:

'(a) primarily to the inventor or joint inventors;
(b) in preference to the foregoing, to any person or persons who, by virtue of any enactment or rule of law, or any foreign law or treaty or international convention, or by virtue of an enforceable term of any agreement entered into with the inventor before the making of the invention, was or were at the time of the making of the invention entitled to the whole of the property in it (other than equitable interests) in the UK;
(c) in any event, to the successor or successors in title of any person or persons mentioned in paragraph (a) or (b) above or any person so mentioned and the successor or successors in title of another person so mentioned;
and to no other person.'

---

1   With apologies to TV star and patent expert Clive Anderson, as in The Patent Office's Laser Disc Patent Training Package (Patent Office, 1992).

The words 'primarily' and 'in preference' simply indicate that the inventor is first and foremost the normal patentee but will sometimes have lost that right, for example to his employer under his contract of employment, as will be seen. By section 7(3) an inventor is simply defined as the actual deviser of the invention.

Where a patent is awarded jointly to more than one inventor it is important to establish the respective entitlements of the holders. Section 36 of the 1977 Act does this by establishing that each joint patentee is entitled to an equal undivided share of the patent, though this may be varied by agreement between the joint patentees. The obvious analogy is with the position of tenants in common of real property. Joint patentees have the right to do anything with the invention without having to consult their fellow patentees with some exceptions, most significantly that the consent of the others is required to any licensing or assignment of the patent.[2] Thus one joint patentee could exploit the invention on his own and pocket the proceeds without any obligation to account in any way to his fellow patentees, in the absence of any agreement to the contrary.

Disposal of the patent can give rise to problems especially if the need for this to happen arises from a dispute between the joint patentees if, for example, one is opposed to, and thus blocks, a proposed licensing arrangement. In *Florey's Patent*[3] the Patent Office was faced with a dispute between a group of medical researchers who had jointly secured a patent for a new form of penicillin. All but one then wished to assign the patent to the National Research Development Council for further development and ultimate exploitation. However the objector, while not opposing the assignment as such, held out for a half share of the proceeds to which he felt entitled. Under what is now the power granted to the Patent Office to determine disputes between joint patentees under section 37(1)(b) of the 1977 Act, the assignment was ordered to proceed with an equal distribution of the proceeds being made as the normal route to follow where, as here, no contrary agreement could be proven.

The main area where disputes arise over entitlement to the grant of a patent is between employers and employees. Many inventions will be made by employees, such as university professors or R & D people in private industry. However, in making their inventions they will in all probability be using the facilities and resources of their employer and this has led the law to declare by section 39 of the 1977 Act that in many instances the employer, not the employee, will be the person entitled to the grant of a patent. Though the current appearance of the law dates from the 1977 Act, there were earlier common law rules covering the same ground and decisions from those cases are said to offer guidance in the interpretation of the

2   Patents Act 1977, s 36(2) and (3).
3   [1962] RPC 186.

statutory rules.[4] Unusually this is purely domestic law; there is no equivalent provision in the EPC. There are two categories of situation where the Act envisages that a grant to the employer is appropriate.

Firstly by section 39(1)(a) of the Act the employer gains the patent if the employee is in the course of his duties and the circumstances are such that an invention might reasonably be expected to result. Put simply if an employee is paid to research he gains his reward in his salary cheque and the employer gains the patent as a reward for his foresight in hiring the researcher in the first place. The second situation where the employer is entitled to the patent is where the invention is made in the course of his duties by an employee who has a 'special obligation to further the interests of the employer's undertaking'[5] by virtue of his duties and responsibilities. So for example the head of a company's R & D division would fit within this category, indeed such a person may fall into both situations.

The first situation is well illustrated by the pre-1977 Act case of *Electrolux Ltd v Hudson*.[6] The defendant was employed as a storeman by the plaintiffs, manufacturers of electrical goods. In the evenings at home he and his wife amused themselves by considering possible inventions and one night devised a new kind of adaptor to facilitate more easily the connection of the dust bag to a vacuum cleaner. The plaintiffs claimed that they were entitled to this invention by reference to a very broad term in their contract of employment which appeared to permit the employer to reap the benefits of all inventive activity. In striking down this clause as being too broad and thus in restraint of trade Whitford J pointed out that Hudson earned a low salary (£1,302 per annum in 1971) and commented:

'It is not the sort of salary that is paid to a research worker. He was not employed to do research or to make inventions'.[7]

It would seem sensible in the light of this for employers in an appropriate case to stipulate that research and invention is part of the duties of a particular employee.

More problems have arisen in deciding just who comes into the other category of employees with a special obligation to the company. Clearly directors and other senior managers who owe a fiduciary duty to the company must come within this category,[8] but precisely where the line is to be drawn is not an easy question. Guidance has been provided by the courts in *Harris' Patent*.[9] Harris was an employee of a company selling valves

4   *Harris' Patent* [1985] RPC 19 at 28, per Falconer J.
5   Patents Act 1977, s 39(1)(b).
6   [1977] FSR 312.
7   Ibid at 323.
8   *Worthington Pumping Engine Co v Moore* (1903) 20 RPC 41.
9   [1985] RPC 19.

under licence from a Swiss firm. He was the manager of the sales department which involved advising potential customers and also providing after-sales service. After learning that he was to be made redundant in five months time Harris designed a new valve which was an improvement on the valves sold by his firm, and sought the grant of a patent for it. His employer claimed that the patent should be theirs, but was unsuccessful in this argument. Falconer J found that his normal duties did not include invention but were concerned with sales and after-sales service thus putting the case outside section 39 (1)(a); this meant that he had to be highly knowledgeable about valves and their use but that is not the same as saying that he was under a duty to invent. An alternative argument based on his position within the company also failed; his title as a manager was not enough in itself and examination of his powers and status in the firm and especially the lack of discretion that he could exercise showed that he did not owe a special obligation to the firm and thus could retain the patent for his own benefit. This leaves open where above Harris' position as manager and below board level the line will be drawn; the presence of a broad duty to the company over and above the day-to-day performance of the duties assigned to an employee seems necessary as an implication of *Harris*.

Harris was also referred to in the more recent case of *Staeng Ltd's Patents*[10] where an employee whose primary role was in the field of marketing was nevertheless expected to generate new ideas for new products as part of his job. This is sensible; marketing and product development are very closely related concepts and it is clear that a senior marketing executive will be expected to participate in product development activity.

The senior status of the employee was also seen as relevant. As a senior executive it was held that he had an obligation towards his employer's business and its development within the terms of section 39(1)(b) of the Patents Act 1997.

On the other hand, the relationship between ordinary work and innovation is less clear. In *Greater Glasgow Health Board's Application*[11] a doctor employed by the Health Board had created a new type of ophthalmoscope on his own initiative and in his own time. The view was taken that the doctor's duty was to treat patients and, although the device in question would improve treatment and diagnosis, it was no part of his duties as an employee to invent such a device.

If this appears to be harsh on employees whose vital inventions are promptly taken over by their employers some relief is at hand in the form of the provisions new to the law in 1977 found in sections 40 and 41 of the Patents Act. These entitle an employee to apply for an award of compensation by the employer if

10   [1996] RPC 183.
11   [1996] RPC 207.

'the patent is (having regard among other things to the size and nature of the employer's undertaking) of outstanding benefit to the employer'.[12]

A similar provision applies where the employee has formally assigned the patent to the employer for an inadequate sum,[13] though these rights do not exist where a collective agreement provides for the payment of compensation to employees,[14] as is quite common.

By section 41 the compensation payable by the employer should represent a fair share of the benefit to the employer of the patent. The fairness of the share will depend on various factors established by section 41(4) as including the nature of the employee's duties, pay, the effort and skill used and the contribution of the employers and of other employees to the invention. It should also be noted that no contract term may diminish these rights,[15] and that for obvious reasons they only apply to employees mainly employed in the UK.[16]

Before employees emboldened by these provisions rush out to buy a new Daimler or two it is clear that this legislation is not designed to produce a bonanza of payments. Outstanding benefits to the employer are one of many obstacles placed in the way of an applicant and recent case law confirms that it will be an uphill struggle to take advantage of these provisions. All three reported cases on this area have resulted in failure by the plaintiff. In *GEC Avionics Ltd's Patent*[17] a claim was made by the inventor of a new method of displaying information to the pilots of aircraft. This resulted in sales valued at US$72m as well as other related contracts and the chance of further future sales. This was not regarded as outstanding in the context of the real profit being around US$10 million and that as part of the turnover of a major international firm regularly making multi-million deals. This shows up the problem of assessing fair compensation too; what is fair to the inventor with his salary and to the employer with this vast turnover will always be very different.

In *British Steel plc's Patent*[18] the decision against the inventor is perhaps more understandable. The claim was by the inventor of a new type of valve that would be of great value in controlling the flow of molten steel. The benefit was regarded as a marginal one, partly because the valve was only used in one steelworks, partly due to the fact that the company had to spend much time and money perfecting the invention into a working product and partly due to the size of British Steel which meant that the proven benefits

12   Patents Act 1977, s 40(1).
13   Patents Act 1977, s 40(2).
14   Patents Act 1977, s 40(3).
15   Patents Act 1977, s 42.
16   Patents Act 1977, s 43.
17   [1992] RPC 107.
18   [1992] RPC 117.

of the invention was only 0.01% of turnover and 0.08% of profits. It was emphasised that the word 'outstanding' is a superlative and hard to prove especially in this case in an application for payment made only seven months after the grant of the patent.

Both these decisions were Patent Office hearings; a similar tale is told by the first case to reach the courts, *Memco-Med Ltd's Patent*.[19] The patent here was for a new door detector unit for passenger lifts and the applicant was a director of the company at the time of the invention. Aldous J found that the employee had the onus of proof in making the application; here it was unclear even that there was a benefit created by the patent since sales of the patented product were all to the Otis Co, with whom Memco-Med had a long-standing record of sales. Although the patented product was in some years responsible for 80% of the sales of the company there was no proof of the profitability of those sales and thus it was impossible to say that it was an outstanding benefit.

. In themselves these decisions are not too surprising. The claim in *Memco-Med* really came to grief for evidential reasons, while in British Steel the benefits of the invention appeared limited and in any event the applicant had received an *ex gratia* payment at the time and had also been awarded the MBE medal. But *GEC* is a reminder that almost anyone working in a large firm, where it is reasonable to assume that the bulk of R & D work goes on, is going to find it next to impossible to make a successful claim under section 40. This suggests that the section was the product of the politics of gesture, rather than of substance.

GRANT AND DEALING

The requirements of patentability have been met; an appropriate patentee is in place. The Comptroller of Patents waves his magic wand and a patent comes into existence for a period of 20 years normally from the date of filing the application.[20] The principal implication of this is that the patent (as well as the application for it) is deemed to be an item of personal property[1] and, subject to what follows, can be dealt with by its owner just like any other item of personal property. In at least one respect it is a somewhat odd example of personal property since it may change its form; there is a process for the amendment of the specification even after grant[2] and this may be a useful way of pre-empting an attack on the validity of the patent.

---

19   [1992] RPC 403.
20   Patents Act 1977, s 25(1).
1   Patents Act 1977, s 30(1).
2   Patents Act 1977, s 27.

■

   The owner of the patent will wish to deal with the valuable commodity that is his patent in various ways. He may wish to assign it to another, perhaps to someone better able than himself to exploit it commercially and this is allowed by the 1977 Act so long as the assignment is in writing and is signed by the parties to the transaction.[3] Similarly the owner of the patent may wish to use the patent as part of a mortgage transaction, perhaps to raise funds with which to develop the patent into a commercial success in his own right; this is permitted subject to the same conditions. All such transactions can, and should, be registered with the Patent Office since registered transactions in relation to patents take priority over those which have not been registered.[4]

LICENSING IN UK LAW

   The most likely form of dealing by the patentee is that he will seek to license out the patent by a formal agreement which allows another party to work the patent without fear of an infringement action. The virtue of this method of exploiting a patent is the flexibility it allows. For instance the patentee may not wish or be able to develop his invention into a perfected commercial product but by licensing it out to someone else this can happen without the patentee losing control as he would do in an assignment of the patent, the precise extent of control being determined by the patent licensing agreement. These agreements are documents that merit careful drafting and are often extremely long and complex. Another common reason for licensing is that it is easier when developing the market for a product in another jurisdiction to use a local firm, with its plant, distribution network, customers and contacts, rather than to seek to create all the necessary infrastructure to one's own account. Licensing of the product or process to a local firm is a sensible way of proceeding. Another possible reason for using a licence is as part of a collaboration between two firms working in the same field who may cross-license each other's patents.
   The alert reader may already have picked up from the foregoing some of the major problems which licences can create. Cross-licensing between collaborators immediately evokes a picture of monopoly while the creation of subsidiaries of other licensees in other jurisdictions reveals that this is an issue which may have international implications. Add to this the fact that many licences are exclusive licences – in other words A only licenses B to work the patent in a given area – then it is clear that the creation of exclusive monopolies in an international setting is bound to attract the wrath of the European Union, devoted to the pursuit of free trade and free competition

3   Patents Act 1977, s 30(3) and (6).
4   Patents Act 1977, s 33.

throughout the Union, and this aspect will form the major part of this section. We will proceed by first looking at some of the different types of licence that exist.

Licences as of right

By section 46 of the Patents Act 1977 the patentee may apply to the Patent Office to enter into the register of patents a statement that licences for a patent are available as of right. Why should a patentee declare 'open house' and allow anyone to come in and work the patent? A typical reason would be where the patentee himself is unable to work up the invention into a viable product or process in the commercial marketplace but is keen nonetheless that the patent should be exploited. Of course the real likelihood of this occurring if the patent is truly of value is low, since an agreement would already be likely to have been made in such a case to assign or license a valuable patent. Thus licences of right are not of the greatest value. A minor incentive to use the process is that patent renewal fees are halved where a licence as of right exists. The only other incentive is that the licensee has to agree terms (or to have them imposed by the Comptroller in the event of a failure to agree) and this will give the patentee an opportunity to secure an appropriate fee or royalty for the licence, but this will of course in reality reflect the dubious value of a patent subject to this procedure.

Compulsory licences

Whereas in the previous section the demand for the licence as of right is initiated by the patentee, here it is the Patent Office itself which imposes the availability of compulsory licences. This seems totally contrary to the picture of the patentee's ownership of a piece of personal property; it is up to the owner to decide whether to use a bicycle or not – surely the same should apply to a patent. That this is not the case in relation to a patent relates to the interests of society which in this part of the law are deemed to take priority over those of the patentee in certain limited circumstances. Some examples of potential problems that can be resolved by compulsory licensing are helpful before looking at the detailed legislation.

A monopoly represents power; all power can be abused. Of course a company which has produced a new drug of great value is entitled to due reward but it could seek artificially to push up the price by closely limiting the amount of the drug that is put on the market. Alternatively the inadequacies of the patentee may mean that, having revealed the existence of a new process through the application process, he is unable to develop it properly himself and in so doing frustrates those of greater ability and/or resources. Possibly a new product could be withheld from the market to protect pre-existing trade; the existence of, say, a reusable condom or a lightbulb of infinite duration might be concealed from the public by an established manufacturer who having invented it realises that it will drastically restrict trade. Of course a sensible manufacturer would see the problem and not apply for a patent.

The legislation thus has to balance the interests of society and inventor. Overall a cautious approach is taken. After three years of a patent's life application can be made for an individual licence or a licence as of right on various grounds.[5] The 1977 Act states that if the patent is capable of being commercially worked in the UK but is not or not fully so worked, that may ground an application, as may the failure to meet the demand for a product on reasonable terms or by domestic production as opposed to imports. The failure to work an invention domestically and the use of imports instead is a further ground, under the UK legislation as is the refusal to grant a licence on reasonable terms to the detriment of the export or domestic market, or the working of another related invention. The imposition of unreasonable conditions attached to licences is a final ground for objection.

The grounds appear fairly wide and as such may be thought to permit frequent intervention against the interests of the inventor, but this impression would be misleading. The decision to grant a compulsory licence is an entirely discretionary one and section 50 of the 1977 Act guides the exercise of that discretion. Consideration must be given to the need to work inventions as much as possible but only insofar as it is reasonably practicable so to do and also reflecting the need for the inventor to receive reasonable remuneration. Regard should be had to the nature of the invention – some may take years to perfect in the light of their complexity – and to the abilities and resources of the proposed licensee seeking to work the unworked invention.

The reality is that few people who go to all the time and effort of obtaining a patent will then ignore it. Even if they do so because of their own ignorance or lack of resources the patent, if of value, will be the likely subject of an assignment or licensing deal. If the difficulties of working a patent are genuine, it is not likely that an applicant can clearly show that his ability and resources will crack problems that the patentee has failed to do. Such relatively few cases which arise in the first place where someone might want to seek a compulsory licence will then have to be decided against the broad discretion imposed by the law.

It may be thought that some aspects of this part of the law have a somewhat protectionist tone but section 53(5) of the 1977 Act makes clear that no order may be made contrary to international obligation, thus including the Treaty of Rome and the Community Patent Convention. It

5   Patents Act 1977, ss 48(1) and (3). See the full analysis of this area in *Therma-Tru Corpn's Patent* [1997] RPC 777.

was argued in *Extrude Hone Co's Patent*[6] that to impose a compulsory licence in the UK was wrong since demand was being met by imports from Ireland, but this argument was rejected on the grounds that the licence had not imposed a restriction on imports but, on the contrary, promoted free competition. However, Hoffmann J took a different view in *Research Co's (Carboplatin) Patent.*[7] Here a licence of right had arisen under transitional provisions connected with the extension of the patent period from 16 to 20 years in the 1977 Act[8] and the licence was drafted in terms of preventing importation of carboplatin from outside the Community. Hoffmann J pointed out[9] that it would not be possible to prevent imports from within the community. This does not as such contradict *Extrude Hone* but is a reminder of the single market in which we live.

Confirmation of this in the context of compulsory licences now comes from the European Court of Justice. In *Re Compulsory Patent Licences: EC v United Kingdom and Italy*[10] the Commission objected to section 48 of the 1977 Act as permitting compulsory licences to be granted in the UK where provision of the product was taking place by importation from elsewhere in the EC, this being contrary to Article 30 of the Treaty. The Court rejected the UK's arguments and found that section 48 of the 1977 Act did run contrary to Article 30. The threat of a compulsory licence was capable of hindering intra-community trade by persuading the patentee to make his product in the UK rather than in other member states,[11] as did the reduction in imports consequent upon a licence being granted,[12] thus contradicting the *Extrude Hone* decision. It is clear that any compulsory licence issued where demand is met by imports from the EU will be ineffective and, arguably, section 48 of the 1977 Act should be amended to take this into account. Exercise of an invention anywhere in the EU and not just domestically must now be the test as in any event it will be under the Community Patent Convention.[13]

A final point to note is that the terms of the compulsory licence will include appropriate compensation for the patentee; this will normally be on a royalty basis.[14] By way of general summary it is clear that compulsory patent licensing is not the threat that it may at first appear to be to the

6   [1982] RPC 361.
7   [1990] RPC 663.
8   Patents Act 1977, Sch 1, paras 3 and 4.
9   [1990] RPC 663 at 694.
10   [1993] RPC 283. Where the importation is prohibited from outside the EU there is no such restriction: See *Generics (UK) Ltd v Smith Kline & French Laboratories (UK) Ltd* [1993] RPC 333. See also n 11, p 115 infra.
11   Ibid at 328.
12   Ibid at 329.
13   Arts 47, 82.
14   *Smith Kline & French Laboratories Ltd's (Cimetidine) Patent* [1990] RPC 203 at 245, per Lloyd LJ .

interests of patentees; they are rarely sought, more rarely granted and in the future will be even less available after the decision of the European Court of Justice.

Crown rights

In one further respect the patentee may find himself forced to share the benefits of the patent with another. Although it is not technically licensing this is a convenient moment to consider the extent to which the Crown can intervene and exploit the patent itself. The fact that the Crown has any such rights is a useful reminder that the grant of a patent is, and has been since the earliest days, an act of the Crown and this area of the law is also significant in showing a very direct way in which the state, and thus society can gain an undoubted advantage from inventive activity.

It is section 55 of the 1977 Act that establishes the basic rights of the Crown in respect of patents. It empowers any government department or person authorised thereby to do various acts in relation to a patent without the consent of the owner, if acting for the services of the Crown. This latter aspect is interpreted broadly and includes the activities of health authorities.[15]

The acts which are authorised by the section include use or sale of either a product or a process or the offer to another of an essential element of the invention with a view to putting the invention into effect. All the actions listed by the section would normally count as infringements of the patent but do not so count as a result of the section in question.

In so far as these provisions may be seen as draconian in their potential impact on patentees, this impression may be tempered by the obligation of the Crown to pay compensation to the patentee on either agreed or court-imposed terms in most instances.[16] This obligation does not arise in the cases of any invention tried or recorded by the Crown before the priority date of the invention and not as a result of information provided by the inventor. So if a private inventor and the Army are simultaneously working on the same invention, the private inventor could be forced to allow the Army to go ahead using the invention without the payment of any compensation. This, however, is clearly a narrow exception and in the normal run of events the inventor will receive compensation. Indeed it is easy to envisage a situation where the inventor will be happy for the Crown to intervene since it will in effect guarantee that there is a market for the invention, thus removing many of the risks inherent in the decision to exploit an invention.

15   *Dory v Sheffield Health Authority* [1991] FSR 221.
16   Patents Act 1977, s 55(4).

The priority enjoyed by the Crown is emphasised by the provisions of section 57 which override third party rights already created in respect of the patent, such as licences in favour of the Crown, though again there is provision for the payment of compensation to those affected.[17] During an official state of emergency the powers of the Crown are increased by section 59 of the 1977 Act and this allows the Crown to exercise its powers to use an invention for a range of reasons from the efficient prosecution of a war to the promotion of industrial productivity.

The Crown enjoys further privileges by virtue of section 22 of the 1977 Act. By virtue of this section any information in a patent application which may be prejudicial to the defence of the realm or to the safety of the public may be prohibited from publication or be restricted in its circulation. The practical effect of this is that any information in a patent application that is, for example, of military significance can be withheld from the documentation available to the public but can still be disseminated to relevant official bodies.

The powers of the Crown in relation to patents are far-reaching particularly when compared with the less draconian powers in most other jurisdictions. While it is true that due compensation is in most cases payable this does not wholly meet the objection that the interests of the patentee are given short shrift across the many areas of activity where the Crown may have an interest in the exploitation of an invention.

Exclusive licences

In many cases the licensing of a patent will be on a basis of exclusivity. This is of benefit to the licensor who will thus only have to make one agreement and deal with one partner and it is of particular benefit to the licensee who thus acquires the monopoly power inherent in the grant of a patent. The law reflects this reality by giving to the holder of an exclusive patent licence the same rights as the original patentee in relation to the bringing of infringement proceedings.[18] As a consequence of the evident power that resides in an exclusive licence, controls have been placed on the contents of all licensing agreements by section 44 of the 1977 Act. Any agreement which ties to the licence further terms which oblige the licensee to acquire other things from the licensor or which prevent the licensee from using the technology of others will, in respect of such terms, be void. Any agreement

---

17 Patents Act 1977, s 57A (added by the Copyright, Designs and Patents Act 1988, Sch 5, para 16(1)).
18 Patents Act 1977, s 67.

of this type which gives the licensee an alternative without such a tie and which is terminable on three months' written notice is however acceptable.[19]

The principal implication of the widespread use of exclusive licences, however, is that their monopoly implications trigger off the interest of the European Union. This therefore is an appropriate time to consider the range of issues that this invokes, not just in patent licences, but across the board of intellectual property law as its propensity towards monopoly clashes with basic principles of EU law. It is also interesting to note that what was at the time of writing still the Competition Bill, but what is expected to have become the Competition Act 1998 at the time of publication of this book, introduces a new competition law regime in English law. This system is more or less a copy of the EU system under Articles 85 and 86 and section 70 of the Bill states explicitly that section 44 (and 45) of the Patents Act 1977 shall cease to have effect.

COMMERCIAL EXPLOITATION IN EUROPEAN LAW

We can see in the text of the chapters of this book that European law has a great influence nowadays on the substantial provisions of intellectual property law. This does not give us the complete picture however, as the free movement and competition law provisions of the Treaty of Rome also have their influence. It is to this influence that we now turn.

The founding fathers of the European Union clearly did not believe that intellectual property was very relevant for their purposes when they negotiated the Treaty of Rome. They therefore did not find it necessary to include a chapter on intellectual property in the Treaty of Rome and during the first ten years virtually no problem related to intellectual property arose. Indeed, the most important obstacles to the creation of the European Economic Community and gradually of a single market were the existence of internal custom tariffs and quantitative restrictions on importations from other member states. The Treaty dutifully set out to remove these obstacles and it was only when a certain level of success had been achieved in this area that intellectual property became a problem. In the absence of European intellectual property provisions it was left to the member states to legislate in this area and to grant intellectual property rights on a national basis. When they were no longer protected by custom tariffs or quantitative restrictions placed on foreign imports certain competitors turned to intellectual property rights to protect their market share or the higher price they could charge in the absence of competition. They tried to invoke infringement of their national intellectual property rights by the importation of the goods or to use their intellectual property right to prevent competition. Infringement of a patent for a pharmaceutical product in member state A was for example

19   Patents Act 1977, s 44(4).

invoked to prevent importation of the same drug from member state B. Or one company applied for parallel patents in all member states and used its one patent per member state to grant one exclusive licence for each of these member states and to exclude as a result all competition. The Community felt it had to react and prevent the use of intellectual property rights to partition the market and to exclude competition. The Court of Justice summarised the situation in *Parke, Davis v Centrafarm* when it stated:

> 'The national rules relating to the protection of industrial property have not yet been unified within the Community. In the absence of such unification, the national character of the protection of industrial property and the variations between the different legislative systems on this subject are capable of creating obstacles both to the free movement of the patented products and to the competition within the Common Market'.[20]

This absence of Community intellectual property provisions does not mean however that intellectual property law is not subject to the general provisions of the Treaty of Rome. The provisions on free movement and competition law apply to all areas and therefore one has to start from the presumption that they also apply to intellectual property rights. Each of these provisions requires specific comments. We will therefore discuss them separately. For each of them we will have a general introduction followed by a patent specific section. It is self-evident that we will come back to these issues when discussing trade marks, copyright and design.

Free movement of goods

The general rule on the free movement of goods is found in Article 30 of the Treaty which sets out to eliminate all quantitative restrictions which hinder the free movement of goods:

> 'Quantitative restrictions on imports and all measures having equivalent effect shall be prohibited between member states'.

This provision is qualified by the first sentence of Article 36 which contains certain exceptions:

> 'The provisions of Articles 30 to 34 shall not prejudice prohibitions or restrictions on imports, exports or goods in transit justified on the grounds of the protection of industrial and commercial property'.

At first sight this would render Article 30 inapplicable in relation to intellectual property, but this cannot be a correct conclusion as the second

---

20   Case 24/67: *Parke, Davis & Co v Probel, Reese, Beintema-Interpharm and Centrafarm* [1968] ECR 55 at 71.

■

sentence of Article 36 limits the exception to the rule in Article 30. The second sentence of Article 36 reads:

'Such prohibitions or restrictions shall not, however, constitute a means of arbitrary discrimination or a disguised restriction on trade between member states'.

There must therefore be cases in which Article 30 applies to intellectual property. Before we attempt to clarify this situation two details need to be mentioned. First, European law should not be interpreted in the same way as an English statute is interpreted. A teleological or purposive interpretation should be given to the provisions of the Treaty rather than a purely literal interpretation. It should therefore be specifically kept in mind that the free movement provisions had as their purpose the creation of a single market within the Community. On the issue of interpretation it is also important to note that exceptions such as those contained in Article 36 should be interpreted restrictively.[21] Secondly, it has been suggested that Article 222 of the Treaty plays, or should play, an important role in relation to intellectual property.

'This Treaty shall in no way prejudice the rules in member states governing the system of property ownership.'

If this really means that the Treaty of Rome does not interfere with intellectual property rights[22] we can stop struggling with Articles 30 and 36. But this is clearly not the case. First, Article 36 would not provide for a partial exception for intellectual property rights if the Treaty was not applicable to them in the first place. Second, Article 222 is not a principle of the Treaty, but a final provision of it. The principles are contained in Articles 1 to 7 and have to be interpreted broadly and the Articles implementing them such as Article 30 also have to be interpreted broadly. The final provisions in Articles 210 to 240 do not override the principles. That is clear from their place in the structure of the Treaty and from their heading. Third, and most important, Article 222 has a very different purpose. It was derived from Article 83 of the European Coal and Steel Community Treaty and both Articles have no other purpose than to emphasise the freedom of the member states to allow companies to be privately or publicly owned.[1] This detail was particularly important because

21 See Pollard and Ross *European Community Law – Text and Materials* Butterworths (1994) at 218-219.
22 Supported wrongly by Miller 'Magill: Time to Abandon the 'Specific Subject-matter' Concept' [1994] 10 EIPR 415 at 421.
1   See Tritton 'Articles 30 to 36 and Intellectual Property: Is the Jurisprudence of the ECJ now of an Ideal Standard?' [1994] 10 EIPR 422 at 423 and Vinje 'Magill: Its Impact on the Information Technology Industry' [1992] 11 EIPR 397 at 398.

many Governments wanted to preserve the possibility to nationalise certain companies, even in a free competition European environment. It is thus impossible to interpret Article 222 teleologically and arrive at the conclusion that it has any role whatsoever in relation to intellectual property. This leaves us with Articles 30 and 36 as the only relevant provisions of the Treaty.

Article 30 lays down the rule that quantitative restrictions are not acceptable. These are defined by the Court as

> 'measures which amount to a total or partial restraint of, according to the circumstances, imports, exports or goods in transit',[2]

but the text of Article 30 makes it clear that this does not necessarily have to be the aim of the measure. Measures which simply have the same effect are also struck down. The effect of Article 36 is to add a further requirement for measures relating to intellectual property and to raise the threshold in Article 30 by requiring that the measure should amount to a means of arbitrary discrimination or a disguised restriction on trade between member states. Only measures which amount to a total or partial restraint of imports, exports or goods in transit and which also constitute a means of arbitrary discrimination or a disguised restriction of trade will fall foul of the Treaty obligations. One should thus distinguish between intellectual property measures which are legitimate under the provisions of the Treaty, and measures which go too far and fall foul of the threshold of Articles 30 and 36.

This system provided by the Treaty is a logical one. The Treaty set out to create a single market based on free competition and as we discussed in section A of this book intellectual property rights are justified as restrictions on competition in furtherance of competition in such a system because competition takes place at more than one level and intellectual property rights, while restricting competition on one level, enhance competition on another level. Intellectual property rights have as a result a place in a European free single market, but only in so far as they fulfil this task. When they are abused to do more than that, they will lead to arbitrary discrimination or to disguised restrictions on trade between member states and fall foul of Articles 30 and 36. It is clear from the above that in such a system the existence of intellectual property rights is a positive element,[3] but that the use that is made of them, the way in which they are exercised, can either be lawful or can constitute an abuse. The Court of Justice summarised the position as follows:

---

2   Case 2/73 *Geddo v Ente* [1974] ECR 865, [1974]1 CMLR 13.
3   The Court explicitly stated that Articles 30 and 36 do not affect the existence of intellectual property rights and leaves the determination of the existence of these rights to the member states in the absence of Community harmonisation. See Case 35/87 *Thetford Corpn v Fiamma SpA* [1990] Ch 339, [1989] 2 All ER 801.

'... whilst the Treaty does not affect the existence of rights recognised by the legislation of a member state in matters of industrial and commercial property, yet the exercise of those rights may nevertheless, depending on the circumstances, be restricted by the prohibitions in the Treaty. Inasmuch as it provides an exception to one of the fundamental principles of the Common Market, Article 36 in fact admits exceptions to the free movement of goods only to the extent to which such exceptions are justified for the purposes of safeguarding the rights which constitute the specific subject-matter of that property'.[4]

In the last sentence of this quotation the Court hints at the tool that will be used to distinguish legitimate forms of exercising intellectual property rights from abusive forms of exercising them. We will have to define what is required for each intellectual property right in order for it to fulfil its task in a system of free competition. The Court calls this the 'specific subject-matter' of an intellectual property right. Once that is done it will be possible to hold that any other use of an intellectual property right which goes further is an abuse and falls foul of Articles 30 and 36, as restrictions on competition through the use of intellectual property rights are only acceptable insofar as they are necessary to maintain an optimal level of competition on the various levels on which competition takes place.

Logically speaking and subject to the analysis that will follow such a specific subject matter will necessarily include the exclusive right to use or exploit the intellectual property right and to oppose infringements. To hold otherwise would render the existence of intellectual property rights meaningless. A theoretical right that cannot be exercised would indeed be absurd. The exploitation of the right must allow the inventor or creator to be rewarded for his or her work and stimulate them to go on inventing or creating. However, this is only one essential element of the economic justification theory which is applicable to intellectual property in a free competition environment. The other essential element is the beneficial effect for society of making the invention or creation available. The Court of Justice strikes the balance between the two elements by including in the specific subject matter of each intellectual property right that the right will be exhausted through first use by or with the consent of the rightholder. This is often referred to as the 'exhaustion' doctrine.[5] And finally the Court also includes the 'essential function' of the intellectual property right in the definition of its specific subject matter.[6] This is done because from the point

---

4   Case 119/75: *Terrapin (Overseas) Ltd v Terranova Industria Ca Kapferer* [1976] ECR 1039, [1976] 2 CMLR 482 at 1061 and 505.
5   See eg Case 15/74 *Centrafarm BV v Sterling Drug Inc* [1974] ECR 1147 at 1162.
6   See eg in *Centrafarm BV v Sterling Drug Inc* ibid.

of view of the economic justification theory the exercise of intellectual property rights is only tolerated in a free competition economic model to perform a specific function. And in turn the performance of that function is required to maintain an optimal level of competition on the various levels on which competition takes place. To use the patent law example, the essential function is to reward the inventor, because that is necessary to stimulate further inventions and create an adequate level of competition on the invention and innovation level. The economic model on which the justification of patents is based would be distorted and the free competition market would no longer operate adequately if the essential function of patents were not to be fulfilled. We will further clarify these principles when applying them to patents.

A last general point relates once more to the teleological interpretation of the relevant Treaty provisions. The interpretation given above is only valid if the provisions are seen as a tool to reach the ultimate goal which is the creation of the single market.[7] The same provisions might not be interpreted in the same way by the Court of Justice in a context where the goal of the creation of a single market is absent. This has its practical importance as the literal text of Articles 30 and 36 is often included in Treaties which the European Union concludes with third countries. This situation arose in *Polydor v Harlequin*[8] and on that occasion the Court did indeed refuse to interpret these provisions in the way it would have interpreted them in an intra-Community case. Caution has to be exercised in relation to the European Economic Area Agreement, as this includes the aim of the creation of a single market and, to a large extent, the interpretation the Court gave to the relevant provision in intra-Community cases.[9] It is submitted that the principle laid down in the *Polydor* case does not apply in relation to the EEA countries. This has now been confirmed by both Advocate General Jacobs and the Court in *Silhouette v Harlauer.*[10] The Agreement on the European Economic Area[11] has effectively made the full exhaustion doctrine applicable to the whole European Economic Area.[12]

7   Case 270/80 *Polydor Ltd v Harlequin Record Shops* [1982] ECR 329 at 349.
8   Case 270/80 *Polydor Ltd v Harlequin Record Shops* [1982] ECR 329, [1982] 1 CMLR 677.
9   See Von Lewinski 'Copyright within the External Relations of the European Union and the EFTA Countries' [1994] 10 EIPR 429 at 433.
10 Opinion of Advocate General Jacobs in Case C-355/96 *Silhouette International Schmied GmbH & Co KG v Hartlauer Handelsgesellschaft mbH* [1998] 2 CMLR 953, at paragraphs 2 and 3 and judgment dated 16 July 1998, unreported.
11 (1994) OJ L1/3, in force since 1 January 1994 (1 May 1995 for Liechtenstein).
12 The European Economic Area is comprised of the EU, Iceland, Liechtenstein and Norway.

Free movement of goods and patents

Many of these criteria were laid down and applied in relation to patents in the *Centrafarm v Sterling Drug* case.[13] This case involved a drug used for the treatment of urinary infections and for which Sterling Drug held parallel patents in the UK and the Netherlands. Due to the tight regulation of drug prices in the UK the drug was sold there at approximatively half the price at which it was sold in the Netherlands. Centrafarm specialised in the parallel import of drugs and bought a large quantity of the drug in the UK and imported it into the Netherlands for resale purposes. Sterling Drug brought a case alleging infringement of its Dutch patent by the importation of the drug.

The Court of Justice ruled that the essential function of a patent was 'to reward the creative effort of the inventor'.[14]

Although it can be argued that the patent system has many other functions, such as making the technological information available to the public, this must indeed be the essential one. Without reward many inventors will or will have to stop their activity and their creative efforts must necessarily precede anything else as, for example, without creation there is no technological information to be passed on.

With that essential function in mind it was necessary to define the specific subject matter in such a way that that function was fulfilled by the patent system and an adequate level of competition was created on the innovation level, while not unduly compromising the adequate levels of competition on the other levels at which competition takes place. The Court defined the specific subject matter of a patent as follows:

'... the guarantee that the patentee, to reward the creative effort of the inventor, has the exclusive right to use an invention with a view to manufacturing industrial products and putting them into circulation for the first time, either directly or by the grant of licences to third parties as well as the right to oppose infringements'.[15]

The patentee has the exclusive right to use the invention to manufacture industrial products and obviously he or she also has the right to oppose infringement. This is the hard core of the patent. If the function of it all is to reward the inventor, this has to be done through the commercial exploitation of the monopoly created by the exclusive right. This is done by allowing the patentee the exclusive right to put the product on the single market for the first time, as that will bring in the profit. But it was felt that

13   Case 15/74 *Centrafarm BV v Sterling Drug Inc* [1974] ECR 1147, [1974] 2 CMLR 480.
14   Case 15/74 *Centrafarm BV v Sterling Drug Inc* [1974] ECR 1147 at 1162.
15   Ibid.

this was sufficient to fulfil the function of rewarding the inventor and that allowing the inventor to control further transactions concerning the industrial product would unduly distort competition at other levels. Sterling Drug had been rewarded when it got its profit when putting the drugs on the market in the UK and they were the only ones that were allowed to use the patent to produce the drug and they could act against any infringing use of the patent. If they were allowed to interfere with the further commercial life of the drug, that would unduly distort competition. They would then be able to partition the single market by relying on their relevant national parallel patent in the importing country each time the drug was imported in another member state,

'where no such restriction was necessary to guarantee the essence of the exclusive rights flowing from the parallel patents'.[16]

Not only was this not necessary to reward the inventor, it went straight against the major aim of the Community. The Court therefore limited the exploitation right that forms part of the specific subject matter to the first marketing of the drug and held that by putting the drug on the single market for the first time all rights under all parallel patents would be exhausted. By putting the drug on the single market through marketing it in the UK Sterling had exhausted all its rights under the parallel patents and could no longer use any right under its Dutch parallel patent to oppose the subsequent importation into the Netherlands of the drugs it had put on the market in the UK. It is also important to note that the essential function is an integral part of the specific subject matter, which stresses the fact that the specific subject matter is defined in such a way that the essential function will be fulfilled.

An important point is that the patentee can undertake the first exploitation himself or can grant a licence to a third party to undertake the first exploitation. The crucial element here is that the first exploitation needs to be undertaken with the consent of the patentee.[17] The first exploitation will only lead to the exhaustion of the rights under all parallel patents if the patentee has consented to the first exploitation. This means in practical terms that a patentee will still be able to block the importation of goods by relying on the patent if these goods have been manufactured by a third party without the consent of the patentee. In such a situation the third party is legally and economically independent and owns the patent in the member states where its manufacturing activities are based.

It is also important to clarify what are parallel patents. As long as national patent legislation is not fully harmonised, it may lead to slightly different

16   Ibid at 1163.
17   Ibid at 1162-1163.

patents, for example, because the claims are worded differently. The Court of Justice therefore adopted the only workable approach. All patents that protect the same invention are held to be parallel patents.[18]

On the basis of this analysis the conclusion on the facts of *Centrafarm v Sterling Drug* was

> '... that the exercise, by a patentee, of the right which he enjoys under the legislation of a member state to prohibit the sale, in that State, of a product protected by the patent which has been marketed in another member state by the patentee or with his consent is incompatible with the rules of the EEC Treaty concerning the free movement of goods within the Common Market'.[19]

Only those ways of exercising the patent right which stay within the specific subject matter of the right are compatible with the Treaty. And as the Treaty has an overriding effect on national law, the national provisions which allow more extensive use of the patent right can no longer be applied in a Community context.

The Court had to analyse the essential function and consent ideas further in *Merck v Stephar*.[20] This case again involved a patent for a drug, this time a drug that was used to treat high blood pressure. Merck held patents relating to the drug in the Netherlands and Stephar was importing the drug into the Netherlands from Italy. The interesting aspect of the case was the fact that at the time there was no patent protection for pharmaceutical products under Italian law. Merck had put the drug on the market in Italy, but argued that to hold that it had thereby exhausted its rights and could no longer rely on its Dutch patent would go against the essential function of the patent as due to the impossibility of patenting the drug in Italy the sale there had not taken place under monopolistic conditions and thus the lower price and profit had not fully rewarded its creative efforts. The Court rejected this interpretation. First of all, no specific reward is guaranteed as the exact amount of the reward depends in all cases on the market conditions. Second, if in these circumstances a choice to put the product on the market without the benefit of a patent is made, the inventor accepts the reward the market will offer. This means that the essential function is fulfilled and that the specific subject matter will indicate the limit of the exercise of the patent rights. In other words, by marketing the drug in Italy Merck had exhausted all rights under the existing parallel patents within the Community and the fact that no patent could exist in Italy did not influence that conclusion. It is up to the patentee to decide whether or not to market the product in a

18   Ibid at 1163.
19   Ibid at 1163.
20   Case 187/80: *Merck & Co Inc v Stephar BV* [1981] ECR 2063, [1981] 3 CMLR 463.

market where weaker forms of protection or no protection at all are available. Needless to say the conclusion would have been the same had Merck decided not to market the drug in Italy themselves, but to have it marketed there with its consent by a third party.

The Court expressed it as follows:

'That the right of first placing a product on the market enables the inventor, by allowing him a monopoly in exploiting his product, to obtain the reward for his creative effort without, however, guaranteeing that he will obtain such a reward in all circumstances. It is for the proprietor of the patent to decide, in the light of all the circumstances, under what conditions he will market his product, including the possibility of marketing it in a member state where the law does not provide patent protection for the product in question. If he decides to do so he must accept the consequences of his choice as regards the free movement of the product within the Common Market, which is a fundamental principle forming part of the legal and economic circumstances which must be taken into account by the proprietor of the patent in determining the manner in which his exclusive right will be exercised.'[1]

Merck had been rewarded for its creative activity and the patent rights had been exhausted by the marketing of the drug in Italy. It could not block the importation of the drug into the Netherlands by Stephar, because that exercise of the patent rights would go beyond the specific subject matter of the patent.

Recently the Court was given an opportunity to overturn its ruling in *Merck v Stephar* in a case relating to the parallel importation of drugs from Spain and Portugal. Its judgment in *Merck v Primecrown*[2] makes it clear though that *Merck v Stephar* is still good law. The Court specifically rejected the argument that the manufacturers of a drug were under a moral obligation to market their products even in countries where no patent protection was available and any suggestion that this took away the free consent of the manufacturers to the marketing of the drugs was rejected.

The consent idea also needs to be applied to compulsory licence cases. The issue is then whether the exploitation and first marketing by the licensee amount to putting the product on the market for the first time with the consent of the patentee and therefore exhausts the rights under all parallel

1   Case 187/80: *Merck & Co Inc v Stephar BV* [1981] ECR 2063 at 2081-2082.
2   Joined Cases C-267/95 and 268/95: *Merck & Co Inc, Merck Sharp & Dohme Ltd, Merck Sharp & Dohme International Services BV v Primecrown Ltd, Ketan Himatlal Mehta, Necessity Supplies Ltd*, and *Beecham Group plc v Europharm of Worthing Ltd* [1997] 1 CMLR 83; see Torremans and Stamatoudi '*Merck v Stephar* Survives the Test' (1997) 22 EL Rev 248 and Torremans and Stamatoudi 'Merck is back to stay: The Court of Justice's Judgement in *Merck v Primecrown*' [1997] 9 EIPR 545.

patents. This situation arose in *Pharmon v Hoechst*.[3] Hoechst owned parallel patents in a drug in the UK, Germany and the Netherlands and a compulsory licence had been granted to a third party in the UK. The Court held that

'such a (compulsory licence) measure deprives the patent proprietor of his right to determine freely the conditions under which he markets his products'.[4]

As a result the product was not put on the market with the consent of the patentee in case this was done on the basis of a compulsory licence and the rights under all parallel patents were not exhausted. Hoechst could rely on the Dutch parallel patent to prevent importation into the Netherlands by Pharmon of the drugs it had bought in the UK from the licensee who had produced these under a compulsory licence.

In *Merck v Primecrown*[5] the Court clarified the consent issue further by ruling that there is also no consent where the holder of a patent is under a genuine, existing legal obligation to market his product or to allow marketing by a third party under a compulsory licence. It is clear from the reasoning of the Court that such a legal obligation is highly unlikely to exist and that it will be difficult to prove. The presence of a legal obligation to market distinguishes the rule in *Pharmon v Hoechst*[6] from that in *Merck v Stephar*.[7] The two rules do not contradict each other.[8]

Articles 30 and 36 were subsequently raised on a couple of occasions in relation to compulsory licences and licences of right. Section 46 of the UK's Patents Act 1977 allowed for licences of right as licences available upon application. As such this does not create a problem, but the law clearly envisaged only production in the UK under such a licence of right. In case the holder of a licence of right imported the products from another member state rather than produce it in the UK an injunction could still be granted. This was exactly what Allen and Hanbury's were asking for when Generics intended to import the products for which it had obtained a licence of right from Italy rather than produce them themselves in the UK. The Court of

3   Case 19/84 *Pharmon BV v Hoechst AG* [1985] ECR 2281.
4   Ibid at 2298.
5   Joined Cases C-267/95 and 268/95: *Merck & Co Inc, Merck Sharp & Dohme Ltd, Merck Sharp & Dohme International Services BV v Primecrown Ltd, Ketan Himatlal Mehta, Necessity Supplies Ltd*, and *Beecham Group plc v Europharm of Worthing Ltd* [1997] 1 CMLR 83.
6   Case 19/84 *Pharmon v Hoechst* [1985] ECR 2281.
7   Case 187/80 *Merck v Stephar* [1981] ECR 2063, [1981] 3 CMLR 463.
8   See Joined Cases C-267/95 and 268/95: *Merck & Co Inc, Merck Sharp & Dohme Ltd, Merck Sharp & Dohme International Services BV v Primecrown Ltd, Ketan Himatlal Mehta, Necessity Supplies Ltd*, and *Beecham Group plc v Europharm of Worthing Ltd* [1997] 1 CMLR 83 at paragraphs 40 and 41.

Justice held that this was a restriction on the free movement of goods in the Community as it blocked certain forms of importation from a member state and encouraged local production rather than importation from within the single market. If all countries were to adopt this measure national markets would in the cases concerned once again replace the single market. This measure amounted to an arbitrary discrimination under Article 36 and could therefore no longer be applied within the Community.[9] Similarly the provision in section 48 of the Patents Act 1977 that allows for the grant of a compulsory licence if the patent is exploited by importing the products from another member state rather than by producing the products in the UK fell foul of Articles 30 and 36 because it is an arbitrary discrimination.[10] It encouraged local production rather than importation from within the single market and therefore hindered the free movement of goods.[11] In neither of these cases were these provisions necessary to safeguard the specific subject matter of the patent.

Patents and competition law – Introduction

Articles 85 and 86 of the Treaty of Rome deal with competition law and neither of these Articles contains an exception for a specific area. Intellectual property must thus be subject to the rules on competition in the European Union. We will first discuss the impact of Article 85 on intellectual property and in a second step we will turn our attention to Article 86.

Patents and competition law – Article 85

Article 85 of the Treaty consists of three paragraphs:

'1. The following shall be prohibited as incompatible with the Common Market: all agreements between undertakings, decisions by associations of undertakings and concerted practices which may affect trade between member states and which have as their object or effect the prevention, restriction or distortion of competition within the Common Market, and in particular those which:

---

9   Case 434/85: *Allen and Hanbury's Ltd v Generics (UK) Ltd* [1988] ECR 1245, [1988] 1 CMLR 701.

10   Case C-30/90: *Commission v United Kingdom* [1992] 2 CMLR 709, see also Case C-235/89: *Commission v Italy* ibid.

11   The provision can still be used if the patent is not exploited by local production and if the goods are instead imported from a non-member state as in these cases the creation of a single market is not affected. See Case C-191/90: *Generics (UK) Ltd v Smith Kline and French Laboratories Ltd* [1993] RPC 333.

(a)   directly or indirectly fix purchase or selling prices or any other trading conditions;
(b)   limit or control production, markets, technical development, or investment;
(c)   share markets or sources of supply;
(d)   apply dissimilar conditions to equivalent transactions with other trading parties, thereby placing them at a competitive disadvantage;
(e)   make the conclusion of contracts subject to acceptance by the other parties of supplementary obligations which, by their nature or according to commercial usage, have no connection with the subject of such contracts.

2. Any agreements or decisions prohibited pursuant to this Article shall be automatically void.

3. The provisions of paragraph 1 may, however, be declared inapplicable in the case of:
(a)   any agreement or category of agreements between undertakings;
(b)   any decision or category of decisions by associations of undertakings;
(c)   any concerted practice or category of concerted practices;
    which contributes to improving the production or distribution of goods or to promoting technical or economic progress, while allowing consumers a fair share of the resulting benefit, and which does not:
    (a)   impose on the undertakings concerned restrictions which are not indispensable to the attainment of these objectives;
    (b)   afford such undertakings the possibility of eliminating competition in respect of a substantial part of the products in question.'

We shall start by analysing this provision briefly.[12] Paragraph 1 outlaws a number of deals because they are anti-competitive and paragraph 2 sanctions that by declaring them void. Paragraph 3 contains an exception clause. When a number of requirements are met a deal which would normally fall foul of paragraph 1 will be exempted and paragraph 1, and consequently paragraph 2 as well, will not be applied to it.

With which deals is paragraph 1 concerned? The obvious category consists of the agreements concluded between undertakings. These will be affected if they have as their object or simply as their effect the prevention of competition, the restriction of competition or the distortion of competition within the Common Market. This provision could easily be circumvented though if it were to stand on its own by avoiding a formal agreement. Competition could nevertheless be affected if the parties were

---

12   For a full analysis from a competition law point of view see Whish *Competition Law* Butterworths (3rd edn, 1993) Ch 7.

to coordinate their actions and replace competition by coordination. The same effect could be reached by replacing an agreement with a decision of an association of undertakings. The drafters of the Treaty avoided this risk by including both concerted practices and decisions of associations of undertakings as separate categories which are covered by Article 85. A last additional requirement is that trade between member states must be affected for Article 85 to operate. Small deals which do not affect trade between member states are not important enough, because they will not have a substantial influence on competition at Community level. National competition authorities may nevertheless decide to pick up these deals and scrutinise them under national competition law.

When a deal is caught by Article 85(1), the sanction provided by Article 85(2) is that it is automatically void. No declaratory decision by a court or competition authority is necessary and in law we act as if the deal never existed. The deal will not bind anyone and no one will be able to rely upon it.

Exemptions which effectively place the deal outside the scope of Article 85(1) can be granted under the authority of Article 85(3) if four conditions, two positive ones and two negative ones, are met. These conditions are applied cumulatively; all four need to be met at any one time. The anti-competitive deal must first of all provide a contribution to the improvement of the production or distribution of goods or to promoting technical or economic progress. It must also allow consumers a fair share of the resulting benefit. Third, no restrictions which are not indispensable to the attainment of these objectives can be imposed and fourth, there should be no possibility of eliminating competition in respect of a substantial part of the products in question. If these four requirements are met an individual exemption can be granted. In practice this is done by submitting the deal to the Commission which implements and polices the Community's competition law as an application for an individual exemption. This individual process is a fairly lengthy process and it causes a lack of legal certainty as the parties to a deal do not know in advance which restrictive clauses will be acceptable to the Commission. In order to solve these problems and to avoid being unable to cope with a flood of applications the Commission issued block exemptions. These take the form of a regulation and contain lists of acceptable and non-acceptable clauses. Agreements that stay within the limits set out by the block exemption are automatically exempted and no further application or other procedure is required.

The next issue to address now that we know what Article 85 is all about is whether agreements concerning intellectual property are caught by it. Licence contracts, or eventually assignments, can restrict competition between the licensor and the licensee or between licensees to a considerable extent. Exclusive licences are prime examples of this. On the other hand there is no provision in the Treaty which provides an exception for the intellectual property area. The conclusion must accordingly be that Article 85 applies unreservedly to intellectual property agreements.[13]

Patent licences: General comments and individual exemptions

The Commission has applied Article 85 to patent licence contracts on several occasions and important guidance can also be derived from the *Windsurfing* case[14] and on the point of exclusivity from the *Maize Seeds* case.[15] Before we look at some clauses, some preliminary points need to be made. Article 85 does not apply to agreements of minor importance. The problem with this provision is that it is difficult to predict the success of certain licences and certain products and a licence agreement which is originally not covered may become such a success that it becomes important enough to be considered under Article 85.[16] This may have very undesirable consequences. Article 85 will not apply if trade between member states is not affected.[17]

A normal exercise of the patent will not infringe Article 85(1). Accordingly the licensor may charge royalties[18] and may try to ensure that his licensee exploits the patent adequately. The latter element implies that minimum royalty clauses[19] under which the licensee is obliged to pay a minimum amount in royalties even if the frequency of its use of the patented technology does not mathematically justify this and clauses that require a licensee to produce minimum quantities of the patented product or to carry out a minimum number of operations using the patented process are acceptable and do not restrict competition.[20] Clauses which go further than that may restrict competition and were held to infringe Article 85(1). Examples are clauses that require the licensee to pay royalties for non-patented products[1] and clauses that require the licensee to continue paying royalties after the patent has expired[2] although it is not an infringement to require the licensee to keep paying royalties for know-how

---

13   See Cases 56 and 58/64: *Consten and Grundig v Commission* [1966] ECR 299, [1966] CMLR 418 and Case 24/67: *Parke, Davis & Co Ltd v Probel* [1968] ECR 55, [1968] CMLR 68.
14   Case 193/83: *Windsurfing International Inc v Commission* [1986] ECR 611, [1986] 3 CMLR 489.
15   Case 258/78: *LC Nungesser KG v Commission* [1982] ECR 2015, [1983] 1 CMLR 278.
16   *Burroughs/Deplanque* (1972) OJ L13/50 and *Burroughs/Geha-Werke* (1972) OJ L13/53.
17   *Raymond/Nagoya* (1972) OJ L143/39.
18   4th Annual Report on Competition Policy, section 20.
19   See *AOIP/Beyrard* (1976) OJ L6/8, where such a clause was not condemned.
20   See the old Patent Licence Block Exemption, Article 2(1)(2) (1984) OJ L219/15.
1   See *AOIP/Beyrard* (1976) OJ L6/8.
2   Ibid.

which the licensee continues to use after the patent has expired if that know-how is still secret and has not yet fallen in the public domain.[3]

The term of the licence agreement may be shorter than the remaining life of the patent,[4] but tie-up clauses[5] which bind the licensee to the licensor once the patent has expired by obliging him or her to take out further licences for other technology do infringe Article 85(1). A licensor may also want to restrict the use the licensee can make of the licensed technology to a certain field of application, particularly if the technology can be used in very different areas, such as for example a drug which can be used both in human and in veterinary medicine. These field of use restrictions will fall outside Article 85(1) if they restrict the use of the licensee to one or more specific and identifiable fields of application.[6] This is in line with the Commission's view that a clause prohibiting the licensee to compete with the licensor or with any connected undertakings in respect of research and development, the so called no-competition clause,[7] or a no-challenge clause[8] that prevents the licensee, who is in this respect particularly well placed as user of the technology, from challenging the validity of the patent are generally[9] speaking bound to infringe Article 85(1).

Clauses that equally infringe Article 85(1) are exclusive grant back clauses[10] which oblige the licensee to grant an exclusive licence to the licensor in relation to all improvements of the technology or to all new and related technology it may develop, or, even worse, to assign these improvements or this technology outright to the licensor. This would deprive the licensee from any incentive to develop its own technology which it will need to compete on the market and give the licensor an unwarranted permanent technological advantage. Only exclusive licences are banned; non-exclusive grant back clauses are acceptable.[11]

The licensor has a legitimate interest in the protection of its brand image and the quality of the products. As a result clauses requiring the licensee to promote the product, to label the product, but not non-patented items as

3   *Kabel- und Metallwerke/Etablissements Luchaire SA* (1975) OJ L222/34.
4   4th Annual Report on Competition Policy, point 29.
5   See *AOIP/Beyrard* (1978) OJ L6/8 and *Velcro/Aplix* [1989] 4 CMLR 157, OJ L233/22.
6   4th Annual Report on Competition Policy, point 28.
7   See *AOIP/Beyrard* (1978) OJ L6/8 and *Velcro/Aplix* [1989] 4 CMLR 157, OJ L233/22.
8   *Windsurfing International* [1983] OJ L229/1 and on appeal from the Commission Decision Case 193/83 *Windsurfing International Inc v Commission* [1986] ECR 611, [1986] 3 CMLR 489.
9   The conclusion may be different in exceptional circumstances, see Case 65/86 *Bayer AG and Maschinenfabriek Hennecke GmbH v Sullhöfer* [1988] ECR 5249, [1990] 4 CMLR 182.
10 See *Kabel- und Metallwerke/Etablissements Luchaire SA* (1975) OJ L222/34; *AOIP/Beyrard* (1976) OJ L6/8, *Velcro/Aplix* [1989] 4 CMLR 157, OJ L233/22 and *Roses* (1985) OJ L369/9.
11 *Re Davidson Rubber Co Agreements* [1972] CMLR D52, OJ L143/31.

well,[12] in a particular way and to comply with certain quality standards fall outside the scope of Article 85(1).[13] A difficult borderline case is presented by a clause obliging a licensee to use the patentee's trade mark and get-up. This type of clause will make it difficult for the licensee to be identified as a separate entity and may make competition unworkable. It is only acceptable if it is combined with a right for the licensee to identify itself while using the patentee's trade mark and get-up.[14] The Commission's approach is that the latter clause may be caught, but may qualify for an exemption.

Tie-in clauses which for example oblige the licensee to buy raw materials from the licensor, will only avoid being caught by Article 85(1) if they are really indispensable for the successful exploitation of the patent.[15] Any other tie-in clause will not even be granted an exemption as this is a perfect tool to control the price at which the licensee can sell, and thus restricting competition.[16] Customer allocation clauses,[17] export bans,[18] vertical price fixing[19] and obligations only to sell the patented product as part of a package[20] will also be caught by Article 85(1).

A number of other clauses are on the other hand considered to fall outside the scope of Article 85(1). Examples of these clauses are obligations of secrecy,[1] most-favoured licensee clauses,[2] obligations to prevent infringement of the patent[3] and restrictions on the assignment and the sub-licensing by the licensee.[4]

Exclusivity is the most difficult issue, as it can be used easily to stop intra-brand competition between the licensor and the licensee and between the various licensees. It can also lead to a compartmentalisation of the market. The bottom line of the debate is that the Commission and the Court will never tolerate absolute closed exclusivity which would oblige the licensor and the licensee not to compete, through an active or even through a passive sales policy, in each other's area and this in combination with a similar obligation between licensees coupled with an obligation not to deal

---

12   Case 193/83: *Windsurfing International Inc v Commission* [1986] ECR 611, [1986] 3 CMLR 489.
13   See the old Patent Licence Block Exemption, Articles 2(6) and 2(9).
14   See the old Patent Licence Block Exemption, Article 1(1)(7).
15   See the old Patent Licence Block Exemption, Article 2(1)(1).
16   See *Vaessen/Moris* [1979] OJ L19/32.
17   See the old Patent Licence Block Exemption, Article 3(7).
18   *AOIP / Beyrard* (1976) OJ L6/8 and *Velcro/Aplix* [1989] 4 CMLR 157, OJ L233/22.
19   See the old Patent Licence Block Exemption, Article 3(6).
20   See Case 193/83 *Windsurfing International Inc v Commission* [1986] ECR 611, [1986] 3 CMLR 489 where the Court upheld the Commission's objections against the obligation to sell the patented rig only as part of a complete sailboard.
1   See the old Patent Licence Block Exemption, Article 2(1)(7).
2   See the old Patent Licence Block Exemption, Article 2(1)(11).
3   See the old Patent Licence Block Exemption, Article 2(1)(8).
4   See the old Patent Licence Block Exemption, Article 2(1)(5).

with parallel importers.[5] All other forms of exclusivity also fall within the scope of Article 85(1), but may be exempted.[6] The Community is particularly keen to keep the parallel import option open and normally requires the licensee to be free to have a passive sales policy in the territories of the licensor and other licensees. The latter means in practice that the licensee, while based in its own territory, can respond to unsolicited orders from these territories. In circumstances where the licensee would not have been prepared to take the risk of taking out a licence and incur the risk and expense in producing the patented goods when not being given some protection against intra-brand competition at the production level in the allocated territory as well, an open exclusive licence exceptionally does not infringe Article 85(1).[7] In practice this means that no one else will be allowed to work the patent in the allocated territory, while leaving the parallel import route whereby an importer buys the patented goods from the licensor or another licensee to import them into the allocated territory unaffected.[8] The Commission has interpreted this exception restrictively.[9]

Patent licences: the block exemption[10]

As we discussed earlier the Commission has not restricted itself to granting individual exemptions, it has also drafted block exemptions. The Patent Licence Block Exemption was issued in 1984, entered into force in 1985 and was bound to expire on 31 December 1994, but its life was extended until 30 June 1995.[11] It applied to patent licences and to combined patent and know-how licences as long as only two undertakings were parties to such an agreement.[12] Patent pool agreements and, to a more limited extent after the 1993 amendments, licence agreements between partners in a joint venture were excluded from its scope, as were reciprocal licence agreements.[13]

5   Case 258/78: *LC Nungesser KG v Commission* [1982] ECR 2015, [1983]1 CMLR 278.
6   See *AOIP/Beyrard* (1976) OJ L6/8.
7   Case 258/78: *LC Nungesser KG v Commission* [1982] ECR 2015, [1983] 1 CMLR 278.
8   See Hoffmann and O'Farrell 'The "Open Exclusive Licence" – Scope and Consequences' [1984] 4 EIPR 104.
9   See *Velcro/Aplix* [1989] 4 CMLR 157, OJ L233/22, *Tetra Pak I* (1988) OJ L272/27 (upheld on appeal: Case T-51/89 *Tetra Pak Rausing SA v Commission* [1991] 4 CMLR 334) and *Delta Chemie/DDD* [1989] 4 CMLR 157, OJ L309/34; but see also Case 27/87: *Erauw-Jacquery SPrl v La Hesbignonne Société* [1988] ECR 1919, [1988] 4 CMLR 576.
10   Commission Regulation 2349/84 of 23 July 1984 on the application of Article 85(3) of the Treaty to certain categories of patent licensing agreements (1984) OJ L219/15, as amended by (1985) OJ L113/34 and (1993) OJ L21/8; see Korah *Patent Licensing and EEC Competition Rules: Regulation 2349/84* ESC (1985).
11   Article 14.
12   Article 1(1).
13   Article 5.

This block exemption introduced a standard format. Article 1 contained a list of clauses that did not come within the scope of Article 85(1) altogether. Article 2 contained a list of clauses that were exempted in case they came within the scope of Article 85(1). These permitted clauses were called the 'white list'. And finally Article 3 contained a list of clauses that were not exempted and the presence of one of these clauses in a licence agreement meant that it could not benefit from the block exemption.

Know-how: the block exemption[14]

This block exemption was issued in 1988, came into force in 1989 and would normally have been in force until the very end of the century.[15] On form and on substance it was clearly modelled on the patent licence block exemption and we will therefore only highlight some differences.

The exemption covered know-how agreements and mixed know-how patent agreements and thus a choice between two block exemptions was offered for the latter category.[16] It required know-how to be a body of technical information that is secret, substantial and identified in any appropriate form.[17] The most obvious example is the know-how that goes with the patent. All that is explained in the patent application is the invention itself. There is of course a most appropriate way to exploit the invention and that knowledge is often kept secret by the patentholder. That body of technical information is quite substantial and can be identified and separated from other general knowledge. The general impression was that the know-how block exemption was slightly more flexible and that it was more advantageous to the licensor.

The Technology Transfer Block Exemption[18]

Rather than replace the old patent licence block exemption by a new one, the Commission preferred to repeal the know-how licence block exemption and to replace both block exemptions at the same time. The new Technology Transfer Block Exemption[19] covers all patent licences, know-how licences

---

14   Commission Regulation 556/89 of 30 November 1988 on the application of Article 85(3) of the Treaty to certain categories of know-how licensing agreements (1989) OJ L61/1, as amended by (1993) OJ L21/8; see Korah *Know-how Licensing Agreements and the EEC Competition Rules: Regulation 556/89* ESC (1989).
15   Article 12.
16   Article 1(1).
17   Article 7(1) to (4).
18   Commission Regulation (EEC) 240/96 on the application of Article 85(3) to certain categories of technology transfer agreements (1996) OJ L31/2.
19   See Robertson 'Technology Transfer Agreements: An Overview of how Regulation 240/96 Changes the Law' [1996] 3 ECLR 157; Kerse 'Block Exemptions under Article 85(3): The Technology Transfer Regulation – Procedural Issues' [1996] 6 ECLR 331.

and mixed patent and know-how licences to which there are only two parties.[20] Just as its predecessors, the block exemption does not cover reciprocal licences, patent or know-how pools and most licences between competing undertakings in the context of a joint venture.[1] In case other intellectual property rights are involved, the block exemption will only operate as long as these other intellectual property rights are ancillary.[2]

Article 1 allows for sole and exclusive licences. This means that an obligation can be imposed upon the licensor not to grant further licences for the territory which is allocated to the licensee[3] or in the latter case that can be coupled with an obligation not to exploit the licensed technology in the licensed territory himself.[4] The licensee can be obliged not to exploit the technology in the territory which is reserved for the licensor.[5] Further permissible restrictions concern the issue where the licensee can manufacture the goods[6] and the issues of active[7] and passive[8] sales. In practical terms this means that a clause in the contract can stop the licensee from manufacturing the licensed product or from using the licensed product or process in those parts of the common market which are licensed to other licensees and that on top of that the licensee can contractually be obliged not to pursue an active policy of putting the patented product on the market in those parts of the common market which are licensed to other licensees[9]. A passive sales restriction adds to that that the licensee is not even allowed to put the patented product on the market in the latter parts of the common market in response to unsolicited orders. The obligation to use the patentee's trade mark and get-up subject to the licensee being identified[10] has also been retained in the format in which it was present in the old block exemptions. An obligation on the licensee to limit the production of the licensed product to the quantities required for the licensee's own products and an obligation to sell the licensed product only as an integral part of or a replacement part for the licensee's own products or otherwise in connection with the licensee's own goods has been added to the list of clauses that do not infringe Article

---

20   Article 1(1).
1   Article 5(1).
2   Article 5(1)(4).
3   Article 1(1)(1).
4   Article 1(1)(2).
5   Article 1(1)(3).
6   Article 1(1)(4).
7   Article 1(1)(5).
8   Article 1(1)(6).
9   Article 1(1)(5) mentions specifically that the licensee can be stopped from engaging in advertising that is specifically aimed at those parts of the common market that are licensed to other licensees and from setting up a branch or distribution centre in the latter parts of the common market.
10   Article 1(1)(7).

85(1), but these obligations are coupled to the requirement that the licensee is free to determine the relevant quantities freely.[11]

These restrictions can only be imposed for a limited time only. For pure patent licences the duration of all these obligations is determined by the term of protection of the patent. The obligations can indeed only be imposed to the extent that and for as long as the licensed product is protected by a patent in the relevant territories. The presence of the patent protection is the sole justification for accepting these restrictions to the competitive freedom of the parties. The obligation not to put the product on the market in territories that are licensed to other licensees in response to unsolicited orders is subject to an even stricter rule. This restriction is only acceptable for a maximum period of five years[12] from the date when the product is first put on the common market by one of the licensees.[13] This five year rule in relation to passive sales applies also to pure know-how licences. In the absence of a patent, the term of which can be used to restrict the duration of the restrictive clauses, the block exemption limits the period of time during which these restrictive clauses are allowed in pure know-how licences to ten years from the date on which the licensed product is first put on the common market by one of the licensees. The fact that the limit of production obligation and the use of trade mark obligation are exempted for the life of the agreement, if and for as long as the know-how remains secret and substantial, forms a significant exception to that rule.[14] The traditional know-how term is prolonged for mixed agreements if the patent which is necessary for the application of the know-how is still in force when the traditional know-how term expires. In those member states where that patent is still in force the term shall expire when the term of the patent expires if the know-how is identified and if it remains secret and substantial.[15]

The white list[16] contains a number of by now well-known clauses. The licensee can be obliged not to divulge confidential know-how, even after the agreement has expired,[17] not to assign the licence or not to grant a sub-licence,[18] not to exploit the licensed technology after the termination of the agreement in so far and as long as the patent is still in force and the know-how is still secret,[19] to assist the licensor in infringement procedures[20]

---

11   Article 1(1)(8).
12   If there is continued patent protection for the product in the relevant territory.
13   Article 1(2).
14   Article 1(3).
15   Article 1(4).
16   Article 2.
17   Article 2(1)(1).
18   Article 2(1)(2).
19   Article 2(1)(3).
20   Article 2(1)(6).

and to mark the product with the licensor's name or with an indication of the licensed patent.[1] Minimum quality clauses that are necessary for a technically satisfactory exploitation of the licensed product or to ensure common quality standards,[2] minimum quantity clauses, minimum royalty clauses,[3] most favoured licensee clauses,[4] and field of use restrictions[5] are also white-listed. A couple of clauses require a more detailed analysis though. Grant back clauses can be imposed upon the licensee only if they are non-exclusive and if the licensor undertakes, eventually even on an exclusive basis, to grant the licensee a licence for all improvements it makes.[6] A licensee can be put under an obligation to keep paying royalties in case the know-how becomes publicly known prematurely or in case patents lose their validity prematurely if this is not caused by any action of the licensor.[7] There is also an obligation for the licensee not to use the licensor's know-how to construct facilities for third parties[8] and an obligation on the licensee to supply only a limited quantity of the licensed product to a particular customer in case a know-how licence was granted at the request of that customer to provide him or her with a second source of supply.[9] The latter clause reflects a common practice in for example the car industry where car manufacturers do not want to be completely dependent upon a single supplier of a particular part.

The white list is followed by a black list[10] that has been shortened substantially in comparison to its equivalent in the old block exemptions. The new black list only contains seven types of clauses. Price fixing clauses that restrict any party in determining its prices or discounts for the licensed products;[11] no competition clauses that restrict any party from competing[12] in respect of research and development, production, use or distribution of competing products;[13] clauses that restrict one party from serving certain customers if the parties were already competing manufacturers before the

---

1   Article 2(1)(11).
2   Article 2(1)(5). This provision also allows checks by the licensor and the imposition of an obligation to acquire certain goods or services from the licensor or an approved third party, if that obligation is imposed for the same reasons.
3   Article 2(1)(9).
4   Article 2(1)(10).
5   Article 2(1)(8).
6   Article 2(1)(4).
7   Article 2(1)(7).
8   Article 2(1)(12).
9   Article 2(1)(13).
10   Article 3.
11   Article 3(1).
12   With the other party, with another undertaking or with an undertaking that is related to the other party. The provision does not prejudice the operation of Articles 2(1)(17) and 2(1)(18).
13   Article 3(2).

grant of the licence,[14] clauses restricting in quantitative terms the use of the licensed technology,[15] exclusive grant back clauses which oblige the licensee to assign all rights in improvements or new applications to the licensor[16] and export restraining clauses which could block the option of parallel imports[17] are still wholly unacceptable as is any attempt to go beyond the maximum terms of the restrictions that are allowed by Articles 1(2), 1(3) and 1(4)[18]. The presence of any one of these clauses in an agreement will deprive it of the benefit of the block exemption.

A special procedure is available if the agreement does consist of white listed clauses and certain other restrictive clauses that are not black listed. This 'opposition' procedure involves the submission under this procedure to the Commission of the agreement. The Commission has then four months to oppose the agreement and the agreement is exempted if no answer from the Commission is forthcoming within this four-month term.[19] The block exemption gives two examples of situations in which the opposition procedure should be used. First, the procedure should be used if the licensee is obliged to accept minimum quality specifications, further licences or an obligation to procure goods or services from a certain source if all these are not necessary for a technically satisfactory exploitation of the licensed technology or for ensuring that the quality standards that have been set by the licensor and the other licensees are observed[20]. Secondly, the procedure should also be used if a clause in the agreement stops the licensee from challenging the secret or substantial nature of the licensed know-how or from challenging the validity of patents that belong to the licensor or to undertakings that are connected to the licensor.[1] The opposition procedure never became a success under the old block exemptions. This may change now, as the shortening of the black list should give rise to a larger number of licences qualifying for the opposition procedure. The fact that the term in which the Commission can oppose the agreement has been shortened from six to four months should also help, by reducing the delay before the agreement can safely be put into practice. The temptation not to notify the Commission in order not to awaken a sleeping dog will remain though. Parties may still think it unlikely that the Commission will find out about their restrictive agreement if the amounts and market shares that are involved are relatively small.

---

14   Article 3(4).
15   Article 3(5).
16   Article 3(6).
17   Article 3(3).
18   Article 3(7).
19   Article 4.
20   Article 4(2)(a).
1   Article 4(2)(b). The patents must be licensed in the common market.

The Commission reserves for itself the right to withdraw any exemption granted under the terms of the block exemption if it thinks that an agreement nevertheless has or has started to have certain effects that are incompatible with the requirements of Article 85(3). [2] This general rule was always part of the block exemptions, but this block exemption lists four situations in which the rule might be applied. These situations are only examples though and nothing stops the Commission from relying on Article 7 in other circumstances. Parallel import is considered to be a vital ingredient of the single market. It therefore does not come as a surprise that a refusal without any objectively justified reason by the licensee to meet unsolicited orders that emanate from the territories of other licensees is found amongst the examples of situations in which the Commission may withdraw the benefit of the block exemption. [3] A second example extends the rule to a refusal by a party to an agreement to deal with third parties in the territory that has been allocated to that party, if these third parties may engage in parallel import into another part of the single market and to any other attempt to obstruct the operations of a parallel importer. [4] A third example concerns the situation where the parties were competing manufacturers when the licence was granted and where the minimum quantity or best endeavours obligations have the effect of preventing the licensee from using competing technologies. [5] These examples refer to certain clauses or practices. The final example is radically different in nature. The Commission originally wanted to link the benefit of the block exemption to market shares. [6] When this proved unacceptable and unworkable the rule was dropped, but it resurfaces here. If the licensee's market share starts to exceed 40 per cent in the licensed territory the Commission can withdraw the benefit of the block exemption. [7] The parties will have more legal certainty though, because the Commission has to take positive action in this case. In the old proposal the protection would have fallen away automatically when a certain market share was exceeded. The whole problem is aggravated, of course, by the difficulty to measure market shares precisely and in a uniform and undisputed way. The new 40 per cent rule is used as an obvious example of a situation in which the effect of the agreement is that there will be no effective competition between the licensed product and interchangeable or substitutable goods or services in the licensed territory. In such a situation the Commission may withdraw the benefit of the block exemption even if the licensee does not reach the 40 per cent market share. [8]

---

2   Article 7.
3   Article 7(2).
4   Article 7(3).
5   Article 7(4).
6   For further details, see the first edition of this book at 112–113 (with further references).
7   Article 7(1).
8   Article 7(1).

The new block exemption entered into force on 1 April 1996 and will remain in force for a period of 10 years.[9]

Patents and competition law – Article 86

This Article prohibits the abuse of a dominant position. We will first examine what constitutes a dominant position for the purposes of the Treaty. It would lead us too far to discuss all issues related to the technical application of Article 86 in detail and we will need to restrict our comments to a couple of essential points.[10] Dominance should not exist in an abstract way, but in the context of a market and three aspects are important. A position needs to be dominant in the relevant product market, it needs to be dominant in the relevant geographical market, and the market is also restricted in time when considering the issue of dominance. The determination of the relevant product market raises issues such as the interchangeability and substitutability of products, while in many cases the relevant geographical and temporal markets are more obvious to determine. Once a dominant position has been established Article 86 requires that that dominant position is held in a substantial part of the Common Market.[11] But dominance as such is not sufficient for the purposes of Article 86 as there also needs to be an abuse of that dominant position. Article 86 does not contain an exhaustive list of what would amount to an abuse, but it gives charging unfair prices, limiting production and discrimination as obvious examples of abuse. We will have to discuss the case law in detail to discover what may amount to an abuse of a dominant position in the context of intellectual property. It is clear that monopoly rights such as intellectual property rights can lead to a dominant position, but an abuse of a dominant position involves a certain action and a certain use of rights. It is therefore correct to assume that as in relation to the free movement of goods the existence of intellectual property rights as such cannot amount to an abuse of a dominant position[12] and neither can certain uses of these rights. We will have to focus our attention on what constitutes an abusive use or exercise of an intellectual property right. As with the free movement of goods, the existence and the normal use of intellectual property rights will not be affected as only the abusive use of intellectual property rights for a purpose which is unrelated to intellectual property, namely the distortion of competition and the distortion of the free movement of goods, will be

---

9   Article 13.
10   For more details see Whish *Competition Law* Butterworths (3rd edn, 1993) Ch 8.
11   Ibid.
12   See Case 238/87: *Volvo v Erik Veng (UK) Ltd* [1988] ECR 6211 (at paragraph 8), [1989] 4 CMLR 122.

targeted by the Treaty provisions. In fact many of these elements transpire already from one of the earliest intellectual property judgments of the Court of Justice.

The Court indicated for the first time that Article 86 could interfere with intellectual property rights in its *Parke Davis* judgment of 1968 when it ruled that the existence of the intellectual property rights granted by a member state is not affected by the prohibition contained in Article 86 of the EEC Treaty and that in the absence of any abuse of a dominant position the exercise of such rights cannot of itself fall under Article 86.

> 'Although a patent confers on its holder a special protection within the framework of a State, it does not follow that the exercise of the rights so conferred implies the existence of the three elements mentioned (the existence of a dominant position on the single market or on a substantial part thereof, abuse of that dominant position and a negative effect on trade between member states). It could only do so if the utilisation of the patent could degenerate into an improper exploitation of the protection.' [13]

In this first case the Court found that a higher sale price for the patented product as compared with that of the unpatented product coming from another member state does not necessarily constitute an abuse of a dominant position. The possibility to ask a higher price for the product as a result of the patent protection was seen as being the normal result of the existence of that patent protection. And even if in this first case no abuse of a dominant position was found, it opened the way for a series of other cases.

A last important preliminary point in relation to Article 86 is that it will only apply if there is an effect on inter-state trade.[14] The Court has held that this requirement will be satisfied where conduct brought about an alteration in the structure of competition in the Common Market.[15]

Article 86 applied to patents

So far only one case, and a rather peculiar case, has arisen when Tetra Pak, which occupies a dominant position in the market for cartons and machines

---

13   Case 24/67: *Parke, Davis & Co v Probel, Reese, Beintema-Interpharm and Centrapharm*
     [1968] ECR 55, [1968] CMLR 47, in relation to copyright see Case 78/70 *Deutsche*
     Grammophon GmbH v Metro-SB-Grossmarkte GmbH & Co KG [1971] ECR 487, [1971]
     CMLR 631 and in relation to trade marks see Case 51/75: *EMI Records Ltd v CBS UK*
     Ltd [1976] ECR 811, [1976] 2 CMLR 235.
14   See Whish *Competition Law* Butterworths (3rd edn, 1993) Ch 8 at pp 247-248.
15   Cases 6/73 and 7/73: *Commercial Solvents Corpn v Commission* [1974] ECR 223, [1974]
     1 CMLR 309.

for packaging milk took over Liquipak. Liquipak had previously obtained an exclusive licence for technology that related to a new method of sterilising cartons that were suitable for long-life milk and Tetra Pak gained access to that technology by taking over Liquipak. The Commission held[16] that it was an abuse for Tetra Pak to take over this company and the exclusive licence. The Commission had particular difficulties in accepting that Tetra Pak held on to the licence and did not attempt to turn it into a non-exclusive licence. On appeal the Decision was upheld by the Court of First Instance.[17] The abuse here seems to be situated in the reinforcement of an already dominant position and to do so on the basis of the acquisition of an exclusive licence. It is submitted that a non-exclusive licence would not have had the same effect. It must also be remembered that this was a very extreme case as Tetra Pak's position was an extremely dominant one and the supplementary exclusive licence concerning a new technology would prevent every new competitor from getting into the market. It would almost eliminate any competition on the relevant market. These extreme factors were clearly important for the Commission and the Court of First Instance in reaching their decision and judgment respectively.

EUROPEAN LAW AND INTELLECTUAL PROPERTY – INTRODUCTION AND PATENTS: AN OVERVIEW

The importance of the preceding section goes far beyond the specific issue of the grant of and dealing in patents. That there is an inherent contradiction between the EU's ideals of free trade and free competition and intellectual property law's blasé creation of monopoly rights is self-evident, but much of the potential force of the clash between these two fundamental principles is tempered by the (inevitable) compromise position adopted. Legitimate use of property rights for their true purpose is condoned and appropriate exemptions are given to reflect this.

The general approach is well-embodied in this area of patent law whereby a patent will be upheld unless its use is for unjustifiable purposes, as shown by such cases as the *Centrafarm* cases. Equally its exclusive licensing, potentially likely to fall foul of anti-trust rules, will be permitted by the sensibly pragmatic block exemption approach.

If nothing else, all this shows that in the context of what is intended to be a free, single market the fact that such concessions are made in favour of intellectual property rights confirms that they are of fundamental economic importance to the effective functioning of a modern capitalist economy.

---

16   *Tetra Pak I (BTG Licence)* Decision [1990] 4 CMLR 47, OJ L272/27.
17   Case T-51/89 *Tetra Pak Rausing v Commission* [1991] 4 CMLR 334.

Chapter 5

Infringement and revocation

As has already been apparent from discussion of many of the leading cases on patentability these two topics are inextricably interlinked. The standard counter-attack of an alleged infringer is to question the validity of the patent itself and seek its revocation, while the initiation of a revocation claim may well be an attempt to clear an inconvenient patent out of the way thus avoiding any threat of claims of infringement. In either event the action will focus sharply on what has been actually claimed for the invention by the patentee in his specification and claims. It will be recalled that the specification must by section 14(3) of the 1977 Act disclose the invention sufficiently that it enables the person skilled in the art to make the invention himself, while section 14(5) insists that the claims clearly and concisely define the subject matter of the patent. Consideration of these documents lies at the heart of all infringement and revocation disputes. It is logical to proceed first to consider revocation since, if no patent exists, it makes little sense to discuss an infringement of it.

REVOCATION

The grounds on which a patent may be revoked are clearly established by section 72 of the 1977 Act. The only grounds for revocation now permitted are:

'(a) the invention is not a patentable invention;
(b) the patent was granted to a person who was not the only person entitled under section 7(2) above to be granted that patent or to two or more persons who were not the only persons so entitled;
(c) the specification of the patent does not disclose the invention clearly

enough and completely enough for it to be performed by a person skilled in the art;

(d) the matter disclosed in the specification of the patent extends beyond that disclosed in the application for the patent, as filed, or, if the patent was granted on a new application filed under sections 8(3), 12 or 37(4) above or as mentioned in section 15(4) above, in the earlier application, as filed;

(e) the protection conferred by the patent has been extended by an amendment which should not have been allowed.'

This is a shorter list than in earlier legislation; former objections on grounds of inutility, inadequate description, failure to claim clearly, falsity or illegality which were permitted grounds for revocation under the 1949 Act[1] are no longer so, at least as such.

The first two of the grounds for revocation under the 1977 Act are straightforward; many of the cases we have considered on patentability and on patent rights have arisen in the context of revocation. The third ground, however, raises issues which relate directly to the wording of the specification itself and to section 14(3) of the Act, and poses a further burden on the patent applicant trying to resolve the perpetual dilemma of how much or how little to disclose in the application. Now there is the added risk that if insufficient disclosure occurs the threat of revocation will loom. Note that it is only the specification and its shortcomings that give rise to this threat; there is no comparable provision to ensure the clarity of the claims made for an invention.

This requirement begs several questions, not least what degree of detail is in fact going to be necessary. Obviously this will ultimately depend on the facts of each case but some guidance is given by *No–Fume Ltd v Frank Pitchford & Co Ltd*.[2] An ashtray designed to retain the smoke inside itself was the subject of this dispute. Romer LJ in the Court of Appeal upheld the validity of the patent even though the application, in describing the various features of the ashtray, failed to indicate the size and relative proportions of the various parts of the ashtray. He stated[3] that it was not necessary that the specification had all the detail in it that might be expected in the detailed specification given to a workman in order to make an article. Rather it was sufficient if the workman could reach the desired result through a combination of the information in the specification and the common knowledge of his trade using trial and error if necessary to achieve the desired result.

---

1   Patents Act 1949, s 32(1).
2   (1935) 52 RPC 231.
3   Ibid at 243 and 245.

The next question to be faced is that of the character of the notional person skilled in the art. Once again the law has to try and put some flesh on the dry bones of this artificial character. The leading case in this context is *Valensi v British Radio Corpn*,[4] a case concerned with the invention of colour television. The Court of Appeal summarised the character of the hypothetical addressee as

'not a person of exceptional skill and knowledge ... not to be expected to exercise any invention nor any prolonged research, inquiry or experiment.'

On the other hand he must 'be prepared to display a reasonable degree of skill and common knowledge in making trials and to correct *obvious* errors in the specification if a means of correcting them can readily be found'.[5]

Applying these principles to the case the problem was that the difficulties faced by the pioneers of colour television were highly technical and it was accepted that an ordinary shopfloor workman was not the appropriate model to consider. Equally, however, the specialist researchers in the field, who the trial judge had used as his model, were also inappropriate. Rather between the two models were the skilled technicians, knowledgeable in their own right but who would equally be reliant on the guidance provided by the specification, and they were the best model to use in considering the question of insufficiency of the information in the specification.

That the *Valensi* test remains good law under the 1977 Act is not in doubt. This has been confirmed by *Mentor Corpn v Hollister Inc*,[6] a decision of the Court of Appeal concerning a patent for a male incontinence device. The court took note of the EPC Rules which by rule 27 state that the description 'shall disclose the invention, as claimed, in such terms that the technical problem ... and its solution can be understood.' Lloyd LJ considered[7] that it was reasonable to expect the addressee to perform routine trials in using the specification to follow and perform the invention and in the light of that the specification disclosed sufficiently the manner of manufacture and should not therefore be revoked.[8] Put simply, the specification should be looked at to see what it teaches the *Valensi* type of reasonable man, who can be expected to carry out at the very least routine trials of this character.

One helpful aspect of the current law is that the applicant does not have to put in his specification the best possible method of carrying out the invention. Formerly this was necessary up until the 1977 Act; the removal of this requirement aids the inventor by enabling him to keep secret the

4   [1973] RPC 337.
5   Ibid at 377.
6   [1993] RPC 7.
7   Ibid at 14.
8   See also *Mölnlycke AB v Procter & Gamble Ltd (No 5)* [1992] FSR 549 at 594–602.

best method and thus retain an additional advantage over his rivals, unless and until, of course, they derive the best method themselves in which case the tables of advantage are turned.

The final two grounds for revocation in section 72 can be dealt with speedily, and were new to the law in 1977 corresponding as they do to EPC provisions.[9] They ensure that no new matter is unfairly added to broaden the scope of the patent, as is forbidden by section 76 of the 1977 Act, by allowing revocation if that has occurred. This upholds the importance of the application date as the starting point of all rights in relation to patents.

INFRINGEMENT

We now turn to the heart of the matter in considering the grounds for and the general approach to the issue of infringement. Section 60 of the 1977 Act is the key provision and unusually makes separate though not dissimilar provisions for patents which are for products and those which are for processes. Section 60(1) states that the following actions are infringements by an infringer in each case they occur without the permission of the patentee.

'(a) where the invention is a product, he makes, disposes of, offers to dispose of, uses or imports the product or keeps it whether for disposal or otherwise;

(b) where the invention is a process, he uses the process or he offers it for use in the UK when he knows, or it is obvious to a reasonable person in the circumstances, that its use there without the consent of the proprietor would be an infringement of the patent;

(c) where the invention is a process, he disposes of, offers to dispose of, uses or imports any product obtained directly by means of that process or keeps any such product whether for disposal or otherwise.'

By section 60(2) it is also an infringement where the unauthorised disclosure takes place of an essential element of the invention such that the recipient will be able to put the invention into effect. This applies to all inventions, whether products or processes but does not apply to the supply of a staple commercial product unless it is supplied with a view to inducing an infringement under the section.[10] These provisions relate to what is commonly described as indirect infringement where the act of infringement consists of enabling another to infringe.

9   Articles 100(c) and 138(1)(c).
10   Patents Act 1977, s 60(3).

It is clear that section 60 covers a very wide range of activities in relation to a patented product or process. Activity before, during or after the unauthorised manufacture of a patented article can count as infringement and actions as diverse as importing and disposing of an article will both fall within the definition. The most significant gap in the law is that it only applies to actions within the UK and thus a sale which takes place abroad of an infringing article does not fall within the provisions, and even an offer made within the jurisdiction to dispose of an article outside it does not fall within section 60.[11] Of course an action will lie under what are likely to be similar rules in that other jurisdiction since the subsections under consideration equates to EPC Articles 29 and 30.

A further, and sensible gap in liability arises from a decision which is of assistance to those who find themselves at risk of liability under these broad provisions while acting in all innocence. In *Smith Kline & French Laboratories Ltd v R D Harbottle (Mercantile) Ltd*[12] the first defendants sought to export the drug Cimetidine from Italy to Nigeria. The consignment was routed via London and while it was in storage in a British Airways cargo warehouse became the subject of a patent infringement claim by the plaintiffs to which the airline were joined as 'keepers' of the offending consignment. Oliver J found in favour of the airline. In his view it was appropriate to consider Article 29 of the EPC and this speaks of 'making, offering, putting on the market, or using' a product and in the light of that it was clearly some form of positive action that was envisaged as amounting to an infringement; the passive warehousing or transporting of an item does not count as positive action in relation to the item. Clearly the commercial implications of any other decision would have been significant, and adverse.

The courts generally seem to take a generous view of legitimate activity, even though there is no general defence of innocence. A useful pre-Act case which would appear to be consistent with the statutory approach is *Solar Thomson Engineering Co Ltd v Barton*.[13] Here the plaintiffs sold a conveyor system the pulleys of which were the subject of a patent. After some years of use the pulleys began to wear out and the defendants repaired them by replacing a vital part with one of their own manufacture though of course as it was part of a broader system it had to be identical to the design of the plaintiffs. It was held by the Court of Appeal that it was quite in order to carry out repairs to an article without this infringing any relevant patents so long as the work of repair could not be said to amount to the manufacture of a new article.

The provisions relating to indirect infringement are not without their problems. The essential concept of 'essential element' goes undefined and

---

11   *Kalman v PCL Packaging* [1982] FSR 406.
12   [1980] RPC 363.
13   [1977] RPC 537.

is bound at some stage to give rise to difficulties in litigation. The exception for the supply of a staple commercial product is also shrouded in uncertainty, at least to UK and European lawyers, but appears to protect the innocent seller of a common product that has obvious non-infringing uses. If A supplies water to B, this may enable B to infringe C's water-powered invention but it would clearly be unfair to burden A with any liability in the absence of any knowledge of the offending use.

There are also statutory defences provided by the 1977 Act in subsection 60(5). Acts which would otherwise count as infringements do not do so if they are done privately for non-commercial purposes. This points to the patent as an item of industrial property; it is only protected in the field of commercial exploitation. Also outside the scope of the infringement provisions are acts done by others for experimental purposes relating to the invention. This is also significant in giving others trading in the same field the right to carry out experiments using the public information made available via the Patent Office as a result of the application procedure, this ensuring the high likelihood of a further patent race hotting up as the patentee's 20-year period of protection draws to a close.

One case has had to consider the experiment defence. In *Monsanto Co v Stauffer Chemical Co*[14] the plaintiffs owned the patent for a herbicide and claimed infringement by the defendants who had carried out some trials of their allegedly infringing product with a view to obtaining official product safety clearances. It was held by the Court of Appeal that experiments permitted by the Act were only those carried out for scientific purposes, for example to test a hypothesis or to discover something unknown[15] about the subject matter of the invention. The tests in question, however, were of a very different kind and tests which were carried out for commercial rather than scientific purposes would not be exempt from the threat of an infringement action.

Other defences also arise from section 60(5) and can be recorded briefly. The extemporaneous preparation in a pharmacy of a medicine under the terms of a prescription is outside section 60; this is again directed to what in fact would be likely to be an innocent infringement. Also outside section 60 are various uses of patented equipment in ships, aircraft and even hovercraft temporarily or accidentally in UK waters or airspace.

A more significant exception relates to prior user, that is user of an article or process without patent protection by A and the impact upon it of a grant of a patent for such an article or process to B. It may seem harsh to penalise A in this example by making his acts into infringements of B's later patent if he continues with his pre-existing use. Section 64 of the 1977 Act deals with this type of situation by allowing the prior user to continue that use

14   [1985] RPC 515.
15   Ibid at 542 per Dillon LJ.

after the grant of a patent to another without it being an infringement so long as the user is in good faith. The problem will only arise where the prior use was secret; if it were not the later actions would not be novel and thus not patentable. The relatively rare instances where the section is thus likely to be invoked mean that it may be some time before the courts have an opportunity to sort out the obvious problem it creates, namely whether the later act, to be permitted to continue, has to be exactly or merely substantially identical to the prior user. Given the steady evolution likely to occur in the history of the development of a product or process to permit only exact replication would deprive section 64 of much of its already limited value.

The right to take action against an infringer is, by section 66, conferred on any one amongst a group of joint proprietors though the others must be joined to the action. As has been seen already, section 67 gives exclusive licensees (but no other licensee) the right to take action against infringers, thus contributing to the popularity of this type of licence.

The legislation also sets out the remedies available to anyone who has rights against an infringer. Section 61 confers an exciting choice of any or all of an injunction, an order to deliver up infringing items, damages, an account of profits (these two are alternatives) and a declaration. It should be noted that both account of profits and delivery up are equitable remedies and thus by definition discretionary in their approach.

The choice between account of profits and damages is not an easy one to make. It is clearly good news for the plaintiff that he is entitled to ask for an account of all the profits and not just that proportion due to infringement,[16] but equally it is a laborious process to prove the profit actually engendered, say, by one product among many produced by a large firm.[17] Seeking damages seems simpler, but in a competitive trading environment precise assessment of the loss caused to the plaintiff by the infringement rather than by any other of a myriad of factors may also prove troublesome. By section 62 damages and account of profits are not available as against an infringer who can prove that they were and should have been unaware of the existence of the relevant patent at the time of the infringing act. Damages in these cases are generally on a royalty basis: the question is what royalties or licensing fees would have been earned by a lawful licensing of the patent.

Patent infringement actions have a reputation for being long and costly, and the breadth of the different activities which can amount to an infringement means that trade in a product even threatened with an

---

16 *Peter Pan Manufacturing Corporation v Corsets Silhouette Ltd* [1963] 3 All ER 402, [1964] 1 WLR 96 (a breach of confidence case).
17 See *Gerber Garment Technology Inc v Lectra Systems Ltd* [1997] RPC 443 noted by Moss and Rogers 'Damages for Loss of Profits in Intellectual Property Litigation' [1997] 8 EIPR 425.

infringement action is likely to be suspended for the often considerable period of time that lapses while the litigation takes its course. In a legitimate case this is acceptable but a more cynical trader may realise the disruptive effect of launching an infringement action against a rival and do so simply to achieve the disruptive effect. Section 70 of the 1977 Act provides protection against this possibility.

The section creates a right for anyone aggrieved to take to court anyone who threatens an action against either the applicant or anyone else for infringement of a patent. A declaration, injunction or damages may be granted unless the defendant can establish that the threats are justifiable. This protection does not however extend to threats to bring proceedings for an infringement in the form of making or importing a product for disposal or of using a process.[18] This is a valuable provision and it is prudent for the plaintiff in an infringement action to bear it in mind before proceeding too far. The law has recognised the adverse effect of even the threat of an infringement action on a wide range of business dealings.

Overall the statutory provisions on infringement appear for the most part to be straightforward and workable, which may make the assertion that such proceedings may well be long and complex somewhat surprising. The problem is that the statute somehow seems to assume that it will be easy to look at the patent and see what it covers and then place that alongside the allegedly infringing act and make a comparison. Section 125 of the 1977 Act makes clear the definition of the invention is that

'specified in a claim of the specification or the application, as the case may be, as interpreted by the description and any drawings contained in that specification, and the extent of the protection conferred by a patent or application of a patent shall be construed accordingly.'

So that tells us in a moderately clear way what the court should be looking at in deciding what the invention is for the purpose of an infringement action. It still does not tell us though how it should be looked at, and here a clash arises between the scientist and the lawyer. The scientist may be caricatured as a bluff commonsense character skilled in his trade who will use his expertise to discern the inventive notion. The lawyer, however, may be caricatured as a wordsmith rather than a blacksmith and will use his interpretative skills, or pedantic ones if preferred, to understand the words that define the inventive notion. Whether the specification should be read with the scientist's purposive outlook or the lawyer's literal one has been the subject of a major battle in recent years which the scientists have won

---

18   Patents Act 1977, s 70(4). See *Bowden Controls Ltd v Acco Cable Controls Ltd* [1990] RPC 427.

with, as will be seen, more than a little assistance from their European friends.

INFRINGEMENT: INTERPRETATION OF SPECIFICATIONS AND CLAIMS

It should be made clear at the outset that the first part of this section describes the law as what it was and not as what it is now. It is valuable though for the purposes of contrasting the old and new positions to start with the earlier approach. A good starting-point is *C Van der Lely NV v Bamfords Ltd.*[19] The House of Lords was faced with a claim against the patentee of a hay rake seeking revocation of that patent, with a cross-claim by the patentee alleging infringement by the claimant. The key part of the litigation centred on a claim that one of the rows of wheels on which the patented hay rake was driven could be removed for different aspects of the haymaker's art. The claim specifically referred to the removal of the hindmost wheels, while the allegedly infringing device for the same reason removed wheels but removed the front ones instead. At this time courts claimed to study the 'pith and marrow' of the invention to see what the true inventive step was but the decision of the House of Lords shows the ambiguity of this phrase. It may be thought to involve a purposive type of inquiry but this was not so. Speaking as one of the majority of the Law Lords who found that there was no infringement Lord Jenkins stated that the patentee had deliberately claimed only the hindmost wheels and that left it open for the rivals to arrange their wheels in any other way,[20] even though the two machines were both achieving the same result by using the same principle. Viscount Radcliffe too said[1] that the words used delimit what the applicant has claimed. Lord Reid dissented on the issue, taking the view that the precise wheels involved were not essential integers of the invention and that there was therefore no infringement.

Then in *Rodi & Weinberger A G v Henri Showell Ltd*[2] the issue returned to the House of Lords. This time the issue was expandable watch straps and in particular the connections between the bands in them. The patented straps were linked together by U-shaped connecting bows; the allegedly infringing straps used C-shaped bows instead. Notwithstanding the obvious point that a U-shape and a C-shape are not exactly dissimilar, the House of Lords found once again that there was no infringement here. Even adopting the essential integers approach, the majority found that those were defined

19 [1963] RPC 61.
20 Ibid at 80.
1   Ibid at 78.
2   [1969] RPC 367.

in the terms of the words of the specification and claim and that therefore the U-shape defined itself, in effect, as an essential integer. Lord Reid this time was joined by Lord Pearce in dissent, seeking to look at the self-evidently similar way in which the two shapes functioned.

Inexorably, at the pace of a constipated tortoise, the House of Lords inched away from the hardest of hard-line literal approaches to patent specifications. In *Beecham Group Ltd v Bristol Laboratories Ltd*[3] Beechams had patent rights in a type of penicillin called Ampicillin while Bristol were importing into the UK Hetacillin which was similar but not identical to Ampicillin. It was derived from it and, once in the bloodstream, it reacted with the water and became Ampicillin, and thus worked as an antibiotic in precisely the same way. The House of Lords found that this was an infringement by applying the 'pith and marrow' test in the broader way we have suggested the phrase properly implies. Lord Diplock accepted[4] that on the most literal approach the two products were different, but that in their actual use they worked in precisely the same way. The variation, he said, was 'evanescent and reversible' and the actual use in Hetacillin was a use of Ampicillin.

This welcome outbreak of common sense is perhaps better seen as a surrender to the inevitable since while the *Beecham* case was being argued in the Lords, Parliament was considering the new Patents Act and the legislation, with its tie-in to the EPC, betokened a very different approach. The way in which this arises is as follows. We have already seen that section 125 of the 1977 Act says that the documents at the heart of the application procedure define the invention and section 125(3) goes on to say that the Protocol on the Interpretation of Article 69 of the EPC should apply to the interpretation of that section of the domestic legislation. Turning then to Article 69 we find that it says simply that the extent of protection given by a European patent shall be determined 'by the terms of the claims'. This seems to advance us little until we find that the Protocol to it states as follows:

'Article 69 should not be interpreted in the sense that the extent of the protection conferred by a European patent is to be understood as that defined by the strict, literal meaning of the wording used in the claims, the description and drawings being employed only for the purpose of resolving an ambiguity found in the claims. Neither should it be interpreted in the sense that the claims serve only as guideline and that the actual protection conferred may extend to what, from a consideration of the description and drawings by a person skilled in the art, the patentee has contemplated. On the contrary, it is to be interpreted as defining a

3   [1978] RPC 153.
4   Ibid at 202.

position between these extremes which combines a fair protection for the patentee with a reasonable degree of certainty for third parties.'

The background to the Protocol merits some explanation. In harmonising any law, let alone an area as complex as patent law, compromises have to be reached and the Protocol is that compromise. It sets out two extremes of interpretation, the mindless literalism typified by cases such as *Rodi and Weinberger* and the 'broad guideline' approach that could be taken to typify the practice at this time in Germany and elsewhere, and requires a court to eschew them both and instead to seek a compromise that balances protection for the patentee's interest in preserving a broad monopoly and regard for the need for others – subsequent inventors, users and other infringers – to know where they stand in a way that, for all its other faults, the literal approach does allow them.

It is important to emphasise the significance of this change. The old UK literal approach gave a narrow protection to the patentee, particularly if he was cautious in his claims, a caution encouraged by the need to ensure that all the claims made for a patent have to be justified during the application procedure. By moving, as we clearly are, to a looser approach with broader methods of interpretation in use we are moving towards greater protection to the patentee. Equally more risk of infringement is placed on others who are now to be offered only a 'reasonable degree of certainty' as opposed to the utter, if at times unpalatable, certainty of the former literal approach.

The problem with all this, however, is that the Protocol is keener to tell us what not to do than how to interpret patents. Thus it fell to the House of Lords to consider yet again the appropriate approach to interpretation in the new era of patent law and the opportunity to do this arose in *Catnic Components Ltd v Hill & Smith Ltd.*[5] It must be emphasised that this was a case under the 1949 Act and no express mention is made of the 1977 Act, the EPC and of the Protocol. But it would be naive to see the developments in *Catnic* as solely the continuing evolution of the UK approach to the issue.[6] The *Catnic* approach represents the first UK answer to the conundrum posed by the Protocol to Article 69 and it provides an answer which it is suggested is entirely compatible with European approaches.

The facts of *Catnic* were simple enough. The plaintiffs had a patent for a type of steel lintel (a load-bearing beam) which specified in its wording that the rear side of the lintel should be vertical. The defendants produced a similar lintel but, presumably in the hope of avoiding an infringement action, made the rear side of their lintel at an angle of 6° from the vertical

---

5   [1982] RPC 183.
6   Cornish & Victoria [1981] JBL 136. Cf Jacob 'The Herchel Smith Lecture 1993' [1993] 9 EIPR 312.

which reduced its load-bearing powers by 0.6%. Did this minor variation avoid the infringement danger?

Lord Diplock gave the sole substantive judgment. He found there was an infringement on the facts. The key passage[7] makes clear that it is the scientists', and Europeans', purposive approach that should take precedence over the old common lawyers' approach because the patent specification is aimed at other workers in the field.

> 'My Lords, a patent specification is a unilateral statement by the patentee, in words of his own choosing, addressed to those likely to have a practical interest in the subject matter of his invention (ie "skilled in the art"), by which he informs them of what he claims to be the essential features of the new product or process for which the letters patent grant him a monopoly. It is those novel features only that he claims to be essential that constitute the so-called "pith and marrow" of the claim. A patent specification should be given a purposive construction rather than a purely literal one derived from applying to it the kind of meticulous verbal analysis in which lawyers are too often tempted by their training to indulge. The question in each case is: whether persons with practical knowledge and experience of the kind of work in which the invention was intended to be used, would understand that strict compliance with a particular descriptive word or phrase appearing in a claim was intended by the patentee to be an essential requirement of the invention so that any variant would fall outside the monopoly claimed, even though it could have no material effect upon the way the invention worked.'

This being the test it then becomes very easy to conclude that no one lintel manufacturer could be imagined as thinking that the vertical rear side was in literal terms essential since this would enable anyone else to use the idea of the patent but by varying it by a degree or two they could avoid an infringement action with impunity. Why bother with a patent if that were so? Of course such arguments will depend very much on the facts of each case. It is easy to imagine a patent where the description of something as being vertical is of great importance for example in some form of new guillotine where a much cleaner cut would be best achieved by a precisely vertical drop.

It is important to put the new purposive test of interpretation derived from *Catnic* in its context. Though new to patent infringement in the UK, purposive methods of interpretation are becoming more and more important; this is because the European influence of the law is also becoming more and more important, both in patents and elsewhere. To a continental

---

7   [1982] RPC 183 at 244. See also *Improver Corpn v Remington Consumer Products Ltd* [1990] FSR 181 at 190, per Hoffmann J.

lawyer purposive or teleological approaches to interpretation are the norm. Within the context of the EU, the Court of Justice takes such a course in its approach to the legal rules of the Union prefaced as they are by extensive preambles spelling out the purposes for which the legislation is being passed.[8]

Of course we do not suggest that the *Catnic* test is of itself perfect. It will still leave some inevitable uncertainty. The volume of litigation and the different approaches taken by the courts in the years since *Catnic* speak eloquently about the difficulties facing common lawyers let loose on continental approaches to statutory interpretation. These cases will be considered shortly. However, if we look at *Catnic* in its own terms, significant changes clearly have occurred to pre-existing case law. *Rodi & Weinberger* would surely now be decided the other way in accordance with the approach of the dissenting minority, but *Van der Lely* poses a problem. On the one hand, the removal of either set of wheels served the same purpose and this factor suggests a different decision post-*Catnic*. On the other hand, however it is surely going further than *Catnic* to move from saying 'vertical equals almost vertical' to saying 'back means front'. The logic of *Catnic* however suggests that where in terms of purpose it is immaterial whether it is the back or front wheels that are removable, 'back' means nothing at all, and could thus be ignored.

However, further discussion of the impact and importance of *Catnic* is best postponed to be resumed in the light of the development and application of the law since the *Catnic* decision. A key moment in its acceptance and use came quickly in *Codex Corporation v Racal-Milgo Ltd*.[9] Here the Court of Appeal was faced with a patent relating to a method of high speed data transmission through a modem. The alleged infringement was by a system of broadly the same type but which was much faster and more complex in its operation. The Court adopted the *Catnic* approach without reservation and consigned previous case law to the outer darkness. They were at pains to point out, however,[10] that the *Catnic* approach was not as radical a change as some had argued, emphasising that the investigation is not of the principle of the patent itself, but of the purposive construction of the relevant documents. This must be right – Article 69, it will be recalled, talks of the 'terms of the claim'.

In the light of this, the Court of Appeal were able to identify three key features in the patented system, namely that it took in a particular sequence of signals, identified that sequence, and signalled that information onwards. Although each of these aspects was carried out in subtly different ways in

---

8   See, inter alia, Neville Brown & Kennedy *The Court of Justice of the European Communities* Sweet & Maxwell (4th edn, 1994) Ch 14, esp pp 311–314 and cases cited therein.
9   [1983] RPC 369.
10   Ibid at 381.

the other system, the same key features were present, carrying out the same sort of functions, and thus there was an infringement.

It is not our intention to look at every case decided on the subject. However the acceptance of the *Catnic* approach meant that, as one would expect, minor variations were now no longer enough to save a later product or process from being an infringing one. So an improved method of loading skips into lorries was still an infringement because it used the same basic idea as the earlier patent,[11] while a dental pin made out of two parts which were put together for use but could be separated with difficulty infringed an earlier patent for a dental pin made in one piece, given that both pins operated in exactly the same way.[12]

Two important post-*Catnic* cases show that the law could function well, finding that there is an infringement where the old law would not. In *A C Edwards Ltd v Acme Signs & Displays Ltd*[13] the Court of Appeal had to consider the familiar digital price display panels typically found outside petrol stations which work by providing seven lines which make up a rectangular figure eight but which by masking or or more of the lines can make up any figure, as prices fluctuate. It is obviously important that the masked lines stay masked and this is where conflict arose between the plaintiffs' patented product and the defendants' allegedly infringing one. The plaintiffs used springs to hold the lines in their required position while the defendants employed a flexible piece of plastic for the same task. It was held that this did infringe; the essential idea of the use of a flexible piece of apparatus to hold lines in place was the same in both products and whether this was done by a spring, as in the patent specification, or by a piece of the plastic which though not a spring acted in the same way as one, was immaterial. The use of the word 'spring' by the plaintiff was not a use of any particular significance.

In *Minnesota Mining & Manufacturing Co v Rennicks (UK) Ltd*[14] the dispute was in connection with reflective sheeting of the kind used in road signs. The patented product was stated to have particularly effective adhesion between its different layers of plastic materials by reason of the layers having undergone a process of curing. The allegedly infringing product also claimed increased adhesion and achieved this by a different method of curing. Again this was found to amount to an infringement since the different methods of curing did not disguise the fact that the essential elements of the two methods were the same.[15]

The cases so far considered exemplify well what the *Catnic* approach is intended to achieve. The more flexible approach embodied by it and

11   *Société Nouvelle des Bennes Saphem v Edbro Ltd* [1983] RPC 345.
12   *Fairfax (Dental Equipment) Ltd v S J Filhol Ltd* [1986] RPC 499.
13   [1992] RPC 131.
14   [1992] RPC 331.
15   Ibid at 346, per Aldous J.

demanded by the EPC means that it will be easier for patentees to secure protection against later infringers, thus increasing the value of their patents, while the infringer in turn will not be able to rely on purely literal interpretations of the specification and claims to disguise the fact that he has stolen the essential idea at the heart of the patented invention. The two cases just described show precisely this pattern. Unfortunately they do not represent an invariable approach and some more restrictive decisions need to be considered.

It is therefore important to consider a second group of such cases to see whether the courts are using *Catnic* properly or whether they are slipping back into older and more literal methods of construction. In *Harrison v Project & Design Co (Redcar) Ltd*[16] the dispute was between a private individual who devised a chair lift to enable his invalid wife to get upstairs, which he patented, and the defendants, a commercial firm who, after dealings with Harrison, began to make their own chair lifts. The case ultimately hinged on whether earlier proceedings were *res judicata* but there was discussion of infringement too. The main difference between the two lifts was that the plaintiff used a weight to balance the progress of the chair lift and ensure the smooth running of the chain mechanism while the defendants had abandoned this approach at an early stage and used an additional length of chain in place of the weight primarily as a safety device. The Court of Appeal found that this did not infringe; this was a different method of achieving the same overall purpose and given that the plaintiff had specified the use of a weight and the defendants' chain did not operate as a weight there was no clash between them. This seems sensible; in purely functional or purposive terms there was a significant difference and no problem arises from the case.

More problematic perhaps is the decision of Hoffmann J in *Improver Corpn v Remington Consumer Products Ltd*.[17] The plaintiffs had a European patent for an electronic hair-removing device known as the Epilady. The defendants had placed on the market a similar device called 'Smooth & Silky'. The principal difference between them was that the plaintiffs' device plucked hairs from the skin by capturing the hairs in a high speed rotating arc-shaped spring while that of the defendants employed a high speed rotating arc-shaped synthetic rubber rod with slits cut in it to capture the hairs. Hoffmann J summarised the *Catnic* approach in clear terms:[18]

'The proper approach to the interpretation of English patents registered under the Patents Act 1949 was explained by Lord Diplock in *Catnic Components Ltd v Hill & Smith Ltd*. The language should be given a

16   [1987] RPC 151.
17   [1990] FSR 181.
18   *Ibid* at 189.

"purposive" and not necessarily a literal construction. If the issue was whether a feature embodied in an alleged infringement which fell outside the primary, literal or a contextual meaning of a descriptive word or phrase in the claim ("a variant") was nevertheless within its language as properly interpreted, the court should ask itself the following three questions:

(1) Does the variant have a material effect upon the way the invention works? If yes, the variant is outside the claim. If no -

(2) Would this (ie that the variant had no material effect) have been obvious at the date of publication of the patent to a reader skilled in the art. If no, the variant is outside the claim. If yes -

(3) Would the reader skilled in the art nevertheless have understood from the language of the claim that the patentee intended that strict compliance with the primary meaning was an essential requirement of the invention. If yes, the variant is outside the claim.

On the other hand, a negative answer to the last question would lead to the conclusion that the patentee was intending the word or phrase to have not a literal but a figurative meaning (the figure being a form of synecdoche or metonymy) denoting a class of things which included the variant and the literal meaning, the latter being perhaps the most perfect, best-known or striking example of the class.'

Applying these criteria, the judge found that the variant had no material effect on the way the invention worked, and that to adopt a rubber rod was obvious to the notional skilled man. However on the vital third question he found that the claim in specifically referring to a helical spring could not be interpreted so broadly as to extend to a rubber rod, which presented many different problems and on which the plaintiff had done no work.

Certainly this promotes the actual words of the patent to a high level of elevation. The fact that the patent only used the helical spring, with no alternatives, also was regarded as significant in adding to the impression that the skilled reader would not think of going beyond it. Given that both products employed a high speed rotating arc-shaped object with gaps in the outer edge it may be thought that the defendants had hijacked the basic inventive concept and that the demand of the Protocol to Article 69 for a balance to be achieved between fair protection for the patentee and reasonable certainty for third parties has not been met, with undue respect still being paid to the form of the words used.

What is more worrying is that parallel litigation in Germany came to the opposite conclusion. Hoffmann J described and referred to this in his judgment,[19] and took consolation from the fact that at an earlier stage of

---

19   Ibid at 197-8. See also Jacob 'The Herchel Smith Lecture 1993' [1993] 9 EIPR 312 at 313.

the litigation there a view similar to his own had been taken. This is frankly shoddy. Here we have a European patent designed to provide Europe-wide protection and yet we have two courts in different states coming to opposite conclusions. The German court found no reason to ask the third question asked by Hoffmann J since the way in which the device functioned was clear and its implications obvious in suggesting that any kind of arc-shaped slitted part would achieve the same result.

The question is then – do we need to ask the third question? It is tentatively suggested that the outcome of the *Improver* case suggests that we should not. The defendants' 'Smooth & Silky' was designed by an engineer whose wife claimed that her 'Epilady' hurt her and he directly adapted the 'Epilady' design to give fewer slits and thus less pain. He thus altered one minor aspect of the 'Epilady' in such a way that would make it unlikely that he could gain patent protection for himself, it being an obvious variation. Yet, by focusing on the words used by the patentee, the *Improver* decision allows an admitted adoption of the patented article with an obvious variant to go unpunished. If this is the effect of the third question, it is suggested it is a bad effect, and thus a bad question.

A further emphasis on the language of the claim was offered by the Court of Appeal in *PLG Research v Ardon International Ltd.*[20] This case concerned an invention of plastic netting for use in civil engineering projects which was described in the patent specification as being 'substantially uniplanar' with the allegedly infringing product being different in appearance but functionally equivalent to the original patented product. In holding that both patents were sustainable Millett LJ[1] referred to the Protocol to Article 69 and claimed that the German courts were at one with domestic jurisprudence in insisting that the scope of the patent has to be determined with direct reference to the language employed in the patent claim and specification. The claim should not be permitted to go beyond those functional equivalents which are deductible from the wording used in the claim. This approach arguably represents a variation from the *Catnic* test but only a minor one affording slightly more protection for the patentee. The *PLG* decision is at least an advance in one respect with the decision being based on an interpretation of the Protocol to Article 69 rather than by reference to the pre-existing common law approach.

Other cases also seemed to concentrate unduly on the precise language employed in the patent claim and/or specification. In *Southco Inc v Dzus Fastener Europe Ltd*[2] the Court of Appeal was faced with a patented latch mechanism and an allegedly infringing one which had many similarities. The key distinction was that the plaintiffs' mechanism worked in a way that

20   [1995] RPC 287.
1   Ibid at 309.
2   [1992] RPC 299.

was foolproof whereas the other at one point in its operation was not. This appears a reasonable decision with both the words used and the overall purpose being considered by the Court. It was also argued by the plaintiffs that the defendants had deliberately designed their product 'down' just so as to achieve the result that they did. Nicholls LJ[3] came to no conclusion on the fact but warned that the Court would take care to ensure that any such attempt would not be rewarded.

A less attractive decision, or rather approach, is that in *Daily v Etablissements Fernand Berchet.*[4] Here an English inventor of an unworked patent for a walking aid which as a safety feature had a pressure-operated 'braking arrangement associated with the rear wheels' (the words of the claim) sought to claim against the French manufacturers of a toy train called the 'Locopousse' which was designed to help young children to walk. This also contained a safety feature, a downward extension of the side at the rear of the toy which slight pressure would bring to contact with the ground thus braking the vehicle's progress, without using the wheels. The Court of Appeal briefly overturned the trial judge's finding that there was an infringement. Nourse LJ referred to no cases and simply relied on the words of the plaintiffs' claim. Balcombe LJ noted[5] that he should proceed in a purposive way but then declared that the ordinary rules of construction should be applied, evidencing some confusion, to say the least, before again relying on the words used. Sir Michael Kerr at least considered the post-*Catnic* threefold test and concluded that there were problems for the plaintiff at every stage and terminal ones at the third stage.

On the facts the decision seems fair enough. Brakes linked to wheels and brakes which act directly on to the ground are tolerably different enough to justify the view that there was no infringement. However the approach of the Court has a smack of older approaches about it (some might say Luddite) and contrasts adversely with the other cases.

Happily a gradual concensus has evolved in the most recent cases which show that the judges are grappling valiantly with the new European-based approach and concentrating more on purpose and less on the precise language employed. Thus in *Glaverbel S A v British Coal Corpn*[6] the Court of Appeal stressed the importance of the purposive approach in patent litigation but, equally, emphasized that examination of the patent claimed should concentrate on the claim rather than on extrinsic evidence of the patentee's intention and his subsequent behaviour. On the facts of the case, it was held that the reasonable skilled man would not have been able to

---

3   Ibid at 323.
4   [1993] RPC 357. See Cole 'Purposive Construction under English Law' [1994] 10 EIPR 455.
5   Ibid at 361.
6   [1995] RPC 255. See Conroy 'The Construction of Claims in UK Patent Litigation' [1995] 4 EIPR 199.

deduce from the earlier patent the solution to the same problem in the allegedly (but in fact not) infringing subsequent activity.

Aldous J encountered the same issue in *Assidoman Multipack Ltd v Mead Corpn.*[7] Here litigation concerned different types of packaging and, in finding that there was an infringement in spite of the different phraseology employed in the applications in question, the judge made clear the point that the Protocol to Article 69 was the proper basis on which to proceed, as a middle way between 'Scylla, the rock of liberal construction, and Charybdis, the whirlpool of guided freedom'. So that's clear then. Jacob J also waded into these murky waters in *Beloit Technologies Inc v Valmet Paper Machinery Inc*[8] and described the *Catnic* approach as a *via media*, the middle way between the two approaches discredited by the Protocol.

At around the same time further support was given to this method of approach by the Court of Appeal in *Kastner v Rizla Ltd.*[9] This dispute arose in relation to two inventions for interleaving cigarette papers used by connoisseurs of self-rolling cigarettes who need the papers to contain the tobacco and any other material in the cigarette. It was held that there was an infringement in this case and Aldous LJ perhaps unsurprisingly followed his view in *Assidoman* and sidestepped the narrower view in *PLG* by expressing it as being obiter and pointing out that *Catnic*, as a House of Lords decision, was to be followed in all cases. The most recent approach to this area has come in *Auchinloss v Agricultural & Veterinary Supplies Ltd*[10] where emphasis was placed on the need for fairness to third parties. Thus a precise claim that a new product claims benefits A, B and C would enable another party using the same product to achieve benefit D to avoid allegations of infringement. On the other hand a more vaguely or broadly worded claim might extend to cover the notional benefit D and would protect the patentee, albeit at risk of the patent being regarded as initially unregistered.

So where are we now? The answer is that the attempt to construe the *Catnic* approach so narrowly as to effectively overrule it has not succeeded. The recent case law suggests that *Catnic* remains as the *via media* with all the uncertainties that such an approach inherently provides. A good recent example is the decision of Jacob J in *Impro Ltd's Patent*[11] where a patent for an invalid lifting hoist was held to be infringed by a laser device with the decision being made with reference to both the purposive interpretation of the claims and, in the light thereof, the wording used in the claims.

7   [1995] RPC 321.
8   [1995] RPC 705 esp at 721.
9   [1995] RPC 585, followed by Laddie J in *Brugger v Medic-Aid Ltd* [1996] RPC 635
10   [1997] RPC 649.
11   [1998] FSR 299.

Doubtless there will still be future litigation which will help to cast light in this area but at least it is clear that the *Catnic* approach will be at the heart of that litigation.

INFRINGEMENT: AN OVERVIEW

Infringement is perhaps the area of patent law most radically transformed by the 1977 legislation. First the old common law rules were replaced by a statutory framework, and this appears to have worked well. The case law in relation to it suggests that there are a few problems, with the potential differences of language between the UK legislation and the European Patent approach being at the heart of the difficulty.

The all important issue is how the courts will approach the interpretation of specifications and claims. *Catnic* clearly represents the dawning of a new era where the patentee is treated more generously and his rivals are more likely to be ensnared in the web of infringement. In so far as it is appropriate to rely on the tip of reported cases that are part of the iceberg of litigation it seems that for the most part the courts have understood the import of what was intended in *Catnic*.

However, the *Improver* litigation is a sorry tale and suggests that the UK courts are yet to fully embrace a continental approach to interpretation, being held back by the third of the three questions that now have to be asked, namely whether the skilled reader, having seen that a variant was obvious, would then still consider that the words of the specification required strict compliance. Thus expressed, the bizarre nature of the question becomes clear; it requires the skilled reader to consciously ignore that which is obvious to him – quite a mental feat. Imposing this bizarre question then leads to the unacceptable situation where, in a case like *Improver*, an EPC patent has differing effects in different states quite contrary to the whole rationale and purpose of international patent co-operation. The *Improver* saga and the *PLG* case seem now to represent a low watermark, however, with the *Catnic* approach restored, however uncertainly, to its central position.

It could be concluded from this that *Catnic* did not intend to go as far as is required by the EPC which, as has been noted, was not on the face of it in the minds of the Law Lords at the time. The better view is that like children on new bicycles judges asked to give purposive interpretations to specifications and claims will be inevitably cautious at first, may make the odd mistake or two, but equally as time passes and the unfamiliar becomes the familiar confidence will grow and mistakes will disappear. With more and more European legislation coming to the courts to be considered it seems likely that the necessary confidence and accuracy will evolve sooner rather than later, and that judges, deprived as they now are of what has been described by Professor Cornish[12] as the rigid 'fenceposts' of literally interpreted patents, will be equally able to gain as much assistance from the guidance of the 'signposts' that represent the results of the new purposive approach. This simply has to occur. If it does not there is an obvious danger that UK patent law will start to become isolated from the mainstream international approach.

12   See Cornish 'Intellectual Property' Sweet & Maxwell (3rd ed, 1996) Ch 6.

Chapter 6

Supplementary protection certificates

BACKGROUND

Pharmaceutical products can attract patent protection just as any other product that satisfies the requirements for patentability. The complicating factor though is that new pharmaceutical products need testing and government authorisation before they can be marketed. All this generally takes place after the patent application has been filed and the whole process may take years rather than months or weeks. As the term of a patent is calculated on the basis of the filing date, patent protection for research and development based products[1] is in practice eroded. The period between the first marketing of the drug and the expiry of the patent was shortened and there have been cases where the patent had expired before marketing authorisation was obtained. As the copying of drugs is in addition to that rather easy, especially when compared with the independent development process, this phenomenon was seriously damaging the pharmaceutical industry.[2]

The situation became particularly pressing when the US and Japan introduced measures to restore the term of patent protection for pharmaceutical products.[3] When France and Italy started introducing national measures aiming to produce a similar effect the Community took

---

1   Generic drugs are not faced with the problem as they do not need the extensive testing
     etc and rely to a great extent on the work done in respect of the original drug of which
     they are a copy.
2   Adams 'Supplementary Protection Certificates: The Challenge to EC Regulation 1768/
     92' [1994] 8 EIPR 323.
3   Two Japanese laws, one dated 1980, the other dated 1987, address the problem and the
     US introduced the Waxman–Hatch Act (35 USC Par 156).

over the initiative and introduced supplementary protection certificates as a *sui generis* intellectual property right for medicinal products.[4]

REGULATION 1768/92

In Europe an extension of the patent term required the amendment of Article 63 of the European Patent Convention. As a number of the contracting parties have a pharmaceutical industry which is almost exclusively based on generics it was felt that the required unanimous vote was out of reach.[5] The Convention does allow for the introduction by the contracting states of other sui generis rights, though only in so far as they grant new and different kinds of industrial property protection. As the extension of the patent term was not an option, the Community took the route of the *sui generis* right and called it the supplementary protection certificate.[6]

The Regulation provides that any product that is protected by a patent in a member state and which is as a medicinal product subject to an authorisation procedure can be the subject of a certificate.[7] A product is defined widely as the active ingredient or the combination of active ingredients of a medicinal product and the latter category comprises substances or combinations of substances which are used to prevent, diagnose or treat a disease or restore, correct or modify physiological functions in humans or in animals.[8] Protection is only granted for the product covered by the original authorisation or by any subsequent authorisation which takes place before the expiry of the patent.[9] This is particularly important in cases where the scope of the patent is wider than that of the authorisation. The various ways in which the active ingredient can be formulated are arguably all covered.[10]

---

4   Regulation 1768/92 concerning the creation of a supplementary protection certificate for medicinal products [1992] OJ L182/1.
5   An amendment to Article 63 EPC which would allow the term of protection for pharmaceutical products to be extended awaits ratification, but it is not likely to be ratified and come into force in the near future.
6   Kunz-Hallstein 'The Compatibility of a Community "Certificate for the Restoration of Protection" with the European Patent Convention' [1990] 6 EIPR 209.
7   Article 2.
8   Article 1.
9   Article 4.
10 This is logical for anyone familiar with chemistry and the pharmaceutical industry. The *travaux préparatoires* of the Regulation seem to spell this out by referring to salts and esters of acids as coming under one product definition. See Whaite and Jones 'Pharmaceutical Patent Term Restoration: The European Commission's Regulation' [1992] 9 EIPR 324 at 325.

Only the patentee of the original patent[11] or any successor in title can file an application for a certificate.[12] Licensees are excluded from this procedure which has to take place at the national patent office that granted the patent. The whole granting procedure takes place at national level.[13] Two statutory instruments translate this into domestic intellectual property law and allow the Patent Office to issue the certificate.[14]

An application for a certificate must be filed within six months of the date on which the marketing authorisation for the medicinal product was granted. The one exception to this rule is formed by the situation where the authorisation is granted before the patent is granted. In that case the application for the certificate must be lodged with the national patent office within six months of the date of the grant of the patent.[15]

If at the date of the application the patent covering the medicinal product is in force and the marketing authorisation is valid, a single certificate[16] can be granted for the medicinal product.[17] It should be noted that the Regulation refers to the first marketing authorisation in relation to the application for and the grant of the certificate,[18] but that any therapeutic use which is authorised before the expiry of the certificate comes within the scope of the protection offered by the certificate.[19] A certificate confers the same rights as the basic patent and is subject to the same limitations.[20] These are granted for a period that runs from the end of the patent term.

11   A product may be covered by more than one patent. In such a case a supplementary protection certificate can be granted for each basic patent (one basic patent and certificate per holder). For further details on this point and on the problems that arise when patents and marketing authorisation are owned by different companies, see Case C-181/95: *Biogen Inc v Smithkline Biologicals SA* [1997] ECR I-717, [1997] 1 CMLR 704.
12   Article 6.
13   Article 9.
14   The two SIs are: Patents (Supplementary Protection Certificates for Medicinal Products) Regulations 1992, SI 1992/3091, which creates the rule-making power for the creation of the certificates and Patents (Supplementary Protection Certificates) Rules 1997 (SI No 64) which contains the rules governing the creation etc of the certificates.
15   Article 7.
16   No second certificate covering the same member state can be granted according to Article 3(c).
17   Article 3.
18   Ibid.
19   Article 4, subject to the general limitation of the protection to anything coming within the scope of the basic patent. See also Whaite and Jones 'Pharmaceutical Patent Term Restoration: The European Commission's Regulation' [1992] 9 EIPR 324 at 325.
20   Article 5. Interesting and outstanding questions are whether and to what extent certificates and patents will be treated in an identical way under national law and how certificates will relate to Article 85 of the EC Treaty and to the block exemptions. See Whaite and Jones 'Pharmaceutical Patent Term Restoration: The European Commission's Regulation' [1992] 9 EIPR 234 at 236. The High Court decided some time ago that the limitations to which both the patent and the certificate are subject must include compulsory licences and licences of right under the Patents Act 1977. (The case is reported as 'In the matter of an application by Faulding Pharmaceuticals plc to settle

The length of that period is calculated in relation to the period for which protection was lost due to the authorisation process. The starting point is the period which lapsed between the date on which the patent application was lodged and that on which the marketing authorisation was granted. This period is reduced by five years. A final restriction is that the resulting term of protection offered by the certificate cannot exceed five years.[1] Once granted the continued existence of the certificate is subject to the payment of an annual fee[2] and the certificate will also expire if the marketing authorisation for that medicinal product is withdrawn.[3]

A certificate becomes invalid if the basic patent is revoked or limited to the extent that the product for which the certificate was granted would no longer be protected by the claims of the basic patent. Once the basic patent has expired, the certificate becomes invalid and anyone has the right to submit an application or bring an action in this respect if grounds exist which would have justified the revocation or limitation of the patent.[4]

Clearly the certificate is very closely linked to the patent covering the medicinal product which is the subject of the certificate. One could even argue that it is in reality nothing else than an extension of the patent term for pharmaceutical products. There are however differences,[5] although one has to admit that the sui generis right was moulded along the lines of the patent model. The certificate is only available for products subject to an authorisation procedure and there is no link to any disclosure. The scope of protection is in no way determined by the patent claims, the patent is only the precondition for the grant of the certificate and it is the authorisation which defines the real scope of the certificate. It is submitted that the certificate constitutes indeed a sui generis right.[6] The argument that it is different from the patent system because it only protects successful inventions[7] cannot be endorsed however. A patented invention is successful in the sense that it fulfils the requirements for patentability and the pharmaceutical industry often finds very lucrative exploitation opportunities even for those patented products that are not granted a marketing authorisation as medicinal products. The real tests for success are the sales figures for the drugs and these will only be known after the

the terms of a licence of right under Supplementary Protection Certificate SPC/GB93/ 032 in the name of Research Corporation Technologies Inc' at [1995] 1 EIPR D-16 and 17.)

1   Article 13.
2   Articles 12 and 14.
3   Article 14(d).
4   Article 15.
5   Kunz-Hallstein 'The Compatibility of a Community "Certificate for the Restoration of Protection" with the European Patent Convention' [1990] 6 EIPR 209.
6   Ibid. See also CLIP Report 'Supplementary Protection Certificates' (1991) p 16 et seq.
7   CLIP Report 'Supplementary Protection Certificates' (1991).

deadline for the filing of an application for a certificate, in general six months after the first authorisation to market the product was obtained.

The Regulation came into force on 2 January 1993. All products that were at that date covered by a patent and for which the first marketing authorisation within the Community was granted after 1 January 1985 qualify for a certificate. A number of other member states were allowed to use another authorisation date and accordingly Spain, Greece and Portugal only made certificates available from 1 January 1998 onwards.[8]

THE EXTENSION OF THE SYSTEM

Industry has lobbied hard to see the system of supplementary protection certificates extended to other products. They argue that the system should be applied to all products that are subject to a marketing authorisation. The Commission has now recognised this argument and it has extended the system of supplementary protection certificates to plant protection products.[9] These products are subject to an authorisation procedure under Directive 91/414[10] and first marketing of these products can only take place once the marketing authorisation has been obtained.

The new Regulation defines plant protection products as 'active substances and preparations containing one or more active substances, put up in the form in which they are supplied to the user,'[11] that have a number of intended uses. Their use can first of all be to 'protect plants or plant products against all harmful organisms or prevent the action of such organisms'.[12] Secondly they can be used to influence the life processes of plants, in as far as they do not do that as a nutrient. They can also be used to preserve plant products, to destroy undesirable plants or to destroy parts of plants or to check or prevent undesirable growth of plants.[13] This is followed in Article 1 of the Regulation by further definitions of substances, preparations, plants and plant products. The rest of the provisions of the Regulation is almost an exact copy of the provisions in the Regulation on pharmaceutical products. The same rules apply if one simply replaces the words pharmaceutical product by plant protection product. It is important to emphasise though that the existence of a patent for the product is once again a prerequisite.[14] If more than one patent exists for one product only

8   Articles 19, 21 and 23.
9   European Parliament and Council Regulation 1610/96 concerning the creation of a supplementary protection certificate for plant protection products [1996] OJ L198/30.
10   [1991] OJ L230/1, as amended by Directive 95/36 [1995] OJ L172/8.
11   Article 1 of the Regulation.
12   Ibid.
13   Ibid.
14   Article 3(1).

one certificate shall be granted in case the patents are owned by the same holder. More than one certificate can only be granted in respect of the same product if there are multiple patents owned by different holders, who apply separately for the certificates.[15]

The Regulation entered into force on 9 January 1997,[16] but it only applies from 2 January 1998 onwards for those member states whose national law did not provide for the patentability of plant protection products on 1 January 1990.[17] The Patents (Supplementary Protection Certificates) Rules 1997[18] provide the procedure under which these certificates will be granted in the UK.

THE CHALLENGE TO THE REGULATION

Spain has a pharmaceutical industry which relies heavily on generic drugs and which is affected negatively by the Regulation. It brought an action in the Court of Justice to annul Regulation 1768/92.[19] The main argument used by Spain was that the Regulation is ultra vires, in that the Community did not have the competence to create the certificate.[20] This argument was based on Articles 36 and 222 of the EC Treaty. Specifically Article 222 provides that the Treaty shall not interfere with the system of property ownership.[1] And Article 36 could be said to deal only with the exercise of existing rights and the extent to which such exercise is acceptable. The arguments comes down to the point that these provisions reserve the power to regulate substantive intellectual property law for the member States and exclude Community action in this area. The Court of Justice flatly rejected this argument.[2] It repeated its ruling that Article 222 'cannot be interpreted as reserving to the national legislature, in relation to industrial and commercial property, the power to adopt measures which would adversely affect the principle of free movement of goods within the common market'[3] and it derived from that ruling that the argument that rules concerning the very existence of industrial property rights fall within the sole jurisdiction

---

15   Article 3(2).
16   Article 21.
17   Article 20.
18   SI 1997/64.
19   Case C-350/92: *Spain v Council of the European Union* [1995] ECR I-1985.
20   See also Adams 'Supplementary Protection Certificates: The Challenge to EC Regulation 1768/92' [1994] 8 EIPR 323.
1   This argument attacks the validity of almost all intellectual property initiatives taken by the Community.
2   Case C-350/92: *Spain v Council* [1995] ECR I-1985 at 2009-2012.
3   Ibid at 2010-2011.

of the national legislature could not be endorsed.[4] The rules of the Treaty must be allowed to interfere in appropriate cases. In relation to Article 36 the Court referred to its judgment in Case 35/76 *Simmenthal SpA v Italian Minister for Finance*[5] and repeated the part of that judgment where it ruled that 'Article 36 is not designed to reserve certain matters to the exclusive jurisdiction of member states'.[6]

Having rejected Spain's main argument, the Court turned to Spain's second argument that concerned the legal basis for the Regulation. The Council had used Article 100a as a legal basis for the Regulation. This meant that the Regulation must pursue the objective of the creation of the single market, as set out in Article 8a of the Treaty. It could be argued that the Regulation does not pursue that objective, because 'as far as the free movement of goods is concerned, the certificate, by its very nature, tends to extend the compartmentalisation of the market beyond the duration of the basic patent, and thus adds to the exceptions provided for in Article 36 of the Treaty, without the extension of the scope of that provision being justified by the Community objective'.[7] Thus, Spain concluded that the introduction of the certificate would create obstacles to the free movement of goods. As the creation of a single market with a free flow of goods was one of the principle aims of the Treaty such a measure must be *ultra vires*. This argument cannot be accepted and it was also rejected by the Court.[8] The Court first started that Article 8a allows the Community to take harmonisation measures to achieve its objective. Such harmonisation measures may be necessary to deal with disparities between the laws of the member states, if and in so far as these are hindering the free movement of goods. In this particular case Italy and France had already been creating their own national certificates and so the only way to avoid the partitioning of the market was the creation of a measure at Community level. Indeed, differences in protection given to one and the same medicine would fragment the common market. The situation in which a product would still be protected in some national markets, but not in others would give rise to different market conditions in different parts of the common market. The Court thus agreed with the draftsmen of the Regulation who argued in the sixth recital that '[t]he regulation thus aims to prevent the heterogeneous development of national laws leading to further disparities which would be likely to create obstacles to the free movement of medicinal products within the Community and thus directly affect the establishment and the functioning of the internal market'.[9] In conclusion, the Court rejected all

4   Ibid at 2011.
5   Case 35/76 [1976] ECR 1871.
6   Case C-350/92: *Spain v Council* [1995] ECR I-1985 at 2011.
7   Ibid at 2013.
8   Ibid at 2012-2016.
9   Ibid at 2014-2015.

arguments that had been put forward by the Kingdom of Spain and the challenge to the Regulation failed.

Another approach which leads to the same conclusion is that taken by Jean-Francois Verstrynghe :

> 'The Court has already given some hint of its thinking in its recent judgment in the Article 169 infringement procedure as applied to compulsory licenses for non-use of patents in the UK. In this judgment of 18 February 1992, it declared a particular feature of the British law to be illegal under Article 30.[10] If this is so, it must then also be accepted that this feature concerning the scope and conditions of patent protection in the UK might affect the establishment and functioning of the internal market under Article 100A, and that therefore the European Community could have harmonised this detail of patent protection – and by implication many other details of national IPR laws [and thus also the certificate] – which affect the establishment and functioning of the internal market.'[11]

The importance of this case is not limited to the issue of supplementary protection certificates. It gives clear guidance in relation to the way in which the Community can operate in the area of intellectual property rights. As we have demonstrated in previous chapters, Community law will interfere with the exercise of intellectual property rights whenever that exercise conflicts with its principles of free movement and free competition. But the role of the Community is not a purely negative one based on Articles 30-36 and 85-86 of the Treaty. This case shows clearly that Article 8a of the Treaty allows the Community to create new right and harmonise the existing national provisions in so far as this is necessary for the creation of the single market. Article 100a will provide a legal basis for such measures. Further measures such as the creation of new supranational rights that are superimposed on national rights,[12] which fall outside the scope of Articles 8a and 100a, can be based on Articles 100 and 235 of the Treaty.[13]

In the case at issue the measure did indeed have as its object the establishment and the functioning of the internal market, because it was introduced as a measure which would replace national measures which would have partitioned the internal market. The use of Article 100a is particularly helpful in such circumstances, because it only requires a

---

10   Case C-30/90 *Commission of the European Communities v United Kingdom* [1992] ECR I-829, [1992] 2 CMLR 709.
11   Verstrynghe 'The Spring 1993 Horace S Manges Lecture – The European Commission's Direction on Copyright and Neighbouring Rights: Towards the Regime of the Twenty-First Century' [1993] 17 Columbia-VLA Journal of Law & the Arts 187 at 194.
12   Eg the Community Trade Mark, see Regulation 40/94 [1994] OJ L11/1.
13   See also Opinion 1/94 [1994] ECR I-5267 (concerning the Community's competence to sign the TRIPs Agreement).

qualified majority. Articles 100 and 235 require unanimity. One can easily
see the political background to the Spanish challenge on these grounds. If
their arguments had succeeded the Council would have been obliged to use
Articles 100 and 235 as a legal basis and Spain would have been able to veto
any supplementary protection certificate scheme it and its generics-based
pharmaceutical industry did not like.

Chapter 7

Section B – an overview

Critics of the patent system have ample ammunition at their disposal. To get a patent much time and energy have to be expended with an uncertain outcome, particularly if others are also in the field, and the best result being the reward of a limited period monopoly. Within the law itself are some real horror stories such as the exposure in *Genentech* of the falsity of the obviousness/inventiveness dichotomy and the inherent uncertainty of the purposive approach to patents being compounded by the additional uncertainty created by common law judges having to learn continental approaches to issues of interpretation. Add to this the uncertainty that attends the basic question of the proper purpose of the patent system and the practical problem of how much and when to claim in an application for a patent and despair may seem an appropriate response.

On the other hand thousands of patents are granted annually. This fact alone may be thought to suggest that all is not lost to despair in the patent system. Much of the law functions well and the time taken to grant a patent is as a result of a painstaking examination to ensure that the invention fits in with the legal criteria. Remember too what the thousands of applicants get from the time and effort of application. It is the triumph of the patent system that the nebulous concept of invention is translated by the law into an item of personal property that can be assigned or licensed to others and used to prevent others from infringing the monopoly it confers. Requiring change to mend some damaged parts of the law does not in any way prevent the conclusion that the patent system works well on both a national and an international level, balancing as it does in different ways at different times the competing interests of all those affected by the law in this area: inventors, their rivals, consumers and society itself.

Insofar as the patent system may be criticised, it is clearly having trouble getting to grips with 'cutting edge' issues such as biotechnology. The extent to which the number of patents granted is not matched by the numbers successfully worked also suggests that there are imperfections in the system. However, the bottom line must be that the patent system, albeit imperfect, is a high quality system involving detailed claims and full examination of them. Critics of the time and cost involved in a patent application forget that these problems arise from the quality of the system. Yes, the system is neither fast nor cheap but it generally succeeds in its aims. It is equally churlish to criticise a Rolls-Royce motor car for being large and expensive – how else can its qualities thrive, uncompromised? It is significant that a government especially keen to promote business efficiency and remove restrictions on commerce failed signally at the height of its power in the mid-1980s to implement proposals made for lower levels of patent protection[1] so as to suit business interests.

1   Cmnd 9117, 1983 esp paras 4.7–4.13.

Section C

Copyright and related issues

Chapter 8

Introduction to copyright

Copyright has two types of roots. It started as an exclusive right to make copies, to reproduce the work of an author. This entrepreneurial side of copyright is linked in tightly with the invention of the printing press which made it much easier to copy a literary work and permitted the entrepreneur for the first time to make multiple identical copies. The other side of this coin is that it became vital to protect the author now that his or her work could be copied much more easily and in much higher numbers. It was felt that the author should share in the profits of this new exploitation of the work, although this tendency was much stronger in continental Europe than in the UK. Before the arrival of the printing press, many original literary, or musical works were commissioned. One copy was written and the author was paid for it by the commissioner. The printing technology resulted in the production of multiple copies and it was almost naturally felt that the author should be paid for each copy that was made. As the technique also reduced the possibility for the author to control the format and contents of the various copies, because the reproduction work was now undertaken by the entrepreneur, it became necessary to think about minimum guarantees for the author in this area. This resulted in the creation of certain so called moral rights, which protected the author against unfair use of his or her work. This double set of roots is still reflected in modern copyright law.

Ever since it was created, copyright was directed towards the protection of a reproduction of the work. It was first of all a right in the production of printed copies of the work. This means that it is exclusively concerned with the material expression of the ideas on which the work is based. Copyright is not about ideas, but about the way in which they are expressed.

Copyright has proven to be a valuable and flexible tool. It could be used to protect various works, as it was merely a reproduction right that could be applied to very different forms of expression of ideas. At various moments in time literary works, musical works, artistic works, such as sculptures and paintings, works of architecture, computer programs etc all started to attract copyright protection. A similar expansion of copyright can be seen in relation to the carriers of the various works, as sound recordings, tapes, broadcasts, films, video, etc all entered the copyright arena. But it is to the essential elements of copyright we must now turn first.

The Copyright, Designs and Patents Act 1988 characterises copyright as a property right. As we have seen above in Chapter 1 there are many types of copyright. First of all we will have to distinguish them and find out which requirements should be fulfilled by the various works and materials to attract copyright protection. In the next stage we will have to consider who becomes the owner of the property right, what will be the duration of the right and what constitutes infringement of this intangible property right?

Does a work attract copyright? This will depend upon the nature of the material involved, produced through intellectual or entrepreneurial activity and upon the qualification issue. The latter element is more international in scope. The copyright and related conventions contain minimum provisions which are translated and implemented by the national copyright acts. The provisions also require that authors and works linked in a certain way to one of the adherents to the conventions will be treated by national copyright legislation in the same way as national authors and works. This link or qualification issue constitutes a separate hurdle and only those works that pass it will attract copyright protection. On the other hand no formalities, such as registration, are required to secure copyright protection.[1]

A last preliminary point is that ideas are not protected, only the particular expression of an idea is protected. It follows that all subject-matter, all works need to exist in some permanent form before attracting copyright. This issue gives in practice rise to interesting interpretation problems in the sphere of artistic activity: is a face make up which is used repeatedly permanent enough in nature,[2] and what about a device used to make sand pictures which contained sand and glycerine?[3] In both cases the answer was negative. For many works however this does not create a problem because the creation and fixation of the work take place at the same time. For example, the idea in a painting is only expressed and can as a consequence attract protection when the work is executed and fixation takes place automatically. But we will have to come back to this issue, because its application to certain other works is more problematical.

---

1   The familiar copyright notice (©, name of the copyright owner and year of first publication) is a formality required not by the Berne Convention, but by the Universal Copyright Convention; it is required if a published work is to attract copyright in a country which adheres only to the UCC.
2   *Merchandising Corpn of America Inc v Harpbond Inc* [1983] FSR 32, the Adam Ant case.
3   *Komesaroff v Mickle* [1988] RPC 204.

Chapter 9

The various types of copyright and the quality issue

Section 1(1) of the 1988 Act lists the various types of copyright which are further defined in the following sections. The case law is also a helpful source of information in this respect. In reality various types of works are defined. Every work that can be classified as one of these types of works will attract copyright, if all the other requirements are met. This classification of works is an important aspect of our copyright system. A work that does not come within the definition of any of the types of works will not be protected by copyright. It could also be argued that each work must be classified in one category. A work cannot get copyright protection at the same time under two different classifications. This is mainly due to the slight differences that exist between the various regimes of copyright protection for each of the types of works. A product may include more than one work for copyright purposes, but each of these works will be classified and protected as a single type of work. The principle could be summarised as follows: '[…] although different copyrights can protect simultaneously a particular product and an author can produce more than one copyright work during the course of a single episode of creative effort, for example a competent musician may write the words and the music for a song at the same time, it is quite another thing to say that a single piece of work by an author gives rise to two or more copyrights in respect of the same creative effort'.[1]

---

1 *Electronic Techniques (Anglia) Ltd v Critchley Components Ltd* [1997] FSR 401, per Laddie J.; see also *Anacon Corpn Ltd v Environmental Research Technology Ltd* [1994] FSR 659.

ORIGINAL LITERARY, DRAMATIC, MUSICAL AND ARTISTIC WORKS

All works in this first category have the originality requirement in common. Originality should not be taken in the normal sense here. Novelty or innovation are not required, the starting point is that the work is not copied and originates from the author.[2] The author must produce his or her own expression of the idea, but the test to establish whether the work originates indeed from the author is only a minimum effort standard. It is not required that the idea is new, because the idea is not covered by copyright at all. A radically new and different expression of the idea of the passionate love story between two people with irreconcilable cultural backgrounds in an outer space setting is equally not required. The author's own expression of the classical *Romeo and Juliet* tale will do. The author must only have expended 'skill, judgment and labour' or 'selection, judgment and experience' or 'labour, skill and capital' in creating the work. In reality two cumulative requirements are involved. First, the work must originate from the author. Second, there must have been a minimum investment by the author of 'skill, judgment and labour'. Both requirements have to be met. The investment of 'skill, judgment and labour' merely in the process of copying someone else's work cannot confer originality.[3] But even if the threshold is low, works that do not meet this minimum standard will not attract copyright protection. A copy which incorporates some minor alterations of a work which is no longer protected under copyright will not attract copyright.[4] And even if the content of a work may be nothing else than a compilation of existing elements, some skill and labour must have been invested in the way in which they are organised and expressed.[5] Football pool coupon lists can be protected, but only if it can be shown that the presentation of the material is special. It must be shown that the author has invested skill and labour in the way in which the table is organised. There must be 'a relation of creation between the work and the author whatever this act of creation (sometimes only presentation) means'.[6] What amounts to a sufficient

2   *Ladbroke (Football) Ltd v William Hill (Football) Ltd* [1964] 1 All ER 465, [1964] 1 WLR 273, at 479 and 291, per Lord Pearce and *University of London Press Ltd v University Tutorial Press Ltd* [1916] 2 Ch 601 at 609, per Peterson J.
3   This was reconfirmed by the Court of Appeal in *Biotrading & Financing OY v Biohit Ltd* [1998] FSR 109 at 116; see also Lord Oliver's opinion in *Interlego AG v Tyco Industries Inc* [1989] AC 217 at 258.
4   See *Interlego AG v Tyco Industries Inc* [1989] AC 217, [1988] 3 All ER 949.
5   See *Cramp v Smythson* [1944] AC 329.
6   Dietz 'The Artist's Right of Integrity Under Copyright Law – A Comparative Approach' (1994) 25 IIC 177 at 182.

amount of independent 'skill, labour and judgment' is not capable of definition in advance. It has to be determined on the facts of each case.[7]

Most other European countries have a slightly higher originality threshold. They define an original work as a work which constitutes the expression of the personality of its author. A work should be the author's own intellectual creation. This version of originality is found in the European Community Copyright Directives[8] which introduced a very partial harmonisation of copyright in the Community.[9] We will have to come back to this issue when we discuss the relevant types of work in detail. Suffice it to say here that this higher originality requirement has now been included in the Copyright, Designs and Patents Act 1988[10] in relation to copyright in databases, as a result of the implementation of the Database Directive.[11] The UK may have to redefine its own originality requirement should a further European harmonisation of copyright take place.

Another essential rule is that copyright does not protect ideas; only a particular expression of an idea is protected. This does not create a specific problem for artistic works, but if one is not to protect the idea in a literary, dramatic or musical work the expression should be recorded in a permanent form. This can be in writing or in any other form and all new technological recording or fixation methods are automatically included. One could see an impromptu speech and a tune devised while playing the guitar which are not recorded as the perfect illustration of this problem. The author can record the work, but this is not required. The requirement mentions only recording, not even the permission of the author is required.[12] This means that the recording requirement will be met as soon as someone records the work.

Literary works

The Act characterises literary works as 'any work, other than a dramatic or musical work, which is written, spoken or sung'.[13] This category should not be restricted to works of literature. As Peterson J put it, this category contains every 'work which is expressed in print or writing, irrespective of

---

7   *Biotrading & Financing OY v Biohit Ltd* [1998] FSR 109 at 116.
8   See eg Article 1(3) of the Council Directive of 14 May 1991 on the legal protection of computer programs (1991) OJ L 122/42.
9   See also the draft Directive ((1993) OJ C 345/14) and Regulation ((1994) OJ C 29/20) on industrial design.
10   As s 3A.
11   European Parliament and Council Directive 96/9/EC (1996) OJ L77/20 and the Copyright and Rights in Databases Regulations 1997.
12   Copyright, Designs and Patents Act 1988, s 3(3).
13   CDPA, s 3(1).

the question whether the quality or style is high'.[14] The case law supplements high quality works with all kinds of compilations and tables.[15] Trade catalogues,[16] street directories,[17] timetable indexes,[18] examination papers,[19] football fixtures lists,[20]a listing of programmes to be broadcast,[1] a racing information service,[2] business letters[3] and consignment notes[4] have all been held to be literary works protected by copyright. Lyrics for songs and computer programs are also protected. An exception is presented by compilations of (only) artistic works. Compilations are protected as literary works, but only if they are written. Most artistic works are not written and such compilations of artistic works will not attract copyright protection.[5] The addition of a substantial quantity of written work will solve this problem, as the originality requirement will be met in these cases.

In practice the originality requirement requires such a low amount of skill, labour and judgment to be invested in a literary work that it operates as a de minimis rule. Only works which are not substantial enough do not attract copyright protection. A first group of works falls in this category because the amount of skill and labour invested in them is almost non-existent. Case law examples are a card containing spaces and directions for eliciting statutory information[6] and an advertisement consisting of four commonplace sentences.[7] Recently it was held that a formula for calculating racing forecasts was not an original literary work, nor were the forecasts produced by using the formula. The calculation was held to be a routine repetitive task which involved feeding the relevant information into a computer and that task did not involve sufficient skill, labour or judgment to produce an original literary work each time the formula was used.[8] A second group of works falls in this category because the volume of these

14   *University of London Press Ltd v University Tutorial Press* [1916] 2 Ch 601 at 608.
15   See also CDPA, s 3(1)(a).
16   *Collis v Cater* (1898) 78 LT 613; *Purefoy v Sykes Boxall* (1955) 72 RPC 89.
17   *Kelly v Morris* (1866) LR 1 Eq 697.
18   *Blacklock v Pearson* [1915] 2 Ch 376.
19   *University of London Press v University Tutorial Press* [1916] 2 Ch 601.
20   *Football League v Littlewoods* [1959] Ch 637, [1959] 2 All ER 546; *Ladbroke (Football) Ltd v William Hill (Football) Ltd* [1964] 1 All ER 465, [1964] 1 WLR 273.
1   *Independent Television Publications v Time Out Ltd* [1984] FSR 64, a subsequent competition law initiative made the copyright owners grant licences and made the listings available to other publishers.
2   *Portway Press v Hague* [1957] RPC 426.
3   *British Oxygen Co Ltd v Liquid Air Ltd* [1925] Ch 383.
4   *Van Oppen & Co Ltd v Van Oppen* (1903) 20 RPC 617.
5   Monotti 'The Extent of Copyright Protection for Compilations of Artistic Works' [1993] 5 EIPR 156 at 160–161.
6   *Libraco v Shaw* (1913) 30 TLR 22.
7   *Kirk v Fleming* MacG Cap Cas (1928–1935) 44.
8   *Bookmakers' Afternoon Greyhound Services Ltd v Wilf Gilbert (Staffordshire) Ltd* [1994] FSR 723.

works is not substantial enough. There is not enough space to distinguish between ideas and expression, if there is an underlying idea at all and copyright should not be used to monopolise words. Obvious examples in this category are trade marks[9] and most titles[10] of books, plays, films, etc.

A literary work based on existing sources can be seen as a different expression of the same idea if no substantial amount of copying is involved and skill and labour has been invested in the new work. As the idea is not protected no infringement problem arises and the new work can attract copyright protection as a literary work. Translations,[11] compilations,[12] selection and abridgment,[13] critical annotation and explanation[14] and editorial work that involves amendments[15] all come under the head of literary works and qualify for protection irrespective whether the material taken from existing sources is in or out of copyright. As for all literary works the de minimis principle applies. On this basis copyright protection for the times of local trains, extracted from a general timetable,[16] and for a collection of existing tables made for the front of a pocket diary[17] was refused.

It may at first seem contradictory, but certain similar works do not fall foul of the de minimis rule. These works involve a sufficient amount of skill and labour in the selection and use of the existing elements on the basis of a commercial judgment. Skill and labour are not restricted to literary selection, expression and presentation. This became clear in *Ladbroke v William Hill*.[18] Copyright protection was granted to a fixed-odds football pool which consisted of a compilation of 16 known forms of bet, when the commercial judgment and skill used in the selection of these forms of bet

---

9   *Exxon v Exxon Insurance Consultants International Ltd* [1982] Ch 119, [1981] 3 All ER 241; copyright should not be used to expand the protection granted by a trade mark to a well-known brand name to an entirely different category of products or services.

10   See *Ladbroke (Football) Ltd v William Hill (Football) Ltd* [1964] 1 All ER 465 at 476, [1964] 1 WLR 273 and 286, per Lord Hodson and *Francis Day & Hunter Ltd v Twentieth Century Fox Corpn Ltd* [1940] AC 112 at 123, per Lord Wright.

11   *Byrne v Statist Co* [1914] 1 KB 622, *Cummins v Bond* [1927] 1 Ch 167.

12   *Portway Press v Hague* [1957] RPC 426, *Football League v Littlewoods* [1959] Ch 637, [1959] 2 All ER 546 and *Ladbroke (Football) Ltd v William Hill (Football) Ltd* [1964] 1 All ER 465, [1964] 1 WLR 273.

13   *Macmillan v Cooper* (1923) 93 LJPC 113; condensation of a single text may not be sufficient, but collecting an anthology of verse is likely to be sufficient: *Sweet v Benning* (1855) 16 CB 459.

14   The notes appended to a condensed text showed sufficient literary skill, taste and judgment in *Macmillan v Cooper* (1923) 93 LJPC 113.

15   *Warwick Film Productions Ltd v Eisinger* [1969] 1 Ch 508, [1967] 3 All ER 367 was concerned with an edited version of a trial transcript.

16   *Leslie v Young* [1894] AC 335; see also *Blacklock v Pearson* [1915] 2 Ch 376.

17   *Cramp v Smythson* [1944] AC 329; see also *Rose v Information Services* [1987] FSR 254.

18   [1964] 1 All ER 465, [1964] 1 WLR 273.

was taken into account and reference was not solely made to the presentation on the pool form.[19]

Works which derive in some way from an earlier source, such as a selection of poetry or a selection of letters written by a celebrity, attract copyright if more than a minimal amount of skill and labour is invested in the choice and presentation of the material.[20] The poems or letters which are reproduced by a substantial amount may still attract copyright which will co-exist with the copyright in the new work. It is obvious that the permission of all owners of a copyright is required to reproduce their work or to deal with the copyright in any other way. Each copyright creates an independent exclusive right in this respect. All this follows logically from the restrictive definition which is given to the originality requirement.

When compared to the wider European originality concept, which would probably deny copyright protection to certain works which are purely functional and do not require creative activity by the author, the UK originality concept makes copyright protection available for works which are only used in a business context. Copyright makes it impossible for the direct business competitor to express his or her business message in an identical way. In these cases copyright is used to remedy the lack of an unfair competition concept. It is arguable that the use of copyright to protect items which are fundamentally different in nature is not desirable and that the continental combination of a tighter originality requirement and an unfair competition concept is a more adequate solution because it creates a suitable and well-defined solution for each of the different problems.

Let us return briefly to the definition the Act gives of a literary work.[1] A literary work is defined widely as any work that is written, spoken or sung and that is not a dramatic or musical work. The exclusion of any work that comes within the definition of a musical or a dramatic work from the category of literary works implements the basic principle that every work can only fall within a single category of types of works. This exclusion slightly narrows the category of literary works, but it remains rather wide. The latter point is demonstrated by the fact that a literary work need not be expressed in words or any particular notation. Any kind of notation can turn a work into a work that is written.[2] As a result of all this a software

---

19   For another example which attracted copyright (a random choice game in a newspaper with grids of letters printed on cards as the only literary material) see *Express Newspapers v Liverpool Daily Post* [1985] 3 All ER 680, [1985] 1 WLR 1089; see also *Mirror Newspapers Ltd v Queensland Newspapers Pty* [1982] Qd R 305 and *Kalamazoo (Aust) Pty Ltd v Compact Business Systems Pty Ltd* [1985] 5 IPR 213.

20   See the comparison in *Ladbroke (Football) Ltd v William Hill (Football) Ltd* [1964] 1 All ER 465, [1964] 1 WLR 273.

1   CDPA 1988, s 3(1).

2   See H Laddie, P Prescott and M Vitoria *The Modern Law of Copyright and Designs* Butterworths (2nd edn, 1995) at 30.

program that is written in any kind a computer programming language will fall within the category of literary works.

That brings us to the types of works that are explicitly included in the definition of a literary work. Section 3(1) of the CDPA mentions specifically that a computer program and the preparatory design material for a computer program are literary works. The same goes for tables and compilations. A table consists of a series of facts or numbers that have been arranged in a systematic way. A compilation is mainly a body of materials that have been brought together. There is no need to distinguish whether a particular work is a table or a compilation, as the Act treats them in exactly the same way. It is important to note that the Act does not require that the author of the table or compilation is also the person from whom the materials, numbers or facts that are included in these works originate. Copyright in a table or compilation consists in protecting the skill and labour employed in selecting, collecting or arranging the materials, numbers or facts. The materials, numbers or facts as such and on their own are not protected by the copyright in the table or compilation. They may, or may not be protected by copyright in their own right; for example five short stories in a compilation may be protected by copyright as five separate literary works. Any copyright in the compilation comes on top of existing separate copyrights in the contents of the compilation and leaves the latter unchanged. And, finally, databases are also defined as literary works for copyright purposes.

Databases have a lot in common with compilations. Most databases could be described as a kind of compilation. The Act makes it clear though that no overlap between the two types of literary works can exist for copyright purposes, by defining compilations as 'compilations, other than a database'. A database – such as the LEXIS legal information system – is the classic example: from legal materials from a range of sources a database is created by the publisher, and used with skill by the subscriber. Section 3A defines a database. The starting point is that a database is a collection of works, data or other materials. First of all these works, data or other materials that form the components of or items of content comprised in the collection need to be independent from one another. A collection of titles and names of authors of all books published in English in the nineteenth century could be a good example. Each title or name of author can stand on its own. This independence is not destroyed when a search facility allows the user of the database to retrieve several of these data from the database at the same time. Each title or name of author is still independent when they are jointly listed on the screen as the search result, for example, of a search for all titles of books that were published in 1830. Such independence does not exist, for example, in relation to a film. A cinematographic film is composed of a succession of still frames. Each frame can stand on its own as a photograph, but in the context of the film the frames are dependent on other frames. The essence of the film is the moving image and that moving image can only be produced by a combination of frames. That means that the individual frames cannot be considered to be independent from one another.

Secondly, a collection will only be a database if the independent works, data or other materials that form the collection are arranged in a systematic or methodical way.[3] In relation to our earlier example of titles and names of authors of books published in English during the nineteenth century this means that the data must for example be organised by year of publication, or alphabetically by name of author, or on the basis of all books published by a certain author in that period. A random collection of names of authors and titles from the nineteenth century will not do. On the other hand, it is sufficient that the data have been given a systematic code in the database and can be retrieved, for example on the screen of the terminal in relation to an electronic database, in a systematic way. The precise way or order in which they are technically stored in any electronic storage medium is irrelevant for this purpose.

Thirdly, the works, data or other materials need to be individually accessible.[4] Access to each individual and independent work needs to be possible. In our example this means that it must be possible to retrieve the data about a specific name of an author or a specific title of a book from the database. Such access can be by electronic or other means. That makes it clear that electronic databases are not the only ones that are protected. Hard copy databases, for example in card or book format, also come under the definition.

An additional hurdle remains, even if a collection meets these three requirements. Such a collection will only be a database if it is original. Originality is defined in a specific way for the purposes of a database.[5] A slightly higher criterion than the normal UK originality criterion is used. The database must constitute the author's own intellectual creation by reason of the selection or arrangement of the contents of the database. The emphasis is firmly placed on the selection or the arrangement of the contents of the database. Copyright in a database is not concerned with the contents of the database as such. The selection and arrangement criterion and the way in which they take place must be the author's own intellectual creation; he or she must have devised them and they cannot, therefore, be commonplace. For example, a standard alphabetical arrangement by name in a telephone directory comprising all people with a telephone connection in a certain area must be commonplace and that arrangement cannot be seen as the author's own intellectual creation.

Any collection that does not meet the three requirements above and the special originality requirement will not be a database for the purposes of the Act. It may nevertheless attract copyright protection as a compilation,

3   CDPA 1988, s 3A(1)(a).
4   CDPA 1988, s 3A(1)(b).
5   CDPA 1988, s 3A(2).

for example, if it only meets the lower standard originality criterion. Those collections that meet the three requirements and the originality criterion will attract copyright protection as a database. That protection does not cover the contents of the database though. What is protected is the structure of the database, because that is the expression of the author's original selection and arrangement of the contents of the database. Other aspects of a database may be protected by a sui generis right. This right is analysed in chapter 26 of this book.

The introduction of a new originality criterion for databases in section 3A(2) of the 1988 Act creates problems in relation to computer programs. Both databases and computer programs are the subject matter of EC Directives.[6] Both Directives contain the same 'author's own intellectual creation' originality criterion,[7] but this criterion has only been transposed into the 1988 Act in relation to databases. After the software directive it could be argued that the Act did not define originality and that we, therefore, did not have to copy the Directive's originality criterion. In the absence of a definition in the Act we could just interpret the level of originality required for computer programs in the light of the Directive and apply our old originality criterion to all other works. Or, one could unconvincingly argue that in practice there was no difference between the Directive's originality criterion and the skill and labour approach in the first place. If either of these explanations were true there was no need to include the 'author's own intellectual creation' originality criterion in the 1988 Act in relation to databases. The only logical conclusion must be that the new originality criterion that is specifically defined for databases departs from the originality criterion that applies to other works. That means that we have failed to implement the Software Directive correctly. The 'author's own intellectual creation' originality criterion should at least apply to databases and computer programs.

Dramatic works

This category shares the same set of general rules with the literary works category from which it is excluded by section 3(1) of the Act. The obvious example is a scenario or script for a play or for a film,[8] but dance and mime are also included in this category.[9] An interesting issue is raised by certain contributions to scripts written by other writers. It is clear that someone

6   European Parliament and Council Directive 96/9/EC on the legal protection of databases (1996) OJ L77/20 and Council Directive 91/250/EEC on the legal protection of computer programs (1991) OJ L122/42.
7   Articles 3(1) and 1(3) respectively.
8   The film itself attracts a separate copyright.
9   Copyright, Designs and Patents Act 1988, s 3(1)

who suggests a series of ideas and key lines for a work written by others will not share in the copyright protection in the work.[10] All he or she contributes are ideas which are expressed by the writer. Only the expression is protected by copyright. This would seem to require a contribution to the precise expression of the ideas, such as the full text of a scene or a number of lines for a scenario, a script or a play. Another relevant rule is the recording requirement. No copyright can be granted if the key lines are not recorded. The same conclusion was reached in a case concerned with an elaborated visual skit for a music hall sketch involving the use of fireworks.[11]

Titles are excluded from protection on the basis of the restrictive UK originality requirement which applies to this category as well and results in a de minimis rule. This rule also covers the names of characters and the typical way in which they behave,[12] unless the link and the characteristics are so strong that they become an independent and recognisable entity.[13] And the protection granted to scripts for plays and movies does not extend to costumes and scenic effects, which will only attract copyright if they are artistic works. Characters and the merchandising rights involved can be protected under passing off, but only in the cases where they benefit from an established trading reputation.[14]

What has become clear from the examples is that dramatic works involve action and movement. This is also reflected in the comment by Lord Bridge that a dramatic work must be capable of performance.[15] It is submitted that a dramatic work can be defined as

'a work created in order to be communicated in motion, that is, through a sequence of actions, movements, irrespective of the technique by which this movement is retrieved or expressed'.[16]

The communication in motion must be required for the proper representation of the work if the work is to be classified as a dramatic work. Any work can but be performed before an audience, for example a literary work can be read, communication in motion is not required for the proper representation of a literary work

---

10   *Tate v Thomas* [1921] 1 Ch 503; see also *Wiseman v Weidenfeld & Nicolson Ltd* [1985] FSR 525 and *Ashmore v Douglas-Home* [1987] FSR 553.
11   *Tate v Fullbrook* [1908] 1 KB 821.
12   See *Kelly v Cinema Houses* MacG Cap Cas (1928–1935) 362 at 368, per Maugham J.
13   *Exxon Corpn v Exxon Insurance Consultants International Ltd* [1982] Ch 119, [1981] 2 All ER 495 which refers to Lewis Carroll's *Jabberwocky* as an example.
14   See Chapter 27 on Character Merchandising.
15   *Green v Broadcasting Corpn of New Zealand* [1989] 2 All ER 1056.
16   Kamina 'Authorship of Films and Implementation of the Term Directive: The Dramatic Tale of Two Copyrights' [1994] 8 EIPR 319 at 320; compare J Phillips, R Durie and I Karet *Whale on Copyright* Sweet & Maxwell (4th edn, 1993) at 27.

This definition implies that a cinematographic or audiovisual work will be a dramatic work as it clearly meets the requirement of a work created to be communicated in motion. This dramatic work is distinct from the script. Various other aspects, such as music, dance, etc, have been added, making the cinematographic or audiovisual work more than a performance of the script. Although based on the script, it will constitute a new (derivative) dramatic work.[17] On the other hand, a proper distinction needs to be drawn between a dramatic work and a performance. Copyright in a dramatic work will only cover the work as such, ie what can be printed and published,[18] and not the interpretation that is given to it by the person who performs it in motion.

Musical works

Lyrics are protected as literary works, so what is left is the music. Every overlap is excluded because a musical work is defined as a work consisting of music, exclusive of any words or action intended to be sung, spoken or performed with it.[19] For copyright purposes music and lyrics are distinct works. They can be owned by different persons, expire at different times, etc. A musical work is 'intended to be performed by the production of a combination of sounds to be appreciated by the ear'.[20]

The general rules governing the two previous categories apply to musical works as well. There is no subjective quality requirement; what is a beautiful piece of music to one person is nothing more than an awful cacophony and noise to another person, and a couple of notes and chords will be sufficient to attract copyright.[1] Secondary musical works based on an existing musical work may attract their own copyright. In this category we find for example arrangements or transcriptions for another type of orchestra.[2] These will attract their own copyright if the minimum amount of skill and labour requested by the originality requirement is invested in them. This does not rule out the possibility of infringement of the copyright in the earlier musical work if for example the arrangement is made without the permission of the owner of the copyright in the earlier work. The situation in relation to arrangements must be distinguished from that in relation to the mere

17 Kamina [1994] 8 EIPR 319 at 320–321.
18 See *Tate v Fullbrook* [1908] 1 KB 821.
19 CDPA 1988, ss 1(1)(a) and 3(1).
20 H Laddie, P Prescott and M Vitoria *The Modern Law of Copyright and Design* Butterworths (2nd edn, 1995) at 43.
1   See *Lawson v Dundas* (1985) Times, 13 June, copyright in the then Channel 4 TV logo music.
2   *Metzler v Curwen* MacG Cap Cas (1928–1935) 127; *Wood v Boosey* (1868) LR 3 QB 223; *Redwood Music v Chappell* (1982) RPC 109.

interpretation in a performance of a work. In the latter case there will be no separate copyright in a (new) musical work, but a right in the performance may arise.

Artistic works

This category of original works is wide in scope and can be subdivided into three parts.[3] First there are the works which are protected irrespective of artistic quality, these are followed by the intermediate group of the works of architecture and the works of artistic craftsmanship. In relation to the latter works artistic quality could play a role. This represents a clear departure from the previous categories of works, for which the possession of artistic quality was irrelevant.

Graphic works, photographs, sculptures or collages are protected as artistic works irrespective of their artistic quality.[4] Graphic works include any painting, drawing, diagram, map, chart, plan, engraving, etching, lithograph, woodcut or similar work.[5] This means that works as different as a painting by Salvador Dali and an engineer's plans and drawings for an electromagnetic train are protected in the same way. No distinction is made between aesthetic, functional and utilitarian works. Casts, moulds or models made for a sculpture are treated as a sculpture.[6] However, the word sculpture should be given its normal plain English meaning. In that sense for a work to be a sculpture in the first place, it must be a three-dimensional work made by an artist's hand. It follows that not every mould is an artistic work. A mould will not be an artistic work if nothing 'suggests that the manufacturers of [this] mould considered themselves, or were considered by anybody else, to be artists when they designed the [mould] or that they were concerned in any way with the shape or appearance of what they were making, save for the purpose of achieving a precise functional effect'.[7] An attempt was also made to keep pace with future technological developments: a photograph was defined as a recording of light or other radiation on any medium on which an image is produced or from which an image may by any means be produced and which is not part of a film.[8] Any conflict with films, which may be seen as a succession of a huge number of photographs, is thus ruled out.

3   CDPA 1988, ss 1(1)(a) and 4(1)(a), (b) and (c).
4   CDPA 1988, s 4(1)(a).
5   CDPA 1988, s 4(2).
6   CDPA 1988, s 4(2).
7   *Metix (UK) Ltd v GH Maughlan (Plastics) Ltd* [1997] FSR 718, per Laddie J.
8   CDPA 1988, s 4(2).

The originality requirement for this first group of artistic works is the same as for all previous types of work. The work should not be copied, should originate from the author and its creation should involve the minimal amount of skill and labour. That minimal amount of skill and labour is clearly present when a photographer makes a photograph from a picture.[9] This is shown by the choice of the angle under which the picture is taken, the exposure time, etc. Other good examples are a woodcut made from a drawing[10] and the label design for a sweet tin.[11] But the skill and labour does not necessarily need to be artistic, a plan for a technical device containing three concentric circles was protected because technical judgment was involved in drawing them to precise measurements which allowed the technical device to work.[12] On the other hand a plan containing a design for Lego toy bricks which was only different from an earlier plan because minor variations were mentioned in words and figures, which are not themselves artistic works, fell foul of the originality requirement and was not awarded distinct copyright.[13]

A second group of artistic works consists of works of architecture.[14] Buildings or models for a building, which are commonly used to attract potential investors, fall in this group, but the architect's plans are protected as a graphic work and fall in the previous group. A model made of a building also falls outside this group.

Section 4(1)(b) does not contain the rule that works in this group are protected irrespective of their artistic quality. This omission means that we have to consider the originality requirement carefully. It is submitted that artistic quality is not required. The addition of the additional line in section 4(1)(a) was necessary to avoid all arguments about the artistic quality of such items as a sculpture which consists only of a rectangular piece of metal. Such arguments do not normally arise concerning buildings and it was not necessary to specify once more that the originality requirement is not an artistic quality test.[15]

---

9   *Graves' Case* (1869) LR 4 QB 715.
10 Or a coin engraved in three dimensions from a drawing: *Martin v Polyplas Manufacturers Ltd* [1969] NZLR 1046; see also *Wham-O Manufacturing Co v Lincoln Industries Ltd* [1985] RPC 127, the New Zealand frisbee case in which wooden models from which moulds for the plastic frisbees were made were protected as sculptures, while the moulds themselves were protected as engravings.
11 *Tavener Rutledge v Specters* [1959] RPC 355.
12 *Solar Thomson Engineering Co Ltd v Barton* [1977] RPC 537 at 558.
13 *Interlego AG v Tyco Industries Inc* [1989] 1 AC 217, [1988] 3 All ER 949.
14 CDPA 1988, s 4(1)(b).
15 Along the same lines H Laddie, P Prescott and M Vitoria *The Modern Law of Copyright and Designs* Butterworths (2nd edn, 1995) at 204–205; and compare W Cornish *Intellectual Property: Patents, Copyright, Trade Marks and Allied Rights* Sweet & Maxwell (3rd edn, 1996) at p 339.

Works of artistic craftsmanship[16]

Works of artistic craftsmanship form the last, but admittedly the most difficult, part of the category of artistic works. Many items or artefacts could be called works of craftsmanship. Jewellery made to a special design, furniture, clothing or cutlery can all be called works of craftsmanship. The Act offers no definition of this term, but through the inclusion of the word 'artistic' makes it clear that only some artistic quality is required if a work of craftsmanship is to attract copyright protection.

The House of Lords was given the opportunity to consider the issues raised by works of artistic craftsmanship in *George Hensher Ltd v Restawhile Upholstery (Lancs) Ltd*.[17] This case was concerned with a prototype for a suite of furniture whose boat shape was said by the House to have given it a particular low-brow appeal. The first important issue is whether artistic quality is required and what level must be attempted or reached. The House of Lords disagreed with the lower court which had held that the work qualified for copyright and the judgment makes it clear that some artistic quality is required. The fact that the work is a work of craftsmanship which is not purely utilitarian is not sufficient. Artistry and craftsmanship are both required, this is the real significance of the judgment, because this is the only point on which their Lordships agreed. Lord Reid and Lord Morris seem to think that a prototype can never satisfy the artistry requirement, because it is by definition not intended to have any value or permanence.[18] It is submitted that the intention of the craftsman is more relevant to a second and separate issue.

Should one look at the craftsman's intention to create something artistic or should one focus on the public's perception of artistic quality? The Court of Appeal had suggested that one should ask whether the public would purchase the thing for its aesthetic appeal rather than for its functional utility.[19] This approach was rejected by the House of Lords. Lord Simon of Glaisdale suggested that the Court of Appeal's approach was wrong because aesthetic appeal was derived from functional utility and vice versa in the English aesthetical tradition.[20] But the speeches do not offer a clear cut alternative approach. Lord Morris and Viscount Dilhorne suggest that an objective approach on the basis of a detached judgment of the work, without giving priority to the craftsman's intention or the perception by the public, is the better approach.[1] Lord Kilbrandon[2] and Lord Simon[3]

16   CDPA 1988, s 4(1)(c).
17   [1976] AC 64, [1974] 2 All ER 420.
18   Ibid at 77, 80, 423 and 425.
19   [1976] AC 64 at 71, [1973] 3 All ER 414 at 419.
20   [1976] AC 64 at 90–92, [1974] 2 All ER 420 at 433–435.
1   Ibid at 81, 86, 426 and 430.
2   Ibid at 97 and 439.
3   Ibid at 95 and 437.

attach more importance to the intention of the craftsman although Lord Simon would also look at the work. And Lord Reid suggested that a work of craftsmanship could only be artistic if a substantial part of the public valued it positively for its appearance.[4] Some further guidance is provided by the *Merlet v Mothercare* case.[5] The criterion suggested by Walton J is whether the craftsman had the conscious purpose of creating a work of art. In his view the work must be a work of art and he considered this to be the common ground in the speeches in the House of Lords in the *Hensher* case. This leads to the conclusion that the intention of the creator prevails. This case was concerned with a prototype of a cape for babies, called 'Raincosy', and provides also helpful guidance by making it clear that only the work itself should be submitted to the test. The use of the work should not be taken into account. In this case this meant that the cape should be considered without a baby in it, and one should clearly not look at the combination of a mother wearing the baby in a baby sling with the baby protected by the 'Raincosy'.

A last interesting point is that the judge can rely on expert witnesses to determine whether the work meets the relevant standards. Their Lordships did not adopt a common position in this respect in the *Hensher* case, but it is clear that they all refer to expert evidence as a determining factor.

All this leaves us with a considerable amount of uncertainty. It is not clear what level of artistic quality is required and no proper and comprehensive test is available. In practice no problems arise for handcrafted jewellery and similar items, but the position for machine-made objects is problematic. In *Hensher* Lord Simon seems to suggest that this should not disqualify an object and that copyright protection would still be possible,[6] but Lord Reid seems to disagree.[7] The problem is potentially aggravated if the object is utilitarian in nature and is produced in mass. This is especially the case because a lot of money is invested in the development of these objects. This situation is particularly regrettable because this category of works is becoming more and more important now that a proper industrial design right has been created. This will create more intellectual property activity in this area and requires a clear delimitation of the copyright and design areas respectively. All this is hampered by the absence of a clear definition of what constitutes a work of artistic craftsmanship.

No clear solution is available either for the situation where one person supplies the craftsmanship, but another one supplies the idea for the work of artistic craftsmanship. An old precedent[8] suggests that no copyright is

---

4   Ibid at 78 and 424; see also *Cuisenaire v Reed* [1963] VR 719 for a similar approach.
5   *Merlet v Mothercare plc* [1986] RPC 115. The case went up to the Court of Appeal, but
      only the point of infringement of the drawing was considered: see [1986] RPC 115.
6   [1976] AC 64 at 90–92, [1974] 2 All ER 420 at 433–435.
7   Ibid at 77 and 423.
8   *Burke v Spicers Dress Designs* [1936] 1 Ch 400.

available in such a case, but it is submitted that this approach is wrong as long as the craftsman's contribution gives the required level of artistic quality to the work.[9]

This situation of 20 years of legal uncertainty is undesirable and unacceptable. The scope of copyright protection is in general extremely wide, which allows it to be used to prevent unfair competition. The stricter requirements for works of artistic craftsmanship are an exception to this rule. But even if, as submitted above, one would prefer a narrower scope of copyright protection coupled with a proper unfair competition tort, it is hard to justify why works of artistic craftsmanship should be treated differently. This is clearly an area where statutory clarification would be desirable.

What we have described above is the generally accepted position. We think the case law allows for an alternative interpretation that may clarify things on a number of points. This interpretation starts from Lord Simon's speech in the *Hensher* case. What is protected is a work of artistic craftsmanship, not an artistic work of craftsmanship.[10] A glazier, a plumber, and others are all craftsmen,[11] though it is clear that the legislator did not seek to protect all their professional activities. The purpose was to protect a certain type of craftsmanship and the legislator attempted to distinguish that activity by calling it artistic craftsmanship.[12] The glazier who makes stained glass windows for example engages in artistic craftsmanship.[13] In making the distinction the judge can rely on the evidence provided by expert witnesses.[14] It follows from this starting point that it is not required that each individual work produced is a work of art, as long as it is the result of an activity which is by the relevant circles considered to be an activity of artistic craftsmanship as opposed to ordinary craftsmanship. This brings this type of work in line with the rest of the copyright works, for which no artistic value of the individual work is required and leads to the application of the normal originality requirement to the individual work.

Or does it? In deciding whether artistic craftsmanship is involved the expert evidence will be directed towards the fact that 'artists have vocationally an aim and impact which differ from those of the ordinary run of humankind'.[15] This covers both the intention of the creator and the result

9   Some more recent decisions expressed disagreement with the case; see *Radley Gowns Ltd v C Spyrou* [1975] FSR 455, per Oliver J, *Bernstein v Sydney Murray* [1981] RPC 303, per Fox J and *Merlet v Mothercare plc* [1986] RPC 115 at 123–124, per Walton J.

10   *George Hensher Ltd v Restawhile Upholstery (Lancs) Ltd* [1976] AC 64 at 94, [1974] 2 All ER 420 at 437, per Lord Simon.

11   Ibid at 91 and 434, per Lord Simon.

12   Ibid at 89–91 and 432–434, per Lord Simon.

13   Ibid at 91 and 434, per Lord Simon.

14   Ibid at 94 and 437, per Lord Simon.

15   Ibid.

of his or her activity.[16] So the work which is produced is taken into account in deciding whether the activity is artistic in nature. But this refers to the work of the author and the relevant kind of activity in general in requiring some artistic level and has the advantage not to refer to the individual piece of work under consideration for the purpose of copyright. Artistic craftsmanship thus involves a type of work with material that requires manual dexterity and that leads to the creation of an object that certain members of the public wish to acquire and retain for its visual appearance, rather than for its functional purpose. In this test the artistic element applies to the type of work carried out by the craftsman and not to the issue of whether each individual work is a piece of art. It is submitted that this approach could remove some of the doubts present in the speeches in the House of Lords and that it would provide us with a workable solution. It would not affect the outcome of the *Hensher* and *Merlet* cases, since both types of activity would be held not to be artistic craftsmanship.

ENTREPRENEURIAL RIGHTS

Section 1 of the Copyright, Designs and Patents Act 1988 also grants copyright protection to sound recordings, films, broadcasts, cable programmes and typographical arrangements of published editions. These are in most cases derivative rights which protect the entrepreneur and the commercial exploitation of copyright. A sound recording of a pop song is a typical example. Original copyrights exist in the lyrics and the music of the song and are, at least in the first stage, owned by their respective authors. An additional copyright is granted to the sound recording, and this copyright is derivative. These rights were introduced to give the entrepreneur his or her own protection. This protection is particularly important because often the financial cost of copyright exploitation is high. Many of the derivative works incorporate a series of original works protected by copyright. A film may incorporate lyrics, music and a script which is a dramatic work. In case of infringement it is extremely helpful that the owner of the copyright in the film can sue. This avoids a series of parallel lawsuits by the owners of the original rights, which may each face the problem of demonstrating that their copyright was infringed. The absence of a derivative right would in practice greatly facilitate film piracy.

In fact all these derivative copyrights are neighbouring rights when compared to the original copyrights. They need in general an original copyright work as their basis. A sound recording of a musical work is a good example and so is the script as the dramatic work as a basis for a film. In a sense they involve a first exploitation of the original work. This distinction

16   Ibid.

is reflected in many provisions of the Act[17] and is not just of theoretical importance. Unfortunately the Act does not adopt this terminology and calls all these rights copyrights, although it is clear that they are in many respects different from the original copyrights.

These works need not be based on works protected by copyright. If we go back to the example of the sound recording and replace the pop song by the noise of the sea unleashing its forces on the Cornish coast, the conclusion is that the recording is still a sound recording for the purposes of the Act and will attract copyright. Whether the derivative work is based on works protected by copyright or not, the originality requirement for original works will not apply to it.

Sound recordings

The Act defines the term sound recording in section 5A(1) as 'a recording of sounds, from which the sounds may be reproduced, or […] a recording of the whole or any part of a literary, dramatic or musical work, from which sounds reproducing the work or part may be produced, regardless of the medium on which the recording is made or the method by which the sounds are reproduced or produced'. It is important to stress that the Act deliberately uses the word sound and not the word music. Not only does this eliminate the discussion on the quality issue, it also means that speech and other noises are included. In brief, all non-musical works are also included. The recording part of the definition is equally wide in scope. All that is required is the recording of the sound and the possibility of reproducing it, the medium on which the recording is made and the method by which the sound is produced or reproduced being irrelevant.[18] This means that all existing formats such as CD, magnetic tape and DAT are included and that all new formats which may be developed in the years to come will automatically be included. It is obvious that the sound which is recorded may include the whole or part of a literary, musical or dramatic work, but copyright will not exist in a sound recording which is, or to the extent that it is, taken from a previous sound recording.[19] In the music industry, or should one say sound industry, this means that copyright will subsist in the master copy of the recording. This master copy is used to produce the copies on sale to the public. The CDs and cassettes do not attract their own copyright, but are protected indirectly through the copyright in the master copy.[20] This technique does not reduce the level of

---

17   See eg CDPA 1988, s 9(2).
18   CDPA 1988, s 5A(1).
19   CDPA 1988, s 5A(2).
20   For more details on the indirect infringement issue see infra the infringement chapter.

copyright protection, but eliminates the possibility that in the absence an originality requirement each new and identical copy would attract copyright and extend the duration of copyright protection.

But each recording made independently will attract copyright. If we take the Cornish example, and many persons make their own recording of the noise of the sea at the same time and place, each of these recordings will attract its own copyright and the person making his or her recording will be able to sue for infringement if someone makes, without permission, a copy of their recording. Such a copy will not only infringe; it will also not attract copyright in its own right.[1]

Films

The Act defines a film in section 5B(1) as 'a recording on any medium from which a moving image may by any means be reproduced'. The essential element here is the recording from which a moving image may be reproduced. The technique used to make the recording, the medium on which it is made and the means of reproduction are irrelevant.[2] All existing formats such as celluloid film, video and laser disc are included and all new formats will also be included, the provisions being drafted in such a way that it will not be outdated by technological developments. Another important point is that only images are referred to. The soundtrack will attract its own separate copyright as a sound recording. Nevertheless, the term 'film' should be taken to include the soundtrack accompanying the moving images. Section 5B(2) makes it clear that the soundtrack shall be treated as part of the film. This solution is unfortunate in as far as it represents a departure from the basic rule that one work should only be classified and protected as a single type of work, but the solution does on the other hand reflect the way in which soundtracks are exploited. They are nowadays on the one hand an integral part of a film and it could be argued that they deserve protection as such and on the other hand they are also exploited as separate sound recordings and people buy them separately on CDs or cassettes. There was therefore no reason either to take away the protection of a soundtrack as a sound recording simply because it is also used in a film.

Only the master copy of a film will attract copyright protection; this rule applies to films in exactly the same way as it applies to sound recordings. Copyright will not subsist in a film which is, or to the extent that it is, a copy of a previous film.[3] Indirect protection for authorised copies is

---

1   *Metix (UK) Ltd v GH Maughlan (Plastics) Ltd* [1997] FSR 718, per Laddie J.
2   CDPA 1988, s 5B(1).
3   CDPA 1988, s 5B(4).

; copying them means indirectly copying the original
\uthorised copy on the other hand will not only not
will also infringe the copyright in the master copy.
sised that this form of copyright in a film is
\es not influence the copyright as a dramatic work
ьтарпıc or audiovisual work that will in many cases be
___ in the film. That copyright as a dramatic work may arise if the
director adds significantly to the scenario or script of an acted film.

The breadth of the references to a recording on any medium and to the
reproduction of moving images in the definition of a film do not only allow
the wording of the Act to cope with further technological developments in
terms of recording medium; it also allows for the classification as films of
certain works that would not necessarily be described as films in the plain
English sense of the word. For example, many multimedia products that
are produced in a digital format seem to fall within the Act's definition of a
film. Digital recording media do not create a problem and the requirement
that a moving image can be reproduced from the recording is also met. Most
of these products do indeed include moving images, in addition to texts,
photographs and sound recordings and computer programs. The latter
additional elements, as well as the potential for interactivity, cannot reverse
the reality that all elements of the definition of a film are met. Once again
the copyright as a film in the multimedia work come on top of and is
independent from the copyright that may exist in any of the works that are
included in it. For example, if a photograph is included in a multimedia
work the film copyright in the multimedia work does not affect the copyright
in the photograph as an artistic work. The maker of the multimedia work
will require a licence to use the photograph if he or she does not own the
copyright in it.

Broadcasts

The Copyright, Designs and Patents Act 1988 grants copyright protection
to broadcasts and cable programmes.[4] This allows us to restrict the scope
of broadcasts to wireless transmission. Wireless transmission means simply
that wires or cables are not used to carry the signal. The Act further defines
a broadcast as a transmission of visual images, sounds or other information
(by means of wireless telegraphy) which is capable of being lawfully received
by members of the public or which is transmitted for presentation to
members of the public.[5] If we analyse this definition further we see that
broadcasts which cannot be lawfully received by members of the public,

4   CDPA 1988, ss 6 and 7.
5   CDPA 1988, s 6(1).

such as certain military broadcasts, do not attract copyright. An interesting problem arises when broadcasts are encrypted. This means that the sound and image are emitted in a way which will result in a distorted image and sound being produced on a normal TV set. This is often done by commercial satellite broadcasters who charge fees to viewers. One needs to subscribe to the service and one then receives a decoder to recreate the normal sound and image. These broadcasts are regarded as capable of being lawfully received if (and only if) decoding equipment has been made available to members of the public by or with the authority of the person making the transmission. The latter can be replaced by the person providing the contents of the transmission.[6] What is meant by transmission for presentation to members of the public? This becomes clear if we contemplate the example of a giant rock concert, say in Hyde Park. Not all fans can attend and giant screens are placed in halls in Edinburgh and Manchester where fans who pay an entrance fee can attend the concert which is displayed on a large screen. The transmission from Hyde Park to Manchester and Edinburgh is a transmission of sound and images for presentation to members of the public and will attract copyright as a broadcast. Reception of a broadcast may be by means of a telecommunications system[7] and copyright does not subsist in a broadcast which infringes (or to the extent that it infringes) the copyright in another broadcast or in a cable programme.[8]

Satellite broadcasting is a form of broadcasting which raises additional problems.[9] The signal is transmitted to the satellite (the 'up-leg') from where it is retransmitted towards the earth (the 'down-leg'). Many countries are covered by the foot of the satellite and the question can be raised which copyright law will be applicable to the broadcasts. The choice is restricted by the fact that the Berne Convention speaks about broadcasting in terms of communication to the public.[10] This could lead to the conclusion that both emission and reception are essential elements and that the copyright law of the emission country and the copyright laws of the countries inside the foot of the satellite should be applied cumulatively.[11] The Copyright, Designs and Patents Act 1988[12] and the EC Council Directive on Satellite

6   CDPA 1988, s 6(2).
7   CDPA 1988, s 6(5).
8   CDPA 1988, s 6(6).
9   See Dietz 'Copyright and Satellite Broadcasts' (1989) 20 IIC 135–150.
10   Article 11bis Berne Convention.
11   This theory is called the 'Bogsch theory'; see Ficsor 'Direct Broadcasting by Satellite and the "Bogsch Theory"' [1990] International Business Lawyer 258. Dr Arpad Bogsch is the former Director General of WIPO, the World Intellectual Property Organisation.
12   CDPA 1988, s 6(4).

Broadcasting[13] reject this approach and focus on the 'up-leg' and apply only the copyright law of the country of emission.[14] Communication to the public occurs in their view solely in the country where the signal is emitted (to the satellite). This approach carries with it the risk that satellite broadcasters will locate their uplink stations in countries with weak copyright laws to evade paying royalties to the largest possible extent. The Directive provides, therefore, for an exception in case the emission takes place in a non-member state that does not provide a sufficient level of copyright protection.[15] That exception has now been implemented by the UK as section 6A of the 1988 Act and its scope has been extended to include the states adhering to the European Economic Area as well as the EU member states. If the signal is emitted to the satellite from the territory of a member state of the EEA the copyright laws of that member state will apply[16] and the person operating the uplink station will be treated as the person making the broadcast.[17] In all member states the level of copyright protection will be at a harmonised level. If the signal is emitted from the territory of a non-member state and that country does not provide a minimum level of protection the exceptional rule comes into operation. The minimum level of protection is defined as equivalent rights for authors of literary, dramatic, musical and artistic works, films and broadcasts to those given to them by section 20 of the CDPA in relation to the broadcasting of their works, plus the requirement that the consent of the performer be obtained before a performance is broadcast live and a right for authors of sound recordings and performers to share in a single equitable remuneration in respect of the broadcasting of sound recordings.[18] The exceptional rule states that, where the emission has been commissioned by a person or a broadcasting organisation established in a member state, then the laws of the member state where the person or the broadcasting organisation has its principal establishment will apply.[19]

The copyright protection for satellite broadcasts is not dependent on the type of satellite used as long as the signals can be lawfully received by members of the public. As a result only point-to-point communication is

---

13   EC Council Directive 93/83/EEC of 27 September 1993 on the co-ordination of certain rules concerning copyright and rights related to copyright applicable to satellite broadcasting and cable retransmission (1993) OJ L248/15 at Article 1(2)(b); see also Kern 'The EC "Common Position" on Copyright Applicable to Satellite Broadcasting and Cable Retransmission' [1993] 8 EIPR 276.

14   On the emission theory see Karnell 'A Refutation of the Bogsch Theory on Direct Satellite Broadcasting Rights' [1990] International Business Lawyer 263; this theory provides in practice a more workable solution.

15   CDPA 1988, s 5A(2).

16   See Article 1(2)(d) of the Directive.

17   See CDPA 1988, s 6A(2).

18   CDPA 1988, s 6A(2).

19   CDPA 1988, s 6A(1).

excluded if it is exclusively meant for reception and retransmission by a local broadcaster.[20]

Cable programmes

A waterproof distinction is made between broadcasts which involve necessarily wireless transmission and cable programme services which involve transmission by cable or another telecommunication system.[1] A cable programme service is a service which consists wholly or mainly in sending visual images, sounds or other information for reception at two or more places[2] or for presentation to members of the public. It must be emphasised that not the cable programme service, but only the cable programmes included in the service attract copyright.[3]

The definition of a cable programme service is followed by a long list of services which are excluded from its scope.[4] Internal business services, including security systems, interactive services where transmission and reception take place at both ends of the system and individual domestic services are the most prominent services on the list. Items included in these services do not attract copyright, nor do cable programmes which infringe another copyright in another cable programme or broadcast.[5] And equally no copyright subsists in cable programmes which are included in a cable programme service by reception and immediate retransmission of a broadcast.[6]

Typographical arrangements

This category of works is concerned with the typographical arrangements of published editions. The type and size of the letters used, the number of words on a page and the place of illustrations in relation to the text are all examples of typographical arrangements. Typographical arrangements have been described as 'graphical images pertaining or relating to printing by which literary, dramatic or musical works may be conveyed to the reader'.[7]

---

20   See Article 1(1) of the Directive.
1   Such as a telephone network or a computer network (eg the internet) whose wires could be used to carry broadcasts.
2   Not necessarily at the same time though; see CDPA 1988, s 7(1).
3   CDPA 1988, ss 1(1)(b) and 7(1).
4   CDPA 1988, s 7(2).
5   CDPA 1988, s 7(6)(b).
6   CDPA 1988, s 7(6)(a).
7   H Laddie, P Prescott and M Vitoria *The Modern Law of Copyright and Designs* Butterworths (2nd edn, 1995) at 486.

The typographical arrangement copyright arises in relation to published editions of the whole or any part of one or more literary, dramatic or musical works.[8] It does not arise in relation to artistic works and does not subsist in the typographical arrangement of a published edition if (or to the extent that) it simply reproduces the typographical arrangement of a previous edition.[9]

8   CDPA 1988, s 8(1).
9   CDPA 1988, s 8(2).

Chapter 10

Qualification

Works that come in one of the categories described above have to pass one more hurdle to secure copyright protection, namely the qualification requirement. This requirement is linked to the principle of national treatment contained in the Berne Convention, in the Universal Copyright Convention and now also in the TRIPs Agreement.[1] Authors connected with another member state are to be treated in the same way as a member states' own authors and should receive the same copyright. The connection with a member state can be provided in two ways. The author can have a personal relationship with the member state or the work can be first published in that member state.[2] The latter option is not available as long as a work remains unpublished.

This principle is implemented in the UK through a two–stage process. First the criteria used to establish a connection with Britain,[3] be it through the author or through publication, are laid down. In a second stage the system is applied to works connected with other member states of both Conventions. The application to another member state is effected by an Order in Council.[4]

Things become further complicated because countries adhere to one or both Conventions at different dates. This creates problems for works published before the date on which the country adheres to the Conventions. Unfortunately the provisions dealing with this issue are not identical in both

---

1   Article 3 Berne Convention, Article 2 Universal Copyright Convention and Article 3 TRIPs Agreement.
2   See also for the implementation of this Convention rule CDPA 1988, s 153.
3   And with dependent territories to which the CDPA 1988 is extended: the Isle of Man, the Channel Islands etc; see CDPA 1988, s 157 and the relevant Orders in Council taken on the basis of that section.
4   CDPA 1988, s 159.

Conventions. The Berne Convention works in part retroactively. If a work is still in copyright under its own national copyright legislation when a country adheres to the Convention, the work will attract copyright protection in the UK for the remaining part of the term of copyright. The Universal Copyright Convention does not work retroactively and a work published before a country, which is not a member of the Berne Convention, adheres to the Convention will not be granted copyright in the UK.

QUALIFICATION BY THE PERSONAL STATUS OF THE AUTHOR

The issue here is whether the author of the work, being the creator of the work,[5] is a qualifying person. This will be the case if the author is a British national,[6] is domiciled or resident in the UK or is a body incorporated under the laws of the UK. Application to a foreign work depends on the question whether the author is a citizen, subject, domiciliary or resident of a Convention country listed in an Order in Council or a company incorporated in such country.[7]

As all these connecting factors can change over time, the connection has to exist at the material time. That is the date on which the work is made for unpublished literary, dramatic, musical and artistic works. If the work is published, reference is made to the date of first publication and the author's status at that date or on the date on which the author died if that occurs before the work is published.[8] There is only one rule for works which do not come within the scope of the 'original' category. The date on which a sound recording or film is made is the material time for these works. The date of transmission is the material time for broadcasts and cable programmes. For typographical arrangements this is the time of first publication.[9] Once qualification has been achieved subsequent events cannot take it away.[10]

QUALIFICATION THROUGH FIRST PUBLICATION

The country of first publication is also a separate connecting factor. A work that is first published in the UK will qualify for copyright protection and

5   To be defined more precisely infra in the section on authorship and ownership of copyright.
6   British Dependent Territories Citizens, British Nationals (Overseas), British Overseas Citizens, British Subjects and British Protected Persons within the meaning of the British Nationality Act 1981 are added to this category, CDPA 1988, see s 154(1)(a).
7   CDPA 1988, s 154.
8   CDPA 1988, s 154(4).
9   CDPA 1988, s 154(5).
10   CDPA 1988, s 153(3).

so will a work first published in another Convention country.[11] The country of transmission is the connecting factor for broadcasts and cable programmes.[12]

Really simultaneous publication does not create a problem if one of the countries in which the work is published is the UK or another contracting state, but a problem may be created if the country in which publication takes place a couple of days before publication in other countries is not a contracting state to one of the copyright conventions. This would normally jeopardise the option of qualification for copyright protection through first publication in a contracting state, but a period of grace of 30 days has been built in. Publication in that period in the UK or another contracting state will be treated as really simultaneous publication and will secure qualification for copyright protection.[13]

But what amounts to publication? The definition of the term publication is first of all relevant for the qualification issue, but in many cases it is also of importance for the term of copyright protection as we will discuss in the next chapter. For copyright purposes publication means issuing copies of the work to the public in sufficient quantities with the intention to satisfy public demand.[14] Copies are issued to the public if they are put into circulation by sale, gift or hire[15] and this takes place where the publisher invites the public to acquire the copies.[16] The intention of the publisher is an important element, since he or she must be prepared to meet public demand.[17] For literary, dramatic, musical and artistic works copies can also be issued to the public through the inclusion of the work in an electronic retrieval system, which makes it available to the public.[18] The number of copies issued is of secondary importance,[19] as shown by the Court of Appeal's decision to accept that the release for sale of six copies of a song which was not (yet) known amounted to publication.[20]

Copies are not issued to the public by the performance of a literary, dramatic or musical work. The same goes for broadcasting or including them in a cable programme, exhibiting an artistic work and issuing graphic works

11   CDPA 1988, s 155(1) and (2).
12   CDPA 1988, s 156.
13   CDPA 1988, s 155(3).
14   CDPA 1988, s 175(1)(a).
15   See *British Northrop v Texteam Blackburn Ltd* [1974] RPC 57 at 67, per Megarry J.
16   Ibid. It would not be workable to take into account the place where the public receives the copies as this would make the country of first publication dependent on where shipments of the work were received first.
17   Compare *Copex v Flegon* (1967) Times, 18 August.
18   CDPA 1988, s 175(1)(b).
19   Mere colourable publication, which is not intended to satisfy public demand is not taken into account: CDPA 1988, s 175(5).
20   *Francis Day v Feldman* [1914] 2 Ch 728, see also *Bodley Head Ltd v Flegon* [1972] 1 WLR 680, [1972] RPC 587.

or photographs of sculptures, works of architecture or works of artistic craftsmanship.[1]

Unauthorised acts are not taken into account when it is established whether a work has been published or not.[2] A related, but fairly specific and exceptional, problem is raised by an adaptation, by the author or with his or her consent, of an unpublished work. Does the translation into English of an unpublished African Swahili literary tale, or does the conversion of an unpublished novel into a play, have the effect of publishing the original if copies of the adaptation are issued to the public? The Act provides no clear guidance, but it seems reasonable to assume that if the adaptation is 'original' enough to attract its own copyright, it is distinct enough from the original to conclude that it does not constitute publication of the original work, which is clearly distinct from the adaptation. If on the other hand the adaptation merely reproduces the older unpublished work, publication of the adaptation will probably have the effect of publication of the older work. An example of the latter case would be a three-dimensional embodiment of a two-dimensional drawing.[3] As we will see later in the infringement chapter this latter example is very similar to cases of copyright infringement.

The Berne Convention has a built-in preference for qualification through the country of first publication to qualification through the personal status of the owner.[4] The latter option will only be taken into account once it has been established that first publication did not take place in a contracting state. This preference is not found in the CDPA 1988. The Act treats both ways of qualification on an equal footing.

---

1   CDPA 1988, s 175(4).
2   CDPA 1988, s 175(6).
3   *Merchant Adventurers v Grew* [1973] RPC 1 at 10.
4   Article 5(4) Berne Convention. Under the Convention this is the normal way to determine the country of origin of a work. First publication is, relatively speaking, easier to determine for any third party and is relatively easily proved in comparison with any aspect of the personal status of the author.

Chapter 11

The term of copyright

GENERAL PRINCIPLES

We have now established which works attract copyright, but what is the duration of copyright? We will mainly have to distinguish between the 'original' works and films on the one hand[1] and all other works on the other hand. The term of copyright in 'original' works used to be 50 years in the UK.[2] In other member states of the European Union longer terms of protection were in force, such as 70 years in Germany and 60 to 80 years in Spain. This was possible because the Berne Convention only imposes a minimum term of protection upon its members,[3] but it could impede the free movement of goods within the Union and was therefore held to be undesirable. A Directive was adopted with the aim of harmonising the term of copyright protection in the European Union.[4] This Directive brought radical change to the relevant sections of the 1988 Act when it was eventually implemented by the Duration of Copyright and Rights in Performances Regulations 1995.[5] In the UK the changes took effect on 1 January 1996.

A preliminary point that affects the transition from a 50-year term to a 70-year term is the issue of the comparison of term. This technique is introduced, or should one say tolerated, by Article 7(8) of the Berne

1   The Directive refers in its Article 1 to works in the meaning of Article 2 of the Berne Convention.
2   CDPA 1988, s 12, as it stood before the amended version that was contained in the Duration of Copyright and Rights in Performances Regulations 1995 (SI 1995/3297) regs 4, 5(1) took effect on 1 January 1996.
3   Article 7(6) Berne Convention for the Protection of Literary and Artistic Works. The minimum term is 50 years.
4   EC Council Directive 93/98/EEC of 29 October 1993 on the harmonising of the term of copyright and certain related rights (1993) OJ L290.
5   SI 1995/3297.

Convention. It means that works whose country of origin has a shorter term of copyright protection will not attract copyright protection in a country with a longer term of protection once their term of protection in the country of origin has expired. In practical terms this means that say an Australian work with an Australian term of protection would not attract 20 extra years of copyright protection in Germany. The Germans are allowed to discriminate and apply the 70-year term only to works whose country of origin is Germany or any other country that allows for a minimum term of protection of 70 years for German works. Article 7 of the Directive makes the application of the comparison of term rule mandatory for all member states. Works originating in third countries that do not offer at least a 70-year copyright term will not benefit from the longer protection in the Union. The obvious aim is to convince third countries to adopt a 70-year term of copyright.

The UK has implemented Article 7 by inserting a provision that stipulates that a work that has a State that is not part of the European Economic Area as its country of origin and the author of which is not a national of a European Economic Area State will only be protected in the UK for the term for which it is granted protection in its country of origin. On top of that the provision stipulate that under no circumstances a term that is longer than the new UK term of protection will be granted. This means, for example, that the UK will only grant a 50-year term of protection to a novel published in New York by a US national. Should the US put in place a copyright system that grants protection for an 80-year term, the UK will still only protect the work for its own 70-year term. The new UK provision applies to all types of copyright works.[6] The country of origin is defined as follows for the purposes of the 1988 Act. If the work is first published in a Contracting State to the Berne Convention, that country of first publication will be the country of origin of the work.[7] For unpublished works and works that are first published in a country which is not a Berne Convention country the country of which the author of the work is a national will normally be the country of origin of the work.[8] Special rules that depart from this latter rule exist for films, works of architecture and artistic works that are incorporated in a building. The country in which the maker of the film has either his headquarters, his domicile or his residence will be the country of origin of the film if that country is a Contracting State to the

---

6   CDPA 1988, ss 12(6), 13A(4), 13B(7) and 14(3); the comparison of term rule is dropped in relation to sound recordings, broadcasts and cable programmes in those cases where its application would be at variance with the UK's international obligations as they stood on 29th October 1993 (CDPA 1988, ss 13A(5) and 14(4)).

7   CDPA 1988, s 15(2); special provisions for cases of simultaneous publication are found in s 15A(3) and (4).

8   CDPA 1988, s 15A(5)(c).

Berne Convention.[9] The Berne Convention country in which the work of architecture is constructed or in which the building or structure in which the artistic work is incorporated is situated will be the country of origin of the work of architecture or the artistic work respectively.[10]

The provision in Article 7(8) of the Berne Convention has strange implications in relation to the Term Directive, due to the transition from a 50-year term to a 70-year term in the majority of member states. Indeed, Article 6 of the Treaty rules out any discrimination on the basis of nationality and this rule applies also to copyright issues.[11] Thus Germany was not entitled to use its comparison of term rule in relation to works of nationals of another member state. These works should have enjoyed a 70-year term of protection in Germany all along. When the Directive came into force the area in which these works enjoy protection became the whole territory of the Union. This had as a strange consequence that all works which were still protected in Germany did benefit from the 70-year term in the whole Union, even if some of these works were out of copyright and in the public domain in a number of member states, eventually including the member state of origin, which used to have a 50-year term. An English literary work, written by an English author who died in 1943 and first published in the UK, did no longer attract copyright protection in the UK under the old provisions of the 1988 Act when the Directive came into force, its term of protection having expired at the end of 1993. It did still attract copyright in Germany though until the end of 2013. The work came back into copyright through the implementation of the Directive and its term of copyright protection will expire at the end of the year 2013 in the whole Union, including the UK. All this is the inevitable result of the combined application of Article 6 of the Treaty, as applied in the *Phil Collins*[12] case, and Article 7 of the Term Directive.[13]

In practical terms, all those works to which a new longer term would now apply if they were created after the date on which the Directive was implemented did see their term of protection increased to the new longer period. For example, the first edition of this book was written in 1995. The old 50-year term applied to it at first, but from 1 January 1996 onwards its term of protection in the UK was increased under the new 70 years rule. If the copyright had already lapsed under the old rules, but the new longer period had not yet expired, the copyright would have been revived for the remaining period of the new longer term. For example, the works of an author such as DH Lawrence, who died in 1930, went out of copyright at the end of 1980, but the copyright in them was revived under the new rules

9   CDPA 1988, s 15A(5)(a).
10   CDPA 1988, s 15A(5)(b).
11   Cases C-93 and 326/92 *Phil Collins v IMTRAT Handelsgesellschaft GmbH* [1993] ECR I-5145, [1993] 3 CMLR 773.
12   Ibid.
13   Dworkin and Sterling 'Phil Collins and the Term Directive' [1994] 5 EIPR 187.

for the period between 1 January 1996 and the end of the year 2000. While this may have been good news for rightholders and those who held copyrights before they lapsed under the old rules, it did create an odd situation for those who had exploited the works, for example by publishing a complete collection of the works of DH Lawrence in 1990, in the understanding that they were out of copyright. This situation has been addressed by the implementing statutory instrument[14] and transition measures have been put in place.[15] Anything done before the UK's implementation date of 1 January 1996 cannot amount to infringement and copies that were made before the Directive's implementation date of 1st July 1995 can be issued to the public without giving rise to copyright infringement even if that effectively takes place once the new system is in force. This means that no royalties will be payable for the collection of the works of DH Lawrence that was published in 1990 in our example and that its publishers can continue to sell existing copies of the collection. On top of that any allegedly infringing acts for which arrangements were made before 1 January 1995 and which are subsequently implemented in relation to works that were out of copyright at that time, will not amount to copyright infringement.

ORIGINAL WORKS

The term of copyright protection is calculated from the end of the year in which the author dies and runs for 70 years.[16] As a result, copyright in original literary, dramatic, musical and artistic works expires 70 years after the end of the year in which the author of the work died. The term of protection for computer-generated works, which have no human author who can die, continues to run for 50 years and the death of the author is replaced by the date on which the work was made.[17] Computer-generated works are virtually unknown outside the UK. Their introduction in the CDPA 1988 was not followed by similar moves in other European countries. The Term Directive does not affect these works and the UK opted to keep their term of protection at 50 years. All terms are indeed for reason of simplicity calculated from 1 January of the year following the event which gives rise to them.[18] In the case of joint authorship the 70-year term of protection for

---

14   See Regulation 23.
15   Bizarre situations remain though, especially since the 1988 Act also contained transitional measures in relation to works created under previous UK Copyright Acts. The combination of the various transition measures can give rise to odd results. See Adams and Edenborough 'The Duration of Copyright in the UK after the 1995 Regulations' [1996] 11 EIPR 590.
16   CDPA 1988, s 12(2).
17   CDPA 1988, s 12(7).
18   Article 8 of the Directive confirms this existing principle in UK copyright law.

the work is calculated from the end of the year in which the last surviving author dies.[19]

Anonymous or pseudonymous works create a problem for the application of these rules. For these works the term of protection runs for 70 years with the lawful publication[20] of the work as the event that gives rise to it. The lawful publication needs to occur within a period of 70 years from the end of the calendar year in which the work was made. If no lawful publication takes place within that period the copyright expires at the end of the 70 years after the work was made period.[1] These rules apply unless the author discloses his identity during the 70-year period or his identity becomes known during that period. In this situation the normal rule for non-anonymous and non-pseudonymous works will apply.[2]

FILMS

Cinematographic and audiovisual works present a different case. The Directive does not simply lay down a term of protection, but also stipulates that the principal director of such a work shall be considered as its author or as one of its authors. Member states are in addition given the freedom to designate other co-authors for these works. The latter provision can be seen as a compromise between the continental tendency to give directors rights in a film and the UK's tradition to give the same rights to producers. It also becomes clear from these provisions that films, to use the UK term, are increasingly associated with or considered as original works, rather than entrepreneurial recording rights. Historically films were very much part of the latter category, which was illustrated by the fact that the original version of the CDPA 1988 dealt with the duration of sound recordings and films in a single section. Originality is still not required for film. Nevertheless, the fact that the 'artistic' creators of a film are now seen as its authors, with the emphasis shifting somewhat away from the 'entre-preneurial' producers, explains why films are now given a duration regime that resembles above all the regime for original works.

From 1 January 1996 onwards the following regime applies. The term of copyright protection for a film will expire 70 years after the end of the year in which the last of the following persons dies: the principal director, the author of the screenplay, the author of the dialogue and the composer of the music specifically created for use in the film.[3] If the identity of one

---

19 CDPA 1988, s 12(8).
20 As defined in s 12(5), CDPA 1988.
1   CDPA 1988, s 12(3).
2   CDPA 1988, s 12(4).
3   CDPA 1988, s 13B(2).

or more of the persons concerned is not known, these persons can be deleted from the list and the death of the last known person will trigger the start of the 70-year term.[4] If the identity of all or the persons concerned is unknown, the film will be protected for 70 years from the end of the calendar year in which it was made. This period is extended to 70 years from the end of the calendar year in which the film was made available to the public if the film is made available before the 70-year period after making expires.[5] A film is made available to the public when it is first shown in public, broadcast or included in a cable programme service, unless it is the consequence of an unauthorised act.[6] If the identity of at least one of the persons concerned becomes known before the 70-year period for anonymous films expires, the normal rules that rely on the death of the author or of the last of the co-authors as the triggering event replace the rules for anonymous films in determining the term of protection for the film.[7] An author's identity shall not be assumed to be unknown simply because the person who wants to find out whether a film is still in copyright does not know it. The criterion is rather that it is not possible to ascertain the identity by reasonable inquiry.[8]

Regrettably the UK took a minimalist approach when implementing the Directive. This means that the list of people that are referred to in relation to the term of copyright in a film does not correspond with that used in relation to the authorship of a film. On the latter point the UK was obliged to let the director in aside the producer who was traditionally there under UK law, but it declined to use the option to add other people too. There seemed to be an unwritten rule that the rules on the term of copyright referred to the authors of the work. This rule has now been set aside in relation to films and the CDPA no longer displays a clear and systematic approach to this matter. Such a political compromise or a bending of the rules in favour of one group of lobbyists does not enhance the transparency and the inherent logic of the copyright system in the UK and is therefore to be regretted. Also a chance to achieve harmonised rules for films that are after all exploited across Europe and not just in the UK has yet again been missed. It is submitted that the better solution would have been the creation of a new heading in the 1988 Act which would cover cinematographic and audiovisual works. These would then be expressly excluded from the scope of the dramatic works provision.[9] This approach would lead to two separate rights, one for, eventually among others, the director in the cinematographical or audiovisual work, and a second right

4   CDPA 1988, s 13B(3).
5   CDPA 1988, s 13B(4).
6   CDPA 1988, s 13B(6).
7   CDPA 1988, s 13B(5).
8   CDPA 1988, s 13B(10).
9   Compare Kamina 'Authorship of Films and Implementation of the Term Directive: The Dramatic Tale of Two Copyrights' [1994] 8 EIPR 319.

for the producer in the film as the recording of the cinematographical or audiovisual work.[10] This is also the approach taken in the new Belgian Copyright Act, which was adopted after the Directive had been adopted.[11] Such an approach would underscore the fact that films are more and more seen as original works. A separate recording right or right in the first fixation would then exist on top of the original right. But maybe such a coherent and systematic approach has too much of a continental flavour to it for the pragmatic UK copyright lawyer!

OTHER ENTREPRENEURIAL WORKS

Sound recordings are the first other type of work. Sound recordings are protected for 50 years from the end of the calendar year in which the sound recording was made. This period is extended to 50 years from release if the recording is released before the 50-year period after making expires.[12] A sound recording is released when it is first published, played in public, broadcast or included in a cable programme service, unless such a release is the consequence of an unauthorised act.[13]

The term of protection for broadcasts and cable programmes is 50 years from first transmission.[14] A broadcast that is a repeat of a broadcast previously made or a cable programme that is a repeat of a cable programme previously included in a cable programme service are not able to prolong the term of copyright in the broadcast or the cable programme or to attract a new copyright after the original term had expired. The copyright in the repeat broadcast or cable programme will expire at the same time as the copyright in the original broadcast or cable programme.[15] For typographical arrangements the term of copyright protection is only 25 years from first publication.[16]

All these terms start to run from the end of the year in which the triggering event takes place.

---

10 The provisions on employer ownership of the copyright in the work and assignment of copyright could still grant the producer most of the rights. Contractual provisions will continue to play an important role in this area.
11 Wet betreffende het auteursrecht en de naburige rechten - Loi relative au droit d'auteur et aux droits voisins of 30 June 1994 [1994] Belgisch Staatsblad - Moniteur Belge 27 July p 19297 et seq; see Articles 2, 14 and 39.
12 CDPA 1988, s 13A(2).
13 CDPA 1988, s 13A(3).
14 CDPA 1988, s 14(2).
15 CDPA 1988, s 14(5) and (6).
16 CDPA 1988, s 15.

Chapter 12

Authorship and ownership of copyright

AUTHORSHIP

The person who creates the work is the author of the work.[1] This hardly creates problems for the original literary, dramatic, musical and artistic works. Thus the writer of a literary work such as a novel will be its author, the composer will be the author of a musical work, the sculptor will be the author of a sculpture and the photographer will be the author of a photograph. For derivative works the application of this principle is not as easy. For instance who creates a sound recording? The Act provides further guidance on this point in section 9(2). The original rule in 1988 was that the person who creates a sound recording and becomes its author is the person who makes the necessary arrangements for the making of the recording. The same solution was adopted for films. In practice this meant that the producer becomes the author of a film as he makes the arrangements for making the film. Most European countries adopted a different approach. From their point of view the director of a film was the creator of the work, even if he or she was not always the sole creator of the work. In an attempt to harmonise these provisions the Community introduced the obligation to consider the principal director of a film as its author and left it to the member states to designate other co-authors if they wished to do so.[2] In the UK the 1988 Act was amended in the light of the Directive by the Copyright and Related Rights Regulations 1996.[3] The original rule in relation to sound recordings and films disappeared entirely. For films it was replaced by a

---

1   CDPA 1988, s 9(1).
2   Article 2(1) of EC Council Directive 93/98/EEC of 29 October 1993 harmonising the term of protection of copyright and certain related rights (1993) OJ L 290/9.
3   SI 1996/2967, regs 4, 18(1).

rule that designates the director and the producer as the co-authors of a film.[4] And the Act now expressly states that the producer is the author of a sound recording.[5]

Who creates a computer-generated literary, dramatic, musical or artistic work? The obvious answer would be the computer, but then the computer becomes the author of the work and it seems rather weird to have a machine as a player in a system that grants property rights. The Act solves this problem by adopting an approach that is identical to the one originally taken in relation to sound recordings and films. The person who makes the necessary arrangements for the creation of the work becomes the author of the work.[6]

The person making the broadcast is its creator, unless this broadcast relays another broadcast by reception and immediate retransmission. In the latter case the person making that other broadcast will be the creator and author.[7] This avoids the unhealthy situation of two equal authors for one work, which one of them created and transmitted and which the other one only retransmits. The application of this principle to cable programmes makes the person providing the cable programme service in which the work is included its creator and author.[8] And the publisher of the typographical arrangement of a published edition is its author.[9]

It is recognised that the identity of the author is not always known; obvious examples of such a situation are presented by anonymous works. A work is of unknown authorship[10] if a person cannot identify the identity of the author by reasonable inquiry.[11] It is not clear which person undertakes this reasonable inquiry. A logical solution would be to make this a subjective test, to be performed by the person who wishes to deal with the work and therefore needs to trace the origin of the work, starting with its author, if he or she wants to obtain the permission to deal with the work.[12]

An increasing number of works are produced by the collaboration of more than one author. The rules outlined above apply to each of the authors as long as it is possible to distinguish and identify their individual contribution to the work. They will be treated as the creator and author of their own individual contribution to the work. This approach does not work when a group of jazz musicians record their own impromptu jazz session.

4   CDPA 1988, s 9(2)(ab).
5   CDPA 1988, s 9(2)(aa).
6   CDPA 1988, s 9(3).
7   CDPA 1988, s 9(2)(b).
8   CDPA 1988, s 9(2)(c).
9   CDPA 1988, s 9(2)(d).
10   If the identity of the author is or becomes known at one stage the work can no longer fall in this category: CDPA 1988, s 9(5) .
11   CDPA 1988, s 9(4) and (5).
12   See R Merkin *Copyright, Designs and Patents: The New Law* Longman (1989) at 50, the alternative option to rely on the concept of the ubiquitous reasonable man is less attractive.

It is impossible to distinguish afterwards between the contribution of one musician and that of another musician. The Act calls this a work of joint authorship.[13] In the latter case all authors are referred to as the author of the work for the purposes of the Act.[14] Rather than become the author of a part of the work each of them becomes (joint) author of the whole work. This has important consequences for the ownership of the copyright in the work. We will discuss this in the next section of this chapter. Section 10(1A) clarifies the relationship between the director and the producer as co-authors of a film. They are to be treated as joint authors and the film is to be treated as a work of joint authorship, unless the producer and the principal director are the same person. Section 10(2) of the Act deals with joint authorship in broadcasts. The person making the broadcast is the person transmitting the programme, if he has responsibility to any extent for its content and any person providing the programme who makes, with the person transmitting it; the arrangements necessary for its transmission.[15] In many cases this results in more than one person making the broadcast and has joint authorship for these persons.

The rule that the creator of the work is the author of it has to be combined with the necessity to record or fixate original literary, musical and dramatic works. Ideas are not protected,[16] while their expression is protected when it is recorded or fixated. This creates problems in a situation such as the one that arose in *Walter v Lane*.[17] Reporters from *The Times* recorded speeches by Lord Rosebery in writing. As we have seen above, the speeches attract copyright as a literary work once they are recorded and it is not necessary that the speaker records them himself. Who is the author of the literary work? In this case it was held that the reporters were the creators of the work and as such the authors. This case was decided before the introduction of the originality requirement.[18] It is submitted that a verbatim report[19] of the complete speech would not pass this originality requirement. The report would not be an original literary work and would not attract copyright, but as they are now recorded the speeches themselves would

13 CDPA 1988, s 10(1).
14 CDPA 1988, s 10(3).
15 CDPA 1988, s 6(3).
16 As shown by the case where a journalist supplied the idea for an article written by his editor. His idea did not attract copyright (he was not the creator of the literary work) and his editor's expression of the idea attracted copyright. The editor was the creator of the expression of the idea and thus as creator of a literary work its author: *Springfield v Thame* (1903) 19 TLR 650.
17 [1900] AC 539.
18 The originality requirement was introduced by the Copyright Act 1911.
19 The case refers to the corrections and revisions made by the reporters. This should be seen as correcting the spelling and other small mistakes while taking down in a hurry the words of the speaker and checking that the report is indeed a full and correct account or written version of the speech.

attract copyright and the speaker would be the author. This situation corresponds to that of a secretary writing down dictation. For the purposes of copyright the person dictating will be the author of the work. The secretary who does the writing can at best be said to be acting as an agent. However if the reporters had edited the work by selecting parts of the speech and had added their own comments, for instance on the venue where the speech was delivered, the situation would have been different. The report would have been an original literary work and would have attracted its own copyright. Skill, labour and judgment would have been applied by the reporters in drafting the report.

A final issue in relation to authorship of copyright is the question of whether a corporate body can be the author of a work. This is particularly relevant in the film and music industry where many arrangements for the making of a sound recording or movie[20] are made by large production companies. It is submitted that this question receives a positive answer under copyright law. Works of a body incorporated under the laws of the UK qualify for copyright protection according to section 154(1)(c) of the Act. There would be no reason to deal with this qualification issue if corporate bodies could not create works which attract copyright. Under the rule agreed at Community level,[1] the term of copyright for films is the life of the author plus 70 years. This results in a never ending copyright in films whose co-author is a production company which never dies. This situation is unacceptable. It could be solved by the introduction of a system where corporate bodies could never be the authors of a work, but their individual employees or directors can. This does not rule out the possibility of an automatic transfer of the ownership and the rights of commercial exploitation of the work to the corporate body.[2] This change is less radical than it may seem. It could already be argued that through downwards delegation within these production companies the real arrangements for making the film are not taken by the company, but by individual producers within the company. An even better example is that of a CNN news crew in a war zone. The practical arrangements for the making of their coverage of the situation there are clearly not made by CNN's Atlanta headquarters, due to the unpredictable nature of a war situation. Even if the company produces the film, the reality is that one or more members of its staff will de facto do the producer's job for a particular film. Their names appear in the credits and they should be taken to be the (co-)authors of the film. The

---

20 Even in the new regime for films the question whether or not they will be co-authors remains.

1 Article 2(1) of EC Directive 93/98/EEC of 29 November 1993 harmonising the term of protection of copyright and certain related rights (1993) OJ L290/9.

2 The employee would not be able to transfer all moral rights in the work to the corporate body and the exercise of these rights could potentially interfere with the commercial exploitation of the work; see infra Chapter 13 for details on moral rights.

■

term of copyright in the film would then be linked to the life and death of these real people, rather than to the 'death of the production-company'.

OWNERSHIP

The general principle is that the author is the first owner of the copyright.[3] A sculptor will be the first owner of his sculpture and I will be the first owner of the copyright in the poems I write for my own enjoyment. Contracts of employment undermine this general principle. The first owner of the copyright in a literary, dramatic, musical or artistic work or in a film[4] created by an employee in the course of his or her employment will be the employer. Agreements to the contrary are possible though.[5] This provision creates some difficulties. Who is an employee? What are the characteristics of the employer/employee relationship? And what is the meaning of this in the course of his employment?

Let us start with some obvious examples. A cleaning lady who writes poetry in her own time will be the first owner of the copyright in her poems. The poems are clearly not written in the course of her employment and she is not in employment as a poet. If on the other hand a purchasing manager of an engineering company writes, during normal working hours, a report on the options open for his company to find an alternative supplier of cylinder valves for the board of directors of the company, this work will obviously have been made in the course of his employment and the employer will be the first owner of the work. The contract of employment and the job description contained in it are important elements in this respect. They can facilitate the application of the test whether the skill, labour and judgment invested by the employee in the creation of the work are part of the employee's normal duties (which can also be implied in the contract) or come within the special duties the employer has assigned to the employee because they reveal the intentions of the parties. If the answer is affirmative the work will have been created in the course of employment and the employer will be the first owner of the copyright in it. This approach is supported by *Stephenson Jordan & Harrison Ltd v MacDonald*.[6] An accountant was employed to advise clients. He started giving lectures and eventually he published them. He owned the copyright in the book because giving lectures was not part of his normal duties and he had not been

---

3   CDPA 1988, s 11(1).
4   This addition to s 11(2), CDPA 1988 was made by the Copyright and Related Rights Regulations 1996 (SI 1996/2967), regs 4, 18(3). Once more copyright in a film was treated as copyright in an original work, rather than in an entrepreneurial work, although the roots of copyright in a film are found in the latter category.
5   CDPA 1988, s 11(2).
6   (1952) 69 RPC 10.

instructed by his employers to give the lectures or produce the book. Two elements complicate this case though. First, his employer had provided secretarial help, which he had used for his project. The court held that the use of the employer's facilities or assistance is not relevant to this copyright test.[7] Second, the accountant had used a report he wrote for a client of his employer in the book. The copyright in this part of the book was owned by his employer.

It is in the interest of both employer and employee that there is no doubt about the ownership of copyright. A clear and detailed job description is required and if the content of a job changes a new description of the employee's duties should be drafted. This does not rule out that a job description can be wide in scope. When someone is employed as a research and development engineer, this description makes it clear that the copyright in every work which is useful to his or her employer will be owned by the employer. But this system depends on the classification of the author of the work as employee. This depends on the existence of a contract of service or apprenticeship between the author and the alleged employer who claims the ownership of the copyright in the work.[8] The establishment of such a relationship is not obvious if the author is a freelance worker or a consultant. It is submitted that these consultants and freelancers have a contract to do a certain job, a certain amount of work, but they are not directly subject to the instructions of the employer. For example a management consultant will be asked to produce a report on the management of a company, but he will decide himself how he will produce the report. His only obligation is to submit a report that meets the standards laid down in the contract by the date agreed in the contract. Employees on the contrary are subject to the instructions of their employer. For them there is a mutuality of agreement in the sense that they are subject to an obligation to accept and perform some minimum, or at least reasonable, amount of work for their alleged employer.[9] The freelance worker and the consultant will own the copyright in their work because they do not come within the definition of an employee.

The employer may allow the employee to become the first owner of the copyright in the work created in the course of employment. This option is left open by section 11(2) of the Act. For normal transfers of ownership of copyright the Act requires the transfer to be in writing and signed by or on behalf of the copyright owner,[10] but this requirement does not apply here. In this situation there is no transfer of copyright ownership, no one owning the copyright before the first owner of the copyright in the work. This case

---

7   It may well have its relevance for other aspects of the employer/employee relationship though (eg breach of the contract of employment).

8   CDPA 1988, s 178.

9   See *Nethermere (St Neots) Ltd v Taverna* [1984] IRLR 240, per Kerr LJ.

10   CDPA 1988, s 90(3).

should be contrasted with the case of a work produced by a consultant or a freelancer. As they are not employees, section 11(1) will apply and the freelancer or consultant will be the first owner of the copyright. Any subsequent transfer of the copyright will have to be in writing and will have to be signed by the owner or on his behalf.[11] A clause in the contract concluded with the freelancer or consultant stipulating that the ownership of the work produced will be transferred is more than advisable. Otherwise one has to rely on the concept of the implied licence. Someone ordering a report from a consultant will have necessarily included in the contract a right to use the result of the consultant's activity. Someone who requests a plan for a house to be built on a certain plot of land from an architect implies in the contract with the architect a clause giving him the right to build the house on that plot since the contract is necessarily for a plan which is to be used to build a house. The architect keeps the ownership of the copyright in the plans, but grants an (implied) licence to use them to build the house.[12]

It is possible that there are two or more joint owners of the copyright in a work if it is a work of joint authorship. The latter possibility was raised above and we will now discuss its implications on the issue of ownership. These owners will own the copyright in the work as tenants in common[13] and will have their own individual rights in the work which they can assign individually. They can also act individually against infringement. But as they will never own the whole copyright individually they will not be able to license someone to exploit the work without the consent of their co-owners.[14] Otherwise they would be able to transfer rights which they did not fully own. The co-owner of the copyright in a book will be able to assign his right to one of his creditors which will allow his creditor to recuperate through the royalties the debt owed to him. The creditor does not deal with the copyright. The same co-owner will not be able to allow a film director to make a movie based on the book without the consent of the co-owners.

Until now we have examined the ownership issue assuming that the author with whom the ownership chain starts is known. An anonymous work would in this system lead to an unknown owner of the copyright in it. This system would endanger the commercial exploitation of the work and would be undesirable. Therefore the Act contains a presumption that the publisher

11   The use of the concept of beneficial ownership was suggested in *Warner v Gestetner Ltd* [1988] EIPR 89. It is submitted that this approach cannot be accepted because it includes a partial assignment of the ownership of copyright which does not satisfy the requirements laid down in CDPA 1988, s 90(3).

12   See *Blair v Osborne & Tomkins* [1971] 2 QB 78, [1971] 1 All ER 468, per Lord Denning MR at 470 and 507.

13   Not as joint tenants, (see *Lauri v Renad* [1892] 3 Ch 402) as this would deny them individual rights and oblige them to act together on each occasion.

14   *Cescinsky v George Routledge & Sons Ltd* [1916] 2 KB 325. The opposite is true in patent law; see Patents Act 1977, s 36.

of an anonymous work is the owner of the copyright in it at the time of publication.[15] This presumption can be rebutted.[16]

The issue of ownership touches upon the commercial exploitation of copyright. We will come back to this issue later. However, not all aspects of copyright are directed to commercial exploitation. Copyright is to a certain extent also an author's right. This will become clear in the next section through the analysis of the new, separate but closely related, moral rights which the 1988 Act grants to authors and which protect them and their works against certain aspects of abusive commercial exploitation.

15 CDPA 1988, s 104(4).
16 For an example of an unsuccessful attempt to rebut the presumption see *Warwick Film Productions Ltd v Eisinger* [1969] 1 Ch 508, [1967] 3 All ER 367.

Chapter 13

Moral rights

GENERAL PRINCIPLES

Copyright in continental Europe is in the first place an author's right. Much attention is paid to the rights of the creator. As copyright law is based on international conventions a compromise with the UK's more entrepreneurial approach was reached in the Berne Convention. This led eventually to the formal inclusion of moral rights in the Copyright, Designs and Patents Act 1988.[1] Previous Acts did not explicitly acknowledge these moral rights although some protection was offered through, for example, the torts of defamation[2] or passing-off.[3]

We submit that the compromise should go much further. The focal points of both approaches work indeed in a complementary manner. Everything starts with the author who has to create works. If there are no works there is nothing to exploit for the entrepreneur. On the other hand if one offers an extremely strong protection to the author-creator this may make the work of the entrepreneur impossible to carry out. If the author has all the rights and the entrepreneur is left with no flexibility or bargaining power based on legal rights the exploitation of the work becomes impossible or at least economically unsound. This could seriously affect the incentive of the author to create works as it would reduce the chances of making a living as an author. It is clear that the volume of the works created would be affected seriously. What is needed in a perfect copyright system is a sound balance between the rights of the author-creator and those of the entrepreneur who exploits the work. We submit that the continental

1 See in general Stamatoudi 'Moral Rights of Authors in England: The Missing Emphasis on the Role of Creators' [1997] IPQ 478.
2 See *Humphreys v Thompson* (1905-1910) Mac CC 148.
3 See *Samuelson v Producers Distributing* [1932] 1 Ch 201.

approach has much to contribute to such a perfect system in relation to the rights of the author, while our traditional approach would be the dominant contributor in relation to the rights given to the entrepreneur. Such a perfect copyright system is not just an ideal. European integration and harmonisation of the provisions dealing with copyright means that inevitably a compromise has to be reached each time between both approaches in an attempt to make copyright in the European Union resemble the perfect model.[4]

How does this relate to the issue of moral rights though? It is submitted that the author-creator should not just become the first owner of the work, and by implication lose control over the work almost immediately afterwards. The possibility of unfair use of the work can deter the author from creating works. He or she should be protected against that possibility. On the other hand a good exploitation of the work requires as much freedom for the entrepreneur as possible. Moral rights reconcile these two aims. They give minimum long lasting rights against manifestly unfair use of the work to the author-creator, while allowing maximum flexibility for the entrepreneur as only manifestly unfair forms of exploitation will be affected. In this approach moral rights are an essential component of the bundle of rights which is given by copyright. That is the reason why we discuss them here and not at the end of the copyright chapter. All the authors of original works and directors of films[5] are given moral rights, while the owners of the entrepreneurial neighbouring rights are not granted any moral rights.[6] This clearly vindicates our approach. The real copyrights are the original ones and moral rights are an essential component of the rights granted by copyright. Neighbouring rights often rely on copyright works and are secondary rights, such as the recording of an original musical work. They are linked to the entrepreneurial exploitation of copyright and therefore moral rights are not needed in relation to them.

There is yet another argument we may wish to consider. The Berne Convention, which is the international basis of our copyright regime, deals with moral rights in article 6bis. This is right in the middle of the articles which deal with the substance of copyright; and it suggests that moral rights are an essential element of copyright, rather than an addendum to it.

Four moral rights are included in the 1988 Act:

---

4   See Verstrynghe 'The Spring 1993 Horace S Manges Lecture – The European Commission's Direction on Copyright and Neighbouring Rights: Toward the Regime of the Twenty-First Century' (1993) 17 Columbia-VLA Journal of Law & the Arts 187 at 206–209.
5   Note that films are treated once more in the same way as original works.
6   CDPA 1988, ss 77, 80 and 84.

- the right to be identified as the author or director of a work (the paternity right);[7]
- the right of the author or a director of a work to object to derogatory treatment of that work (the integrity right);[8]
- the right for everyone not to have a work falsely attributed to him;[9]
- the commissioner's right of privacy in respect of a photograph or film made for private and domestic purposes.[10]

Only the first two rights are full moral rights, while the latter two are hybrid in nature as they do not confer special rights on the creator of the work. All these rights aim to restore the balance between the interests of the commercial exploitation of the work and the interests of the creator of the work. This cannot be done through contractual negotiations in which the author or director quite often occupies a weak bargaining position. To protect the author or director as the weaker party, moral rights are inalienable to others; but they are transmissible on death.[11] As they are coupled to the commercial rights granted by copyright the term of moral rights is coupled to that of copyright in the work to which they relate.[12] The one exception to the latter rule is the right to object to false attribution which expires 20 years after a person's death.[13]

THE PATERNITY RIGHT

The creator of a work has the right to be identified as its author; this is the basic concept behind this right. As this right has to restore the balance with the commercial exploitation of the work which attracts copyright protection, it is also restricted to those works which attract copyright. The scope of the right is further restricted to literary, dramatic, musical or artistic works and films and identification should only take place in certain cases.[14] These cases are different for the various categories of works and the categories themselves are different from the ones used in relation to the existence of copyright. In particular lyrics for songs are not treated as literary works, but as musical works and films are the only category of non-'original' works to be included.

7   CDPA 1988, ss 77–79.
8   CDPA 1988, ss 80–83.
9   CDPA 1988, s 84.
10   CDPA 1988, s 85.
11   CDPA 1988, ss 94 and 95.
12   CDPA 1988, s 86(1).
13   CDPA 1988, s 86(2).
14   CDPA 1988, s 77(1).

The author of a literary work which is not intended to be spoken or sung with music and the author of a dramatic work both have the right to be identified whenever the work is published commercially, performed in public, broadcast or included in a cable programme or whenever copies of a film or sound recording of the work are issued to the public.[15] Non-commercial exploitation, such as the private performance of a play, does not give rise to the obligation to identify the author. This fits in with the logic that this moral right only restores the balance with the commercial exploitation of the work. Another interesting point is the meaning given to 'issuing copies of the work'. It cannot be restricted to the narrow meaning it has in section 18(2) of the Act. Every commercial publication, every public performance requires the identification of the author and not just the first publication or first performance. Issuing copies is mentioned together with publication and performance and should mean making copies available, not just making them available in the UK for the first time. Only this interpretation conforms to the logical sense of the system.

Musical works and lyrics are subjected to the same regime. Commercial publication of them and the issuing of copies of a sound recording of the work to the public give rise to the obligation to identify the author.[16] Performance of the work, which was included in relation to literary and dramatic works, is not included here because it would in practice not be feasible to require that for example a disc jockey identifies the author of every song before or after playing it. On the other hand if a film, the soundtrack of which includes the work, is shown in public or copies of the film are issued to the public the author of the musical works and their lyrics should be identified. This provision fits in with the rules for films. Indeed, the director of a film has the right to be identified each time the film is shown in public, broadcast, included in a cable programme service and when copies of the film are issued to the public.[17] The director of the film gets preference over the producer in relation to moral rights. The creative activity is the director's contribution which deserves the special moral rights protection, while the entrepreneurial contribution of the producer does not deserve that. The provisions for artistic works are similar but include also public exhibition of the work.[18]

Identification should take place in a clear and prominent way for instance in or on each copy of the work,[19] or in any other way which brings the identity of the author or director to the attention of the person who acquires

---

15   CDPA 1988, s 77(2).
16   CDPA 1988, s 77(3).
17   CDPA 1988, s 77(6).
18   CDPA 1988, s 77(4); see also s 77(5) on works of architecture.
19   The obvious technique for, eg, books.

■

a copy of the work.[20] The author or director also has the right to be identified in relation to an adaptation of the work. When a textbook on public international law written by an English professor is translated into Russian, the English author has the right to be identified in the Russian translation. If we assume that it is not the whole work that is translated but only a couple of chapters, the right to be identified would still apply, because it applies in relation to the whole work or to a substantial part of it.[1] The test to determine whether or not a part is substantial is probably the same as the one used in relation to copyright infringement. We will discuss that test in the next chapter, which deals with copyright infringement.

This leaves us with one major precondition and some exceptions to the right to be identified. The paternity right is not granted automatically. The author or director who wants to benefit from it has to assert it.[2] Such an assertion can be general in nature or can be in relation to specified acts only. This can be done in the form of a statement which is included in an instrument assigning copyright in the work. Such a document has to be in writing and has to be signed by or on behalf of the author.[3] This method of asserting the paternity right has to be recommended because it will not only bind the assignee, but also anyone claiming through him, such as the person to whom the assignee assigns part of his rights, even if those other persons did not receive notice of the assertion.[4] The assertion can also be made by another written instrument signed by the author or director, but this assertion will only bind those with notice of it.[5] The paternity right can be asserted at any time during the life of the author, but it is not retrospective in nature. The right only arises once it has been asserted.[6] The assertion does not cover past use of the work. Any delay in asserting the right can only work to the detriment of the author or director as it should be taken into account in determining whether an injunction should be granted and in the determination of damages and other relief.[7]

There is also a long list of exceptions to the paternity right contained in section 79 of the Act. Some of them are particularly important. No paternity right exists in relation to computer programs, computer-generated works and typefaces[8] and publications in newspapers, periodicals, encyclopædias

---

20   Eg when a play is performed the programme can contain the name of the author of the
      play.
1   CDPA 1988, s 89(1).
2   CDPA 1988, s 78(1).
3   CDPA 1988, s 78(2).
4   CDPA 1988, s 78(4).
5   CDPA 1988, ss 78(2) and (4).
6   CDPA 1988, s 78(1).
7   CDPA 1988, s 78(5).
8   CDPA 1988, s 79(2).

and dictionaries are excluded.[9] The first category is clearly too much linked to technical and technological elements and too far away from the moral rights idea of the artist-creator who should be identified, while in the latter category identification of the author of each article or contribution would overload the works and be impractical as editors edit and each edition of a newspaper may change dramatically. All these identifications could effectively take up a substantial percentage of the whole work. The employer/first owner of the copyright in a work created in the course of employment, or anyone acting with his authority, is not obliged to identify the creator employee.[10] This avoids the considerable problem that would have been created had an employee-engineer, or later eventually an ex-employee engineer, been allowed to interfere with the exploitation of the drawings he made for a series of products through the exercise of his moral rights. The paternity right will under certain circumstances not be infringed by acts done in relation to the reporting of current events or by incidental inclusion of the work.[11]

RIGHT TO OBJECT TO DEROGATORY TREATMENT

The beneficiaries of this moral right, the integrity right, are the same as those of the paternity right: authors of literary, dramatic, musical and artistic works and directors of films. The integrity right applies only to the extent that works are and remain in copyright.[12] Derogatory treatment of the work involves addition, deletion, alteration or adaptation which amounts to distortion or mutilation of the work or which is otherwise prejudicial to the honour or reputation of the author or the director.[13] This would be the case if a tale for young children written by a reputed children's author was turned into a pornographic story through addition and alteration. On the other hand, criticism of a work is in no way complicated by this integrity right. Criticism does not involve distortion or mutilation and does not affect the honour or reputation of the author. It takes place at a different level and derogatory criticism should not be called criticism, but it should be called by its true name: derogatory treatment.

The critical issue is when does an act amount to distortion or mutilation of the work or when is it otherwise prejudicial to the honour or reputation of the author or the director. The integrity right can clearly not be exercised at the discretion of the author or the director. It has to be proven

9   CDPA 1988, s 79(6).
10   CDPA 1988, s 79(3)(a).
11   The fair dealing and incidental inclusion concepts will be analysed fully in the chapter
     on copyright infringement where they find their roots; see CDPA 1988, s 79(4).
12   CDPA 1988, s 80(1).
13   CDPA 1988, ss 80(1) and (2).

'that the distortion or other mutilation of [the] work really prejudices [the author's] lawful intellectual or personal interests in the work'.[14]

This involves the balancing of all relevant interests involved. In this process the nature and the purpose of the work to which the allegedly infringing act is done is an important factor. It is submitted that for example an act done to a drawing containing technical details and a draft plan for an industrial product will less easily infringe the integrity right of the author than a similar act done to a work of fine art such as a painting. The author of the drawing knows that his or her work is just the starting point for a long process of development and change involving many other people. The painter who delivers the painting to an art dealer, however, readily assumes that the painting will not be changed at all. A first criterion in the balancing test is thus whether the work is relatively speaking more utilitarian or more artistic in nature.[15]

'Additional criteria could be, for example, the nature and the extent of the alteration of the work and also how far the latter is reversible or irreversible; the number of people or the size of the public addressed by the user of the work in altered form; the fact whether the author created the work in an employment relationship or as a self-employed author, or else whether a commissioning party did not have a decisive influence on the final result of the creation[. A]lso the possible consequences for the professional life of the author and, of course, for his or her reputation have to be taken into consideration.'[16]

Since the integrity right and other moral rights very strongly involve the issue of fundamental fairness between the author and the user of the work one could add the purpose and the character of the use of the work as another relevant criterion. Finally, certain well established customs and traditions in certain parts of industry may also be taken into account.[17]

All these elements point towards a rather objective test. It is submitted that the determination whether the author's or the director's honour or reputation has been prejudiced by the treatment of the work by a third party is to be effected by answering the question whether right thinking members of the public would think less of him as a result of the treatment.[18] This test bears similarities to the one that is applied in cases of defamation, and

14   Dietz 'The Artist's Right of Integrity Under Copyright Law – A Comparative Approach' (1994) 25 IIC 177 at 183.
15   Dietz (1994) 25 IIC 177 at 184–185.
16   Ibid at 185.
17   Ibid at 185–187.
18   See *Tidy v The Trustees of the Natural History Museum* [1996] 3 EIPR D-81.

the view that a 'certain subjective element or judgment on the part of the author so long as it is reasonably arrived at'[19] is involved needs to be rejected. The latter view would push the integrity right beyond its role as a fundamental right that preserves the balance of rights between the author/ director and those exploiting the work.

The courts in the UK have not yet decided any major case on moral rights since the introduction of the 1988 Act.[20] However, German and Swiss courts have used the balancing test on the basis of similar provisions.[1] The Swiss Federal Supreme Court used it to rule that the proposed alterations to a school building, which involved among other things the replacement of the original flat roof by a saddleback roof, did not amount to a mutilation of the architectural work and did not infringe the integrity right of the architect.[2]

Authors and directors can invoke this right to object to derogatory treatment of their work which occurs when copies of the work are published commercially, when copies of a sound recording or film are made available to the public, when the work is performed, played or shown in public and when it is broadcast or included in a cable programme service.[3] The right also applies to parts of works which were previously adapted or translated by someone else. When a French translation of a novel by Dame Barbara Cartland is subjected to derogatory treatment, she will still be able to object to the infringement of her integrity right.[4]

The wide scope of the right is subject to a series of exceptions though. The integrity right is not infringed if the treatment of the work does not go further than the translation of a literary or dramatic work or the arrangement or transcription of a musical work involving no more than a change of key or register.[5] Furthermore the integrity right does not apply to computer programs and computer-generated works. Nor does it apply in relation to publication in a newspaper, periodical, encyclopædia or yearbook and any subsequent unmodified re-publication thereof. Should the author or director of a work made in the course of employment that is altered be identified, the right is restricted to a sufficient disclaimer of association with

19   *Snow v The Eaton Centre* 70 CPR 105 (2d) (a Canadian High Court decision).
20   For a first timid attempt see *Tidy v The Trustees of the Natural History Museum* [1996] 3 EIPR D-81.
1   German Supreme Court Decision of 31 May 1974 [1974] GRUR 675, see also German Supreme Court Decision of 2 October 1981 [1982] GRUR 107, both cases cited by Dietz 'The Artist's Right of Integrity Under Copyright Law – A Comparative Approach' (1994) 25 IIC 177 at 188.
2   Swiss Federal Supreme Court Decision of 24 September 1991 [1992] GRUR 473, cited by Dietz 'The Artist's Right of Integrity Under Copyright Law – A Comparative Approach' (1994) 25 IIC 177 at 188.
3   CDPA 1988, s 80(3)-(6).
4   CDPA 1988, s 80(7).
5   CDPA 1988, s 80(2)(a).

the altered work.[6] The impact of the right is further compromised by the introduction of a special remedy for this moral right. By means of an injunction the court may allow the act complained of to continue once a disclaimer dissociating the author or director from the altered work is made.[7] A clear example of this is that an architect's integrity right is restricted to him being allowed to request the removal of his identification from the building.[8]

A broadcasting authority may in certain circumstances wish to censor certain works and make excisions and alterations as its broadcasts should not incite crime, offend good taste and decency, lead to disorder or be offensive to public feeling. Because this could eventually amount to derogatory treatment of the works concerned, the Act explicitly allows the BBC, but, oddly, not the commercial channels, to censor the works by stipulating that this will not infringe the integrity right in the work.[9]

The scope of the right and its effectiveness are on the other hand widened by the fact that the right is also infringed by possessing in the course of a business or dealing with an infringing article if such a person knows or has reason to believe that there is a false attribution.[10] It may be easier to find someone in possession of or dealing with the infringing article than to find the person responsible for the alterations. An action for infringement is now more readily available which makes it easier to enforce the integrity right.

FALSE ATTRIBUTION OF THE WORK

The author or director has the right to be identified. The other side of the coin is that he should also have a right only to be identified if he really is the creator of the work. This right is laid down by the Act as the right to oppose false attribution of the work. It applies to literary, dramatic, musical and artistic works and to films. Any person to whom such a work is attributed falsely and who is not its creator may object to it.[11] This right can be useful, for example if someone plagiarises the style of a famous novelist such as Jeffrey Archer in producing a mediocre novel in which he or she advocates the imposition of mafia style taxes (extortion!) to generate funds for a political party and prints Jeffrey Archer's name on the cover page. We may assume that the famous novelist would like to object to the attribution of this work to him. The opportunity to object arises when copies

6   CDPA 1988, ss 81 and 82.
7   CDPA 1988, s 103(2).
8   CDPA 1988, s 80(5).
9   CDPA 1988, s 81(5)(c).
10   See the section on copyright infringement for a proper definition of the concepts of possessing or dealing with an infringing copy; CDPA 1988, s 81.
11   CDPA 1988, s 84(1).

of the work containing the false attribution are issued to the public, when an artistic work or a copy of it in or on which there is a false attribution is exhibited in public, when a literary, dramatic or musical work is performed in public, broadcast or included in a cable programme service as being the work of the plaintiff and when a film is shown in public, broadcast or included in a cable programme service as being directed by the plaintiff.[12] The plaintiff is also given a right of action against anyone possessing a copy of the work in the course of business or dealing with a copy of the work if such a person knows or has reason to believe that there is a false attribution.[13] A special problem arises in relation to an artistic work which is left in the possession of a dealer before it is altered. When such a work is dealt with afterwards as the unaltered work of the author he will have the right to object to this as being a false attribution.[14]

The right also applies to adaptations which are falsely being presented as adaptations of the work of a person. In the case of an artistic work this means a copy of a work which is falsely presented as being a copy made by the author of the artistic work.[15]

The right expires 20 years after the death of the person to whom the work is attributed falsely.[16] In this sense it forms an exception to the rule that the term of moral rights and commercial copyright are the same. This rule cannot be applied here as there is no equivalent copyright for the person to whom a work is attributed falsely.

The right to object to false attribution is particularly relevant in relation to certain forms of parody. By definition a parody has to resemble the original work closely in order for people to make the link between the two. It is easy to see how the impression can be created that the parody is the work of the author of the original work in this context. A good example of such a situation is found in *Clark v Associated Newspapers Ltd*.[17] Alan Clark famously published his diaries some years ago and it is believed that further similar publications are in the pipeline. The defendants published a parody of the diaries as a column in the *Evening Standard* newspaper. The newspaper columns were written by a Mr Peter Bradshaw and they carried the headings 'Alan Clark's Secret Election' and 'Alan Clark's Political Diary'. The headings were accompanied of a photograph of Mr Clark and Mr Bradshaw's name, albeit in capital letters, appeared only in the introductory paragraph. That paragraph mentioned the fact that the column was in fact all about how Mr Bradshaw imagined Mr Clark might record certain events. Mr Clark brought a case in passing-off and he relied also on

12   CDPA 1988, s 84(2)-(4).
13   CDPA 1988, s 84(5).
14   CDPA 1988, s 84(6).
15   CDPA 1988, s 84(8).
16   CDPA 1988, s 86(2).
17   [1998] 1 All ER 959.

section 84 of the 1988 Act. In relation to the latter point he argued that the readers of the *Evening Standard*, or at least a large number of them, would assume that he was the author of the column. In his view confusion as to who is the author was sufficient for the purposes of section 84. The court started its analysis of section 84 by stating that

> '[t]wo distinctive features of the statutory tort are: (a) that it is unnecessary that the plaintiff be a professional author and accordingly that he has any goodwill or reputation as an author to protect or which may be damaged by false attribution; and (b) consequently the tort is actionable per se without proof of damage. In short s 84 confers a personal or civic right on everyone not to have authorship of any literary work falsely attributed to him.'

However, it is up to the plaintiff to establish that the work contains what is a false attribution of authorship. It is not sufficient that some or more people may understand it to be a false attribution.[18] On this basis the court ruled that '[t]he proper approach [...] is to determine what is the single meaning which the literary work conveys to the notional reasonable reader'. On the basis of the facts of this case the court concluded that the articles contained in their title and through the addition of a photograph a clear and unequivocal false statement attributing their authorship to Mr Clark. The court accepted that such a statement could in certain cases be neutralised by an express contradiction, but such a contradiction had to be as bold, precise and compelling as the false statement and this requirement had not been met in this case. Similarly, section 84 could also be used to object to the attribution to an interviewee of the comments made in an interview in circumstances where the interviewer added or made up 90 per cent of the comments.[19]

RIGHT TO PRIVACY IN RELATION TO COMMISSIONED PHOTOGRAPHS

When someone commissions a photograph the photographer gets the ownership of the copyright as creator of the work. He can use the negatives for all kinds of purposes and does not need the consent of the commissioner.[20] This can be undesirable if the photograph is commissioned

18   Support for the single meaning view can be found in *Moore v News of the World Ltd* [1972] 1 All ER 915 at 921-922 and [1972] 1 QB 441 at 451-452.
19   See *Moore v News of the World Ltd* [1972] 1 All ER 915 and [1972] 1 QB 441; see also *Noah v Shuba* [1991] FSR 14.
20   See Gendreau 'Copyright Ownership of Photographs in Anglo-American Law' [1993] 6 EIPR 207 at 211–213. See also Chapter 27 on character merchandising.

for private and domestic purposes, for example one would not like to see one's own wedding pictures as part of a billboard advertising campaign for life-insurance policies or on the front page of the tabloids next to a story under the title 'How many husbands are unfaithful right from the start?'. The right to privacy grants the commissioner some protection in this respect. The commissioner has the right not to have copies of the photograph issued to the public, not to have them exhibited in public, and not to have the photograph included in a broadcast or a cable programme service. Anyone who does or authorises these acts infringes the right to privacy. Two further requirements have to be met. The photograph has to be commissioned for private and domestic purposes and needs to attract copyright. An identical right exists in relation to films commissioned for private and domestic purposes.[1] There are no other requirements for the existence of the right, it is for instance immaterial whether the commissioner hired a professional photographer at an enormous price or an unpaid friend or relative.

The term of the right is equal to that of the copyright in the photograph or film[2] and the right is given independently to each joint co-commissioner.[3] It applies to the whole work or to a substantial part of it.[4] There are some minor exceptions to the right.[5] The most important one is that the right to privacy is not infringed in case of the incidental inclusion in an artistic work, film, broadcast or cable programme.[6]

This right compensates in this particular area the lack of a general right to privacy. This became necessary because the 1988 Act no longer gives the commissioner any ownership of the copyright in the commissioned work. An interesting case in this respect was decided before the 1988 Act came into force. In *Mail Newspapers plc v Express Newspapers plc*[7] wedding pictures were at the centre of the debate. The wife had suffered a brain haemorrhage and was kept alive artificially to give birth. The husband had sold the exclusive right in the pictures to one newspaper and the other newspaper tried to obtain copies from the photographer. Under the new provision the husband could have stopped the photographer from giving copies of the picture to the newspaper. This case is also interesting because it illustrates that the right is not just a negative right; in practice it will often be used to secure exclusivity and gain a higher price for the use of the photographs or films. In the example it is clear that the husband could stop the photographer

---

1   CDPA 1988, s 85(1).
2   CDPA 1988, s 86(1).
3   CDPA 1988, s 88(6). This must mean that the right does not disappear when the commissioner dies, but is transmissible on death.
4   CDPA 1988, s 89(1) .
5   CDPA 1988, s 85(2).
6   CDPA 1988, s 85(2)(a).
7   [1987] FSR 90.

■

without having to rely on the consent of his wife. The interesting point is whether the photographer-owner of the copyright can interfere with the exclusivity contract. It is submitted that the commissioner has an implied licence to use the photographs and the privacy right does not play any special role.

Interestingly, the right is given to the commissioner rather than to the person in the photograph or film, whilst in most cases it is the latter's privacy that is at issue. The problem obviously only arises when the commissioner is not the person in the photograph or film. The rule can be justified though on the basis that it is much easier to identify and contact the commissioner whose name and address will be know to the photographer or the maker of the film. There may also be a single commissioner, but many people may figure in the photograph or film. Names and addresses of the latter parties may also not necessarily been known to the owners of the copyright in the work.

CONSENT AND WAIVER

It could be accepted that the moral rights of a person who consented to an act being done are not infringed.[8] When the author consents to the publication of his novel without being identified, he cannot complain about the infringement of his identity right afterwards. But the Act goes further and allows moral rights to be waived. The person entitled to any of the four moral rights can surrender them in a written and signed instrument.[9] Contractual consideration is not required. This can be done before an issue arises. Such a waiver may relate to one or more specific rights or to all moral rights. It may relate to one specific work, to a class of works, to all works and even to future works. The waiver can be conditional or unconditional and can also be expressed to be subject to revocation.[10] This possibility for the author to waive his or her moral rights substantially weakens the impact and value of the moral rights. An author or director quite often occupies a weak bargaining position in negotiating the conditions for the creation and the commercial exploitation of the work and can be leaned upon to waive all moral rights. It is submitted that the possibility of waiving moral rights contradicts the essence of the concept of moral rights as essential safeguards for the author or director as the weaker party.

Even worse is the possibility of an informal waiver under the general principles of contract or estoppel.[11] The enforcement of the identity right

---

8   CDPA 1988, s 87(1).
9   CDPA 1988, s 87(2).
10   CDPA 1988, s 87(3).
11   CDPA 1988, s 87(4).

may become impossible if conduct of the author or director leads another person to believe that he or she will not insist upon identification.

The introduction of moral rights in the Act was clearly a step in the right direction. The protection of the weaker party cannot be left entirely to the contractual freedom of the parties. But the flexible waiver facility undermines the whole system. It becomes clear that the concept of moral rights is not yet fully integrated in the UK's entrepreneurial style copyright system.[12]

---

12   See Stamatoudi 'Moral Rights of Authors in England: The Missing Emphasis on the Role of Creators' [1997] IPQ 478.

Chapter 14

Copyright infringement

The owner of the copyright in a work is given a property right according to the first section of the Copyright, Designs and Patents Act 1988. What is the content of this property right though? The owner is given the exclusive right to perform certain acts in relation to the work. With an intangible right it is easier though to approach things from an infringement perspective. Anyone who performs an act that has been reserved exclusively for the copyright-owner will infringe the copyright in the work if he or she has not in advance obtained the permission of the copyright owner to perform that act. This chapter will therefore be concerned with the various acts that can infringe copyright and the content of the property right of the copyright-owner will be defined in this indirect way.

Essentially, copyright is a right to make copies. Copyright infringement can be seen as making unauthorised copies of a work. This was the historical starting point. Now much refinement has taken place and a distinction is made between primary and secondary infringement.

PRIMARY INFRINGEMENT

One way or the other all forms of primary infringement involve copying, whether through reproduction or through performance of the work. According to section 16(1) the rights of the copyright owner are infringed if:

— the work is copied;
— copies of the work are issued to the public;
— the work is lent or rented to the public;
— the work is performed, shown or played in public;

- the work is broadcast or included in a cable programme service and;
- an adaptation is made of the work or any of the above is done in relation to an adaptation.

It is an infringement to do these acts, but also to authorise someone else to do them.[1] These acts are called restricted acts, only the owner of the copyright or someone with his or her consent can do them.

Copyright infringement is the infringement of an intangible right in the expression of an idea. The idea is not protected and copying the idea is not an infringement of copyright. The work should also be dissociated from its physical, tangible carrier. When you buy a wooden sculpture you buy the piece of wood, the ownership of the copyright is not transferred though.[2]

INFRINGEMENT REQUIRES MISAPPROPRIATION

The causal link

Appropriation of the expression of the copyright work is an essential element of copyright infringement. As only the particular expression of an idea is protected by copyright, a work expressing the same idea is not necessarily an infringement. This will be the case and no infringement will arise if the result is reached independently[3] or if a common source is relied upon.[4] This will for instance be the case if two authors describe the Venice Marathon Race in a very similar way, while sitting at opposite sides of the Rialto bridge over the Canal Grande. They will reach the similar result independently. A common source may be found in two very different tables of matches on football pool coupons, which have to rely on the list of matches provided by the Football Association. It is necessary to demonstrate that the alleged infringement is linked to the original work and that part of its expression has been taken.

Recent case law provides a straightforward example in relation to a film. The plaintiff had shown the defendant an advertising film. The defendant had declined the offer to utilise the film, but he had afterwards taken the idea that was contained in it to make his own film. It was held that copyright in the original film is not infringed when the defendant does not make an exact copy of the film itself, but makes another film in a way which is

---

1   CDPA 1988, s 16(2).
2   This does not exclude a separate transfer of copyright.
3   See *Francis Day & Hunter Ltd v Bron* [1963] Ch 587, [1963] 2 All ER 16.
4   Eg factual, scientific and historical data which are readily available and form the basis of a number of works; see *Harman Pictures NV v Osborne* [1967] 2 All ER 324 at 328, [1967] 1 WLR 723 at 728.

designed to and which does closely resemble and imitate the film in which copyright subsists.[5]

The owner who alleges infringement of his or her copyright is given the burden to prove that the similarity between his or her work and the alleged infringement is explained by this causal connection. Part of the evidence required is that the plaintiff's work was created before the alleged infringement, which rules out the possibility that it borrowed subject-matter from the alleged infringement. In practice it is extremely difficult to demonstrate the causal link fully. In most cases strong similarities between the earlier work and the allegedly infringing work are coupled with evidence that the defendant had the opportunity to know the plaintiff's work. If the defendant does not provide another convincing explanation for the similarities, most judges will accept that the plaintiff has discharged the burden of proof and will find copying proved.

The intention of the infringer and subconscious copying

The intention of the defendant is not relevant. The fact that he believed that for whatever reason he was allowed to reproduce or perform the work does not influence the finding of infringement. Here the defendant does not realise he is infringing copyright. One also finds situations in which the defendant does not realise he is copying. We all frequently come into contact with copyright works. Some of them leave untraceable impressions in our memory. Unconsciously we may copy these works or parts of them when creating our own work. This will also constitute infringement, since copying does not need to happen consciously.[6] The obvious example is that of a composer who listens to hundreds of melodies and when composing his own music unconsciously copies fragments of the melodies he heard. Full proof of a causal link will be even more difficult in cases of unconscious copying. Judges will consider

'the degree of familiarity (if proved at all, or properly inferred) with the plaintiff's work, the character of the work, particularly its qualities of impressing the mind and memory, the objective similarity of the defendant's work, the inherent probability that such similarities as found could be due to coincidence, the existence of other influences on the

5   The fact that the work was a film explains certain peculiarities of the case: *Norowzian* v *Arks Ltd* [1998] FSR 394.
6   See *Rees v Melville* (1911–1916) Mac CC 168; *Ricordi v Clayton & Waller* (1928–1935) Mac CC 154; *Francis Day & Hunter Ltd v Bron* [1963] Ch 587, [1963] 2 All ER 16; and *Industrial Furnaces v Reaves* [1970] RPC 605 at 623.

defendant ... the quality of the defendant's ... own evidence on the presence in his mind of the plaintiff's work'.[7]

Indirect copying

The causal relationship can be turned into a causal chain. A copy of a copy indirectly copies the original work and constitutes an infringement.[8] Drawings are often made before a three-dimensional object is made. If someone makes his or her own drawing after having seen the object, but without having seen the original drawing the copyright in that drawing will nevertheless be infringed.[9] This chain can be long, but it must be uninterrupted and run in the same direction. The final infringing copy must be linked to the original work, the copyright in which it is infringing. It is not required though that all intermediate acts produce works which can attract copyright.[10] To go back to our example it is not required that the three-dimensional object attracts copyright. A recent case law example concerned parts of cartridges for laser printers and photocopiers.[11] The copying by the defendant of parts of the plaintiff's cartridges constituted an indirect reproduction of the plaintiff's drawings, in which artistic copyright existed. The fact that the cartridges were functional three-dimensional objects was irrelevant. The provision cannot be used though if two similar objects are created and drawings of each of these objects are made. In that situation there is no indirect infringement of the drawing of the first object, as the objects are the starting point in the chain, not the drawing.[12]

SUBSTANTIAL COPYING

Not every act of copying is actionable. The defendant must have copied either the whole work or a substantial part of it.[13] Cases where the whole work has been copied are not problematic, but what is a substantial part of a work? This is not determined on a quantitative basis. It is not possible to

---

7   *Francis Day & Hunter Ltd v Bron* [1963] Ch 587 at 614, [1963] 2 All ER 16, per Willmer LJ, adopting the words of Wilberforce J at first instance.

8   CDPA 1988, s 16(3); this provision is based on the case law of eg *King Features Syndicate v Kleeman* [1941] AC 417 and *British Leyland Motor Corpn v Armstrong Patents Co Ltd* [1986] RPC 279.

9   See *LB (Plastics) v Swish Products Ltd* [1979] RPC 551.

10 CDPA 1988, s 16(3).

11 *Canon Kabushiki Kaisha v Green Cartridge Co (Hong Kong Ltd)* [1997] 3 WLR 13, [1997] FSR 817 (Privy Council).

12 *Purefoy v Sykes Boxall* (1954) 71 RPC 227 at 232. Compare the Court of Appeal's approach in the same case, which is differently worded: (1955) 72 RPC 89 at 99.

13 CDPA 1988, s 16(3)(a).

■

derive from the Act and the case law a rule that the copying of X% of a work will not be substantial copying while the copying of Y% of the work will be substantial copying. Although obviously the quantity taken from the original work plays a certain role, it is much more a qualitative approach which is taken to determine whether the copying was substantial.[14] This is linked to the fact that copyright is used in the UK as a tool against unfair competition. Copying will be allowed only in so far as it does not lead to unfair competition. A qualitative approach fits this purpose much more easily. Another relevant factor is the principle that ideas are not protected. A substantial part of the expression of the idea can be copied, but it is not possible to translate that into a percentage of the work as one does not know the balance between idea and expression in the work.

Whether or not a substantial part of the work has been copied will have to be determined case by case. It is a matter of fact and degree and will depend on the circumstances of the case.[15] Some guidance can be given though.

The court will have to concentrate on the similarities between the part of the work that has allegedly been copied and the equivalent part in the alleged copy. Differences between them can only be used to ascertain the similarities.[16] The qualitative approach to determining whether a substantial part of the work has been copied means that particular weight will be given to the copying of the most important and interesting parts of the original work. In a case that was concerned with cacao crop reports the copying of the pod count summary from the much longer report was held to constitute the copying of a substantial part of the work for this very reason. If parts of more than one work, for example a series of articles, are copied in the allegedly infringing work, each of the original works must be considered separately for the purposes of determining whether a substantial part of it has been copied.[17]

Once the court is convinced that unfair competition is taking place,[18] it will be hard to convince them that the alterations made are so substantial that the part of the original work which is copied is no longer substantial.[19] This should also be seen against the background of the vague dividing line

---

14   *Ladbroke (Football) Ltd v William Hill (Football) Ltd* [1964] 1 All ER 465 at 469, [1964] 1 WLR 273 at 276, per Lord Reid; see also Lord Pearce's speech at 481 and 293.

15   Eg in *Hawkes & Sons (London) Ltd v Paramount Film Service Ltd* [1934] Ch 593 it was held that the inclusion of a 20-second portion of the main melody of the march 'Colonel Bogey', which lasts for four minutes, in a newsreel amounted to substantial copying.

16   *Biotrading & Financing OY v Biohit Ltd* [1998] FSR 109 at 121.

17   *PCR Ltd v Dow Jones Telerate ltd* [1998] FSR 170.

18   Especially if the judges adhere to the hardline approach suggested by Peterson J that 'what is worth copying is prima facie worth protecting': *University of London Press v Universal Tutorial Press* [1916] 2 Ch 601 at 610 (quoted in *Ladbroke (Football) Ltd v William Hill (Football) Ltd* [1964] 1 All ER 465, [1964] 1 WLR 273 at 279).

19   An excellent example is found in *Elanco Products v Mandops (Agrochemical Specialists) Ltd* [1980] RPC 213.

between idea and expression. Judges in the type of case described often take the view that the idea is restricted to the thought underlying the work, such as a joke underlying a cartoon.[20] The only way in which the defendant can avoid copying the expression is by drawing a different cartoon starting from the same joke, but not from the completed original cartoon.[1] This extremely wide interpretation of what is expression facilitates of course the finding that a substantial part of it has been copied. The case law contains various examples of this approach in relation to scripts for plays or films based on plots found in a play or a novel.[2] The actual words were often not copied, just the plot as such was taken and eventually slightly adapted.[3] The courts decided that substantial copying had nevertheless taken place. In their view the idea was confined to the thought which was the starting point for the development of the plot, such as making a play about the home-coming of a husband who was presumed dead.[4] It is submitted that this approach should be confined to cases where there is a very strong sense of unfair competition or where the starting point is the essential element of the work which determines its economic value. The economic value of a plot and the play or film based on it are often determined on the basis of the value of the initial starting point. This is less so for a novel, where literary style is also extremely important, or for an artistic work, for which eye appeal is the other extremely important factor.[5]

In all other circumstances the idea is wider in scope. Under these circumstances other elements become prominent to determine whether substantial copying has taken place. One obvious element is the unaltered copying of a key element of the original work, such as the refrain of a song.[6] This amounts qualitatively speaking to substantial copying, even if the amount taken is not large in comparison to the whole work.[7]

A smart copier alters and reworks the part he has copied. Does this still amount to substantial copying? The test is whether a substantial part of the original work survives in the new work.[8] It has been suggested that this

---

20   *McCrum v Eisner* (1917-1923) Mac CC 14, (1917) 87 LJ Ch 99, 117 LT 536.
1   Ibid; see also *Krisarts SA v Briarfine Ltd* [1977] FSR 557 (defendant painting independently a scene which the plaintiff painted at an earlier time, resulting in a similar process of creation, while only the idea was borrowed).
2   *Corelli v Gray* (1913) 30 TLR 116 and *Vane v Famous Players* Mac CC (1928-1935) 394, are good examples of this approach.
3   *Kelly v Cinema Houses Ltd* (1928-1935) Mac CC 362; *Dagnall v British and Dominion Film Corpn* (1928-1935) Mac CC 391 and *Fernald v Jay Lewis* [1975] FSR 499 (case decided in 1953).
4   An example given in *Vane v Famous Players* Mac CC (1928-1935) 394, per Scrutton LJ.
5   See *Bauman v Fussell* [1978] RPC 485 at 487, per Somervell LJ.
6   Cf *Hawkes & Sons (London) Ltd v Paramount Film Service Ltd* [1934] Ch 593.
7   On the other hand one line taken from the refrain of a popular song did not amount to substantial copying in *Joy Music Ltd v Sunday Pictorial Newspapers (1920) Ltd* [1960] 2 QB 60, see infra.
8   *Schweppes Ltd v Wellington Ltd* [1984] FSR 210 and *Redwood Music v Chappell & Co Ltd* [1982] RPC 109.

means that no substantial and actionable copying will occur if the copier
has invested enough skill and labour in the alteration of the copied parts[9]
for the result to attract its own copyright.[10] This is however not the real
test and it should be emphasised that the skill and labour approach should
in any case be restricted to the parts based on the copying. Other parts of
the allegedly infringing work and the skill and labour invested in them
should not be taken into account when discussing the infringement issue.
Two excellent examples of circumstances in which alterations lead to
difficulties in this respect are satirical versions of works and summaries of
works. The satirical version has to stay close enough to the original for
people to recognise the link and for reasons of accuracy a summary has to
contain the essential elements of the original work. A song, the lyrics of
which had been altered and parodied in pursuit of Prince Philip, was held
not to be an infringing copy, because only one repeated phrase had been
taken from the original lyrics.[11] Selection of the essential elements of the
work,[12] condensation and revision must amount to enough skill and labour
to attract copyright for a summary to escape the infringement sanction.[13]

The work that has been copied may also contain unoriginal parts. This
leads to special problems if the part that was copied included the unoriginal
parts. It was held that where an unoriginal part was taken and that part was
used in a similar context and way as in the original copyright work, the latter
aspect meant that also part of the work of the author that provided originality
was taken. It is likely that in these circumstances the amount taken would
be likely to amount to a substantial part of the work.[14] Industrial drawings
are a good example in this context. They often consist of unoriginal shapes
that are copied from earlier drawings in combination with new original
shapes. When such an industrial drawing is copied, the copying of the
unoriginal shape may not amount to the copying of a substantial part, but
substantial copying may be involved when the amount copied included the
context in which the shape was portrayed. The latter conclusion is reached

9   It is essential that the copied work does not rely exclusively on information gathered by
       the plaintiff, using his skill and judgment; see *Elanco Products v Mandops (Agrochemical
       Specialists) Ltd* [1980] RPC 213; it must be remembered though that this was a case in
       which there were strong indications of unfair competition as the first version of the
       instruction leaflet was an exact copy of the plaintiff's leaflet and the
       second version was only revised to such extent as to give the same information in other
       words; the judgment can be criticised because it gives the plaintiffs, authors of a trivial
       work, an almost absolute monopoly in the only possible way to express these instructions
       efficiently, concisely and accurately.
10   *Joy Music Ltd v Sunday Pictorial Newspapers (1920) Ltd* [1960] 2 QB 60, [1960] 1 All
       ER 703 and *Glyn v Weston Feature Film Co* [1916] 1 Ch 261.
11   Ibid in the *Joy Music* case.
12   This aspect is essential, because the Court of Appeal held in *Elanco Products v Mandops
       (Agrochemical Specialists) Ltd* [1980] RPC 213, that the defendant could not rely
       exclusively on the plaintiff's effort and judgment in selecting the information.
13   See *Sweet v Benning* (1855) 16 CB 459 at 483, per Jervis CJ.
14   *Biotrading & Financing OY v Biohit Ltd* [1998] FSR 109 at 121.

because the copier has also taken much of the work of the author in deciding how and in what way the unoriginal shape should be combined with the original shape. The inclusion of the unoriginal shape in what is copied has little relevance in deciding whether or not a substantial part has been copied.[15]

It cannot be the aim of copyright to give the plaintiff a wide-ranging monopoly. This could happen if works involving substantial copying of a part of a work which itself involves only the minimum amount of skill and labour to attract copyright are held to be infringements. This would be an undesirable consequence of the low requirements for a work to attract copyright and judges have fortunately responded to it by taking the extent of the effort invested by the plaintiff into account when deciding whether substantial copying has occurred. The answer will only be affirmative if an exact copy of the work which itself involved an extremely low level of creativity is produced.[16]

A particular problem arises when a work which is itself an edited version or which consists of selected and compiled material is allegedly copied to a substantial extent. This occurs in relation to a collection of selected poems of which some poems are copied together with some of the annotation. It occurs also in relation to cases of tables where the commercial judgment in selecting the material secures copyright and where that selection is copied. Copyright arises in the whole work but it is obvious that the real skill and labour expended by the plaintiff are located in the areas of selection, editing and annotation. This is taken into account when determining whether the amount copied amounts to a substantial part of the work.[17] The infringement of the plaintiff's contribution must be substantial as well.

COPYING THE VARIOUS TYPES OF WORKS

The technical definition of copying depends on the type of work. But once such a case arises the principles laid down above apply to it.

Original literary, artistic, dramatic and musical works

An original work is copied through reproduction in any material form.[18] This includes storing the work in any medium by electronic means, such as storing the content of a book on a CD-Rom. It also includes

15 Ibid at 122.
16 *Kenrick v Lawrence & Co* (1890) 25 QBD 99 (a drawing of a hand, showing voters where to cast their vote).
17 *Warwick Film Productions Ltd v Eisinger* [1969] 1 Ch 508, [1967] 3 All ER 367.
18 CDPA 1988, s 17(2).

materialisation on a TV monitor.[19] A special option arises for artistic works.[20] A two-dimensional copy can be made of a three-dimensional work, or a three-dimensional copy can be made of a two-dimensional work. The work is also reproduced in a material way in these cases. Such a case arises for example when a cartoon is enacted.[1]

Films, television broadcasts and cable programmes

Films, television broadcasts and cable programmes are copied when they are reproduced.[2] This can take place when a film is made of a film, a broadcast or a cable programme. It also takes place when a photograph of the whole or any substantial part of an image forming part of the film, broadcast or cable programme is made.[3] The courts held that making a photograph of a single frame of a *Starsky and Hutch* film was an infringement.[4] This situation also covers the case where a photograph of a television screen, on which the work is momentarily displayed, is made.

Typographical arrangements of published editions

Copying a typographical arrangement involves making a facsimile copy of that arrangement.[5] That copy can be enlarged or reduced in scale,[6] which means that infringement quite often takes place through photocopies or through a fax.

All works

Copying of any kind of work also includes making copies which are transient or incidental to some other use of the work.[7] The prime example here is making a series of photographs while copying a film.

19   *Bookmakers' Afternoon Greyhound Services Ltd v Wilf Gilbert (Staffordshire) Ltd* [1994] FSR 723.
20   CDPA 1988, s 17(3).
1   *Bradbury, Agnew & Co v Day* (1916) 32 TLR 349; the dimensional shift rule does only apply to artistic works; it does not apply when eg a literary work is involved: see *Brigid Foley Ltd v Eliott* [1982] RPC 433.
2   CDPA 1988, s 17(4).
3   On a conceptual basis copying needs to be distinguished from making another film in a way which is designed to and which does closely resemble and imitate the film in which copyright subsists, if no exact copy is made in the latter case: see *Norowzian v Arks Ltd* [1998] FSR 394.
4   *Spelling Goldberg Productions Inc v BPC Publishing Ltd* [1981] RPC 283.
5   CDPA 1988, s 17(5).
6   CDPA 1988, s 17(8).
7   CDPA 1988, s 17(6).

ISSUING COPIES TO THE PUBLIC

Copying is not the only restricted act. Copyright is also infringed when copies of a work are issued to the public. This applies to all works, no distinction is made between the various categories. Copies are issued to the public when they are put into circulation for the first time. It is essential that copies of the work were not previously available and that they are now put into circulation. A distinction is made between putting copies into circulation in the UK or in any other member state of the European Economic Area on the one hand and putting copies into circulation outside the member states of the European Economic Area on the other hand. Copies are issued to the public by putting them into circulation in the territory of the European Economic Area if these copies have not previously been put into circulation in that territory by or with the consent of the copyright owner. Copies are also issued to the public when they are put into circulation outside the territory of the European Economic Area if they have not previously been put into circulation in the European Economic Area or elsewhere. All this reflects also in the fact that subsequent dealings with a copy which is put into circulation do not constitute the restricted act of issuing copies to the public. When a book that has not been published is put into circulation this will be an infringement of the copyright in the book, but subsequent importation of copies of the book and the loan of these copies will not constitute issuing copies to the public.[8] Rental and lending are subject to special provisions and it is to these provisions that we now turn.

RENTAL AND LENDING OF THE WORK TO THE PUBLIC

Rental and lending of a work[9] mean that a copy of the work is made available for use, on terms that it will or may be returned. Hire purchase type deals are therefore also included. In the case of rental the work is made available for direct or indirect commercial or economic advantage. The activities of video shops come to mind as an obvious example. Lending covers all cases where no direct or indirect commercial or economic advantage is involved[10] and the copy of the work is made available through an establishment that is accessible to the public, such as a library.[11] Unauthorised rental or lending of copies of certain types of works to the public will constitute an infringement of the copyright in the work. The types of works involved are

---

8 CDPA 1988, s 18.
9 CDPA 1988, s 18A(2).
10 This does not exclude the payment of an amount to cover the operating costs of the establishment: CDPA 1988, s 18A(5).
11 Interlibrary transactions are excluded from the scope of lending: CDPA 1988, s 18A(4).

literary, dramatic and musical works, films and sound recordings. Artistic works are only involved in so far as they are not a work of architecture in the form of a building or a model for a building, or a work of applied art.[12]

The right to object to unauthorised rental and lending does not apply to a limited number of cases, because they have been excluded from the scope of the definition of rental and lending. These exclusions cover making a copy of the work available for the purpose of public performance, playing or showing in public, broadcasting or inclusion in a cable programme service, and making a copy available for the purpose of exhibition in public, as well as making the copy available for on-the-spot reference use.[13] The latter excludes for example all use of a work inside a library without taking it out.

PUBLIC PERFORMANCE OF THE WORK, SHOWING OR PLAYING THE WORK IN PUBLIC

In this category of restricted acts public performances apply to literary, dramatic and musical works only. The copyright in these works is infringed by the public performance of the work. This includes any visual or acoustic presentation of the work, even if the presentation is done by means of sound recordings, films, broadcasts or cable programmes. Lectures, speeches and addresses obviously come within this category.[14]

It is an infringement of copyright too to play or show a sound recording, film, broadcast or cable programme in public.[15] This kind of infringement arises for instance when background music is played in a shop or restaurant.[16] The application of this provision is not without problems. How do we define 'in public'? It is clear that this is not a reference to the public at large. Showing the work to a group of ten members of the public can be an infringement. Private showings are not caught, even if to a larger number of people. To avoid infringement the audience has to be of a domestic nature. Copyright will not be infringed when a father plays a record and the rest of the family is listening in the lounge of the family home. This distinction is not always clear though. Is the showing of a film in a hotel equipped with a central video recorder and a TV set in every room private or public? People will watch the film in the private atmosphere of their room, but the work will be available to a large group of people. Judges seem to attach a lot of importance to the question whether the economic interests of the copyright

---

12 Interlibrary transactions are excluded from the scope of lending: CDPA 1988, s 18A(1).
13 Interlibrary transactions are excluded from the scope of lending: CDPA 1988, s 18A(3).
14 CDPA 1988, s 19(1) and (2).
15 CDPA 1988, s 19(3).
16 Blanket licences are available from collecting societies; see chapter 17 .

owner are harmed.[17] If the answer is positive the showing or playing will be public and will infringe. This will often be the case where everyone can gain access to the place where the showing or playing takes place, with or without payment.

When a work is performed, played or shown by means of apparatus receiving visual images or sounds which are conveyed by electronic means, the infringer will not be the person who sends the sounds or images (and the performer in case of a performance),[18] but the person who makes the arrangements for the infringing act to take place.

BROADCASTING AND INCLUDING IN A CABLE PROGRAMME SERVICE

Copyright in literary, dramatic, musical and artistic works as well as sound recordings, films, broadcasts and cable programmes is infringed when these works are broadcast or included in a cable programme service.[19] It is important to note that the exceptions to the definition of a cable programme service or broadcasts are also applicable here.[20] Inclusion in a cable programme service which does not come within the definition given in the Act will not be an infringement.

MAKING AN ADAPTATION

Making an adaptation of a literary, dramatic or musical work is also a restricted act.[1] Adaptations of artistic works are excluded. The adaptation is made when it is recorded, in writing or otherwise. Examples are the translation of a literary work into a foreign language, adapting a novel into a play or making an arrangement of a musical work. The making of an adaptation of an adaptation or doing any other restricted act to an adaptation, for example include it in a broadcast, is also an act restricted by the copyright in the work and will constitute an infringement.[2]

---

17   See *Duck v Bates* (1884) 13 QBD 843; *Ernest Turner Electrical Instruments Ltd v Performing Right Society Ltd* [1943] 1 Ch 167; see also *Performing Right Society Ltd v Harlequin Record Shops* [1979] FSR 233.
18   CDPA 1988, s 19(4).
19   CDPA 1988, s 20.
20   CDPA 1988, ss 6 and 7.
1   CDPA 1988, s 21(1).
2   CDPA 1988, s 21(2).

SECONDARY INFRINGEMENT

Copyright can also be infringed by dealing commercially with copies of works that attract copyright.[3] This is called secondary infringement because in all forms of primary infringement an infringing copy of the work is made while here these copies are only exploited commercially. The other main difference with primary infringement is found in the mental element on the infringer's side. The intention to infringe or the fact that one is infringing copyright knowingly is irrelevant for primary infringement, it is possible to infringe copyright unconsciously. This is very different in cases of secondary infringement. The alleged infringer must have had knowledge or reason to believe that his or her activity is a secondary infringement of copyright.[4] This requirement is approached objectively. It should have been obvious to the defendant that his or her activity would infringe copyright. Obviousness may be tested by taking the reasonable man approach.[5] Would it have been obvious to a reasonable man that the activity would infringe?

Knowledge of infringement proceedings is not sufficient to establish that the alleged infringer must have had knowledge or a reasonable belief that the activities would be an infringement. And setting aside money for a fighting fund does not change that. This is a logical conclusion because in certain cases the reasonable man might expect the alleged infringer to win the case.[6] On the other hand, the alleged infringer must make the reasonable man assessment in all the circumstances and cannot escape liability for secondary infringement simply by relying on a representation to the extent that no infringement is involved made by a business partner that has a self-interest in the case. In a recent case it was indeed held that a distributor of records could not rely on a representation that everything was in order, made by the recording company involved, to escape secondary infringement liability. Newspaper stories and an interlocutory injunction in a foreign court should have led any reasonable man to the obvious belief that the activity would infringe.[7]

Various types of secondary infringement in the exploitation of copies of a work are listed in the Act. All apply in relation to any kind of work that attracts copyright. Included in the list are:

---

3   CDPA 1988, ss 22–26 .
4   CDPA 1988, ss 22–26, each section *in fine*.
5   See *Infabrics Ltd v Jaytex Shirt Co* [1978] FSR 451 at 464–465, per Whitford J (a case interpreting the similar provisions of the previous Copyright Act). This approach adopted by the courts before the introduction of the new criteria in the 1988 Act will be continued. See also *LA Gear Inc v Hi-Tech Sports Plc* [1992] FSR 121.
6   *Metix (UK) Ltd v GH Maughan (Plastics) Ltd* [1997] FSR 718 and see also *Hutchison Personal Communications Ltd v Hook Advertising Ltd* [1995] FSR 365.
7   *ZYX Music GmbH v King* [1997] 2 All ER 129.

– The importation into the UK of an infringing copy of the work, if this copy is not imported for the importer's private and domestic use.[8] If we assume that a novel is translated without the consent of the copyright owner, you can import an infringing copy to read it at home, but you cannot import ten copies to sell them as exclusive pieces in your bookshop without infringing copyright.

– Possessing an infringing copy in the course of a business, selling it, letting it for hire, offering or exposing it for sale or hire, exhibiting it in public in the course of a business or otherwise to such an extent that it affects the copyright owner prejudicially.[9]

– Providing the means to make infringing copies of the work. These means, such as machines, have to be designed specifically for this purpose.[10] The double casette or video-recorder for example is not specifically designed for the purpose of copying films from one cassette to the other as it can also be used to record legally something which is not protected by copyright, but whose length exceeds the maximum recording time of one cassette.[11]

– Transmission of the work by means of a telecommunications system when it is likely that infringing copies of the work will be made due to the reception of the transmission. Broadcasting the work or including it in a cable programme service will not constitute transmission of the work for the purposes of this provision.[12]

– Permitting the use of a place of public entertainment for an infringing performance of the work. The person permitting the use of such a place will escape liability if he or she believed on reasonable grounds that the performance would not infringe copyright.[13]

– The provision of material or equipment required for the infringing performance if the person providing the material or equipment knows or has reason to believe that it will be used for an infringing performance.[14]

These provisions refer to the concept of an infringing copy of the work. This concept is defined in section 27 of the Act. An article, the making of which constituted an infringement of copyright, is an infringing copy. Articles, the making of which would have constituted an infringement of

8   CDPA 1988, s 22.
9   CDPA 1988, s 23.
10   CDPA 1988, s 24(1).
11   *CBS Songs Ltd v Amstrad Consumer Electronics plc* [1988] AC 1013, [1988] 2 All ER 484.
12   CDPA 1988, s 24(2).
13   CDPA 1988, s 25.
14   CDPA 1988, s 26.

copyright if they would have been made in the UK or a breach of an exclusive licence agreement and which have been or will be imported into the UK are also infringing copies. So are copies which are infringing copies by virtue of several provisions relating to the acts permitted in relation to copyright.[15] The latter are defences to copyright infringement and will be analysed in the next chapter.

Chapter 15

Defences to copyright infringement

Certain acts that constitute infringements of copyright on the basis of the provisions analysed in the previous chapter are permitted acts. In particular circumstances copyright will not be infringed because a defence is available, making the allegedly infringing act a permitted act. These defences exist in order to restore the balance between the rights of the owner of copyright and the rights of society at large. They restrict the exclusive rights granted by copyright in cases where it is felt they go too far. This is particularly useful as copyright is extremely wide in scope and its term of protection is long. Before we start our analysis of the permitted acts or the exceptions to copyright infringement, it has to be emphasised that these exceptions are exceptions to copyright infringement only.[1] If a case involves a breach of confidence too, the exception will not apply to the breach of confidence. The first two defences are of a general nature and are not listed in Chapter III of the Copyright, Designs and Patents Act 1988 as permitted acts.

AUTHORISATION OR CONSENT OF THE OWNER

Copyright in a work is not infringed if the owner of the copyright in the work authorised or consented to the allegedly infringing act.[2] No formal contractual licence to do these acts is required. Informal or even implied[3] licences are acceptable. An amateur musician does not infringe the copyright in a musical work when he makes a copy of it with the authorisation of the

1   CDPA 1988, s 28(1).
2   CDPA 1988, s 16(2).
3   Although the use of an implied licence may lead to problems, see *Warner v Gestetner Ltd* [1988] EIPR 89 and *Blair v Osborne and Tomkins* [1971] 2 QB 78, [1971] 1 All ER 468.

composer of the musical work who owns the copyright in it. In cases of joint ownership of copyright a licence from all the joint owners is required.[4]

PUBLIC INTEREST

If the allegedly infringing act is in the public interest this will provide a valid defence against the alleged infringement. This defence does also apply to the law of confidence, but it remains difficult to determine precisely what is in the public interest. It still is a nebulous concept.

In the copyright context the defence is often used to justify publication of information in breach of copyright and confidence in the information.[5] Especially when that information is embarrassing for someone, an attempt to use copyright to stop the publication of the information will be launched. It is submitted that the principles involved are identical to those formulated by the courts in relation to breach of confidence. We will discuss these substantially later, in Chapter 25 which deals with breach of confidence.

This is the most common aspect of the concept of public interest. It presents the concept as a defence against allegations of copyright infringement in cases where copyright information is published. There is also another aspect to it. It can be used to punish anyone who acts against the public interest and who has a copyright interest that results from that act. The public interest concept will allow the courts in such a case not to enforce that copyright and infringers will no longer be liable for copyright infringement. The concept was applied this way in the *Spycatcher* case.[6] The House of Lords held that the book's author, Peter Wright, had acted against the public interest in revealing details about the operations of the secret service, as it is in the public interest that the operations of the nation's secret service are kept secret. His conduct could harm national security. The courts in this country would as a result, or perhaps as a punishment, not enforce the copyright in his book *Spycatcher*.[7] In terms of the facts of the case everyone was free to publish substantial extracts from the book without being liable for copyright infringement. The rule can be phrased in a slightly wider way. The public interest can also be used to back positive action, rather than purely negative non-enforcement. It can be said that it is against the public interest that a convicted criminal should benefit from his or her crime and should therefore not be allowed to receive or retain profit directly derived from the commission of the crime. Copyright royalties for the

4   CDPA 1988, s 173.
5   See *Beloff v Pressdram Ltd* [1973] 1 All ER 241 at 259.
6   *A-G v Guardian Newspapers Ltd (No 2)* [1990] 1 AC 109, [1988] 3 All ER 545, see also *A-G v Times Newspapers Ltd* [1992] 1 AC 191, [1991] 2 All ER 398.
7   *A-G v Guardian Newspapers Ltd (No 2)* [1990] 1 AC 109, [1988] 3 All ER 545.

publication of a book in which the crime is desribed should therefore not be paid to the offender and the courts are authorised to use the public interest principle to grant an injunction to that extent (upon the application of the Attorney-General).[8]

Alleged infringement of copyright by the plaintiff does not warrant the operation of the public interest principle though. Here the private interest of a copyrightholder is at stake, rather than the public interest. The (alleged) infringement of the copyright of a third party by the plaintiff when he made his adaptation of the original work is therefore not a public interest defence to the infringement of the plaintiff's copyright in his adaptation by the arrangement of adaptation by the defendant of that first adaptation.[9] If the concept of originality is satisfied the author of the first adaptation will receive copyright in it, notwithstanding the fact that he may at the same time have infringed the copyright in the original work.[10] Any damages for copyright infringement that he recovers from the author of the second adaptation will have to be shared with the author of the original work.[11] The concept of public interest needs to be described narrowly.

FAIR DEALING

The Act allows fair dealing with the work that attracts copyright. This means roughly that there will be no copyright infringement if the use made of the work is fair. The defence only becomes relevant when the part taken from the work is substantial, otherwise no copying arises in the first place and any defence is without purpose.[12]

The fairness issue will have to be determined by the judge taking into account all circumstances of the case. The Act provides no definition, but restricts the defence to fair use for a number of purposes. In *Hubbard v Vosper*, a case on fair dealing for the purposes of review and criticism, Lord Denning described the scope of the fair dealing defence and how a judge should assess it when he said:

---

8   See *A-G v Chaudry* [1971] 3 All ER 938 and *A-G v Blake (Jonathan Cape Ltd, third party)* [1998] 1 All ER 833.
9   *ZYX Music GmbH v King* [1995] 3 All ER 1.
10   See also *Redwood Music Ltd* v *Chappell & Co Ltd* [1982] RPC 109 at 120.
11   *ZYX Music GmbH v King* [1995] 3 All ER 1.
12   Contra, but with respect arguably wrong. Whitford J: 'Indeed once the conclusion is reached that the whole or a substantial part of the copyright work has been taken, a defence under (the fair dealing provisions) is unlikely to succeed' in *Independent Television Publications Ltd v Time Out Ltd* [1984] FSR 64. In this view only insubstantial copying would be justified by the defence, but insubstantial copying is no infringement. It cannot be accepted that Parliament included a useless and unneeded defence in the 1988 Act.

'You must first consider the number and the extent of the quotations
... Then you must consider the use made of them. If they are used as a
basis of comment, criticism or review, that may be fair dealing. If they
are used to convey the same information as the author, for a rival purpose,
they may be unfair. Next you must consider the proportions. To take
long extracts and attach short comments may be unfair. But short extracts
and long comments may be fair. Other considerations may come to mind
also. But ... it must be a matter of impression.'[13]

There is no reason to restrict the scope of this quote to one particular
type of fair dealing, it applies to fair dealing in general. A couple of factors
are extremely important in the assessment. For which purpose was a
substantial part of the work copied? What is the proportion of the copied
part in relation to the whole work? What motive led to the copying? If the
motive was to compete with the original work, this is likely to make the
dealing with the work unfair and the defence unavailable.[14] And finally, what
is the status of the work from which a substantial part is copied? If that work
is not published or confidential the defence is unlikely to succeed. The same
conclusion is reached in case of a 'leak'.[15]

Although a number of quantitative elements are taken into account the
final assessment will be qualitative in nature. In practice this means that
depending upon the circumstances of the case the fair dealing defence may
be unavailable for someone who copies only marginally more than the
minimal substantial part of a work or may be available in the other extreme
case to someone who copies almost the whole work.

Research and private study

Fair dealing with a work may be for the purposes of research and private
study.[16] This defence applies first of all to substantial copying in relation to
literary, dramatic, musical and artistic works. It will allow me to copy a
passage of a book on the history of Crete by hand, but a problem may arise
if I use a photocopier to make the copy as the typographical arrangement
will be copied as well. Therefore, the defence applies also to typographical
arrangements. This becomes particularly relevant in cases where the work
as such is out of copyright, but the typographical arrangement is not. There
will be no infringement through the fair dealing with the published edition,

---

13   *Hubbard v Vosper* [1972] 2 QB 84 at 94, [1972] 1 All ER 1023, per Lord Denning MR.
14   *Wheatherby & Sons Ltd v International Horse Agency and Exchange Ltd* [1910] 2 Ch 297.
15   *British Oxygen Co Ltd v Liquid Air Ltd* [1925] Ch 383 and *Beloff v Pressdram Ltd* [1973]
      1 All ER 241, [1973] RPC 765, [1973] FSR 33.
16   CDPA 1988, s 29.

indirectly affecting the copyright in the typographical arrangement, nor will there be infringement through fair dealing with the typographical arrangement itself.[17]

The research involved may be commercial or industrial in nature, but in these cases other elements need to demonstrate the fairness of such use convincingly. If the purpose of the commercial research is for example to produce a competing work, the defence will not be available.[18] On the other hand the publication in breach of copyright of a student textbook was held not to be fair dealing for the purposes of research and private study.[19] This book involved substantial copying to facilitate someone else's research and private study, the defendant itself not being involved in research or private study. This does not mean that the researcher or student has to make his or her own copies though, but the person who makes the copies should not know or have reason to believe that the copying will result in copies of substantially the same material being provided to more than one person at substantially the same time and for substantially the same purpose.[20]

It is submitted that even the copying of a fairly large part of a work can amount to fair dealing with the work for the purposes of research and private study. Very large parts of books and eventually whole articles may be copied if the number of them needed for one's research and private study in combination with the limited direct use of the information contained in them for the purposes of that research and private study makes it unpracticable to buy all books and to subscribe to all the periodicals containing these articles. The situation will be entirely different when one book is used and a photocopy is made where it would still be possible to buy a copy of the book (at a slightly higher price). In the latter case the dealing with the book would be unfair. The defence clearly aims to facilitate research and private study. Copyright should not become a financial and practical obstructing factor for research and private study. There needs to be a balance between the interests of copyright owners and society in the well functioning of the copyright system and the interest of society for its development in research and private study of its members.

Review and criticism

Fair dealing for the purpose of review and criticism applies to any form of work or to a performance of a work.[1] Copyright will not be infringed if a

---

17   CDPA 1988, s 29(1) and (2).
18   See *Independent Television Publications Ltd v Time Out Ltd* [1984] FSR 64 (a case on fair dealing for the purposes of review and criticism).
19   *Sillitoe v McGraw-Hill Book Co (UK) Ltd* [1983] FSR 545.
20   CDPA 1988, s 29(3).
1   CDPA 1988, s 30(1).

sufficient acknowledgment,[2]comprising the title, or another description, of the work and the identification of the author, is given.[3] The identification has to be to the audience and any wording or other indication that would make the reasonably alert member of the audience realise that the person that is indentified is the author of the work will be sufficient.[4] It is fair to deal with one work in order to criticise another work or a performance of the work. There is no requirement that parts of only the work that is reviewed or criticised should be used. This book can be reviewed or criticised using parts and quotes from other textbooks on intellectual property. On the other hand there is a requirement that the dealing with a work should be for the purposes of review and criticism, be it of the subject-matter of the work or of its style. The defence does not cover those cases where only ideas, doctrine, philosophy and events contained in the work are criticised. Laddie J repeated this in the *Pro Sieben* case when he ruled that '[t]he Act does not provide a general defence to the effect that it is permissible to fairly deal in any copyright work for the purpose of criticising or reviewing that work or anything else[;] the defence is limited to criticising or reviewing that or another work or a performance of a work'.[5] In *Pro Sieben* the plaintiffs, Pro Sieben, had conducted an interview with Mandy Allwood and her boyfriend about Ms Allwood's decision to carry on with her pregnancy after it had been revealed that she was carrying eight live embryos, and a TV programme had resulted from this. The defendants copied parts of the German TV programme and included it in one of their own programmes. It was held that the defendants could not rely on the fair dealing defence to justify their copying, because their programme did not criticise or review the Pro Sieben programme, but rather Pro Sieben's decision to pay for an interview. Similarly, when the *Sun* newspaper copied and published a photograph of Princess Caroline of Monaco without having obtained the prior authorisation of the photographer, Mr Banier, they could not successfully invoke the defence. The photograph was not used to illustrate any review or criticism of the copyright work (ie the photograph itself).[6] The aim of the defence is to give a critic or a reviewer a reasonable freedom of quotation or copying for the purpose of criticism or review. This means that one has to take the state of the reviewer or critic's mind at the time of the alleged infringement into account, while the effect of the derivative work on the audience is irrelevant for this purpose.[7] The dealing

---

2   See *Sillitoe v McGraw-Hill Book Co (UK) Ltd* [1983] FSR 545.
3   Ibid, and see also CDPA 1988, s 178; there is no need to include the name of the author if the work is published anonymously (see *PCR Ltd v Dow Jones Telerate Ltd* [1998] FSR 170) or if the name of the author cannot be ascertained by reasonable enquiry.
4   *Pro Sieben Media AG v Carlton UK Television Ltd* [1998] FSR 43.
5   Ibid.
6   *Banier v News Group Newspapers Ltd* [1997] FSR 812.
7   Ibid and *Pro Sieben Media AG v Carlton UK Television Ltd* [1998] FSR 43.

with the work must also be fair, even in those cases where the reviewer or critic had the right state of mind in that he intended to deal with the work for the purposes of review or criticism. This does not mean that the judge should decide whether the criticism or the review is fair, but it does mean that the extent of the copying must be fair in all the circumstances to support or illustrate the criticisms or the review. The dealing or copying must be directed at supporting or illustrating the review or criticism. The defence cannot justify any other dealing with the work or any dealing with the work that goes further. However, the examination of this point should not involve a requirement for the defendant to demonstrate that no alternative way to review or criticise the work was available.[8]

Thus this defence will not apply in cases of copying where there is no review or criticism or where there is only review and criticism to a minimal extent. It is not fair dealing with the correspondence between the Duke and Duchess of Windsor when extracts are published without review or criticism.[9] The defence covers any type of review or criticism, from the most polite and laudatory forms to the most scathing ones.

If the defence is to have any proper value it has to apply to cases where the review and criticism involve a substantial part of a work. In *Hubbard v Vosper* substantial parts of confidential as well as non-confidential works, such as books and letters, written by the plaintiff were used in a book written by the defendant who was an ex-member of the cult of Scientology. The book was highly critical of the cult and reviewed and criticised its views. The defence of fair use for the purpose of review and criticism was raised successfully against the alleged copyright infringement.[10] The proportion of the work which can be taken may be large, but review and criticism do not require such large amounts of the work to be taken as what is possible for the purpose of research and private study.[11] Recently further clarification on this point was provided by the *Time Warner v Channel 4* case.[12] Channel 4 wished to use fragments from Stanley Kubrick's notorious film *A Clockwork Orange* in an arts documentary. Time Warner had withdrawn the film from British theatres 20 years ago at the request of the director himself and was not prepared to give Channel 4 a licence to show the fragments. When Channel 4 proceeded without a licence they obtained an injunction which was lifted by the Court of Appeal which accepted that Channel 4 were engaging in fair dealing for the purpose of the review and

---

8   *Pro Sieben Media AG v Carlton UK Television Ltd* [1998] FSR 43.
9   *Associated Newspapers Group plc v News Group Newspapers Ltd* [1986] RPC 515.
10 [1972] 2 QB 84, [1972] 1 All ER 1023.
11 See *Hubbard v Vosper* [1972] 2 QB 84, [1972] 1 All ER 1023 and *Walter v Steinkopff* [1892] 3 Ch 489.
12 *Time Warner Entertainments Company v Channel 4 Television plc* (1993) Independent, 23 October (Court of Appeal, 22 October 1993), [1994] EMLR 1.

criticism defence. In this case the fragments shown by Channel 4 amounted to almost 10% of the film. It is submitted that this high percentage of allowed copying under the defence was reached because of the very large amount and high quality of review and criticism equally included in the programme and the fact that a documentary is particularly suited for review and criticism. But it gives an impression of how far reaching the defence can potentially be.

The defence includes fair dealing with a work in order to report current events. Copyright will not be infringed unless the work is a photograph. Newspapers quite often copy stories published 24 hours earlier by another newspaper. This is covered by the defence, but without copyright permission they will not be able to copy the photograph accompanying the story. A sufficient acknowledgment is required.[13] Due to practical problems and the speed at which these media work an acknowledgment is not required in connection with the reporting of current events by means of a sound recording, film, broadcast or cable programme.[14] It is hard to understand why the special treatment accorded to photographs should not be applied to broadcasts and films. The definition of the concept of current events is an important issue in this respect. That concept must include all matters of current interest or concern, as opposed to matters of historical interest or concern. On top of that the concept should be construed liberally and the fair use of copyright material cannot be restricted, for example, to the reporting of news events that are less than 24 hours old.[15] In a case where the defendant copied substantial parts of the plaintiff's reports of the current status of cacao crops around the world[16] the defendant could argue that the following points came within the concept of current events: the fact that the reports had been published, the broad substance of the reports and the impact of the reports on the market. The defendant could copy parts of the reports to report these issues. But once more the nature and the extent of the copying should not go beyond what is reasonable and appropriate to report these current events. The latter decision is ultimately one of impression. In the cacoa reports case it was held that the copying of the full pod count report went beyond what is fair dealing to report the current events as described above. In this case the concept of fair dealing involved a balancing of the interests of the owner of the copyright and those of the news reporter.[17]

---

13   CDPA 1988, s 30(2).

14   CDPA 1988, s 30(3). See *BBC v British Satellite Broadcasting Ltd* [1992] Ch 141, [1991] 3 All ER 833.

15   *Pro Sieben Media AG v Carlton UK Television Ltd* [1998] FSR 43.

16   *PCR Ltd v Dow Jones Telerate Ltd* [1998] FSR 170.

17   CDPA 1988, s 36A.

INCIDENTAL INCLUSION

When a foreign tourist visits London and takes some photographs it is almost inevitable that at least one of the photographs will include a work protected by copyright, such as a building, an artistic work or just the front page of a newspaper. The same applies when a television news crew films a demonstration in the City and the report is broadcast. It is not feasible to require that on each of these occasions copyright permission is obtained in advance or it would be impossible to make these photographs, films and broadcasts. The Act gets around this problem by introducing a rule that copyright in a work which is accidentally included in an artistic work, a sound recording, a film, a broadcast or a cable programme will not be infringed.[18]

Subsequent dealings with the work in which another work was accidentally included are exempted as well.[19] Copies can be issued to the public, the work can be shown or played, it can be broadcast or included in a cable programme service. The film made in the City can be broadcast and can be included in a cable programme service without infringing indirectly the copyright in the works accidentally included in it.

The inclusion must be accidental. This defence will not be available if a work is included deliberately. If we go back to our news crew, they may decide to add some background music to the soundtrack of their film. The background music will not be included accidentally and if the copying through the inclusion is substantial copyright in the musical work will be infringed if no advance copyright permission was obtained. The latter rule applies to all musical works, lyrics and all works embodying them.[20] In *Hawkes & Sons (London) Ltd v Paramount Film Service Ltd*[1] copyright infringement took place and the accidental inclusion defence did not apply because the 28 bars of the march 'Colonel Bogey' were included deliberately in the newsreel as background music. The outcome of the case would have been different if the newsreel's topic had been a parade by a band playing the march. Then the inclusion of part of the march, recorded live during the parade together with the images, would have been accidental.

18   CDPA 1988, s 31(1).
19   CDPA 1988, s 31(2).
20   CDPA 1988, s 31(3) .
1   [1934] Ch 593.

■

EDUCATIONAL USE[2]

Instruction and examination

Copyright will not be infringed if a literary, dramatic, artistic or musical work or a substantial part of any of them is copied in the course of instruction or while preparing instruction if two preconditions are met. The copying must be done by the person giving instruction or the person receiving instruction and it may not be done by means of a reprographic process.[3] When a student writes down a substantial part of a legal article in his essay in support of his or her own point of view, copyright in the article as a literary work will not be infringed. Neither will it be infringed when a lecturer writes down the same quote on his whiteboard for discussion with the students during a tutorial.

In the same circumstances copies of a sound recording, a film, a broadcast or a cable programme can be made in making a film or soundtrack for the purpose of instruction, without infringing copyright.[4]

In an exam situation copyright will not be infringed by anything done in setting the questions, communicating them to the students or answering them.[5] The question can thus contain a large quote taken from a literary work before asking students to analyse it and comment on it. The only exception to this rule is the making of reprographical copies of a musical work which is to be performed by the students during the examination.[6] Here copyright permission is required.

This educational exception does not cover any subsequent dealings in the copies made for educational use. Copyright will be infringed when they are sold, let for hire, or offered or exposed for sale or hire.[7] A poem may be copied for the purpose of setting an exam question, but the subsequent sale of the exam paper containing the poem will infringe the copyright in the poem.

Anthologies

Short passages of published literary and dramatic works may be included in a book which consists of a collection of passages, mainly taken from works

---

2   See Copyright (Educational Establishments) (No 2) Order 1989.
3   CDPA 1988, s 32(1).
4   CDPA 1988, s 32(2).
5   CDPA 1988, s 32(3).
6   CDPA 1988, s 32(4).
7   CDPA 1988, s 32(5).

which are not or no longer protected by copyright. The book, called an anthology, has to be clearly intended for educational use.[8]

Performing, playing or showing a work

Literary, dramatic and musical works can be shown, played or performed at an educational establishment without infringing copyright. This can either be done by the students and teachers in the course of the activities of the educational establishment or by a third person in the course of instruction. Students, teachers and other persons directly connected with the activities of the establishment may form part of the audience.[9] Parents and any other persons that are only connected indirectly to the activities of the educational establishment may not form part of the audience.[10] School plays to which parents are invited will require copyright permission to perform the work.

Copyright will not be infringed either if a sound recording, film, broadcast or cable programme is played or shown before a similar audience as long as the event takes place at the educational institution for the purposes of instruction.[11]

Recording, reprographic copying[12] and lending

An educational establishment[13] may record for educational purposes and for its own use broadcasts and cable programmes.[14] Under the same preconditions they can copy reprographically, in practice with a photocopier, passages of published works. The latter copying is restricted to one per cent of each work per term.[15]

---

8   CDPA 1988, s 33(1).
9   CDPA 1988, s 34(1).
10 CDPA 1988, s 34(3).
11 CDPA 1988, s 34(2).
12 See Copyright (Certification of Licensing Scheme for Educational Recording of Broadcast and Cable Programmes) (Educational Recording Agency Limited) Order 1990, SI 1990/879; Copyright (Certification of Licensing Scheme for Educational Recording of Broadcast and Cable Programmes) (Educational Recording Agency Limited) (Amendment) Order 1993, SI 1993/193; Copyright (Certification of Licensing Scheme for Educational Recording of Broadcasts) (Open University Educational Enterprises Limited) Order 1993, SI 1993/2755; Copyright (Certification of Licensing Scheme for Educational Recording of Broadcast and Cable Programmes) (Educational Recording Agency Limited) (Amendment) Order 1994, SI 1994/247.
13 As defined in CDPA 1988, s 174.
14 CDPA 1988, s 35(1).
15 CDPA 1988, s 36(1) and (2).

■

If the educational institution stays within the framework of these two exceptions copyright in the recorded or copied works will not be infringed. But these two exceptions have two further aspects in common. Copyright will be infringed if the authorised recordings and copies are subsequently dealt with and both exceptions can in practice be superseded by a licensing scheme allowing the educational institutions to make recordings and reprographic copies subject to certain conditions.[16]

There is also a special exception to the lending right of copyright owners. Lending of copies of the work by an educational establishment[17] will not infringe the copyright in the work.

LIBRARIES, ARCHIVES AND PUBLIC ADMINISTRATION

Further exceptions to copyright infringement are provided for the benefit of libraries, archives and public administration.[18] We will only refer generally to a couple of these detailed exceptions. None of the acts specified underneath will give rise to copyright infringement.

The exceptions for libraries and archives only apply to those libraries and archives that are prescribed by statutory instrument.[19] A librarian can make one copy of an article in a periodical for a person who requires it for the purposes of research and private study. It is essential that no person is supplied with more than one copy of the article at the same time[20] and that not more than one article from the same issue of the periodical is supplied.[1] Under the same conditions librarians can copy part of a published edition of a literary, dramatic or musical work.[2] The person supplied with the copies must pay the costs. The readers of this book will all be familiar with the system of inter-library loans and will recognise the legal basis for this system and the particular format of the copyright declaration accompanying them. The librarian or archivist may rely on the contents of the declaration. If the declaration is false, the person making the declaration will have infringed the copyright in the work of which he obtained copies, as if he made them himself, and the copies will be infringing copies.

The lending of copies of a work by libraries or archives is also subject to a special regime.[3] The copyright in any work is not infringed by the lending

---

16   CDPA 1988, ss 35 and 36.
17   Ibid.
18   CDPA 1988, ss 37 to 50.
19   See Copyright (Librarian Archivists) (Copying of Copyright Material) Regulations 1989, SI 1989/1212.
20   Multiple copies are banned by the Act.
1   CDPA 1988, s 38.
2   CDPA 1988, s 39.
3   CDPA 1988, s 40A.

of a book that is within the public lending right scheme if the lending takes place through a public library. Copyright in a work is not infringed either through the lending of copies of the work by a prescribed library or archive[4] if that lending is not conducted for profit.

Librarians can also supply each other with copies of articles in periodicals or, if the identity of the person who can authorise the copying is unknown and cannot be ascertained by reasonable enquiry, the whole or part of a published edition of a literary, dramatic or musical work.[5] Copies can also be made to replace copies of works which have been lost, destroyed or damaged or to preserve the original.[6] The latter will only be possible if it is not reasonably practicable to buy another copy of the work.[7]

Acts done for the purposes of public administration will not infringe copyright. In copyright infringement cases copies of the respective works can be made in the course of the proceedings, judicial proceedings can be reported,[8] entries in the Trade Marks Register can be copied, etc.

MISCELLANEOUS

Copyright infringement does not occur if buildings, or sculptures, works of artistic craftsmanship or models for buildings which are permanently situated in a public place or premises open to the public, are photographed. One may also make a graphic work of them, ie a drawing or painting, film them and include a visual image of them in a broadcast or a cable programme service.[9]

When artistic works are put up for sale copies made for advertising purposes will not infringe the copyright in the artistic work. This will only occur if the copies are subsequently dealt with for other purposes,[10] for example if they are sold themselves.

The reconstruction of a building will not involve an infringement of the copyright that exists in the building or in the plans for the building.[11]

Video recorders are quite useful if you want to watch a broadcast or a cable programme that is emitted when you have something else to do or when you are not at home. You let the video recorder do its work and you can watch it any time you want. There is only one small problem; you have recorded the broadcast or cable programme and your activity may infringe

4   Other than a public library.
5   CDPA 1988, s 41.
6   Which may be particularly valuable or fragile.
7   CDPA 1988, s 42.
8   Obviously this does not cover the copying of published reports of judicial proceedings.
9   CDPA 1988, s 62; copies may also be issued to the public.
10 CDPA 1988, s 63.
11 CDPA 1988, s 65.

copyright. The Act solves this problem by allowing anyone to record a broadcast or cable programme for private and domestic use if this recording is made for the purpose of time shifting.[12] In other words the recording may only be made if it is made in order to view the broadcast or cable programme at a (more) convenient time. Only in these particular circumstances is the recording exempted.

If anything done to an adaptation is excepted on the basis of the provisions analysed above, the copyright in the original work will not be infringed either.[13]

COPYRIGHT INFRINGEMENT AND DEFENCES: AN OVERVIEW

Once we have ascertained that copyright does subsist in the work we examine the allegedly infringing act:

- Is it a restricted act, such as copying?
- Has the act been done to a substantial part of the work? Only if these two questions are answered affirmatively can there potentially be infringement.

There will nevertheless be no infringement if any of the next stages of our examination receives a positive answer:

- Did the owner of the copyright in the work authorise the act or consent to it, be it expressly or impliedly?
- Is the copyright infringement in the public interest?
- Is the act covered by any of the permitted acts?

Only a negative answer to these three further questions will allow us to conclude that the copyright in the work has been infringed.

---

12   CDPA 1988, s 70.
13   CDPA 1988, s 76.

Chapter 16

Rights in performances

THE PROBLEM

Luciano Pavarotti adores live performances in front of mass audiences. Imagine him performing, live at Wembley, a series of songs taken from Gaetano Donizetti's famous opera *Lucia di Lammermoor*. Someone in the audience makes a bootleg recording of Pavarotti's performance and sells it to a record company other than Decca, with whom Pavarotti has a recording contract. There is very little that can be done on the basis of the copyright rules described above. Donizetti died in 1848, the copyright in the music and the libretto have long expired. The Decca recording is not copied or dealt with, the bootleg recording is an entirely separate and independent recording. No copyright infringement can be found and both Pavarotti as the performer and Decca as the recording company are left unprotected.

This was felt to be undesirable as both performers and recording companies[1] make a substantial contribution and would be less inclined to do so if they are unable to secure a proper return for their contribution. Apart from the financial implications the performer contributes to the artistic value of the work in bringing it to life and the recording company's entrepreneurial investment is considerable. To remedy the absence of protection for these groups under traditional copyright rules the Convention for the Protection of Performers, Producers of Phonograms and Broadcasting Organisations was concluded in Rome in 1961. Before the Copyright, Designs and Patents Act 1988 entered into force the old rules[2]

1 See Boytha 'The Intellectual Property Status of Sound Recordings' (1993) 24 IIC 295-306.
2 See the Dramatic and Musical Performer's Protection Act 1925, the Dramatic and Musical Performer's Protection Act 1958, the Performer's Protection Act 1963 and the Performer's Protection Act 1972; criminal penalties were made available.

in the UK tried to offer some protection. The performers were given a right to civil remedies on top of the statutory criminal penalties in *Rickless v United Artists Corpn.*[3] The defendant took clips and discarded excerpts from old Pink Panther films starring the late Peter Sellers to make a new film without obtaining the permission of the actor's executors. The Court of Appeal argued that the statutory provision of criminal penalties created an obligation or prohibition for the benefit of the performers. Any aggrieved performer thus had a cause of action. The same Court of Appeal felt obliged however to deny similar civil remedies to a recording company that wished to act against the making of a bootleg recording.[4] Effective protection is only achievable when the interested parties can enforce their rights themselves and have access to civil remedies. The old system could not provide that in all cases. It was replaced by Part II of the Copyright, Designs and Patents Act 1988.[5]

SUBSISTENCE OF RIGHTS

Rights in performances are given to the performers and to the person who has recording rights in relation to the performance. A performance in this context means a live performance by one person or a group of persons. It can be a musical performance, such as Pavarotti's performance in our example, a dramatic performance, dance or mime. It can also be the reading or recitation of a literary work, a performance of a variety act or a similar presentation.[6] This definition is extremely wide in scope. The consent of the performer or performers of such a performance is required for any exploitation of the performance.[7]

No film or sound recording can be made of a performance without the consent of the performer or the person having recording rights in relation to the performance. The latter will have an exclusive recording contract, such as the one Pavarotti has with Decca, under which he alone has the right to make the recording. The Act covers recordings made directly from the live performance, recordings made from a broadcast of, or a cable programme including, the performance as well as any recording made, directly or indirectly, from another recording of the performance.[8] Once again this is a definition which is very wide in scope.

3   *Rickless v United Artists Corpn* [1988] QB 40, [1987] 1 All ER 679.
4   *RCA Corpn v Pollard* [1983] Ch 135, [1982] 3 All ER 771.
5   For a detailed analysis see R Arnold *Performer's Rights* Sweet & Maxwell (2nd edn, 1997).
6   CDPA 1988, s 180(2).
7   CDPA 1988, s 180(1).
8   CDPA 1988, ss 180(1), 180(2) and 185(1).

TERM OF PROTECTION

These rights in performances come on top of the rights conferred by copyright and they are independent rights[9] which expire after a 50-year term. The rights in the performance expire normally 50 years after the end of the calendar year in which the performance to which they relate took place. But if a recording of the performance is lawfully released during this normal 50-year period the rule changes and the rights shall only expire 50 years after the end of the calendar year in which the first release of the recording of the performance took place.[10] The concept of release includes the first publication, showing or playing in public, broadcasting or inclusion in a cable programme service of a recording. Unauthorised acts cannot be taken into account to determine whether or not a recording has been released or to determine the date of release.[11] These rules are different from the normal ones in copyright which refer to the life of the author. Here no reference is made to the life of the performer. On the other hand, the restriction of the term of protection to the one offered in the country of which the performer is a national for performers who are not nationals of a European Economic Area state shows strong similarities with the copyright comparison of term regime.[12]

If we go back to Pavarotti's Wembley performance, his performer's right will expire 50 years after the end of the year in which the concert takes place. The situation changes when Decca makes a lawful recording of the concert. This constitutes a fixation of the performance and, assuming that no other communication to the public takes place, Pavarotti's performer's right will expire 50 years after the end of the year in which the recording was released. Decca's recording right expires 50 years after the end of the year in which the recording of the performance is released, assuming that the recording will be released before the period of 50 years from the end of the year in which the performance that was recorded took place expires.

THE QUALIFICATION REQUIREMENT

The qualification requirement also exists for rights in performances.[13] The performance must be a qualifying performance, ie a performance given in a qualifying country or by a person who is a citizen or a subject of such a

9 CDPA 1988, s 180(4).
10 CDPA 1988, s 191(2).
11 CDPA 1988, s 191(3).
12 The new term can only be shorter than the one put in place by s 191(2), CDPA 1998; see CDPA 1988, s 191(4).
13 CDPA 1988, s 181.

■

qualifying country. A country qualifies if it offers reciprocal protection.[14]
The UK, the other member states of the European Union, and some other
countries designated by Order in Council are qualifying countries, but the
complete list is much shorter because the Rome Convention for the
Protection of Performers, Producers of Phonograms and Broadcasting
Organisations has only been adhered to by approximately one-third of the
states that adhere to the Berne Convention. This weakens the international
protection for rights in performances, performers and recorders.

CONTENT AND INFRINGEMENT

The content of the intangible right in a performance is best examined by
means of the list of those acts that will constitute an infringement of the
right. In general the rights in performances are infringed whenever a
performance is exploited without the consent of the performer or whenever
the performance is recorded without the consent of the person who owns
the exclusive recording right. The consent of the owners of the rights in
the performance is essential.[15] Helpfully consent given in respect of one
particular use does not mean that no consent is given for any other use unless
there are special indications that further consent was required.[16]

The performer's right is infringed when certain acts are done to the whole
or a substantial part of the performance. Within the scope of these acts fall:

–   making a recording of the live performance[17] which is not exclusively
    for private and domestic use;[18]
–   broadcasting the performance live or including it live in a cable
    programme service;[19]
–   making, otherwise than for private and domestic use, either directly
    or indirectly,[20] a copy of a recording of the performance[1] (this is the
    reproduction right[2]);

---

14   CDPA 1988, ss 206–208.
15   CDPA 1988, see s 197.
16   See *Grower v British Broadcasting Corporation* [1990] FSR 595, consent given for the
     broadcasting of a recording of a performance in a radio programme does not exclude
     consent for other use of the recording in the absence of special indications to the contrary.
17   CDPA 1988, s 182(1)(a).
18   CDPA 1988, s 182(2).
19   CDPA 1988, s 182(1)(b).
20   CDPA 1988. s 182A(2).
1   CDPA 1988, s 182A(1).
2   CDPA 1988, s 182A(3).

- issuing copies or the original[3] of a recording of the performance to the public[4] (this is the distribution right[5]);
- renting or lending copies of a recording of the performance to the public;[6]
- making a recording of the performance directly from a broadcast of, or a cable programme including, the live performance;[7]
- showing a recording of the performance in public, broadcasting it or including it in a cable programme service;[8]
- importing into the UK an illicit recording of the performance if the person importing it knows it is an infringing copy or has reason to believe that;[9]
- possessing in the course of business, selling or letting for sale, offering or exposing for sale or hire, or distributing an illicit recording of the performance if the person importing it knows it is an infringing copy or has reason to believe that.[10]

The performer is also given a right to equitable remuneration for the exploitation of a sound recording of the whole or of a substantial part of the performance.[11] This remuneration is to be paid by the owner of the copyright in the commercially published sound recording when it is played in public or when it is included in a broadcast or a cable programme service. The determination of the exact amount payable is to be determined in negotiations between the parties and in default of agreement the amount will be determined by the Copyright Tribunal. The right to equitable remuneration cannot be assigned, except to a collecting society that will enforce the right on behalf of the rightholder.[12]

The rights of a person who has the exclusive recording right of a performance are infringed when the same acts are done to the whole or a substantial part of the performance, but the person having recording rights

---

3   CDPA 1988, s 182B(4).
4   CDPA 1988, s 182B(1). Issuing to the public is defined in ss 182B(2) and (3). It includes exclusively 'the act of putting into circulation in the EEA copies not previously put into circulation in the EEA by or with the consent of the performer' or 'the act of putting into circulation outside the EEA copies not previously put into circulation in the EEA or elsewhere'.
5   CDPA 1988, s 182B(5).
6   CDPA 1988, s 182C, rental and lending are defined in the section.
7   CDPA 1988, s 182(1)(c).
8   CDPA 1988, s 183.
9   CDPA 1988, s 184(1)(a).
10 CDPA 1988, s 184(1)(b).
11 CDPA 1988, s 182D.
12 Ibid.

■

is not given the rights of reproduction, distribution, rental and lending.[13] There is one further exception to this rule that his rights are similar to those of the performer. The recording rights are not infringed by a live broadcast of the performance or by the live inclusion of the performance in a cable programme service.[14] One could argue that this does not involve the recording of the performance, nor any dealings with illicit copies.

These lists contain forms of primary and secondary infringement and bear similarities with the regime for normal copyright infringement.

DEFENCES AGAINST ALLEGED INFRINGEMENTS

The defences available are very similar to those available in cases of alleged copyright infringement. They are contained in Schedule 2 to the Copyright, Designs and Patents Act 1988: review and criticism, reporting current events,[15] educational use (slightly less extensive), incidental inclusion, public administration, etc. It has to be noted that there is no exception for research and private study.

THE NATURE OF THE PERFORMER'S RIGHTS AND THEIR TRANSFER

Two types of rights are given to the performer. Some rights are property rights and others are non-property rights. The reproduction right, the distribution right and the rental and lending right fall in the first category. They are the performer's property rights.[16] These property rights can be assigned and they are transmissible just as any other item of personal or moveable property. Just as any other assignment, this type of assignment can be partial and needs to be in writing and signed by or on behalf of the assignor.[17] Normally such an assigment cannot be presumed. However, the Act contains an exception to this rule. This exception operates where an agreement concerning film production is concluded between a performer and a film producer. To avoid a situation in which too many persons, each of whom has made a small contribution to the film, need to give their approval for the exploitation of the film, the performer shall be presumed

---

13   These will nevertheless exist in relation to the copyright in the sound recording (or film) that results from the exercise of the recording right. In practice the owners of these various rights will often be the same persons.
14   CDPA 1988, ss 185-188.
15   These three defences do not seem to require a sufficient acknowledgment, at least in cases where it is not required by copyright itself.
16   CDPA 1988, s 191A.
17   CDPA 1988, s 191B.

to have transferred to the producer any rental right in relation to the film. That rental right would arise due to the inclusion of the recording of the performer's performance in the film. The presumption is overturned in case the agreement provides to the contrary.[18] In any event, the performer retains always a right to equitable remuneration when he has transferred his rental rights concerning a sound recording or a film to the producer of the latter works.[19]

Secondly, the performer is also given certain non-property rights.[20] The rights granted by sections 182 to 184 CDPA 1988 are included in this category, which comprise all rights that are not specifically listed as property rights. The non-property rights in performances are normally not assignable or transmissible.[1] But the right given to the performer is transmissible *ex mortem* , by testamentary disposition or otherwise, and the exclusive recording licence, as the benefit of the rights in the performance, can be assigned, eg from one recording company to another.[2]

FUTURE DEVELOPMENTS

At the international level the Rome Convention of 1961, on which the rights in performances are based, never attracted the level of support that is enjoyed by the Berne Convnetion in the copyright area. WIPO tried to remedy this lack of international recognition for rights in performances. That attempt resulted on 20 December 1996 in the signing of the WIPO Performances and Phonograms Treaty. This treaty offers enhanced levels of international protection and it is hoped that its link with the Berne Convention will convince the vast majority of countries to sign up to it and ratify it. When it comes into force, the performer will be given inalienable moral rights. In the case of live preformances and performances fixed in phonograms performers will be given the right to be identified and the right of integrity. In addition the Treaty provides for enhanced protection at the level of the economic rights. These will include an exclusive right to authorise or prohibit reproduction, communication to the public, rental and distribution of performances and their recordings.[3] Most elements of the Treaty are to be transposed into EU law through the draft European Parliament and Council Directive on the harmonisation of certain aspects

---

18   CDPA 1988, s 191F.
19   CDPA 1988, s 191G.
20   CDPA 1988, s 192A.
1   Ibid and CDPA 1988, s 192B.
2   CDPA 1988, s 192A(2), s 192B(2) and s 185(2)(b) and (3)(b).
3   See R Arnold *Performer's Rights* Sweet & Maxwell (2nd edn, 1997) at 33-34 and Reinbothe, Martin-Prat and von Lewinski 'The New WIPO Treaties: A First Resumé' [1997] 4 EIPR 171.

of copyright and related rights in the information society.[4] After its adoption at Community level, the Directive will in turn be transposed into national law by each of the member states. It might take a couple more years before the UK will put the provisions of the WIPO Performances and Phonograms Treaty into operation.

4   COM(97) 628 final, dated 10 December 1997.

Chapter 17

Dealing in copyright

CROWN COPYRIGHT

It is clear in principle that works made by Her Majesty or by officers or servants of the Crown will attract copyright if they come within the normal copyright rules described above. The 1988 Act contains a few special provisions though in relation to Crown copyright. These rules apply to works made by Her Majesty and, if the works are made in the course of his or her duties, works made by an officer or servant of the Crown.[1] It is clear that the Crown will own the copyright in these works.[2] If no special rules exist, the normal copyright rules apply. A first rule affects literary, dramatic, musical and artistic works. The term of copyright protection for such a work is 125 years from the end of the calendar year in which they were made if the work is not published commercially.[3] The term of copyright protection is however reduced to the more standard 50-year term if the work is published commercially during the first 75 years of the 125-year term. This reduced 50-year term, which the UK may in due course decide to harmonise with the new standard term of 70 years, starts running from the end of the calendar year in which first commercial publication took place.[4] As we know, commercial publication is defined by the 1988 Act as

> 'issuing copies to the public at a time when copies made in advance of the receipt of orders are generally available to the public [or] making the work available by means of an electronic retrieval system'.[5]

1   CDPA 1988, s 163.
2   CDPA 1988, s 163(1)(b).
3   CDPA 1988, s 163(3)(a).
4   CDPA 1988, s 163(3)(b).
5   CDPA 1988, s 175(2).

■

Most works which are protected by Crown copyright will be published as soon as they are created. In practice the 50-year term therefore seems to be the rule rather than the 125-year term.

Acts of Parliament and Measures of the General Synod of the Church of England present us with another copyright particularity. They will attract copyright protection, owned by Her Majesty, for a 50-year term which will start running from the end of the calendar year in which they received Royal Assent.[6] Parliamentary copyright is copyright in works which are made by or under the direction or control of the House of Commons or the House of Lords. They will own the copyright in the works so produced. In general these works are subject to the normal copyright rules, but the term of protection for literary, dramatic, musical or artistic works is 50 years from the end of the calendar year in which the work was made.[7] In these categories we find works such as reports of select committees, only Parliamentary Bills are catered for separately. Copyright in them will expire when they receive the Royal Assent,[8] when they are rejected or withdrawn at the end of the session.[9]

COMMERCIAL EXPLOITATION OF COPYRIGHT IN THE UK

Copyright, as a form of intellectual property, has the same kind of commercial value as any other property right. Its contracual exploitation can take various forms, such as a sale or a more restricted right to do something in relation to the subject matter of the right. Authors can exploit their works themselves, but they may not be interested in doing so. Often they do not have the financial, material and organisational means to exploit their works or to exploit them efficiently. They can then leave the exploitation to a third party. This normally involves the transfer of some or all rights in the work to that third party.[10] Some aspects of copyright are slightly peculiar though. First of all, exploitation of copyright takes place through a material item in which the work is recorded. This implies that if one acquires that material item, one does not normally acquire the intellectual property right as well. If I buy a book, as a recording of a literary work, I buy the paper and the ink, but not the copyright in the book or any right in relation to the copyright, such as the right to reproduce the work. This separation between the copyright and the right in the carrier is a special characteristic of intellectual property rights. Second, copyright works are normally still created by an individual author or by a couple of individuals.

6   CDPA 1988, s 164.
7   CDPA 1988, s 165.
8   The copyright in the Act commences at this point.
9   CDPA 1988, s 166.
10 On the economic importance of the exploitation of copyright see Cohen Jehoram 'Critical Reflections on the Economic Importance of Copyright' (1989) 20 IIC 485–497.

They will normally rely on a third party to exploit their work and that third party is often a corporate body. This results in the fact that the balance of bargaining and negotiating powers tilts almost necessarily in favour of the party exploiting the work, while the author is left behind as the weaker party. Third, copyright offers only a weak form of protection as only the reproduction of expression is protected. This leaves the idea of the work unprotected and leaves the author powerless to act against various things that can be done to his work, such as the production of a satirical work which clearly through the borrowing of the idea refers to the author's work. This reinforces the view that the author is in a weak position.

In the UK we are historically not too bothered about this, as we see copyright as an entrepreneurial right which primarily protects the interests of the person who exploits the work. In contrast continental copyright emphasised the role of the artist, the creator of the copyright work. The focus on moral rights is a good example of this emphasis on the artist. Now we have seen the introduction of moral rights in the 1988 Act in the UK and we see the European Union develop initiatives in the copyright area. Have we therefore arrived at a compromise? It is submitted that the use of the word compromise is misleading in this context, as it implies that concessions were made on both sides. We have rather moved ahead towards a better and more complete set of copyright rules. It is logical to start with the author. If the author does not create copyright works, there will be nothing to exploit and performing artists will have no works to perform. We may encounter the odd artist who does keep all his or her works to themselves, but the vast majority of creators of copyright works want to see their works exploited. This can be explained by the desire to disseminate their work and the ideas behind it, or simply through the need for remuneration to allow them to keep creating works. The role of the person who exploits the copyright work is therefore in no way secondary in importance to the role of the author.

If we go back to the author who comes first, he or she becomes the first owner of the copyright in the work. The author is also given certain moral rights to compensate for the weak position in which he or she finds themselves and which we described above. These moral rights are minimal rights and as such they do not in any way obstruct the normal exploitation of the work as they only allow the author to act against forms of abusive exploitation of the work. It is therfore extremely important, taking also the weak position of the author into account, that these moral rights are inalienable. It is submitted that the possibility for the author to waive the moral rights has no place in this system.[11]

---

11   See Verstrynghe 'The Spring 1993 Horace S Manges Lecture – The European Commission's Direction on Copyright and Neighbouring Rights: Toward the Regime of the Twenty-First Century' (1993) 17 Columbia-VLA Journal of Law & the Arts 187 at 206-208.

■

The person who exploits the rights should also have an exclusive right. There should be a transfer of all economic rights if each of these rights has been contracted against an equitable remuneration. A producer who has acquired exploitation rights from authors or performers has to posses all exclusive rights which are required for an efficient exploitation in the interest of all rightholders. Clearly a right to act independently against infringers should form part of these exclusive rights. This should be the starting point of the legislation and it should be left to the contractual freedom of the parties to add to this set of rules or to derogate from it.[12]

The essential feature of this system is that neither party gains total control over each other. Both of them would be given parallel exclusive rights and this should incite them to co-operate which is in the best interests of both parties and in the best interest of copyright.[13] It is probably also the only system that will be able to cope with the challenge of the digital exploitation of copyright, which will make worldwide high speed exploitation of copyright in various formats possible and which offers the opportunity to play around with an original work and to amend it efficiently, speedily and in practice on a worrying number of occasions.[14]

Assignment of copyright and copyright licences

These are the two forms of contract involved in the exploitation of a copyright work by a third party.[15] Each of them has its own characteristics.

Assignment

An assignment involves the disposal of the copyright. The copyright is assigned by the author to another person. The 1988 Act requires that an assignment is in writing and is signed by or on behalf of the assignor.[16] The standard type of assignment involves the transfer of the complete copyright, but this need not be the case. Two forms of partial assignment are possible. It is possible to assign only certain aspects of the copyright or certain rights and not the whole copyright and it is also possible to restrict the assignment to a certain period.[17] This makes it possible to assign for example the copyright in the novel, to assign only the public performance right or the

---

12   See ibid at 206–207.
13   See ibid at 206–207.
14   Dreier 'Copyright in the Age of Digital Technology' (1993) 24 IIC 481.
15   CDPA 1988, s 90(1).
16   CDPA 1988, s 90(2).
17   CDPA 1988, s 90(2).

translation right or to assign all or any of these rights only for a period of 10 years. The assignor will normally receive a lump sum in return for the assignment of the copyright in the work.

An assignment can also take place in relation to a work that has still to be created. The Act calls this the assignment of future copyright, this is copyright that will come into existence once the potential author decides to create the work and the work is effectively created. The author will then become the first owner of the copyright and the assignment will take effect immediately.[18]

A difficult point is presented by the assignment of copyright in equity. The courts have on a couple of occasions accepted that an assignment can take place even if the formal requirements of section 90 are not met. In *Warner v Gestetner*[19] the court held that there had been an assignment of copyright in equity only. Warner had produced drawings of cats for Gestetner. These drawings were to be used to produce a new product at a fair and Warner would remain the owner of the copyright in the drawings. They were later used by Gestetner in promotional literature. The court decided that Gestetner was entitled to use the drawings and implied a clause assigning beneficial ownership of the copyright to Gestetner. In this construction there is a legal owner of the copyright and an owner at equity who is free to use the work. It seems to be the case that an equitable owner of copyright cannot bring an infringement case without the assistance of the legal owner of the copyright in the work though.[20]

Licences

A licence does not involve a transfer of the copyright in the work. The owner of the copyright simply grants permission to the licensee to do certain acts in relation to the copyright work which would constitute an infringement of the copyright in the work in case no licence had been granted. An obvious example is a licence to perform a play. Without the licence being granted the performance would have constituted an infringement of the copyright in the play. A licence can be granted in return for the payment of a lump sum or the licensor can be paid by royalties. This involves the payment of a fixed sum or a percentage of the return each time the act allowed by the licence takes place.

In the same way as an assignment the licence can be restricted in relation to its scope, ie the acts that are allowed, or in relation to its term.[1] It is indeed quite common to grant various licences, eventually in combination with partial assignment, to various persons in relation to the exploitation of a

18   CDPA 1988, s 91(1) and (2).
19   (1988) EIPR 89.
20   *Performing Right Society Ltd v London Theatre of Varieties Ltd* [1924] AC 1.
1   CDPA 1988, s 90(2).

work. Let us consider a novel as an example. The owner of the copyright in the novel can assign the publication rights in the UK to a publisher, license the performing rights, license another publisher to produce a translation in French, license a German producer to make a sound recording, assign the film rights to MGM in the USA, etc.

A licence can be exclusive or non-exclusive. An exclusive licence is subject to certain additional provisions. It is the only type of licence for which the 1988 Act requires a written format which has to be signed by or on behalf of the copyright owner-licensor.[2] And it allows the exclusive licensee to exercise certain rights in relation to the copyright work on an exclusive basis. This means that all other persons, including the licensor, will be excluded from exercising that right. The exclusive licensee can also bring an independent infringement action after joining the owner or by leave of the court, while a non-exclusive licensee needs the assistance of the licensor to do so, because in that case only the owner can sue. And the exclusive licensee has the same rights against a successor in title who is bound by the licence as he has against the original licensor.[3]

This brings us to the question who is bound by a licence. In principle every successor in title to the licensor is bound by the licence and there is only one exception to this rule. A purchaser in good faith and for valuable consideration, or someone deriving his or her title from such a purchaser, is not bound by the terms of the licence if he or she had no actual or constructive notice of the licence.[4] These requirements are extremely difficult to meet in practice because once exploitation has taken place it is almost impossible for a purchaser to prove that he or she did not even have constructive notice of the licence. Nevertheless this rule is one of the reasons why publishers prefer an assignment of copyright to an exclusive licence.

A prospective owner can license future copyright, just as it can be assigned.[5] Here again though the purchaser in good faith is granted protection.[6]

It is clear that it is extremely difficult to distinguish certain copyright licences from certain assignments of copyright. This is a matter of construction and the actual words used by the parties are not conclusive.[7] The payment of royalties points towards a licence and the difference regarding the right to sue independently is also an important factor in this respect.

---

2   CDPA 1988, s 92(1).
3   CDPA 1988, s 92(2).
4   CDPA 1988, s 90(4).
5   CDPA 1988, s 91(3).
6   CDPA 1988, s 91(3).
7   *Jonathan Cape Ltd v Consolidated Press Ltd* [1954] 3 All ER 253, [1954] 1 WLR 1313.

Collecting societies

The normal way of exploiting copyright by way of licences involves the grant of a licence for every use that is made of the copyright work. In cases where the work is a record that would involve a licence every time that record is played. It is probably not very convenient for the copyright owner to collect a minimum fee on every occasion. The overhead costs would be tremendous, it would take up all his or her time and he or she would in practice only be able to collect a fraction of royalties owed to him or her. The user of these records is in a similar position. If a restaurant owner wants to play background music in the restaurant that requires a separate licence for every work which is played. How is he going to find all the rightowners in the first place? This problem is addressed by the creation of collecting societies, such as the Performing Right Society (PRS) or Phonographic Performance Ltd (PPL). There is normally one collecting society per type of work and per country. Owners of the copyright become members of this body, which will license the use of their works and collect the royalties for them. The PRS takes an assignment of the copyright in the performance and broadcasting of musical works, grants licences, collects royalties and distributes these amongst its members after the deduction of administration costs. This presents a tremendous advantage to copyright owners, but it is also advantageous for the users of the works. They now have to deal with one body only and they will be able to get a blanket licence which will allow them to use any work in the repertoire of the society.

The fact that a society has a double monopoly creates some problems though. Copyright owners are obliged to deal with the one existing society if they want to exploit their works effectively. This situation can give rise to discrimination by the society against certain of its members by imposing different membership rules for example for foreign owners of copyright or by the adoption of discriminatory royalty distribution rules for certain types of works or certain classes of members. The society is also an unavoidable partner for the users of copyright works and abuse could consist here for example in charging exorbitant royalties. The 1988 Act took this into account and gave the Copyright Tribunal jurisdiction to deal with such cases.[8]

Licensing schemes

The owner of the copyright in a work may be willing to set standard conditions on which licences to do certain acts are available. This is for example the case in relation to the photocopying of literary works. Every

---

8   See also *Association of Independent Radio Companies Ltd v Phonographic Performance Ltd* [1994] RPC 143.

owner knows that this is happening and that it is unrealistic to expect every person who engages in photocopying the work to apply for a separate licence for each work of which he or she wishes to copy a part. It is also unrealistic to assume that the copyright owner could act effectively against this form of infringement in case no licence is applied for. The solution is to pool resources and to arrive at standard conditions on which licences are available and to do so with a large group of copyright owners. More copiers will be prepared to take a licence and the body administering the licence will be more effective in acting against infringement. The Act also sees this from another perspective. By giving the Copyright Tribunal jurisdiction over these schemes, it can prevent the abuse of monopoly powers by the copyright owners.

A licensing scheme is defined as

> 'a scheme setting out the classes of case in which the operator of the scheme, or the person on whose behalf he acts, is willing to grant copyright licences, and the terms on which licences would be granted in those classes of case', [9]

whereas a licensing body

> 'means a society or other organisation which has as its main object, or one of its main objects, the negotiation or granting, either as owner or prospective owner of copyright or as agent for him, of copyright licences, and whose objects include the granting of licences covering works of more than one author'.[10]

The Copyright Tribunal

The Copyright Tribunal has a wide jurisdiction. The following cases can be referred to it:

- the determination of the royalty or other remuneration to be paid with respect to the re-transmission of a broadcast that includes the work;
- an application to determine the amount of the equitable remuneration that remains payable in those cases where the author has transferred his rental rights concerning a sound recording or film to the producer;
- a proposed or existing licensing scheme that is operated by a licensing body and that covers works of more than one author (such an action can for example be brought by an organisation that represents persons

9   CDPA 1988, s 116(1).
10   CDPA 1988, s 116(2).

which require licences that are covered by the scheme). The licences must cover[11] the copying of the work, the rental or lending of copies of the work, the performing, showing or playing of the work in public, the broadcasting of the work or its inclusion in a cable programme service;

- an application in relation to entitlement under such a licensing scheme (for instance if someone is refused a licence);
- a reference in relation to licensing by a licensing body (for example a case in relation to the terms of a licence). The licences must cover the same acts as those listed above in relation to licensing schemes;[12]
- an application or reference in relation to the use as of right of sound recordings in broadcasts or cable programme services;
- an appeal against the coverage of a licensing scheme or a licence;
- an application to settle the royalties for the rental of sound recordings, films or computer programs in cases where the Secretary of State uses the exceptional powers contained in section 66 of the 1988 Act;
- an application to settle the terms of a copyright licence which has become available as of right.[13]

Appeals on a point of law from the decisions of the Copyright Tribunal can be made to the High Court, or in Scotland to the Court of Session.[14]

The rental and the lending right

If we take video cassettes containing a copy of a film as an example it is easy to understand that exploitation through rental of a film has become one of the leading ways to exploit a film. Rental and lending of copyright works have indeed acquired an important status in the field of copyright exploitation and as they have replaced in a number of cases the acquisition of a copy of the work and the royalty payment that goes with it, it was felt that the authors of the works that are exploited in this way were entitled to some form of remuneration. Section 66 of the 1988 Act provides for the payment of a reasonable royalty in rental cases, but this provision is in fact a last remedy against abuse by the owners of copyright in sound recordings, films and computer programs of their copyright and it is unlikely that the Secretary of State will ever use his power under this section to grant licences and ask the Copyright Tribunal to determine the reasonable royalty in default of agreement. In the absence of any substantial rental or lending

---

11   CDPA 1988, s 117.
12   CDPA 1988, s 124.
13   CDPA 1988, s 149.
14   CDPA 1988, s 152.

provisions in many of the member states the European Union took the initiative to introduce these rights in a harmonised way and this resulted in a Council Directive.[15]

The implementation of the Directive[16] in the UK added the rental and lending of the work or of copies of it to the list of restricted acts.[17] The fact that these acts are now restricted to the owner of the copyright in the work enables the copyright owner to charge royalties for the rental and lending of the work and to receive payment for this new way of exploiting his work. The general structure of the relevant provisions has been discussed above and need not be repeated here. We also discussed the introducion of rental and lending rights as part of the rights in performances. We therefore turn our attention to a few special aspects of the rental and lending rights regime.

As the credits that appear on the screen at the end of the showing of a film demonstrate, a long list of people is generally involved in the making of a film. The list of those people that will possess rental rights is significantly shorter, but can nevertheless still be rather long. Once the film is made, each of them will normally go his or her own way. It might therefore be rather unpractical to impose a system whereby the film can only be exploited through rental if the authorisation of each contributor has been obtained. Some of the contributors may be hard to trace or even a single one could hold the whole project to ransom. The Directive and the Act therefore provide the possibility to concentrate the rental rights in a single pair of hands. The Act contains a presumption[18] that, unless the agreement provides to the contrary, the conclusion of an agreement concerning the production of a film between the producer and an author of a literary, musical, dramatic or artistic work[19] is presumed to include a transfer to the producer of any rental right in relation to the film arising by virtue of the inclusion of a copy of the author's work in the film. As we have seen above, an identical provision exists in relation to performers.[20] Due to the higher level of bargaining power of the producer, such a presumption could be to the detriment of authors and producers who would hardly be able to secure a proper remuneration for the transfer of their rental rights in the production agreement. The Act tries to overcome this problem by introducing a rule that the authors or performers remain entitled to an equitable remuneration

15   Council Directive 92/100 on rental right and lending right and on certain rights related to copyright in the field of intellectual property (1992) OJ L346/61.
16   A challenge against the Directive in which its validity was questioned, was rejected by the Court of Justice on 28 April 1998 in Case C-200/96 *Metronome Musik GmbH v Music Point Hokamp GmbH*, not yet reported.
17   CDPA 1988, s 16(1)(ba).
18   CDPA 1988, s 93A.
19   Screenplays, dialogues or music that are specifically created for and used in a film are excluded according to s 93A(3), CDPA 1988.
20   CDPA 1988, s 191F.

for the rental, even after the transfer of their right.[1] The producer may be the only person that can authorise the rental of the work, but he has to provide an equitable remuneration for those whose rights have been transferred to him. That right of equitable remuneration cannot be assigned, except to a collecting society that will enforce the right on behalf of the rightholder.[2] For the purposes of this rule the category of authors also includes the principal director of the film, in addition to the author of a literary, dramatic, musical or artistic work.[3]

The amount payable by way of equitable remuneration is to be agreed between the author and performers on the one hand and the producers or his successor in title as assignee of the rental rights in the film on the other hand.[4] In default of an agreement the amount will be determined by the Copyright Tribunal upon application.[5]

These provisions successfully overcome the problems that arise when too many persons potentially get rental rights in relation to a single work. The general conclusion must therefore be that the system of rental rights enhances the copyright position of the people involved and constitutes an appropriate and necessary response to the change in the way in which certain copyright works are exploited commercially. The position of the performers is especially enhanced by this change, as their protection was until now rather weak.

The exploitation of copyright works through hard copies has further been eroded through the rise of the internet. Many works are now available on-line and their use on-line reduces the use of hard copies. The existing provisions of copyright, including those concerning rental and lending, are perhaps not entirely capable of successfully tackling the problems that arise. The European Commission has therefore suggested further amendments to the copyright legislation of the member states. These amendments are contained in the proposal for a European Parliament and Council Directive on the harmonisation of certain aspects of copyright and related rights in the information society.[6] It would lead too far to discuss every aspect of the draft, but the proposed distribution right[7] is particularly relevant in this respect. Authors would be given the exclusive right to authorise or prohibit any form of distribution to the public of their work or of copies thereof. This clearly includes the on-line distribution of copyright works and enables authors to claim royalties for that form of distribution. Other forms of exploitation of copyright works in this area, in addition to on-line services,

1   CDPA 1988, s 93B(1).
2   CDPA 1988, s 93B(2).
3   CDPA 1988, s 93B(1).
4   CDPA 1988, s 93B(4).
5   CDPA 1988, ss 93C and 191G.
6   COM(97) 628 final, dated 20 December 1997.
7   Article 4.

■

include pay-TV, video or music on demand and electronic publishing. These can be called conditional access services. Authors can only be paid properly in this context if unauthorised (pirate) access without payment to these services is prohibited and prevented. Another EU Directive that deals with conditional access services and their protection is about to be adopted.[8]

Copyright exploitation and free competition

The position in the UK under domestic law in relation to the conflict between copyright exploitation and free competition is clear in that it gives priority to copyright exploitation. Section 66 of the 1988 Act could lead to compulsory licences in a restricted area, but as discussed above the provision will probably never be used. This leaves us with the licences of right as the only effective tool to act against an abuse during the exploitation of the rights granted by copyright law. A report of the Monopolies and Mergers Commission may lead to the creation of licences of right, which means essentially that licences become available to anyone who applies for them. What is required is that the public interest is or has been or may be prejudiced. This can be on the basis of conditions in licences restricting the use of the work or the right of the owner to grant other licences or on the basis of a refusal of the copyright owner to grant licences on reasonable terms.[9] Of real practical importance are the provisions of the Treaty of Rome and it is to these that we now turn.

COPYRIGHT EXPLOITATION UNDER EUROPEAN LAW

Copyright and the free movement of goods

Article 36 of the Treaty refers to 'industrial and commercial property' and this clearly includes patents and trade marks, but does it include copyright as well? Does it really mean the same as 'intellectual property'? The Court has now given a positive answer to these questions[10] and all the general principles which we outlined in the patent chapter can be applied to copyright subject to what follows.

Copyright is a difficult area, because its scope is so extremely wide and because it protects as a result very different types of works. This makes it extremely difficult to define the specific subject matter of copyright and

---

8   Proposal for a European Parliament and Council Directive on the Legal Protection of Services based on, or consisting of, Conditional Access (1997) OJ C 314/7 (COM(97) 0356 final).
9   CDPA 1988, s 144.
10 Case 57/80 *Musik-Vertrieb Membran GmbH v GEMA* [1981] ECR 147, [1981] 2 CMLR 44.

the Court of Justice has not yet made an attempt to do so. It is submitted that for these purposes there are two types of copyright, which probably have a different specific subject matter. The first category comprises all non-performance copyrights, such as those in books, paintings and sound-recordings, while the second category comprises all performance copyrights. The latter category includes live performances, but also all performances of films. We will discuss both categories separately.

Non-performance copyrights

These are treated very similarly to patents. In fact the oldest case in which the exhaustion doctrine was applied was a case relating to records. In *Deutsche Grammophon v Metro*[11] the Court was faced with the following issue. Deutsche Grammophon sold the same records in Germany and in France, but its French subsidiary, Polydor, could only charge a lower price due to market conditions. Metro bought the records in France for resale in Germany at a price below the price Deutsche Grammophon charged. Deutsche Grammophon invoked its copyright[12] in the records to stop this practice. The Court ruled that Deutsche Grammophon had exhausted its copyright in the records by putting them on the market in France with its consent and could not oppose the importation of the records by Metro.[13]

This approach was confirmed in the *Musik-Vertrieb Membran v GEMA* case.[14] Once more records and cassettes were being imported into Germany after they had been put on the market in another member state with the consent of the copyright owner. The German collecting society GEMA tried to rely on the German copyright in the works to levy the difference between the low royalty that had been paid abroad and the higher German royalty. The Court reiterated that by putting the records and cassettes on the market with its consent the owner of the copyright had exhausted all copyright in them. They could as a result not rely on any copyright to prevent the importation, nor could they rely on it to charge an additional royalty. In the Court's view, the copyright owner who markets its works in member states where the royalties are low has to abide by that decision and accept the consequences of it. The approach sounds identical to that taken in the patent case of *Merck v Stephar*.[15]

11 Case 78/70 *Deutsche Grammophon GmbH v Metro-SB-Grossmarkte GmbH & Co KG* [1971] ECR 487, [1971] CMLR 631.

12 For the purposes of our discussion of the case we can assume that the German exclusive distribution right is akin to copyright.

13 Case 78/70 *Deutsche Grammophon GmbH v Metro-SB-Grossmarkte GmbH & Co KG* [1971] ECR 487 at 500.

14 Joined cases 55 and 57/80 *Musik-Vertrieb Membran v GEMA* [1981] ECR 147, [1981] 2 CMLR 44, see also case 58/80 *Dansk Supermarked A/S v Imerco A/S* [1981] ECR 181, [1981] 3 CMLR 590.

15 Case 187/80 *Merck & Co Inc v Stephar BV* [1981] ECR 2063, discussed supra in chapter 4.

In *Warner Bros v Christiaensen*[16] a difficult problem arose. Video cassettes which were put on the market both in the UK and Denmark were being imported from the UK into Denmark. It is clear that the plaintiff could not rely on its Danish copyright to stop the importation of the video cassettes, as this only requires a normal application of the dictum in the two previous cases. The problem arose because Danish law granted a rental right to the author or the producer, while such a right did not exist in the UK and Christiaensen imported the cassettes to hire them out afterwards. Christiaensen argued that the rights in the cassettes had been exhausted because they had been marketed in the UK with the consent of the owner, but the Court rejected this argument. Indeed the rental right has to be treated as a separate right and as it did not exist in the UK, it could not have been exhausted.[17] Warner Bros could invoke the Danish rental right to stop Christiaensen hiring out the video cassettes.[18] It is easier to understand why the rental right should be treated as a separate right by looking at the consequences of not doing so. That would effectively have rendered the rental right worthless, as it would have been exhausted by sale in a member state where the right is not known. As we discussed in relation to patents in chapter 4, Articles 30 and 36 are construed in such a way that they must leave the existence of the right and a certain exercise untouched as any other interpretation would render them senseless. The approach taken by the Court must thus be correct.

It may be tempting to argue that this case presented similar features to those of the *Merck v Stephar* case[19] in patents and that as a result the Court should have ruled that Warner Bros could not rely on the Danish rental right as they should accept the consequences of their decision to market the video cassettes in a country where no rental right is available. It is submitted that this approach is wrong. In *Merck* Italy had a patent law, but excluded pharmaceuticals from its scope. The Court argued that Merck should accept the consequences of a weaker or absent patent protection in Italy and could not invoke its Dutch patent. Only one right was involved. In the *Warner* case two rights were involved. The copyright had been exhausted, but was not relied upon as only the Danish right was used. This allows us to distinguish the cases.

A problem relating to the term of copyright arose in *EMI Electrola v Patricia*[20] because the term of copyright protection for records in Denmark was shorter than the one in Germany. Patricia bought Cliff Richard sound recordings in Denmark once they were out of copyright and imported them

16   Case 158/86 *Warner Bros Inc v Christiansen* [1988] ECR 2605.
17   See Henry 'Rental and Duration Directives: Issues Arising from Current EC Reforms' [1993] 12 EIPR 437 at 439.
18   Ibid.
19   Case 187/80 *Merck & Co Inc v Stephar BV* [1981] ECR 2063, discussed supra in chapter 4.
20   Case 341/87 *EMI Electrola GmbH v Patricia Im-Und Export* [1989] ECR 79.

into Germany, where EMI Electrola tried to stop them by relying on the German copyright in the recordings which had not yet expired. The Court of justice held that the German copyright had not been exhausted because the marketing in Denmark had not occurred with the consent of the copyright owner, but was due to the fact that the term of copyright had expired. This case can now be described as legal history, because the term of copyright has now been harmonised in the Community and because the Phil Collins judgment[1] would result in the work in a similar case remaining in copyright in the whole of the European Union, as discussed in relation to the term of copyright. The problem will therefore not re-occur.

The essential function of copyright was first described by the Court of First Instance in the *Magill* cases, which are concerned with competition law, as being

'to protect the moral rights in the work and to ensure a reward for the creative effort, while respecting the aims of, in particular, Article 86'.[2]

This definition is not precise enough, though it rightly indicates the two essential elements of copyright, moral rights and economic rights, which are granted to the author. The reference to creativity must be understood against the background of the low originality requirement in copyright. This definition should be treated with caution.

The *Warner Bros* case[3] shows clearly that there are many facets to the essential function of copyright and especially to the specific subject-matter of copyright. The rental right point was clearly a separate aspect within the latter. This should not come as a surprise. Copyright is a broad right that protects a wide variety of products. It may in each case, broadly speaking, be the aim to protect the author and the subsequent rightholders because it is felt that their creative efforts deserve encouragement and protection, but the exact way in which this is put into practice by including different aspects within the specific subject-matter of copyright is not always as easy to determine as it is with the narrower patent right. While it can be understood that rental as a separate way in which the work is exploited may have been entitled to be promoted to a separate aspect of the specific subject-matter, one should not construe the latter too broadly either. The *Dior* case[4] illustrates this point. Dior had exhausted all copyrights in the box in which

1   Case C-92/92 *Phil Collins v IMTRAT Handels-GmbH* [1993] 3 CMLR 773, where the parallel case Case 362/92 *Patricia v EMI Electrola* concerning Cliff Richard's work is also reported, see also Dworkin and Sterling 'Phil Collins and the Term Directive' [1994] 5 EIPR 187.
2   Cases T-69/89 *Radio Telefis Eireann v Commission* [1991] ECR II-485, [1991] 4 CMLR 586, T-70/89 *BBC v Commission* [1991] ECR II-535, [1991] 4 CMLR 669 and T-76/89 *Independent Television Productions v Commission* [1991] 4 CMLR 745.
3   Case C-158/86 *Warner Bros v Christiansen* [1988] ECR 2605.
4   Case C-337/95 *Parfums Christian Dior SA v Evora BV* [1998] RPC 166

■

it sold its perfume bottles by putting the perfumes, in the box, on the market for the first time. This is normal copyright exhaustion and the reward for the copyright in the design of the boxes is seen as being included in the sales price of the perfume. Any further use of the copyright in the design of the boxes would therefore go beyond the specific subject-matter of copyright in this case. A problem arose because the parallel importer wanted to reproduce the design of the boxes in its publicity. Printing a photograph of the boxes to advertise the fact that the perfume is now available at a lower price from certain outlets certainly involves copying. Could Dior stop this on the basis of its copyright? The Court of Justice ruled that it could not. The exhaustion of the copyright by putting the product on the market exhausted all rights. Reprinting for publicity purposes is clearly not a separate aspect of the specific subject-matter of the right; it is part of the main aspect of copyright. It could rather be argued that the parallel importer who has the right to import the perfume bottles which Dior put on the market in another member state must also have the right to advertise these products. Otherwise the consumer will not be informed and in the absence of real sales the whole system of parallel import will de facto collapse. Any use of copyright to stop the advertising of the products would therefore be a use to block parallel imports of legitimately acquired products. This cannot be part of the essential function of copyright. It must be an abusive use of the right. It must therefore be treated as falling outside the specific subject-matter of the right and the right must be treated as having been exhausted for this purpose.[5]

Performance copyrights

This category is concerned with plays and films and their performance. The exploitation of these works takes place through public exhibitions which can be repeated an indefinite number of times. It is like rendering a service and the whole area has more links with the free movement of services provided for in Article 59 of the Treaty of Rome than with the free movement of goods. This implies that this category of rights should be treated differently.

The Court was confronted with this problem in the *Coditel* case.[6] This case made the French film *Le Boucher*, the copyright in which was owned by the French company 'Les Films la Boétie', famous. A seven-year exclusive licence to exhibit the film in Belgium had been given to Ciné Vog. One of the clauses of the licence stipulated that Ciné Vog could only allow the film to be broadcast on Belgian television 40 months after its first cinema

5   See also Stamatoudi 'From drugs to spirits and from boxes to publicity: Decided and undecided issues in relation to trade mark and copyright exhaustion' [1998] IPQ Issue 4, December.

6   Case 62/79 *Coditel v Ciné Vog Films SA* [1980] ECR 881, [1981] 2 CMLR 362.

showing. A different exclusive licensee was appointed for Germany and that licence contract did not restrict the showing of the film on television. The film was shown on German television before it could have been shown on Belgian television and the Belgian cable company Coditel picked up the German signal and retransmitted it on its cable network. This required the authorisation of the Belgian licensee under Belgian copyright law because it was held to be a communication to the public. Because no authorisation had been applied for and because they feared loss of revenue because the Belgian television stations would be less interested in acquiring the right to broadcast a film that many of their viewers had already seen in the German version, Ciné Vog sued Coditel for infringement of copyright. Coditel based its defence inter alia on the freedom to provide services and argued that as the film had been shown with the consent of the owner of the copyright all copyright in it had been exhausted.

The problem with the free movement of services provision of the Treaty, however, is that it does not provide for an exception for intellectual property. This did not prevent Advocate-General Warner suggesting that Article 36 applied by analogy in this context. The Court must have agreed with this suggestion because it ruled that:

> 'Whilst Article 59 of the Treaty prohibits restrictions upon the freedom to provide services, it does not hereby encompass limits upon the exercise of certain economic activities which have their origin in the application of national legislation for the protection of intellectual property, save where such application constitutes a means of arbitrary discrimination or a disguised restriction on trade between member states. Such would be the case if that application enabled parties to create artificial barriers to trade between member states'.[7]

In a next step the specific subject-matter of the performing right in a film was defined as the right of authorities to forbid each and every performance of the film, including the right of it being televised. As the retransmission of the film by Coditel amounted to a new performance, the performing right in the film had not been exhausted and Ciné Vog could rely on it. The restriction on the showing of the film which Ciné Vog claimed was necessary in order to guarantee it the benefit of the essence of the exclusive performing right. The remaining issue was whether the practice to have one exclusive licensee per member state was an example of the artificial barriers to trade to which the Court objected. The Court did not see it as such an example and accepted that such an approach was objectively

7   Case 62/79 *Coditel v Ciné Vog Films SA* [1980] ECR 881 at 903.

justifiable because at that time all television services were organised on the national basis of a legal broadcasting monopoly.[8] Its conclusion was

'... that the provisions of the Treaty relating to the freedom to provide services did not preclude an assignee of the performing right in a cinematographic film in a member state from relying upon his right to prohibit the exhibition of that film in that State, without its authority, by means of cable diffusion if the film so exhibited is picked up and transmitted after being broadcast in another member state by a third party with the consent of the original owner of the right'.[9]

Copyright and competition law

Article 85

Agreements related to copyright may restrict competition and thus may fall within the scope of Article 85. Such infringing agreements will involve an improper or abusive exercise of copyright, as confirmed by the Court of Justice in the *Coditel (No 2)* case.[10] It cannot be said that many cases arose in this area, but the practice of the Commission shows that its approach is similar to its approach in patent licence cases. For example no-challenge clauses, royalty clauses which were extended to non-protected goods or works, non-competition clauses which were to continue after the expiry date of the agreement, an exclusive grant back clause,[11] export bans[12] and attempts to guarantee absolute exclusivity[13] were disputed by the Commission and the relevant agreements were modified at the Commission's request so that no formal decisions were issued.

Article 86 - Collecting societies

The largest number of cases in which Article 86 has been applied to copyright concern collecting societies. The Court of Justice has indicated

---

8   Arguably this is no longer the case now that Directive 93/83 on copyright and neighbouring rights relating to satellite broadcasting and cable retransmission has been adopted ((1993) OJ L248/15, see supra). For example Article 7(3) on co-production agreements shows that licences may have to be granted on a Community scale, thereby excluding territorial licensing. See Kern 'The EC "Common Position" on Copyright Applicable to Satellite Broadcasting and Cable Retransmission' [1993] 8 EIPR 276 at 280.
9   Case 62/79 *Coditel v Ciné Vog Films SA* [1980] ECR 881 at 904.
10 Case 262/81 *Coditel v Ciné Vog Films SA* [1982] ECR 3381 and [1983] 1 CMLR 49.
11 *Neilsen-Hordell/Reichmark* 12th Annual Report on Competition Policy, points 88-89.
12 *Re Ernest Benn Ltd* 9th Annual Report on Competition Policy.
13 *Knoll/Hille-Form* 13th Annual Report on Competition Policy, points 142-146.

that there is nothing intrinsically objectionable about the establishment of collecting societies, which may be necessary in order that individual artists can obtain a reasonable return for their endeavour.[14] But usually these collecting societies occupy a dominant position as they operate as a de facto monopoly in the member states, this is on a substantial part of the Common Market. Trade between member states is affected by the fact that the creation of a single market for copyright services is prevented. So the way these collecting societies exploit their dominant position will be closely examined and improper exploitation will be an infringement of Article 86.[15]

The internal rules of the collecting societies have to take account of all the relevant interests and the result must be a balance between 'the requirement of maximum freedom for authors, composers, and publishers to dispose of their works and that of the effective management of their rights'.[16] Every exaggeration towards one side can imply an abuse of dominant position. This abuse takes the form of discrimination against nationals of other member states and among members or the binding of members with excessive obligations.[17]

There is no doubt that any discrimination on grounds of nationality is an abuse of dominant position. The Commission made that clear in its *GEMA* decision.[18] Membership cannot be made dependent on the establishment of a tax domicile in the member state where the collecting society operates and special forms of membership or membership of the organs of the society cannot be denied to persons or companies which have the nationality of a different member state than the collecting society. Account should also be taken of income received from other collecting societies in order to determine if a member qualifies for a special form of membership.[19] GEMA did not appeal to the Court of Justice, but the Court approved of the Commission's point of view by giving judgment against GVL when it refused to represent anyone not resident in Germany because secondary exploitation rights in other member states were generally less comprehensive and more difficult to assert.[20]

14   Case 127/73 *Belgische Radio en Televisie and Société Belge des Auteurs, Compositeurs et Editeurs v SV SABAM and NV Fonior* [1974] ECR 313, [1974] 2 CMLR 238.
15   See Bellis 'Collecting societies and EEC law' in D Peeperhorn and C van Rij (eds) *Collecting societies in the music business (reports presented at the meeting of the International Association of Entertainment Lawyers, Midem 1989, Cannes)* Maklu (1989) at 78, and B Cawthra *Industrial Property Rights in the EEC* Gower Press Limited (1973) at 70-71.
16   Case 127/73 *Belgische Radio en Televisie and Société Belge des Auteurs, Compositeurs et Editeurs v SV SABAM and NV Fonior* [1974] ECR 313, [1974] 2 CMLR 238.
17   Bellis 'Collecting societies and EEC law' in D Peeperhorn and C van Rij (eds) *Collecting societies in the music business (reports presented at the meeting of the International Association of Entertainment Lawyers, Midem 1989, Cannes)* Maklu (1989) at 78.
18   (1971) OJ L134 15. GEMA is a German collecting society.
19   Ibid.
20   Case 7/82 *Gesellschaft zur Verwertung von Leistungsschutzrechten mbH (GVL) v Commission* [1983] ECR 483, [1983] 3 CMLR 645.

Discrimination amongst members in relation to the distribution of income is also an abuse. Every classification procedure has to be cost-justified and without cost-justification an undertaking in a dominant position cannot pay loyalty bonuses,[1] especially not to certain members with funds coming from all members. The Commission found that GEMA was infringing these principles.[2] But if royalty income from all sources is taken into account, a collecting society is still permitted to set a reasonable level of royalty income as a condition of membership.[3] It was stated:

'The abuse also lies in the fact that GEMA binds its members by obligations which are not objectively justified and which, in particular, unfairly complicate the movement of its members to another society.'[4]

It cannot be accepted that members are required to assign their rights for all categories of works and for the entire world to the collecting society, especially not if the assignment period and the waiting period for the acquisition of certain benefits are excessive and if future works have to be assigned as well. The two latter points are already abuses when considered on their own.[5] The Commission held that members should be free to assign all or part of their rights for the countries in which the collecting society does not operate directly to other societies and that they should be equally free to assign only certain categories of rights to the collecting society and to withdraw from it the administration of certain categories at the end of a three year period.[6]

Members must have the opportunity to choose another collecting society to represent them outside the Community. And an abuse which relates only to performance outside the Community stays an infringement of Article

1   See case 85/76 *Hoffmann–La Roche & Co AG v Commission* [1979] ECR 461, [1979] 3 CMLR 211.
2   *GEMA* decision (1971) OJ L134 15.
3   Bellis 'Collecting societies and EEC law' in D Peeperhorn and C van Rij (eds) *Collecting societies in the music business (reports presented at the meeting of the International Association of Entertainment Lawyers, Midem 1989, Cannes)* Maklu (1989) 78 at 79.
4   *GEMA* decision (1971) OJ L134 15.
5   Ibid.
6   The original period was one year and seven categories were defined. This option is still open (*GEMA* decision (1971) OJ L134 15). The Commission's decision of 6 July 1972 ((1972) OJ L 166 22) offered the alternative of a three year period compensated by these narrower categories : the general performance right, the radio broadcasting right, the public performing right of broadcast works, the right to transmit by television, the public performing right of televised works, the motion picture performance right, the right of mechanical reproduction and distribution, the public performing right of mechanically reproduced works, the motion picture production right, the right to produce, reproduce and distribute on videotape, the public performing right of works reproduced on videotape and the utilisation rights arising in the future as a result of technical development or a change in legislation.

86 if the contract was concluded in the Community by parties within the jurisdiction of one of the member states.[7]

A couple of final details can be added, such as the rule that the right of judicial recourse may not be excluded by an undertaking occupying a dominant position[8] and that if this is essential to strengthen the position of the collecting society in negotiations with powerful large customers such as national radio and television stations, restrictions imposed on members can be accepted.[9]

The relationship between collecting societies and third parties can also be problematic and raises certain issues in relation to Article 86. The first abuses to be found in this area were the imposition of a higher royalty on imported tape and video recorders than on equipment produced in the member state where the collecting society is established and the contractual extension of royalty payments to works that are no longer protected.[10]

A series of recent cases allowed the Court of Justice to work out a more detailed point of view. In the *Basset v SACEM* case[11] the Court ruled that it is no abuse in the sense of Article 86 if a collecting society charges a royalty called a 'supplementary mechanical reproduction fee', in addition to a performance royalty, on the public performance of sound recordings. This only amounted to a normal copyright exploitation and no act of arbitrary discrimination nor a disguised restriction on trade between member states could be seen in it as the fee was charged for all sound recordings, regardless of their origin. The fact that such a fee did not exist in the member state where the sounds recorded were lawfully placed on the market did not influence this conclusion.

Even more important in that case was an obiter dictum:

'It is not impossible, however, that the amount of the royalty, or of the combined royalties, charged by the copyright-management society may be such that Article 86 applies'.[12]

The Court elaborated this *obiter dictum* further by laying the burden of proving that an appreciably higher scale of royalty fees is justified by a better copyright protection on the collecting society. If such proof is not brought

7   Case 22/79 *Greenwich Film Production, Paris v SACEM and another* [1979] ECR 3275, [1980] 1 CMLR 629.
8   *GEMA* decision (1971) OJ L134 15.
9   Case 127/73 *Belgische Radio en Televisie and Société Belge des Auteurs, Compositeurs et Editeurs v SV SABAM and NV Fonior* [1974] ECR 313, [1974] 2 CMLR 238.
10 *GEMA* decision (1971) OJ L134 15, but collecting societies have the right to round off the playing time to the nearest minute.
11 Case 402/85 *G Basset v Société des Auteurs, Compositeurs et Editeurs de Musique (SACEM)* [1987] ECR 1747, [1987] 3 CMLR 173.
12 Ibid at [1987] ECR 1769. This dictum fell outside the scope of the prejudicial question referred to the Court by the French judge.

the imposition of the higher fees forms an abuse of dominant position. In the subsequent *Lucazeau* case the Court rule :

'When an undertaking holding a dominant position imposes scales of fees for its services which are appreciably higher than those charged in other member states and where a comparison of the fee levels has been made on a consistent basis, that difference must be regarded as indicative of an abuse of a dominant position. In such a case it is for the undertaking in question to justify the difference with reference to objective dissimilarities between the situation in the member state concerned and the situation prevailing in all the other member states'.[13]

The Court had reached the same conclusion some weeks earlier in the *Tournier* case.[14] But in *Tournier* the Court ruled also that a collecting society that refuses to grant the users of recorded music access only to its foreign repertoire does not abuse its dominant position in the sense of Article 86

'unless access to a part of the protected repertoire could entirely safeguard the interests of the authors, composers and publishers of music without thereby increasing the costs of managing contracts and monitoring the use of protected musical works'.[15]

The main issues with a Community interest in relation to collecting societies have now been addressed. *BEMIM*[16] and *Tremblay*[17] showed that the outstanding issues lack a Community interest and fall therefore under the jurisdiction of the national courts. This may suit the Union well, since it becomes clear that it will need the co-operation of the collecting societies if these are to be increasingly involved in collecting royalties for the exploitation of copyright works in the information society.[18] However, these developments do not involve a change in policy as far as the points of substantive law are involved.

---

13   Cases 110/88, 241/88 and 242/88 *François Lucazeau v Société des Auteurs, Compositeurs et Editeurs de Musique (SACEM)* [1989] ECR 2811 at 2831.
14   Case 395/87 *Ministère Public v Jean-Louis Tournier* [1989] ECR 2521.
15   Ibid at 2580.
16   Case T-114/92 *Bureau Européen des Médias de l'industrie Musicale (BEMIM) v EC Commission* [1995] ECR II-147, [1996] 4 CMLR 305.
17   Case T-5/93 *Roger Tremblay v EC Commission (Syndicat des Exploitants de Lieux de Loisirs (SELL), intervening)* [1995] ECR II-185, [1996] 4 CMLR 305 and Case C-91/95P *Roger Tremblay v EC Commission* [1996] ECR I-5547, [1997] 4 CMLR 211.
18   See Torremans and Stamatoudi 'Collecting Societies: Sorry, the Community is no longer interested!' (1997) 22 E L Rev 352. See also Stamatoudi 'The European Court's Share – State Relationship with Collecting Societies' [1997] 6 EIPR 289-297.

Article 86 - Does dominance force an undertaking to grant a licence?

The central issue involved here is whether an undertaking in a dominant position can be forced to grant a 'licence' of an intellectual property right it holds and if a refusal to do so implies an abuse of its dominant position. In recent years this issue arose on three occasions in the areas of design and copyright. We discuss these cases here together as they strongly draw upon each other.

The issue arose for the first time in two cases which were concerned with designs for spare parts for cars, the *Maxicar v Renault* case[19] and the *Volvo v Veng* case.[20] Maxicar and Veng were involved in car repairs and maintenance and wanted to obtain a licence to produce spare parts themselves. When unsuccessful in obtaining these licences they argued that Volvo and Renault occupied a dominant position in the relevant market and that by refusing to grant licences they abused their dominant position. They wanted to see Volvo and Renault obliged to grant the licences and submitted that the Court should interpret Article 86 accordingly. The Court of Justice started its analysis by ruling out the possibility that the existence of the fact that an intellectual property right was obtained could be an abuse of a dominant position. The Court held that the existence and the issue of obtaining an intellectual property right is a matter for the national rules of the member states, which rules determine the nature and extent of the protection.[1] In the *Maxicar v Renault* case the Court stated that

'the mere fact of obtaining protective rights ... does not constitute an abuse of a dominant position within the meaning of Article 86'.[2]

The obligation for a dominant undertaking to grant a licence[3] was ruled out in the *Volvo v Veng* case :

'the right of the proprietor of a protected design to prevent third parties from manufacturing and selling or importing, without its consent, products incorporating the design constitutes the very subject-matter of his exclusive right. It follows that an obligation imposed upon the proprietor of a protected design to grant to third parties, even in return

19 Case 53/87 *Consorzio italiano della componentistica di ricambio per autoveicoli and Maxicar v Régie nationale des usines Renault* [1988] ECR 6039, [1990] 4 CMLR 265.
20 Case 238/87 *AB Volvo v Erik Veng (UK) Ltd* [1988] ECR 6211, [1989] 4 CMLR 122.
1   Ibid, with reference to case 144/81 *Keurkoop BV v Nancy Kean Gifts BV* [1982] ECR 2853, [1983] 2 CMLR 47.
2   Case 53/87 *Consorzio italiano della componentistica di ricambio per autoveicoli and Maxicar v Régie nationale des usines Renault* [1988] ECR 6039, [1990] 4 CMLR 265; this quotation at [1988] ECR 6073.
3   See Korah 'No Duty to Licence Independent Repairers to Make Spare Parts : the Renault, Volvo and Bayer Cases' [1988] 12 EIPR 381.

for a reasonable royalty, a licence for the supply of products incorporating the design would lead to the proprietor thereof being deprived of the substance of his exclusive right, and that a refusal to grant such a licence cannot in itself constitute an abuse of a dominant position'.[4]

The situation may however be different if the owner of the right refuses to supply spare parts, fixes prices at an unfair level[5] or discontinues production. Provided that such conduct is liable to affect trade between member states such exercise of the intellectual property right is prohibited by Article 86 and in this situation the grant of a 'compulsory' licence becomes possible.[6] But it is clear from the cases that more than the existence of the right creating a dominant position and the simple refusal to grant a licence is required if an abuse is to be proved. The starting point must be that the power to decide whether or not to grant licences is an essential component of the right with which Article 86 does not interfere. The *Volvo v Veng* case dealt with designs, but the Court's ruling in the *Maxicar v Renault* case does not permit any difference when patents are concerned.[7]

In the *Magill* cases[8] the problem arose when Magill wished to publish the listings of programmes of BBC, ITV and RTE in a single weekly publication. The three companies refused to supply those listings and invoked their copyright in the listings to do so. It should be noted that they published their own guides, which thus enjoyed a form of monopoly, and supplied, free of charge, the weekly listings to foreign publications. They also supplied daily listings to the press. The Commission[9] ruled that the three companies abused their dominant position in exercising their copyright in such a way and required that advance information was supplied

---

4   Case 238/87 *AB Volvo v Erik Veng (UK) Ltd* [1988] ECR 6211, [1989] 4 CMLR 122 at 6235.

5   Products protected by an intellectual property right may be sold at a higher price than similar unprotected products if the price-difference forms a reasonable return of the investments made, see Case 24/67 *Parke, Davis & Co v Probel, Reese, Beintema-Interfarm and Centrafarm* [1968] ECR 55, [1968] CMLR 47, confirmed in case 53/87 *Maxicar and another v Régie nationale des usines Renault* [1988] ECR 6039, [1990] 4 CMLR 265.

6   Case 238/87 *AB Volvo v Erik Veng (UK) Ltd* [1988] ECR 6211, [1989] 4 CMLR 122 and case 53/87 *Maxicar and another v Régie nationale des usines Renault* [1988] ECR 6039, [1990] 4 CMLR 265.

7   Ibid and see C Bellamy and G Child *Common Market Law of Competition/First Supplement to the Third Edition* Sweet & Maxwell (1991) at 86.

8   Case T-69/89 *Radio Telefis Eireann v Commission (Magill TV Guide Ltd intervening)* [1991] 4 CMLR 586; case T-70/89 *British Broadcasting Corporation and BBC Enterprises Ltd v Commission (Magill TV Guide Ltd intervening)* [1991] 4 CMLR 669 and case T-76/89 *Independent Television Publications Ltd v Commission (Magill TV Guide Ltd intervening)* [1991] ECR II-575, [1991] 4 CMLR 745.

9   *Magill TV Guide/ITP, BBC and RTE decision* [1989] OJ L78/43.

to Magill. The decision on this point was upheld by the Court of First Instance.[10]

The judgment of the Court of First Instance reads:

'Conduct of that type (the exercise of the copyright in the way described above) ... clearly goes beyond what is necessary to fulfil the essential function of the copyright as permitted in Community law'.

After failing to find an objective and specific justification for this conduct the Court of First Instance continued:

'... the aim and effect of the applicant's exclusive reproduction of its programme listings was to exclude any potential competition ... in order to maintain the monopoly enjoyed ... by the applicant on that market. From the point of view of outside undertakings interested in publishing a television magazine, the applicant's refusal to authorise, on request and on a non-discriminatory basis, any third party to publish its programme listings is therefore comparable ... to an arbitrary refusal by a car manufacturer to supply spare parts ... to an independent repairer ...'[11]

The Court of First Instance applied the *Volvo v Veng* doctrine to copyright. This situation falls under the exception in the doctrine where the grant of a 'compulsory' licence is possible because the intellectual property right is exercised in a way which is prohibited by Article 86.[12]

The Court of First Instance also stressed that it is enough in order for Article 86 to be applicable that the abusive conduct is capable of affecting trade between member states. No present and real effect on such trade is requested.[13]

The *Magill* cases went on to be appealed before the Court of Justice.[14] The main problem with the approach taken by the Commission and the

10 Case T-69/89 *Radio Telefis Eireann v Commission (Magill TV Guide Ltd intervening)* [1991] ECR II-485, [1991] 4 CMLR 586; Case T-70/89 *BBC and BBC Enterprises Ltd v Commission (Magill TV Guide Ltd intervening)* [1991] ECR II-535, [1991] 4 CMLR 669 and Case T-76/89 *Independent Television Publications Ltd v Commission (Magill TV Guide Ltd intervening)* [1991] ECR II-575, [1991] 4 CMLR 745.
11 Case T-69/89 *Radio Telefis Eireann v Commission (Magill TV Guide Limited intervening)* [1991] ECR II-485, [1991] 4 CMLR 586 at 618; similar rulings are found in the other *Magill* cases.
12 Compare R Whish *Competition Law* Butterworths (3rd edn, 1993) at 648, differently: C Bellamy and G Child *Common Market Law of Competition/ First Supplement to the Third Edition* Sweet & Maxwell (1991) at 87 could not reconcile the Commission's decision with the *Volvo v Veng* doctrine.
13 Case T-69/89 *Radio Telefis Eireann v Commission (Magill TV Guide Ltd intervening)* [1991] ECR II-485, [1991] 4 CMLR 586; case T-70/89 *BBC and BBC Enterprises Ltd v Commission (Magill TV Guide Ltd intervening)* [1991] ECR II-535, [1991] 4 CMLR 669 and case T-76/89 *Independent Television Publications Ltd v Commission (Magill TV Guide Ltd intervening)* [1991] ECR II-575, [1991] 4 CMLR 745.
14 Joined cases C-241/91 P and C-242/91 P *Radio Telefis Eireann and Independent Television Publications Ltd v Commission* [1995] ECR I-743, [1995] 4 CMLR 718.

Court of First Instance is that it could suggest that once an undertaking occupies a dominant position the simple refusal to grant a licence could constitute an abuse of that dominant position.[15] This cannot be a correct interpretation of Article 86. As suggested in *Volvo* and *Renault*, the interpretation of Article 86 develops along the lines of the interpretation of Articles 30 and 36. This is the approach we advocated above in relation to the free movement of goods and it was also the approach taken by Advocate-General Gulmann in his conclusion which was delivered in June 1994.[16]

In a controversial judgment, the wording of which strongly resembles the *Commercial Solvents* line of thought,[17] the Court of Justice declined to overrule the Court of First Instance. The reasons given by the Court and the implications of the judgment require some careful examination though.[18] The main principle is that a refusal to licence intellectual property rights can contravene Article 86 in 'exceptional circumstances'. In those cases compulsory licensing is an available remedy.[19]

When it established that the broadcasters occupied a dominant position, the Court indicated first of all that it accepted that the relevant product and geographical market should be defined as the market in comprehensive TV listings guides in Ireland and Northern Ireland. The Court went on to confirm that the mere ownership of an intellectual property right, here the copyright in the programme listings, does not confer a dominant position.[20] That dominant position did however exist in the particular circumstances of the case. This was derived from the fact that the broadcasters were the only source of the basic programming information, that they had a de facto monopoly over the raw material which that programming information constituted[1] and that they could therefore prevent effective competition in the secondary market of weekly TV magazines.[2]

Even so, the question remained whether the refusal to licence amounted to an abuse of that dominant position. The exisiting case law pointed towards the fact that the mere existence of the intellectual property right and its use that stays within the specific subject-matter of the right cannot amount to an abuse. If the possession of the immaterial right is to have any value, its owner must be free to decide under which circumstances and under which

---

15 See Haines 'Copyright Takes the Dominant Position: The Advocate General's Opinion in Magill' [1994] 9 EIPR 401 at 401.
16 See ibid.
17 See *ICI and Commercial Solvents v Commission* [1974] ECR 223.
18 See Stamatoudi 'The Hidden Agenda in *Magill* and its Impact on New Technologies' (1998) 1 JWIP 153.
19 Joined cases C-241/91 P and C-242/91 P *Radio Telefis Eireann and Independent Television Publications Ltd v Commission* [1995] ECR I-743, [1995] 4 CMLR 718.
20 Ibid, at para 46.
1 Ibid, at para 53.
2 Ibid, at para 47.

financial conditions he is prepared to grant a licence. A right to refuse to grant a licence must be part of such a system and must therefore come within the specific subject-matter of the right. In normal circumstances such a refusal can therefore not be in breach of Article 86. However, there may be circumstances where the intellectual property right is used improperly and to serve purposes that have nothing to do with the real purpose and essential function of the right. If the right is abused, the refusal to grant a licence is no longer used to implement the essential function of the right and, just as anything else in relation to an exclusive or monopoly intellectual property right, exposes itself to the sanction of Article 86. This approach is endorsed by the Court's judgment. The Court argued that a refusal might in exceptional circumstances constitute an abuse.[3] These exceptional circumstances involved the following in this case. The broadcaster's main activity is broadcasting; the TV guides market is only a secondary market for them. By refusing to provide the basic programme listing information, of which they were the only source, the broadcasters prevented the appearance of new products which they did not offer and for which there was a consumer demand. The refusal could not be justified by virtue of their normal activities. And, by denying access to the basic information which was required to make the new product, the broadcasters were effectively reserving the secondary market for weekly TV guides to themselves. The use of copyright to block the apprearance of a new product for which the copyright information is essential and to reserve a secondary market to oneself is an abuse and cannot be said to be necessary to fulfil the essential function (reward and encouragement of the author) of copyright. This is especially so if one is the only source of the copyright information or material. Especially the latter element is of vital importance. It may not be part of the abuse, but the availability of other sources for the material would take away the element of dominance. And without dominance there can simply be no abuse of a dominant position.

Looking at it this way, the Court has allayed the fears that had arisen on the basis of the problematically worded judgment of the Court of First Instance. It is also clear that the Court's judgment in *Magill* is by no means a departure from its exisiting case law. It is rather an application of that case law in an extreme set of circumstances. All intellectual property rights still have their role in a free market economy, but as we explained earlier that role is restricted to their capacity to enhance overall levels of competition. This means that intellectual property rights can only be used to fulfil their essential function. This point has been overlooked on too many occasions and the specific subject-matter of a right has too often been seen as a list, written in stone, of things that the rightholder is allowed to do. Refusing a licence had to be on that list. *Magill* has shown that that list is by no means

---

3   Ibid, at paras 54 and 57.

written in stone and that the items on there are only there in as far as they fulfil the essential pro-competitive function of the intellectual property right involved. They will be caught by the operation of competition law if they are (ab)used for other purposes. This will be the case in what the Court described as 'exceptional circumstances' and the essential facilities doctrine which is so prominently present in the judgment provides just one, but admittedly a poignant, example of exceptional circumstances in which the use of an intellectual property right falls outside what is required for the fulfilment of the essential function of the intellectual property right concerned.

One can find criticism of the fact that the UK and Ireland grant copyright to basic programme information listings that have such a low level of originality between the lines of the *Magill* case. This point will have to be addressed though by the member states concerned or by means of a Parliament and Council Directive. The Court has no power to interfere with issues such as what is original enough to attract copyright or in trade marks terms, with the point whether there is de facto confusion between two trade marks. It made this clear in the *Deutsche Renault* v *Audi* case.[4] These issues of substantive law are part of the sovereign powers of the member states in the absence of Community harmonisation measures on the points concerned.

It must be obvious that these exceptional circumstances will rarely be found and that the operation of the rule in *Magill* will be restricted to unusual and special cases. The essential function is by no means a narrow concept. *Magill* must also be seen against the background of the fact that a weak copyright was involved. Most other member states would not even have given copyright in the basic programme information concerned. Basic information is more easily an indispensible raw material for new products than the more traditional highly creative personal expressions of certain ideas by authors. This means that the Magill rule will more easily bite in the former cases. The more original the work is, the more creative expression that has gone in a particlar expression of an idea, the more unlikely it is that a refusal to licence will be an abuse. The refusal to grant a licence for the TV listing became abusive, among other things, because without the licence Magill could not publish any guide. The whole market and the emergence of a new product were blocked. A refusal to grant a licence to turn a novel into a movie is clearly not in the same league. Plenty of other films can be made and the monopolisation of any secondary market is simply not present.

The conclusion that *Magill* needs to be confined to a small number of extreme cases is also supported by the Court of First Instance's judgment in one of the many *Ladbroke* cases.[5] This case was concerned with the

---

4   Case C-317/91 *Deutsche Renault v Audi* [1993] ECR I-6227, [1995] 1 CMLR 461.
5   Case T-504/93 *Tiercé Ladbroke SA v European Commission (Société d'Encouragement et des Steeple-Chases de France intervening)* [1997] 5 CMLR 309.

question whether a refusal by the French copyright owners to license sound and pictures of French horse races to a Belgian betting agency amounted to a *Magill*-style abuse of a dominant position.[6] The emphasis lies in this case squarely on the issue of abuse. That abuse must be found on the relevant geographical market and any activity or decision outside that market is irrelevant. The Court of First Instance rules that no *Magill*-style abuse could be found. It reached this conclusion for a couple of reasons.[7] First, Ladbroke was not prevented from entering another market by the refusal to licence. It was already an important player on the market concerned and it could not be argued that the French horse racing organisations reserved that betting market for themselves, especially since they were not even present on it. The pictures were not essential for the exercise of the activity in question. And secondly, the emergence of a new product was not blocked and in any case the sound and pictures were not the essential ingredient of such a product. Ladbroke rather wanted to offer an additional service to its clients for its main betting activity. Only a refusal to licence that concerned either a new product whose introduction might be prevented, despite specific, constant and regular potential consumer demand, or a product of service that was essential, due to the absence of a real or potential sustitute, for the activity concerned, would fall foul of Article 86.

Ladbroke was also not excluded from a market in which the French horse racing organisations were operating by the refusal to licence and neither was it discriminated against on the Belgian market.[8]

Magill had left open the question whether or not the prevention of the emergence of a new product and the monopolisation of another market were seperate instances of abuse in this type of case or whether they were conditions that needed to be met cumulatively. *Ladbroke* provides a reassuring answer to that question.[9] The case was dismissed on the basis that no monopolisation of a separate market had taken place. The Court found it unnecessary to examine the prevention of the emergence of a new product issue in detail. This can only mean that the two conditions must apply cumulatively. A dominant undertaking is not obiged to allow a second player onto the market by licensing its intellectual property rights to it. The *Commercial Solvents* decision[10] imposes a different conclusion if the only

6 See Fitzgerald 'Magill Revisited: Tiecé Ladbroke SA *v* The Commission' [1998] EIPR 154.

7 See Case T-504/93 *Tiercé Ladbroke SA v European Commission (Société d'Encouragement et des Steeple-Chases de France intervening)* [1997] 5 CMLR 309 at paras 129 to 131.

8 Ibid at paras 124 to 128 and 133.

9 See Fitzgerald 'Magill Revisited: Tiecé Ladbroke SA *v* The Commission' [1998] EIPR 154.

10 See *ICI and Commercial Solvents v Commission* [1974] ECR 223.

thing involved is the monopolisation of a secondary market. That is an abuse as such; even a new product is not prevented from appearing on that market.

It must therefore be clear that *Magill* is anything but an authorisation to compel any intellectual property rightholder in a dominant position to licence the intellectual property right concerned to any potential licencee.

Chapter 18

Copyright – an overview

Copyright is a right of diversity. We started our analysis by referring to the dual roots of the right and this element proved to be omnipresent in the rest of our analysis. Copyright is a constant balancing act between the author and his or her rights and the entrepreneur who exploits copyright works and his or her rights. This is inevitable as they are heavily interdependent.

We discussed the wide variety of sometimes very different types of works that attract copyright protection. The one point they have in common is that they form the original expression of an idea or that, if they are derivative works, they are a technical format which allows the exploitation of that expression.

The essence of the copyright in a work is the exclusive right to make copies of the work. This right is often transferred to the entrepreneur who undertakes the commercial exploitation of the work. The author maintains then his or her moral rights to prohibit any abusive form of exploitation of the work and the transfer of rights normally also involves a form of remuneration for the author.

The constant evolution in the way in which copyright works are exploited resulted in rights for performers and producers of phonograms on the one hand and in things such as rental and lending rights on the other hand. The exploitation of copyright is also linked very strongly to the evolution of the reproduction technology.

As copyright is a rather weak right that only protects the expression and not the idea, it offers as a form of compensation a rather long term of protection. In general this term is now 70 years from the death of the author, although some 50-year terms still exist.

Copyright has over the years proved to be a flexible and extremely useful tool. It plays also an important economic role. New technical developments in the computer area are stretching it to the limit though. We will discuss some of these developments in the chapter on computers and intellectual property rights. Suffice it here to say that it is essential that copyright sticks to the core elements of the right which we described above, because bending these too strongly would turn a flexible right into a hollow right. We have to preserve the common core that is formed by the essential copyright requirements.

Designs

Chapter 19

Design and copyright

INTRODUCTORY REMARKS

Various definitions of what is a design could be given. Design law sees design as features of shape or configuration which can either be of an aesthetic or of a functional nature. For each of them there is now a separate design right. Aesthetic designs are protected under the provisions of the Registered Designs Act 1949, while the functional designs are governed by the provisions of the Copyright, Designs and Patents Act 1988. This has always been an area of substantial complexity, amongst other elements due to the influence of copyright.

THE WALL BETWEEN DESIGN AND COPYRIGHT

There seems to be a natural overlap between design law and copyright, as in the majority of cases designs are laid down in drawings, plans or blueprints that attract copyright protection. A copy of an article incorporating the design involves making a three dimensional copy of the drawing, plan or blueprint and infringes the copyright in them.

The problems involved became very clear in the famous *British Leyland Motor Corpn Ltd v Armstrong Patents Co Ltd* case,[1] which deals with functional designs. British Leyland owned the copyright in the drawings for exhaust pipes for its vehicles which were built to a functional design. Armstrong reverse engineered the exhaust pipes. They made their own exhaust pipes by taking the original apart and using the information acquired to make identical copies and they wanted to sell them as spare parts for

---

1   [1986] AC 577, [1986] 1 All ER 850.

British Leyland cars. On the basis of our above analysis British Leyland could successfully bring a case for copyright infringement. This would lead to the undesirable situation though that a manufacturer has a de facto monopoly in the supply of spare parts for the life of the author plus (then) 50 years and could eventually abuse that monopoly. The House of Lords attempted to get around the problem by applying the land law principle of non-derogation from grant to soften the exaggerated strength of copyright protection for functional designs. By selling cars, British Leyland had impliedly promised to make spare parts available during the life of the car to facilitate its maintenance. It was clear that law reform was needed.

The Copyright, Designs and Patents Act 1988 tried to remove the overlap between copyright and designs once and for always. Section 51 is the provision which is supposed to take care of that. Section 51(1) reads:

> 'It is not an infringement of any copyright in a design document or model recording or embodying a design for anything other than an artistic work or a typeface to make an article to the design or to copy an article made to the design.'

The section goes back to the old method of protecting a design through the copyright in the design drawings. It does not abolish copyright in these drawings or in any other design document, but it provides an exception in relation to copyright infringement. It is no longer an (indirect) infringement of the copyright in the design document or in a model recording or embodying the design to make an article to that design or to copy an article made to that design. This means that a photocopy of the design document will still infringe the copyright in the design document, but that an article made on the basis of that design document will no longer infringe the copyright in the design document as a three dimensional copy of a two dimensional work. Instead the infringement action will now have to be brought under the new design right provisions. In a case such as *British Leyland* the copyright in the two dimensional drawing of the three dimensional product would not be infringed. An action for infringement of the design right in the copied design is the only available option.

A couple of points in this system need clarification and a number of details need to be added. A design document includes any record of a design. This can for example take the format of a literary work, a set of computer data, a model or a photograph apart from the obvious drawing format.[2] It has to be a design document or model which records or embodies the design. This clearly refers to a document or model made for that purpose. Taken on its own a drawing of Mickey Mouse made for a comic strip is not made for the production of articles, such as toy figures, to that design. It is

2   CDPA 1988, s 51 (1) and (3).

submitted that such drawings are not design documents for the purposes of section 51. Otherwise all kinds of drawings and photographs would lose a substantial part of their copyright protection, especially the possibility of infringement by making a three dimensional copy of the two–dimensional original, just because someone may at one stage want to use them for design purposes. More importantly, section 51 excludes design documents or models for artistic works or typefaces from its scope. Copyright in them will still be infringed if an article is made to their design or if an article made to that design is copied. A good example may be found in the production of furniture.[3] It will not be an infringement to make furniture to someone else's design without having obtained permission to do so unless the furniture as such is an artistic work. Furniture can indeed qualify for copyright protection as an artistic work, be it a sculpture or a work of artistic craftsmanship, and if this is the case the exclusion clause in section 51 will apply and copyright will still be infringed.[4] In everyday life most cases of furniture production rely on mass industrial production and artistic copyright protection is unlikely to exist in these cases. Items which are not infringing copyright can also be issued to the public or included in films, broadcasts or cable programme services without infringing copyright.[5] This completes the copyright exception, which would otherwise have little practical economical importance.

If section 51 is to be really effective in reducing the overlap and the confusion it should cover both the overlap between copyright and unregistered-functional design and the overlap between registered-aesthetic design and copyright. There is no doubt that it covers the overlap with unregistered designs as cases such as *British Leyland* did arise in relation to functional designs. And we will see that the definition of an unregistered design is identical to the one found in section 51. Though it is submitted that that definition is at first glance wide enough in scope to encompass the definition of registered designs,[6] there are a number of elements which complicate things. First of all most design documents which are copied in aesthetic designs will be artistic works and this category of copyright works is excluded from the scope of section 51. Second, surface decoration is also excluded from the scope of section 51, while it may come inside the scope of the definition of a registered design where no similar exclusion is found. It is not necessary to go into the detail of the various definitions right now before we discuss the two design rights in substance. It is indeed clear that in practice section 51 is almost exclusively restricted to cases of unregistered

3   CDPA 1988, s 51 (1).
4   See MacQueen 'A Scottish Case on Unregistered Designs' [1994] 2 EIPR 86 on
    Squirewood Ltd v Morris & Co Ltd at 87. The case was not reported, but is available on
    Lexis.
5   CDPA 1988, s 51(2).
6   Registered Designs Act 1949, s 1, discussed infra.

design. This creates the impression that the overlap between copyright and registered design is left untouched and may still create problems, but this impression is not correct.

Indeed, for purposes of completeness a brief reference should be made to section 52 of the 1988 Act. This section refers to authorised use of an artistic work and restricts the term of copyright protection in these works to 25 years if copies of the work are made by an industrial process or if such copies are marketed.[7] Articles to the description of the artistic work can be made without infringing copyright, starting 25 years after the end of the calendar year in which the first marketing of the articles authorised by the owner of the artistic copyright were first marketed.[8] This effectively reduces the duration of copyright to that of the registered design right, as we will see. The two rights co-exist, but no substantial problems arise as the two forms of protection have the same coverage and will disappear together.

But what was the influence of the law reform on the defence created in the *British Leyland* case? The provisions of the Copyright, Designs and Patents Act 1988, and especially sections 51 and 52, effectively replaced the existing law in this area. One of the reasons why Parliament introduced new legislation in this area was that the old law was not satisfactory. It is submitted that the British Leyland defence does in practice no longer exist under the regime of the 1988 Act. Section 171(3) keeps the defence alive in theory as it stipulates that the provisions of the 1988 Act do not affect any rule of law that prevents or restricts the enforcement of copyright. The British Leyland defence clearly had that effect. But for the defence to operate there must first of all be a case of copyright infringement and the effect of section 51 is exactly that this will no longer be possible in design related cases. The copyright in the design document will not be infringed, so in practice there is no use for a rule restricting the enforcement of copyright. Making articles, such as the famous exhaust pipes, to the design contained in the design document, such as the drawing of the exhaust pipe, will not infringe the copyright in the design document.[9] The alleged copyright infringer does not infringe and the production can go ahead. There is no need for the British Leyland defence against copyright infringement to arrive at this conclusion.

Nevertheless, the Act has not abolished the British Leyland defence. Maybe the defence can still play a role, when defined properly. That proper

---

7   In the UK or elsewhere, s 52(1)(b).
8   CDPA 1988, s 52.
9   Contra, *Flogates Ltd, USX Corpn and USX Engineers and Consultants Inc v Refco Ltd and Graham Peter Briggs* [1996] FSR 935. The comments by Jacob J were obiter, as the case was concerned with the transitional provisions of the 1988 Act. (Schedule 1, Para 19(9) to the 1988 Act keeps the defence alive for cases which come under the transitional provisions.)

definition was provided by the Privy Council in the *Canon* case.[10] The Privy Council ruled that the British Leyland spare parts exception must be seen as a proper exception from copyright infringement. It is the expression of the public policy rule that will prevent manufacturers using their copyright to control the aftermarket in spare parts. That public policy rule will operate if two requirements are met. First, there must be a manifest unfairness to the consumer, who is using the original product for which the spare part is intended. Secondly, the monopoly must plainly be anti-competitive in nature. The Privy Council added that the jurisprudential and economic basis for the doctrine of the exception becomes very fragile if these requirements are not met.

The *Canon* case applied this to a situation where replacement ink cartridges for photocopiers and laserprinters infringed the copyright in the drawings of the original Canon cartridges. It was held that the defence did not apply, because the replacement of a cartridge was not a repair which an ordinary purchaser would assume he could carry out himself in order to have the continuing enjoyment of the product he purchased. The manufacture of the cartridges was an infringement of the copyright in the drawings and the defence could not change that position (the provisions of the 1988 Act did not apply in this case), because the purchaser accepted that he would every so often need to buy a replacement cartridge. The interests of the consumer were not affected unfairly and the practices of Canon were not anti-competitive.[11]

It is submitted that the decision to found the British Leyland spare parts exception on grounds of public policy needs to be applauded. It must indeed be the case that even in a purely domestic context intellectual property rights need to be fitted in with the overall principle of the enhancement of free competition. Public policy rules should be able to stop the operation of intellectual property whenever these rights are put to inproper use, whenever they are abused and used for an anti-competitive goal for which they were not intended. Although narrowly focused on the spare parts issue, the decision of the Privy Council could open the door for a wider application of this exceptional public policy safeguard in other cases of abuse. It could eventually be developed into a rule that fulfils the same role in domestic competition law as that fulfilled by the essential function - specific subject matter doctrine in the *Magill* case at European level in relation to intellectual property rights. It is now time though to look at the substantive provisions on registered designs.

10   *Canon Kabushiki Kaisha* v *Green Cartridge Co (Hong Kong) Ltd* [1997] AC 728, [1997] 3 WLR 13.
11   Ibid.

Chapter 20

Registered designs

STARTING POINTS

One could be forgiven for thinking that a design is a plan or blue-print which shows how an item is to be constructed or how the elements of the item are arranged. Intellectual property law however has never accepted that simple definition. For our purposes a design is concerned with aspects of an article or with features applied to it, and is never concerned with the article itself. To complicate things further two types of designs exist in the UK: registered designs, based on the Registered Designs Act 1949, as amended, and (unregistered) designs, based on the Copyright, Designs and Patents Act 1988. In this chapter we will examine the registered designs system.

Registered designs are aesthetic designs which are intended to appeal to the eye. Decorative features or articles such as a beautifully decorated crystal vase or patterns applied to household porcelain will attract registered design protection. On the other hand designs may be functional in nature. Exhaust pipes for cars are the prime example,[1] but there are plenty of other examples such as kitchen utensils which fall within the scope of the (unregistered) design right. Oversimplification leads to the rule that aesthetic designs are covered by the registered design while functional designs are covered by the (unregistered) design right. In reality there is a considerable overlap. Many aesthetic designs are also functional and may meet the requirements of the (unregistered) design right, such as food containers of a particular shape made to distinguish the product of one manufacturer from the identical product of a competitor which also contains the product, while some primarily functional designs may have eye appeal as well. As indicated

1   Spare parts occupy a special position in design law, see *British Leyland Motor Corpn Ltd v Armstrong Patents Co Ltd* [1986] AC 577, [1986] 1 All ER 850.

above we will now start our analysis of the registered designs,[2] which were introduced approximately a century ago in response to a demand from the textile industry.

REQUIREMENTS FOR THE GRANT OF A REGISTERED DESIGN

A design means 'features of shape, configuration, pattern or ornament' that are 'applied to an article by an industrial process' and that are 'features which in the finished article appeal to and are judged by the eye'.[3] Such a design should also be new.[4]

Features

Features that are registrable are features of shape, configuration, pattern or ornament. Red crystal grapes on a crystal vase form a good example. Two-dimensional designs as well as three-dimensional designs attract protection. Surface decoration and designs applied to textiles and materials from which dresses are made are placed on the same footing as the shape of a suite of furniture.

Novelty

Such a design must also be new. The first basic rule is that the design should not be the same as any design registered in a prior application.[5] As a design should be seen as something applied to an article, the nature of the article to which the design was to be applied is irrelevant in this respect. The second basic rule is that prior to the date of the application the design should not have been published in the UK.[6]

Some detail needs to be added to the framework provided by these basic rules. They will also apply to designs which are not really fully but almost fully identical to an existing design if the differences are only to be found in immaterial details or in features that are commonly used as variants of the original features inside the relevant area of trade. There is one exception to this rule. When I want to extend the registration of my design to other articles a couple of years after the initial registration for one article the prior

2   We will refer to the Registered Designs Act 1949 (RDA), as amended by the Copyright, Designs and Patents Act 1988.
3   RDA 1949, s 1(1).
4   RDA 1949, s 1(2).
5   RDA 1949, s 1(4)(a).
6   RDA 1949, s 1(4)(b).

registration or publication of the design is ignored. The proprietor of a design will have no problem in passing the novelty hurdle if he wishes to register his design in respect of other articles, even if the design is altered slightly.[7] A similar rule applies when an application is made for the registration of a design that is based on or copied from an artistic work. Such a corresponding design will be treated as new as long as the prior use does not include any form of commercial exploitation of articles to which the design has been applied industrially.[8] A last rule relates only to the prior publication of the design. A design will still be considered to be new if the prior publication was made contrary to good faith or in breach of confidence.[9]

This novelty requirement bears many similarities with the novelty requirement in patent law. In *Rosedale Associated Manufacturers Ltd v Airfix Products Ltd*[10] the patent anticipation rules were held to apply to registered designs. This shows clearly that registered designs are seen as belonging in the category of industrial rights.

Eye appeal

This is an essential requirement. A design has to appeal to the eye if it is to be registered. To use the example mentioned above, the red crystal grapes on the crystal vase have to appeal to the eye. The visual appearance of the design should be aesthetic but no artistic quality is required. As we have seen in our analysis of copyright, artistic works will attract copyright protection. It was never the purpose of the Registered Designs Act 1949 to duplicate that protection. On the contrary registered design protection should be seen as an industrial right. Inventions are protected by the patent system, but apart from the technological value of a product, there is also its appearance. It is worth protecting a design which is different from the existing ones and which distinguishes the article to which it is applied from other similar articles, not on technological grounds, but on grounds of appearance. To fulfil this distinguishing function, a design needs to attract attention; it needs visual qualities that catch the eye. This visual attractiveness is what the word aesthetic means in this context - nothing more is required.

A direct consequence of all this is that features of shape or configuration which are internal can only be registered if the outer surface of the article to which they are applied is transparent. They cannot have eye appeal if

---

7   RDA 1949, s 4(1).
8   RDA 1949, s 6(4) and (5).
9   RDA 1949, s 6(1).
10   [1957] RPC 239.

they cannot be seen. It is however necessary to circumscribe the concept of eye appeal further and that is exactly what section 1(1) and (3) of the Registered Designs Act 1949 does.

The features should, in the finished article, appeal to the eye and they should be judged by the eye.[11] Designs which lead to the article being chosen by the consumer because of its usefulness do not pass this test.[12] An alternate coloured bands design for computer printout paper presents a good example. It was not registrable because consumers would buy it for its utility as it facilitated the reading of the printout and allowed the information to be printed more closely spaced.[13] The appearance of the article must also be material[14] and this tightens the eye appeal rule. One could start the interpretation of this concept by stating that the appearance of the article must be of importance. Whether or not the appearance of an article is material depends on the outcome of a two-stage test. The first stage of the test focuses on the group of articles that are of the same type as the article to which the design has been applied. One has to examine whether persons acquiring or using such articles do normally take into account aesthetic considerations. If that is indeed the case then the appearance of the article is material. If the outcome of the examination is negative, one goes on to consider the second stage of the test. This stage of the test focuses exclusively on articles to which the design for which registration is sought has been applied. The question is whether persons acquiring or using such articles would take aesthetic consideration into account to a material extent when making their choice. If the answer is yes the appearance of the article is material despite the fact that this is not the case for other articles of the same type or for the category of similar articles as a whole.[15]

This test is not as draconian as it may seem to be at first sight. Even if the article is acquired or used for almost entirely functional reasons the aesthetic considerations and the appearance of the article may have their importance, especially when a choice is made between various brands of the same article. One does not normally buy vinegar because the bottle in which it is contained appeals to the eye but a bottle made to a new attractive design which would look attractive on your dining table or in your kitchen may appeal to you and may make you decide to buy that particular brand of vinegar. Such a design would pass this test and certain specific features

---

11 RDA 1949, s 1(1).
12 Compare *Amp Incorporated v Utilux Pty Ltd* [1972] RPC 103 at 108, per Lord Reid; it should be noted that the RDA 1949 referred to designs judged solely by the eye before it was amended by the Copyright, Designs and Patents Act 1988.
13 *Lamson Industries Ltd's Application* [1978] RPC 1, per Whitford J.
14 RDA 1949, s 1(3).
15 It is submitted that certain pre-1988 decisions would fall foul of this new test; eg a design including the underside of a shower tray that is no longer visible when installed would not pass this test, not as a category of article and neither as that particular shower tray: *Gardex Ltd v Sorata Ltd* [1986] RPC 623.

of the vinegar bottle could be registered. It should be emphasised that the test refers not only to acquisition, but also to use. Appearance will be particularly important in terms of purchase and usage of wallpaper, curtains, wrapping paper and the like. This too makes the test easier to pass.

Application to an article by an industrial process

We have mentioned already that a design as such is not protected. It must be applied to an article or at least there must be an intention to do so. That application must be done by means of any industrial process. It is submitted that this requirement refers to the fact that registered designs are industrial property rights and thus tries to avoid an overlap with artistic copyright. Individual and unique copies are excluded, but they may fall within the scope of copyright protection. The design needs to be applied to a series of articles.[16] The industrial process reference further indicates that that application should be done by a process which can be repeated in an identical way such as a hot metal stamp applied by hand or a computer operated laser printing or cutting system on a mass production line. In this respect the requirement bears a lot of similarity with the industrial application requirement for patents. It is clear that the Act only refers to the application of the design to the final article, storage of the design in a computer program or any other intermediate step in the industrial application of the design will not, as such, give rise to registered design protection.

Things are complicated further by the definition of the term article. Any article of manufacture and any part of an article, if that part is made and sold separately, are included in the definition.[17] And only these articles coming within the definition can be considered for design protection. Difficulties specifically arise in relation to parts of an article. It is submitted that the separate sale involved is a sale to the end user and that this provision should be taken to operate on this level only. If sales to the assembling manufacturer are included as well all these parts become articles themselves and the distinction loses its meaning. This approach corresponds with that taken by Graham J in *Sifam Electrical Instrument Co Ltd v Sangamo Weston Ltd*,[18] a case that was concerned with a design on the front of an electric meter that was held not to be an article because no separate sale was envisaged. He said:

'... on the whole I think the intention must be to grant registration only for such articles as are intended by the proprietor of the design to be

16   See RDA 1949, s 6(6); see also Rule 26 Registered Design Rules 1995 (SI 1995/2912).
17   RDA 1949, s 44(1).
18   [1971] 2 All ER 1074, [1973] RPC 899.

put on the market and sold separately, such as for example a hammer handle, or a bit of a bradawl'.[19]

Afterwards he went on to state that '... both the sale and the manufacture of the part in question must be operations which are distinct from the manufacture and sale of the whole article of which the "part" forms a component'. The problem becomes worse when we consider the issue of spare parts. For example designs for door panels for vehicles can be seen as parts that are made separately, but are sold as part of the vehicle. That approach was taken by the High Court in *Ford Motor Co Ltd & Iveco Fiat SpA's Design Application*[20] and the design was held not to be registrable. The counter-argument here is that the spare part is also sold separately. The door panels are sold as part of the vehicle, but they are also sold separately as spare parts.

The *Ford* case led to a judicial review procedure which sought to clarify this issue.[1] A distinction was made between two types of components or spare parts. First there are those that form part and contribute to the overall shape and appearance of the product, such as the door panels, the windscreen and the boot lid if we stick to the motor vehicle as an example of a product. Secondly there are those components or spare parts that are contributing features to the appearance of the product, but are only subsidiary to its essential shape, such as seats and steering wheels in our example. The first type of component is only sold separately to allow someone to replace a damaged or deteriorated part of the product. They are not sold separately in the sense that someone who does not own a particular type of product would buy a spare part for that particular product for general use. These components have no general use. No one would buy a Ford Escort door panel for general use, one only buys it to replace a damaged or deteriorated door panel of a Ford Escort. The second type of component can be substituted without radically affecting the appearance or identity of the product. In our example seats or steering wheels can be substituted by sportier ones without producing that effect. These components are made and sold separately. You may buy light alloy wheels, sporty wheel covers and steering wheels irrespective of the original ones on your car, so these components are bought for general use. McCowan J concluded that the essential point is whether an article or part is made and sold separately and

'to be that, an article has to have an independent life as an article of commerce and not merely be an adjunct of some larger article of which

19   Ibid at 914.
20   [1993] RPC 399.
1   *R v Registered Designs Appeal Tribunal, ex p Ford Motor Co Ltd* [1994] RPC 545.

■

it forms part. ... The selling of a mere replacement part is not separate from the sale of the article as a whole.'[2]

The first type of component does not come within the definition of section 44(1) and will not attract design protection, but the second type of component does come within the definition and may, if all other requirements are met, attract design protection.

When the case went before the House of Lords their Lordships declined the invitation to overrule the decision.[3] Their Lordships' judgment excludes both parts which will only ever form part of a finished product and parts which are intended for dual use as part of a larger object and as replacement parts from registration. Only parts that are subsidiary to the overall shape of the object escape the exclusion, because they have an independent life as an article of commerce. Dual use parts could arguably also have an independent life as an article of commerce, but the House of Lords ignored this argument. In severely limiting the scope for registration the House of Lords clearly attempted to avoid undue monopolies as a result of registration of design rights for spare parts. It can be doubted whether the 'must match' exception was not more suited to take care of that concern and whether the decision does not unduly restrict the scope for registration.[4] The term article seems in any case to have been defined extremely restrictively.

Exceptions to registration

Registered designs aim to confer an exclusive right in certain aesthetic features. They are not meant to prevent anyone from making a new design along the same lines. Therefore methods or principles of construction are excluded from registration.[5] An exclusive right in them would prevent anyone from arriving through them at a similar but new design.[6] Similar articles to other designs could in that case no longer be made. Such a monopoly would be excessively wide in scope. For similar reasons features of shape or configuration of an article that are dictated solely by the function which the article has to perform are also excluded.[7] An exclusive right in them would effectively pre-empt every attempt to design and make an article

---

2   Ibid.
3   *R v Registered Designs Appeal Tribunal, ex Ford Motor Co Ltd* [1995] RPC 167.
4   See H Laddie, P Prescott and M Vitoria *The Modern Law of Copyright and Designs* Butterworths (2nd edn, 1995), stop press insert and at 1071-1077 and compare W Cornish *Intellectual Property* Sweet & Maxwell (3rd edn, 1996) at 489-490.
5   RDA 1949, s 1(1)(a).
6   Compare the exclusion of scientific theories and mathematical methods from the scope of patent protection.
7   RDA 1949, s 1(1)(b)(i).

that performs the same function. This exception does not cover those cases where different features of shape or configuration are possible, only cases where only one option is left open to the designer if the article is to perform a certain function are covered.[8] This exception was invoked in a case concerned with rubber hot water bottles. A design for a rubber hot water bottle with a series of diagonally arranged ribs on both sides of the bottle had been registered. An alleged infringer raised as a defence that the registration was defective as it involved a method or principle of construction (the ribbed construction of the bottle) and that its features of shape or configuration were dictated solely by function (the ribs were necessary to facilitate the heat transfer). This defence was rejected. The development of other designs for hot water bottles was not prevented as ribs could still be used in other designs and horizontal ribs would also do the job.[9]

The other important exception is the 'must match' exception.[10] It covers design features which are dependent upon the appearance of another article if it is the intention of the author of the design that his article will form an integral part of that other article. The other article involved has to be taken as a whole. If we take design features of door panels for motor vehicles once more as an example, the other article is the motor vehicle including the door panels.[11] This exception can be seen as allowing independent manufacturers to produce spare parts[12] where normally a registered design right would have prevented this. Things are not that easy though and the exception is fairly narrow in scope. A body panel for a car will obviously be covered by the exception. It is designed to form part of a car and its design is determined by the fact that it has to fit in with the chassis and other body panels of the car. The designer has no design freedom. Mirrors and steering wheels on the other hand can be designed more freely; only the features of one contact point are dependent upon the appearance of another article. All their other features may be registrable as a design[13] as the designer has a great deal of design freedom. It is possible to replace the original parts by parts made to a different design. The design is in this case not dependent upon the appearance of another article, even if the owner may wish to blend the design of the new part in with the general style of the vehicle.[14] The same principles apply to all other kinds of products.[15]

8   See *Amp Incorporated v Utilux Pty Ltd* [1970] RPC 397.
9   *Cow (PB) & Co Ltd v Cannon Rubber Manufacturers Ltd* [1959] RPC 240.
10 RDA 1949, s 1(1)(b)(ii).
11 *R v Registered Designs Appeal Tribunal, ex p Ford Motor Co Ltd* [1994] RPC 545.
12 See *British Leyland Motor Corpn Ltd v Armstrong Patents Co Ltd* [1986] AC 577, [1986] All ER 850.
13 See *Ford Motor Co Ltd & Iveco Fiat SpA's Design Application* [1993] RPC 399.
14 *R v Registered Designs Appeal Tribunal, ex p Ford Motor Co Ltd* [1994] RPC 545.
15 Seen in combination with the definition given to the concept of an article this results in a very weak registered design protection for spare parts, even if the 'must match' exception is a rather narrow one.

The Registrar has also a general discretion. He will refuse registration of a design which is, in his opinion, contrary to law or morality.[16] Morality can only be invoked though if the design would offend the moral principles of right thinking members of society; the fact that some people might find the design distasteful is not sufficient.[17]

Multiple applications

Many designs are applied to various items. A pattern of lines and colours can be applied to wallpaper as well as to material for curtains and dresses. In principle multiple applications for registration of the design should be made[18] and when the design is registered separate fees should be paid. The Registered Designs Act provides one exception to this rule. A design may be registered for a set of articles. This implies that these articles have the same general character, are usually on sale together or are intended to be used together. This could be the case with a set of dishes or a set of glasses consisting out of one type of glass for wine, water glasses, port glasses and whisky glasses. The Act allows that the design applied to each of these types of glasses is slightly different, as long as the modifications or variations of the original design are not sufficient to alter the character of the design and as long as they do not affect the identity of the design substantially.[19] A set of decorative vases would not qualify if a different design was applied to each individual vase.

OWNERSHIP OF A REGISTERED DESIGN

The author of a design, this being the person who creates the design,[20] will be the first owner of the registered design.[1] There are only two exceptions to this rule. The employer of the employee who creates a design will be the first owner of the registered design if the design is created in the course of employment.[2] And the person who commissions a design will be the first owner of the registered design if the design was commissioned for money

---

16   RDA 1949, ss 3(3) and 43(1).
17   *Re Masterman's Design* [1991] RPC 89 (a design for a Scots doll with a kilt which exposed male genitalia when lifted); a design which shows directly representations of genitalia may still infringe morality though.
18   See Rule 13 Registered Design Rules 1995, SI 1995/2912.
19   RDA 1949, s 44.
20   RDA 1949, s 2(3).
1   RDA 1949, s 2(1).
2   RDA 1949, s 2(1B).

or money's worth.[3] A specific problem arises when a design is computer-generated. The computer is not a person and cannot become the first owner of the registered design, but there is no human author. The ownership of the registered design is then attributed to the nearest person involved in its creation, the person who made the arrangements necessary for the creation of the design.[4]

The ownership of a registered design right or the right to apply the design to any article can be transferred. This can be done by an assignment or any other form of transmission.[5] The transferee can either become the full owner of the right or he or she can become joint owner of the right together with the assignor.[6] Licences can also be granted.[7] Partial transfers, such as of the right to apply the design to one specific article, and transfers to more than one party, resulting in joint ownership, are possible. But all assignments of a registered design right must be registered. This means that in practice it is advisable that assignments and licences be in writing although this is in theory not an express requirement.[8]

RIGHTS OF THE OWNER AND INFRINGEMENT

Designs are registered in respect of certain articles. The registered owner of a design is given the exclusive right to do certain things in relation to articles which embody the design and in respect of which the design has been registered. The owner has the exclusive right to make or import these articles for sale or for hire or for use for the purposes of a trade or business. He or she also has the exclusive right to sell, hire or offer or expose these articles for sale or hire. These rights are extended to articles to which a design which is not substantially different from the registered design has been applied.[9]

This obviously means that anyone who does any of the above-mentioned acts without the consent or licence of the owner of the registered design infringes the rights in the registered design.[10] Infringement can only be avoided if the design used is substantially different from the registered design. The test for infringement is that of substantial taking from the allegedly infringed registered design. It has to be emphasised that only the specific design features of the article, which are protected by the registered

3   RDA 1949, s 2(1A).
4   RDA 1949, s 2(4).
5   RDA 1949, s 2(2).
6   Ibid.
7   See RDA 1949, s 19(4).
8   RDA 1949, s 19.
9   RDA 1949, s 7(1).
10   RDA 1949, s 7(2).

design right because they appeal to and are judged by the eye, will be taken into consideration, not the entire article. The case law shows this in an example concerned with baking trays. Not all the differences between the baking trays were in issue, but only those between the separating wires, the original design of which had been registered. In that case a design involving right-angled-goal-post shaped separating wires did not infringe a design involving semi-circular separating wires.[11] All features composing the design should be taken into consideration in order to arrive at a global judgement, similarities in one or more features being not of determining importance.[12]

The representation of the design that is part of the application for registration provides guidance and can be used for the comparison with the allegedly infringing design. The test should be applied by someone buying or using the article, basically the interested consumer. It has been suggested that such a person should first look at both designs together and in a later stage only to the allegedly infringing design. At that stage only the features that really struck the eye and deserve protection would be remembered and a decision whether the two designs are substantially different could be made at that stage.[13] In order to circumscribe the concept of substantial difference it may be helpful to examine whether the interested consumer with an imperfect recollection would be confused between the two designs. This was done in a case where a design involving horizontal grooves on the backrest of a plastic garden chair and sideway grooves on its seat was held not to infringe a registered design whose features were vertical grooves on the backrest and grooves running from front to back on the seat, because the interested consumer would not confuse the chairs with one another.[14]

In practice the approach differs between cases where the allegedly infringing design comprises novel features which relate to the overall shape and cases where the novel features are related to details. In the former case the comparison focuses on the general form of the designs, similarities on a couple of details will be rather unimportant. The contrary is true in the latter case, where the comparison obviously focuses on the details.[15]

The Act also lists a couple of other forms of infringement. All of them lead indirectly to an article that embodies the registered design. It is an infringement of a registered design:

–   to make anything for enabling an infringing article to be made anywhere;[16]

---

11   *Matthew Swain Ltd v Thomas Barker & Sons Ltd* [1967] RPC 23.
12   See *Best Products Ltd v F W Woolworth & Co Ltd* [1964] RPC 226 and *Benchairs v Chair Centre Ltd* [1974] RPC 429.
13   *Gaskell & Chambers Ltd v Measure Master Ltd* [1993] RPC 76.
14   *Sommer Allibert (UK) Ltd v Flair Plastics Ltd* [1987] RPC 599.
15   *Gaskell & Chambers Ltd v Measure Master Ltd* [1993] RPC 76.
16   RDA 1949, s 7(3).

- to do anything in relation to a kit which would infringe if it were done to the assembled article;[17]
- to make anything for enabling a kit to be made or assembled anywhere if the assembled article embodies the design;[18]

if in each case this is done without the licence of the owner of the registered design. In essence this removes the possibility of working with parts of the article which can be assembled; a kit is defined as a complete or substantially complete set of components which is intended to be assembled into an article. But, of course, only the registered features are protected and can be infringed, these forms of infringement do not extend design protection to other features.

The traditional remedies will be available in cases of infringement, but it should be noted that damages will not be available if the defendant can show that at the time of the infringement he was unaware of the registration of the design and had no reasonable grounds for supposing that the design was registered.[19] This provision bears strong similarities to section 62(1) of the Patents Act 1977. The owner of a registered design can rule out this option if he places a notice which comprises the registration number and the word registered or an abbreviation thereof on the articles that embody the design. It may be added that the most frequent defence against an allegation of infringement of a registered design involves an attack on the validity of the design. This defence is also available in patent and trade mark law. If the original design did not meet the requirements for registration and can be declared invalid, no design which can be infringed will exist. When successful this is probably the best possible defence.

DURATION OF THE REGISTERED DESIGN RIGHT

If the design is registered and published[20] after the examination of the application by the Designs Registry, a branch of the Patent Office, it will initially be valid for a period of five years[1] from the date of registration.[2] The registration of the design can be renewed four times, bringing the maximum term of protection to 25 years.[3] In practice the commercial life of an aesthetic design will often be shorter than 25 years and it can be

---

17   RDA 1949, s 7(4)(a).
18   RDA 1949, s 7(4)(b).
19   RDA 1949, s 9(1).
20   See RDA 1949, s 5 though, which contains exceptional rules.
1   RDA 1949, s 8(1).
2   Earlier applications will have a priority right that can be claimed for up to six months.
3   RDA 1949, s 8(2).

expected that many registered designs will be allowed to lapse because no further renewal is requested by their owners. Fashions do indeed exist in eye appealing designs. Many features of shape or ornament that were very popular around 1975 are no longer popular as we enter a new millennium, so there was no need to renew the design registration. In doing so one would have incurred a cost that could no longer be recuperated by profits through sales of items made to the design.

The application for renewal of the registered design right needs to be addressed to the Registrar during the last six months of the previous five-year period. In the absence of such an application the right will cease to exist upon expiry of the previous five-year period.[4] However the owner of the right is given an additional six-month period during which he can renew his right,[5] although a restoration fee will be payable on top of the normal renewal fee. If the right is restored it shall be treated as if it had never expired.[6]

COMMERCIAL EXPLOITATION

A design should be applied to the articles for which it is registered and this should be done to a reasonable extent. If this is not the case anyone can apply to the Registrar and be granted a compulsory licence. The Registrar has however a discretion. The grant of a compulsory licence does not take place automatically.[7] This system is very similar to the regime in relation to patents, but the regime applicable to licences of right is special. On the basis of a report by the Monopolies and Mergers Commission the appropriate minister or ministers can make an application to the Registrar. In situations where the rules on free competition are infringed this procedure allows the Registrar to make an entry in the Register indicating that licences of right will become available in respect of a certain registered design.[8] It should be repeated here that exploitation of a design can also take place through assignment of the design right or through the grant of licences in respect of the design right.

International exploitation of registered designs is facilitated by the fact that this area is covered by the Paris Convention for Industrial Property 1883 to which the UK is a party. A design application in one of the Contracting States will result in a priority right, the term of which is six

---

4   RDA 1949, s 8(3).
5   This is not an automatic right; the Registrar has a discretion.
6   RDA 1949, s 8(4).
7   RDA 1949, s 10.
8   RDA 1949, s 11A.

months, in relation to applications made in other Contracting States.[9] On the other hand substantial problems in relation to the international exploitation of a registered design are created by the tremendous international disparity in design protection systems. So, contrary to the UK system, many foreign systems do not provide for a search, but operate a deposit system, which means that designs are entered into the register upon application, with a possibility for all interested parties to object to the validity of the design and to request its removal from the register. The latter option was also taken by the Contracting Parties to the Hague Agreement 1925 which aimed at creating a unified registration system for designs, but this system never managed to attract much international support (and obviously the UK never adhered to it). Many Commonwealth countries copied the principles of the UK's registered design system. A large group among them extends protection to UK registered designs without requiring local registration.[10] They even request local applicants to register their designs in the UK. Some other countries and territories[11] require local re-registration before they extend protection to the design. We will come back to the difficulties regarding the international exploitation of design rights and the potential (partial) solution offered inside the European Union by the draft design right at the end of the chapter on (unregistered) designs.

REGISTERED DESIGNS – AN OVERVIEW

Aesthetic features applied to an article by an industrial process can be protected as a registered design if the design is new and appeals to the eye. The creator will normally own the design right. Designs created by employees and commissioned designs may present exceptions to this rule though.

The owner of the registered design right will be in a position to oppose infringement in relation to goods in respect of which the design has been registered. All the rights granted by a design registration expire after five years, unless the term of protection is renewed for further five year periods, up to a maximum of 25 years.

Designs which appeal to the eye can be of a tremendous commercial value. They do not amount to an invention and are not necessarily a trade mark. Copyright does not protect the idea behind the design. So, there is a

---

9   RDA 1949, s 14; a resident of the UK can only make a second application six weeks after the application in the UK was made. See RDA 1949, s 5.
10 Antigua, Bermuda, Botswana, Cyprus, Fiji, Ghana, Gibraltar, Hong Kong, Kenya, Malaysia, Sierra Leone, Singapore and Uganda all form part of this group.
11 Eg The Channel Islands, Malta and Tanzania.

very real need to register the design as a registered design. It is the only way to prevent competitors from cashing in on a good and valuable design by using a substantially identical design.

Chapter 21

Unregistered designs

INTRODUCTION

This type of design right was introduced by the Copyright, Designs and Patents Act 1988 in an attempt to overcome various problems. Functional non-aesthetic designs, such as those for exhaust pipes for cars, did not qualify for registered design protection and were not covered either by a special intellectual property right before 1988. But there was an overlap with copyright, as in the majority of cases functional designs are laid down in drawings, plans or blueprints that attract copyright protection. A copy of an article incorporating the design involves making a three-dimensional copy of the drawing, plan or blueprint and infringes the copyright in them. This system provided indirect protection for the majority of functional designs. It is hard to see why a certain category of designs, the aesthetic ones, deserve the creation of a special intellectual property right, while the other designs, which are purely functional in nature, should only be protected indirectly through copyright.

This argument becomes even more forceful if one considers that in theory all design rights, aesthetical and functional ones, benefit potentially from the overlap with copyright. In practice designs which met all the requirements for registration were often not registered because the non-bureaucratic and fee-free copyright offered long term protection. Parliament tried to remedy this by a series of arbitrary measures. First in the Copyright Act 1956 copyright protection was denied to designs that could have been registered. In the Design Copyright Act 1968, copyright was once again permitted but the term of copyright protection in such cases was restricted to the term of the registered design right.[1] This created absurd situations

---

1   At that stage 15 years, now extended to 25 years, as discussed supra.

such as the one in *Dorling v Honnor Marine*.[2] This case was concerned with a sailing dinghy. The design for the dinghy met the requirements for registration, but had not been registered. Before their relationship turned sour the defendant built the dinghies, both in complete and in kit form, under a licence granted by the plaintiff. The case arose when the defendant went on to assign his licence to a limited company he had formed. The company became the co-defendant in the case. Drawings of the dinghy and of all its parts existed and theoretically speaking the copyright in them was infringed by making three-dimensional copies. In practice the Copyright Act 1956 had removed copyright protection for designs that could have been registered, so no intellectual property right had been infringed in building the dinghies. But kits of parts were also made. The design of each of the parts was purely functional and could not be registered. As a result copyright protection in the drawings for them was not excluded by the provisions of the Copyright Act 1956 and the production of the parts formed an indirect infringement of the copyright in the drawings by making three-dimensional copies of these two-dimensional drawings. The functional design of the parts enjoyed protection for the life of the author plus 50 years, while no protection was available for the aesthetical design of the complete dinghy.[3] This discrepancy in protection for the two types of designs could not be justified.

It is not just the discrepancy that caused problems though. Copyright protection for functional designs proved also to be an inadequate solution. This became clear in the famous *British Leyland Motor Corpn Ltd v Armstrong Patents Co Ltd* case[4] which we discussed above. The case most strongly indicated the need for design law reform.

Action needed to be undertaken on two points. A specific intellectual property right needed to be created for functional designs. This would mean that the whole design area would be covered by two specific design rights: aesthetical designs would still be protected by the registered design right and the non-aesthetical functional designs would be covered by the new design right. The second point which needed to be addressed is the overlap with copyright. A clear delimitation of both the copyright and the design area was required. The Copyright, Designs and Patents Act 1988 reform attempted to reach that conclusion and created the (unregistered) design right. Officially it is called design right, but in order to distinguish it from the registered design and as there is no registration requirement we will describe it as the (unregistered) design.

---

2   *Dorling v Honnor Marine Ltd* [1965] Ch 1, [1964] 1 All ER 241.
3   Even if the design had been registered, the term of protection would have been much shorter.
4   *British Leyland Motor Corpn Ltd v Armstrong Patents Co Ltd* [1986] AC 577, [1986] 1 All ER 850.

SUBSISTENCE OF THE (UNREGISTERED) DESIGN RIGHTS

A design

The technical definition of a design which is given is that it is 'the design of any aspect of the shape or configuration (whether internal or external) of the whole or part of an article'.[5] This means that various aspects of the shape or configuration of an article can be the subject of different design rights, and that a design does not necessarily relate to the whole article. The case law offers an example in a case concerning pig fenders for use in pig arks which provide shelter for a single sow and her piglets. A two inch tube protected the teats of the sow. This two inch tube was held to be an aspect of the shape or configuration of a part of the fender. The tube element constituted a design.[6] However, a clear distinction must be made between the design and the article to which it is applied. The design is protected, while the article is not. The right protects the design itself and not the article on which it has been recorded or to which it has been applied.[7]

Aspects of the internal shape or configuration of the whole or part of an article can also be taken into account. This marks a clear difference with the eye appeal requirement for registered designs. (Unregistered) designs are intended to offer protection for functional designs; eye appeal is not required. The worth and ingenuity of such a design might be found in its detailed relative dimensions. A design might even exist (and be different and new) if the eye is not able to distinguish the shape (over other designs).[8] Larger, and clearly visible, shapes are obviously also possible and remain eligible for protection.

An original design

The design right will only subsist in designs that are original. This clearly means that the design should not be copied and that it should be the result of its creator's own work. But that is not all. Section 213(4) specifies that

'a design is not "original" if it is commonplace in the design field in question at the time of its creation'.

---

5   CDPA 1988, s 213 (2).
6   *C & H Engineering v Klucznik & Sons Ltd* [1992] FSR 421 at 428 per Aldous J and see Turner 'A True Design Right: C & H Engineering v Klucznik & Sons' [1993] 1 EIPR 24 at 24.
7   *Electronic Techniques (Anglia) Ltd v Critchley Components Ltd* [1997] FSR 401.
8   *Ocular Sciences Ltd & ANR v Aspect Vision Care Ltd; Geoffrey Harrison Galley v Ocular Sciences Ltd* [1997] RPC 289 at 423.

Laddie J has defined as commonplace any design that is 'trite, trivial, common or garden, hackneyed or of the type which would excite no particular attention in those in the relevant art'.[9] For example, in a case which was concerned with designs for leather cases for individual models of mobile phones, it was held that those aspects of the design that were found in industry standard cases were commonplace.[10] They were therefore excluded from the design right. However, it is possible to arrive at a design that is not commonplace through the combination of commonplace and trite ingredients. The test applies to the design. If the design is a combination of ingredients, that combination itself must not be commonplace.

The provision that is contained in section 213(4) makes the originality requirement for designs clearly more stringent than the one for copyright. Indeed, an objective component akin to the novelty consideration in patents is introduced.[11] A design that is already known and is in reality nothing more than a copy of an existing design will not be original. Mere changes in scale will not produce a different or new design either.[12] It is submitted that the design must be innovative, although the fact that it is new does not carry with it any qualitative judgement. The design must not be good or better than all existing designs, nor should it present a technical advantage. This does not imply that one should simply use the novelty requirement as applied in patent law though. First, the Act itself restricts the scope of the provision to the design field in question. Nothing outside that specific design field will influence the decision regarding the originality of the design. A design which is known in another unrelated design field will still be original. Patent anticipation is clearly much wider in scope. Secondly, by pointing out that the design should not be commonplace the Act clearly does not deprive of the required level of originality any design which has been circulated to a limited extent. Showing a limited number of articles incorporating the new design at a trade fair or consulting colleagues or potential customers on the qualities of the new design by showing them a drawing of it will not necessarily make the design commonplace. And thirdly, the relevant moment in time is the creation of the design rather than the filing date of the application used in patent law. This is of course a consequence of the fact that there is no registration requirement for this design right. Arguably this originality requirement comes close to the

---

9   Ibid at 429. In that case there was a reference to semiconductor products and the design right in them. The definition was repeated in *Mayfair Brassware* v *Aqualine International Ltd* [1998] FSR 135, in a context which refers to design rights.
10   *Philip Parker* v *Stephen Tidball* [1997] FSR 680.
11   Ibid.
12   *Ocular Sciences Ltd* v *Aspect Vision Care Ltd*; *Geoffrey Harrison Galley* v *Ocular Sciences Ltd* [1997] RPC 289 at 423.

novelty requirement for registered designs, although there is a clear difference in relation to anticipation by publication for certain purposes in restricted circles.

The tangible form requirement

No registration is required before a design can attract design protection, but one cannot protect something if the content, and thus the precise subject of protection of it, is not known. Therefore a design has to have a tangible form if it is to attract design protection.[13] This requirement can be met in two ways. The design can be recorded in a design document, as defined above, or an article can be made to the design. The design right will subsist from the moment of recording or from the moment of incorporation onwards.[14] And it is clear that the recording does not need to be made by the designer for this requirement to be met.[15] In the case of registered designs the tangible form is evidently required for the purposes of registration. One cannot materially speaking put together an application if the design does not exist, in the application, in a tangible form. In the registration system the date of registration is the starting point for the term of protection. As that element is not available in a system without registration, the date of recording is substituted for it.

The commencement date for the new design regime was 1 August 1989. Designs which were recorded in a design document or which were applied to an article before that date will not attract design right protection.[16]

Exceptions to the design right

Design rights will not subsist in a number of items. These are listed in section 213(3) of the 1988 Act. The first ones on the list are 'methods or principles of construction'.[17] This is an obvious exception, which also exists in relation to registered designs.[18] Particular features of shape or configuration, as applied to an article or a part of it, are protected, but not general, theoretical and eventually underlying principles. This exception is similar in nature to the scientific theories and mathematical methods exceptions in relation to patentable subject matter.[19] Also on the list is

---

13   CDPA 1988, s 213 (6).
14   Ibid.
15   *C & H Engineering v Klucznik & Sons Ltd* [1992] FSR 421 at 428, per Aldous J.
16   CDPA 1988, s 213 (7).
17   CDPA 1988, s 213(3)(a).
18   See Registered Designs Act 1949, s 1(1)(a).
19   Patents Act 1977, s 1(2)(a).

surface decoration,[20] which does not come within the category of functional rather than aesthetical design which the 1988 Act set out to protect. Surface decoration includes two things. First, it includes decoration lying on the surface of the article. And, secondly, it includes decorative features of the surface itself. Surface decoration cannot be confined to features that are essentially two-dimensional and it includes potentially also those features that also serve a functional purpose. Accordingly, the painted finish, cockbeading and V-grooves, which were all aspects of the external appearance of a single wall unit in a range of kitchens, were excluded from the scope of the design protection that was held to exist in the unit. The exclusion of certain aspects of the design as surface decoration does not mean that the rest of the aspects of the shape of the kitchen unit could not attract an (unregistered) design right.[1] The most important exceptions on the list are the 'must fit'[2] and 'must match'[3] exceptions though.

The 'must fit' exception excludes

'features of shape or configuration which enable the article to be connected to, placed in, around or against another article so that either article may perform its function'[4]

from the scope of the design right. The exception, which is also referred to as the interface provision, is confined to these situations where two articles, produced by one or two producers, are linked and certain features of shape or configuration enable either article to perform its function. However, it also applies to the interface features of two interfitting articles that are later assembled together to form the whole or part of another, larger, article.[5] The exception is also confined strictly to those features that play this enabling role, and must be of a certain precise shape or configuration to be able to play it. Other features of shape or configuration of the same article may well attract design protection. No feature of shape of configuration will escape from the scope of the exception because it also performed some other purpose, for example because it was also attractive.[6] In certain cases two or more different designs would enable the articles to be fitted together in a way which allowed one or all of them to perform their function. In those cases all these designs fall within the exclusion and no (unregistered) design right will exist in them. This indicates the wide scope of the exception, which

20 CDPA 1988, s 213(3)(c).
1   *Mark Wilkinson Furniture Ltd v Woodcraft Designs (Radcliffe) Ltd* [1998] FSR 63.
2   CDPA 1988, s 213(3)(b)(i).
3   CDPA 1988, s 213(3)(b)(ii).
4   CDPA 1988, s 213(3)(b)(i).
5   *Electronic Techniques (Anglia) Ltd v Critchley Components Ltd* [1997] FSR 401.
6   *Ocular Sciences Ltd v Aspect Vision Care Ltd; Geoffrey Harrison Galley v Ocular Sciences Ltd* [1997] RPC 289 at 424.

has as its purpose to prevent 'the designer of a piece of equipment from using design right to prevent others from making parts which fitted his equipment'.[7] That purpose will only be met if the drafting in wide terms of the exception is given its proper wide and extensive interpretation. The word 'article' can therefore be applied to living and formerly living things, as well as to inanimate things. This means that in a case concerning contact lenses the back radius, the diameter and the parallel peripheral carrier of the contact lens were all excluded from the design right, because they were features that enabled the lens to fit against the eyeball so as to allow the lens to perform its function of correcting the focusing ability of the eye and to remain in a stable position in the eye.[8] Another example is found in an electrical currency adaptor which allows you to use equipment built for 110 volts on our 220 volts system and which has many peculiar functional features of shape, but also rods that fit into a wall socket. This example may well result in design rights for the various features of shape, but no design right will subsist in the shape of the rods as this shape will be dependent upon the shape of the socket and will enable the adaptor to be connected to the socket and the electricity network and allow the socket and the adaptor to perform their functions. Those features of the shape of leather cases for individual mobile phones that enable the cases to be placed around the phones so that either the phones or the cases may perform their functions are yet another example of design features that fall foul of the exception.[9] This exception has an equivalent in section 1(1)(b)(i) of the Registered Designs Act 1949, but the latter refers to the 'purpose solely dictated by function' and is therefore wider in scope.

The 'must match' exception covers all features of shape or configuration that

'are dependent upon the appearance of another article of which the article is intended by the designer to form an integral part'.[10]

The classical example here are the doors of a car. Their design is determined by the appearance of the bodywork of the car. If I buy a door as a spare part for my car, it is rather essential that it fits in the gap left in the body for it to fit in. The exception, like the 'must fit' exception, of course does not extend to other features of the same article. It does apply where an article was not intended to form an integral part of another article. For example, the features of a kitchen unit were not caught by the exclusion , because the complete kitchen unit was a series of matching articles, none of which formed an

7   Ibid, per Laddie J.
8   Ibid at 425–428.
9   *Philip Parker* v *Stephen Tidball* [1997] FSR 680.
10   CDPA 1988, s 213(3)(b)(ii).

integral part of another article.[11] The fact that an article could incidentally be made to form an integral part of another article is not relevant. This makes it also clear that things made in sets, such as plates and glasses, are not covered by the exception. In these cases one design will be applied to the whole set.

The example concerning the design of the doors of a car that was given above already indicates that spare parts occupy a special position in relation to the design right. Not only do they cover a very substantial part of the whole design activity; the exceptions also seem to exclude them almost entirely from design protection. This meets the need for competition in this area. The legislature found it unacceptable that the producer of an article could, through copyright (at one time) and design protection regimes, monopolise the spare parts market. This market is opened up for competition through these exceptions to the design right. The fact that other features are not covered by the exception can create some difficulty though. The alternative producer of spare parts should be careful not to infringe the design right in these features should it exist. On the other hand it can be seen as a tool for the original producer to distinguish its spare parts from those of alternative producers.

Qualification

Designs which meet all previous requirements will only be protected if they meet one additional requirement. The design should also qualify for protection. This requirement is very similar to the qualification requirement in copyright and forms an inherent part of any intellectual property right which is not subject to a registration requirement and which is after all granted on a national basis. The qualification requirement is met if the designer,[12] the commissioner of the design[13] (if the design is commissioned for money or money's worth)[14] or the employer of the designer[15] (for designs created in the course of employment) is a qualifying person. The position of the designer is only relevant if the design is not created in the course of employment, nor in pursuance of a commission.[16]

The system starts with the definition of what is a qualifying country.[17] This is defined as the UK and the other member states of the European Union, eventually supplemented by other countries by an Order in

---

11   *Mark Wilkinson Furniture Ltd v Woodcraft Designs (Radcliffe) Ltd* [1998] FSR 63.
12   CDPA 1988, s 218(2).
13   CDPA 1988, s 219(1).
14   CDPA 1988, s 263(1).
15   CDPA 1988, s 219(1).
16   CDPA 1988, s 218(1).
17   CDPA 1988, s 217(3).

Council.[18] A qualifying individual is a citizen of or an individual habitually resident in such a qualifying country. Together with any corporate body or any body having legal personality which is formed under the law of a qualifying country or which has at least a place of business at which substantial business activity[19] is carried out in a qualifying country, the qualifying individuals form the category of the qualifying persons.[20]

The qualification requirement can also be met by reference to the country and person of first marketing of articles made to the design if the designer, and eventually the commissioner or employer do not qualify.[1] This is the case if the first marketing takes place by a qualifying person in a qualifying country. On top of that, the qualifying person must be exclusively authorised by the person who would have been the first owner of the design right, if it came into existence, to put the articles made to the design on the market in the UK and that exclusivity must be enforceable by legal proceedings in the UK. For qualification purposes the place where the design was created is utterly irrelevant.

THE SUBSTANCE OF THE DESIGN RIGHT

The design right is a property right[2] that grants its owner the exclusive right to reproduce the design for commercial purposes. The obvious way to do so is by making articles to the design, but the owner can also make a design document in which the design is recorded and which enables such articles to be made by a third party.[3] An article is reproduced for 'commercial purposes' if the reproduction is undertaken with a view to the article being sold or hired in the course of business.[4]

THE PERSON BEHIND THE DESIGN

The preceding analysis refers often to the person behind the design. It is now time to fill in that notion.

The designer is the person who creates the design.[5] Should this rule lead us to a computer, then the person that undertakes the necessary

18 See Design Right (Reciprocal Protection) (No 2) Order 1989, SI 1989/1294.
19 'Dealings in goods which are at all material times outside the country' shall not be taken into account, CDPA 1988, s 217(5).
20 CDPA 1988, s 217(1).
1   CDPA 1988, s 220.
2   CDPA 1988, s 213(1).
3   CDPA 1988, s 226(1).
4   CDPA 1988, s 263(3).
5   CDPA 1988, s 214(1).

arrangements for the creation of the design by the computer will be regarded as the designer.[6] Creation should be interpreted as having the idea for the design, it does not necessarily include the recording of the design.[7]

This leads us to the issue of who will be the first owner of the design. Where the design is not commissioned and not created in the course of employment, the designer will be the first owner of the design right in it.[8] The commissioner and the employer are the first owners of the design right in the design created in pursuance of a commission or in the course of employment respectively.[9] These rules apply in all circumstances except in those of section 220 of the 1988 Act. If the design qualifies through first marketing only, the first owner of the design right will be the person that markets the articles made to the design.[10]

Joint creation, which will arise when the contribution of two or more designers is not distinct and cannot be distinguished, and joint ownership are possible and do not create specific problems. It is worth pointing out though that in cases where not all persons involved are qualifying persons only those who do qualify will be entitled to the design right,[11] although the design will meet the qualifying requirement as soon as any of the persons involved is a qualifying person.[12] A design jointly created by eight designers for example will qualify for design protection as long as one of the designers is a qualifying person. In that case that one (qualifying) person alone will be entitled to the design right. In case four of the designers qualify, the four of them will be jointly entitled to the design right. In any case, designers that are not qualifying persons will not be entitled to the design right.

THE TERM OF (UNREGISTERED) DESIGN PROTECTION

We have already discussed the fact that the design right comes into existence at the moment when it is either recorded in a design document or when an article is made to the design. As with most terms in copyright, the duration of the design right is then linked to the end of the calendar year in which such recording or production takes place. We will call this important point the 'end of the creation year'.

Most designs will be exploited before the end of a five-year period which starts running from the end of the creation year. If such exploitation takes

---

6   CDPA 1988, s 214(2).
7   *C & H Engineering v Klucznik & Sons Ltd* [1992] FSR 421 at 428, per Aldous J.
8   CDPA 1988, s 215(1).
9   CDPA 1988, s 215(2) and (3).
10   CDPA 1988, s 215(4).
11   CDPA 1988, ss 218(4) and 219(3).
12   CDPA 1988, ss 218(3) and 219(2).

the form of articles made to the design being made available for sale or hire, the term of (unregistered) design protection is ten years. This term starts running at the end of the calendar year during which the exploitation first occurred.[13] The exploitation can take place anywhere in the world, as long as it is done by the owner of the design right or with its licence.[14]

No exploitation, as defined above, within the first five years does not lead to unlimited design right protection though. In that case the term of (unregistered) design protection expires 15 years after the end of the creation year.[15]

These terms of protection are substantially shorter than the ones used in copyright and are much more in line with the ones used in patent law. This is probably a recognition of the fact that functional designs are in general an industrial property right and that a fair return on the investment they require can be obtained in a relatively short period. As we have seen in Chapter 1 of this book, the term of protection should indeed be linked to the determination of the correct balance between the innovation (creation of new designs) and production level (articles produced to the design). Approximately 10 years of design exclusivity will allow for the ongoing creation of new designs and will not unduly restrict the free use of the design.

INFRINGEMENT AND REMEDIES

Primary infringement

As the owner of the design right has the exclusive right to reproduce the design for commercial purposes, the design right will first of all be infringed by anyone making an article to the design without the licence of the owner of the design right and by anyone making a design document that records the design for the purpose of enabling someone to make articles to it, once again if this is done without the licence of the design right owner. One can immediately add to this the case where someone authorises someone else to do one of these two things. Design right infringement is subject to the same principles as copyright infringement.[16] This means, first of all, that an objective similarity between the allegedly infringing article and the design must exist. All features that are covered by an exclusion, such as the interface exclusion, should be disregarded for this purpose. Secondly, a causal

---

13   CDPA 1988, s 216(1)(b).
14   CDPA 1988, s 216(2).
15   CDPA 1988, s 216(1)(a).
16   *Mark Wilkinson Furniture Ltd v Woodcraft Designs (Radcliffe) Ltd* [1998] FSR 63.

connection between the design and the allegedly infringing article needs to be established.[17]

The act of making articles to the design is circumscribed more precisely. The design has to be copied in such a way that articles exactly or substantially similar to the design are produced. This latter element involves an objective test which should be decided through the eyes of the person to whom the design is directed.[18] This is the person who will use the articles made to the design. In a case that was concerned with design rights in the features of shape of a kitchen unit, the design was held to be directed to the person interested in buying a fitted kitchen.[19] That person should look at the similarities and differences between the two designs. Infringement will arise if the allegedly infringing article is simply made to the plaintiff's design or if it is made substantially to that design. The latter situation will definitely cover all occasions on which all the elements linked to the functional role of the design have been copied and the differences are not relevant for that role. It is submitted that the approach should bear important similarities to the one adopted in relation to patent law in the *Catnic* case, but only the case law can shed some more light on this issue in a decisive way over the next few years. In addition it should be emphasised that the objective test through the eyes of the person to whom the design is directed may involve the article being dismantled to allow him or her to compare the designs if they apply to a internal part of the article, as design rights can exist in features of shape or configuration of an internal part of the article.

It is extremely important though to see what is being compared in the objective test and it is respectfully submitted that the approach taken obiter[20] in the *Klucznik* case is not detailed enough.[1] Infringement is situated in the fact of making articles to the design without having obtained a licence to do so. But the design right covers features of shape or configuration of the whole or part of the article and the test is directed to see whether the design right has been infringed. It is submitted that section 226 (2) directs us to look at the similarities and differences in the designs rather than in the articles. If the design right covers features of shape or configuration of the whole article, the result will not necessarily vary, but the importance of the nuance is found in the fact that the design right can also cover features of

---

17   As in the equivalent copyright cases, it is not required that the infringer has the protected design in front of him when the allegedly infringing article is made. See *Philip Parker v Stephen Tidball* [1997] FSR 680.

18   *C & H Engineering v Klucznik & Sons Ltd* [1992] FSR 421 at 428, per Aldous J.

19   *Mark Wilkinson Furniture Ltd v Woodcraft Designs (Radcliffe) Ltd* [1998] FSR 63.

20   Klucznik's claim to the design right failed because Aldous J was unable to reach the conclusion that they were the owners of the design (had they thought of it or had C & H Engineering thought of it?), thus their infringement action accordingly also failed. Aldous J nevertheless considered the infringement issue, but that part of the judgment is thus obiter.

1   *C & H Engineering v Klucznik & Sons Ltd* [1992] FSR 421 at 428, per Aldous J.

shape or configuration of a part of the article. Making reference to the whole article would in such a case reduce the number of cases in which infringements would be found substantially and weaken the design right as such. It would also be absurd to take into account additional non-protected features and eventually features which form the subject of another design right and which are applied to another part of the same article in deciding whether a design right has been infringed. The test should only take into consideration those parts of the article to which the design refers, although this can eventually be the whole article.[2] Otherwise there could almost never be an infringement when only the design for part of an article is reproduced. The emphasis on the design does not change the fact though that the observer is forced to compare the original design to the article in which allegedly a substantial part of the design has been copied. One should 'ask oneself what by way of comparative design would be suggested to the interested observer'.[3] This should be done in the light of the entirety of the allegedly infringing article.

In the *Klucznik* case[4] the test was indeed described as an objective one, having the pig farmer, as the person to whom the design is directed, look at the similarities and differences between the two pig fenders. The conclusion reached was that the designs were not substantially the same, but it is submitted that this conclusion could be wrong because it relies on an additional feature of the allegedly infringing fender. This feature was not part of the design right which was allegedly infringed and the features of shape covered by the design right, the two inch tube, were only features of shape of a part of the fender. Attention should in this case primarily be directed to that part of the fender and other additional features should be left aside. One should only turn to the whole of the allegedly infringing article in a second stage to determine whether the overall features of the article allow for a conclusion that the overall impression of the observer is not that the allegedly infringing article has been made to the original design. This should only be the case if the other features have become the essential features of the article. In that case the article is no longer produced to the original design, even if they have certain aspects in common. This slightly more complicated test follows from the fact that design infringement is not completely similar to copyright infringement and that additional emphasis is put on the point that the copying must lead to the production of article exactly or substantially to the design. That judgment in relation to the allegedly infringing article comes on top of the copyright style substantial

---

2   Compare Turner 'A True Design Right: C & H Engineering *v* Klucznik & Sons' [1993] 1 EIPR 24 at 25.

3   *Philip Parker v Stephen Tidball* [1997] FSR 680.

4   *C & H Engineering v Klucznik & Sons Ltd* [1992] FSR 421.

∎

copying test (from one design to another, or to the relevant part of the allegedly infringing article).

The enabling recording of a design document as an infringing activity bears strong similarities to its equivalent in copyright, but it is slightly harder to prove the design version. The recording should be made for the purpose of enabling someone to make articles to the design. The only purpose one needs to establish for its copyright infringement alternative is the purpose to copy.[5] The design intention should be present at the time the recording was made, otherwise the recording was not made for that purpose. It is indeed not sufficient that the recording can eventually later be used to enable someone to make articles to the design.

The reproduction of the design may be direct or indirect. Indirect reproduction will still infringe, even if the intervening acts do not infringe the design right themselves.[6] This has important consequences in relation to the reverse engineering of designs. One can easily take apart an article made to the design, analyse the design and copy the non-protected elements. Eventually this can lead to the creation of a new original design. But if reverse engineering simply precedes reproduction, making an article to the design will still infringe.

Innocent infringement is possible. This clarification is made indirectly in section 233 of the 1988 Act. If at the time of the infringement the defendant was unaware and had no reason to believe that design right subsisted in the design, the plaintiff will not be entitled to damages against the defendant. Other remedies remain available though.[7] This provision offers a limited amount of protection to the reasonable bona fide user of the design who thought there was no design right he could be infringing. This is bound to happen on a number of occasions such as when a user cannot check in any register of designs in order to pre-empt this situation.

Secondary infringement

The design right will also be infringed if a person does any of the following acts in relation to an infringing article without the licence of the owner of the design right. The design right will be infringed if they import the article into the UK for commercial purposes,[8] or if they have the article in their possession for commercial purposes.[9] The design right will also be infringed if they sell, hire, or offer or expose for sale or hire, the article in the course

---

5   MacQueen 'A Scottish Case on Unregistered Designs' [1994] 2 EIPR 86 at 87.
6   CDPA 1988, s 226(4).
7   CDPA 1988, s 233(1).
8   CDPA 1988, s 227(1)(a).
9   CDPA 1988, s 227(1)(b).

of a business.[10] Apart from the possession for commercial purposes, similar provisions are found in section 7 of the Registered Designs Act 1949.

First of all, what is an infringing article? An article is an infringing article if the making of the article to the design constituted an infringement of the design right in the design.[11] Articles which have been imported into the UK or are proposed to be imported into it and the making of which would have constituted an infringement of the design right (or a breach of an exclusive licence agreement) had the articles been made in the UK, are also infringing articles.[12] In addition an action for secondary design infringement can only be successful if it is proven that the defendant knew or had reason to believe that the article was an infringing article.[13] This additional knowledge requirement is identical to the one found in copyright and does not exist for registered designs.[14]

This knowledge requirement taken in combination with the fact that only designs created after the commencement date of the design provisions of the 1988 Act attract design protection, could create a problem for the plaintiff in proving that the article was made at a time when the right subsisted and is thus an infringing article. The Act therefore introduced a presumption in favour of the plaintiff. The article made to the design is presumed to have been made at a time when the design right in the design subsisted, unless the contrary can be proved.[15] This is even more favourable for the plaintiff as he or she will be quite often the only person able to prove when the design right first arose.

If the defendant in an action for secondary infringement is able to show that the infringing article was acquired innocently by him or her or by a predecessor in title this will not imply that the action is bound to fail. Rather it only restricts the remedies available to damages up to what would be a reasonable amount of royalties in respect of the act complained of.[16]

Defences

A defendant in a design right infringement action can try to argue that the design right has expired or that it was not valid in the first place because one of the requirements was not met and that the design right thus never came into existence. Apart from these arguments it is obvious that the defendant will try to argue that the requirements for primary and secondary

10   CDPA 1988, s 227(1)(c).
11   CDPA 1988, s 228(2).
12   CDPA 1988, s 228(3).
13   CDPA 1988, s 227(1).
14   See pp 236–238 and 309–311 above.
15   CDPA 1988, s 228(4).
16   CDPA 1988, s 233(2).

infringement to take place are not met. A last defence could, in relevant cases, be based on section 236.

These relevant cases are those in which copyright exists in a work that consists of or includes a design in which a design right subsists. Anything which is an infringement of the copyright in the work will not be an infringement of the design right.[17] This provision clearly aims to complete the separation between copyright and design right. It applies to design right infringement cases whereas section 51 applies to the copyright infringement cases.

COMMERCIAL EXPLOITATION

Assignment and licences

As is the case with most other intellectual property rights, an (unregistered) design right can be exploited commercially in various ways. Owners of the design right can exploit the right themselves by making an article to the design, but can also leave the exploitation or part of it to a third party. In such cases the design right can be assigned or a licence can be granted. An assignment can be compared to a sale and is particularly appropriate if the owners of the design right do not want to exploit the design themselves. Granting a licence is more like hiring out the right to use the design. If the licence is not exclusive it allows the owners to exploit the design themselves too and even the exclusive licence may ultimately expire and then the exploitation right will return to the owners. This is of course only a rough description of assignments and licences. They can be moulded to perform special functions through the insertion of special clauses in the contract. A future design right, that will or may come into being, can be the subject of an assignment or of a licence. The same rules apply to the exploitation of both the existing design right and the future design right.[18]

When the design right is assigned this must be done in writing and the assignment must be signed by the owner-assignor or it must be signed on his or her behalf.[19] An assignment effectively transfers the design right to the assignee. An assignment can be partial in two ways though.[20] The assignment can be limited in terms of its duration. This implies that the design right returns to the assignor after the expiry of the term agreed in the assignment contract. It can also be limited in scope in the sense that not all the exclusive rights of the owner are assigned to the assignee. In relation

17   CDPA 1988, s 236.
18   CDPA 1988, s 223.
19   CDPA 1988, s 222(3).
20   CDPA 1988, s 222(2).

to the rights assigned to him or her the assignee has exactly the same rights as the ones the owner-assignor had before the assignment and would have had if the assignment had not taken place. Apart from by assignment, the design right can also be transferred by testamentary disposition or by the operation of law,[1] such as in the case of a liquidation of a company that owned a design right.

The alternative to an assignment is a licence. This authorises the licensee to do certain things in relation to the design right. The owner can grant an exclusive licence or a non-exclusive licence. An exclusive licence gives the licensee the exclusive right to exploit the design right in a certain area and/ or the exclusive right to exploit the design right in a certain way. All other persons, including the owner-licensor, are excluded from exploiting the design right in the area and or form of exploitation covered by the exclusive licence. It has to be in writing and it has to be signed by the owner-licensor of the design right or on his or her behalf[2] and it gives the exclusive licensee the same rights and remedies as an assignment. There is one exception to the latter point though, the rights and remedies are not the same in relation to the owner-licensor. The exclusive licensee can, as can the assignee, act independently against infringers.[3] But as the licensor retains certain rights in relation to the design right, there will be cases where the two parties have a right of action. The Act calls this a concurrent right of action and requires that the other party is either joined as a plaintiff or added as a defendant before the action proceeds.[4]

One or more non-exclusive licences can also be granted and they may give the licensee the non-exclusive right to exploit the design right in a certain area and/or the non-exclusive right to exploit the design right in a certain way. The licensor will remain free to exploit the design right himself and may also appoint other licensees. There are no requirements regarding the format of a non-exclusive licence and the licensor will have to rely on the contract in infringement cases. No rights to act independently are transferred, the licensee will have to request the licensor to take action against the infringer. A licence granted by the owner of the design right shall normally bind him or her and every successor in title. It will not bind a purchaser of the design right who purchases in good faith, for valuable consideration, and has no actual or constructive notice of the licence.[5] An assignor who meets the additional requirements could be such a purchaser. This clearly puts the licensee in a weaker position than the licensor and makes an assignment theoretically more attractive than a licence. It remains to be seen however whether an assignment is available in practice and even

1   CDPA 1988, s 222(1).
2   CDPA 1988, s 225(1).
3   CDPA 1988, s 234.
4   CDPA 1988, s 235(1).
5   CDPA 1988, s 222(4).

if that is the case the higher price linked to it may well outweigh the advantage.

Licences of right are available during the last five years of the term of protection offered by the design right. This weakens the value of the design right, but opens another opportunity for the exploitation of the design right. The Comptroller-General of Patents, Designs and Trade Marks will settle the terms of the licence if the parties fail to agree upon it.[6] It will not always be easy for the potential licensee to find out when these licences of right become available, as in cases where the design is recorded some time before it is exploited the owner of the design right is often the only person to know the real date on which the design right came into existence.

One design, two design rights

Some designs meet the requirements of the Registered Designs Act 1949 as well as those for the (unregistered) design right. If they are registered they will attract double design protection. An example may be a teapot, the spout or handle of which is both aesthetically pleasing and also fulfils a functional role. This could create problems when only one right is assigned or licensed and commercial exploitation of the design takes place. This could constitute an infringement of the other design. The Act therefore provides that if the owners of both design rights are the same persons, an assignment of the registered design will include an assignment of the (unregistered) design right unless an intention to the contrary appears from the transaction or its circumstances.[7] The opposite situation is covered by section 19(3B) of the Registered Designs Act 1949 which provides that if the owners of both design rights are the same persons, an assignment of the (unregistered) design right will include an assignment of the registered design unless an intention to the contrary appears. This is of course only a partial solution. The presumption may be rebutted and the rights may become separated because they are owned by different persons. The latter risk is reduced by the fact that the Registrar is not supposed to register a registered design if the application is not made by the person who claims to be the owner of the design right.[8] The legislature clearly attempts to keep the ownership of both design rights in the same hands, while leaving it up to the parties to negotiate the terms of the licences, which are just a temporary right to use. It can indeed be accepted that no one will agree to a licence for one of the rights, if the use of that right would infringe the second design right and even if

---

6   CDPA 1988, s 237.
7   CDPA 1988, s 224.
8   Registered Designs Act 1949, s 3.

that were the case, the courts might imply a licence for the second design right.

Crown use

The 1988 Act also contains provisions on Crown use of design rights. It refers to the use by the Crown without a licence but with a form of remuneration of designs protected by design rights for purposes such as health and other needs of the services of the Crown. There are also provisions on the supply of articles made to the design for foreign defence purposes.[9]

Competition law

Agreements on the exploitation of design rights may infringe competition law. In relation to UK competition law the 1988 Act allows action to be taken in such cases.[10] The most relevant provisions are to be found though in the EC Treaty. Licence agreements in relation to design rights may infringe Article 85 of the Treaty. We may refer here to our discussion of this Treaty provision above as it applies in the same way to all intellectual property rights. Suffice it to say that no block exemption covers design rights. In theory there is also no reason why Article 86 on the abuse of a dominant position could not apply in relation to a design right, although it is not too likely that such a case will often arise in practice.

The Court of Justice was invited to rule on the relationship between design rights and the free movement provisions of the EC Treaty in the *Keurkoop v Nancy Kean Gifts* case.[11] The judgment makes it clear that designs form an intellectual property right for the purposes of these provisions and that the exhaustion doctrine applies to them. The Court found it not necessary, however, to define the specific subject matter of designs, as it could reach its conclusion without doing so. It said that in the absence of Community harmonisation it is left to the member states to decide which system of design rights they have and to decide accordingly on the terms and conditions under which protection is granted. The existing disparity did not influence the applicability of the free movement provisions to design rights. This means that there is nothing special about design rights

---

9   CDPA 1988, see ss 240 to 244.
10   CDPA 1988, s 238.
11   Case 144/81 *Keurkoop BV v Nancy Kean Gifts BV* [1982] ECR 2853, [1983] 2 CMLR 47.

in this context and that the principles which we discussed in relation to other intellectual property rights apply equally to them.

European designs[12]

This leaves us with the remark in the *Keurkoop v Nancy Kean Gifts* case that there is a great disparity in design law between the member states. It was felt that a European harmonisation initiative was necessary. This developed along the lines of the trade marks initiative. So a harmonisation Directive, coupled with the creation of a Community Design Right, is the plan from which the European Union is working.[13] It must be said that at the time of writing this project is still in a draft stage.[14] The texts have been amended on various occasions and a reconciliation procedure between the Council and the Parliament needs to resolve their major differences, primarily over spare parts.[15] The impression has been created that two scenarios are possible. An agreement between the Council and the Parliament would see the harmonisation Directive through, while discussions on the Regulation seem to be at a halt, at least until the Directive has been approved. Secondly, in the absence of an agreement in the near future the whole design project will collapse and a fresh start in one form or another may then be at least a few years away.

We will restrict our comments mainly to the Community Design Right. This European initiative does not use the UK's distinction between aesthetical and functional designs; rather it opts instead for one industrial design right. In practice most of the designs that are currently covered by either of the two UK design rights would qualify, apart from the purely functional designs.[16] Suffice it to say that the harmonisation Directive addresses issues such as the conditions of protection, the duration of

---

12   For more details see Horton 'European Design Law and the Spare Parts Dilemma: The Proposed Regulation and Directive' [1994] 2 EIPR 51.

13   EC Draft Directive on the Legal Protection of Designs [1993] OJ C345/14, as amended (see eg COM(96) 66 final), and EC Draft Regulation on Community Design (1994) OJ C29/20.

14   For a detailed commentary on the proposed Directive and Regulation, see M Franzosi (ed) *European Design Protection: Commentary to Directive and Regulation Proposals* Kluwer Law International (1996). The latest developments are, obviously, not included in this commentary, because it was published in 1996. It is the authors' declared intention to write further updates.

15   The Council had deleted the spare parts clause from the proposal for a Directive. While this move had opened the way to an agreement within the Council, the Parliament vehemently opposed it and demanded the re-introduction of the clause. The conciliation procedure should have yielded its results by the end of July 1998.

16   See the Regulation's definition of a design underneath. The latest version of the text of the Directive adds that the design is concerned with the 'outwardly visible' appearance of the product.

protection, the interconnections and repair-spare parts exceptions and the one-year grace period for registered protection and is only concerned with registered designs, as many member states have no unregistered design right. There would accordingly not be a great deal to harmonise in that area.

In the draft Community Design Regulation a design is defined as

'the appearance of the whole or a part of a product resulting from the specific features of the lines, contours, colours, shape and/or materials of the product itself and/or its ornamentation'.[17]

For the purposes of this definition it is irrelevant whether the design is of an aesthetic or a functional character. It is also immaterial whether the appearance of the product is material to the user.

The system recognises that there are two kinds of designs: those with a long life and those with a very short life, say a couple of months to a year or two.[18] The latter kind of designs are found frequently in industrial sectors, for example in the case of textiles and fashion whose commercial life is often restricted to one season. These designs will not be registered. The registration procedure will take longer than the commercial life of the design and for some of them the whole system will be too time-consuming and costly. With these designs in mind an unregistered design was created. It allows for three years of protection and comes into being automatically when the design is made available to the public.[19] The unregistered design right only protects its owner against unauthorised reproduction, which is defined as deliberate copying of the design.[20]

The alternative system is the registered design. Normally any design will start as an unregistered design, offering protection before and during the registration period. An unregistered design can be registered within the first 12 months of its existence.[1] The registered design will be administered by the European Design Office, which will be a branch of the European Trade Mark Office in Alicante.[2] The right will have a renewable five-year term of protection, with a maximum duration of 25 years.[3]

In order to attract protection the design has to pass a high threshold. The novelty requirement refers to an objective test of absolute worldwide novelty.[4] In addition there is a requirement of distinctiveness. This means that the design should have an individual character. This is tested against

17   Article 3.
18   See Article 1.
19   Article 12.
20   Article 20.
1   Article 8.
2   Articles 2 and 101–123.
3   Article 13.
4   Article 5.

the background of all designs commercialised in the Union at the date of reference and all published designs both at the European Design Office and national level and the test refers to the overall impression the design produces on the informed user.[5]

A number of items are excluded from design protection. They are for example designs for which the need to realise a technical function leaves no freedom as regards the features of appearance and interconnections which allow the connection of a product to which the design is applied to another product.[6]

Spare parts were an issue of major controversy. The draft suggests that the issue is solved through the introduction of a repair clause.[7] Although a Community Design can be obtained for spare parts, the original producer will not be allowed to use that right against another producer of the spare parts after the expiry of a three-year period from the moment on which the product incorporating the design or the product to which the design was applied was first put on the market. This clause applies provided that

'(a)   the product incorporating the design or to which the design is applied is part of a complex product upon whose appearance the protected design is dependent, and
(b)   the purpose of such a use is to permit the repair of the complex product so as to restore its original appearance'.[8]

These requirements assure that the exception will only apply to spare parts. The compromise allows for some protection for spare part designs (three years), while opening up the spare parts market to a great extent and avoiding it being monopolised by the original producers.

Once past this hurdle the design as such will be protected. There is no reference to the products to which the design is applied, as is the case in the existing UK system.

A key feature of the existing UK system is the exclusion of copyright from the design area. This is clearly based on previous bad experiences in cases such as *British Leyland v Armstrong*. It is important to note that both the harmonisation Directive[9] and the Community Design Regulation[10] explicitly provide for the co-existence of copyright and design right. Cumulative protection is even one of the main features of the whole European initiative. It is submitted that this is indeed a healthy approach

5   Article 6.
6   Article 9.
7   Article 23.
8   Ibid.
9   Draft Directive on the Legal Protection of Designs (1993) OJ C345/14, Article 18.
10   EC Draft Regulation on Community Design (1994) OJ C29/20 Article 100, see also Cohen-Jehoram 'Herschel Smith Lecture 1994' [1994] 12 EIPR 514.

and that our past problems had more to do with the (then) underdeveloped UK design system than with the co-existence of copyright and design right. It will nevertheless be quite a change for the UK and require a complete change of mentality. But it is worth putting in the effort if it will result in a better design right.

The harmonisation Directive has been amended on regular occasions since it was passed. Whether or not it will be approved and in which form is currently still uncertain. The main issue of contention is still the spare parts clause, which the Council deleted and which the Parliament wants to see reinstated.

Chapter 22

Designs – an overview

Registered design is the little brother of patents and trade marks, but that does not mean that design rights are not valuable for industry. On the contrary, enormous amounts of money are spent on designs. Registration alone is simply not the best way of protecting designs and it would be wrong to disregard anything smaller than the giants patents and trade marks as not important.

It is submitted that the right way forward for the UK is to adopt a substantial part of the scheme contained in the draft Regulation. Our existing systems of registered and unregistered designs show strong similarities as has become clear in the analysis above and we demonstrated that the definition of unregistered design is wide enough in scope to contain almost all the designs covered by the definition of registered design. Much confusion would be eliminated by having one design right which could serve both aesthetic and functional designs. It is more important for industry to have an unregistered copyright based design right to protect these designs that do not have a commercial life that is long enough to warrant their registration as a registered design. Ironically almost all these designs are aesthetic in nature. Does the UK require registration for the wrong kind of designs? Or would many of the functional designs never be registered if there was a need to do so in order to attract design protection?

Not much would change in relation to the requirements that have to be met to attract design right protection. The term of protection for functional designs would go up to 25 years though and that may be slightly long. After all a patent comes only with a 20-year term. On the other hand the owner will only renew the protection if the exploitation income can support this and have we not agreed that what is worth copying is worth protecting?[1]

---

1   *University of London Press Ltd v University Tutorial Press Ltd* [1916] 2 Ch 601 at 610, per Peterson J (in a copyright context).

Caution should also be exercised when protecting the design as such, as suggested in the draft Regulation, rather than the design as applied to certain articles. This could widen the scope of the design right protection substantially. On the other hand the spare part repair clause seems to be an appropriate solution for the crucial spare parts problem because it is a good compromise between all parties involved.

Section E

Image rights

Chapter 23

Trade marks

Today the trade mark industry is a vital component of the whole structure of the advertising and marketing that is such a strong feature of the commercial scene. Logos, catchphrases and images all fall within the ambit of the trade mark and form a valuable part of the goodwill of the business with which they are associated. In law, however, trade marks have in recent years been the subject of increasing controversy; this has culminated in an entirely new legislative framework for them, in the form of the Trade Marks Act 1994.

TRADE MARKS – DEVELOPMENT

The earliest form of trade mark is both the most obvious and the type that is still at the heart of the law of trade marks today. Even in Roman times, pottery was made (and has survived) bearing the name of the potter responsible for it. Then, as now, the trade mark was an important badge of origin for the product, the origin of course also being indicative of the quality of the product associated with it. Many major brand names are the names of the founder of the brand – Ford for cars or Kelloggs for breakfast cereals are obvious examples. Exceptionally the name may even become synonymous with the product itself; people will often refer to any brand of vacuum cleaner as a 'Hoover', for instance.

However, throughout history, with only a couple of minor exceptions, trade marks were essentially a part of the private sector, attracting legal protection by use, rather than by formal grant by the state. This was unacceptable in a society that was rapidly changing and industrialising and it became clear both that a more formal system was required and that the central authority of the state should form a central feature of that system.

In 1862 a Trade Marks Bill was considered but did not go ahead for various reasons. There were doubts about whether a formal and transferable legal right was appropriate to reflect the personal nature of the typical trade mark, and the common law of passing-off was, as will be seen in the next chapter, already in a process of development. Deliberate counterfeiting was seen to be more of a problem abroad than at home, and this called into question the effectiveness of the proposed new law. However, pressure continued to mount in favour of a statutory system of trade marks and that demand was ultimately fulfilled, in the first place, by the Trade Marks Act of 1875.

This Act created a central Trade Marks Registry (now subsumed within the Patent Office) which could award a proprietary right in the form of a trade mark and also register its existence and ownership for the benefit and guidance of future prospective applicants. Then, as now, at the heart of the notion of the trade mark lay the idea that it should be distinctive, thus going far beyond the notion of the mark as being a badge of origin. From 1875, then, the essence of the modern system of trade mark law and practice was in place, but the law was never to stay in a settled form for too long. New Acts extended the law in 1883, 1905 and 1919, the latter splitting the Register into two sections, while the keynote Act until recently was that of 1938. This too, however, did not survive unadorned with some of the recommendations of the Mathys Committee of 1974[1] being enacted by the Trade Marks (Amendment) Act of 1984, creating, among other things, a mark for services as well as for goods. More change, however, was thought to be needed.

THE NEED FOR REFORM

Reform was canvassed in a Government White Paper, 'Reform of Trade Marks Law'[2] in 1990. It recognised that many of the recommendations of the Mathys Committee had never been taken up, but that there were other factors which tended to suggest that more fundamental reform was needed. First and foremost amongst these factors was the 'Europeanisation' of yet another area of intellectual property.

The influence of the EU on trade marks law takes two separate but related forms. Firstly, a Directive was passed as far back as 1988,[3] seeking to harmonise the national laws relating to trade marks so as to remove potential barriers to freer trade. The terms of the Directive required compliance with its terms by the end of 1991 (later extended by a year), a deadline well missed

---

1   Cmnd 5601.
2   Cm 1203.
3   89/104 EC, (1989) OJ L40/1.

by the UK. However, the 1994 Act appears now to fulfil this requirement, at least in almost all respects.

The second aspect of EU activity which has had a significant impact on the reform process is the establishment of a community-wide trade mark, distinct from the individual national marks. After interminable discussion and the traditional haggling, the Regulation approving the creation of such a mark was finalised in 1994.[4] The Community Trade Marks Office is sited in Alicante in Spain and it has been confronted with a(n unexpected) flood of applications ever since it opened its doors to the public. This new mark is of course not subject to amendment by domestic legislation, but, on the converse, this has been a sensible opportunity to try and match the domestic and European procedures so as to minimise both conflict and duplication between the two systems.

A third international fact was also at play in the formulation of the 1994 legislation. Trade, and thus trade marks, takes on an increasingly international dimension all the time, and thus the international protectability of trade mark rights takes on an even greater importance. For over a century an international register of trade marks has been maintained under the provisions of the Madrid Agreement[5] with an International Register maintained by WIPO in Geneva. This system was not entirely successful as reflecting continental rather than common law approaches to the topic but the era of harmonisation meant that change was not only appropriate but also necessary. In consequence, a Protocol[6] was added to the Madrid Agreement enabling the UK and many other countries to fall within its scope, and the 1994 Act had the further task of adapting domestic law to this new international agreement. Finally, further implementation of the Paris Convention for the Protection of Intellectual Property of 1883 is facilitated by the new legislation.

Other, domestic, factors also shaped the new law of trade marks. There is no doubt that the old law was in a messy state. The 1938 Act, far from clear in certain aspects even from day one, had been changed by successive amendments in 1984, 1986 and 1988 and divining the precise text of the legislation on service marks, in particular, was not an easy task. This alone suggested that an urgent clarification of the law was required. However, broader political forces were at play too. The Government was consistently in favour of the promotion of the interests of business groups and this in its own right coupled with the related drive towards deregulation meant that a simpler, clearer and more market-related system of trade marks law was

---

4   Regulation 40/94 (1994) OJ L11/1.
5   Madrid Agreement Concerning the International Registration of Marks of 14 April 1891.
6   Protocol Relating to the Madrid Agreement Concerning the International Registration of Marks of 28 June 1989.

deemed to be a necessity.[7] An efficient and less costly system should emerge from the 1994 reforms.

As part of this process of simplification, there were mysteries created by the law which it was opportune to resolve. Some examples follow. The fact that the shape of a container such as a Coca-Cola bottle could not be registered[8] may or may not be objectionable, but it is difficult to justify such a view when the entire surface of a two-coloured pill could be registered;[9] such narrow distinctions may have been the stuff of life to medieval philosophers but were less familiar to provincial solicitors.

Equally arcane distinctions between the different types of trade mark, the Part A and Part B mark, were also found to pose problems. The need in a Part A mark was to establish its distinctiveness by considering whether it was 'adapted to distinguish' the goods of its proprietors from those of others. This was to be done[10] with reference to its inherent adaptability to distinguish and the extent to which its use in fact adapted it to distinguish. For a Part B trade mark, the test of distinctiveness was whether the mark was capable of distinguishing the goods from others,[11] but this was done with reference to inherent capability and factual capability. The difference between 'adapted' and 'capable' was at once vital and obscure. Any thoughts that a Part B mark could be identified by the presence of 100% factual distinctiveness was scotched by the House of Lords in *York Trailers Holdings v Registrar of Trade Marks*[12] where the fact that the applicant was the only manufacturer of trailers in York, Canada (or indeed, it seems, any other York) did not justify the grant of a trade mark on the grounds that it would be to create too great a monopoly to allow the claim by one manufacturer to use as a trade mark the name of a substantial chunk of territory. Thus additional rules of law were created to complicate further an already tangled web.

A third example can be given from the world of infringement. It is obvious that it is wrong to claim the trade mark of another for your own use on rival goods or services. However, the old law also treated as an infringement the situation where the use of another's mark in some way connoted that the use of the mark was with the proprietor's permission or otherwise, in the words of section 4(1)(b) of the 1938 Act, that the use 'imported a reference to some person having the right as proprietor to use the trade mark'. A good example of the perhaps surprising consequences

7   Cm 1203, p 2.
8   *Re Coca-Cola Co's Applications* [1986] 2 All ER 274, [1986] 1 WLR 695.
9   *Smith, Kline & French Laboratories v Sterling-Winthrop Group* [1975] 2 All ER 578, [1975] 1 WLR 914.
10 TMA 1938, s 9(3)(b).
11 TMA 1938, s 10(2).
12 [1982] 1 All ER 257, [1982] 1 WLR 195.

of this is given by the comparative advertising case of *News Group Ltd v Mirror Group Ltd.*[13]

Here the publishers of the *Daily Mirror* decided to exploit the unpopularity of the Conservative Government and its then leader and the slavish support that was nevertheless afforded to it by most other newspapers by launching an advertising campaign. One poster featured, under the words 'Yes, Prime Minister', the masthead logos of all the pro-Conservative papers, including the plaintiff's organ, the *Sun*. Another poster, under the words 'No, Prime Minister', featured in solitary splendour the masthead logo of the *Daily Mirror*. In spite of the context in which the *Sun* was appearing to be criticised for its editorial stance, it was still found that its trade-marked logo had been infringed through the 'importing a reference' route.

But all this will soon become part of history, once cases arising from the old law and the various transitional provisions have worked their weary way through the system. The Trade Marks Act 1994 summarily repeals the 1938 legislation in its entirety and replaces it with a new code. It is also clearly the case that the myriad complexities of the case law arising from earlier legislation are now of little value, since the new law is based on different principles. Therefore reliance will not, for the most part, be placed on the old law as such, though, of course, there will be ample occasions to cite past cases as examples of areas of difficulty which may have been resolved (or not!) by the new law.

WHY TRADE MARKS?

Before examining the detail of the new law it is appropriate to investigate the rationale of a system of trade marks. It is clear that trade marks law has to achieve a balance between various potentially competing interests. The trader seeks to protect the image and reputation of his goods but the rival trader, in a society based on free competition, has every reason to wish to compete on level terms within the same market and will, at the very least, hope that the monopoly conferred by the grant of a trade mark is confined to reasonable limits so as not to inhibit legitimate competition. The consumer also has an interest; he associates the product or service and its quality with the brand name or logo that is associated with it, and will not wish to be confused by similar names or logos placed on different, especially inferior, products.

As has been seen, the trade mark originally evolved in the private sector at the behest of the traders themselves and this generally has been the principal interest given protection by the trade marks system. The

13   [1989] FSR 126.

protection afforded has centred on the origin of the goods and, while this has also been of benefit to consumer interests, this has been first and foremost in the interests of the proprietor of the trade mark. In indicating origin the mark, being distinctive, differentiates that product from another and, in turn, by so doing, guides the consumer in the exercise of choice. This, it is suggested, may now be seen as the 'core' function of trade marks and it will be pertinent to bear this view in mind, in particular when considering the direction taken by the new law of trade marks.

There can be no doubt as to the commercial significance of trade marks in modern society. Brand names or product identities such as that of Guinness or Coca-Cola are hugely valuable assets to their owners and are vigorously protected by them. It may be confidently predicted that the advent of a new and more flexible law of trade marks will create a flood of new registrations of previously unregistrable marks, thus adding further to the value of this sector.

TRADE MARK RECOGNITION – THE UK FRAMEWORK

The Register of Trade Marks is a public document which can be consulted by interested parties. Joining it, and thus gaining access to the alleged prosperity that will then ensue, is a matter of formal application and examination before a registration is awarded. The applicant must provide, by virtue of section 32 of the Trade Marks Act 1994 a request for registration of the mark and a statement of the goods or services in relation to which the mark is sought, a representation of the mark and a statement that the mark is used or is intended to be used, whether by the applicant himself or with his consent, in connection with those goods or services. Non-use of a mark will prevent registration of it. On receipt of all bar the last of these items, the application receives an official filing date which may be of importance in deciding which of two rival marks has priority, a problem already encountered in the system for the registration of patents.

The Registrar of Trade Marks then examines the application to see that the proposed mark fulfils the legal requirements necessary for a trade mark and, in so doing, he is likely to search pre-existing trade marks to ensure that there is no duplication.[14] The Registrar must ask for further details from the applicant[15] if not satisfied and must[16] publish the application so that other interested parties can oppose or make comments on the proposed mark. If the necessary criteria have been met, the Registrar 'shall accept the

---

14   TMA 1994, s 37(2).
15   TMA 1994, s 37(3).
16   TMA 1994, s 38.

application',[17] but only 'if it appears to the Registrar' that the criteria have been fulfilled. This suggests that some discretionary powers remain with the Registrar and it would seem that registration is not automatic since it is for the Registrar to determine, in his own opinion, whether the at times vague requirements for registration have been met before permitting it to take place. If and when it occurs, the registered trade mark is deemed (by section 2 of the Act) to be a property right.

A trade mark is granted not for all purposes but only for those classes of goods and services for which an application has been made, though one of the advantages of the 1994 Act is to make multiple applications easier by allowing one application to be made for more than one class, unlike in the old law. The classification of goods and services is carried out in accordance with an international agreement, the Nice Classification, 6th edition, which splits goods and services into, respectively, 34 and 8 classes. These are incorporated into domestic law by reference to the 'prescribed system of classification' which is referred to in section 34 of the 1994 Act, but new Rules have had to be promulgated to incorporate the classification into the law, they formerly having been a Schedule to the old Trade Marks Act.[18] Internationally there is also the 1985 Vienna Agreement Establishing an International Classification of the Figurative Elements of Marks; this however does not form part of the domestic law.

The classification is designed to be comprehensive and by definition covers the whole range of manufacturing and service industry. Thus, as a random example, all vehicles form Class 12 of the classification while firearms, ammunition, explosives and fireworks form Class 13. Inevitably there are anomalies, so by Class 32 beers and soft drinks form one class, while all alcoholic drinks other than beers form Class 33.

Clearly the requirements for registration lie at the heart of this process and it is to these and, first and foremost, to the key question of what is a trade mark, that we now turn.

TRADE MARKS DEFINED

The basic definition of a trade mark is given by section 1(1) of the 1994 Act and appears alarmingly straightforward. The Act states that a 'trade mark' is:

> 'any sign capable of being represented graphically which is capable of distinguishing goods or services of one undertaking from those of another'.

---

17   TMA 1994, s 37(5).
18   SI 1994/2583, Sch 4.

It should be immediately stated that certain marks which fall within this broad definition are nevertheless refused registration in accordance with sections 3, 4 and 5 of the 1994 Act, considered subsequently. On its own, section 1(1) contains three elements. The graphical representation point and the distinctiveness point will be discussed in more detail later on, but it is important to mention the third element at this stage. A trade mark is described as 'any sign'. This concept is very wide in scope and should be taken to mean 'anything which can convey information'.[19]

Once it is decided that a mark may fall within section 1(1) it is necessary to consider whether it will fall foul of the inherent bars to registration, in sections 3 and 4 of the 1994 Act, and then go on to see whether there are problems relating to the existence of other marks which may also present a difficulty in the way of registration, as per section 5 of the Act. Meanwhile, the initial section of the Act continues:

> 'A trade mark may, in particular, consist of words (including personal names), designs, letters, numerals or the shape of goods or their packaging.'

These provisions closely follow, and clearly equate to the words of Article 2 of the Harmonisation Directive.[20]

These definitions need to be examined closely, but their import is clear. A mark, to be registrable, can consist of anything, with the items in the second paragraph of section 1(1) clearly being no more than illustrations. However, it is clear that no mark can be registered unless it satisfies the two vital, but related, factors of being capable of being represented graphically and also capable of distinguishing one trader's products from those of others. The concept of distinctiveness will in due course warrant further examination, but the requirement of capability of graphical representation may in certain cases create more of a problem than was first thought. Swizzels Matlow's trade mark application for a chewy sweet on a stick[1] illustrates that point clearly. The application was rejected because it was not possible to understand the mark precisely without reference to samples of the goods. This meant that the mark in all its aspects was not capable of being represented graphically. These issues can be addressed further in the context of what a mark can be, but it is first appropriate to consider the significance of the use of the word 'trade'.

---

19   *Phillips Electronics NV v Remington Consumer Products* (1998) Times 2 February, per Jacob J.
20   89/104 EC, (1989) OJ L40/1.
1   [1998] RPC 244.

People's signatures may quite appropriately be regarded as their 'mark', but although anyone's signature is both graphic and distinctive,[2] it is not a trade mark because no trade is normally likely to be involved. That is not to say that it could never be, however. The 1938 Act[3] expressly permitted registration of a signature of the proprietor of a mark or his predecessor in business. And this last word is the clue; personal marks are not registrable, and only those that are used in trade are. By section 103(1) of the 1994 Act, trade is unhelpfully stated to 'include any profession or business', but this nevertheless gives some indication that this whole area is once again concerned solely with the commercial exploitation of the relevant intellectual property rights. Footballer Paul Gascoigne, like many others with a similar name has the nickname 'Gazza' – this as such is not registrable. However, once this particular 'Gazza' attains fame or notoriety and can enter trade, for example in the character merchandising industry, then the name or signature can be registered as a *trade* mark (so long as all other criteria are satisfied). Thus there has to be trade, but, unlike in the old law,[4] there does not appear to be any need for the trade in question to be for valuable consideration. This is not to say though that the registration of a name or a signature as a trade mark is now a straightforward issue. The distinctiveness requirement can still create major problems if the mark is not adapted to distinguish the goods of the applicant from those of other traders. The *Elvis Presley* case graphically illustrates these problems. In that case a cursive rendition of the singer's name was held not to be distinctive. Laddie J ruled that the public bought memorabilia carrying the Elvis name because they referred to the singer. The public did not assume that these goods came from one source that was linked to the singer. The proposed mark was therefore not capable of distinguishing memorabilia marketed by the applicant from those marketed by other traders. A famous name refers to the person and as such it does not necessarily possess the distinctiveness required to distinguish goods from one source from those of another source.[5]

From this, then, we can return to the issue of the kinds of marks which will attract registration. The 1938 Act, by virtue of section 68(1) gave a list of things which could count as marks and most of these have been retained on the similarly non-inclusive list in section 1(1) of the new law. (Those which have not, such as devices or headings are not incapable of trade mark registration but must simply satisfy the general requirements of the first

---

2   Laddie J's judgment in the Elvis Presley case correctly qualifies this basic starting point and argues that signatures, although prima facie distictive, are not inevitably distinctive. Only those signatures that are stylistically unique are really distinctive. In practice the latter are often a highly distorted way of writing a name and can be seen as a private graphic tied to one person: *Re Elvis Presley Trade Marks* [1997] RPC 543.

3   TMA 1938, s 9(1)(b).

4   See *Re Dee Corpn plc's Application* [1990] RPC 159.

5   *Re Elvis Presley Trade Marks* [1997] RPC 543.

paragraph of section 1(1).) However, it must be emphasised that even the types of marks listed must also satisfy these requirements. It is not every word or numeral which can now be registered as a trade mark, only those which can be both graphically represented and are product-distinctive, the latter point often giving difficulty.

However, it is important to point out at this stage that the list of potential marks does expressly include an important new area. By clarifying that 'the shape of goods or their packaging' can be registrable in appropriate circumstances, the 1994 Act at once removes not only such awkward cases as *Re Coca-Cola*[6] thus allowing registration of a suitably distinct bottle and other containers (a picture of the container will count as a graphic representation), but also appears to go even further back to overrule cases such as *James v Soulby*[7] which prevented the registration of the distinctive shape of the thing itself, registration of the shape, if distinctive, now being permissible under the 1994 Act.

It is appropriate to consider some of the problems that dogged the old law here and to use some examples from the previous case law to illustrate those problems. The use of a name *per se* may well not be distinctive, if the name is relatively common. The old law, by section 9(1)(a) of the 1938 Act, insisted that a name could only be registered if in a special or particular manner, as demonstrated by *Re Standard Cameras Ltd's Application*[8] where the name Robin Hood was used for a camera, registration being allowed since the first letter was shaped as an archer similar to the well-known historical figure and the last letter in the name portrayed as a target. Now the answer would appear to be the same but by the simpler route of the clear factual distinctiveness that such a mark would appear to enjoy.

The category of words has given rise to various problems since the courts were constrained by the 1938 Act[9] to allow only invented words or words which conveyed no connection with the object itself and which were not either a geographical name or a surname. The name of the game for trade mark proprietors was to sail as close to the wind as possible so as to try and associate the goods as directly as possible with the name chosen. Thus in *De Cordova v Vick*,[10] a chest rub was named 'Vaporub'. The claim that was made was that this was an invented word and thus registrable. In a narrow sense the word was not to be found in any dictionary but was too obvious in its origins to be regarded as invented, and thus registrable. On the other hand, in *Re Hallgarten*[11] a whisky-based liqueur marketed as 'Whisquer' was seen as sufficient of a variant from the new word's origins that it was to

6   [1986] 2 All ER 274, [1986] 1 WLR 695 discussed at p 346 above.
7   (1886) 33 Ch D 392.
8   (1952) 69 RPC 125.
9   Section 9(1)(c) and (d).
10   (1951) 68 RPC 103.
11   (1948) 66 RPC 105.

be regarded as invented and thus could be registered. Now, under section 1(1) of the 1994 Act, the test is whether the names distinguish their product from others and it would seem likely that the presence of other products of that type on the market would mean that 'Vaporub' would remain unregistrable while 'Whisquer' might survive in the absence, so far as is known, of any similar product name or description in the market place.

The law has taken and, it seems likely, will continue to take cognisance of the problem of phonetic equivalence. This is shown by the case of *Re Exxate Trade Mark*[12] where the use of Exxate on petrochemical products was allowed not as an invented word, the origin being too obvious, but as a mark nevertheless distinctive bearing no obvious relation to the goods. This would seem still to represent the conclusion that the law will reach even after its rewriting. This argument is reinforced by the decision of the appointed person in the *Froot Loops Trade Mark* case.[13] Trade mark registration for 'Froot Loops' in respect of cereals and cereal preparations was refused because it was the phonetic equivalent of fruit loops. As such the mark lost its distinctiveness and became a description of the goods involved. The law's concern to restrict the use of laudatory epithets, lest an over-extensive monopoly be created, is perhaps harder to retain under the new law. In *Re Joseph Crosfield & Sons Ltd*,[14] the name 'Perfection' was denied trade mark registration for a soap as being too broad a monopoly and as being, in the future, potentially misleading. It seems difficult to argue today that such a general word could be distinctive even within a particular category of goods, though of course distinctiveness will ultimately be a question of fact. In the first case to raise this issue under the 1994 Act Jacob J denied trade mark protection to the laudatory epithet 'Treat' which was used in relation to dessert sauces and syrups.[15]

However, the law may be more helpful to a laudatory epithet less likely to be in common use. The case of *My Mums Cola Trade Mark*[16] was decided in relation to a Part B mark and thus should be relevant in the new era where factual distinctiveness is at the heart of all marks. The mark was held to be registrable notwithstanding its laudatory character since its use of the words 'My Mums' was not a use that other traders would have any reason to employ. Now we simply look to see whether any trader had in fact used such an epithet.

Greater difficulties arise in relation to other types of potential marks on which the 1994 Act is silent as to their registrability. Certainly nothing is excluded from registrability as the list in section 1 of the Act simply indicates

12   [1986] RPC 567.
13   [1998] RPC 240.
14   [1910] 1 Ch 118 (High Ct), [1910] 1 Ch 130 at 142-3 (Court of Appeal).
15   *British Sugar plc v James Robertson & Sons Ltd* [1996] RPC 281.
16   [1988] RPC 130.

that the examples given are just that. Doubts, however, exist in relation to various types of potential marks. Many things make a product or service distinctive in the minds of its customers. A preference for one type of malt whisky over another will be based on taste, while the choice of a favourite perfume or aftershave may be a response to its particular unique smell. Likewise the choice of a new shirt may be governed by the customer's reaction to the feel or texture of the garment. There is no doubt that such features of a product are just as distinctive of them as is their name or logo. The problem with such features, however, lies in the need for those distinctive attributes to be represented graphically for the purposes of trade mark registration. It is one thing to know that you enjoy a particular brand of, say, mustard rather than another; it is much harder, however, to represent that particular flavour in graphic terms.

It is suggested that any attempt to register marks[17] of this type will meet with considerable difficulty. It is hard to be precise in using words to convey such vague notions as taste and smell. It is difficult to vocalise such things in any way other than one which is too vague – 'it smells like almonds' is surely not a sufficient graphical representation to be registrable, being too vague and also uncertain: someone else may disagree and describe the smell in different terms. The only mark that may be registrable would be a factual statement itemising the ingredients which make up the flavour (for example, two ounces of almonds and three ounces of thyme), but this would amount to a description of the contents of the product and, as will be seen, may run into problems with section 3 of the 1994 Act and in any event, be descriptive of the product itself rather than the mark associated with it.[18] It is clearly arguable that a mark which merely describes goods or their composition is not capable of distinguishing those goods from other goods of the same composition. It may be that in the case for example of a perfume a graphic representation of separate chemical elements may be obtainable by chromatographic or other such process, but this also appears to be no more than purely descriptive.

However, there will clearly be commercial pressure to seek registration of distinctive tastes and smells, for example in the context of the 'wars' between the various rival Cola drinks. The express intention behind the recent launch of Virgin Cola has been to replicate the taste of the market

17 For a list of colourful applications under the 1994 Act see [1998] 1 IP Business 22-23.
18 Two examples illustrate this point. Sumitomo successfully registered 'a floral fragrance smell similar to roses as applied to tyres' for use in realtion to tyres and vehicles wheels. Here the trade mark is not the product itself and can distinguish Sumitomo tyres from tyres produced by other manufacturers. Chanel on the other hand was obliged to withdraw its application for 'the scent of aldehydic-floral-fragrance product, with an aldehydic top note from aldehydes, bergamot, lemon and neroli; an elegant floral middle note from jasmine, rose, lily of the valley, orris and ylang-ylang; and a sensual feminine base note from sandal, cedar, vanilla, amber, civet and musk' because it simply described its No 5 perfume. See [1998] 3 IP Business 15.

leader Coca-Cola and such intangibles as taste and smell are clearly valuable aspects of a product's identity. Likewise the availability of cheap perfumes designed to replicate the smell of expensive brands shows that the pressure to try and obtain registrations for smells and other such intangibles is considerable and it is a fairly safe prediction that there will be intensive litigation in this area in years to come. When the 1994 Act came into force in October of that year there were over 800 applications on the first day of the new law, many of which were for marks of this type.

Some marks are easier to get registered. Music associated with a product whether by way of incidental music or jingles clearly can be capable of graphical representation in the form of the musical notation. Likewise the feel or texture of a product could be illustrated by a graphical representation of the surface features of the product that create the feel in question. Here too, however, there is the risk that the representation will be merely descriptive of the product itself rather than be a separate mark which is associated with, rather than is, the product.

Most products do not rely on just one aspect to attain their distinctive status. If consumers of, say, Coca-Cola, are asked to identify what they find to be distinctive of the product, some may cite its taste, others its red tin and/or the logos thereon while yet others may recall the many adverts over the years which have invariably featured smiling, happy young people usually singing the praises of the drink. The most typical response will probably be to refer to some combination of all these elements. This poses a problem for the trade marks lawyer since it is clear that this subtle combination which amounts to a product's overall image and reputation cannot obtain registration as not being capable of graphical representation (a cynic might add that most Cola drinks, their presentation and their marketing are so similar that they might not be distinctive either) and so resort will have to be had in such cases to the rules of passing-off, discussed in the following chapter.

A final area of potential difficulty lies in the issue of registration of colour as a trade mark – again the 1994 Act is silent as to this. The old law seemed willing to allow the registration of combinations of colours, at least where they were not a necessary feature of the product, as in *Smith, Kline & French Laboratories Ltd v Sterling-Winthrop Ltd*,[19] concerning a capsule in two colours which were not derived from the chemical elements therein. However claims for functional colours have not succeeded,[20] and neither have claims for a single colour which in *Smith, Kline & French Laboratories Ltd's CimetidineTrade Mark*[1] was found not adequately to act as an identification of the particular drug product in question. Under the 1994

---

19   [1976] RPC 511.
20   *Re Unilever plc's Trade Mark* [1984] RPC 155.
1   [1991] RPC 17.

Act with the test of de facto distinctiveness being easier to satisfy, there is no doubt that the combination of non-essential colours is likely to be distinctive if market conditions so permit, but it will be much harder for any purely functional colour to meet that requirement given that other producers are highly likely to be using the same materials. The single colour example is harder to work out in the new law but there seems no reason in principle why a single colour should not in fact be distinctive for the first person in the field to use a non-essential colour on the category of product in question. A good example may be the distinctive colouring of gas bottles and containers by the various makers thereof.

Some trade marks may be created from more than one image, for example a distinctive name written in a distinctive manner; the way Coca-Cola is written on its tins is an obvious example. The question which arises is whether a problem is created if one of the elements is not distinctive and thus in itself not able to gain trade mark protection. This problem is at least in part dealt with by the system of disclaimers whereby an applicant can disclaim parts of his trade mark by denying any claim to the exclusive use of that element.[2] The classic illustration of this is the old case of *Re Diamond T Trade Mark*[3] where a mark had three distinct elements, namely the word 'diamond', the shape of a diamond and the letter 'T'. None of these were in themselves distinctive and each of the individual items was thus the subject of a disclaimer. However, a trade mark was held to subsist in what was left, namely the (distinctive) combination of the three items.

The 1994 Act varies from its predecessor in one vital way where the use of disclaimers is concerned. Formerly disclaimers could be imposed by the Registrar, but now it is a voluntary matter for the applicant. However there is a clear incentive for the applicant to avail himself of this facility since there is always a risk that the failure so to do will often be counter-productive since, as will be seen, a mark may be refused or may subsequently be struck down at the instigation of a rival trader if, for example, it is thought to be likely to cause confusion with other similar marks or other similar goods, and clearly the incorporation of non-distinctive matter will readily raise such potential confusion.

That said, the use of the disclaimer enables trade marks to incorporate, albeit under the disclaimer, much valuable descriptive matter. The proprietor of 'Torremans' Fresh Orange Juice' cannot monopolise the description of the product. However if the name is printed in distinctive purple spiky lettering a trade mark can be obtained in the overall mark and it may then be as a matter of fact that the public associate the general product description with the particular trade marked product.

2   TMA 1994, s 13.
3   (1921) 38 RPC 373.

Unregistrable marks

Fulfilling the basic requirements of trade mark registration does not guarantee that a trade mark will be obtained. The 1994 Act makes clear that certain marks are either never registrable or are unregistrable in the light of market conditions. It is the first category that we now examine.

Absolute grounds for refusal of registration

Section 3 of the 1994 Act establishes the principal rules relating to absolute unregistrability. It lists a range of different grounds and by subsection (1) states that the following marks shall not be registered:

'(a) signs which do not satisfy the requirements of section 1(1),
(b) trade marks which are devoid of any distinctive character,
(c) trade marks which consist exclusively of signs or indications which may serve, in trade, to designate the kind, quality, quantity, intended purpose, value, geographical origin, the time of production of goods or of rendering of services, or other characteristics of goods or services,
(d) trade marks which consist exclusively of signs or indications which have become customary in the current language or in the bona fide and established practices of the trade;
provided that a trade mark shall not be refused registration by virtue of paragraph (b), (c) or (d) above if, before the date of application for registration, it has in fact acquired a distinctive character as a result of the use made of it.'

These complex provisions go to the heart of the issue of distinctiveness already flagged up as crucial by section 1 of the Act. The first paragraph of section 3 is self-evident. Paragraph (b) denies trade mark registration to trade marks that are devoid of any distinctive character. It basically repeats the requirement in section 1 that the trade mark must be capable of distinguishing. A trade mark must at the very least be able to serve as a guarantee of trade origin, ie it must be capable of distinguishing the goods that originate from one trader from similar goods that originate from another trader.[4] A mark that is devoid of any distinctive character can never convey the message 'these are the goods of a particular trader'. That conclusion is reached by considering the mark on its own, considering no use. It was for example held that the word 'treat' was devoid of any distinctive character, when looked at on its own.[5] The same applied to the PREPARE mark which

---

4   *Philips Electronics NV v Remington Consumer Products Ltd* (1998) Times 2 February.
5   *British Sugar plc v James Robertson & Sons Ltd* [1996] RPC 281.

as such was unable to distinguish the teaching aids of one trader from those of another trader and only referred to the work 'prepare'.[6] 'Eurolamb'[7] as an abbreviation of European lamb and 'Froot Loops'[8] as the phonetic equivalent of fruit loops (cereals) were also held not to be distinctive and therefore excluded from registration through the operation of section 3(1)(b). And when Philips tried to register its three-headed rotary shaver as a trade mark, it was held that the shaver as a 'sign can never only denote shavers made by Philips and no one else because it primarily says "here is a three headed rotary shaver"' and that the sign 'is not "capable" of denoting only Philips goods'.[9] The mark was therefore invalid. It is important to note that the Philips sign did not include the name Philips and that any other three-headed rotary shaver design would have infringed the mark if it had been granted. It was also irrelevant that no other manufacturer had hitherto made such shavers. Similarly Lego was denied trade mark registration for its toy plastic bricks when it tried to register them without the name Lego stamped on them.[10] This does not mean that trade mark protection for shapes of goods is to be ruled out altogether. The distinctive Coca-Cola bottle is probably a good example of a successful case.

Paragraph (c) of section 3(1) is designed to deny trade mark registration to descriptive marks which, as such, are likely not to be distinctive. Once more the *Treat* case can serve as an example.[11] 'Treat' was held to be a sign that designated exclusively the kind, quality and intended purpose of the product. Similarly Philips' shaver head fell foul of this provision in as far as the public took it as a picture of the goods[12] and not as a trade mark.[13] It is important to note that the bar on registration applies only where the mark is exclusively composed of these types of descriptive matter and marks can be registered which among other elements include matters of this sort, whether the subject of a disclaimer or not.

Obviously, certain, but not all, marks can become distinctive and capable of distinguishing through use[14] and through educating the public that the sign is a trade mark.[15] If there is evidence that this has happened before an

6   [1997] RPC 884.
7   *Eurolamb Trade Mark* [1997] RPC 279.
8   *Froot Loops Trade Mark* [1998] RPC 240.
9   *Philips Electronics NV v Remington Consumer Products Ltd* (1998) Times 2 February, per Jacob J.
10   *Interlego AG's Trade Mark Application* [1998] RPC 69 (a case under the 1938 Act).
11   *British Sugar plc v James Robertson & Sons Ltd* [1996] RPC 281.
12   See also *Froot Loops Trade Mark* (the trade mark is understood as fruit loops and as such describes the cereals involved)[1998] RPC 240 and *Eurolamb Trade Mark* (the trade mark means European lamb and that is a description of the product) [1997] RPC 279.
13   *Philips Electronics NV v Remington Consumer Products Ltd* (1998) Times 2 February.
14   The Coca-Cola bottle may be seen as an example. The shape of the bottle clearly became a sign that refers uniquely to the Coca-Cola Company.
15   See Jacob J's comments concerning the 'Treat' mark in *British Sugar plc v James Robertson & Sons Ltd* [1996] RPC 281.

application is made to register them, then there is no problem. Indeed in such a case the position of the applicant is further enhanced by the proviso to paragraphs (b), (c) and (d) which provides that in such a case registration of the trade mark shall not be refused.[16] This fits in with the new Act's emphasis on factual distinctiveness as being the test for trade mark protection and irrevocably overturns the *York Trailers*[17] decision that had occasioned so much controversy. Thus, whether the mark in question is not distinctive, is exclusively descriptive or has become a common or generic name will not be a bar to registration if it can be proven that at that time the mark was already 100% factually distinctive. This meets head-on one of the strongest objections to the old law of trade marks. But if the mark is registered while still not being distinctive, the registration can normally be declared invalid. However, the proviso to section 47(1) allows for the mark to stay on the register and for it not to be declared invalid in those cases where the mark has after registration acquired a distinctive character in relation to the goods or services for which it is registered. It needs to be added though that in the case of descriptive or laudatory words the burden of proof will be very high. Evidence of the fact that 60 per cent of the public would recognise the word 'Treat' as a British Sugar Silver Spoon trade mark was held to be insufficient in this respect.[18]

Section 3(2) creates further instances of unregistrability arising directly from the extension of trade mark protection to shapes of articles. Clearly there is a risk of overlap between trade marks and other intellectual property rights and this is addressed by the provision that shapes (in each case exclusively) resulting from the nature of the goods themselves[19] and shapes necessary to achieve a technical result[20] shall not be registered. How does one determine though whether a sign consists exclusively of a shape which results from the nature of the goods themselves? The definition that is given to the concept of the goods themselves is vital in this respect. If the goods are defined narrowly, for example as three-headed rotary shavers in the Philips case, any shape mark would be rendered invalid. It could, of course, be argued that the goods should be taken to mean the specification of goods for which the mark is intended to be registered. Jacob J rejected that argument in the Philips case and called the whole issue 'a practical business matter'. He arrived at his ruling that the goods in the case at issue were electric shavers on the basis of the criterion that this was how things were in practice as articles of commerce. Alternatively the problem under section 3(2) may lie in the fact that the shape of the goods is necessary to achieve a

---

16   For an application see *Waterford Wedgwood plc v David Nagli Ltd* [1998] FSR 92.
17   [1982] 1 All ER 257. See p 346 above.
18   *British Sugar plc v James Robertson & Sons Ltd* [1996] RPC 281, however Jacob J was happy to accept that 90 per cent would clearly do.
19   TMA 1994, s 3(2)(a).
20   TMA 1994, s 3(2)(b).

technical result. This was held not to mean that there was no other route to that result. It rather means that in substance the shape is motivated by function. The test was established as whether in substance the shape solely achieves a technical result.[1] The Philips three-headed rotary shaver shape was held to have been chosen to achieve a technical result and it therefore fell foul of section 3(2)(b).[2] Patent and design law may offer alternative routes to intellectual property protection in appropriate cases that are excluded from trade mark law through the operation of section 3(2).

More difficulty is provided by the third exclusion in this group namely the exclusion of a shape 'which (exclusively) gives substantial value to the goods' by section 3(2)(c). This is an entirely new provision in the law and has its origins in the trade marks law of the Benelux countries. Taken at face value, it appears to exclude a significant range of products from trade mark protection since those involved in marketing will obviously seek to attract customers to a product by, among other things, its distinctive shape and if this ploy succeeds they will have enhanced the value of the product.

Examples are manifold. The success of the film *Jurassic Park* caused many manufacturers of such foodstuffs as fish fingers and burgers to shape their products so as to resemble dinosaurs. It is a reasonable assumption to make that this helped the sales of the products and thus the shape gave added value (though query whether substantial added value) to the product. Many articles of designer clothing or jewellery also seem to fall within this exception and significant litigation has occurred in the Benelux countries from where this new provision is derived. The guidance provided by Benelux decisions may not be followed in the UK – the 1994 Act does not require reference to be made to it. Nevertheless it would seem sensible to see what issues this provision can raise. The need for the value conferred by the shape to be substantial has been emphasised,[3] and it must be the shape itself rather than the overall image of the product that must be responsible for the extra value.[4]

The section was invoked in the Philips case and this gave an English court the opportunity to express itself on the matter for the first time. It was held that the provision excluded 'shapes which exclusively add some sort of value (design or functional appearance or perhaps something else [...]) to the goods *disregarding* any value attributable to the trade mark [ie source identification] function'.[5] In the case at issue the shaving head had an engineering function which rendered it very effective and this was seen as adding substantial value to the product, especially since it had already been

1   *Philips Electronics NV v Remington Consumer Products Ltd* (1998) Times 2 February.
2   Ibid.
3   *Adidas v De Laet*, Benelux Court, 23 December 1985.
4   *Superconfex v Burberrys*, Benelux Court, 14 April 1989.
5   *Philips Electronics NV v Remington Consumer Products Ltd* (1998) Times, 2 February, per Jacob J.

held that the shape was not distinctive and could therefore not have a source identification function. The exception is only logical in as far as it targets the trade mark protection of the sign when it does not fulfil the traditional trade mark function of source identification. The Philips case is an extreme example of such a case, since the sign was held not to be distinctive and capable of identifying a source at all. A case where the shape does allow source identification, but nevertheless gives substantive value to the goods, presents more of a dilemma. Trade mark protection will necessarily apply to both aspects, comprised in a single shape, and not just to the trade mark function. Jacob J's ruling in the Phillips case seems to suggest that this case will not be covered by the exception, because the shape does not 'exclusively' add some other value to the goods. This approach is to be supported. Only those extreme cases were the trade mark protection would be granted to a shape that would have no, or almost no, value as a source identification function should be targeted by the exception. Those extreme cases do not belong in trade mark law, because the basic function of a trade mark is not fulfilled by such a mark and perhaps such shapes should seek protection in the various design rights, reflecting their success in coming up with an aesthetically pleasing design for their product.

The next part of the Act, section 3(3) adds further restrictions. No mark may be registered if, firstly, it is contrary to public policy or accepted principles of morality or, secondly, if it would have the effect of deceiving the public. The first category will of course be one that will be hard to predict given the inherent changeability of such issues as public policy and morality. The Registrar has taken the view that the religious connotations of the word 'Hallelujah' meant that it was inappropriate to allow it as a trade mark for women's clothing,[6] and presumably there would be similar protection granted to, for example, symbols of significance to Muslims or Buddhists. On the other hand, claims that the use of the mark 'Oomphies' for footwear should be refused because of its connotations of sex appeal and even its potential encouragement for foot-fetishists were ignored and registration allowed in *Re La Marquise Footwear's Application*.[7]

The second category of prohibited mark in section 3(3) has given rise, in its earlier but similar formulations, to more extensive discussion. The subsection itself points out, inter alia, that the deception may arise in connection with the nature of the goods or services, their quality or their geographical origin. In *Re Royal Worcester Corset Co's Application*[8] trade mark registration was refused for the use of the company's name as a trade mark on corsets, since the application did not distinguish between corsets made by the company in Worcester, Massachusetts, and other corsets and,

6   *Re Hallelujah Trade Mark* [1976] RPC 605.
7   (1946) 64 RPC 27.
8   (1909) 26 RPC 185.

in any event, no royal patronage had been conferred on the goods.[9] Thus the proposed mark was doubly deceptive. Likewise the word 'Orlwoola' could not be registered for use on goods which were not all wool;[10] here the phonetic equivalence gave rise to the deception. More fortunate was the proprietor of the *Queen Diana Trade Mark*[11] used on Scotch whisky. The typical consumer may have assumed that there had been royal patronage of a drink named after the then likely future designation of Diana Princess of Wales. However, it was held that there was no deception since, by what at the time must have seemed to the proprietor a remarkable stroke of good fortune, the name had been in use since 1971 and this honest use, during which time a reputation had been gained, was sufficient to deny any allegation of deception. Clearly section 3(3) represents a sensible and necessary set of controls.

It is not possible to register any mark use of which is forbidden by other laws, according to section 3(4). The best example of this is the provision preventing the use of red crosses or red crescents for any purpose apart from the humanitarian activities of the Red Cross and related organisations.[12] Section 3(5) prevents registration of specially protected emblems. This is a reference to section 4 of the 1994 Act which establishes that the use of a wide range of royal arms and insignia is only allowed with the permission of royalty, and also makes clear[13] that a representation of either the Union Jack or of the national flags of the component countries of the UK shall not be registered if that use would be either misleading or grossly offensive. There is analogous protection, conferred by section 4(3) for national emblems and other such insignia of all signatory states to the Paris Convention[14] and of international agencies of which any Paris Convention state is a member.[15] Thus the unauthorised use of a wide range of insignia is controlled as a matter of law, rather than as one of discretion. The 1994 Act has in this and other ways fulfilled the Government's aim of reducing the (inherently unpredictable) discretionary powers of the Registrar.

Having said that, however, the final part of section 3 appears to lead in an entirely opposite direction. By section 3(6), a trade mark shall not be registered if the application is made in bad faith. This seems to introduce a considerable degree of uncertainty into the law, at least until such time as litigation occurs to test the parameters of this rule. Possible examples may be where the mark is sought solely to obstruct someone else's planned

---

9   See also *Waterford Wedgwood plc v David Nagli Ltd* [1998] FSR 92 (a case decided under the 1994 Act).
10   (1909) 26 RPC 185.
11   [1991] RPC 395.
12   Geneva Conventions Act 1957, s 6.
13   TMA 1994, s 4(2).
14   TMA 1994, s 57.
15   TMA 1994, s 58.

registration, or where there is no intention to use the mark in trade. Section 3(6) of the 1994 Act was raised in *Mickey Dees (Nightclub) Trade Mark*,[16] a case that came before the Trade Mark Registry and in which to a certain degree involved both examples. MD, known as Mickey Dee, had applied for a trade mark in the name Mickey Dees in respect of 'provision of nightclub services; presentation of live music performances'. He only provided the latter of the range of services listed in the application though and at the same time he was employed as manager of a nightclub which his employer had baptised Mickey Dees. It was held that he acted in bad faith when he applied for the mark in respect of the provision of nightclub services.[17] His application resulted in his employer being unable to register the trade mark. A similar result was reached when a sole distributor for the UK registered the Travelpro trade mark in the UK for goods that were very similar to those which he distributed under the contract and in respect of which his American partner had obtained a trade mark registration in the US. The distributor's application was held to have been made in bad faith.[18] Section 3(6) presents a clear overlap with the earlier provisions of the section; an application for a mark which is clearly deceptive or which implies without permission some royal connection will also be an application not made in good faith. It also overlaps with the protection conferred by section 5 on owners of previous marks, since clearly a later attempt to register an already registered name is likely to be one made in bad faith. Thus the 'bad faith' exception has potential for considerable use; it may best be regarded as a general catch-all provision.

Relative grounds for refusal of registration

It is now necessary to turn to the second group of unregistrable marks, namely those which cannot be registered not because of their own inherent problems but because of the pre-existing presence in the market of other similar or identical marks on other similar or identical goods or services. Section 5 of the 1994 Act and its related provisions provide the relevant provisions.[19]

The first thing to establish is that in looking at the pre-existing marks which may affect the registrability of a new mark it is necessary to cast the net widely and look beyond merely what trade marks have been registered in the UK. Section 5 refers to an 'earlier trade mark' and this key phrase is explained by the following section as including all UK marks, the Community trade mark and trade marks registered through the provisions

16   [1998] RPC 359.
17   Ibid.
18   *Travelpro Trade Mark* [1997] **RPC** 867.
19   See *Wild Child Trade Mark* [1998] RPC 455.

■

of the Madrid Protocol and also applications for trade marks[20] in each case where that mark has, in effect, an earlier priority date. Even marks which have lapsed are protected for a year after their expiry unless they have not been used in the two years prior to their expiry, according to section 6(3) of the Act. The phrase, by virtue of section 6(1)(c) of the 1994 Act, also covers well-known trade marks, that is those marks explained by section 56 of the Act as being well-known for the purposes of the Paris Convention, namely a mark of a person or business from any signatory country who, although not in business or even in possession of business goodwill in the UK nevertheless has a mark which is well-known. It is not clear from the wording of the legislation whether the mark in question has to be well-known in the UK or merely in one or more other signatory state. If the latter is the case then an example of such a mark may be the logo of a major airline, but one which does not fly into the UK. However if the former is the case,[1] the airline, in order to benefit from this protection, would have to show that their mark was well-known in the UK which is difficult to disassociate from the presence of goodwill. If the airline is in fact used by many UK travellers this will suggest that it has goodwill in the UK and is also well known, but if it confines itself primarily to flying citizens of its own state, it seems that it will neither be well-known in the UK nor have goodwill here, and thus will not be protected by these provisions.

If there is goodwill in the UK, which will therefore be protected separately by the tort of passing-off, a further route exists to protect that goodwill against the possibility of the subsequent registration of an overlapping trade mark. Section 5(4) of the 1994 Act makes clear that registration of a later trade mark will be denied if its use will be prevented by any prior legal right, including by a specific reference the tort of passing-off (and also copyright and design law).[2] Thus the holder of a non-proprietary right in goodwill is also regarded as the holder of a relevant 'earlier right', though not an 'earlier trade mark', and this will give rights not under the rest of section 5 but, for example, in section 7.

Having ascertained what is an 'earlier trade mark', it is now necessary to consider the ways in which such a mark will intervene so as to prevent a subsequent registration. The Act offers a three-tier system of protection. Firstly, and most simply, no trade mark can ever be registered if it is identical to an earlier mark and is used on identical goods or services,[3] this being perhaps a relatively unlikely scenario. The more likely situation is where either or both of the mark or the goods or services are not identical but

---

20   TMA 1994, s 6(2).
1   As suggested by Annand & Norman *Blackstone's Guide to the Trade Marks Act 1994* (Blackstone Press, 1994) at p 31. See also Blakeney '"Well-known" Marks'(1994) 11 EIPR 481.
2   See *Wild Child Trade Mark* [1998] RPC 455.
3   TMA 1994, s 5(1).

merely similar. So, secondly, a mark must also not be registered if it is *either* identical with an earlier mark and to be used on similar goods and services *or* similar to an earlier mark and to be used on identical *or* similar goods and services.[4] However, this is subject to a proviso, namely that the overlap must cause confusion on the part of the public. So the essential question to ask is whether the similarities in question are likely to confuse. Obviously there is a likelihood that any such proposed mark may already have hit trouble under section 3 as being either a deceptive mark or one sought in bad faith.

What will be regarded as 'similar' for the purpose of section 5(2) is unclear. However, the courts have experience of considering this type of issue under section 12 of the 1938 Act. It is clear from the old case law, which still appears to be relevant here, that the question of similarity cannot really be untangled from the necessary presence of confusion. So, in *Re Revue TM*[5] 'Revue' had been registered for a range of photographic equipment, including cameras, light meters, exposure meters, binoculars and other apparatus, and the applicants for a mark in 'Revuetronic' sought to remove it from the register on the grounds of non-use. However there was clear use at the least in relation to binoculars and exposure meters and this was regarded as evidence of user in the photographic trade. However, the Registrar pointed out that exposure meters were the same type of goods as cameras, flashguns and other items used in the actual process of photography but that goods such as projectors and enlargers used in the process of developing the film were in a separate category. Clearly there may be some confusion between the various items used to take a photograph, but not between those items and the physically quite separate items used to develop the film, elsewhere, later, and often by someone else.

Another illustration of this is the splendid case of *Re Seahorse Trade Mark*.[6] 'Seahorse' was already registered for marine engines but its proprietor was in the business of making outboard motors for dinghies and suchlike with a horse-power ranging from 1 to 115. A new application was made to register 'Seahorse', again for marine engines, but this time the engines were huge engines designed to power large sea-going ships of over 5,000 horsepower. The registration was allowed since the different character of the products ensured that there would be no confusion. A final instance where the similarity of the goods was the subject of discussion is provided by *Re Hack's Application*.[7] The mark 'Black Magic' had already been registered for what remains a widely recognised box of chocolates and the proprietors of that mark objected to the proposed use of the same words on

---

4   TMA 1994, s 5(2).
5   [1979] RPC 27.
6   [1979] RPC 27.
7   (1940) 58 RPC 91.

a new brand of laxatives. Evidence that some laxatives were sold with a chocolate flavouring and further evidence that many shops sold both chocolates and laxatives combined to enable Morton J to find that there was a clear risk of confusion and thus that the application in respect of laxatives should not be registered.

From cases concerned with the similarity of goods we can now turn to cases which consider similarities between marks. Again this will be a question of fact, and relevant factors may include not just the mark itself, but the surrounding circumstances of its use. Clearly the marks 'Lancia' and 'Lancer' are in themselves very similar and if the products in question were sold in a crowded market or a busy pub registration of one would not be appropriate if there was a prior registration of the other. In *Re Lancer Trade Mark*,[8] however, the products in question were two types of car. Cars are bought with care, and with the likelihood of inspections, detailed brochures and guidance (or persuasion) by attentive sales staff. In those circumstances, both could be registered since all the circumstances indicated that confusion would not be caused.

There is a third level of protection also. In certain circumstances prior use of a mark, whether similar or identical, will prevent a subsequent registration even for totally dissimilar goods or services. This arises where the earlier mark has gained a reputation and the subsequent use of the same mark in a different context would either take unfair advantage of or be detrimental to the distinctive character or repute of the earlier trade mark.[9] This is an entirely new provision in the UK trade marks law[10] and its effect is therefore not entirely clear. It seems to revolve around the mark having developed a reputation such that people associate the mark with that proprietor. It is less clear what form the subsequent use might take. Clearly if a subsequent trade mark applicant uses a renowned mark such as, say, the masthead logo of the *Independent* newspaper, and sought to use it as a trade mark on a range of violent videos, clear detriment will be caused to the newspaper proprietors. However, the phrase 'unfair advantage' appears to go much further.[11] Arguably, any use of a renowned trade mark by another is making an unwarranted and unfair use of the mark to the repute of which the later applicant has done nothing to contribute.

Thus identical marks used on identical goods lead to immediate unregistrability. Where similarities are concerned it is the presence of confusion which leads to unregistrability. And where identical or similar marks are used on dissimilar goods and services, it is the presence of harm

---

8   [1987] RPC 303.
9   TMA 1994, s 5(3).
10 Though cf the passing-off case of *Lego System A/S v Lego M Lemelstrich* [1983] FSR 155, discussed below at p 425.
11 See Carty [1997] 12 EIPR 684.

to the reputation of the earlier mark that will prevent registration of the later mark. In all cases, the consent of the proprietor of the earlier mark negates the operation of the section.[12]

This clear framework, designed to ensure that there is no damaging duplication of trade marks, has, however, one clear and surprising exception. This is created by section 7 of the 1994 Act. This provides that the Registrar can still register a trade mark even when there is already an earlier trade mark as designated by section 5(1), (2) or (3) or an earlier right as defined by subsection (4). This possibility arises in cases where there has been 'honest concurrent use'[13] of the two marks and this phrase is stated to have the same meaning as in section 12(2) of the 1938 Act.[14] In deciding whether the honest concurrent use should be allowed the principles laid down by Lord Tomlin in *Re Alex Pirie & Sons Ltd's Application*[15] remain relevant. The extent of confusion, the honesty of the parties, the length of the user and the size of the applicant's trade are all factors to be brought into the equation. Longer use and larger trade will both help the honest applicant.

Problems are caused by this provision. First, the very fact that honest concurrent user may be permitted means that the risk of confusion to the consumer remains a clear possibility and this clearly undermines and devalues the entire concept of the trade mark as a clear badge of origin and as a valuable trading asset. Second, the effect of the section is limited in that the presence of earlier rights of all kinds in respect of which there has been honest concurrent user, though no bar to a registration as such, is stated[16] to confer on the proprietor of those earlier rights a right to object to the later registration. The Registrar, in the first place will then have to decide whether confusion or harm to reputation will ensue from the prospective dual registration. So considerable extra uncertainty will arise from the operation of the section.

The third problem is, however, more fundamental. There is no provision whatsoever in the EU Directive[17] for an exception of this type. Indeed the position is quite the opposite with article 4, the basis of section 5 of the 1994 Act, stating clearly that a mark shall not be registered in the cases to which section 5 of the 1994 Act applies while section 7 of the 1994 Act specifically applies as an exception to cases where section 5 of the Act would otherwise apply. It is hard to see any reason why the proprietor of an earlier mark whose interests are harmed by a subsequent registration based on the honest concurrent user exception should not jump on the first plane to Luxembourg and require that the European Court of Justice (assuming that

12 TMA 1994, s 5(5).
13 TMA 1994, s 7(1).
14 TMA 1994, s 7(3).
15 (1933) 50 RPC 147, at 159-160.
16 TMA 1994, s 7(2).
17 89/104 EC, (1989) OJ L40/1.

no domestic tribunal is so willing) strike out section 7 of the 1994 Act as being wholly incompatible with the Directive that it ostensibly seeks to implement and, for good measure, with the Community trade marks system as well.

A final issue of much broader relevance is thrown up by this provision, which is stated[18] not to apply when there is an order in force made under section 8 of the Act. The implications of this are both less than clear and also far-reaching. Fuller explanation is necessary. The UK system of trade marks registration, both prior to and after the 1994 Act, depends ultimately on an exercise of judgment by the Registrar as to whether the mark is registrable. However, the system in several other European states is that a mark will be registered unless other traders register their opposition to it and the Community trade marks system will follow the latter type of system,[19] with the objection by the proprietor of an earlier mark being the only reason for triggering a consideration of the relative relationship between the earlier mark and that for which registration is now being sought.

For the moment, then, the provisions of section 7 are the only area where the onus is on the proprietor to initiate discussion of the relationships of the two marks. However, section 8 reflects the fact that the usual approach of the UK may not be compatible with the future evolution of pan-European trade mark law and that there may be at some stage in the future a general move towards a system of registration where opposition to marks being registered can only arise on the initiation of an earlier mark's proprietor with the Registrar no longer able to initiate such objections himself. Accordingly, section 8 allows the Secretary of State to make an order that only opposition by an owner of an earlier trade mark or right is permissible, but such an order cannot be made until, at the earliest, ten years after the introduction of a working Community trade marks system. If such an order would ever be made, section 7's exceptional procedure would become the norm, hence there would no longer be any need for its express provisions.

The examination system

Thus the present system of examination by the Registrar of the registrability of a mark in the context of the existence of other marks appears to have within it the seeds of its own destruction. The Registrar's right of intervention could be terminated at the stroke of the pen of the Secretary of State early in the new century, if political, legal and economic considerations so dictate at that time. However, this is not an entirely true picture. The Community rules merely prevent its own implementation of searches and there is nothing to stop a reference being made to the UK (or

18   TMA 1994, s 7(5).
19   Regulation 40/94, (1994) OJ L11/1 art 8.

any other state) if that state requests that such a reference be made, as the UK presumably has and will continue to do so.

Much of the new law on unregistrable marks is nothing but sensible, for the most part building on previous good practice. However, the new law provides in places for great potential uncertainty, for example in denying registration for shapes which add value to a product and in creating the bad faith exception. The added irony is that after a decade to grow accustomed to the new trade mark system, it has within itself the possibility of a further radical change of approach if the decision is made, under section 8, to move towards a more European type of approach to trade mark registration, especially in relation to methods of opposing registrations in view of the pre-existing presence of earlier marks.

SPECIAL MARKS

So far we have been concerned entirely with registration by a proprietor of the trade mark he uses himself on his own goods. However, there are now two quite distinct ways in which groups of traders, rather than individuals, can seek a form of joint trade mark which protects their joint, rather than individual, reputation. The 1994 Act retains the pre-existing category of certification marks but adds the new concept of the collective mark.

Certification marks are unique in that, until 1994, they were the only way in which a group of traders could obtain trade mark protection as a group and also unique in that, then and now, they are the only form of trade mark where the quality of the product is testified to by the existence of the trade marks. Of course many trade marks in reality make a link in the consumer's mind between the mark and the quality of the goods or services provided, but a mark can equally be created in respect of poor quality goods or services, other than in this field.

The principal provision of the 1994 Act in respect of these marks is section 50. This defines a certification mark as an indication that the goods or services in question are, by the mark,

'certified by the proprietor of the mark in respect of origin, material, mode of manufacture of goods or performance of services, quality, accuracy or other characteristics'.

Note that this is a mark rather than a trade mark; their appears to be no requirement that the mark is used in the course of trading activity under the 1994 Act.[20] Indeed no such mark can be granted if the proprietors of the certification mark are in the business of supplying goods or services of

20   Cf *'Sea Island Cotton' Certification Trade Mark* [1989] RPC 87.

the kind certified.[1] It will thus normally be a trade association who will seek this type of mark.

Detailed regulations adapting the general trade mark regime to the needs of this different type of mark are found in Schedule 2 of the 1994 Act, but the general principles remain applicable. The main change of any significance is that the geographical origin of goods or services, normally unregistrable unless prior factual distinctiveness can be shown,[2] can be appropriately, indeed typically, registered as a certification mark since the origin of goods or services is often the hallmark of their quality. Champagne, from that region of France, would be an excellent example.

Problems of geographical origin arose in one of the few reported cases on these marks. In *Re Stilton Trade Mark*[3] a certification trade mark was sought by an association of manufacturers of Stilton cheese, a business long associated with the area around the Leicestershire town of Melton Mowbray. The problem arose, though, that Stilton is itself a village some 50 miles away. However, the court was satisfied that no cheese of any kind had been made in the village for many years and that there was ample evidence of the connection between the cheese and the Melton Mowbray area so as to justify the award of a certification trade mark.

Unfortunately the other grounds for refusal of registration in section 3(1)(c) of the 1994 Act have not been waived and apply equally to certification marks. Thus a certification mark certifying the quality of the goods, as did the mark in the *Stilton* case for instance, which is a criterion in section 50 of the Act for the grant of such a mark will fall foul of section 3(1)(c) which excludes quality if a trade mark exclusively consists of a mark indicating the quality of the goods unless prior factual distinctiveness can be shown. Thus the need to show either such distinctiveness or to include other material in the mark, which may not fall within the rules on certification marks, will pose further problems which will in all likelihood further restrict the already limited use made of certification marks.

This is then an appropriate moment to introduce the new Collective Mark. This is introduced into UK law (the concept having long been familiar in Europe and the USA) by section 49 of the 1994 Act. This states that a collective mark is one which:

'distinguishes the goods or services of members of the association which is the proprietor of the mark from those of other undertakings'.

Thus the only lawful proprietor of this type of mark will be a trade association.

1   TMA 1994, Sch 2, para 4.
2   TMA 1994, s 3(1)(c).
3   [1967] RPC 173.

Again there are detailed rules applying to such marks, found in Schedule 1 of the 1994 Act but again these adapt the mainstream rules to this type of mark. As with certification marks, an indication of geographical origin (but no other matter excluded by section 3(1)(c)) can be registered as a collective mark but this does not entitle the proprietor to prohibit others from using such indications themselves, so long as that use is 'in accordance with honest practices in industrial or commercial matters'.[4] No definition of this phrase is provided.

Such marks, being easier to obtain, may well replace the certification mark over a period of time. In any event it is easy to envisage situations where a group of small traders decides to pool their energies and resources and seek to obtain a collective mark where it would be beyond them to gain individual trade mark registration, either through lack of resources or, if all in a common trade, potential problems with lack of distinctiveness.

The 1994 Act has sought to ease the burden placed on the applicant for a trade mark. To a great extent the criteria for registration have been eased in favour of the applicant and against the exercise of discretion by the registrar. It is, however, clear from this area of the law in particular that fuller thought could and should have been given to the precise drafting of the 1994 Act.

USE OF TRADE MARKS

If a trade mark is registered in accordance with the foregoing rules, it confers on the proprietor of the mark exclusive rights in the mark and the right to bring actions for infringement of the mark;[5] the mark becomes an item of personal property.[6] The effect of the registration is to confer these exclusive rights for a period of 10 years, which is renewable for further periods of ten years,[7] this being an extension of the seven-year period provided by the law prior to 1994, and bringing UK law into harmony with that of most other countries.

Given that a trade mark is an item of property, naturally proprietors of trade marks will wish to trade with them and the 1994 Act understands that this is the case. Clear provisions exist permitting (relatively) unrestricted dealing with trade marks.

The first major provision is found in section 24 of the 1994 Act, which permits assignment or other disposition of a trade mark in just the same way as is the case with any other items of personal property. This right to

---

4   TMA 1994, Sch 1, para 3.
5   TMA 1994, s 9.
6   TMA 1994, s 72.
7   TMA 1994, s 42.

assign is expressly stated to exist irrespective of whether business goodwill is assigned at the same time or not, and is also capable of being exercised in part rather than wholly, for example in respect of particular uses of the mark or its application to particular goods. However, assignments must be made in writing or, in case of an English company, by the affixing of the company's seal. Though clearly a sensible provision, and one which reflects commercial reality, the ease by which assignment is permitted clearly goes far to break down the traditional link between the mark and its proprietor. This is echoed by section 32(3) of the 1994 Act which, as has been seen, insists that the proposed use of the mark has to be declared as part of the registration procedure, but that use does not have to be by the applicant himself, but may merely be with his consent. Thus use by an assignee will count as use for these purposes, as will use by a licensee.

Licensing of trade marks is permitted by section 28 of the 1994 Act and the sections that follow it. The restriction placed by the old section 28 (of the 1938 Act) on the registration of a mark being unavailable where the purpose of the registration is to facilitate trafficking or dealing in the mark has been completely swept away,[8] again reflecting the commercial need to use a trade mark as a tradable asset. A licence may be granted in whole or in part but, in any event, there is a requirement that, to be valid, the licence must be put in writing by its grantor.[9] A licensee of a trade mark is entitled, subject to any agreement to the contrary, to require the proprietor of the mark to take infringement proceedings if his interests are threatened and, in the case of inaction by the proprietor, after two months the licensee is granted the right to take proceedings in his own name.[10] This approach fits in with the fact that a trade mark licence is traditionally seen as a right to use the trade mark, which remains owned by the licensor. Any goodwill created through the use of the trade mark accrues in the mark and is owned by the rightholder-licensor.[11]

In many cases the parties will wish to restrict the number of licences so that the licensee gains the monopoly benefits normally enjoyed by the

---

8   For criticism of this provision see *Re American Greeting Corpn's Application* [1984] 1 All ER 426, [1984] 1 WLR 189.
9   TMA 1994, s 28(2).
10 TMA 1994, s 30(2) and (3).
11 The latter point seems to have been doubted in the recent Scandecor case. It is submitted that this case must be seen as a special case though, due to the fact that the rights in the mark were at first owned by one company and that the licence deal formed part of the splitting-up process of that original company. In general, there is an absolute lack of cases in this area relating to licence contracts: *Scandecor Development AB v Scandecor Marketing AB* [1998] FSR 500 (High Court) and Court of Appeal (23 July 1998, unreported).

proprietor of a mark. This can be done in the form of an exclusive licence, where the licensee has the sole right to use a trade mark excluding even exploitation by the proprietor of the mark himself.[12] An exclusive licensee has his own right to bring infringement proceedings, not contingent on any action by the proprietor, and is in effect in the same position as an assignee of the trade mark,[13] subject again to the terms of the agreement.

The fact that rights of action may be enjoyed by both assignees and licensees means that care needs to be taken to alert others to the existence of their interests. This is achieved by section 25 of the 1994 Act which insists that various transactions relating to trade marks can be registered alongside the mark itself. The process is voluntary in that it is up to, for example, an assignee or licensee to seek registration of the transaction in question but there is, to put it mildly, an incentive to register the transaction since by virtue of section 25(3) rights against persons claiming a conflicting interest in the mark in ignorance of any such transaction and all the rights of licensees are ineffective in the absence of an application to register the relevant transaction. So, in reality, all affected transactions are likely to be formally registered.

There is of course a further problem with exclusive licences. Any such licence has the effect of moving the monopoly right from the originator of the trade mark, who may in broad terms be regarded as having deserved such a privilege, to another. Such extensions of monopoly rights have naturally attracted the interest of the EU, but in this area there are no block exemptions, making the likely interest of EU competition law all the stronger at first glance.

TRADE MARKS: INFRINGEMENT AND REVOCATION

In trade mark law, just as in patent law, the issues of infringement and revocation, though separate, inevitably are interlocked in many examples of litigation. It is typical for a claim that a trade mark has been infringed to be countered by the argument that the trade mark has been wrongly registered in the first place. Equally a revocation claim may be met by the counter-threat of an infringement allegation. The 1994 Act understands this symbiosis, and the two separate concepts are the subject of well co-ordinated legislation. It can be added that in defining what will amount to an infringement the act also indirectly defines the scope of the rights that are given to the trade mark owner.

---

12   TMA 1994, s 29(1).
13   TMA 1994, s 31(1).

Infringement

Section 10 of the 1994 Act establishes the basic criteria for an infringement action. It is written to accord with the provisions of section 5 of the Act which, as has been seen, is designed to prevent the concurrent use of duplicate or similar marks. If a mark is already on the register it is an infringement to use the same mark for the same goods or services.[14] Where either or both the two marks and the product in question are similar rather than identical there will be an infringement if the later use of the earlier mark will be likely to cause confusion to the public.[15] Finally unauthorised use of an identical or a similar mark on totally different goods will also be an infringement if the repute of the mark would be harmed by such a use.[16] This crucial section is worded as follows:

'10(1) A person infringes a registered trade mark if he uses in the course of trade a sign which is identical with the trade mark in relation to goods or services which are identical with those for which it is registered.

(2) A person infringes a registered trade mark if he uses in the course of trade a sign where because –

(a)   the sign is identical with the trade mark and is used in relation to goods or services similar to those for which the trade mark is registered, or

(b)   the sign is similar to the trade mark and is used in relation to goods or services identical with or similar to those for which the trade mark is registered,

there exists a likelihood of confusion on the part of the public which includes the likelihood of association with the trade mark.

(3) A person infringes a registered trade mark if he uses in the course of trade a sign which –

(a)   is identical with or similar to the trade mark, and

(b)   is used in relation to goods or services which are not similar to those for which the trade mark is registered,

Where the trade mark has a reputation in the United Kingdom and the use of the sign, being without due cause, takes unfair advantage of, or is detrimental to, the distinctive character or the repute of the trade mark.'

The application of each of these three subsections gives rise to a number of issues.

---

14   TMA 1994, s 10(1).
15   TMA 1994, s 10(2).
16   TMA 1994, s 10(3).

Section 10(1)

Section 10(1) refers to a 'sign' that is allegedly infringing and that is used by the alleged infringer. It is first of all necessary to define what is a sign in any particular case. In the *British Sugar* case[17] Jacob J took the sign to be the word 'Treat'. The defendant, Robertson, had also used the phrase 'Robertson's Toffee Treat', but the two first words were regarded as added matter which described the goods. 'Treat' was the sign, or label, that was used to distinguish the goods. Additionally section 10(1) requires that the sign is used in the course of trade. That does not mean though that the sign should be used in a trade mark sense, ie as a distinctive sign. In the *British Sugar Treat* case Jacob J gave the example of the phrase 'give your child a treat, give it Robertson's marmalade'.[18] He argued that the use of the word treat in that sentence, while clearly not used in a trade mark sense, could still come within the provisions of section 10.[19] The main point in section 10(1), and the test for infringement, is the comparison that needs to be made between the use of the plaintiff's trade mark in a normal and fair manner in relation to the goods for which it has been registered and the way in which the defendant actually used its allegedly infringing sign, discounting added or surrounding[20] matter or circumstances.[1] Firstly, this test will have to determine whether the sign and the trade mark can be considered to be identical. And, secondly, as the section requires use of the sign in relation to goods or services that are identical to those for which the mark has been registered, one must also determine whether the goods or services in relation to which the allegedly infringing sign is used fall within the specification contained in the trade mark registration.[2] In the *Treat* case[3] that meant answering the question whether Robertson's product was a dessert sauce or a syrup. Jacob J adopted a pragmatic approach on this point. He argued that the words in a trade mark specification should be construed in a practical manner, taking into account how the product is regarded for the purposes of trade. A trade mark specification was after all concerned with use in trade. Robertson's spread would hardly be used on desserts; despite the comments on the label, it was marketed in a jam jar and supermarkets regarded it as a spread. The pragmatic conclusion had indeed to be that for the purposes

---

17 *British Sugar plc v James Robertson & Sons Ltd* [1996] RPC 281.
18 Ibid.
19 It had been accepted in the Scottish case *Bravado Merchandising Services Ltd v Mainstream Publishing (Edinburgh) Ltd* [1996] FSR 205 -the Wet Wet Wet case- that s 10(1) required use in a trade mark sense. While applauding the outcome of the case Jacob J disagreed with that view.
20 See *United Biscuits (UK) Ltd v Asda Stores Ltd* [1997] RPC 513.
1 *Origin Natural Resources Inc v Origin Clothing Ltd* [1995] FSR 280, repeated obiter in *British Sugar plc v James Robertson & Sons Ltd* [1996] RPC 281.
2 See also *Avnet Incorporated v Isoact Ltd* [1998] FSR 16.
3 *British Sugar plc v James Robertson & Sons Ltd* [1996] RPC 281.

of trade it was not a dessert sauce or a syrup. Isolated and rare use of the product as a dessert sauce could not change that conclusion. The product was not identical to the goods in relation to which the trade mark was registered and the infringement claim based on section 10(1) failed.

Section 10(2)

Section 10(2) resembles section 10(1). The term sign and the concept of use in the course of trade are used in the same way here as they were in relation to section 10(1). And once more the comparison that needs to be made is between the use of the plaintiff's trade mark in a normal and fair manner in relation to the goods for which it has been registered and the way in which the defendant actually used its allegedly infringing sign, discounting added or surrounding[4] matter or circumstances.[5] The essential difference is that section 10(2) deals either with a similar, rather than identical, sign that is used in relation to identical or similar goods or services or with an identical sign, but this time in relation to similar rather than identical goods or services. And the use of the allegedly infringing sign must give rise to a likelihood of confusion, because of the similarity. If we restrict the analysis to section 10(2)(a) in a first stage, it could be said that the section came down to a three point test.[6]

• Is the sign used in the course of trade?
• Are the goods or services for which the sign is used similar to those in relation to which the trade mark has been registered?
• Is there a likelihood of confusion because of that similarity?

The first point of the test requires no further comment. The question of similarity needs some further analysis. That question is wholly independent of the particular mark or of the defendant's sign and similarity constitutes a separate issue that needs to be established independently before one considers the third point of likelihood of confusion. The category of similar goods needs to be defined narrowly, since the trade mark owner should as a starting point be encouraged to register the mark for all classes of goods for which he wants to use the mark. A comparison of the use, users and physical nature of the plaintiff's and the defendant's goods or services, the way in which they were sold or offered and the extent to which they were competitive were the relevant factors in considering similarity. When

4   See *United Biscuits (UK) Ltd v Asda Stores Ltd* [1997] RPC 513.
5   *Origin Natural Resources Inc v Origin Clothing Ltd* [1995] FSR 280, repeated obiter in *British Sugar plc v James Robertson & Sons Ltd* [1996] RPC 281.
6   *British Sugar plc v James Robertson & Sons Ltd* [1996] RPC 281.

applying these criteria in the *Treat* case[7] Jacob J arrived at the conclusion that Robertson's spread was not similar to dessert sauces and syrups, because it was different in physical nature (hardly pourable and in need of spooning out, as opposed to pourable), because market research put it in a different sector and because it was sold in another location in the supermarket. In another case it was held that television programmes with an adult content were not similar to videotapes and video discs, which were the products in relation to which the plaintiff had registered his trade mark.[8] In that case the products were distributed in a different way.

The third point of confusion has created grave difficulties. What is clear though is that it can only been treated separately from similarity and once the latter has been established.[9] Otherwise stronger marks would get protection for a greater range of goods or services than weaker marks, since the use of a strong mark in relation to dissimilar goods might create confusion in the heads of the consumers. Confusion requires that the consumer will be confused. Traditionally this has been interpreted as meaning that the consumer, when confronted with the similar goods or services that are labelled with the sign, is confused about the origin of these goods or services and thinks that they originate from the trade mark owner. The major problem that arises in relation to this traditional link between confusion and origin is created by the Benelux law based addition in the 1994 Act that confusion must now include the likelihood of association with the trade mark. Laddie J ruled in *Wagamama*[10] that the traditional approach could remain unchanged and that the addition did not change anything in English trade mark law. That conclusion must now be doubted, even though the practical outcome in the *Wagamama* case must be correct. The reason for the doubt is found in the Court of Justice's decision on the confusion-association point in *Sabel v Puma*. That case concerned two bounding feline trade marks and the German Bundesgerichtshof (Supreme Court) asked the Court of Justice to explain the relevant provisions of the Trade Mark Directive.

A careful analysis of the *Sabel* case is required in an attempt to clarify the situation.[11] Two views were put to the court. The Benelux countries argued that their concept of association had been incorporated into the wording of the Directive and should be followed.[12] That meant that in an extreme case likelihood of association may arise 'where the public considers the sign to be similar to the mark and perception of the sign calls to mind

7   Ibid.
8   *Baywatch Production Co Inc v The Home Video Channel* [1997] FSR 22.
9   See ibid.
10   *Wagamama Ltd v City Centre Restaurants* [1995] FSR 713.
11   See further Torremans [1998] IPQ 295-310.
12   Case 251/95: *Sabel BV v Puma AG* [1998] 1 CMLR 445, at paras 14 and 15.

the memory of the mark, although the two are not confused'.[13] For example, the Sabel mark would infringe if, when confronted with the Sabel mark, the public would associate it with the Puma mark in the sense that the Puma mark would come to mind, without leading the public to confuse the two marks and think that it saw the Puma mark. Sabel, the Commission and the UK strongly opposed this view. They argued that the wording of the Directive excluded this interpretation. The court agreed and argued that 'it follows from th[e] wording ["there exists a likelihood of confusion on the part of the public, which includes the likelihood of association with the earlier trade mark"] that the concept of likelihood of association is not an alternative to that of likelihood of confusion, but serves to define its scope[; t]he terms of the provision itself exclude its application where there is no likelihood of confusion on the part of the public'.[14] The Directive only uses the concept of association to define the scope of the concept of confusion. For the purposes of the Directive there can be no likelihood of association if there is not at least a certain form of confusion. The Court backs its view up with a reference to the 'tenth recital in the preamble of the Directive, according to which 'the likelihood of confusion ... constitutes the specific condition for such protection'.[15] However, two types of likelihood of confusion need to be distinguished.[16] The straightforward type of direct consumer confusion (confusion as to origin) arises in the situation where the public sees the sign and links the goods labelled with it to the trade mark and its owner. In the *Sabel v Puma* example such a situation would arise if the public was confronted with the Sabel mark and thought that it saw the Puma mark and assumed that the Sabel goods originated from Puma. The second type of likelihood of confusion is somewhat more sophisticated. Here the public is not directly confused, but it makes a connection between the proprietors of the sign and those of the mark and confuses them. This type of confusion can be described as indirect confusion or association and it is here that the inclusion of the concept of association in the concept of confusion plays its widening role. An example would be the situation where the public connects the Sabel mark with the Puma mark due to the similarity between the two marks and assumes that there is a link between the two trade mark owners. The public might unjustifiably suspect the existence of a licence or any other kind of business link between the two companies involved.[17] It is submitted that both types of confusion are now covered by the Directive and the 1994 Act, because whereas the prerequisite of the likelihood of confusion needs to be adhered to, the limitation of the concept

13 Ibid at para 16.
14 Ibid at para 18.
15 Ibid at para 19.
16 Ibid at paras 16 and 17.
17 Case C-39/97: *Canon Kabushiki Kaisha v Metro-Goldwyn-Mayer Inc* (29 September 1998, unreported).

of confusion to confusion in relation to the origin of the product or service can no longer be sustained. To do so would be to empty the concept of association of its content. The argument that European trade mark law must now include a finding of infringement in cases where there is strictly speaking no confusion in relation to origin and therefore offers an increased level of protection to the trade mark owner is supported by a number of factors. Firstly, the court's judgment does at no point refer to the notion of confusion in relation to origin, even if the Advocate General had made such a reference in his conclusion. Secondly, in a couple of recent cases[18] the court has given the trade mark owner a right under the trade mark to oppose shoddy advertising of his product or shoddy repackaging of it, even if no doubt is created in relation to origin. That must mean that trade mark law must protect more than the origin function of the trade mark and that the quality guarantee function of the trade mark is now also protected. In turn that means that the trade mark must be infringed by confusing associations that affect that guarantee of a certain level of quality.

A number of elements can be taken into account when determining whether or not there exists a likelihood of confusion. In *Sabel v Puma* the Court of Justice elaborated on this point.[19] The Court of Justice lists, in a non-exhaustive way, a number of factors that are to be taken into account by the national courts in arriving at their decision on the point of likelihood of confusion, but adds that account must be taken of all factors that are relevant in the circumstances of each individual case. The degree of recognition of the trade mark on the market,[20] the degree of similarity between the sign and the trade mark and between the goods and services that are labelled, as well as the possibilities to make associations with the registered trade mark are factors which the court borrows from the preamble to the Directive. It adds that the national court is to take the perspective of the average consumer and that the mark must be considered as a whole. It is clear that in this perspective a more distinctive mark will more easily give rise to a likelihood of confusion.[1] The court specifically cited the German Bundesgerichtshof with approval on the point that the overall impression of a mark as a whole, while giving proper weight to special distinctive characteristics, must be the starting point of the analysis.

That brings us back to section 10(2) of the 1994 Act and in particular to section 10(2)(b). Only the second point of the test changes here. The similarity test now applies to the sign and eventually also to the goods or

---

18 Cases C-427/93, C-429/93 and C-436/93: *Bristol Myers Squibb v Paranova* [1996] ECR I-3457; Case C-337/95: *Parfums Christian Dior v Evora* [1998] 1 CMLR 737.
19 Case 251/95: *Sabel v Puma* [1998] 1 CMLR 445, at paras 22–25 of the judgment.
20 See also Case C-39/97: *Canon Kabushiki Kaisha v Metro-Goldwyn-Mayer Inc* (29 September 1998, unreported).
1 Case C-39/97: *Canon Kabushiki Kaisha v Metro-Goldwyn-Mayer Inc* (29 September 1998, unreported).

services. Similarity in relation to the sign was held to be a question of degree. A degree of similarity is tolerable, provided that the mark and the sign were not confusingly similar.[2] Once more all surrounding matter needs to be disregarded, both in relation to the mark and to the sign.[3] There may also be cases where the mark and the sign are visually different, but phonetically similar.[4] The aural effect of the mark is particularly relevant to the comparison in those cases, but nevertheless such an aural effect cannot be relied upon by the plaintiff to disregard those distinctive features of its mark which could be seen but not be heard.[5]

Section 10(3)

And finally there is section 10(3), which deals with use in relation to dissimilar goods or services. The section will only apply when dissimilar goods or services are involved, but there are other requirements that need to be met for there to be infringement of the trade mark under this section. Firstly, the sign that is used in relation to the dissimilar goods or services must at least be similar to the trade mark. Obviously, the use of an identical sign will also be covered. It can be argued that the similarity of the mark must give rise to a likelihood of confusion on the part of the public. Otherwise the arguably illogical result that greater protection was granted in relation to dissimilar goods or services would be reached if in comparison to section 10(2) the confusion requirement was dropped.[6] But the requirement that likelihood of confusion is required was doubted by the Court of Appeal in the *One-in-a-Million* case.[7] Secondly, the mark must have also have a reputation in the UK. Not all marks can benefit under this section. The mark must be a strong mark. This may also explain why likelihood of confusion may not be required and why that is not that illogical after all. Strong or famous marks may be entitled to a stronger protective regime. Thirdly, the use of the sign must be without due cause. An example of use which is not without due cause could be found in the car repair business. An independent repairer may be entitled to use a sign that corresponds to the trade mark of a car manufacturer to indicate to the public that he specialises in repair work in relation to cars of that particular make.

---

2   See the guidance given in *Conran v Mean Fiddler Holdings Ltd* [1997] FSR 856.
3   *United Biscuits (UK) Ltd v Asda Stores Ltd* [1997] RPC 513 (the supermarket lookalike brands case)
4   See *Conran v Mean Fiddler Holdings Ltd* [1997] FSR 856 (zinc and the chemical symbol Zn).
5   *The European Ltd v The Economist Newspaper Ltd* [1998] FSR 283.
6   *Baywatch Production Co Inc v Home Video Channel* [1997] FSR 22.
7   *British Telecommunications plc v One In A Million Ltd* [1998] 4 All ER 476. Aldous LJ was prepared to accept that confusion is required for the purposes of this case.

He may, for example, wish to describe himself as an 'independent Mercedes specialist'.[8] And, fourthly, that use of the sign must take advantage of, or must be detrimental to, the distinctive character or the repute of the mark.[9] This requirement effectively adds to the similarity requirement and can be seen as a more flexible alternative to the likelihood of confusion requirement. For example, when cyberpirates registered domain names comprising the trade marks of well-known companies, this use of a similar sign (eg sainsburys.com) was held to come under section 10(3) and the use was held to be detrimental to the marks by damaging the plaintiff's exclusivity. It was accepted that the domain names were registered to take advantage of the distinctive character and reputation of the mark and that this was unfair and detrimental. It was also held in that case that use in the course of trade meant use in the course of business, without requiring use of a trade mark. The use of a trade mark in the course of a business of a professional dealer for the purposes of making domain names more valuable through registration and extracting money from the trade mark owner before handing over the registration was clearly use in the course of trade.[10]

Another example of a case that would fit in well under section 10(3) is the controversial Benelux case *Claeryn/Klarein*.[11] Because of their phonetic similarity in Dutch these were similar signs and they were used in relation to gin and a toilet cleaner respectively. That means that there was use in relation to dissimilar use. The finding of infringement in the case was primarily based on the fact that the strong mark was diluted and suffered detriment because a sign once exclusively associated with gin would now also be associated with a toilet cleaner. Also, no due cause for the use of the sign could be established in this case.

Further examples and an extension of infringement rules

The 1994 Act goes on to give examples (non-inclusively) of the kind of acts that may equate to an infringement. The use of a sign on goods or on their packaging and the offer or sale of goods under the sign in question will both

8 See the Opinion of Advocate General Jacobs in Case C-63/97: *Bayerische Motorenwerke AG and BMW Nederland BV v Ronald Karel Deenik* (2 April 1998, unreported).
9 *Baywatch Production Co Inc v The Home Video Channel* [1997] FSR 22, see also Jacob J's obiter comments in relation to s 10(3) in *British Sugar plc v James Robertson & Sons Ltd* [1996] RPC 281.
10 *British Telecommunications plc v One In A Million Ltd* [1998] 4 All ER 476, CA; and the first instance decision that was approved of: *Marks & Spencer plc v One In A Million, Ladbrokes plc v One In A Million, J Sainsbury plc v One In A Million, Virgin Enterprises Ltd v One In A Million, British Telecommunications plc v One In A Million* [1998] FSR 265.
11 Benelux Court of Justice, 1 March 1975, [1975] NJ 472, see also Torremans [1998] IPQ 295–310 and the comment made by Jacob J in *British Sugar plc v James Robertson & Sons Ltd* [1996] RPC 281.

amount to an infringement. So also will the import or export of goods under the sign and the use of the sign on any business papers or in advertising amount to a potential infringement.[12] A loophole that needed to be plugged is duly done so by the provision of section 10(2) whereby the use of a mark can still be capable of being an infringement even if the use is other than by a graphical representation. This means that, unlike under the previous law, it will be an infringement to speak the name of a trade mark registered in its written form perhaps, as an example, in a radio advert criticising a rival product.

It is clear from the careful matching of the phraseology of sections 5 and 10 that the definitions of confusion, through similar marks or goods, and of reputation, in the case of dissimilar products, should be the same and the discussion of these points in the context of section 5 need not be repeated here.

An extension to the normal infringement rules arises under section 10(5). This extends the protection of the trade mark proprietor to include a right to act against anyone who applies a trade mark to labels or packages of goods, business papers or advertising material if that person either knew or else had reason to believe that the use of the mark was not authorised by its proprietor. Accordingly it is now not just the person who makes the decision to infringe who will be liable; as an example, the printer who fails to act on his suspicions as to the unauthorised use of a trade mark will also be at risk of infringement litigation.

Comparative advertising

A final element of the law in this area is significant in that it offers liberalisation of the approach to comparative advertising, that is the practice of promoting one's own product with reference to its rivals and the alleged lack of quality in their goods.[13] As has been seen, the convoluted approach of the old law, as exemplified by *News Group Ltd v Mirror Group Ltd*,[14] meant that the use of other marks in seemingly harmless comparative advertising activity could give rise to infringement actions.

Now, however, section 10(6) specifically addresses this issue. Its primary objective is to allow comparative advertising.[15] Section 10(6) allows the use by anyone of a mark to take place without there being an infringement if the use is to identify any goods or services as being those of the proprietor of the mark. So the use as in the *News Group* case of a rival paper's logo so as to emphasise the difference between the papers would seem, as such,

---

12   TMA 1994, s 10(4). On the latter point see also *Cheetah Trade Mark* [1993] FSR 263.
13   See Mills [1995] 9 EIPR 417.
14   [1989] FSR 126. See p 397 above.
15   *Barclays Bank plc v RBS Advanta* [1996] RPC 307, at 315.

legitimate.[16] The subsection has a proviso though. It will continue to be an infringement if the use is not 'in accordance with honest practices in industrial or commercial matters' and also takes unfair advantage of or is detrimental to the reputation of the mark.

To start with that proviso, because that is the area where the problems are found, the owner of the registered trade mark has been given the onus to show that the factors indicated in it exist.[17] But as long as the use of the mark is honest, there is nothing wrong in telling the public of the relative merits of competing services and using trade marks to identify these competing services.[18] Advanta was in this sense entitled to use Barclays Bank's Barclaycard trade mark to identify it as a competing service in a publicity leaflet in which a table comparing the features and advantages and disadvantages of the various credit cards, including the Barclaycard and its own card, were detailed.[19] There will therefore be no trade mark infringement unless the use of the registered trade mark is not in accordance with honest practices.[20] The test that is applied in this respect is an objective one. Would a reasonable man be likely to say, upon being given the full facts, that the advertisement is not honest?[1] Or would a reasonable trader have made the statement contained in the advertising based on the information he had at the time?[2] Obviously, a person who knowingly put forward a false claim is not honest and his activity is not in accordance with honest practice.[3] A comparative advertisement is also not in accordance with honest practices if it is objectively misleading to a substantial proportion of the reasonable audience.[4] Statutory or industry codes of conduct on the other hand are not helpful to decide whether or not the advertisement is honest.

Honesty also has to be gauged against the reasonable expectations of the relevant public in relation to advertisements for the particular type of goods or services.[5] These expectations of the public form the benchmarks in this area. It should be borne in mind in this context that the general public is

---

16 See *MacMillan Magazines Ltd v RCN Publishing Company Ltd* [1998] FSR 9.
17 *Barclays Bank plc v RBS Advanta* [1996] RPC 307, at 315 and see also *Vodafone Group plc v Orange Personal Communications Services Ltd* [1997] FSR 34.
18 Ibid.
19 *Barclays Bank plc v RBS Advanta* [1996] RPC 307.
20 Ibid, at 315.
1   *Barclays Bank plc v RBS Advanta* [1996] RPC 307, at 315 and see also *Vodafone Group plc v Orange Personal Communications Services Ltd* [1997] FSR 34.
2   *Cable & Wireless plc v British Telecommunications plc* [1998] FSR 383.
3   Ibid.
4   *Vodafone Group plc v Orange Personal Communications Services Ltd* [1997] FSR 34. The 'one meaning rule' that is found in the law of malicious falsehood is not applicable in trade mark cases.
5   *Barclays Bank plc v RBS Advanta* [1996] RPC 307, at 316.

used to the ways of advertisers and that they expect hyperbole.[6] This leads nevertheless to the inevitable conclusion that an advertisement that is significantly misleading is not honest for the purposes of section 10(6).[7] But in examining an advertisement it should also be borne in mind that the public will not normally engage in a minute textual examination[8] and the advertisement must be considered as a whole.[9]

The second half of the proviso to section 10(6) seems to introduce the additional requirement that the use of the trade mark in a comparative advertisement without due cause must take unfair advantage of, or must be detrimental to, the distinctive character or repute of the mark. It has been held though that in most cases this adds nothing of significance to the first half of the proviso.[10] Any form of misleading comparative advertising and any dishonest use of the trade mark in this context must almost by definition be seen as detrimental or taking unfair advantage of the distinctive character or repute of the trade mark.

The *Advanta* case was concerned with comparative advertising practices in relation to credit cards, but most other recent cases deal with the battle for marketshares in the telecommunications market. *Vodafone v Orange*,[11] for example, was concerned with a campaign in which Orange claimed that its users on average saved £20 per month in comparison with someone that used the equivalent Vodafone tariffs. Obviously, not every user saved in practice £20 per month and transfer costs to Orange had not fully been taken into account. Vodafone's claim for dishonest use of its trade mark was nevertheless rejected, because the ordinary man would expect some hyperbole in this type of market. He would have interpreted the slogan at face value and not literally. He would not have assumed that the saving would apply to every single customer, but just to an average customer. Looked at in that way the claim of falsity and dishonesty had not been made out.

The EU has now also taken an interest in the issue of comparative advertising. A recent EU Directive[12] also accepts the principle that comparative advertising should be allowed in principle. It defines comparative advertising as 'any advertising which explicitly or by

6   *Barclays Bank plc v RBS Advanta* [1996] RPC 307, at 315 and see also *Vodafone Group plc v Orange Personal Communications Services Ltd* [1997] FSR 34.

7   *Barclays Bank plc v RBS Advanta* [1996] RPC 307, at 316 and see also *Vodafone Group plc v Orange Personal Communications Services Ltd* [1997] FSR 34.

8   *British Telecommunications plc v AT & T Communications (UK) Ltd* (18 December 1996 unreported), High Court.

9   *Barclays Bank plc v RBS Advanta* [1996] RPC 307, at 316–318.

10   *Vodafone Group plc v Orange Personal Communications Services Ltd* [1997] FSR 34.

11   Ibid.

12   Directive 97/55/EC of the European Parliament and of the Council of 6 October 1997 amending Directive 84/450/EEC concerning misleading advertising so as to include comparative advertising (1997) OJ L290/18.

implication identifies a competitor or goods or services offered by a competitor'.[13] As this definition already indicates, the European approach is wider in scope than just the use of a competitor's trade mark. The provisions of the Directive are in general also more detailed in nature and their implementation will probably require the introduction of additional legislation in the UK. Member states have been given time until June 2000 to introduce the necessary measures.

Exceptions to infringement

There are of course some exceptions to the foregoing where what would otherwise be an infringement is exempted. Section 11(1) refuses an infringement action to the owner of a mark which has also been registered. Obviously in a properly functioning system of examination of trade marks this situation should never arise. Indeed it is a second proprietor who will be in difficulty facing the prospect of revocation of his mark.[14]

Section 11(2) of the 1994 Act also removes the threat of an infringement action from a range of different situations in each case subject to a proviso that the use that would otherwise be an infringement is a use that is, once again, 'in accordance with honest practices in industrial or commercial matters'.[15] This fits in well with section 3(6) which, as has been seen, may prevent an application for a mark from succeeding if made in bad faith, though of course this would not prevent the possibility of a mark being registered in good faith and then being used in bad faith, in which case infringement actions will still be available.

The activities exempted by section 11(2) include, first, the use by a person of his own name or address. Though this seems obvious and only fair, the use in trade of a sign including name and address is not an essential feature of many trades and may well therefore not be honest. If Ronald McDonald of Leicester wants to open a burger bar, there are many burger-related names that would be more appropriate than his own name and the only reason for using it would be the less than honest desire to steal trade from his better known namesake; but if Herbert Smith of Leicester wants to set up a solicitor's firm this may be honest given that a solicitor normally trades under his own name if a sole practitioner.

Second, the subsection allows the honest use of all the descriptive matter that cannot be registered under section 3(1), unless entirely factually distinctive prior to registration. Thus a trade mark granted on the basis of distinctive but descriptive words cannot be protected when the

13   Article 1 of the Directive.
14   TMA 1994, s 47(2).
15   See *Philips Electronics NV v Remington Consumer Products Ltd* (1998) Times, 2 February, per Jacob J.

distinctiveness is lost by subsequent usage, so long as that use was honest. It is the purpose of section 11(2)(b) to permit the fair use of the plaintiff's mark to indicate the characteristics of goods or services of the user of the sign. However, that purpose does not extend to performing the dual function of indicating both the characteristics and the trade origin of the goods.[16] Use of a sign as a trade mark can indeed never constitute descriptive use that is authorised under section 10(2)(b).[17] In *Philips v Remington* Jacob J held that the use by Remington of the shaver mark was use as an indication as to the kind, quality, etc of the goods. Remington could therefore rely on the exception in section 10(2)(b).[18] The third exception relates to the use of a mark to indicate the purpose of goods or services, for example as spare parts or accessories. Thus if I am free to make spare parts for Ford cars it will not be an infringement to use (as ever, honestly) the name or even mark of Ford to indicate the suitability of my parts for Ford cars.

A further area covered by these provisions that permit what would otherwise be infringements is created by section 11(3). This is a somewhat odd provision which protects the use in a particular locality of an earlier right applicable only in that locality. Such a right must be enjoyed continuously prior to the first use of the registration of the mark by its user. No assistance is given as to the definition of a 'locality' and, once again, the use of this provision should be infrequent given that the earlier local mark should in an effective system of examination be unearthed and thus deprive the later mark of the necessary distinctiveness. Because of this, it is far from easy to think of an example of the operation of the provision, but a possible example may be if a trade mark is granted in respect of a scotch whisky named after an island and it is then discovered that a small local firm on the island has been brewing whisky for the locals using the island's name as part of the brand name.

Exhaustion

Section 12 of the Act creates an important and different restriction of the right to bring infringement actions. This brings into this area of the law the 'exhaustion of rights' principle familiar from other areas of intellectual property. In brief this is the principle whereby goods which bear, here, a trade mark go beyond the control of the proprietor of the mark once they are put on the market – his rights in them are exhausted once the goods are in circulation and he cannot object to any use of them. This has a particular relevance in the European context where the principle of the single market

---

16 *The European Ltd v The Economist Newspaper Ltd* [1998] FSR 283, obiter per Millett LJ.
17 *British Sugar plc v James Robertson & Sons Ltd* [1996] RPC 281.
18 *Philips Electronics NV v Remington Consumer Products Ltd* (1998) Times, 2 February, per Jacob J.

has obliged community law to assert that the circulation of goods in any one member state equates to their circulation in all such states,[19] unless any of the standard objections to free movement principles apply, as exemplified by the *Hag II* case.[20]

The problem arises primarily in the context of parallel imports where a company makes goods bearing a mark both in, say, the UK and, more cheaply, through a subsidiary in Portugal. Ideally such a company would like to prevent goods from Portugal being imported cheaply into the UK thus undermining the home market, but the two principles of exhaustion and single market now combine to make this impossible.

This situation is given effect in UK law by the aforementioned section 12. This removes the right to bring an infringement action in relation to goods put on to the market anywhere in the European Economic Area by the proprietor with his consent. However section 12(2) removes this where the proprietor has legitimate reasons to oppose further dealings, such as a change in the conditions of the product, again reflecting the jurisprudence of the European Court of Justice.[1] Clearly however, UK trade mark law can still be used to stop parallel imports from countries elsewhere in the world. This confirms the approach taken under the former law as exemplified by *Colgate-Palmolive Ltd v Markwell Finance Ltd.*[2] Here the US Colgate company operated through subsidiaries in both the UK and Brazil. Toothpaste from Brazil of an inferior quality was imported into the UK under the Colgate name, causing complaint and confusion, and both trade mark law and passing-off combined to defeat the importer's appeal.

Consequences of trade mark infringement

The consequences of there being a trade mark infringement are far-reaching. The proprietor of the mark is entitled to bring infringement proceedings,[3] as is, as has been seen, the exclusive licensee or, in certain cases, a non-exclusive licensee.[4] The only specific rule to note is that in trade mark cases where the infringement is innocent, damages can be awarded but no account of profits may be ordered.[5] In addition to the usual remedies in the form of damages, injunctions and accounts of profits which are available in the usual manner, specific additional remedies are made available to the victim of trade mark infringement.

19   See eg Case 78/70: *Deutsche Grammophon Gesellschaft mbH v Metro-SB-Grossmärkte GmbH & Co KG* [1971] ECR 487.
20   Case C-10/89: *CNL-Sucal NV SA v Hag GF AG* [1990] ECR I-3711.
1   Case 3/78: *Centrafarm BV v American Home Products Corporation* [1978] ECR 1823.
2   [1989] RPC 497.
3   TMA 1994, s 14.
4   See p 373 above.
5   *Gillette UK Ltd v Edenwest Ltd* [1994] RPC 279.

■

By section 15 of the 1994 Act, the court is given a discretionary power to order that the infringing sign be erased, removed or obliterated from the offending goods. Naturally this will not always be possible; if this is the case the court can go to the next stage and order that the goods in question be destroyed. In the alternative, section 16 enables the proprietor to request the court to order any person that the infringing material be delivered up to him though this right is then lost if six years have elapsed since the infringing act took place – a period which may be extended if there has been concealed fraud or other such disability.[6]

If goods are thus delivered up then an order must be made by the court under the provisions of section 19 of the Act. This may be for the destruction or forfeiture of those goods or, alternatively, no order may be made, in which event the property will be returned to its source. Regard has to be had to the availability of other remedies in making such orders. This remedy appears to apply irrespective of the guilt or otherwise of the recipient of the order for delivery up, thus potentially affecting, say, an innocent shopkeeper unaware that goods he has obtained from a manufacturer infringe a trade mark. There seems to be no provision for the proprietor to take possession of the infringing goods himself.[7]

What goods are infringing goods? Section 17 of the Act makes clear that goods, material or articles can all infringe and all are referred to in all the remedies provisions. The section provides full definitions in this respect. By section 17(2) infringing goods must bear a sign identical or similar to the mark and must be either an infringement or are about to be imported and would then (subject to EC rules) infringe or, finally, if the goods infringe in any other way – it is far from clear what is achieved by this last part of the provision. Infringing material may include labelling or packaging of goods, use of the mark on business paper or in adverts while infringing articles are those which are specifically designed or adapted for making copies of the mark or something similar to it where the person in possession, custody or control of it is or should be aware of its use in the process of infringement.

A new range of criminal offences concerning the unauthorised use of trade marks has also been created by the 1994 Act by section 92 and other offences about false claims about registration are created by sections 94 and 95 . Also, goods, material or articles which may come into the possession of anyone in connection with the investigation or prosecution of these and related offences may be the subject of forfeiture if it appears to the court that such offences have been created.

Why are these extra remedies necessary in trade mark law? The answer is simple. The production of counterfeit goods has proceeded apace both

6   TMA 1994, s 18.
7   TMA 1994, ss 16(3), 19(1), 19(5).

in the UK and elsewhere. The value of the trade mark is under general threat from a tidal wave of counterfeit goods which, in order to succeed on the market, are very likely to infringe the trade marks on 'real' products. Wide-ranging measures, including those directed against importation and illicit manufacture are thus necessary to protect the very real economic interests of the proprietors of trade marks.

However the draconian nature of infringement proceedings means that they represent a real threat to anyone innocently accused and thus also give a real motive to rivals to make groundless threats of infringement proceedings. Thus, for the first time, the 1994 Act makes provision for remedies for the victim of such groundless threats[8] as has been the case for some time in patent law.[9] This right is given only to what may be described as 'secondary infringers', that is to say not the person who actually applies the mark to the goods, or imports them, or supplies the infringing service but rather people such as shop owners and distributors in the wholesale network. Such plaintiffs may seek redress in the form of declaration, injunction and/or damages and the onus is on the defendant to show that the claim of infringement is justified. This is useful, if limited, protection for innocent parties.

Revocation and invalidity

The grant of a trade mark lasts initially for 10 years from the date of its registration[10] and this may be renewed for a seemingly indefinite number of further periods of 10 years thereafter on payment of the appropriate fee,[11] currently £250 for a renewal in one class and £200 in any extra classes for which the renewal of the registration is sought.[12] These are small prices to pay for the maintenance of a famous trade mark on the register and thus the retention of a commercially valuable monopoly.

However, as ever, there is a problem. Such rights may be lost in two ways, either through a successful application for the revocation of the trade mark or, alternatively, a claim that the initial registration was invalid. Either of these routes will, if pursued successfully, lead to the sudden end of the trade mark and the rights therein.

There are four grounds listed in section 46(1) of the 1994 Act as being reasons for revocation. Firstly five years of lack of genuine use of the mark in the UK[13] without cause can lead to revocation of the registration and it

8   TMA 1994, s 21; see *Prince plc v Prince Sports Group Inc* [1998] FSR 21.
9   Patents Act 1977, s 70.
10   TMA 1994, s 42(1).
11   TMA 1994, ss 42(2), 43.
12   Trade Marks (Fees) Rules 1994, SI 1994/2584.
13   See *United Biscuits (UK) Ltd v Asda Stores Ltd* [1997] RPC 513.

■

is for the proprietor to prove that there has been use.[14] Secondly a suspension for the same period (after initial use) is a ground for revocation. A third ground is that, whether due to the acts or the inactivity of the proprietor, the mark has become the common name for the product in question and, finally, revocation of a mark is also appropriate if it has been used in a misleading manner, especially as to the nature, quality or origin of the goods or services in question. In effect the first two grounds penalise non-use, while the latter two grounds are aimed at confusing use of a mark.

Use seems to be generously defined by the new law. Use by someone other than the proprietor, though with his consent, will suffice – this is an obvious corollary of the more relaxed approach to the licensing of trade marks. Similarly use of a mark not identical, but equally not different in its essential character will count as use of the mark, as will the use of it in the UK solely for export purposes.[15]

A good example from the old law of the first type of revocation is provided by the facts of *Imperial Group Ltd v Philip Morris & Co Ltd*[16] where the word 'Nerit' was registered for cigarettes by the defendants who were hoping in due course to launch the 'Merit' brand of cigarettes which of course was unregistrable as a laudatory epithet but use of which by others could be blocked by the 'Nerit' mark. A tiny number of cigarettes were sold under the name, but the subterfuge was seen through by the Court of Appeal. There was no genuine use of the mark and it was accordingly expunged from the register. This case would appear to be one that would be decided similarly under the new law.

The 'confusing use' grounds for revocation pose separate issues. The fact that the acts, in particular, of a proprietor leads to his trade mark becoming a household or generic name may be thought to be grounds for acclaim rather than for the revocation of the mark. But the fact that this ground for revocation only arises from the acts or omissions of the proprietor is the explanation for the provision, the scope of which is quite narrow, and justifies its presence. If the public habitually refers to all vacuum cleaners as Hoovers no ground for revocation arises. It is only if the proprietors cause the confusion, perhaps by failing to make clear that their use of 'Hoover' is as a trade mark, that this ground arises. Misleading use is the most obvious ground for revocation, given that if the intention was present at the time of registration such a mark would never be allowed in the first place.

Generally, the 1994 Act allows anyone to apply for revocation[17] though the burden of proof is placed on the objector to overcome the presumption that the registration is valid.[18] The only restriction on this appears to be that

14   TMA 1994, s 100.
15   TMA 1994, s 46(2).
16   [1982] FSR 72.
17   TMA 1994, s 46(4).
18   TMA 1994, s 72.

five years of acquiescence in the use of a trade mark by the holder of an earlier right will debar such a person from objecting to the validity of the trade mark.

Turning to removal of a trade mark from the register on the grounds of its invalidity, it is section 47 of the 1994 Act that provides the relevant rules. It is important to note that the key distinction between revocation and invalidity is that in the latter case the registration is deemed to have never been made and thus amounts to a complete legal nullity except with respect to transactions that are past and closed.[19]

The grounds for claiming invalidity are straightforward and refer back to the rules on unregistrable marks created by sections 3 and 5 of the Act. Any mark gained in contradiction to those provisions is an invalid mark. The sole exception to this is in relation to marks that should not have been registered on the grounds of non-distinctiveness, descriptiveness or customary or generic use.[20] These will not lose their validity if after registration by their use they acquire the necessary distinctive character which, had it been present at the time of registration would have, in any event, justified their valid registration at that time. Any person may once again object to the validity of a mark and if registration has been obtained in bad faith the Registrar may himself initiate the application for a declaration of invalidity.

In general, it is clear that the symbiotic relationship of infringement and revocation arguments has been well understood by the authors of the new trade mark legislation. The same basic ideas stemming from the basic notion of trade mark registrability run through both infringement and revocation provisions. This makes for a generally cogent piece of legislation, especially by contrast with its (much-amended) predecessor.

TRADE MARKS – INTERNATIONAL ASPECTS

We have noted in the introductory section of this chapter that one of the reasons for a new law of trade marks in 1994 was the need for the UK to bring its system into accord with the various international and European obligations of the country. It is Part II of the 1994 Act that seeks to do this by, in turn, making provision with regard to the EU's Community Trade Mark, the new Protocol to the long-standing Madrid Agreement and, third, the provisions of the Paris Convention of 1883. The latter two are long-standing examples of the traditional incompatibility of aspects of the common lawyer's approach to trade marks with the general international approach.

---

19   TMA 1994, s 47(6) and (7).
20   TMA 1994, s 3(1).

The Act itself deals with each of these matters in an apparently cursory manner. By section 52 of the 1994 legislation, the Secretary of State is simply given the power to make such regulations that he feels are appropriate in connection with the operation of the Community Trade Mark Regulation.[1] In particular, issues such as applying for a Community mark through the Patent Office, the interrelationship of domestic and Community marks and jurisdictional issues are flagged up as particular issues in respect of which regulations may need to be made.[2]

However this low-key legislative approach should not be allowed to disguise the significance of the developments taking place under this heading. The Regulation establishing the new Community trade mark is, of course, binding in itself and this creates an entirely new trade mark system in parallel to the domestic one. The new system is not to be seen as a rival, however. Rather proprietors have a choice. If they are active across Europe the Community trade mark will provide valuable comprehensive and consistent coverage from a single application. But for many applicants only a domestic registration will be needed and this will be the (presumably) cheaper way forward preferred for many.

The language of the Regulation is almost identical to that of the Harmonisation Directive which, in turn, the 1994 Act implements, and the basic structure of the system and its key definitions are the same in the Regulation, Directive and Act. It is not therefore proposed to go through the Regulation article by article, since to do so would simply be to repeat much of what has been said. However, it is useful to refer to the overall structure of the Regulation for the sake of reference.

Article 1 of the Regulation[3] establishes that the mark shall have a unitary character; in other words it will be equally effective and be equally treated throughout the Community – a single mark in a single market. Article 4 gives the basic definition of a mark which must be a sign capable of being represented graphically and be capable of distinguishing goods or services from those of other traders. Article 7 provides the absolute grounds for non-registration, closely similar to those in section 3 of the domestic legislation while Article 8 provides the so-called relative grounds for refusal of a mark, this approximating to section 5 of the UK legislation. Article 29 creates a priority date system and there is a full examination and search procedure.[4] The mark lasts for 10 years and is renewable for further decades thereafter.[5]

---

1   Regulation 40/94 (1994) OJ L11/1.
2   Community Trade Mark Regulations 1996 (SI 1996/1908).
3   Ibid, Art 1, para 2.
4   Ibid, Arts 36–39.
5   Ibid, Arts 46–47.

There are of course some points of distinction between the Regulation and other trade mark legislation. The unitary nature of the Community Trade Mark is reinforced by the provision[6] that the grounds for absolute unregistrability apply across the whole Community even if they are applicable in only a part of the Community. So if a UK company uses a mark which happens, in Greek, to be a word regarded as being against public morality, no Community mark can be granted and resort would thus have to be had to individual national registrations of the mark. Protection is given for prior rights even in unregistered marks, but only if they are 'of more than mere local significance'.[7] Perhaps of more significance is that all the relative grounds for not registering a mark apply only when they are raised in opposition proceedings.[8] There is a Community collective mark, but there is no provision for a Community certification mark.

As soon as the new Community trade mark system came into being the sceptics were proved to be wrong. The system has in its first couple of years in operation been highly successful. It has attracted more registrations than expected and it clearly has taken away business from the national trade mark registries. Its procedures are complex, but this is mainly due to the international nature of the whole operation and its fees are not unduly high especially when compared to the fees of the European Patent Office in Munich as the other transnational Intellectual Property office. The Community Trade Mark Office will not make searches itself, but will depend on rivals to initiate opposition proceedings, thus alleviating the examination process and reducing it to purely administrative checks. The functioning of a system which has to consider the meaning and significance of words in all the languages of an expanded Community is bound to be difficult; and the fact that enforcement of rights conferred by Community trade marks is to a large extent left to national courts will surely hinder, rather than aid, the creation of a unitary system. In any event national registrations will continue and may well still have the effect of distorting the single market. In any event, and more significantly, there is an alternative method of obtaining international registrations, and to this we now turn.

The second part of the 1994 Act with international repercussions concerns the international registration of marks. Once again the legislation itself adopts a minimalist approach, section 54 of the Act allowing the Secretary of State to make 'such provisions as he thinks fit' for giving domestic effect to the provisions of the Madrid Protocol. Again, though, the significance of this is far-reaching.

As has been explained in the first part of this chapter, there has for long been an International Register of Trade Marks, maintained by WIPO,

---

6   Ibid, Art 7, para 2.
7   Ibid, Art 8, para 4.
8   Ibid, Art 8, para 1. Cf TMA 1994, s 8.

established under the Madrid Agreement. An international registration lasts for a period of 20 years, with provision for recurrent renewals for the same period. Only one application needs to be made nominating the signatory countries where the applicant wishes to be granted registration. If an international registration is secured the national trade mark offices in the nominated countries must recognise it unless it falls foul of a domestic provision that would prevent a domestic registration. The effect is that a single application leads to a collection of domestic marks.

The Madrid Protocol of 1989 is designed to create a similar parallel system which enables many more countries to join the international system. The basis of an international registration may, under the Protocol, be a domestic application and not just, as hitherto, a domestic registration and the period of registration and renewal is down to ten years. The overall picture, however, is the same as under the Agreement in that a single international application should confer a collection of national trade marks.[9]

When provision is made under section 54 of the 1994 Act, it will have to provide for two things. Firstly it must allow a UK application or registration to be directed on to the international level by establishing appropriate rules. Secondly there must be provision for the recognition by the UK of an international registration that has originated in another jurisdiction – this will be known as an 'international trade mark (UK)'.[10]

It is tempting to view the Madrid Protocol system and the Community trade mark as being rivals to each other. This is indeed so for a business trading in a limited number of European countries, say France and the Benelux states. However for a true multinational company, it seems likely that both systems may be employed, with a Community application being made and this then forming the basis of an international registration (the Community trade mark will be recognised for this purpose) allowing a registration to be secured for non-EU states such as Switzerland and Norway. The only real advantage that the Madrid system enjoys is that, by having registration on a national rather than an international level it avoids the problem that the unacceptability of a mark in one particular state would entirely prevent the registration of a Community trade mark but would simply allow registration to occur in all other states under the Madrid system.

The third and final area of the international aspects of trade mark law dealt with by the 1994 legislation concerns the changes made to the law in order to bring the UK into line with provisions of the Paris Convention for the Protection of Industrial Property 1883. The 1994 Act extends the

---

9   For an excellent full account of the workings of the Madrid Protocol see Kunze 'The Madrid System for the International Registration of Marks as applied under the Protocol'(1994) 6 EIPR 223.

10   TMA 1994, s 53.

protection of the law, as has been seen, to cover well-known trade marks held by nationals of or businesses domiciled in signatory countries, irrespective of whether there is business activity or goodwill in the UK.[11] This is the principal change and has significant implications for both trade mark law and also for the tort of passing-off, considered in the next chapter.

Additional provisions in the 1994 Act also clearly fulfil Paris Convention obligations; section 57 protects flags and other state insignia of a signatory country which shall not be registered without appropriate permission. Similar protection is granted to any international organisation of which one or more Paris signatories are members; such emblems cannot be used as, or as a part of, trade marks if the use suggests a misleading connection between the organisation and the trade mark. Thus entrepreneurs will not be able to sell WIPO sweatshirts, but WIPO apparently can.

A final Paris-related provision is found in section 60 of the 1994 Act. This allows the holder of an overseas mark to render invalid a mark registered in respect of it in the UK by an agent or representative who has acted without the appropriate authority. An example of this under similar provisions of the old law is provided by *K Sabatier Trade Mark*[12] where a distributor had registered the mark of a French manufacturer of knives; this was expunged from the register.

There is an obligation under the Paris Convention[13] to provide protection against unfair competition. Clearly much of trade mark law and the tort of passing-off has this effect. However, the absence of any action for unfair competition as such is bound to raise a potential clash which may arise in the future.

The internationalisation of the trade mark scene is an inevitable reflection of multinational companies and multinational trade. Clearly such interests need protection as a reflection of their commercial value. But there must be a slight note of caution. The promotion of image through trade marks is not an abstract exercise but one which interacts with the citizen who is being persuaded to buy a product or use a service. Individual perceptions vary from state to state and are nurtured in different ways by different languages. International co-operation may be essential, but international conformity is not and indeed may be unwise. The permissive Madrid approach may be thought to reflect this more satisfactorily than the single Community trade mark. But on the other hand, more and more companies do business across the EU and treat it as a single market in which they market their goods or services under a single trade mark. For them the Community trade mark may be the ideal tool and they may use the Madrid system to expand protection to certain non EU member states.

11   TMA 1994, ss 56, 6(1)(c).
12   [1993] RPC 97.
13   Article 10 bis.

UK TRADE MARKS – AN OVERVIEW

That the old law needed reform was undoubted. Its convolutions and complexities were considerable and became worse as amendment after amendment was made. Its failure to slot in with internationally recognised approaches was regrettable too. Does the 1994 Trade Marks Act then meet the objective of redressing these difficulties? The answer must be that in broad measure it does. A simpler, clearer and better internationally co-ordinated approach is created by the new law and this is obviously to be welcomed. There is a pleasing symmetry too to the interrelationship and overlap between the principal provisions on registrability, infringement and revocation. It reflects an understanding of reality in terms of the need to assign or licence trade marks.

That there will turn out to be gremlins in the drafting of the new law is inevitable and that there will have to be considerable litigation to mark the boundaries of the new law in relation to new types of mark such as shape and, in particular, tastes and smells is unavoidable. Less justifiable perhaps are some of the inherently vague items of terminology which for the most part are, unsurprisingly, inherited from the Directive. Clearly it will take some time before a clear picture emerges as to what, for instance, will be a shape that gives value to a product or in what circumstances registration will be refused on the grounds of bad faith. Some clarifications have already been provided, but we are not yet there entirely. The retention of honest concurrent use as a defence seems particularly unfortunate as it is flying in the face of the words of the Directive itself.

In terms of requirements for registration the 1994 Act represents a move away from the role of trade mark law as a method of consumer protection and does not have the traditional assurance provided by the mark as a badge of quality. It offers registration to those trade marks that function (as a minimum) as a badge of origin, protecting a business against predatory rivals often engaged in cynical counterfeiting activity. Indeed, in this respect the best litmus test of the new law, both in its pure domestic context and in its promotion of international accord, is whether it is successful in going at least some way to stemming the tidal wave of blatantly counterfeit goods that form a major blot on our trading landscape.

A slightly different picture emerges in relation to trade mark infringement and the scope of trade mark protection. In these areas the legal system now extends its protection beyond the origin function of the trade mark, even if the latter is still the primary function of the trade mark. This evolution is clearly based on the influence of the Directive, it is not always reflected clearly in the 1994 Act and it is not necessarily readily accepted by the Courts in this country. Nevertheless, it clearly emerges from the case law of the Court of Justice of the European Communities. *Sabel v Puma*[14]

14   Case C–251/95: [1998] 1 CMLR 445.

provided a first indication in this respect and this has now been followed up by a ruling that confusion can exist where the public perceives the goods or services as being produced in different places and by economically linked undertakings rather than necessarily by the same undertaking.[15] This clearly goes beyond the protection of the function of origin.[16] The trade mark owner also gets protection for some of the non-origin uses of its trade mark.

TRADE MARKS AND THE FREE MOVEMENT OF GOODS

We discussed in relation to patents how the provisions on free movement and competition law in the Treaty of Rome apply to intellectual property rights. The principles we set out there obviously also apply to trade marks and this section will only be concerned with the specific application of these principles.

Towards a definition of the specific subject matter and the essential function

The first case decided by the Court of Justice is a parallel case to the *Centrafarm v Sterling Drug*[17] case in patents. The trade mark case is *Centrafarm v Winthrop*.[18] As in the patent case Centrafarm was buying drugs in the UK and importing them into the Netherlands for resale. In both countries the drug was marketed under the trade mark Negram. Winthrop, the Dutch subsidiary of Sterling owned the trade mark in the Netherlands and tried to exercise its rights under it to block the importation and resale operation in the Netherlands. Unfortunately the Court of Justice did not spell out fully the essential function of a trade mark in this case, although it is fair to say that the approach taken is identical to the one in patents as the court went on to define the specific subject matter which included a reference to the exhaustion doctrine. The specific subject matter of a trade mark is:

'the guarantee that the owner of the trade mark has the exclusive right to use that mark, for the purpose of putting products protected by the trade mark into circulation for the first time, and is therefore intended to protect him against competitors wishing to take advantage of the status

---

15   Case C-39/97: *Canon Kabushiki Kaisha v Metro-Goldwyn-Mayer Inc*, 29 September 1998, unreported.
16   Torremans [1998] IPQ 295-310.
17   Case 15/74: *Centrafarm BV v Sterling Drug Inc* [1974] ECR 1147, [1974] 2 CMLR 480, see supra.
18   Case 16/74: *Centrafarm BV v Winthrop BV* [1974] ECR 1183, [1974] 2 CMLR 480.

and reputation of the trade mark by selling products illegally bearing that mark.'[19]

The owner of the trade mark has the exclusive right to use the trade mark for commercial purposes and can oppose infringement. He can exercise the right by putting products (or services) labelled with the trade mark on the market for the first time, but afterwards his rights are exhausted. These are all rights under parallel trade marks in the Community. The comments we made concerning the similar specific subject matter of a patent apply here as well. Any exercise of the trade mark that goes further will fall foul of Articles 30 and 36. Obviously the trade mark owner can put the products on the market himself or he can allow a third party to exploit the trade mark with his consent. Which option is taken does not influence the application of the exhaustion doctrine. Winthrop could thus not be allowed to exercise its Dutch trade mark rights to block the importation and resale operation Centrafarm was setting up for Negram as the marketing in the UK had been done by the Sterling group, meeting the consent requirement, and had exhausted all rights under parallel trade marks in the Community. Such exercise of its trade mark rights by Winthrop would go beyond the specific subject matter of a trade mark and it therefore falls foul of Articles 30 and 36. In the words of the court:

'the exercise, by the owner of a trade mark, of the right which he enjoys under the legislation of a Member State to prohibit the sale, in that State, of a product which has been marketed under the trade mark in another Member State by the trade mark owner or with his consent is incompatible with the rules of the EEC Treaty concerning the free movement of goods within the Common Market'.[20]

The fact that the product has been manufactured outside the EU, before it was put on the market inside the Union, is irrelevant as long as the product was put into circulation in the EU by or with the consent of the trade mark owner.[1] The consent for the marketing within the Union is the crucial element.

The essential function of the trade mark was spelled out in the next trade mark case to reach the Court. In *Hoffmann–La Roche v Centrafarm*[2] the Court said that the essential function of a trade mark was

---

19   Ibid at 1194 and 5080.
20   Ibid at 1195 and 510.
1   Case C-352/95: *Pytheron International SA v Jean Bourdon* [1997] ECR I-1729.
2   Case 102/77: *Hoffmann–La Roche v Centrafarm* [1978] ECR 1139, [1978] 3 CMLR 217.

'to guarantee the identity of the trade marked product to the consumer or ultimate user, by enabling him without any possibility of confusion to distinguish that product from products which have another origin'.[3]

This has to be read in conjunction with the partial statement on the subject in *Centrafarm v Winthrop* where the protection of the goodwill of the owner of the trade mark was emphasised. Why this seemingly odd combination? It is submitted that in relation to trade marks it is impossible to say that one function is more essential than the other as was the case in relation to patents. Goodwill is an essential element of a trade mark for its owner, but it will only exist if the consumer distinguishes the product or service labelled with the trade mark from other products or services. The guarantee for consumers or users that the product or service labelled with the trade mark is of a standard quality is essential in order for the goodwill, be it negative or positive goodwill, to be created. The combination of these two elements forms the essential function of a trade mark which is fulfilled by the exercise of the rights within the specific subject matter of a trade mark.

The repackaging and relabelling saga

Further complications arose when certain trade marked drugs were sold in different packing formats in various Member States. In the *Hoffmann–La Roche* case the drug Valium was sold in packs containing a different number of pills in the UK and in Germany. Centrafarm bought the drugs in the UK, removed the outer packing and repacked the drug for the German market in packs containing the number of pills which was normal on the German market. It applied the Valium trade mark which Hoffmann–La Roche owned all over Europe to the packs destined for the German market. Hoffmann–La Roche wanted to rely on its German Valium trade mark to stop Centrafarm. It argued that it had not exhausted its rights in the trade mark because it had not applied it to the repacked goods. The Court of Justice rejected the argument. Hoffmann–La Roche had marketed the drugs in the UK under the Valium trade mark and thereby exhausted its rights in all parallel trade marks. The way in which Hoffmann–La Roche wanted to use its trade mark went beyond the specific subject matter of the trade mark and fell foul of Articles 30 and 36. The interesting element in this case relates to the essential function of trade marks, as this needs to be fulfilled by the exercise of the rights under the specific subject matter of the trade mark. The goodwill of Hoffmann–La Roche and the interest of the consumers had therefore to be protected. This is the reason why the court

3   Ibid at 1164 and 241.

laid down additional requirements. It specified that there needs to be a guarantee that the repacking has no adverse effect on the original condition of the goods because tampering with the goods would affect the goodwill of the owner of the trade mark and undermine the identity guarantee the consumer is entitled to. The fact that the goods have been repacked means the identity of the repacker should also figure on the repacked goods for the information of the consumer. And the owner of the trade mark should be informed of the intention to repack the goods so that it can keep an eye on the market to safeguard its goodwill and act when that is threatened. If these conditions are met, the essential function of the trade mark is fulfilled and every exercise that goes beyond the specific subject matter of the trade mark will fall foul of Articles 30 and 36.[4] The court confirmed this approach in *Pfizer Inc v Eurim-Pharm GmbH*.[5]

Not only repacking caused problems though. A company could also use different trade marks for one product in different member states. This can of course be done for legitimate reasons as it may not be possible to register the same trade mark in certain member states because a similar mark already exists or because the trade mark has a negative connotation in the language of that member state. The trade mark owner can have less legitimate reasons though. One trade mark per member state in effect partitions the single market. The owner of the trade marks can operate freely in each of the national markets from a dominant position. A challenger should be entitled to use the trade mark which the owner uses in that market in order to mount an effective challenge and the owner will try to prevent this by relying on the trade mark and alleging infringement. This is what happened in *Centrafarm BV v American Home Products Corpn*.[6] American Home Products marketed the same drug in the UK under the trade mark Serenid, while using the trade mark Seresta in the Benelux countries and Germany. Centrafarm bought the drug in the UK and sold it in Holland after changing the trade mark to Seresta because Dutch consumers were familiar with this trade mark. American Home Products objected to this practice and argued that it infringed its Dutch Seresta trade mark. In this case there was no legitimate reason to use a different trade mark in the Netherlands.[7] The goodwill of American Home Products was not affected and the interests of the consumers were unharmed, safeguarding the essential function of the trade mark. The rights conferred by the trade mark were exercised to serve one function, to restrict the free movement of goods and to partition the single market. Therefore this exercise of the trade marks should fall foul of

4 Case 102/77: *Hoffmann–La Roche v Centrafarm* [1978] ECR 1139, (1978) 3 CMLR 217.
5 Case 1/81: *Pfizer Inc v Eurim-Pharm GmbH* [1981] ECR 2913, [1982] 1 CMLR 406.
6 Case 3/78: *Centrafarm BV v American Home Products Corpn* [1978] ECR 1823, [1978] 1 CMLR 326.
7 For an example of a case where there was such a legitimate reason see Case C-313/94: *Fratelli Graffione SNC v Ditta Fransa* [1996] ECR I-6039.

Articles 30 and 36 because it constitutes a disguised restriction of trade and this was indeed what the Court decided.[8] To be precise, the specific subject matter of the trade mark as a description of what is allowed was preserved as the trade mark owner still put all products concerned on the market for the first time. This case has been criticised because it introduces a subjective criterion by relying on the intent of the owner of the trade marks.[9] Subsequent developments in the case law of the court have shown that the court never intended to introduce a subjective element. The parallel importer does not have to prove that the rightholder set out to partition the market deliberately. We now turn to the detailed analysis of these subsequent developments, which have clarified a number of points.

This was the position before the harmonisation of national trade mark laws. The court's case law dealt with the apparent clash between the national trade mark laws of the member states and Articles 30 and 36 of the EC Treaty. The First Harmonisation Directive changed that picture.[10] It deals with exhaustion in its Article 7 and on the basis of that article the pharmaceutical industry challenged the validity of court's case law.[11] The issue whether *Hoffmann–La Roche v Centrafarm*[12] was still good law was brought before the court as a preliminary question on the interpretation of Article 7 of the Directive after a series of cases had been brought in the national courts by pharmaceutical companies that objected to the repackaging activity of parallel importers.[13]

8   Case 3/78: *Centrafarm BV v American Home Products Corpn* [1978] ECR 1823; [1978] 1 CMLR 326.
9   Baden Fuller 'Economic Issues Relating to Property Rights in Trade Marks' (1981) 6 EL Rev 162.
10   Council Directive 89/104 EC (1989) OJ L40/1.
11   The real reason why parallel imports of pharmaceutical products are such a problem in the Community, and especially in the eyes of the main pharmaceutical companies, is the difference in prices between the different member states. This would not be such a problem if the different prices were determined entirely freely by the pharmaceutical companies that produce the drugs, but in practice there is also a lot of government regulation around in the area. It is however not allowed to circumvent the absence of a harmonisation in the national rules regulating the prices of pharmaceutical products and the perceived lack of political will to achieve it by breaching the rules on free movement. National trade mark law cannot be allowed to disregard Community law in this area, the purpose of trade marks is not to remedy the market distortions caused by the national price regulating regimes. What needs to be done is harmonising those different national regimes.
12   Case 102/77: [1978] ECR 1139.
13   Cases C-427, 429 and 436/93: *Bristol-Meyers Squibb*; *CH Boehringer Sohn, Boehringer Ingelheim KG, Boehringer Ingelheim A/S* and *Bayer AG, Bayer Danmark A/S v Paranova A/S* [1996] ECR I-3457; Cases C-71, 72 and 73/94: *Eurim-Pharm Arzneimittel GmbH v Beiersdorf AG*; *Boehringer Ingelheim KG* and *Farmitalia Carlo Erba GmbH* [1996] ECR I-3603 and case C-232/94: *MPA Pharma GmbH v Rhone-Poulenc Pharma GmbH* [1996] ECR I-3671; see also Torremans 'New Re-Packaging under the Trade mark Directive of Well-Established Exhaustion Principles' [1997] 11 EIPR 664.

The Directive grants the trade mark owner the exclusive right to affix the trade mark to the product or its packaging,[14] subject to the impact of the exhaustion principle. That principle is said in Article 7.1 not to 'entitle the proprietor to prohibit (the trade mark's) use in relation to goods which have been put on the market within the Community under that trade mark by the proprietor or with his consent'. Article 7.2 adds to that that Article 7.1 will not stop the trade mark owner from opposing the continued marketing of the goods if he does so on reasonable grounds. Obvious examples of such grounds are cases in which the goods have been impaired or altered after having been put on the market by the trade mark owner or with his consent.

The pharmaceutical companies argued that Article 7.1 should be interpreted in such a way that the goods are the goods in the format and the unit in which they have been put on the market. This would mean, for example, 20 tablets of the pharmaceutical product in a box with certain dimensions, colours, etc. The parallel importer would be free to buy these boxes in another member state and resell them as they are. Any repacking and re-affixing of the trade mark would constitute an infringement of the trade mark. Article 7.2 would only operate for example to allow the trade mark owner to stop the marketing of damaged products. The same result is achieved if one admits that Article 7.1 results in the exhaustion of the trade mark as soon as the trade-marked product has been put on the market in any form, while giving a broad interpretation to Article 7.2 by including any change of the brand presentation and ie any form of repacking and/or re-affixing of the trade mark as a reasonable ground to exclude the operation of the exhaustion principle in Article 7.1.[15]

This would of course involve a radical change in the definition of the exhaustion principle and it would reverse the court's case law. Can the Directive be interpreted in this way? Or should one stick to the interpretation that Article 7.1 results in the exhaustion of the trade mark as soon as the trade marked product has been put on the market in any form, while the only reasonable ground on the basis of which the trade mark owner can object involves a change to the product which is actually consumed, ie the tablets in our earlier example?

Before jumping to any conclusion, one should start with the basics. The starting point of all Community law in this area is Articles 30 and 36 of the EC Treaty. Any secondary Community legislation can only apply and not change the Treaty and should therefore be interpreted in a way which is in

---

14   Article 5.3(a) of the Directive.
15   See Dyekjaer-Hansen 'The Trade Mark Directive and the Protection of Brands and Branding' [1996] 1 EIPR 62 at 63.

line and compatible with the provisions of the Treaty.[16] The provisions of the Directive must thus be interpreted in the light of articles 30 and 36 EC.

What is not under discussion is that Article 36 EC only provides for a partial exemption of trade mark rights from the application of Article 30 EC and its free movement rule. What is exempted is the specific subject matter of the trade mark. The trade mark can play its competition enhancing role[17] in the economy, but any other use is caught by Article 30 EC. What then is the essence of a trade mark? A trade mark is essentially an indication of origin. The trade mark guarantees the consumer that a certain product has been manufactured by or under the control of a certain company that bears responsibility for the fact that the product meets certain standards or expectations of quality. The trade mark is the means by which the product is identified. That identification by customers leads to the establishment of goodwill for the company which is able to bind the customers to it.[18]

The next question that needs to be answered is then the origin of what is indicated by the trade mark. The obvious answer is of the goods that are labelled with the trade mark, but that does not solve our problem if one considers that marketing experts might suggest that the whole trade dress of a carefully marketed product forms part of the goods. A return to the basic principles of trade mark law provides the solution to this problem. A trade mark is a sign to distinguish goods which is registered in relation to a certain category or certain categories of goods. That means that a trade mark is, for example, registered in relation to pharmaceutical products. No one will pretend that anything else than the product that is actually used for medicinal purposes is covered by this category. The trade dress is not part of the goods. The goods or products are, for example, the tablets, but they do not include the box in which they are packed by the manufacturer. This is the maximum coverage of trade mark law before the Treaty provisions interfere with it. That interference can only reduce the level of protection and the options offered to the trade mark owner due to the fact that Article 30 rules out restriction to the free movement and Article 36 only partially alleviates that ban. The outcome of the process can therefore not be that

---

16 See Case C-47/90: *Etablissements Delhaize Frères v Promalvin* [1992] ECR I-3669 at para 26 and Case C-315/92: *Verband Sozialer Wettbewerb* [1994] ECR I-317 at para 12 referred to in joined Cases C-427, 429 and 436/93: *Bristol-Meyers Squibb v Paranova A/S* [1996] ECR I-3457, at para 27.

17 The Court explicitly recognised that trade mark rights (within the constraints of their specific subject matter) form an essential element of the system of free competition on the Common Market which the Treaty set out to establish, joined cases C-427, 429 and 436/93: *Bristol-Meyers Squibb v Paranova A/S* [1996] ECR I-3457, at para 43.

18 Joined Cases C-427, 429 and 436/93 *Bristol-Meyers Squibb v Paranova A/S* [1996] ECR I-3457, at para 43, with reference to case C-10/89: *CNL-SUCAL NV SA v Hag GF AG* (Hag II) [1990] ECR I-3711, at para 13 and Case C-9/93 *IHT Internationaler Heiztechnik GmbH v Ideal Standard GmbH* [1994] ECR I-2789 at paras 37 and 45.

trade dress is now included in the definition of the goods to which a trade mark is applied and in relation to which it creates certain exclusive rights.

Let us now turn to the Directive. It must be clear that the Directive or any other piece of secondary Community legislation cannot introduce quantitative restrictions if it can only apply the provisions of the Treaty. Any other conclusion would involve a violation of Articles 30 and 36 EC.[19] These articles can only be changed by a new Treaty.

The final step brings us to the national trade mark laws. These must obviously be interpreted along the lines of the Directive. As the Directive was supposed to harmonise the trade mark laws of the member states and the protection of trade marks as allowed in the context of Article 36, one should first of all turn to the Directive when the compatibility of a provision of national trade mark law with Community law is at issue.[20] The Directive is supposed to offer more detailed rules and guidance, which is fully in line with the provisions of the Treaty.

Where does all this theory lead us in practical terms? The question whether or not national trade mark law can allow a trade mark owner to oppose the repackaging of pharmaceutical products and/or the re-affixing of the trade mark needs to be answered on the basis of the provisions of the Directive.[1] Article 7 deals with the exhaustion issue in a complete way. The trade mark owner can oppose the activities of the parallel importer if Article 7 does not exhaust his right to object to these activitities. On the basis of the text of Article 7.1 it could be suggested that the term goods can be said to include the goods as packed. It has been shown above though that this would involve an unjustifiable expansion of trade mark protection. Such an interpretation of the Directive would not be in line with the Treaty provisions. That leaves us with the question whether a change of packaging can be a reasonable ground under Article 7.2 of the Directive. If so, no exhaustion would take place. Once more the text of the Directive does not provide a conclusive answer. We have to turn to the provisions of the Treaty[2] and analyse whether such a wide interpretation of the reasonable ground concept is required to guarantee that the trade mark can fulfil its essential role.

19   See Case C-51/93: *Meyhui NV v Schott Zwiesel Slaswerke AG* [1994] ECR I-3879, at para 11, refered to in joined Cases C-427, 429 and 436/93 *Bristol-Meyers Squibb v Paranova A/S* [1996] ECR I-3457, at para 35.
20   See Case 5/77: *Tedeschi v Denkavit Commerciale srl* [1977] ECR 1555, at para 35; case 227/82: *Van Bennekom* [1983] ECR 3883, at para 35 Case C-37/92: *Vanacker and Lesage* [1993] ECR I-4947, at para 9 and Case C-323/93: *Société Civile Agricole du Centre d'insémination de la Crespelle* [1994] ECR I-5077, at para 31; refered to in joined Cases C-427, 429 and 436/93: *Bristol-Meyers Squibb v Paranova A/S* [1996] ECR I-3457, at para 25.
1   Joined Cases C-427, 429 and 436/93: *Bristol-Meyers Squibb v Paranova A/S* [1996] ECR I-3457, at para 26.
2   See joined Cases C-427, 429 and 436/93: *Bristol-Meyers Squibb v Paranova A/S* [1996] ECR I-3457, at para 40.

It is submitted that the court rightly decided that this was not the case. The trade mark should function as an indication of origin. For the consumer this means that he needs to be sure that when he buys the trade marked product he buys the original pharmaceutical product, for example the tablets, produced by the trade mark owner or under his control. No other products should be marketed under the trade mark to achieve this aim. In the cases under discussion there was no evidence that the pharmaceutical products had been tampered with or that any product was passed off as the product of the trade mark owner. Indeed, in the one instance where a vaporiser was added by the parallel importer that item did not bear the trade mark and it was made clear that the item had been added by and under the sole responsibility of the parallel importer.

The consumer should also be able to rely on the trade mark to be sure that the pharmaceutical product he buys is of a certain quality. This requirement is met as long as the original product is not tampered with.

The trade mark owner should also be allowed to preserve the goodwill created by the trade mark. The indication of origin points indeed towards certain goods, of a certain quality coming from one source or at least with one party, the trade mark owner, controlling the system. This requirement is met as long as no other goods are labelled with the trade mark and as long as the goods are not tampered with.[3] To guarantee this further additional rules have been added. The packaging should clearly indicate who produced the goods, so as not to create the impression that the parallel importer or any third party has any right to the trade mark.[4] The parallel importer that is responsible for the repackaging needs also to be identified clearly on the packaging in order to show that that party and not the trade mark owner is responsible for the packaging. The straightforward way to do so is to print on the new packaging in a prominent way a message that X manufactured the product, while Y, the parallel importer, imported and repacked the product.[5] Even so, the packaging should not be of a low standard, as that association with materials of a low quality would damage the high quality standard that is associated with pharmaceutical products.[6] The trade mark owner should also be allowed to control the use of the trade mark and to prevent any damage to the goodwill associated with the trade mark which any inappropriate use of the trade mark could cause. This means that the trade mark owner should be advised in advance of any repackaging activity

---

3   Joined Cases C-427, 429 and 436/93: *Bristol-Meyers Squibb v Paranova A/S* [1996] ECR I-3457, at para 59–64.

4   Joined Cases C-71, 72 and 73/94: *Eurim-Pharm v Beiersdorf* [1996] ECR I-3603, at para 64, with reference to case 1/81: *Pfizer v Eurim-Pharm* [1981] ECR 2913, at para 11.

5   Joined Cases C-427, 429 and 436/93: *Bristol-Meyers Squibb v Paranova A/S* [1996] ECR I-3457, at para 70.

6   Ibid, at para 65–66 and 75–76.

■

and should be given the opportunity to request a sample copy of the repacked product to inspect it.[7]

Under these conditions the trade mark can fulfil its role as an indication of origin. Any further requirement goes beyond that role and would therefore be out of line with Article 36 EC. A requirement that the fact that the repackaging took place without the consent of the trade mark owner should be mentioned explicitly on the packaging, for example, would create the impression that there might be something wrong with the product.[8]

Article 7.2 of the Directive is really only a way to restate the rule contained in Article 36 of the Treaty.[9] The interpretation the court had previously given to that article in a repackaging context is still good law. All these new cases have added to it is the fact that the court seized the opportunity to clarify the rule and to provide the national court with more detailed guidance.

The parallel importer of pharmaceutical products is not free to repack them in any circumstances. Repackaging only becomes an option if the product is de facto marketed in different quantities in different member states. The right of the trade mark owner to oppose repackaging is only exhausted if the repackaging is necessary for the product to be marketable in the country of importation,[10] for example because health insurance legislation prescribes a standard size.[11] This can be seen as a prerequisite for any repackaging and reaffixing of trade mark operation.

On the other hand there is no need for the parallel importer to prove that the trade mark owner set out to partition the market deliberately by marketing the product in different quantities in different member states. By requiring an artificial partitioning of the market to be demonstrated before allowing the repackaging of products the court only left the option to oppose the marketing of parallel imported products by the trade mark owner open in those cases where this is necessary to preserve the specific subject matter of the trade mark. A de facto use of different packaging sizes is all the parallel importer needs to demonstrate initially to justify its activity.[12]

---

7   Joined Cases C-427, 429 and 436/93: *Bristol-Meyers Squibb v Paranova A/S* [1996] ECR I-3457, at para 78.

8   Ibid, at para 72.

9   Joined Cases C-427, 429 and 436/93: *Bristol-Meyers Squibb v Paranova A/S* [1996] ECR I-3457, at para 40.

10 The fact that the product is, apart from the size in which it is bought by the parallel importer, also available in the country of exportation in the size in which it is repacked does not alter this conclusion; see joined cases C-427, 429 and 436/93: *Bristol-Meyers Squibb v Paranova A/S* [1996] ECR I-3457, at para 54.

11 Joined Cases C-427, 429 and 436/93: *Bristol-Meyers Squibb v Paranova A/S* [1996] ECR I-3457, at para 53–56.

12 Ibid, at para 57.

This set of cases could create the false impression that the parallel importer has an almost absolute freedom to repack and relabel the products. The analysis above shows that this is not the case and that the parallel importer's activity is restricted to what is required and necessary to allow parallel imports. The *Ballantines* case[13] illustrates this point too. The parallel importer was given a certain freedom to bring the labelling of the bottles of whisky in line with the requirements of each member state and to identify itself, but the court did not approve of the removal of the identification numbers from the bottles. The latter was not required to allow parallel import to take place. Obviously, the presence of these numbers would also allow the producer of the whisky to trace the suppliers of the parallel importer. The court argued that competition law would provide a remedy in case the producer decided to take action against the supplier of the parallel importer in an attempt to stop the parallel importation.[14]

Exhaustion covers publicity

Parallel importation can only work in practice if the parallel importer can sell the goods successfully. This requires that he can advertise the fact that the original product is now also available through his outlets and that his prices are lower. Can the parallel importer reproduce the trade mark for the purposes of this advertising? The answer can only be affirmative if the exhaustion of the trade mark by putting it on the market in the member state from which it was imported by the parallel importer also covered the trade mark's reproduction for advertising purposes. This should indeed be the case, since normal advertising practices will not damage the goodwill of the trade mark owner, if it only informs the public about the availability of the public. The consumer is not mislead either, since the original product is advertised rather than any similar product. The advertising does not normally create the impression that the parallel importer manufactures the product. On the contrary he will try to emphasise that he sells the real thing, ie the original product, from the original producer, but only at a lower price. That is his best strategy to maximise his sales. This means that the essential function of the trade mark is fulfilled, and that there is no need to allow the trade mark owner to use his trade mark to stop the advertising, since the goods concerned have been marketed with his consent.

---

13   Case C-349/95: *Frits Loendersloot v George Ballantine & Son Ltd* [1998] 1 CMLR 1015.
14   For further details see Stamatoudi 'From Drugs to Spirits and from Boxes to Publicity: Decided and Undecided Issues in Relation to Trade Mark and Copyright Exhaustion' [1998] IPQ December issue, in print.

The Court of Justice approved this approach in the *Dior* case,[15] when it stopped Dior from relying on its trade marks to stop the parallel importer from advertsing its goods by reproducing in its publicity the boxes in which the perfumes were sold. These boxes obviously carried the trade marks. The adverising took place in the format that was normally used by the parallel importer and others in the same type of trade. Dior argued that that form of advertising did not meet its high standards and could therefore affect the reputation of its trade marks in a negative way. The court ruled that any form of advertising in the way and quality in which the parallel importer normally advertised its goods could not damage the goodwill of Dior. The court expressed it as follows:

> 'The proprietor of a trade mark may not rely on Article 7(2) of Directive 89/104 to oppose the use of the trade mark, by a reseller who habitually markets articles of the same kind, but not necessarily of the same quality, as the trade-marked goods, in ways customary in the reseller's sector of trade, for the purpose of bringing to the public's attention the further commercialisation of those goods, unless it is established that, given the specific circumstances of the case, the use of the trade mark for this purpose seriously damages the reputation of the trade mark'.[16]

The only reason why Dior could stop the use of its trade marks was the fact that its goodwill would be affected. This had to be demonstrated on the basis of the facts of the case. Advertising of a very low and sloppy quality, far underneath the normal standards of the type of business concerned, could be an example of such an exceptional case. In that case the essential function of the trade mark could no longer be fulfilled, which justifies the use of the trade mark to stop such a practice.

International exhaustion

The Agreement on the European Economic Area expanded the area in which exhaustion applies to the whole of the European Economic Area, which means that, apart from to the EU, it applies to Iceland, Liechtenstein and Norway.[17] However, until recently it was unclear whether the EU would opt for the principle of international exhaustion or not. In very simple terms international exhaustion means that all trade mark rights are exhausted once

15 Case C-337/95: *Parfums Christian Dior SA and Parfums Christian Dior BV v Evora BV* [1998] RPC 166.
16 Ibid and see Stamatoudi 'From Drugs to Spirits and from Boxes to Publicity: Decided and Undecided Issues in Relation to Trade Mark and Copyright Exhaustion' [1998] IPQ December issue, in print.
17 [1994] OJ L1/3.

the product labelled with the trade mark has been put on the market anywhere in the world by or with the consent of the trade mark owner. Trade mark owners in the EU would no longer be able to stop parallel importation of their products from outside the European Economic Area by relying on their parallel trade marks in the member states if the principle of international exhaustion applied.

Traditionally certain member states, such as Austria, had incorporated the principle of international exhaustion into their domestic trade mark system. Recently, the majority of the member states and the Commission seemed to have abandoned the principle of international exhaustion though. One could take a cynical view and argue that this was a symptom of the 'Fortress Europe' mentality and that they only wanted to protect themselves from cheap imports. The crucial issue was whether the Trade Mark Directive[18] had decided the issue or not.

Article 7 of the Directive deals with the issue of exhaustion and refers to goods that have been put on the market in the European Economic Area. It is clear that this provision does not oblige the member states to operate an international exhaustion rule. In as far as it imposes a system of exhaustion the provisions restricts its scope to the European Economic Area. Two conclusions seemed possible on this basis. First, it could be left to the member states to decide whether or not they wanted to adopt an international exhaustion rule. This argument sees Article 7 as the minimum, but a minimum that can be added to. Secondly, one could argue that Article 7 is a restriction on the rights of trade mark owners and that the Directive does not allow the member states to add further restrictions, which an international exhaustion rule would necessarily carry with it.

The *Silhouette* case[19] gave the Court of Justice the opportunity to decide the issue. Silhouette had sold a large number of its spectacle frames in Bulgaria and these had been reimported into the European Economic Area by Harlauer, a parallel importer, for sale in the latter's outlets in Austria. Silhouette sued for infringement of its Austrian trade mark and the Austrian court asked the Court of Justice whether it could still operate an international exhaustion rule. The Court of Justice argued that the Trade Mark Directive set out to harmonise fully all those elements of trade mark law that may distort competition within the common market and the functioning in general of the common market. The court derives from this starting point the rule that 'Article 5 to 7 of the Directive must be construed as embodying a complete harmonisation of the rules relating to the rights conferred by a trade mark'[20] and that member states can add only those rules that are

---

18   [1989] OJ L40/1.
19   Case C-355/96: *Silhouette International Schmied GmbH & Co KG v Hartlauer Handelsgesellschaft mbH* [1998] All ER (EC) 769, [1998] 2 CMLR 953.
20   Ibid, at para 25.

included as optional provisions in this article. Any other additions would destroy the aim of the Directive. Member states are therefore no longer free to operate a rule of international exhaustion, because such a rule was not included in the Directive as an option. The court effectively declared international exhaustion dead under the existing legislation.

This decision is highly political and regrettable. There is nothing in the essential function of a trade mark that can justify the fact that exhaustion needs to stop at the borders of the European Economic Area. On the contrary, the logic of the system is that the sytem of exhaustion should operate on all occasions where the original product is concerned and where that product has been marketed by or with the consent of the trade mark owner, irrespective of the place of first marketing. Exhaustion should only be put aside in exceptional cases, for example where the product has been tampered with or where the quality of the parallel imported product is inferior to the product marketed under the same name by the original producer in the area into which parallel importation takes place. In those examples the operation of the exhaustion rule would impinge on the goodwill of the producer and the interests of the consumers would be harmed. The essential function of the trade mark would be affected in these exceptional cases.

It is submitted that the Directive does not rule out this radically different conclusion either. The full harmonisation in Article 7 could be restricted to the operation of a European Economic Area wide exhaustion rule. All points that have not been decided by what is after all called a 'first' harmonisation Directive should be left to the discretion of the member states. Any member state would then be free to introduce an international exhaustion rule. And arguably any use of a trade mark to block parallel importation under the laws of a member state that had opted against international exhaustion would amount to an abusive use of the rights granted by a trade mark, because it would obstruct the operation of the common market. Alternatively, the free circulation of the parallel imported goods that were first marketed outside the European Economic Area could be restricted to the member state under whose international exhaustion rule their importation took place, because they were not put on the market in the European Economic Area by or with the consent of the trade mark owner. In either case, this solution would have fitted in much better with the current climate of worldwide free trade and the expectation for the latter that was created by the WTO agreement signed in Marrakesh.

The real context

Although the impression might be created that the interference of the Court and of European law in relation to trade marks is enormous, this is not correct and the whole issue must be seen in its real context. Generally, the grant of trade marks and the right to take action against infringement are national (harmonised) competences. The Court will only interfere when these provisions are applied in a discriminatory manner.[1] This was emphasised in the recent *Audi* case[2] where the Court verified whether the German requirements for trade mark protection were equally applied to trade marks of national and foreign origin, while leaving it to the German courts to decide whether under German trade mark law the use of the name Quadra by Renault created confusion with Audi's Quattro trade mark.[3] The court merely focuses on the abusive exercise of trade mark rights.

The doctrine of common origin

The Court of Justice set out the doctrine of common origin in the *Hag I* case.[4] This was a rather peculiar case. A German company, Hag AG, owned the trade mark Hag in Germany, Belgium and Luxembourg, but after the war its Belgian and Luxembourg property was sequestrated and the trade mark was assigned to the Van Zuylen Frères company. Both companies produced coffee under the Hag trade mark and a problem arose when Van Zuylen tried to rely on its Belgian trade mark to prevent Hag AG from importing coffee into Belgium. The argument was that Van Zuylen had not consented to the use of its trade mark and had thus not exhausted its rights and could stop Hag AG from using the Hag trade mark in Belgium. This would have been the logical conclusion under the free movement rules as we discussed them above, but the court arrived at a different conclusion by focusing on the common origin of the trade mark in the period before the war. The court held that

> 'one cannot allow the holder of a trade mark to rely upon the exclusiveness of a trade mark right – which may have the consequence of a territorial limitation of national markets – with a view to prohibiting the marketing in a member state of goods legally produced in another member state under an identical mark having the same origin'.[5]

---

1   See Würtenberger 'Determination of Risk of Confusion in Trade Mark Infringement Proceedings in the European Union: The Quattro Decision' [1994] 7 EIPR 302 at 304.

2   Case C-317/91: *AG Deutsche Renault v Audi AG* [1993] ECR I-6227, [1995] 1 CMLR 461.

3   See Würtenberger 'Determination of Risk of Confusion in Trade Mark Infringement Proceedings in the European Union: The Quattro Decision' [1994] 7 EIPR 302 and see also Reich 'The "November Revolution" of the European Court of Justice: *Keck, Meng* and *Audi* revisited' (1994) 31 CMLR 459 at 463.

4   Case 192/73: *Van Zuylen Frères v Hag AG* [1974] ECR 731, [1974] 2 CMLR 127.

5   Ibid at 744 and 143-144 (different translations to the same effect).

■

If the trade marks have a common origin one cannot rely on the trade mark to prevent the other party from using it in the member state in which one owns the trade mark. Van Zuylen could not exercise any right under its Hag trade mark to prevent the use of it in Belgium by Hag AG. The Court feared the partitioning of the single market. This approach did not make sense however as it endangered the essential functions of the trade mark by putting both the goodwill of the trade mark owner and the interests of the consumers at risk because confusion would inevitably arise when two coffee producers started marketing their coffee Hag in the same market. The court never used the doctrine in any other decisions until the *Hag II* case made its way to it. More than 15 years after the *Hag I* case had been decided Van Zuylen had been acquired by Jacobs–Suchard and they intended to market the Belgian Hag coffee in Germany. Under the doctrine of common origin Hag AG could not object to this as the trade marks had a common origin. The Court used the *Hag II* case[6] to admit it had made a mistake in *Hag I* and repealed the doctrine of common origin. Hag AG was consequently allowed to rely on its German trade mark that had not been exhausted to stop the importation into Germany of the Belgian coffee Hag. The court expressed it as follows:

> 'Articles 30 and 36 of the EEC Treaty do not preclude national legislation from allowing an undertaking which is the holder of a trade mark in a member state from opposing the importation from another member state of similar products lawfully bearing an identical trade mark in the latter state or liable to confusion with the protected mark even though the mark under which the contested products are imported originally belonged to a subsidiary of the undertaking which opposes the importation and was acquired by a third undertaking as a result of the expropriation of that subsidiary'.[7]

This created some doubt as to whether the doctrine of common origin had really been repealed or whether it might still apply in a case where there was a common origin of the trade mark followed by a voluntary assignment rather than by a forced expropriation. This issue was solved in the *Ideal Standard* case[8] in which the court applied its dictum in *Hag II* to a case involving the voluntary assignment of a trade mark. The doctrine of common origin is now legal history as the dictum in *Hag I* has now been repealed fully by the combined effect of the *Hag II* and the *Ideal Standard* decisions.

6   Case C-10/89 *CNL-SUCAL NV SA v Hag GF AG* [1990] ECR I-3711, [1990] 3 CMLR 571.

7   Ibid at paras 22 and 609 (different translations to same effect).

8   Case C-9/93 *IHT International Heiztechnik GmbH v Ideal Standard GmbH* [1995] FSR 59.

TRADE MARKS AND COMPETITION LAW

Article 85

Trade mark licence agreements can restrict competition and are in that respect not different from patent licence agreements. The Commission will use its powers to enforce Article 85 if an agreement has as its effect or as its object to restrict competition and compartmentalise the single market. The Commission's prime target is the so-called absolute territorial protection. It is based on the grant of a single exclusive trade mark licence per member state coupled with an obligation for each exclusive licensee (and for the licensor) not to pursue any active or passive sales policy outside its licensed territory. Its aim is to produce full exclusivity resulting in the product being available from a single source in each part of the single market which is covered by an exclusive licence and it fully excludes parallel imports. The Commission is not prepared to grant an exemption for this type of trade mark licence and on two occasions an appeal to the court on this point failed. This was the case in *Consten and Grundig v Commission*[9] and in *Tepea BV v Commission*.[10] The Commission is however prepared to grant an exemption if at least parallel imports remain possible even if the licence is exclusive and licensees are prohibited to pursue an active sales policy outside their territory.[11] An exemption is also possible if the agreement has a positive effect on intra-brand competition and widens the consumer's choice.[12]

Article 86

Certain ways of using a trade mark can amount to an abuse of a dominant position, but in practice few if any problems have arisen in this area up to now.[13]

---

9   Joined cases 56 and 58/64: *Consten and Grundig v Commission* [1966] ECR 299, [1966] CMLR 418.
10 Case 28/77: *Tepea BV v Commission* [1978] ECR 1391, [1978] 3 CMLR 392.
11 *Re Davide Campari-Milano SpA Agreement* [1978] 2 CMLR 397, OJ L70/69.
12 *Moosehead/Whitbread* [1991] 4 CMLR 391, (1990) OJ L100/32, this was a combined trade mark/know-how case in which the trade mark aspect was clearly dominant.
13 See *Chiquita/Fyffes plc* Commission Press Release dated 4 June 1992. The Commission invoked both Arts 85 and 86 although it seems this was more an Art 85 case dealing with an agreement between the parties whereby one of them would restrict the use of its trade mark in continental Europe.

Chapter 24

Tortious protection of intellectual property rights

Now we move away from the creation of formal rights in intellectual property to consider the various ways in which the common law, in the form of the law of tort, creates rights of action, as opposed to proprietary rights, which have the effect of protecting activity in the area of intellectual property. Passing-off and malicious falsehood will be the principal torts considered, though attention will also be paid to the ways in which defamation can assist. It must be emphasised that these rights are supplementary, and complementary, to the statutory formal rights. In particular, trade mark law and passing-off closely overlap, though section 2(2) of the Trade Marks Act 1994 preserves passing-off as a separate cause of action. That said, the extensions to the range of protection afforded by the trade mark regime by the 1994 Act inevitably diminish the role of these tortious rights, especially in the absence of proprietary rights arising from them.

PASSING-OFF

As will be clear to any student of patent law, some areas of the law of intellectual property appear on the surface to be deceptive in their simplicity. The tort of passing-off, however, stands at the opposite end of the spectrum. Much heat and noise has been generated in the quest for definitions of the tort. However, it is useful to assert at the outset that the essence of the tort is the protection of both consumers and other traders from the effect of confusion on their goodwill in trade, that confusion being generated by the activity of a trader in causing his goods or services and/or their presentation to become confused with those of the plaintiff, and that protection being afforded by the grant of a right of action to the trader whose economic interests and trading goodwill are harmed by the confusion.

Historical development

The 'informal' protection of rights by the tort of passing-off closely parallels the formal rights created by trade mark law. However, it is significant that the tortious right came into existence long before the establishment of a trade mark system. It appears that the law first began to address the problem of trade confusion in the late sixteenth century. Reference is made in *Southern v How*[1] to a case in the 1580s where an action on the case was successfully maintained by a cloth manufacturer whose distinguishing mark was used by a rival trader on his greatly inferior cloth. The use of the term 'passing-off' can be traced back to *Perry v Truefitt*,[2] an unedifying dispute between two hair oil manufacturers both selling their brands of 'Medicated Mexican Balm', where the plaintiff was refused an injunction but not denied a legal right to protect his original use of the trade name in question.

A key point in the development of the tort appeared early in the twentieth century. *Spalding & Brothers v A W Gamage*[3] was a consideration by the House of Lords of a dispute between rival football sellers, the plaintiff manufacturer objecting to the sale of their balls by the defendants at a greatly reduced price in adverts which failed to disclose that the balls under offer were of an older and inferior design by comparison with the plaintiffs' current model. Lord Parker emphasised, in finding for the plaintiffs, that the essence of a passing-off action was the protection of rights in the business and its goodwill that may be harmed by the defendants' conduct. It was equally clear, however, that this right in goodwill was not a property right as such, but rather a right to seek a remedy during such period of time as the goodwill continues to exist. From this, the tort of passing-off comes to exist in its modern form.

Passing-off defined

Attempts to define the tort have been, at times, confusing, particularly after the decision of the House of Lords in *Erven Warnink V v J Townend & Sons (Hull) Ltd*[4] offered two separate definitions. However, the case is worth a moment's pause: the plaintiffs produced Advocaat, a blend of spirit and eggs, while the defendants entered the market with 'Keeling's Old English Advocaat', a concoction of Cyprus sherry and egg powder. This attracted a lower rate of duty, being wine-based and not spirit-based. It was found that this was a case of passing-off because, in so far as common ground could

1   (1618) Poph 143 at 144, 79 ER 1243.
2   (1842) 6 Beav 66; 49 ER 749.
3   (1915) 32 RPC 273.
4   [1979] AC 731, [1979] 2 All ER 927.

be found between the leading judgments, damage could be caused to the plaintiff's goodwill by the confusion engendered by the activities of the defendants. This analysis explains, if not defines, the essence of this action.

Various attempts were made to apply this case[5] but a definitive answer has now been provided by the famous *Jif Lemon* case, *Reckitt & Colman Products Ltd v Borden Inc,*[6] aspects of which will be considered later in this chapter.

Lord Oliver offered a clear and concise definition of the three elements which, in his view, were the essential ingredients of the tort.

> 'First, he must establish a goodwill or reputation attached to the goods or services which he supplies in the mind of the purchasing public by association with the identifying "get-up" (whether it consists simply of a brand name or a trade description, or the individual features of labelling or packaging) under which his particular goods are offered to the public, such that the get-up is recognised by the public as distinctive specifically of the plaintiff's goods or services. Second, he must demonstrate a misrepresentation (whether or not intentional) leading or likely to lead the public to believe that goods or services offered by him are the goods or services of the plaintiff. Whether the public is aware of the plaintiff's identity as the manufacturer or supplier of the goods and services is immaterial, as long as they are identified with a particular source which is in fact the plaintiff. For example if the public is accustomed to rely upon a particular brand name in purchasing goods of a particular description, it matters not at all that there is little or no public awareness of the identity of the proprietor of the brand name. Third, he must demonstrate that he suffers or, in a *quia timet* action, that he is likely to suffer damage by reason of the erroneous belief engendered by the defendant's misrepresentation that the source of the defendant's goods or services is the same as the source of those offered by the plaintiff.'[7]

This is the starting point of the law as it stands now. We will now analyse it in further detail. Obviously, in so doing, reference will often be made to the case law developed in the area over the last century, not least because they show the flexibility of the passing-off action.[8]

---

5   See eg *Anheuser-Busch Inc v Budejovicky Budvar Narodni Podnick* [1984] FSR 413 (and on this Budweiser litigation also *Re Bud Trade Mark* [1988] RPC 535); *Consorzio del Prosciutto di Parma v Marks & Spencer plc* [1991] RPC 351, especially at 386.

6   [1990] 1 All ER 873, [1990] 1 WLR 491.

7   Ibid at 880 and 499.

8   Historically the five-stage test that was put forward by Lord Diplock in the Advocaat case (*Erven Warnink V v J Townend & Sons (Hull) Ltd* [1979] AC 731, [1979] 2 All ER 927) has also been important. The test involved 1) a misrepresentation 2) made by a trader in the course of trade 3) to prospective customers of his or ultimate consumers of goods or services supplied by him 4) which is calculated to injure the goodwill of another trader and 5) which causes actual damage to a business or goodwill of the trader by whom the

Goodwill

The leading case of *Spalding & Brothers v A W Gamage*[9] identifies, as has been seen, the element of goodwill as being at the heart of an action in the tort of passing-off. On its facts, it was clear that the footballs made by the plaintiffs under the brand-name 'Orb' had been on the market from 1910 and that goodwill in the name was well-established by August 1912, when the defendant began to market 'Orb' balls which were in fact discarded stock rejected by the plaintiffs, and far below the standard (and price) of the improved balls that were now being produced by the plaintiffs still under the 'Orb' name. This is a clear and straightforward case of passing-off but the question of goodwill is not always so easy to answer and will always ultimately hinge on factual considerations.

Duration of goodwill

As a business is started, as a question of fact it is clear that it may take time to establish its goodwill. The courts appear reasonably generous in providing support for relatively new traders against their predatory rivals. This is shown by two contrasting cases in 1967. Firstly, in *Stannard v Reay*[10] both parties independently decided to establish a mobile fish and chip shop business in the Isle of Wight. Both hit upon the name 'Mr Chippy' as being appropriate for the venture, but the plaintiffs had a headstart of about five weeks. Once the rival operation began, the plaintiffs sought an injunction and this was granted on an interlocutory basis by Buckley J, in the light of the fact that the evidence showed that the plaintiffs had built up a substantial trade very quickly and could thus be said to have developed goodwill in the use of the name.

By contrast, in *Compatibility Research Ltd v Computer Psyche Co Ltd*[11] two companies independently set up the then new business of running a computer dating agency. The plaintiffs began one month earlier than the defendants and with both companies using the biological male and female symbols in their publicity, the plaintiffs sought to establish that their one month headstart had been sufficient to confer upon them goodwill in that pair of symbols. Their claim was rejected by Stamp J. He took the view that

> 'where a trader seeks to say that the name descriptive of his trade has become distinctive of his trade and no other, he assumes a heavy burden'.[12]

---

action is brought. It is submitted that this test is not substantially different from the three-stage *Jif Lemon* test and that the latter summarises it in a more convenient way.

9   (1915) 32 RPC 273.
10   [1967] RPC 589.
11   [1967] RPC 201.
12   Ibid at 207.

It is clear, however, in deciding against the plaintiffs that much emphasis was placed on their use of a commonplace and partly descriptive symbol that would make it much harder to develop goodwill than if they had thought up their own original logo which was then copied by a subsequent rival. It was not so much the short time that they had traded but the lack of a distinctive image that flawed their claim.

That these cases hinge on factual issues is well shown by the contrast between the *Compatibility* case and that of *BBC v Talbot Motor Co Ltd*.[13] The heavy launch publicity in the media arranged by Compatibility Research did not avail them in their goodwill argument yet, in the BBC case, goodwill was found to exist for the 'Carfax' service of radio traffic information broadcasts from television and specialist press coverage even though the service had not (and still has not!) come into being. The BBC were thus held entitled to prevent the defendants from using the same name for their spare car part sales operation.

Clearly where neither the project or its preliminaries are under way there is no chance that a passing-off action can succeed. *Marcus Publishing plc v Hutton-Wild Communications Ltd*[14] where the two parties were rushing to be first into the market with identically-named journals but neither had yet reached the news-stands or, indeed, just gone beyond the stage of producing a pilot edition for advertisers. The Court of Appeal found that neither party had done enough to establish any goodwill, even for the purposes of an interlocutory injunction, although both parties had been planning their projects for the best part of a year.

Similar problems arise at the end of a business' life in assessing the time at which goodwill finally dissipates. *Ad-lib Club Ltd v Glanville*[15] is instructive. The Ad-Lib Club was a trendy London nightspot that operated from 1964 to early 1966 when it was closed due to complaints about noise and no substitute premises could be found. Late in 1970 the defendant proposed to open his own Ad-Lib Club and, in spite of the five-year gap, the plaintiffs were held entitled to object to this. The issue was not the lapse of time, but rather whether the plaintiff's goodwill had lapsed. The fact that the press confused the two operations in stories concerning the 're-opening' of the famous club and the strong suspicion that the defendant's choice of name was quite deliberate were helpful factors in the plaintiffs' case, but ultimately it was the retention of goodwill in their name and their right to exploit that while it still lasted that was crucial to the success of the claim, even though they had no precise plans for re-opening. Of course the presence of such plans would always be helpful to a plaintiff, as evidenced

13 [1981] FSR 228.
14 [1990] RPC 576.
15 [1972] RPC 673.

by *Levey v Henderson-Kenton (Holdings) Ltd*[16] where trade by the plaintiff under the name 'Kentons' was held to retain goodwill during a temporary closure caused by two fires and a compulsory purchase.

Geographical extent of goodwill

The next section covers the question of the geographical area over which goodwill may be regarded as extending. The *Levey* case just mentioned provides a simple example in that the plaintiff's shop was well-known in Newcastle only while the defendants were successfully trading under the same name but primarily in the Midlands with no store within 120 miles of Newcastle until the proposed opening of a store in Newcastle which triggered off the plaintiff's action. The interlocutory injunction only extended to Newcastle and, if the plaintiff had sought to trade in the defendants' heartland in the Midlands the position would inevitably be completely the opposite.

However this case may be the exception rather than the rule where the geographical separation was so clear-cut. A more complex, and perhaps more typical, set of facts arose in *Chelsea Man Menswear Ltd v Chelsea Girl Ltd*.[17] The plaintiffs sold clothes under the 'Chelsea Man' label in their shops in Leicester, Coventry and London; the defendants proposed to extend their business from women's clothing to that for men also and naturally wanted to use 'Chelsea Man' themselves in this venture. The defendants argued that any injunction against them should be confined to the areas of the plaintiffs' pre-existing business, but this was rejected by the Court of Appeal who allowed an injunction covering all of England and Wales, regard being paid to the fact that both people and goods move around the country and also to the desire of the plaintiffs themselves to extend their business in the future (though no specific plans appear to have been made). Nourse LJ noted[18] that the *Levey* case was the only reported case to have imposed a geographical limit, and that only at a pre-trial stage. The desire of businesses to expand legitimately in the future may well make the *Chelsea Man* case the model for the future.

Goodwill can, it seems, transcend international boundaries too. Many companies, such as for example the international oil companies, trade in dozens of countries and clearly have international goodwill. This area of the law needs to be considered in two different ways. Firstly the approach taken by the case law in recent years will be considered. Then it will be necessary to review the impact of the new protection of internationally well-

---

16   [1974] RPC 617.
17   [1987] RPC 189.
18   Ibid at 208.

known marks introduced into UK law for the first time by the Trade Marks Act 1994.

The problem that has arisen in litigation is whether in the absence of trade, goodwill can nevertheless be established within the jurisdiction. The case law suggests that this is possible at least in some cases. The principal support for such a proposition comes from *Maxim's Ltd v Dye*[19] where the owners of one of Paris' grandest and most prestigious restaurants succeeded in preventing the use of the name 'Maxim's' for a bistro in Norwich. Graham J refused to follow an earlier High Court decision[20] where the owners of Paris' 'Crazy Horse Saloon' nightclub failed to stop the use of the same name on London premises because, he insisted, goodwill could transcend frontiers, and indeed was more likely so to do in an era of international integration, and in particular within the Common Market.[1] Here there was ample evidence that the Paris restaurant was known in the UK, was patronised by its citizens and (though no weight seems to have been attached to this factor) was owned by a British registered company. The judge also considered that to fail to protect the goodwill enjoyed by a French company in the UK was discriminatory under the Treaty of Rome as being a disguised restriction on trade, a distortion of level competition and a restriction on the free supply of services within the European Union,[2] and it seems that the goodwill of a company trading elsewhere within the EU will be treated henceforth on equal terms with that of a domestic business with the factors noted above being relevant to the scope of the injunction awarded geographically.

However it is equally clear that *Maxim's* is not a wide open door for any foreign business to mount a passing-off action in the UK. *Athletes Foot Marketing Associates Inc v Cobra Sports Ltd*[3] shows this well. The plaintiffs are a leading American business franchising a chain of sports shoe shops under the brand name 'The Athlete's Foot' – presumably the foot infection of that name bears a different appellation across the Atlantic. Beyond abortive discussions, no steps had been taken to develop the chain in England, so the defendants filled the gap by christening their London store 'Athlete's Foot Bargain Basement', a name apparently coined while watching a rugby match from the bar at Twickenham Rugby Stadium. After a full survey of the authorities, Walton J concluded that passing-off does not confine its protection to those currently carrying on a business within the jurisdiction, so long as they have a reputation from which goodwill can arise. On these facts, however, the plaintiffs did not even have a reputation,

---

19   [1977] FSR 364.
20   *Alain Bernardin et Cie v Pavilion Properties Ltd* [1967] RPC 581.
1   [1977] FSR 364 at 368.
2   EU Treaty, Articles 36, 3 (f) and 59 respectively.
3   [1980] RPC 343.

having provided no evidence of any transactions with British citizens. It was impossible to say that there was the necessary goodwill within the jurisdiction. This is a significant point of distinction with the *Maxim's* case.

A further twist is provided by *My Kinda Bones Ltd v Dr Pepper's Stove Co Ltd*.[4] This on the face of it looks like the *Athlete's Foot* case with an American firm intending to open, for the first time, one of their now successful 'Chicago Rib Shack' restaurants in London, only to find to their irritation that the defendants were also proposing to operate a 'Rib Shack'. The plaintiffs sued and the defendants sought to strike out the claim as giving no grounds for action, in the light of the *Athlete's Foot* case. Slade J refused to strike out the claim, which of course is not to say that it would succeed at trial. He felt that the lack of customers in the UK for the plaintiffs' business could not be the sole test since there was evidence that the plaintiffs had begun to promote their new venture not least in their pre-existing chain of pizzerias. In the light of this, there was at least a triable issue under the principle established in *BBC v Talbot*[5] that they had carried out enough preparation and interested enough people in their forthcoming product that goodwill had been created; though it is hard to disagree with Slade J[6] that the plaintiffs' prospects of success were slender.

In summary, it seems clear that the starting point of the court in considering passing-off will be to give protection across the whole of the relevant jurisdiction to anyone with a reputation within that jurisdiction. Such a reputation is most easily established by evidence of customers within that jurisdiction, so going a long way to show goodwill there. But equally clearly other acts such as self-promotion or work done preparatory to the product launch may also be helpful to showing goodwill within the jurisdiction.

The position at common law has, however, now been altered by section 56 of the Trade Marks Act 1994. This section brings into our law for the first time the protection given by Article 6bis of the Paris Convention for the Protection of Intellectual Property 1883. This creates an obligation on signatory states to protect well-known marks belonging to any national of any Convention state. This allows such a person to act within this jurisdiction by obtaining an injunction against the use in the UK of a trade mark (or an essential part thereof):

'identical or similar to his mark, in relation to identical or similar goods or services, where the use is likely to cause confusion'.[7]

---

4   [1984] FSR 289.
5   [1981] FSR 228; above at p 418.
6   [1984] FSR 289 at 303.
7   TMA 1994, s 56(2).

This right arises irrespective of whether the claimant has any business or even any goodwill in the UK, though the mark must be 'well-known'.

The implications of this are far from clear. The key case to reconsider is *Athlete's Foot*. The claim there failed through lack of goodwill on the part of the plaintiff. This in itself would no longer bar them from opposing the use by their UK counterpart of the same name as a trade mark. However it seems that it would still be necessary to establish that theirs was a 'well-known' mark and it is not clear whether it is necessary to show that the mark is well-known in the applicant's country or here in the UK. Clearly there is no problem in the former event but if the latter is the case[8] it will be an unusual mark indeed that has no goodwill but is nonetheless well-known. It seems that section 56 is unlikely to make any great difference.

Goodwill in trading

In this section we consider the activities in respect of which goodwill may arise or be protected. Just as in trade mark law protection is not given universally, but rather only for the class or classes of activity in which trade is carried out, so a parallel restriction applies in passing-off. But first a further parallel needs exploring. Where in trade mark law there must be trade before any protection is conferred, so also in a passing-off action there must be a recognisable trading activity.[9]

So professional bodies[10] and political parties are unlikely to succeed in a passing-off claim.

From here it is appropriate to return to the question of what activities by a company or individual admittedly in trade are protected by the passing-off action. To take an example, Butterworths through their name and logo have a reputation for and consequent goodwill in the production of leading legal tomes, and could accordingly use the tort of passing-off to prevent a newcomer to the field from using the name and logo or anything close thereto. But if a new dairy products business decides to use the Butterworth name, it is far from clear that any harm will be done, since confusion is unlikely to arise, the publishers not being engaged in and therefore enjoying no goodwill in the dairy business. The way in which this has traditionally been considered is in the form of the need for there to be a representation by the defendant to the customers of the plaintiff. If the customers are different, or are in entirely distinct areas of activity, then no goodwill is

---

8   Annand & Norman *Blackstone's Guide to the Trade Marks Act 1994* (Blackstone Press, 1994) p 31. See p 395 above.
9   *Erven Warnink V v J Townend & Sons (Hull) Ltd* [1979] AC 731, [1979] 2 All ER 927, per Lord Diplock, at 742 and 932.
10   *British Association of Aesthetic Plastic Surgeons v Cambright* [1987] RPC 549. Cf *The Society of Incorporated Accountants v Vincent* (1954) 71 RPC 325.

harmed and no action in passing-off will lie. It is a common field of activity that traditionally is necessary.

An easy example of this is shown by *Granada Group Ltd v Ford Motor Co Ltd*.[11] The plaintiffs had a solid reputation in the television and cinema industry and became concerned when they found out that the defendants were intending to christen their new luxury car the Ford Granada. The plaintiffs argued that the use of this well-known name would cause boundless confusion but the defendants replied that the name had been chosen with regard to its Europe-wide effectiveness and that their business was in so different a field of activity that no impact on Granada's goodwill would be discernible. Graham J found for the defendants refusing even an interlocutory injunction. No confusion would arise in the public mind between the very different companies and their very different products. Some of their customers may be the same, but there was no common field of activity to cause confusion even to those common customers. Likewise, in *Wombles Ltd v Wombles Skips Ltd*[12] the plaintiffs had the rights in the Wombles, fictitious furry creatures who, *inter alia*, were devoted to cleansing Wimbledon Common of litter, and their popularity meant that the plaintiffs enjoyed the fruits of a successful merchandising programme. The defendants were a new company providing domestic rubbish skips and chose their name precisely because of both its popularity and its connotations of cleanliness. Walton J was clear that no injunction should be awarded since there was no common field of activity, and thus no common customers to be confused, as between toys and other merchandising terms on the one hand and rubbish removal on the other.

In considering whether there is a common field of activity and therefore a representation by the defendant to the customers of the plaintiff, some tenuous connections are sometimes made to assist the plaintiff's cause of action. In *BBC v Talbot Motor Co Ltd*,[13] the differences between the plaintiffs' proposed Carfax radio traffic information services and the defendants' Carfax car parts appear to be obvious yet Megarry V-C found the dangers of confusion to be real since both operations were concerned with motor vehicles and confusion could particularly attend car radio purchases (although Talbot had offered in court to exclude car radios from their parts service). In *Annabel's (Berkeley Square) Ltd v Schock*,[14] the plaintiffs were (and are) a top London nightspot frequented by the social elite. The defendant operated a business under the name 'Annabel's Escort Agency' providing young ladies to escort clients to dinner, dances, etc. The Court of Appeal, fortified by evidence of men ringing the nightclub in search

11   [1973] RPC 49.
12   [1977] RPC 99.
13   [1981] FSR 228.
14   [1972] RPC 838.

of escorts and women arriving there seeking an escort job, found that there was a common field of activity in the field of night entertainment, that confusion could arise and had arisen, and that the public image of escort agencies was such that harm may be caused to the nightclub, and an injunction was obtained by them against the defendants.[15]

The courts have seemed more willing to uphold this type of case when the whiff of fraud is in the air. *Eastman Photographic Materials Co Ltd v John Griffiths Cycle Co Ltd*[16] is such a case. Eastman made Kodak cameras while the defendants sought to sell a new brand of bicycle, the Kodak cycle. In the light of the fact that the plaintiffs sold special 'Cycle Kodaks', cameras specially adapted for use on bicycles, and the deliberate conduct of the defendants, an injunction was awarded. Also, in *Harrods Ltd v R Harrod Ltd*,[17] the plaintiff department store succeeded in preventing the defendants from using their name for a money lending business. The plaintiffs did have a small banking section but did not lend money. However the Court of Appeal awarded an injunction, in part because of the closeness of the two businesses, in part because of evidence of customer confusion, and in part because of the fact that there was no legitimate reason for the defendants to use that name, no one called Harrod being in any way involved with the business.

Another Harrods case was concerned with the use of the name 'Harrodian School' for a school that was unrelated to Harrods, but that was established in the buildings of the former 'Harrodian Club', membership of which had at one stage been restricted to employees of Harrods. Harrods alleged passing-off, but, unlike the first case, this action failed. In relation to the common field of activity it was held by the court of Appeal that there was no requirement that the plaintiff should be carrying on a business which competed with that of the plaintiff or which would compete with any natural extension of the plaintiff's business. It was added, however, that the absence of a common field of activity was an important and highly relevant consideration in deciding whether there was a likelihood of confusion. Passing-off will only protect goodwill against damage resulting from misrepresentations if there is a likelihood of confusion that makes damage to goodwill plausible. In this case there was no common field of activity between the defendant who was running a school and the defendant who was running a department store. The only question was whether there was a real risk that members of the public would be deceived into thinking that a school called 'Harrodian School' was owned or managed by Harrods or under Harrods' supervision or control. Did the public believe that the goods or services offered by the defendant were the goods or services of the

15   For a similar decision, on less interesting facts, see *Walter v Ashton* [1902] 2 Ch 282.
16   (1898) 15 RPC 105.
17   (1923) 41 RPC 74.

plaintiff? Only if this was established could the plaintiff's reputation for excellence potentially suffer damage. This was a matter of fact and in this case no likelihood of confusion had been established.[18]

In summary, reasonably clear guidelines have been established to set the boundaries of goodwill created by trade. First there must be trade; then there must be trade by both parties to the same customers and in the same or at least broadly similar fields of activity, with the level of broad similarity being required that is the area of greatest uncertainty or, if preferred, discretion. However one significant decision appears to erode the clarity of the picture as far as the need for a common field of activity is concerned. In *Lego Systems Aktieselskab v Lego M Lemelstrich Ltd*[19] the plaintiffs, well-known manufacturers of toy plastic bricks, took action against the sale by the defendants of Lego brand water sprinklers and other such items of gardening irrigation equipment. Falconer J allowed an injunction to be granted. He rejected the argument that the common field of activity was essential here by pointing to the great fame of the Lego name and the assumption that would be made by customers of Lego sprinklers that they were buying products made by the Danish toy brick firm. In other words, Lego's goodwill is so great that it extends beyond their sole trading field into related and, here, unrelated areas of activity. People would be misled into thinking that any defect in the sprinklers was the fault of the toy firm, and Lego would be prevented from using the goodwill in their name to diversify in the future into the garden sprinkler trade.

This is a bold decision. It surely stretches the notion of goodwill in trade close to its breaking point. It goes far beyond cases where there has been protection afforded by passing-off for an active intention on the part of the plaintiff to diversify into related areas,[20] let alone those cases where the courts have refused relief because the activities, though obviously related in a broad sense have not amounted to a common field of activity (eg ice lollies/ bubble gum).[1] However, it does not seem unacceptable.

The phrase 'common field of activity' has never been part of the mainstream of the vocabulary of passing-off[2] and the approach now seems entirely compatible in principle with the language and approach of the Trade Marks Act 1994, s 5(3).[3] Where the *Lego* decision still has a role, arguably, is where the threat of damage to the plaintiff's reputation is as vague (or illusory) as in the case itself, as opposed to the statute's requirement of

---

18 *Harrods Ltd v Harrodian School Ltd* [1996] RPC 697.
19 [1983] FSR 155.
20 Eg *LRC International Ltd v Lilla Edets Sales Co Ltd* [1973] RPC 560.
1   *Lyons Maid Ltd v Trebor Ltd* [1967] RPC 222.
2   *McCollough v Lewis A May Ltd* [1947] 2 All ER 845. See Phillips & Coleman 'Passing-Off and the "Common Field of Activity"' (1985) 101 LQR 242.
3   See above p 366.

■

detriment to the mark or its reputation, or, of course, if the plaintiff does not have trade mark protection.

Meanwhile, some of the earlier case law may need rethinking. Are not *Granada* and were not *Wombles* equally the possessors of the widest amount of goodwill? The first *Harrod's* decision would now seem unduly cautious and narrow. Clearly in the light of *Lego*, there is the potential for well-known brand names to establish broader goodwill than in the past if no longer confined to any type of common field of activity in bringing claims of passing-off. Any *Lego*-based approach must be subject to one restriction though. There must be a likelihood of confusion or deception and in this respect any indication of a common field of activity may still be a very relevant factor.[4]

Goodwill in real names

We have just seen in the *Harrod's* decision that the unnecessary use of the name by another business amounted to passing-off. What would have happened if the proprietor of the rival business was indeed a Mr Harrod? Clearly just as much confusion and thus harm to goodwill may arise but it may seem harsh to restrict the fictitious Mr Harrod from proudly using his own name for his business. However, the courts do seem prepared to so order. In *Baume and Co Ltd v A H Moore Ltd*[5] the plaintiffs sold watches under the trade mark 'Baume' and had done so for well over a century. The defendants began to import Swiss watches made by Baume and Mercier Ltd of Geneva, a fact marked both on the watches and their boxes. This was held to amount to passing-off, although the use of the name was genuine in every respect (there had previously been a family connection between the two firms). The use of a real name could be actionable if it is used in such a way as to cause confusion with another's business and

> 'the defence of innocent and honest user of the manufacturers' name on the watches which the defendants have sold will not avail them as a defence if the other ingredients of passing off are established.'[6]

Confusion was likely given the similarity of both the name and the type of product.

If this seems harsh, it is worth reflecting that the importers of Baume & Mercier watches had taken no steps deliberately to distinguish them from the watches already on the market. This explains the opposite conclusion

---

4   *Nice and Safe Attitude Ltd v Piers Flook (t/a 'Slaam! Clothing Company')* [1997] FSR 14; *Harrods Ltd v Harrodian School Ltd* [1996] RPC 697.
5   [1958] Ch 907. [1958] 2 All ER 113.
6   Ibid, per Romer L J at 917 and 117.

reached by Hoffmann J in *Anderson & Lembke Ltd v Anderson & Lembke Inc.*[7] A specialist advertising agency in Sweden set up and then sold off international subsidiaries, including the parties to this litigation, based respectively in London and Connecticut. However, the American firm gained contracts in Europe and decided to open an office in London. The plaintiffs' complaint was rejected; the defendants had taken steps to change the name under which they traded to 'A & L Europe' and then to 'Business Advertising Europe' and while there was reference in some documents to the connection with the American parent firm, this was regarded as inevitable and appropriate and did not amount to passing-off. It seems that honesty, though not a formal defence, is not unhelpful to a defendant's cause.

Another possible way of getting round *Baume* is to emphasise that the other ingredients of passing-off need to be satisfied and it is far from clear that the defendants in that case had made any misrepresentation; they were after all selling watches made by Baume & Mercier and it is customary for watches to bear the name of their manufacturer. It seems that the courts are more generous in allowing the honest use of a name for a business than for its products,[8] where greater care must be taken to distinguish one article from another.

In summary, if your name is McDonald and you want to open a burger bar, the tort of passing-off will be reluctant to prevent the use of your name for your business. However, if you invite McDonald to join your business just so as to be able to use his name, this is unlikely to be regarded as bona fide, after *Harrod's* and in any event it may be prudent to make your business as distinct as possible from that of your namesake, to avoid the problems of *Baume*. Likewise, use of the name or variants thereof on products rather than for the business at large is less likely to escape legal objection. In passing, use of the 'Mc' prefix seems to be regarded as a popular marketing weapon in the fast food trade. It would seem difficult, without more, for McDonalds to prevent this, unless other steps were taken to confuse customers.

An unusual case in this area is the recent case of *Alan Clark v Associated Newspapers*[9] where the distinguished, if controversial, politician succeeded in a complaint against the *Evening Standard* for a spoof column based on his diaries style of writing and using his name (though the columns were attributed to the journalist who wrote them). It was held that the use of Alan Clark's name, prominently, would be seen by the public as associating him with the articles and thus would amount to passing-off.

---

7   [1989] RPC 124.
8   *Marengo v Daily Sketch & Sunday Graphic Ltd* (1948) 65 RPC 242, especially per Lord Simonds at 251.
9   [1998] RPC 261. See also Ch 27.

■──■

Goodwill in real words

Similar risks of granting an over-generous monopoly arise in respect of the use of real words, especially those descriptive of a product. Clearly the first person to make ice cream should not have a monopoly on those words that are descriptive of his product, and this is reflected by the legal position. *County Sound plc v Ocean Sound plc*[10] is a good contemporary example. The parties are both local radio stations in Southern England broadcasting to adjacent but overlapping catchment areas. The plaintiffs decided to launch a new service, broadcasting old records on their medium wave/AM frequency; this they christened 'The Gold AM'. Six months later, the defendants began to broadcast a similar service and used the same name for it. The Court of Appeal refused to grant an injunction against the defendants on the grounds that, although the plaintiffs had had time to develop the necessary goodwill, no goodwill could develop around 'The Gold AM' since 'Gold' was in the view of Nourse LJ[11] a word 'descriptive of popular hits of the 1950s, 1960s and 1970s and AM was simply the description of the frequency on which the service could be found'. Descriptive words could only develop goodwill by the use of that name and no other for goods over a substantial period of time, the old case of *Reddaway v Banham*[12] being cited as authority for this, a case where more than a decade's usage of 'Camel Hair Belting' was held sufficient to generate the necessary goodwill; this is clearly the exception rather than the rule and here too the question must arise as to whether there is anything in the nature of a misrepresentation in a subsequent use by another of purely descriptive wording.

The name 'Farm Fluids', a description of an agrichemical product has likewise been held to be unable to be used by a rival producer because the name was known in the relevant market as synonymous with the plaintiff's business.[13]

Collective goodwill

In most of the cases so far examined the plaintiff trader has generated by his trading endeavours his own goodwill. However this is not a requirement of the tort of passing-off. It is equally possible for the necessary goodwill to be generated by a group of traders collectively, as the group of cases colloquially known as 'The Alcohol Cases' clearly shows.

---

10   [1991] FSR 367.
11   Ibid at 373.
12   [1896] AC 199. This approach is now reflected in the proviso to TMA 1994, s 3(1)(c).
13   *Antec International Ltd v South Western Chicks (Warren) Ltd* [1998] FSR 738.

The first of these cases is *Bollinger v Costa Brava Wine Co*[14] heard first on preliminary points of law and subsequently[15] as a full trial. The plaintiffs were a group of French producers of Champagne from that region of France and they were seeking to prevent the defendants from marketing their sparkling wine from Spain as 'Spanish Champagne'. Obviously no single producer has any sort of exclusive right to the word 'Champagne' but the argument was that, together, the French manufacturers of the drink had developed a collective goodwill and reputation in the name. This then novel argument was successful. Danckwerts J felt[16] that the nature and purpose of passing-off was to prevent unfair trading and to control unfair competition and the necessary goodwill could just as easily be developed by, as here, a group of persons producing particular goods in a particular locality although each of the plaintiffs is separately entitled to bring their own legal action in respect of harm to their own share of the goodwill.[17] The decision represented both a substantial advance for the tort of passing-off and a growing recognition of the potential the tort has as a tool for regulating unfair trading – this latter aspect will be considered later in this chapter.

The lead given in *Bollinger* was followed in *Vine Products Ltd v Mackenzie & Co Ltd*.[18] This time the drink in question was sherry, or to be precise British sherry, and the action was brought by a group of manufacturers seeking to establish their right to use the name 'sherry' against the objections of Spanish producers of the drink from the Jerez region from where traditional sherry comes. Cross J upheld the objections to a limited extent insofar as the word 'sherry' itself was not to be used on its own on any drink other than that from Jerez. However, the long usage of British sherry and other non-Spanish varieties such as sherry from South Africa and Cyprus was permitted to continue. So 'British sherry is good' would be a permitted form of advert but 'British sherry is good sherry' would not be.

Cross J appeared to regard[19] *Bollinger* as creating a new tort of unfair competition rather than as passing-off since the normal requirements of representation and confusion were absent – this appears to be an odd remark since the drinks described as champagne and sherry were not from the relevant geographical areas and this surely may amount to a misrepresentation and thus cause confusion. However, these remarks were expressly adopted by Foster J in the third case in this group, *John Walker & Sons Ltd v Henry Ost & Co Ltd*[20] where the plaintiffs were a group of

---

14   [1960] Ch 262, [1959] 3 All ER 800.
15   *Bollinger v Costa Brava Wine Co Ltd (No 2)* [1961] 1 All ER 561, [1961] 1WLR 277.
16   [1960] Ch 262 at 284, [1959] 3 All ER 800 at 811.
17   [1961] 1 All ER 561 at 563, [1961] 1 WLR 277 at 281.
18   [1969] RPC 1.
19   Ibid at 23 and 28.
20   [1970] 2 All ER 106, [1970] 1WLR 917.

Scotch whisky producers who were held able to prevent the name of Scotch
whisky from being besmirched by its use on a blend of whisky and cane
spirit that was available in Ecuador. However, the *Advocaat*[1] case restores
the cases to the fold of passing-off albeit 'in an extended form'[2] and also
bearing in mind that the larger a group claiming collective goodwill the
harder it will be to show the public recognition of distinctiveness which a
word such as 'Champagne' had attracted.[3] (The action was only brought
by one manufacturer so these comments are presumably obiter.)

The continuing relevance of this area of case law, and its continuing
existence within the tort of passing-off is confirmed by a more recent case,
still concerned with alcohol. Once again the highly litigious champagne
industry came to the courts, this time to restrain the use of 'their' word in
a non-alcoholic product made from elderflowers known as Elderflower
Champagne. In *Taittinger v Allbev Ltd*,[4] the Court of Appeal held that they
could so restrain the use of 'champagne'. After consideration of mainstream
passing-off case law, the view was taken that there was a clear threat to the
collective goodwill of the champagne industry if this cheap non-alcoholic
drink could continue to bear the hallowed name.

The plaintiffs also sought and gained an injunction on the alternative
ground that the defendants were in breach of EC Regulation 823/87.[5] These
regulations insist on correct wine labelling and there was a clear breach of
them, and an injunction was appropriate in view of the fact that the purpose
of the Regulation was to avoid the very confusion which the use by the
defendants of 'Champagne' had caused. Collective goodwill thus remains
a valid method of satisfying the first requirement of the tort of passing-off,
but *Vine Products* reminds us that it may only receive limited protection by
a restrictively drawn injunction, while the *Advocaat* case suggests that use
of collective goodwill may not be widely available except in the clearest of
cases.

The most recent example of this type of claim is the successful action
by Swiss chocolatiers to prevent the UK-based Cadbury's from using the
name and image of Swiss chocolate in promoting a doubtless fine product,
but which was made in Birmingham, through the use of the 'Chocosuisse'
name.[6] This case illustrates the difficulties that surround the use of
descriptive words as names in which collective goodwill is claimed to exist.
The case makes it clear that a passing-off action can only get off the ground
if these descriptive words, here the reference to Swiss chocolate, are taken

1   Above at p 416.
2   [1979] AC 731 at 739, [1979] 2 All ER 927 at 929 per Lord Diplock.
3   [1979] AC 731 at 744, [1979] 2 All ER 927 at 934 per Lord Diplock.
4   [1994] 4 All ER 75.
5   Incorporated into UK law by the Common Agricultural Policy (Wine) Regulations 1992,
    SI 1992/672).
6   *Chocosuisse Union des Fabricants Suisse de Chocolat v Cadbury Ltd* [1998] RPC 117.

by a significant part of the public to be used in relation to and indicating a particular group of products having a discrete reputation as a group. The requirement does not go as far as demanding that the goods that fall into the group and that are protected by the name must be distinguishable in fact from all competing goods. In the case at issue, the public clearly identified Swiss chocolate as a group of products with a separate reputation, despite the fact that it is not possible to point towards a particular recipe that is used for all Swiss chocolate and that is used nowhere else in the world.

The new collective trade mark, created by s49 of the Trade Marks Act 1994 will of course meet many of these problems, but only if the plaintiffs are part of a formal association of traders rather than simply being a group of rivals with, nonetheless, a common interest in seeing off outside competition.

Range of goodwill protected

In most of the cases considered so far the attack on the plaintiff's goodwill has been straightforwardly aimed at some feature of the heart of the plaintiff's business such as brand name, company name or, in the last section, distinctive product description. In this section the question arises as to how broadly the notion of goodwill can extend towards more peripheral parts of the plaintiff's trading activity. A notable extension of the range of goodwill protected by the tort of passing-off has been provided by the Privy Council in *Cadbury Schweppes Pty Ltd v Pub Squash Co Pty Ltd*.[7] This litigation arose when the plaintiffs and, subsequently, the defendants both entered the Australian drinks market with lemon flavoured soft drinks. There was no doubt that the defendants were seeking to exploit the large market which the plaintiffs' product, called Solo, had shown existed for this type of product, but the defendants chose a very different name, Pub Squash, for their product. The problem arose in the two firms' respective marketing campaigns. Both used a broadly similar strategy; both tried to associate their drink with two separate themes – heroic masculine endeavour and nostalgia for tasty drinks in the past – and both products were sold in a yellow can. The issue then was plain – would the tort of passing-off extend to more general imagery associated with the product?

The answer given by Lord Scarman was clearly that passing-off could so extend. The tort may have originated with the name and description of the product itself but it was not in any way constrained to remain there. Rather, it was now capable of conferring protection on goodwill created by many other types of descriptive material:

---

7   [1981] 1 All ER 213, [1981] 1 WLR 193.

'such as slogans or visual images, which radio, television or newspaper advertising campaigns can lead the market to associate with a plaintiff's product, provided that such material has become part of the goodwill of the product. And the test is whether the product has derived from the advertising a distinctive character which the market recognises'.[8]

So in allowing the protection of passing-off to be thus extended, Lord Scarman is being doubly cautious. First not all advertising and other such imagery will be protected – only that which is part of the company's goodwill. So a standard advert of a contented family group or a sunny tropical isle will never attract the necessary goodwill, but an innovative advert or campaign as here, associating unlikely concepts with the product – rugged masculine endeavour is not obviously linked to lemonade. They also appear to fulfil Lord Scarman's second constraint, namely that of distinctiveness. Only those brands are thus advertised and there is no inherent reason why they should be: creativity has been employed so as to establish distinctiveness.

After this a successful conclusion to the plaintiffs' claim may be anticipated. However they were unable to restrain Pub Squash's use of their marketing material. As a matter of policy, Lord Scarman expressed concern that to allow the claim would be to blur the line between fair and unfair methods of competition:

'a defendant, however, does no wrong by entering a market created by another and there competing with its creator'.[9]

Passing-off was not to be confused with a wider tort of unfair competition, and here the defendants, though consciously trying to grab part of the plaintiffs' market share, were not trying to make the public think their product was that of the plaintiffs: there was thus no deception, no misrepresentation and no infringement of the rights of the plaintiffs.

In spite of its outcome, *Cadbury Schweppes* is clearly a decision of potentially great significance. Its broadening out of the range of goodwill protected is a major advance on the previous position. However its practical effect may well be limited. After the initial expansion, Lord Scarman is cautious to dampen down expectations by emphasising that only that material which is both distinctive and becomes part of goodwill is protected and the need for fair competition to be preserved clearly also reduces the chance of claiming successfully. Indeed arguments based on this expansion of goodwill have been notable only by their absence in ensuing years. A likely explanation of this is that goodwill in such cases is generated so far away

8   Ibid at 218 and 200.
9   Ibid.

from the product itself that no misrepresentation is likely.[10] The basic differences, for example in the product name, far outweigh the broad similarity found in the marketing campaign.

Notwithstanding this, it is still appropriate to conclude the entire section on goodwill with such a case for it typifies in its own way the continuing development and expansion of the notion of goodwill which has been a common feature of many of the areas discussed. Granted that findings of fact can diminish their overall impact, it is significant that in few areas is the concept of goodwill being contracted, and in many it has expanded or is expanding or, at the least, has the potential to expand.

Misrepresentation

The next vital element in any passing-off action is that the defendant must represent his goods or services to be those of the plaintiff. The representation must create a false belief of connection between the two products in the mind of the consumer and accordingly it is appropriate to refer to it as a misrepresentation. To sell orange-flavoured cakes as 'Jaffa Cakes' does not amount to passing-off since that is no more than a description of the product and does not create any form of confusion in the mind of the consumer. However to market the Jaffa Cakes in packs of similar design to that of the market leader may be actionable in passing-off, since by using that design customers may be likely to confuse the two products and it may be a misrepresentation so to do.[11] In recent years supermarket look-alike products have tried to resemble the original, but supermarkets have at least claimed[12] that they made every effort to avoid giving rise to confusion by making a misrepresentation. To put it another way, a true representation of a product, quite apart from being unlikely to attract goodwill, will not cause any confusion and will not therefore be actionable. The hallmark of the misrepresentation is that confusion is the result of it. Of course not all confusion in trading is necessarily the result of a misrepresentation; confusion is inevitable whenever a monopoly is first broken. There must be a representation that the newcomer's goods are, or are connected with, those of the original seller.[13] A simple belief, for example, that the plaintiff had sponsored or given financial support to the defendant would not

---

10 Some authors have argued that a strict approach is the only correct approach and that the three traditional requirements should be adhered to strictly. Passing-off should remain a misrepresentation tort. See Carty [1996] 11 EIPR 629.

11 See *United Biscuits (UK) Ltd v Burton Biscuits Ltd* [1992] FSR 14.

12 Asda did not succeed in this respect though in *United Biscuits (UK) Ltd v Asda Stores Ltd* [1997] RPC 513. They were held to have passed off their look-alike 'Puffin' biscuits as United Biscuits' 'Penguin' biscuits.

13 *My Kinda Town Ltd v Soll and Grunts Investments* [1983] RPC 407.

ordinarily give the public the impression that the plaintiff had made himself responsible for the quality of the defendant's goods or services. Such a connection would not constitute a misrepresentation.[14] There has to be deception. Mere confusion or likelihood of confusion is not sufficient. A full misrepresentation must take place and such a misrepresentation is a necessary ingredient of a cause of action of passing-off.[15]

The range of misrepresentations is very broad. They may relate to the nature of the product itself; the cases on champagne noted above exemplify this well. In many other cases the get-up of the product, ie its packaging and presentation, may be the source of confusion. It may be more remote; the *Cadbury Schweppes* case just considered shows that goodwill may extend to cover general aspects of the marketing campaign and thus misrepresentations may exist in that context too.

Misrepresentation by get-up

The most common category appears to be cases concerning the get-up of a product. The courts do not seem to object to essential similarities in appearance dictated, for example, by the function that a product has to perform. In *JB Williams Co v H Bronnley Co Ltd*[16] the separate brands of shaving stick were sold in similar containers. The Court of Appeal found that the plaintiffs' container was not distinctive; all its features were either dictated by the shape of the stick or were common to many other types of container in everyday use. On the other hand *William Edge & Sons Ltd v William Niccolls & Sons Ltd*[17] was a case where the similarity was not necessary and therefore did amount to a misrepresentation. The plaintiff had for long sold laundry blue, a type of dye, in bags with a wooden stick attached, to enable it to be lowered into a sink of washing without the hands of the user coming into contact with the water and dye. The defendants then began to sell a similar product of almost identical appearance. The House of Lords found that this amounted to passing-off since there was nothing essential about the size and shape of the stick – any stick would perform the same useful function and there was no justification for the defendants to have used the same type of get-up.

The principal case of this type is now *Reckitt & Colman Products Ltd v Borden Inc.*[18] This concerns the sale of Jif Lemon juice in lemon-shaped containers, which had been going on successfully and profitably for over thirty years. The defendants then decided to market their lemon juice in similar though not identical containers, different models of container being

14   *Harrods Ltd v Harrodian School Ltd* [1996] RPC 697.
15   *Barnsley Brewery Co Ltd v RBNB* [1997] FSR 462.
16   (1909) 26 RPC 765. See also *Scott v Nice-Pak Products* [1989] FSR 100.
17   [1911] AC 693.
18   [1990] 1 All ER 873, [1990] 1 WLR 491.

of a different size from that of Jif, or with a different coloured cap and/or label. None of these refinements detracted from the essential lemon shape and colour that was at the base of Borden's marketing strategy. Lord Oliver emphasised[19] that the key questions in a passing-off action 'were always ones of fact, and the vital finding of fact made by the trial judge, Walton J, was that there was a likelihood of confusion in the market place if both firms sold their juice in similar containers. This conclusion was reached with regard to the way in which this particular product was purchased by a busy shopper rushing around a busy supermarket making an occasional low price purchase of an ordinary item; in such circumstances no great care can be expected to be taken and confusion can readily ensue.

Several points arise from the significant *Jif* case. Firstly, it shows the tort of passing-off to be in good health, offering protection beyond that given by the trade mark registration which at that time did not extend to goods and/or containers following *Re Coca-Cola Co's Application.*[20] It also stands out as a rare instance of the House of Lords in recent times extending the scope of monopoly. Lord Oliver addressed this issue by asserting.[1]

'the principle that no man is entitled to steal another's trade by deceit is one of at least equal importance to the alleged need to curtail monopolies.'

Lord Bridge, however, clearly regretted[2] that the judge's findings of fact left him with no option but to grant an injunction in the case.

Jif is also notable for its confirmation that the identity of likely customers is an element in the equation. Were great care taken habitually by lemon juice purchasers, no confusion would arise and no action would have succeeded but Walton J confirms that in practice care is not taken in such a minor and routine transaction (incidentally enabling Jif to be sold at a far higher unit price than bottled lemon juice). On the other hand if the differences are so great that the reasonable man will be able to discern them, the fact that a few still may get confused is not sufficient to ground an action. This was well illustrated by Foster J in *Morning Star Co-operative Society Ltd v Express Newspapers Ltd*[3] when he observed that the differences between the austere broadsheet 'Morning Star' and the racy tabloid 'Daily Star' were such that 'only a moron in a hurry would be misled',[4] and thus no passing-off had occurred. The knowledge, actual or imputed, of the customers is also relevant; separate firms trading as 'JSB Motor Policies at Lloyds' and 'BJS Motor Syndicate at Lloyds' did not generate any confusion since the

19 Ibid at 880 and 499.
20 [1986] 2 All ER 274, sub nom *Coca Cola, Re* [1986] 1 WLR 695 cf TMA 1994, s 1(1). See p 346 above.
1   [1990] 1 All ER 873 at 889, [1990] 1 WLR 491 at 509.
2   Ibid at 877 and 495.
3   [1979] FSR 113.
4   Ibid at 117.

defendants only traded with insurance brokers whose expertise included knowledge of the separate nature of the two operations.[5]

The *Jif* case also highlights a most important practical point in passing-off litigation, namely how to obtain the all-important evidence that confusion has been or is likely to be engendered. This is particularly difficult in a case where the offending new project is yet to be launched, so no members of the public have as yet been confused. The vital evidence in *Jif* itself came from tests carried out by the plaintiffs, stopping shoppers in the street offering them one of the defendants' lemons, holding interviews with shoppers and displaying the defendants' lemon in a supermarket on Shrove Tuesday, when much lemon juice is sold for use on pancakes; each of these tests showed a great degree of confusion with shoppers believing that the defendants' lemon was in fact a Jif lemon.

However such unequivocal evidence is rare. Too often survey evidence is not found to be convincing by the courts because of flaws in the survey itself. Useful guidelines were set out by Whitford J in *Imperial Group plc v Philip Morris Ltd*.[6] He insisted that in order to be of any value in court a survey should be of an adequately large size and be fairly conducted. Full details of results and methods should be made available to the defence. Care should be taken about the use of questions which lead or otherwise direct the target of the question. A good example of survey evidence failing this test is provided by *United Biscuits (UK) Ltd v Burtons Biscuits Ltd*.[7] This was a dispute between rival brands of Jaffa Cakes. A straw poll questionnaire and a survey were regarded as worthless by Vinelott J as being ill-defined and capable of misinterpretation, while a tachistoscope test, which tests the operator's recognition of a brand by quickly flashing an image of it was also of no help because the false recognition of the defendants' package as that of the plaintiffs could be equally explained by the fact that the plaintiffs were the clear brand leader. Clearly care needs to be taken by the parties in the collection of survey evidence and caution will be the hallmark of the courts in their use of it;[8] however its dramatic impact in the *Jif* case shows that in an appropriate case it will have great value. Equally the courts are also unwilling to hear evidence from marketing 'experts' where the issue is of potential confusion amongst the public at large.[9]

A few other examples of passing-off by confusing get-up may be helpful. In *Rizla Ltd v Bryant & May Ltd*,[10] the plaintiffs' longstanding business

5   *John Hayter Motor Underwriting Agencies Ltd v RBHS Agencies Ltd* [1977] FSR 285. The lack of confusion at the point of sale prevented a passing-off claim in *Bostick Ltd v Sellotape GB Ltd* [1994] RPC 556.
6   [1984] RPC 293 at 302.
7   [1992] FSR 14.
8   See Morcom 'Survey Evidence in Trade Mark Proceedings' [1984] 1 EIPR 6.
9   *Dalgety Spillers Foods Ltd v Food Brokers Ltd* [1994] FSR 504.
10 [1986] RPC 389.

of selling packs of cigarette papers faced a serious threat of competition from the defendants. They proposed to market three different types of paper, as did the plaintiffs, and were proposing to use the same colour as their rivals for each type of paper. There, however, the similarity ceased with the defendants' 'Swan' brand name being prominently displayed, preventing any confusion with the Rizla papers arising. Likewise, the inclusion of a pink paper section for business news in the tabloid evening newspaper the *Evening Standard* was not thought likely to cause any confusion with the broadsheet morning pink paper newspaper the *Financial Times*.[11] Nor too could the proprietor of the magazine *Gourmet* restrain the introduction of a new journal *BBC Gourmet Good Food* when their get-up was different and they would be typically purchased from a rack on the basis of their get-up and not orally purchased from behind the newsagent's counter.[12]

Misrepresentation by name

In other cases it is not the get-up of the goods but the name being used that is the source of potential confusion. In *Newsweek Inc v BBC*[13] the publishers of the international news magazine sought to prevent the use of *Newsweek* as the title of a current affairs television programme. The Court of Appeal rejected the claim since the BBC would broadcast the programme with their usual logos, etc, and there would be no risk of confusing it with the plaintiffs' magazine. The mere use of a name used by another trader does not necessarily create the impression that the businesses are in some way connected, it seems.

However, the use of the same name in a related field of activity is more likely to be restrained. *Island Trading Co v Anchor Brewing Co*[14] is instructive. The plaintiffs sold 'Newquay Real Steam Bitter' with a steam theme used as part of its promotion. The defendants then began to import from California for the first time their 'Anchor Steam Beer' and the plaintiffs feared that confusion would arise. Knox J found that the Newquay brand was often referred to by customers as 'Steam Beer', and he awarded an injunction against the sale of Anchor Steam Beer in kegs, but allowed it in bottles. The reasoning was that kegs of beer in pubs might well cause confusion when a drinker asks for a 'pint of Steam', but bottled beer sold from the shelves of off-licences would not give rise to such confusion, the bottles being very different in appearance, the customer being more likely to be sober, the sales staff less under pressure and the noise level likely to be lower.

11   *The Financial Times Ltd v Evening Standard Co Ltd* [1991] FSR 7.
12   *Advance Magazine Publishing Inc v Redwood Publishing Ltd* [1993] FSR 449.
13   [1979] RPC 441.
14   [1989] RPC 287.

A particular problem arises when the same name is used on two similar products in cases where a real name is being used. Can the use of your own name amount to a misrepresentation, given that goodwill may attach, as we have seen, to a person's name? Well-known families appear to be particularly susceptible to this kind of dispute. In *Tussaud v Tussaud*,[15] the plaintiffs ran the famous Madame Tussaud waxworks in London; this had been a family business but had just been sold to an outsider. Young Louis Tussaud had worked in the family business but was now intending to open his own rival waxworks as Louis Tussaud Ltd. An injunction was awarded to the plaintiffs registering a company of that name because of the confusion that would arise and also because Louis Tussaud was not in the process of incorporating a pre-existing business of his.

Similar decisions have been reached in other cases. *Parker-Knoll Ltd v Knoll International Ltd*[16] saw a clash between the plaintiffs, manufacturers of traditional furniture, and the defendants, making more modern designs primarily for industrial use. The proprietor of the defendants was the wife of the nephew of the original Knoll who lent his name to the plaintiff firm. The House of Lords found by a majority that the defendants could be prevented by injunction from using their name because of the likelihood that they would be referred to as Knoll and the confusion that would arise thereby. More recently the Gucci family have also resorted to litigation. In *Guccio Gucci SpA v Paolo Gucci*,[17] the defendant was also prevented from trading under his own name because the evidence was that the buyers of designer label clothes may be confused by the use of the Gucci name by anyone other than the plaintiffs. These decisions may appear harsh on defendants legitimately using their own name but they are a reminder that the first in the field has the opportunity to develop a reputation and thus acquire goodwill, and this inevitably confers on him an advantage over later entrants into the market who, after all, do not have to use their own name in their trading activities and only do so because of the cachet that their (well-known) name may confer.

The development of the internet has in recent years given rise to a new type of case in which misrepresentation by name takes place. 'Cyberpirates' have tried to register the names of famous companies as domain names in order to be able to sell them to the companies involved for a profit. Some would call it extortion, but actions in passing-off have proved useful to stop this practice. The goodwill of the famous companies is not in doubt and it was held that the registration of the names by cyberpirates amounted to a

15   (1890) 44 Ch D 678.
16   [1962] RPC 265.
17   [1991] FSR 89.

misrepresentation. The least that could be said was that the registration amounted to the creation of an instrument of deception.[18]

Misrepresentation of the product itself

Another form of misrepresentation may arise when the product itself appears to be that of the plaintiffs. This particularly can arise in cases of parallel imports, where goods made elsewhere by a multinational firm are imported and compete with their home-grown product, at a lower price because of the cheaper manufacturing costs elsewhere. In *Colgate-Palmolive Ltd v Markwell Finance Ltd*,[19] the plaintiffs made and sold toothpaste in the UK as a subsidiary of its American parent company. There was also a Brazilian subsidiary which made toothpaste of poorer quality; it was not intended to compete in the markets of other members of the Colgate group but the defendants succeeded in circumventing the restrictions that had been placed on the trading activity of the Brazilian firm. It was clear that confusion was caused – complaints were made to the plaintiffs about what was in fact toothpaste from Brazil. The Court of Appeal found that this amounted to passing-off, even though both types of Colgate product derived from a common origin – it was not the origin but the quality of the goods that was at issue and the use by the defendants of products bearing the Colgate name amounted to a misrepresentation to their customers of the quality to be expected from those goods. A similar decision was reached much earlier in *Gillette Safety Razor Co v Franks*[20] where the defendant was prevented from selling second-hand imported Gillette razor blades in Gillette packaging as new blades.

Developments in misrepresentation

It is evident that the law is willing to recognise a variety of different ways whereby trading activity can amount to a misrepresentation. Where there is such flexibility, it is always open to litigants to try and exploit that flexibility by seeking to gradually extend the frontiers of liability. There is evidence from two recent decisions of this happening in respect of misrepresentations in passing-off cases.

---

18   *Marks & Spencer plc v One in A Million Ltd; Ladbroke's plc v One in A Million Ltd; J Sainsbury plc v One in A Million Ltd; Virgin Enterprises Ltd v One in A Million Ltd; British Telecommunications plc v One in A Million Ltd* [1998] FSR 265 at 271, confirmed on appeal *British Telecommunications plc v One in A Million Ltd* [1998] 4 All ER 476. Other cases are concerned with the registration of company names in bad faith: *Glaxo plc v Glaxowellcome Ltd* [1996] FSR 388; *Direct Line Group Ltd v Direct Line Estate Agency Ltd* [1997] FSR 374.
19   [1989] RPC 497.
20   (1924) 41 RPC 499.

■

Bristol Conservatories Ltd v Conservatories Custom Built Ltd[1] was a case of what may be described as reverse passing-off. Usually the representor seeks to establish that his goods are the goods of the plaintiff but here the opposite was the case and the claim was that the goods of the plaintiff were in fact his. This arose in relation to the erection of ornamental conservatories as extensions to buildings. The plaintiffs were engaged in this business when an employee left and joined the defendants' newly formed business. He then touted for business showing prospective customers pictures of conservatories erected by the plaintiffs conveying the impression that they had been the work of the defendants. The Court of Appeal ruled on a preliminary point that these facts disclosed a good cause of action. The basis of the decision is in essence that any confusion, however caused, even if indirect in origin, will be enough to ground a misrepresentation claim, and clearly here customers would become confused as to the true origin of the conservatories. In fact the defendants' salesman had been silent as to the basis of the pictures, so inferences drawn from a silence can amount to a misrepresentation, which is a long way from traditional definitions of misrepresentation. Ralph Gibson LJ also specifically endorses[2] the view that the common law should seek to parallel the legislative trend towards ever higher standards of commercial integrity and this invitation, if taken up, will only strengthen the expansionist tone adopted in recent times by the tort of passing-off.

More recently, the existence of this type of claim has been confirmed by the sale of 'Welsh Whiskey' which was in fact based on a blend of Scotch whisky and herbs. This was found to be an abuse of the name and reputation of Scotch whisky by dressing it up as being Welsh.[3]

The other case that again shows a broad approach to misrepresentation is that of *Associated Newspapers plc v Insert Media Ltd.*[4] The plaintiffs, newspaper proprietors, sought to prevent the unauthorised insertion of advertising material into copies of their newspapers. Just as in *Bristol Conservatories*, the problem was that in one sense there was no misrepresentation because nothing was said to the readers to indicate that the inserts were not by or with the permission of the proprietors. The Court of Appeal found for the plaintiffs. While accepting that the mere act of inserting copy into the papers may not in itself amount to a misrepresentation, it would do so if all the surrounding circumstances suggested that the inserts were there with the permission of the proprietor and in particular if as a result the public is likely to be confused because of what has been done. On these facts the defendant had himself, in his

1   [1989] RPC 455, noted Holyoak 'Reverse Passing-Off – A New Liability' (1990) 106 LQR 564.
2   [1989] RPC 455 at 466.
3   *Matthew Gloag & Sons Ltd v Welsh Distillers Ltd* [1998] FSR 718.
4   [1991] 3 All ER 535, [1991] 1 WLR 571.

publicity, pointed to the link that would be made by people associating the insert and the product it promoted with the quality newspaper that accompanied it; thus confusion would be generated with members of the public thinking that the publishers of the paper were responsible for the insertion and that was sufficient to say that the conduct of the defendants amounted to a misrepresentation, and one which could cause harm to the reputation of the plaintiffs in appropriate circumstances.

Unintentional misrepresentation

Throughout the entire discussion of misrepresentation in the tort of passing-off, there is one common element which may be emphasised here. In common law actions for misrepresentation much depends on the state of the defendant's mind in making the statement, but that is not the case in passing-off claims. Rather it is merely necessary, as Lord Diplock put it in the *Advocaat* case,[5] that the misrepresentation is 'calculated to injure' the goodwill of the other trader. However, even this formulation is prone to mislead since 'calculating' is normally thought to involve some element of deliberate conduct but this is not the case here. The view has long been taken that all that is needed is to show that the misrepresentation is likely to harm the plaintiff's interests and that may be the case even where the defendant is innocent and does not intend to cause harm.[6] The only exception to this clear rule arises where the misrepresentation arises through the actions of a third party on facts such as those of *Bovril Ltd v Bodega Co Ltd*[7] when the defendant served Oxo in response to requests for Bovril; clearly in such a case the innocence of the manufacturers of Oxo would count in their favour although their goods were in fact being passed off as the goods of another. Perhaps the simplest way of explaining such a case is that Oxo have made no representation at all. The innocent passer-off may be at a slight advantage when remedies are considered; any account of profits may be limited to the time after the defendant becomes aware of the situation and continues with the misrepresentation,[8] but there seems to be no ground for differentiating between innocent and other defendants where the award of damages is concerned. This has been an area of controversy in the past[9] but this view is now confirmed by the decision of Blackburne J in *Gillette UK Ltd v Edenwest Ltd*.[10]

The failure to require any intention on the part of the defendant can lead to ironic results. On the one hand the defendants in the *Cadbury Schweppes*

5   [1979] AC 731 at 742, [1979] 2 All ER 927 at 933.
6   See eg *Baume & Co v A H Moore Ltd* [1958] Ch 907 at 916, [1958] 2 All ER 113 at 116.
7   (1916) 33 RPC 153.
8   *Spalding & Brothers v A W Gamage Ltd* (1915) 32 RPC 273 at 283, per Lord Parker.
9   See eg *Marengo v Daily Sketch & Sunday Graphic Ltd* (1948) 65 RPC 242.
10 [1994] RPC 279.

case intentionally copied the marketing ideas of the plaintiffs, but were not liable since no one was deceived. On the other hand in the *Jif* case, clear attempts were made to differentiate the products (though admittedly without abandoning the basic lemon shape) yet their failure to avoid confusion led to the defendants being found liable. The failure to provide a defence of innocence adds to the force of the tort of passing-off, and shows that traders must be continually on their guard not to generate confusion between their product and that of other traders.

Damage

All the various proferred definitions of the elements of the tort of passing-off include the necessity for damage to be incurred by the plaintiff or, in a case where injunctive relief is sought, the likelihood of damage. Passing-off is therefore not actionable per se and harm to goodwill resulting from the misrepresentation has to be proven – or does it?[11] Isolated instances of case law show that the courts may be prepared to assume the existence of damage.

In *Draper v Trist & Tristbestos Brake Linings Ltd*[12] the trial judge was only prepared to award nominal damages in the absence of proof that the passing-off caused any specific damage. The Court of Appeal, however, substituted an award of £2,000. Sir Wilfrid Greene MR noted[13] that the

'right which is infringed in a passing-off case is one which was regarded at law as one the mere violation of which led to damage ... it was not regarded at law as a case in which damage was of the gist of the action'

while Goddard L J commented[14] that the law

'assumes ... that if the goodwill of a man's business has been interfered with by the passing-off of goods, damage results therefrom.'

Although the plaintiff could not show direct loss of trade from the passing-off, he was able to show that this was a 'real business possibility'[15] and thus succeeded.

---

11   It is at least not clear whether the plaintiff must identify some specific head of pecuniary loss in order to succeed. See *Law Society of England and Wales v Society of Lawyers* [1996] FSR 739.
12   (1939) 56 RPC 429.
13   Ibid at 435.
14   Ibid at 442.
15   Ibid at 440, per Sir Wilfrid Greene MR.

This case was followed in *Procea Products Ltd v Evans & Sons Ltd*[16] where the defendants were selling a type of loaf known as 'process bread' which the plaintiffs thought would engender confusion with their product name. There was no evidence of actual loss of trade and only nominal damages were being sought. Roxburgh J followed the *Draper* decision and awarded £1 in damages. (This was an innocent misrepresentation and the judge was clearly troubled by the same doubt as noted above[17] as to whether anything more than nominal damages should be awarded in a case of innocence – as has been seen this has been resolved and full damages may now be awarded.)

The status of these two cases is somewhat hazy. They have not been the subject of attack or criticism but may appear inconsistent with the demands that damage be proven. It is suggested that they can be reconciled. Clearly a plaintiff has to show damage has occurred,[18] but the exact loss of trade is very often difficult to pinpoint. If a firm's business declines, a whole range of factors quite apart from passing-off by rivals – poor product, high price, etc – as well as legitimate as opposed to illegitimate forms of competition may be to blame. As a result of this in a case such as *Draper* the court is requiring proof of likely losses rather than actual losses and the assumption being made is not that any passing-off always causes damage but that the particular circumstances are such that damage of some kind is likely to occur. A case such as *Procea* is different again; where no damage has (yet) been shown to occur, though some may be likely to result, nominal damages is clearly all that can be awarded (as well as the injunction that was granted). In deciding whether the facts show the likelihood of damage, the scope of the goodwill of the plaintiff and the way in which confusion may arise will be of importance to the court in deciding whether there is liability by inferring the risk of damage from those elements.[19]

A useful case demonstrating this process and showing that damage remains of importance is *Stringfellow v McCain Foods (GB) Ltd*.[20] The plaintiff owned a top London nightclub while the defendant named their new brand of long thin oven chip 'Stringfellows' and advertised it on television with a disco scene set in a domestic kitchen. Clearly the plaintiff was possessed of goodwill, and it may be thought that the name and imagery suggested that the chips were in some way connected with the nightclub. However the Court of Appeal rejected the claim. This was in part due to its view that there was no misrepresentation in the use of the name but also because even after the television adverts, which may have amounted to a

16   (1951) 68 RPC 210.
17   See p 441 above.
18   *Reckitt & Colman Products Ltd v Borden Inc* [1990] 1 All ER 873 at 880, [1990] 1 WLR 491 at 499, per Lord Oliver.
19   See eg *Annabel's (Berkeley Square) Ltd v Schock* [1972] RPC 838 at p 423 above. Cf *Miss World (Jersey) Ltd v James Street Productions Ltd* [1981] FSR 309.
20   [1984] RPC 501.

misrepresentation, there was no actual evidence of goodwill being damaged. Although the plaintiff feared loss of goodwill, that was not enough; there was no evidence of trade declining and the argument that his future merchandising activity may be compromised was short-circuited by Stringfellow's admission that it was only this action that had alerted him to the possibility of merchandising. No damage was therefore found likely to occur and the claim was as a result found not to succeed.

The damage requirement also proved to be problematical when the tort was used to combat the practices of 'cyberpirates' who register the names of famous companies as domain names. The Court of Appeal was prepared to accept that the registration of a domain name that included the famous name would amount to an erosion of the exclusive goodwill in the name and it was assumed that damage was likely to result from the registration as such. Use of the registered name would definitely lead to damage and the Court was prepared to grant interlocutory relief to stop damage from occurring. Aldous LJ ruled that :

> 'In my view there be discerned from the case a jurisdiction to grant injunctive relief where a defendant is equipped with or is intending to equip another with an instrument of fraud. Whether any name is an instrument of fraud will depend upon all the circumstances. A name which will, by reason of its similarity to the name of another, inherently lead to passing-off is such an instrument. If it would not inherently lead to passing-off, it does not follow that it is not an instrument of fraud. The Court should consider the similarity of the names, the intention of the defendant, the type of trade and all the surrounding circumstances. If it be the intention of the defendant to appropriate the goodwill of another or enable others to do so, I can see no reason why the Court should not infer that it will happen, even if there is a possibility that such an appropriation would not take place. If, taking all the circumstances into account the Court should conclude that the name was produced to enable passing-off, is adapted to be used for passing-off and, if used, is likely to be fraudulently used, an injunction will be appropriate.'[1]

When can an action be brought?

The above ruling of the Court of Appeal is also helpful in another respect. It shows clearly in which different situations the passing-off action can be used. Aldous LJ summarised it as follows:

---

1   *British Telecommunications plc v One in A Million Ltd* [1998] 4 All ER 476.

'It follows that the Court will intervene by way of injunction in passing-off cases in three types of case. First, where there is passing-off established or it is threatened. Second, where the defendant is a joint tortfeasor with another in passing-off, either actual or threatened. Third, where the defendant has equipped himself with or intends to equip another with an instrument of fraud. This third type is probably mere quia timet action.'[2]

It should be added, though, that merely providing assistance is not sufficient to become a joint tortfeasor.[3]

Remedies

There is little that needs to be said specifically about remedies in the context of passing-off. Injunctive relief is often sought, particularly to prevent the alleged passing-off from ever occurring given the speculative nature of the damage in fact caused by the passing-off, as has just been noted. Alternatively, but unusually, a declaration may be sought by the plaintiff instead, for example where the defendant has already ceased his wrongful trading.[4]

As far as monetary compensation is concerned, the plaintiff is faced with a choice of a claim for damages or an account of profits. The latter is of course discretionary and as has been seen previously not available in respect of innocent passing-off. That said, if available to a plaintiff it is clearly advantageous since the account will be for profits from all sales of the offending product even if the passing-off does not contribute to the sales in question.[5]

Damages are awarded on standard tortious principles to reflect the harm caused to the goodwill of the plaintiff with all the attendant difficulties of deciding what harm is attributable to the conduct of the defendant. Perhaps as a response to that, an alternative approach has been canvassed in the case of *Dormeuil Frères SA v Feraglow Ltd*[6] where the defendants had been quite extensively engaged in the manufacture of cloth which contained and thus infringed the trade mark of the plaintiffs. The difficulty of assessing the losses of the plaintiff led to the argument that damages should be awarded on a royalty basis as in patent cases and relevant licensing agreements could be examined to come up with an appropriate figure. Knox J reviewed the

2   *British Telecommunications plc v One in A Million Ltd* [1998] 4 All ER 476.
3   See *Crédit Lyonnais Bank Nederland NV v Export Credit Guarantee Department* [1998] 1 Lloyd's Rep 19.
4   Eg *Treasure Cot Co Ltd v Hamleys Bros Ltd* (1950) 67 RPC 89.
5   *Lever v Goodwin* (1887) 36 Ch D 1.
6   [1990] RPC 449.

law in detail and concluded that it was possible but not certain that a royalty-based claim could be made and, since this was a preliminary hearing, it was not appropriate at this stage to create a new royalty-based approach. The key question is whether the analogy suggested with patent cases is appropriate; there of course it is the plaintiff's proprietary right that is being usurped by the defendant whereas the rights created by the tort of passing-off are not proprietary in character. It would therefore be something of a jump to allow passing-off damages to be calculated in this manner and would enhance the protection of the plaintiff's goodwill considerably. This may be too big a leap for the tort to take, though equally recently it has not been noted for its timidity.

Passing-off: an overview

In reviewing the contemporary role of this tort, several issues arise:
(1) why has it expanded in so many ways in recent years?
(2) will it still have a role in the light of the Trade Marks Act 1994?
(3) does it have the effect of being a tort of unfair competition?

The first question can easily be answered with reference to two factors. The most obvious is the shortcomings of the, at times, ill-thought-out trade marks legislation at the time of the key developments in the tort's recent development. Most of the expansion of the tort has been in response to these difficulties; an analogy might be made with the way the tort of negligence, in its expansionist period, rushed in to fill some of the holes in contract law and public law.

The second factor to bear strongly in mind is that goodwill, though not as such a proprietary interest, is nevertheless a real, and tradeable, commodity. If, say, I decide to sell my cruise ship, that will cost the buyer £x. However, if I decide to make available to the new owner of the ship the business that it has been operating, I would expect a further £y to reflect the goodwill of that business. Only passing-off can protect that goodwill interest, it is suggested.

This all leads logically to our second question. Clearly the broader scope of the new legislative approach reduces the role of the tort. As we have seen, several problems hitherto the exclusive province of passing-off, are now broadly, though not precisely, covered by the 1994 Act. Examples would include the *Bollinger* type of case (Trade Marks Act 1994, s 49) and the *Lego* type of case (Trade Marks Act 1994, s 5(3)).

But both these examples have gaps and a provisional list of instances where the law of tort still has a role to play might be:
(1)   cases of attack on general goodwill rather than on the mark itself, especially where no mark has been registered, in that area (*Lego*) or at all.

(2) cases of attack on general image which is not capable of being protected by a trade mark - *Cadbury Schweppes* is the classic example.

(3) it is not clear that the odd facts of a case like *Bristol Conservatories* can be resolved in any other way than through the tort of passing-off, unless a trade mark had been, on those facts, registered in the pictures of the conservatories, which seems unlikely.

We may add to this list the likelihood that a claim in passing-off will continue to be co-pleaded with a trade mark action due to a combination of the uncertainties still attaching to the 1994 Act and the understandable conservatism in these matters of the legal professions.

In relation to the tort of unfair competition, the claims that there may be one in the 'Alcohol cases' have been soundly and authoritatively refuted in *Cadbury Schweppes*. The absence of such an immediate remedy distinguishes the UK jurisdiction from that of may others, such as, for instance, the broad approach of Australia's Trade Practices Act 1974. So, as so often in the common law, the question has to be whether the sundry elements of the law provide adequate protection for the parties: this question is best left until after we have considered the other elements of tortious protection of intellectual property rights.

Meanwhile, as to passing-off, it clearly still has a role. As we have seen it has a role, albeit a diminished one, in filling the gaps in trade mark law. It also stands out in the world of tort law as a protector of economic interests, directly those of traders, and indirectly those of consumers too. Also as a tort, created by the courts and developed by them, it has an inherent flexibility which is not a quality normally associated with statutory provisions. This tort will not fade away.

DEFAMATION AND MALICIOUS FALSEHOOD

The law of defamation – libel and slander – provides protection for the reputation of an individual while malicious falsehood, which is also sometimes referred to as injurious falsehood or slander of goods, provides a parallel protection for the reputations of businesses. It is thus convenient to consider them in the same section.

Defamation

It is clear that in its protection of an individual's reputation, the tort of defamation will extend its coverage to the professional or business aspects of that individual's life. The classic instance of this is provided by *Tolley v JS Fry Ltd*[7] where the plaintiff, a (genuinely) amateur golfer was appalled

---

7   [1931] AC 333.

to discover that a likeness of him was appearing in the newspaper adverts for the defendants' chocolate bars, accompanied by a banal limerick comparing the excellence of Tolley's golf with that of the defendants' product. Tolley complained not on grounds of taste or with regard to the as yet unconceived notion of character merchandising but because he felt that his status as an amateur would be hopelessly compromised in the minds of readers because they would assume that, contrary to the then rules, he must have been paid to lend his name to the adverts. The House of Lords found that that was an appropriate conclusion for them to reach and thus the adverts amounted to defamation by innuendo, and were thus actionable.

However, the role of defamation in this field goes further than that. There is also clear authority that a business can sue in defamation where its reputation is falsely impugned, and this amounts to a backdoor method of protecting a trading reputation against false allegations. Cases of this nature have been few and far between and not always accompanied by success, but it seems reasonably clear that such a cause of action exists.[8] In *South Hetton Coal Co v North-Eastern News Association Ltd*[9] criticism was published of the insanitary state of the housing provided by the coal company for its employees. Lord Esher MR was quite clear[10] that the laws of libel gave a company the same rights as an ordinary person, but that this was not an actionable libel as being legitimate fair comment on a matter of public interest. In *Lewis v Daily Telegraph Ltd*,[11] a company and its chairman brought an action in libel against the defendants for a news story reporting that the police had raided the company's premises in a fraud inquiry. The House of Lords seemed to accept that a company could sue in libel without demur but ruled that the stories were not libellous since they only referred to the investigation of possible crimes and did not state or imply that actual crimes had been committed. The House of Lords recently denied the availability of libel to a local authority[12] but this was on the particular ground of the public interest in democratic free speech and cases in the *South Hetton* line of authority were approved and it is difficult to see how public interest would act so compellingly to prevent any claim in libel by a company.[13]

Malicious falsehood

It is evident that the role of defamation in this field is peripheral and most cases are more likely by companies within the more appropriate but also

---

8   See eg *Berkoff v Burchill* [1996] 4 All ER 1008, CA.
9   [1894] 1 QB 133.
10   Ibid at 138.
11   [1964] AC 234, [1963] 2 All ER 151.
12   *Derbyshire County Council v Times Newspapers Ltd* [1993] AC 534, [1993] 1 All ER 1011.
13   Cf Patfield 'Defamation, Freedom of Speech and Corporations' [1993] Jur Rev 294.

more restrictive tort of malicious falsehood. This is a classic example of an action on the case which evolved and developed a long way from its initial roots to the role which it now plays. It began to deal with wrongful allegations of unlawful claims to proprietary rights in land[14] but now extends to cover the trading reputation of a business and its product. It is only in the latter part of the nineteenth century that the tort came to fulfil this type of need. Two significant cases in its development at this time were *The Western Countries Manure Co v Lawes Chemical Manure Co*[15] and *Riding v Smith*.[16] In the *Manure* case the quality of the plaintiffs' product was wrongly impugned by the defendants and this attack on the goods was found to give a novel cause of action to the plaintiffs while in *Riding* it was the business itself that was the subject of criticism. In this enchanting case the defendant alleged that the plaintiff's wife (who helped in his shop) had committed adultery in the shop with the new vicar. Whereas today the tabloids would encourage flocks of their readers to visit the shop in those stern times there was evidence of a falling-off in the trade of the plaintiff following the allegations, and this too was held to represent a good cause of action.

The strands of this emergent tort were pulled together in *Ratcliffe v Evans*[17] where the defendant falsely alleged that the plaintiff's business had ceased to exist. This was clearly harmful to the interests of the plaintiff but was inaccurate rather than defamatory. In spite of this, Bowen LJ found the statements to be actionable stating[18] that

'an action will lie for written or oral falsehoods, not actionable *per se* nor even defamatory, where they are maliciously published, where they are calculated in the ordinary course of things to produce, and where they do produce, actual damage.'

The House of Lords confirmed that this was so in *White v Mellin*[19] but added that it was necessary for the plaintiff to establish that special damage had been suffered and for this reason and also for the reason that the facts did not reveal the necessary denigration of the plaintiff's goods (White sold Mellin's baby food but put on the wrappers a notice stating that another brand in which he had an interest was more nutritious) no action was found to exist on the facts as then found.

In the light of these cases it can be established that several elements go to make up this tort and all need to be established if a claim is to succeed. It

14   *Gerard v Dickenson* (1590) 4 Co Rep 18a, 76 ER 903.
15   (1874) LR 9 Exch 218.
16   (1876) 1 Ex D 91.
17   [1892] 2 QB 524.
18   Ibid at 527.
19   [1895] AC 154.

is necessary to show that the defendant has made a false statement which is derogatory of the plaintiff's goods or business, the statement being made with malice and resulting in damage to the plaintiff.

It is also worth noting that in recent years an action in defamation in an intellectual property case has been brought in combination with an action for trade mark infringement.[20] A pattern similar to that in relation to passing-off and trade marks is being established.

Falsity

This is a simple requirement. As with defamation, the statement must not be true. If the plaintiff cannot prove falsity, he will not succeed.[1] This contrasts with the position in mainstream defamation cases where it is for the defence to justify the truth of statements made. In determining the falsity of a statement the 'one meaning rule' applies. This means that the single natural and ordinary meaning of the words used must be determined.[2]

Denigration

For this tort it is not sufficient that the statement be false; it must go further and damage the reputation of the goods or business by denigrating it, in other words making derogatory statements which harm the reputation of the goods or business. As we have just seen, this was a problem in *White v Mellin* where there was no derogatory comment about the plaintiff's product but rather only a suggestion that that of the defendant was superior. It would have been different if it had been stated that White's product was in some way harmful to children.

The context in which the statement is made will be an important factor in deciding whether it is derogatory or not. *De Beers Abrasive Products Ltd v International General Electric Co of New York Ltd*[3] demonstrates this well. The defendants circulated to the trade results of tests which, in a highly technical manner only comprehensible to people within the trade, purported to demonstrate that the defendants' synthetic diamond abrasive (used for cutting concrete) was of a superior quality to the natural diamond abrasive of the plaintiffs. Walton J found the defendants would be liable if the facts as assumed at that stage of the proceedings were proven and in so doing emphasised that the offending statements were not mere puffs but detailed technical information aimed solely at people expert in the field who would

20   See *Vodafone Group plc v Orange Personal Communications Services Ltd* [1997] FSR 34; *Macmillan Magazines Ltd v RCN Publishing Co Ltd* [1998] FSR 9.
1   *Anderson v Liebig's Extract of Meat Co Ltd* (1881) 45 LT 757.
2   *Vodafone Group plc v Orange Personal Communications Services Ltd* [1997] FSR 34.
3   [1975] 2 All ER 599, [1975] 1 WLR 972.

understand it and its significance, and who would clearly see the alleged inferiority of the plaintiffs' goods.

Statements which on the face of it are innocuous may come to be regarded as denigratory once placed in context. In *Lyne v Nicholls*[4] the defendant stated falsely that his newspaper's circulation was 20 times that of any local rival. This was found to denigrate rivals in potentially causing advertisers to switch away from other papers to that of the defendant. An odd case is *Serville v Constance*.[5] Here the plaintiff was the official welterweight boxing champion of Trinidad who on arrival in London discovered that the defendant was claiming that title. Harman J found that, had malice been proven, that would amount to a malicious falsehood against the plaintiff, presumably in suggesting that his claims to the title were false and that he was therefore a liar. Other more obvious examples of the tort are claims that a plaintiff had departed from the address used for his business[6] and claims by the defendant that the goods of the plaintiff were infringing a trade mark.[7]

A significant recent case showing how the denigration can arise indirectly and/or by conduct is *Kaye v Robertson*.[8] The plaintiff, a well-known actor, suffered life threatening head injuries in an accident during a gale which blew a plank through the windscreen of his car. While lying in hospital, still very ill, representatives of the *Sunday Sport* newspaper broke in and took photographs of the actor and recorded his delirious utterances, with a view to running a major feature in their next edition. An injunction was sought and granted to prevent publication. The Court of Appeal thought that the publication, with the implication that Kaye had consented to its tasteless content, would amount to defamation, but felt constrained from injuncting it on this basis, following a long line of authority restricting the use of injunctions in libel cases.[9] However no such caution attended Kaye's alternative claim in malicious falsehood. By implying his consent the proposed feature amounted to denigration of Kaye's trade as a celebrity;[10] he may have wished to publish his story of the incident himself, and in a more salubrious forum, and this expectation was harmed by the conduct of the defendants. The case both shows the inherent flexibility of the tort and also the great ease with which injunctions can be obtained.

---

4 (1906) 23 TLR 86.
5 [1954] 1 All ER 662, [1954] 1 WLR 487.
6 *Joyce v Motor Services Ltd* [1948] Ch 252.
7 *Greers Ltd v Pearman and Corder* (1922) 39 RPC 406.
8 [1991] FSR 62.
9 From *William Coulson & Sons v James Coulson & Co* (1887) 3 TLR 846 onwards.
10 See Ch 27 on this aspect of the case.

∎

Malice

The element of malice is at the core of this tort and, in insisting that the plaintiff proves this element, it greatly reduces the impact of the tort since in many cases a defendant will be able to claim accidental mistake rather than deliberate malice as the reason for the false statement. This element also makes this tort stand out from its neighbours, passing-off and defamation, where it is not a necessary element of the cause of action.[11]

Given the importance of malice, it is perhaps surprising that the courts have over the years had some difficulty in deciding how precisely to define it. In *Shapiro v La Morta*[12] the plaintiff musician lost her claim against the defendants who had claimed wrongly that she would be performing at their music hall because she could not prove malice defined by Atkin L J[13] as being an intentionally or recklessly made statement. However earlier in one of the leading cases, *Royal Baking Powder Co v Wright, Crossley & Co*,[14] Lord Bankes[15] had defined 'malice' as meaning the absence of any 'just cause or excuse'– clearly a much less rigorous definition, but one that seems not now to be followed,[16] thus adding to the burden placed on the plaintiff.

A more recent case to touch on this area is *McDonald's Hamburgers Ltd v Burgerking (UK) Ltd*.[17] As we have already seen in the *De Beers* case, this tort has great potential in cases of comparative advertising. Here the defendants advertised their Whopper burger under the slogan 'It's Not Just Big, Mac' and went on to claim that their product was 100% beef 'unlike some burgers'. The plaintiffs saw this as an attack on their Big Mac burger, described[18] memorably by Whitford J as the 'flagship of the McDonald's range, though not, I apprehend, with reference to the ease with which it can be sunk'. The plaintiffs' claim in passing-off was successful because readers may have deduced from the overall appearance of the advert that Big Macs could be purchased from Burgerking outlets, but their claim in malicious falsehood that Big Macs were wrongly imputed to be less than 100% beef did not succeed, partly because it required a sophisticated analysis of a kind not normally reserved for adverts in Underground trains to reach this conclusion so was probably not denigratory, and also because there was no evidence of malice which Whitford J regarded as,[19] at the least,

---

11   Many defamation cases fail because the plaintiff cannot prove the element of malice in a convincing way; see *Vodafone Group plc v Orange Personal Communications Services Ltd* [1997] FSR 34.
12   (1923) 40 TLR 201.
13   Ibid at 203.
14   (1900) 18 RPC 95.
15   Ibid at 99.
16   See eg *Balden v Shorter* [1933] Ch 427.
17   [1986] FSR 45, [1987] FSR 112 (on another point).
18   Ibid at 47.
19   Ibid at 61.

a reckless indifference as to whether harm may be caused to the interests of the plaintiff.

Damage

Traditionally there has been the need for the plaintiff in actions based on this tort to have to prove special damage ie bring distinct evidence of harm to their business. This requirement is however no longer present in most cases following the Defamation Act 1952, s 3(1) which establishes in respect of this tort that special damage is not necessary if the words used are

'calculated to cause pecuniary damage to the plaintiff and are published in writing or other permanent form'

or alternatively are

'calculated to cause pecuniary damage to the plaintiff in respect of any office, profession, calling, trade or business'.

Given the requirement of malice and the way it is interpreted by the courts, most likely cases of malicious falsehood will fall within this exception.

Guidance on quantum in such cases was provided in *Fielding v Variety Inc*[20] where the *Variety* newspaper singled out a musical promoted by the plaintiff as being a disastrous flop. This was not the case; it was and continued to be a great success. It was difficult to see what loss the plaintiff had suffered as a result of the falsehood and a nominal figure of £100 was awarded in respect of the malicious falsehood.

TORT - AN OVERVIEW

Malicious falsehood's impact on intellectual property law is limited to a great degree by the requirement of malice but it is a notable recognition that businesses and products have reputations too, which the tort will in its terms protect, just as do the proprietors of businesses, whose personal reputation falls within the ambit of the tort of defamation. Clearly, however, the notion of a business' reputation overlaps extensively with the notion of its goodwill, and much more effective protection is afforded by the tort of passing-off, most significantly because of its focus on the likely consequences of words and acts, not the intention of those making them. Equally, passing-off requires there to be the all-important confusion between the goods or services of the parties where malicious falsehood goes wider to cover any

20   [1967] 2 QB 841.

attack on the quality of those goods or services. Together the torts provide vital back-up to the proprietary intellectual property rights in covering the vague but vital areas of goodwill and repute.

It may be argued, however, that between them the two torts come close to the idea of a tort of unfair competition. It is accepted that maliciously unfair competition needs to be proven, but in more severe cases than *McDonalds* this is not impossible. In vaguer cases of unfair taking advantage of the repute of others, passing-off clearly has a valuable role to play, not to mention the new, improved, Trade Marks Act.

Issues in intellectual property

This section merits a brief explanation. So far we have been concerned with identifying the nature and scope of the individual rights that make up intellectual property law. In this section however, we are concerned with some broader issues in intellectual property law and practice that can only be understood with reference to a wide range of different rights which collectively provide, or at least go some way to providing, a resolution of these important issues.

Chapter 25

Confidentiality and trade secrets

The laws protecting the confidentiality of information arise in a broad range of decided cases. It is inevitable that discussion of the current state of the law will reflect this fact but it is important to assert at the outset that the remit of this chapter is to consider the use of actions for breach of confidence as a means of protecting intellectual/industrial property rights. The ramifications of the case law with implications for personal privacy and governmental secrecy are matters on the periphery of the scope of this work, and will only receive passing attention. It is also important from the outset to establish why this action is relevant, indeed vital, to an understanding of intellectual property law. A right of action for breach of confidence underpins and, in many cases, predates a more formed intellectual property right. As an example, it is obvious that I have no copyright protection in my idea for a new film until the idea is translated into concrete form. However, if I discuss the idea with you secretly, and then discover subsequently that you have created a film using the same idea then, in principle, an action for breach of confidence may lie. Equally, the idea for a new invention may be protected by this area of law long before I achieve a working and thus patentable model. In trade mark law too, discussions about marks prior to their registration, rough drafts, etc may all give rise to an obligation on the part of anyone privy to such discussions.

A final preliminary point is important to make. In all these actions, the plaintiff is seeking to restrict the propagation of information which is true. Clearly the law has an interest in protecting both an individual victim and society more generally from falsity and, for example, the various torts such as passing-off and injurious falsehood exist to achieve this purpose. However, where truth is concerned, the interest of the individual and that of society may part company. The individual will wish to keep information close to his chest, whether for commercial or personal reasons. Society, however, may be thought to have an interest in the free availability of all true information.

HISTORICAL DEVELOPMENT AND CONCEPTUAL BASIS[1]

The law of breach of confidence took its modern form in the middle of the nineteenth century. Perhaps the leading case from this period is *Prince Albert v Strange*.[2] This action, oddly reminiscent of the excesses of modern tabloid journalism, was an action brought by the husband of the reigning monarch, Queen Victoria. It appeared that the royal couple had been in the habit of, privately, making drawings and etchings. Some of these works were sent away. Some of the drawings were sent away to be printed professionally and it seemed that this printer (Strange) made unauthorised copies which he then intended to display for gain in a public exhibition, Strange claiming that such an event would add to the reputation of the royal couple by showing their 'eminent artistic talent.' The outcome of such a case was inevitably a finding in favour of the plaintiff, but the reasoning of the court is important too.

Clearly the action against Strange was not an action based on any contract, for reasons of privity. The House of Lords, in the speech of Lord Cottenham LC, seemed to take the view that the action arose as an aspect of the plaintiff's proprietary rights in the drawings, but he was keen to point out[3] that the action was equally sustainable on grounds of equity, confidence and (presumably as against the printer only) contract law. It should be noted that there have been attempts subsequently to use contract as the basis of breach of confidence actions,[4] and clearly confidentiality will often arise, whether expressly or impliedly, as a term of a contract. However, the leading *Spycatcher* case[5] has made clear that the obligation may arise independently of any contractual relationship.[6]

The nature of an action for breach of confidence was further considered in another of the pioneer cases, namely *Morison v Moat*.[7] The parties and families had jointly been involved in the development of a commercial medicine rejoicing in the name of 'Morison's Universal Medicine.' Subsequently the partnership arrangements ended, and the defendant continued to make the medicine. The plaintiff claimed that this was improperly using information gained during the period of the partnership,

---

1 For a fuller discussion, see Gurry *Breach of Confidence* Clarendon Press (1984).
2 (1849) 2 De G & SM 652, Mac & G 25, 64 ER 293; affd (1849) 41 ER 1171.
3 1 Mac & G 25 at 44, 41 ER 1171 at 1178.
4 Eg *Vokes v Heather* (1945) 62 RPC 135.
5 *A-G v Guardian Newspapers (No 2)* [1990] 1 AC 109, [1988] 3 All ER 545.
6 Ibid at 255 and 639, per Lord Keith.
7 (1851) 9 Hare 241; 68 ER 492.

and sought an injunction. This was granted with the court accepting that the basis of the action was far from certain but may well be based on trust or confidence creating an obligation on the defendant's conscience not to breach that confidence – clearly a distinct equitable tinge to the obligation. An important point was also made in this case: faced with the claim that to allow the plaintiffs' claim would give him patent-style protection for non-patentable subject matter, it was made clear that the key distinction was that Morison was protected only against Moat, and not against the world at large.

Returning to the precise basis of the obligation, *Robb v Green*[8] is also instructive. Here the defendant secretly copied a customer list from his employer. The Court of Appeal found that this conduct was in breach of an implied contractual term, but the basis of that term was the good faith that must exist between employer and employee. Kay LJ[9] made clear that it was immaterial whether the action was founded on breach of trust or on breach of contract since in either event an injunction should be granted.

The *Spycatcher* case[10] confirms this approach. In the words of Lord Keith, '[the obligation] may exist independently of any contract on the basis of an independent equitable principle of confidence'.[11]

The equitable nature of the action appears to be an important part of its foundation with obvious consequences for anyone seeking to bring an action who has himself behaved in an unconscionable manner.

ELEMENTS OF THE ACTION

The leading modern case to formulate the ingredients of a successful action for breach of confidence is *Coco v AN Clark (Engineers) Ltd*.[12] Here, once again, what began as a co-operative venture between the parties, in respect of a new moped engine, ended in tears when the parties went their separate ways, the defendant allegedly then making use of confidential information acquired during the period of co-operation. In the High Court, Megarry J pointed to the absence of any formal contractual relationship and concluded that he was dealing with 'the pure equitable doctrine of confidence unaffected by contract'.[13] He went on to state[14] that there were three essential elements necessary in a claim for breach of confidence. First, the information must be, in itself, of a confidential character. Second, the imparting of the information must occur in circumstances or on an occasion of confidence.

8   [1895] 2 QB 315.
9   Ibid at 319.
10   *A-G v Guardian Newspapers (No 2)* [1990] 1 AC 109, [1988] 5 All ER 545.
11   Ibid at 255 and 639, per Lord Keith.
12   [1969] RPC 41.
13   Ibid at 46.
14   Ibid at 47.

Finally the information must be used in an unauthorised way and so as to cause detriment to the plaintiff. Clearly the same principles will be applicable in a contractual context, subject of course to any contrary express terms of the contract. Each of these elements will be considered in turn but the *Coco* saga should first be concluded; Megarry J held that the claim should not succeed. Although the information was passed on an 'occasion of confidence', it was not clear that the nature of the (rather vague) information was confidential, nor could the plaintiff establish clear misuse of the information.

When is information confidential?

It is clear that a very wide range of different items of information may be regarded as confidential in character. Examples include items of considerable commercial significance, such as sales lists,[15] or information of a personal and private character.[16] What these, and many other, examples have in common is that people generally would recognise that such information was not intended for the public domain and that fact alone is sufficient to give the information in question the cachet of confidentiality. It is best regarded as an objective test, dependent upon the expectations of ordinary or reasonable men[17] who will with an unerring instinct be aware that commercially valuable lists of customers or the secrets of the boardroom should not be spread beyond those persons who have to know of the facts in question. However, the cachet of confidentiality may be bestowed upon the most trivial bit of information if it is not yet in the public domain. In such cases it is sufficient that the reasonable man realises (or is told about) the confidential character of the information.[18]

A more subjective element is however imported into the equation by the decision of Megarry V-C in *Thomas Marshall (Exports) Ltd v Guinle*.[19] Here a company's managing director set up rival operations in a similar field. Unsurprisingly the company gained an injunction and it was observed that information in this type of case became confidential when the owner of the information believes that its release would be harmful to him and when he believes that it remains outside the public domain, in each case that belief being reasonable, with regard to the relevant area of activity and its practices.

15   As in *Robb v Green.*
16   Eg *Argyll v Argyll* [1967] Ch 302.
17   For an application in an employment context see *Ocular Sciences Ltd v Aspect Vision Care Ltd Geoffrey Harrison Galley v Ocular Sciences Ltd* [1997] RPC 289.
18   See *PCR Ltd v Dow Jones Telerate Ltd* [1998] FSR 170. Arguably the claim based on breach of confidence also failed in this case because the information had not been passed on on an occasion of confidence.
19   [1979] 1 Ch 227, [1978] 3 All ER 193.

This simply suggests that the decision as to whether information is confidential or not will include the beliefs of the owner of that information, but the requirement that only reasonably held beliefs are considered means that it is not likely that the subjective views of the owner of the information are likely to contradict the objective view of the reasonable man.

It is clear that the private, or at least restricted, nature of information is an essential element if it is to become confidential. In *Woodward v Hutchins*,[20] lurid revelations by a former employee of the management company of a group of pop stars under such headlines as 'Tom Jones, Superstud' could not be the subject of an injunction since several of the incidents described took place in public, for example on board an airliner. On the other hand, information may go beyond its initial source to other people, while still remaining confidential. An example of this is provided by *Stephens v Avery*.[1] In this case the plaintiff sued in relation to a newspaper story telling of her lesbian relationship with the wife of a notorious criminal. She had revealed this to a friend, who unhelpfully passed on the information to the press. It was argued that by telling her friend she had removed the label of confidentiality, but this claim did not succeed. The High Court held that information could retain its secret character even while being passed on. In the words of Sir Nicolas Browne-Wilkinson V-C,[2]

'the mere fact that two people know a secret does not mean that it is not confidential. If in fact information is secret, then in my judgment it is capable of being kept secret by the imposition of a duty of confidence on any person to whom it is communicated. Information only ceases to be capable of protection as confidential when it is in fact known to a substantial number of people.'

Further litigation has to be awaited to find out how 'substantial' this group must be.

One group of cases, now clarified by and large, appears to suggest that an action for breach of confidence may lie in respect of information which is in the public domain. This apparently contradictory notion first arose in *Terrapin Ltd v Builders Supply Co (Hayes) Ltd*.[3] The defendants made portable buildings designed by the plaintiffs and, in due course, began to sell their own buildings made to a markedly similar design. The problem for a breach of confidence action was that these buildings were widely

---

20   [1977] 2 All ER 751, [1977] 1 WLR 760.
1   [1988] Ch 449, [1988] 2 All ER 477.
2   Ibid at 454 and 481.
3   [1967] RPC 375 (High Ct), (1960) 71 RPC 128 (Court of Appeal).

available and could be inspected by anyone who so desired. However, Roxburgh J at first instance found in Terrapin's favour. He stated[4] that

> 'the essence of this branch of the law is that a person who has obtained information in confidence is not allowed to use it as a spring-board for activities detrimental to the person who made the confidential communication.'

Here the technical information disclosed while the parties were in collaboration would assist the defendants materially in making their own design of portable building. The Court of Appeal upheld the trial judge's judgment.

Likewise, in *Cranleigh Precision Engineering Ltd v Bryant*,[5] the defendant was the managing director of the plaintiff company which made and sold a unique type of swimming pool who set up his own business selling similar pools. These pools were made under an assigned Swiss patent that had been known to Bryant (but not his employer) for some years and which incorporated features of Cranleigh's pools. In spite of this information being, albeit obscurely, in the public domain, an injunction was awarded since Bryant had gained his knowledge of the Swiss patent in his capacity as managing director of Cranleigh and thus it should be regarded as confidential information. In effect, Bryant had gained a springboard which put him in a uniquely advantageous position when he set up his own business.

Speed Seal Products Ltd v Paddington[6] provides a further more recent example. The defendant had been employed by the plaintiffs on the design of oil pipe couplings, and then set up his own company in the same trade. Paddington ran the defence that the information he had used was not confidential in that it appeared in his publicity brochures and in a patent application that he had filed and was thus known to the world. This did not succeed; the first disclosure was by the defendant and this could not prevent the plaintiffs from taking action, with *Cranleigh* expressly followed.

This surprising trio of cases have now happily been reviewed by the House of Lords in the *Spycatcher* case.[7] Since it will be mentioned so often it is appropriate here to recall the basic facts of *Spycatcher*. A former British spy, Wright, produced a book detailing clearly confidential information gleaned during his career. The British Government, in this action, sought to prevent newspapers from printing extracts from it but failed, basically because the book was widely available in other jurisdictions and the

---

4   [1967] RPC 375 at 391.
5   [1964] 3 All ER 289, [1965] 1 WLR 1263.
6   [1986] 1 All ER 91, [1985] 1 WLR 1327.
7   *A-G v Guardian Newspapers (No 2)* [1990] 1 AC 109, [1988] 3 All ER 545.

information contained in the book had lost its confidential character as a result of its widespread availability. The defendant newspapers offered as one of their defences the fact that the information was no longer confidential since it was widely available for instance in the many countries where the Spycatcher book was freely available in open sale. Lord Goff of Chievely addresses the issue directly.[8] He considers the *Cranleigh* decision as being merely an example of the 'springboard' principle derived from the earlier *Terrapin* decision. He refuses to allow the case to stand as a general principle and denies that there is any rule that disclosure by a third party releases the confidant from his obligations. It then follows that *Speed Seal*, based as it is on *Cranleigh*, cannot stand either. So it seems that, after all, information must remain private and outside the public domain if it is to be subject to the obligation of confidence. Lord Goff discusses at length whether this is tantamount to allowing the holder of confidential information to rid himself of the obligation of confidence by disclosure but points to the existence of other remedies such as copyright and criminal law. He reserves his position on the question left unanswered by his analysis of *Cranleigh* viz the scope of any 'springboard' type of obligation imposed on a confider who benefits from his destruction of a confidence. This, added to the obiter character of Lord Goff's views and the failure of the other Law Lords to address the issue in detail given that they were of the view that the obligation of confidentiality was ongoing, means that a conclusive view of the law in this area cannot yet be reached.[9] The understandable reluctance of the courts to allow a confidant to benefit by breaching his confidence stands in the way of a clear unequivocal statement by the law that, as would seem sensible, information which is confidential cannot be public. The point that information which is supposed to be confidential cannot be public was however emphasised by Laddie J in a case where the element of reluctance was almost absent due to the vexatious nature of the proceedings brought by the plaintiff and the oppressive way in which these proceedings had been conducted by the plaintiff.[10]

One clear example does exist whereby confidential information ceases so to be. This is when the confider himself discloses the information, as in the 1928 case of *Mustad & Son v Allcock & Co Ltd and Dosen*[11] where an employer was held unable to sue an employee for breach of confidence once they had themselves applied for a patent thus disclosing the relevant information.

8   Ibid at 285–6 and 661–2.
9   See the Law Commission's view, Cmnd 8388, para 4.30. See also Patfield '*Attorney-General v The Observer Ltd; Attorney-General v The Times Newspapers Ltd* – The Decision of the House of Lords in the Spycatcher Litigation' [1989] EIPR 27.
10 *Ocular Sciences Ltd v Aspect Vision Care Ltd Geoffrey Harrison Galley v Ocular Sciences Ltd* [1997] RPC 289 at 368 and 373–375.
11 [1963] 3 All ER 416, [1964] 1 WLR 109.

Equally it seems clear that lapse of time may cause there to be an erosion of the obligation of confidentiality. This appears from *A-G v Jonathan Cape Ltd*,[12] the case arising from the publication of the diaries of the late Richard Crossman written when he was a Cabinet minister a decade previously. The information contained in them was held to have lost its confidentiality simply because of the years that had passed, though with due regard also paid to the nature of the information and its likely effect. Crossman's chronicling of political gossip had long lost the chance of causing any serious harm.

Finally, in looking at what is not confidential information it is worth recording the comment of Megarry J in *Coco v Clark*[13] that it is not appropriate for protection to be given to 'trivial tittle-tattle'; such matters of little consequence do not deserve the mighty protection of equity. Whether this should raise a question about the role of confidence in cases involving lesbian relationships with prisoners' wives[14] or the active sex life of an arms-dealer's wife[15] is not, it seems, the point for in these cases no such objection has been taken. In any event, information which is of commercial significance is hardly likely to fall within the category of 'tittle-tattle'.

The public interest exception

A major gap, but a justifiable one, is opened up in the law's protection of confidential information by the exception created to allow the dissemination of information where that dissemination is seen as being in the public interest. Thus the truth will come out in an appropriate case. One of the earliest cases to use this approach was *Gartside v Outram*[16] when a firm of wool-brokers sought to prevent their former sales clerk from using customer information gained by him during his period of employment, while he, in turn, alleged that their business was conducted in a fraudulent manner. It was held that, if proven, these allegations would wipe out any obligation of confidence since 'there is no confidence in the disclosure of an iniquity'.[17]

Over the years, a wide range of differing instances have been found to fall within this exception. Sometimes the exception is used where upholding confidence would have the effect of concealing evidence of wrongdoing. A

12   [1976] QB 752, [1975] 3 All ER 484.
13   [1969] RPC 41 at 48.
14   See *Stephens v Avery* at p 461 above. Sir Nicolas Browne-Wilkinson V-C said that the question could only arise at the trial and not at the interlocutory injunction stage.
15   See *Khashoggi v Smith* (1980) 124 S J 149.
16   (1856) 26 L J Ch 113.
17   Ibid at 114, per Wood V-C.

classic example is provided by *Lion Laboratories Ltd v Evans*.[18] The plaintiffs here were the manufacturers of the intoximeter device used by the police for measuring alcohol consumption by road users. The defendants were ex-employees of the firm who revealed to the press documents obtained while they were employees which indicated that the devices were erratic and unreliable. An action against them for breach of confidence failed, on the grounds that the faulty intoximeters represented a serious threat to the fair administration of justice and that it was essential to ventilate public disquiet about the accuracy of the evidence provided by the machines.

W v Egdell[19] also illustrates this area well. W was a mental patient who had been convicted of multiple manslaughter and who had been examined by the defendant. His concern at W's condition was such that he sent a copy of his report to the Home Secretary. W sued, alleging breach of confidence, the doctor-patient relationship clearly being one where an obligation of confidence can normally be expected to arise. However, the Court of Appeal found that, exceptionally, the interests of the public outweighed the interests of the patient and the doctor was justified in disclosing the report so as to minimise the chances of W being freed and thus the public being put at risk of further attacks.[20]

This case followed on from *X v Y*,[1] though here a different answer was reached. In this case two doctors were revealed in the press as sufferers from AIDS, the story being based on internal health authority documents. The paper's argument that the public had an interest in knowing of these facts was not enough to overturn the vital confidentiality of patient records and an injunction was granted to restrain the information from being published. The same vital confidentiality exists in the relationship between the police and the accused in relation to statements made by the accused under caution to the police. The information contained in those statements could only be used for the purposes for which it was provided and not for extraneous purposes.[2] It is likely that *W v Egdell* and its extreme facts will be the exception rather than the rule.

---

18   [1985] QB 526, [1984] 2 All ER 417.

19   [1990] Ch 359, [1989] 1 All ER 1089.

20   This approach was confirmed in *R v Chief Constable of the North Wales Police, ex p AB* [1998] 3 All ER 310, [1998] 3 WLR 57, where the Court of Appeal accepted that confidential police information concerning paedophiles who had served their sentences could be released to the owner of a campsite in order to allow him to take precautionary measures to safeguard the children that were to arrive on the campsite over the Easter holidays. Once more the interests of the public prevailed over the obligation of confidence.

1   [1988] 2 All ER 648.

2   *Bunn v BBC* [1998] 3 All ER 552. However, the action for breach of confidence failed in this case and no injunctive relief was granted, because the information had been read out in open court and it had also been published in a book of which 2,000 copies had already been distributed. These facts had brought the obligation of confidence to an end.

In other cases the harm cited to justify the breach of confidence may be less tangible. In *Hubbard v Vosper*,[3] the defendant left the cult of Scientology and subsequently wrote a book denouncing it which drew heavily on material issued by the cult itself. The Court of Appeal found that the disclosures were justified as revealing what Lord Denning MR described[4] as 'medical quackeries of a sort which may be dangerous if practised behind closed doors', while Megaw LJ[5] highlighted evidence that the cult was prepared to use violence against those who had criticised it.

An attractive if simplistic argument which has the effect of widening the likely scope of this exception was proposed in *Woodward v Hutchins*.[6] An ex-employee was selling stories about the private lives of rock stars, clearly in prima facie breach of his obligations of confidence. Nevertheless, the Court of Appeal found that no injunction should be granted because of the fact that the stars were keen to manage and manipulate their own images so as to appear in the best possible light, and therefore they could not object if what were presumed to be true, but less flattering, tales about them were released. In the words of Lord Denning MR,[7] as there should be 'truth in advertising', so there should be 'truth in publicity', while Bridge LJ sternly warned:[8]

'it seems to me that those who seek and welcome publicity of every kind bearing on their private lives so long as it shows them in a favourable light are in no position to complain of an invasion of their privacy by publicity which shows them in an unfavourable light.'

While not normally sympathetic to people such as the plaintiffs in this case, it may be thought harsh to offer less protection against breaches of confidence to those who are most likely to be the subject of such breaches. There seems no reason in principle why this argument should not also be used to justify breaches of confidence about heavily advertised goods or services, though it is fair to note that the approach in *Woodward* has not been expressly adopted in subsequent cases.

Just as the breach of confidence action does not extend to protect lightweight gossip, so also the public interest exception is curtailed. In *Beloff v Pressdram Ltd*,[9] the plaintiff was a senior journalist who had sent a memo to her colleagues concerning a senior government minister and allegations

3   [1972] 2 QB 84, [1972] 1 All ER 1023.
4   Ibid at 96 and 1029.
5   Ibid at 100–101 and 103.
6   [1977] 2 All ER 751, [1977] 1 WLR 760. See also *Lennon v News Group Newspapers Ltd* [1978] FSR 573.
7   Ibid at 754 and 764.
8   Ibid at 755 and 765.
9   [1973] 1 All ER 241.

of possible misconduct. This memo subsequently was reprinted in the satirical magazine *Private Eye*. The action was framed in breach of copyright, but the same principle of public interest applies there too. Ungoed-Thomas J found that the exception did not apply. This was not a case involving grave misdeeds, but was rather only the re-telling of current political gossip and, as such, did not attract the public interest exception.

Naturally, as time goes by, so do public perceptions of conduct change. This reflects itself when a court has to decide what amounts to 'iniquity'. In *Stephens v Avery*,[10] the court was faced with an attempt to use confidence to protect a story of a lesbian relationship. Sir Nicolas Browne-Wilkinson V-C took the view that there was no widespread view within society that sexual activity, even homosexual acts, between consenting adults was grossly immoral and thus appears to suggest that only universally deplored activity would count as being iniquitous for the purposes of the public interest exception.

Ironically, perhaps, *Stephens* suggests that the heart of the public interest exception, namely claims of iniquity, is diminishing in importance just as the broader exception seems to expand into an ever-increasing range of different instances. The courts seem willing to subordinate confidentiality to the public interest in a wide range of cases, with perhaps *W v Egdell*[11] the clearest indication that the rights of the public can take priority over one of the longest established relationships of confidence, that between doctor and patient. The inherent flexibility of the public interest immunity is an obvious asset in aiding its sensible and flexible use. The purpose for which the confidential information may be used will be relevant; in *Lion Laboratories*, for instance the defendants were motivated by a sense of civic responsibility and the decision may well have been different had they simply been seeking to sell the information for a personal profit.

The clash between the interests of the owner of the information in keeping it confidential and the interests of society in making it accessible in the interests of the general public may be seen as a clash between private and public interests. However, a case such as *W v Egdell* adopts the view that both of the conflicting interests are public; the interest of W in keeping his medical record to himself and his doctor is part of the general public interest in knowing that private information is able to retain its confidentiality, and the decision in the case merely reflected that one aspect of public interest in the freedom from threats of attack by W - was so important that it should take priority over the confidentiality of the relationship.

All cases where this exception comes into play have this inherent clash in them. The *Spycatcher*[12] case's facts illustrate it well. As a society, it may

10   [1988] Ch 449, [1988] 2 All ER 477. See p 461 above.
11   [1990] Ch 359, [1989] 1 All ER 1089.
12   *A-G v Guardian Newspapers (No 2)* [1990] 1 AC 109, [1988] 3 All ER 545.

be argued that we have an interest in having a secret service which is just that, so we can argue that its working should be protected by confidentiality, but equally in a democratic society we want openness so that we can learn and act upon information that the intelligence community is acting (or threatening to act) against the elected government of the country. In resolving this difficult choice, the House of Lords made one important pro-disclosure point in following the High Court of Australia in *Commonwealth of Australia v John Fairfax & Sons Ltd*[13] by ruling that a government must prove that any disclosure is harmful to the public interest, although the force of this is reduced by the assertions, particularly by Lord Keith,[14] that wholesale disclosure of information about the workings of the secret service was obviously against the public interest and far more significant than that small part of the book which suggested that there had been improprieties.

Perhaps the most pointed of clashes comes when use is sought to be made in legal proceedings of information which the law would normally regard as being confidential in character. The leading case on this is now *R v Licensing Authority, ex p Smith, Kline & French Laboratories Ltd*.[15] The statutory function of the authority is to award product licences for drugs which have been appropriately tested and proven to be safe. Smith, Kline & French had secured a licence for the drug Cimetidine and in the course of their application had revealed various items of confidential information to the authority. They were concerned that rival firms were now seeking product licences for generic versions of the same drug and that the authority would make use of, and thus possibly reveal, the information provided earlier, and so brought an action against the authority. The claim did not succeed. The House of Lords held that the statutory duty of the authority should take priority and that it had both the right and the duty to make whatever use it saw fit of all information that was available to it. This was, it must be said, not a particularly meritorious claim by Smith, Kline & French who, by making objections to the grant of licences for generic counterparts of their drug, were in effect seeking to extend the life-span of their own patent monopoly. That the interests of justice and the merits of the claim thus came together to defeat the company's claims is a pleasing coincidence.

The use of confidential information in court proceedings themselves has been at the heart of two recent cases. In *Marcel v Metropolitan Police Commissioner*,[16] the police had obtained documents from the plaintiffs under Police and Criminal Evidence Act 1984 powers. The plaintiffs then found that the defendants in a civil fraud case in which they were also plaintiffs subpoenaed the police to give evidence from the documents in question.

13   (1980) 147 CLR 39.
14   [1990] 1 AC 109 at 259, [1988] 3 All ER 545 at 642.
15   [1990] 1 AC 64, [1989] 1 All ER 578.
16   [1992] 1 All ER 72, [1992] 1 WLR 50.

The Court of Appeal held that the plaintiffs could not succeed in an action claiming that the documents contained confidential information and therefore they should not be used. While accepting that an obligation of confidentiality was imposed on the police in respect of evidence obtained pre-trial,[17] except in so far as disclosure was intended to occur for the purpose of the statute, that obligation was overcome by the subpoena issued to the police and which, equally, could have been issued against the plaintiffs if still in possession of the documents themselves. In *Hoechst UK Ltd v Chemiculture Ltd*,[18] these principles were applied when information supplied to the Health & Safety Executive was given to Hoechst who promptly used it as the basis of an Anton Piller order in trade mark and passing-off litigation against the defendants. Morritt J found that disclosure of this information, which related to use of an unauthorised pesticide, was not in breach of confidence as being within the purposes envisaged by the relevant legislation, the Food & Environment Protection Act 1985.

Thus disclosure of information otherwise confidential is quite likely to occur in legal and related proceedings. The statute may authorise disclosure for all or, more likely, limited purposes; the duty of the court or other agency may be to make the fullest use of all information before it and, finally, a subpoena will take priority.

Generally, the public interest exception is vital to the health of the action for breach of confidence. It recognises that simple assertions of secrecy or privacy do not do enough to resolve the inexorable contradiction between one person's right to confidentiality and one person's right to knowledge. The outline of the exception is to try and split situations up between the genuinely private, which can be kept secret, and the increasingly wide range of cases where the public has interests and rights too, and where confidentiality has to be curtailed. To assess whether the balance is right is not easy and risks trespassing into the domain of the right of privacy debate. But no one can deny that the public has rights too and has an interest in the outing of truth and to the extent that that right or interest is recognised, it is recognised by this exception. The balancing of the interests involved is also reflected in the provisions of the European Convention on Human Rights. On the one hand Article 8 seeks to guarantee a right of respect for an individual's private and family life, his home and his private correspondence. On the other hand there are clearly limitations to this right, as evidenced by the text of the Article itself and for example by the freedom of expression that is guaranteed by Article 10 of the Convention. This is clearly an area where further discussion and case law are bound to arise.

---

17   For the position in relation to statements made to the police during an interview under caution see *Bunn v BBC* [1998] 3 All ER 552.

18   [1993] FSR 270.

■

Equally, although some of the case law has arisen from sexual or criminal conduct, this area is also important in reminding commercial interests too that their private activity may have public interest implications. Firms such as drug or food companies may wish to keep their manufacturing problems secret, but the public may need to know about those problems. Any attempt to conceal the problems behind a cloak of confidentiality may in turn be overcome by an allegation of iniquity, as the *Lion Intoximeters* case has vividly shown.

The obligation of confidence

The second element in the action as defined by Megarry J in *Coco v Clark*[19] is the issue of what circumstances give rise to an obligation of confidentiality. This question focuses not on the nature of the information itself but on the relationship between the parties and, in particular, whether the relationship is one which should give rise to the obligation of confidentiality. Megarry J[20] makes it quite clear that the test is an objective one, with the ever-popular judicial device of the reasonable man being employed to encapsulate the appropriate tests:

> 'it seems to me that if the circumstances are such that any reasonable man standing in the shoes of the recipient of the information would have realised that upon reasonable grounds the information was being given to him in confidence, then this should suffice to impose upon him the equitable obligation of confidence.'

The judge also emphasises the independence of this element from the confidentiality of the information itself.

> 'However secret and confidential the information, there can be no binding obligation of confidence if that information is blurted out in public or is communicated in other circumstances which negative any duty of holding it confidential.'[1]

Equally, if the circumstances do support the existence of a duty of confidentiality, it will be hard for the recipient of information to deny the existence of the obligation; the type of case in this category envisaged by

19   [1969] RPC 41.
20   Ibid at 48.
1   Ibid at 47-48.

Megarry J is where information is of commercial value and is passed on in a business context such as a joint venture.[2]

Many different types of relationship may give rise to the obligation of confidence. As has just been noted, business dealings will often create obligations of confidentiality even where no contract is ultimately concluded, as in *Coco v Clark*[3] itself. On the other hand, private and personal relationships such as marriage may also create an obligation not to divulge confidences, as in *Argyll v Argyll*,[4] where the plaintiff Duchess was able to prevent her ex-husband from revealing personal matters in the tabloid press, doubtless to the regret of millions. It is obviously not sensible to list every possible relationship where the reasonable man may decree that an obligation of confidence is created, but certain types of case have given rise to frequent litigation and it is therefore appropriate to proceed by giving detailed consideration to cases arising from fiduciary relationships, contractual relationships (especially in the context of employment) and third party relationships where parties outside the initial bond of confidence are nonetheless caught up in its obligations.

Fiduciary relationships

The essence of a fiduciary relationship is that equity imposes a strong obligation on the trustee to act not in his own interests but in those of the beneficiary. The close relationship between the parties is inevitably one where information will pass between the parties and this information is likely to be regarded as confidential. The obligation can arise in a range of different cases; company directors and top managers owe a fiduciary duty to their company; professionals such as accountants and lawyers may owe fiduciary duties to their clients. A useful example is provided by *Jarman & Platt Ltd v I Barget Ltd*[5] where the plaintiff company, engaged in the reproduction furniture trade, commissioned a report on its somewhat parlous financial condition. One of the defendants, Hutchins, then the sales manager of the plaintiffs, appears to have taken the report from the desk and then circulated it to other sales representatives of the company, seemingly so as to lure them to a rival firm which Hutchins was intending to join. This was held to be a clear breach of confidence by a senior employee and was accordingly held to be actionable.

Not every fiduciary duty necessarily gives rise to liability for breach of confidence. A simple example of this is *Baker v Gibbons*[6] where a director

---

2   Ibid at 48.
3   Ibid.
4   [1967] Ch 302, [1965] 1 All ER 611.
5   [1977] FSR 260.
6   [1972] 2 All ER 759, [1972] 1 WLR 693.

of a cavity wall insulation firm set up a rival operation and solicited some of the company's agents in the hope of persuading them to transfer their allegiance to him. This was clearly contrary to his fiduciary obligations towards the company, but the action did not succeed for the simple reason that the name and addresses of the agents concerned were in the public domain and thus did not represent confidential information.

Contractual relationships

Parties to contracts are naturally free to make whatever provision is felt to be appropriate in relation to information passing as a result of the contractual nexus. It is common to expressly stipulate that information is not to be passed beyond the parameters of the contract; a good example of the potential effect of this is provided by *Exchange Telegraph Co v Gregory & Co.*[7] The plaintiffs operated a news agency service providing up-to-date share price information to its subscribers. The defendants were originally subscribers but the contract was not renewed by the plaintiffs since the Stock Exchange, the source of the information, did not want the service offered to parties such as the defendants who were 'outside brokers', not subject to the rules of the Stock Exchange. In pique, the defendants arranged to obtain the information service from another subscriber and then sold it on to their own subscribers. The terms of the plaintiffs' subscription contract included a provision that information was not to be passed on to non-subscribers. Clearly, had they been identified, the subscriber who was prepared to allow the defendants access to the service would have been liable directly for breach of contract; the defendants, as past subscribers, knew of the terms of the agreement and so knew of the confidentiality obligation and accordingly were held to be liable for infringing the plaintiffs' rights of confidentiality.

In many other cases it will be an implied term rather than an express one which is relied upon, since many contracts will only be workable if information passed under their arrangements remains confidential, for example as between doctor and patient or between the manufacturer of a new product and his advertising agency. A clear illustration is provided by *Tournier v National Provincial & Union Bank of England*[8] where the plaintiff banked with the defendants and was overdrawn. The bank kept a careful eye on Tournier's affairs, and noted that he had endorsed a cheque payable to his account over to someone else's account, this party being a bookmaker.

7   [1896] 1 QB 147.
8   [1924] 1 KB 461.

The bank accordingly rang his employer and revealed this nugget of information, resulting in his dismissal. The Court of Appeal found for Tournier; it was an implied term in the banker-customer relationship that information derived from that contract should not be disclosed by the bank, unless the law compels such a disclosure.

Just as a contract can create an obligation of confidence, so of course it can deny that obligation as the plaintiff in *Fraser v Evans*[9] discovered. He wrote a report for the Greek Government (then a military junta) on its public relations. A copy of the report found its way back to Britain, and the *Sunday Times* proposed to write an article featuring the report and making criticisms of Fraser, who objected that it was a confidential report. On examination of the contract under the terms of which the report had been written, the Court of Appeal found that while Fraser was expressly bound by an obligation of confidentiality, there was no such obligation placed on the Government of Greece. In effect they had bought the information from Fraser and were free to use it as they saw fit; if the disclosure had been unauthorised, then the Greek Government would be able to restrain publication, but they had taken no steps so to do.

The employment relationship

Particular problems arise in relation to the inevitably large amount of information of a confidential character that passes between employer and employee – information about working methods, manufacturing processes, etc. Express terms may frequently be used,[10] but it is clear that the courts in any event regard the employee as being under a duty of fidelity towards his employer and will use this to enforce the obligation of confidentiality.

The basic duty of fidelity arises throughout the course of the employment relationship, and can be far-reaching in its effect. The leading case is *Hivac Ltd v Park Royal Scientific Instruments Ltd.*[11] The plaintiffs employed Mr and Mrs Davis as production engineer and forewoman respectively at their plant which made midget valves which were in great demand during the war. The defendants started a business nearby, also making midget valves and the evidence was clear that Mr Davis had been involved in the foundation of the business, albeit only in his spare time, and Mrs Davis, who had left Hivac on health grounds, was soon well enough to work for Park Royal. They also encouraged several of their colleagues to join them in their 'moonlighting'. Hivac sought an injunction to prevent the Davis

9   [1969] 1 QB 349, [1969] 1 All ER 8.
10   Eg *Bents Brewery v Hogan* [1945] 2 All ER 570.
11   [1946] Ch 169, [1946] 1 All ER 350.

couple from working for the rival firm. The trial judge found as a fact, perhaps surprisingly, that no confidential information had been used in setting up and operating Park Royal, though it was clear that there was an ongoing risk that this would happen, for example if Hivac improved their process there would be an obvious temptation for that improvement to be made at Park Royal too. In the light of this, the Court of Appeal were prepared to award an interlocutory injunction, having regard to several other factors too. The duty of fidelity owed by an employee was said to be variable depending on the status of the employee with Morton L J[12] noting that these were skilled employees, and it was also relevant that their activities, even without (yet) breaking confidences, were clearly harmful to their employers, putting at risk the lucrative monopoly that they had enjoyed, and that those activities were carried out in a highly secretive manner was also a factor militating against the defendants.

This important decision ultimately is resolved with close reference to the specific facts of the case. However it does seem to imply that any employee who discloses confidential information is in breach of his obligations given that an injunction was awarded with reference to what was merely a risk of future disclosure, albeit a significant risk. This is illustrated too by *Printers and Finishers Ltd v Holloway*[13] where the defendant was dismissed for inviting an employee of a rival firm to inspect a testing room; indeed that employee was also the subject of an injunction preventing him from using any confidential information he may have gleaned while there.

Clearly also the more senior the employee the greater and more onerous the duty that is imposed upon him. Indeed, at the more senior end of the scale the duty is probably best regarded as fiduciary in character.[14] On the other hand, more lowly employees are less likely to be affected, as illustrated by *Nova Plastics v Froggatt*[15] where an 'odd-job man' was allowed to work for a rival in his spare time, given that there was no evidence of any harm to his main employer having occurred or even being likely. More questionable is the decision in *Laughton v Bapp Industrial Supplies Ltd*[16] where a warehouse manager and a driver used their knowledge of the company's suppliers to write to them requesting price lists and other information with a view to setting up their own competing business. It was held that their dismissals were unfair, in circumstances where they had acted in their own time and not that of the firm, and where there was no clear evidence of present or future breach of confidence by them. This seems a generous

12   Ibid at 181 and 356.
13   [1964] 3 All ER 731, [1965] 1 WLR 1.
14   *Boardman v Phipps* [1967] 2 AC 46, [1966] 3 All ER 721.
15   [1982] IRLR 146.
16   [1986] ICR 634.

decision in the light of the status of the warehouse manager within the firm and in the light of the fate of the employees in *Hivac*. However, it is clear that subsequent cases are prepared to make use of the *Laughton* decision, though on rather different facts.

In *Balston Ltd v Headline Filters Ltd*[17] an employee-director gave notice in March 1986 that he would leave in that July. He had already agreed to lease his own premises. In fact he resigned as director and ceased work in April 1986 and then moved quickly, making contact with his former employer's customers and workforce with a view to establishing a rival business. Falconer J held that there was no breach of his duties as both director and employee in respect of the minimal acts carried out prior to his resignation as a director, but that he was in breach of his employee's duty of fidelity in actively competing with the plaintiffs while still on their payroll, even though not actually working for them. *Laughton* was used as the basis of this decision and also that of *Marshall v Industrial Systems & Control Ltd*[18] where a managing director, while still in his post, made active plans to set up a rival business and contacted employees and customers of his firm to that end. His status and his actions were both the opposite of the facts of *Laughton*, which was duly distinguished, and Marshall was held to be fairly dismissed. This decision is in line with the earlier case of *Sanders v Parry*,[19] where an assistant solicitor negotiated a deal with one of the law firm's main clients whereby he was to set up on his own and handle all the client's legal work in his own right. By doing this while still employed by the firm, he was held to be clearly in breach of his implied duties of good faith and fidelity.

Taken together, these cases show an awareness that the company's whole business – its plans, its customers, its employees – is given clear protection by the law. An action for breach of confidence or the broader *Hivac*- type action for breach of fidelity duty almost has the effect of protecting the current trading activity of the business in the same way as the tort of passing-off protects its business goodwill, and it will be interesting to see whether there grows a clearer conception of what is protectable trading activity, the use of which is improper, and what is just fair competition as in *Laughton* itself. Meanwhile, the courts provide further support for the protection of trading activity by restricting the use that can be made by former employees of information gained during the period of employment.

17 [1990] FSR 385.
18 [1992] IRLR 294.
19 [1967] 2 All ER 803, [1967] 1 WLR 753.

The former employee's obligations

Once an employee has left, his duties as regard confidential information diminish but do not disappear. It may well be that the contract itself has laid down stipulations as to future conduct, perhaps restricting the nature and location of subsequent work to avoid the risk of prejudicial competition or limiting the use that may be made of information learnt during the period of employment. In imposing such terms, however, great care needs to be taken by the employer since there is a clear risk that a court will strike them down as being void for restraint of trade. This is a complex issue of contract law but, in short, the courts will uphold clauses that are seen as being legitimately necessary to protect the employer's interests while, on the other hand, seeking to preserve as far as possible free and fair competition.

However, quite irrespective of any contractual stipulations, the law of confidence may also be prepared to intervene; the leading case in this area is now *Faccenda Chicken Ltd v Fowler*.[20] Fowler was the company's sales manager and established a surprisingly successful aspect of the company's operation running a fleet of vans around the streets selling fresh chickens. On leaving the firm (he resigned after being charged with stealing company property; he was later acquitted), he set up his own business which also was to sell fresh chickens from vans in the same area. Clearly Fowler was aided by his prior knowledge of the identity and requirements of regular chicken customers and he also recruited his staff from among Faccenda's employees.

At first instance,[1] Goulding J categorised information which an employee may acquire into three types. Some information will not be regarded as confidential at all, given its easy accessibility from the public domain, and the employee is always free to disclose this – the logos used by the company would be a good example. Secondly, there is information which is confidential during the period of employment but is not after the employment has ceased, when the ex-employee is entitled to use it as part of the package of skills which he brings to the workplace; examples would include the basic manufacturing processes used or customer information remembered by the ex-employee after he has finished employment (though not lists deliberately copied during employment).[2] Thirdly is a category of information best described as a trade secret such as secret manufacturing processes - this information remains confidential even after employment has ceased.

Both Goulding J and, subsequently, the Court of Appeal ruled that Fowler had only used information in the second category and, no longer being in Faccenda's employment, was therefore at liberty to make use of it,

---

20 [1987] Ch 117, [1986] 1 All ER 617.
1   [1984] ICR 589.
2   *Robb v Green* [1895] 2 QB 315.

there being no express stipulation in his contract of employment. The Court of Appeal provided some useful guidance as to what should be regarded as a trade secret. Consideration should be given, according to Neill LJ,[3] to the nature of the employment, habitual handling of confidential information giving rise to a higher burden on the employee because its importance is more likely to be realised, the nature of the information and the aura of secrecy (or otherwise) which surrounds it, whether the employer has stressed the secret nature of the information and whether the information is separate or whether it forms an inevitable part of the employee's package of skills which he is entitled to take to his next post. On this latter matter, the Court of Appeal left open the question of whether the answer would be different had Fowler not been legitimately using his skills but simply selling the customer information to another for profit.

It is clear from *Faccenda* that the number of instances where an obligation of confidence will survive will be significantly limited, and this represents a stark contrast with the wide-ranging character of the duty of fidelity while the course of the employment continues. Subsequent case law indicates that the courts appear to be reluctant to characterise information as being in the trade secret category. In *Roger Bullivant Ltd v Ellis*,[4] a company's managing director left and set up in competition using a copy of the firm's customer card index. This was regarded as being confidential only during employment, but this was when he had misappropriated it, so it might be expected that an injunction might be awarded against him. The trial judge did so award, and the Court of Appeal agreed that this was right and rejected Ellis' argument that much of the information in the index was also in his memory. However the injunction was discharged solely on the grounds that the benefit of the information was shortlived, providing no more than a quick bounce on the springboard. In *Beverly Administration Inc v McClelland*,[5] use by former employees of figures in a company's business plan was not grounds for an injunction; the information was really little more than assumptions made in the plan and were not accurate figures of turnover and profitability and did not attain any level of protection. Some figures were in the public domain; others represented the kind of guess anyone in the relevant trade (currency exchange bureaux) would know as part of their ordinary experience of that trade. Similarly, in a case concerning contact lenses it was held that the use by the former employees-defendants of formulations within the ranges of the target figures of the plaintiff's master formulae was not a breach of confidence. This was so because every skilled man in the area would have spent a significant part of his working life

---

3   [1987] Ch 117 at 137–138, [1986] 1 All ER 617 at 626–627.
4   [1987] FSR 172.
5   [1990] FSR 505.

working with the specific class of polymers concerned and he would know how to adjust the mix of reagents in order to make the various polymers differing in their water-absorbing qualities. These things could easily be worked out on the basis of details that were in the public domain.[6] In *Mainmet Holdings v Austin*[7] too, the information used by the defendant, documenting defects in his former employer's products, was not even confidential information.

In reviewing these cases, two things are clear. Firstly the courts seem to be reluctant to hold that information is in the second category of confidentiality during the period of employment, let alone amounts to being a trade secret and thus protectable beyond the period of employment. This is good news for ex-employees who will often be free to transfer their skills, knowledge and experience to other firms without fear of legal redress, and thus good news for those enthused by free competition. The law, however, does not provide any great protection for the original employer unless he goes out of his way to expressly declare matters to be confidential in nature, thus helping them to become trade secrets. A second point is very different; several of the cases in this area of the law are notable for the length of the hearings involved, which may suggest that the courts are finding this area difficult to apply, perhaps because of the evidential difficulties of deciding what category each item of information belongs in, and in seeing what advantage, if any, has been gained by its use.

In determining whether a certain piece of information should be classified as a trade secret the courts seem to use a variant of the objective test that is generally used in relation to breach of confidence. The notional reasonable man reappears to assess what forms part of the employee's acquired general skill and knowledge which he is free to use and to distinguish that part from the information which is a trade secret. The test is whether 'the information in question can fairly be regarded as a separate part of the employee's stock of knowledge which a man of ordinary honesty and intelligence would recognise to be the property of his employer, and not his own to do as he likes with'.[8]

Restricted as the idea of the trade secret has become, it is still important to assert its value in what may be described as its 'core' area, namely that where the employer has gone out of his way to establish that secrecy of work is vital. A classic example of this is during the development work pre-dating

---

6   *Ocular Sciences Ltd v Aspect Vision Care Ltd, Geoffrey Harrison Galley v Ocular Sciences Ltd* [1997] RPC 289 at 385–386.
7   [1991] FSR 538.
8   *Ocular Sciences Ltd v Aspect Vision Care Ltd Geoffrey Harrison Galley v Ocular Sciences Ltd* [1997] RPC 289 at 371; applying *Printers & Finishers Ltd v Holloway* [1965] 1 WLR 1, [1965] RPC 239.

a patent application. Key employees will know of the vital need for secrecy even without any added reminders from the management. The employee who leaves with information vital to the proposed patent, and who prevents its registration by giving or, worse, selling such information to a rival, thus disclosing it, is an obvious example where his use of trade secrets will be grounds for an injunction. Equally, the example shows the vital importance of trade secret law in protecting the steps taken prior to the application for a patent.

Third party relationships

If I tell you some information in confidence you will be bound by that confidence. But what if you tell someone else? Can the obligation of confidentiality extend onwards to third parties? The short answer is 'Yes' and the leading case is *Saltman v Campbell*.[9] This was a 1948 decision[10] in which the plaintiffs were the owners of drawings of a type of tool used for making leather punches. They instructed another linked company, Monarch, to arrange with the defendants to manufacture tools from the drawings and the defendants did this but also retained the drawings for their own use. In finding that there had been a breach of confidence, the Court of Appeal ruled that it made no difference that the parties had not been in a direct contractual nexus, since the confidentiality of the drawings, and the rights of Saltman in respect of them were obvious to the defendants. Cases involving disclosure to newspapers also illustrate the proposition. In *Argyll v Argyll*[11] what the Duchess told the Duke, the Duke was now telling to the Sunday papers but clearly the papers were aware from the nature of the information that it was of a private and confidential character and thus they too were restrained by the confidentiality; the *Spycatcher*[12] case can be analysed in similar terms though of course the element of confidentiality had been lost by the time of hearing. Were this the first disclosure of such information its nature was such as to render it obviously confidential in character.

It must be emphasised that the third party only enters the liability picture when the information is not only known, but is also known to be of a confidential nature. *Fraser v Thames Television Ltd*[13] shows this well; the plaintiffs had the idea for a television drama series concerning the exploits

---

9   [1963] 3 All ER 413n.
10 Contemporaneously reported at (1948) 65 RPC 203.
11 [1967] Ch 302, [1965] 1 All ER 611.
12 *A-G v Guardian Newspapers (No 2)* [1990] 1 AC 109, [1988] 3 All ER 545.
13 [1984] QB 44, [1983] 2 All ER 101.

of an all-female rock group, and this was discussed confidentially with a scriptwriter, who discussed it with a producer and Thames themselves were fully aware of these discussions. The project did not proceed but shortly afterwards the producer, scriptwriter and Thames collaborated on a series called *Rock Follies*, which closely resembled the plaintiffs' original proposal. All were held liable for breach of confidence because at every stage both the identity of the originators of the proposal and the need for confidentiality were clearly known and therefore all the defendants were aware of those matters and thus in breach of their obligations. The case is also a useful reminder of a point made at the outset of this chapter: no final scripts were ever produced by the plaintiffs being still at the ideas stage, so no copyright protection could exist. However, the ideas stage was protectable by an action for breach of confidence.

Particular difficulty is caused by unauthorised acquisition of confidential information by a third party: the two main cases involve information gained by the use of unauthorised telephone tapping, and do not appear to tell a consistent tale so consideration must be given to both *Malone v Metropolitan Police Comr*[14] and *Francome v Mirror Group Newspapers*.[15] In *Malone* the prosecution in a handling stolen goods case made use of authorised phone taps by the police and the plaintiff applied to the courts for a declaration that use of the taps was unlawful. This Megarry V-C refused to give. In discussing whether a breach of confidence had occurred, he stated[16] that in any situation a speaker had to recognise that there is a risk of an unknown person overhearing the conversation and that in the case of telephone calls there is always the risk of being overheard by a crossed line or by a deliberate tapping of the telephone; in such cases the speaker takes the risk that any confidences which he divulges may be intercepted and no obligation of confidence is created on that third party. In any event, in such a case as *Malone* it may well be that the public interest in the revelation of iniquity would in any event overcome the obligation of confidentiality.

In *Francome* the facts were rather different. The plaintiff was a well-known jockey whose phone was tapped by an unknown party. The tap appeared to reveal evidence that Francome was breaching various rules of the racing business and the recordings made were made available to the *Daily Mirror* with a view to making their contents public. This time an interlocutory injunction was granted restraining publication of the recordings on the grounds that there appeared to be a breach of confidence, and any suggestion that the public interest defence was relevant could be dealt with at a subsequent full trial.

14 [1979] Ch 344, [1979] 2 All ER 620.
15 [1984] 2 All ER 408, [1984] 1 WLR 892.
16 [1979] Ch 344 at 376, [1979] 2 All ER 620 at 633-4. There are significant differences between the two reports.

It is possible to reconcile these two decisions, either by pointing to *Francome* as being purely an interlocutory proceeding and thus easy to distinguish, or to *Malone* as hinging on a remedies point as discussed later in this chapter, or, more satisfactorily, by emphasising, as was done in *Francome*, the words of Megarry V-C in *Malone*[17] that he was only seeking to lay down principles to govern the use of authorised police phone taps in criminal proceedings and did not purport to be dealing with other categories of cases. This is a convenient let-out but is surely not satisfactory. The basis of *Malone* is clearly flawed. While it is acceptable to argue that there is a risk of any conversation being overheard, it does not in any way follow logically from this that any hearer should be freed automatically from an obligation to help the information gleaned stay confidential. The basic approach in cases of third parties from *Saltman v Campbell*[18] onwards is that a third party is bound if he receives confidential information in circumstances where he is aware of that confidentiality. If you overhear me and my counsellor discussing my private sexual problems you will realise that this is confidential information and will become enveloped in the web of confidence that already binds me and my counsellor. It surely makes matters worse not better for the third party if the information is gained not by an inadvertent overhearing but by a deliberate telephone tap. And this is not a charter for criminals; if my statements include confessions of criminal behaviour, it is clear that the defence of iniquity will act to justify the breach of confidence, as shown by the practice of reputable film developers of disclosing to the police photographs they develop which appear to show evidence of illegal conduct. *Malone* does not sit within the general principles of third party confidentiality, does provide a quite unnecessary breach in the web of confidence that protects individuals, and should be regarded as incorrectly decided.

When an occasion is one of confidence an obligation is created. Overall, the law has developed clear guidelines to deal with the principal examples of such an occasion and the attempts to balance free access to and use of information which have clearly been made by the law have generally reached an acceptable compromise. However, it should always be borne in mind that these are merely examples of the general principle, and that the judicial cypher of the reasonable man is always at hand to vary the balance, particularly in novel situations.

---

17   Ibid at 384 and 651.
18   [1963] 3 All ER 413n.

■   ■

Unauthorised use of confidential information

Several elements come together at this stage of the definition. Firstly, and obviously, there has to be use of the information but it is clear that not every use will be sufficient. In *Amber Size & Chemical Co Ltd v Menzel*,[19] the defendant was an ex-employee who had been misusing a trade secret in his subsequent employment. The trade secret in question was a scientific process involving various materials, the proportions as between them, the density of the ensuing mixture and the timing of the operation. Menzel knew which materials were involved, but did not know the proportions and density precisely. However, he knew that the plaintiffs used a particular type of hydrometer in the process, and this, coupled with his knowledge of the materials and the timing, were brought to bear in his new employment. The High Court found that this was enough to ground a breach of confidence action; Menzel had been aware of the principal features of the process and he and his new employers were expecting him to be able to recreate the process from his stolen knowledge, even though not all the details were known to him. It seems to follow from this that use of a minor or unimportant part of the information may not ground a breach of confidence action, but that might seem to dent the protection afforded by the law to confidentiality. A better view may be to assume that the approach in *Amber Size* was calculated to consider merely whether it was usable information that the plaintiff had acquired. On this basis, too, *Fraser v Thames Television Ltd*[20] is also explicable; the mere idea of a drama series about a female rock group may not have been usable as such, but considerable plot and character development had taken place and this was directly used in the subsequent unauthorised (by the plaintiffs) programme.

Next it is important to note that the law does not seek to concern itself with the way in which the information is used and, in particular, with the state of mind of the person using, or rather misusing, the information. In other words, the law will intervene to protect not only deliberate but also innocent uses of confidential information. This is important because often it will be tempting for the user to claim that the use of information is subconscious or coincidental. To adapt the facts of *Fraser v Thames*, it would be easy for someone in the position of the defendants to say, 'Yes, now you mention it I do recall a conversation about a female rock group series; it must have been lurking at the back of my mind all this time', but the law will still act to control such apparently innocent uses of confidential information.

---

19   [1913] 2 Ch 239.
20   [1984] QB 44, [1983] 2 All ER 101. See above at p 479.

The clearest example of this is provided by the decision of the Court of Appeal in *Seager v Copydex Ltd (No 1)*,[1] when scandal and intrigue rocked the world of stair carpet grip manufacture. Seager designed a new type of stair carpet grip and he and the defendants discussed its possible manufacture to no avail. Soon after this, the defendant company produced a new type of stair carpet grip which embodied the key design features of Seager's grip, though not so as to infringe Seager's patent. The name used, 'Invisigrip', had also been suggested by Seager. However, the company claimed that it was all their own work; the court took the view that this was subconscious copying and so found in Seager's favour, awarding him damages.

The latter aspect is not entirely compatible with the case of *Nichrotherm Electrical Company Ltd v Percy*.[2] This was a dispute about a machine for artificially rearing pigs. It was a notably unsuccessful machine but this was no bar to (indeed the possible cause of) litigation. The defendant was found to have misused the plaintiffs' confidential information in making his own rival and equally unsuccessful pig rearing machine but the problem arose that the second defendants gave Percy the plaintiffs' plans for the machine, apparently in innocence, they having received them from the plaintiffs, with a view to their involvement in the manufacture of the devices. In the view of Harman J at first instance, the second defendants were liable in breach of confidence, but their innocence should mean that they were not obliged to pay damages, thus presumably suggesting that an innocent breach of confidence is only remediable by an injunction if appropriate.[3] Since only Percy appealed, the Court of Appeal gave no consideration to the position of the second defendant.

Nichrotherm was not considered in *Seager*, and the latter case bears the stamp of the Court of Appeal's authority. It may also be suggested that *Nichrotherm* is not entirely compatible with the provisions in Lord Cairns' Act 1858 which allows a court to award damages in its equitable jurisdiction 'in lieu of or in addition to' an injunction; at best Harman J was not willing to exercise this discretion. In any event the fact that Harman J nevertheless ordered an inquiry into damages against both defendants suggests that there was some confusion present and it is suggested that *Seager* is the more reliable authority at least where there has been a change of position following the innocent use of the confidential information.

Sometimes an issue arises as to whether the use of the confidential material is unauthorised. This happens particularly where the confidential information is the result of a joint effort and the alleged breach of confidence

---

1   [1967] 2 All ER 415, [1967] 1 WLR 923.
2   [1956] RPC 272 (High Ct), [1957] RPC 207 (Ct of Appeal).
3   Such an injunction was awarded by Cross J in *National Broach & Machine Co v Churchill Gear Machines Ltd* [1965] RPC 61.

is committed by one or more members of the team that put in the joint effort. Typically the plaintiff is a member of the team that did not authorise the use that was made of the information. *Murray v Yorkshire Fund Managers Ltd*[4] was such a case. Mr Murray had contributed a vital section on marketing to a business plan that was drafted by a team of people that sought to take over a company. At a later stage Mr Murray had been excluded from the team. Nevertheless, the takeover went ahead on the basis of the business plan and Mr Murray sued for breach of confidence. He argued that his section on marketing was protected by an obligation of confidence and that unauthorised use had been made of the information. The action failed in the Court of Appeal, because the Court ruled that there had been no unauthorised use of the information. Nourse LJ relied on a dictum of Kekewich J in *Heyl-Dia v Edmunds*[5] when he considered that when a team of people had collaborated in the production of confidential information, they were co-owners of it, and in the absence of any contractual restraint, each co-owner was free to deal with the information.[6] In this case it meant that Mr Murray's former partners were free to use all of the confidential information when they took over the company, because they were the co-owners of the property right in the information. This outcome is perfectly acceptable in the sense that a single person should not be given a veto over the use of the confidential information in such a situation. That would be an abusive use of the law of confidence. Such a person should rather pursue an action in restitution for the value of his contribution. On the other hand though, the outcome raises some questions concerning the nature of the action for breach of confidence. The Court of Appeal treated information as property and drew parallels with co-ownership cases concerning patents and the proprietary aspects of the latter. This may have provided a neat solution in this case, but clearly one cannot simply ignore the equitable nature of the action for breach of confidence. It is hard to see how on this point *Murray v Yorkshire Fund Managers Ltd*[7] could have provided the final and conclusive answer.

The final element that makes up this head of the law of confidentiality is the question of whether the plaintiff has to suffer a detriment as a result of the breach of confidence. Clearly the presence of such detriment is of great assistance in a case where damages are sought and its presence will strengthen the case for an injunction, but is it essential? Certainly Megarry J in *Coco v AN Clark Engineers Ltd*[8] referred to detriment as being part of

4   [1998] 2 All ER 1015.
5   (1899) 81 LT 579 at 580.
6   *Murray v Yorkshire Fund Managers Ltd* [1998] 2 All ER 1015.
7   Ibid. We are grateful to our colleague Professor Mark Thompson for letting us have a copy of his note on this case, which will in due course appear in the *Conveyancer*.
8   [1969] RPC 41 at 48.

the definition of the breach of confidence action, though he accepted there may be arguments for a broader approach to the action without the requirement of detriment. The issue has been discussed in two significant recent cases.

In *X v Y*[9] discussion on the point was obiter because the doctors who were the subjects of the newspaper story about doctors with AIDS did suffer detriment, in the form of distress caused by the unwarranted intrusion into their lives of reporters in hot pursuit of the story. Nonetheless Rose J addressed the issue and concluded that detriment in the use of the information was unnecessary and that an injunction at least could be awarded where there was no actual or likely detriment. He emphasised[10] that the cause of action related to the initial disclosure and not the subsequent publication which was the effective cause of the distress suffered.

In *Spycatcher*[11] too, the issue is considered but a less than clear picture emerges. The failure of the Government to restrain the publication of extracts from the book could be seen as reflecting the lack of detriment due to the pre-existing wide knowledge of the book and its contents. However, this factor simultaneously removed the confidentiality of the information itself and it is not therefore clear evidence for the essential role of detriment. Lord Keith[12] took the view that the disclosure of that which was intended to be kept a secret was itself a detriment, so there would thus always be a detriment present, neatly sidestepping the question, though he adds that in a case brought by the Government harm to the public interest must be demonstrated anyway. Lord Griffiths adopted[13] the *Coco* test as his basic definition and thus appeared to embrace detriment as being essential, and agreed with Lord Keith on the special position in claims by government. Lord Goff[14] felt that it was still an open question.

In attempting to resolve this conundrum, the first thing to reiterate is the value of detriment in strengthening a claim, whether for damages or for an injunction. Beyond this, it is tempting to follow Rose J and deny the vital nature of detriment in a breach of confidence action. This would help in cases where confidential information about two people is to be leaked, where it would disclose negative information about one, who may therefore be reluctant to take the public action of litigation, but would still permit the other to take action. If a police document is about to be leaked, revealing that A & B have been questioned about a murder and A's answers were satisfactory and B's were not, A suffers no detriment by its disclosure yet

9   [1988] 2 All ER 648. See above at p 465.
10 Ibid at 658.
11 *A-G v Guardian Newspapers (No 2)* [1990] 1 AC 109, [1988] 3 All ER 545.
12 Ibid at 256 and 640.
13 Ibid at 269-270 and 650-651.
14 Ibid at 282 and 659.

clearly still ought to have a right of action. The same conclusion can of course be reached courtesy of Lord Keith's intellectual acrobatics and the tentative conclusion is offered that no detriment beyond that created by the fact of disclosure per se is necessary to be proven in bringing a breach of confidence action and that, in particular, this should justify injunctive relief with substantial damages available if greater harm ensues.

REMEDIES FOR BREACH OF CONFIDENCE

Injunctions

Little needs to be said here about injunctive relief; the law and practice in relation to breach of confidence is in most ways no different from that in other areas of intellectual property and the general coverage of remedies in Chapter 29 is fully relevant here. However, Megarry J in *Coco v Clark*[15] laid down some guidelines as to factors which may be relevant in exercising the discretion whether or not to issue an injunction in actions of this type and suggests that damages alone may suffice in a case of subconscious copying (as in *Seager* two years earlier). He also suggests that the use made by the defendant in reliance on the information may make an injunction to restore the status quo difficult (if not impossible) to award. Clearly in business-related cases, it may be relatively easier to award damages rather than an injunction since the damage may be readily quantifiable where, say, business has been lost, as opposed to cases involving personally confidential matter, where the distress caused by the disclosure will be far harder to quantify, and injunctive relief thus more appropriate. Nevertheless, injunctive relief may still be an appropriate remedy in commercial cases, especially if pre-empting the defendants (often former employees in this case) from disclosing the confidential information is the vital aim of the case.[16]

Damages

In considering the award of damages in an action for breach of confidence, the first question to consider is what is the precise nature of the action. Where the breach of confidence is also a breach of an express or implied term of a contract, an award of damages is appropriate and should be based on the standard contractual principles on which those damages are assessed,

---

15   [1969] RPC 41 at 49 and 50.
16   See *Ocular Sciences Ltd v Aspect Vision Care Ltd, Geoffrey Harrison Galley v Ocular Sciences Ltd* [1997] RPC 289 at 409.

as in *Nichrotherm Electrical Company Ltd v Percy*.[17] Where the action is not based on contract but on the more general equitable principle of confidence, it is clear that damages may also be awarded under the modern successor to Lord Cairns' Act, section 50 of the Supreme Court Act 1981. This permits the court to award damages 'in addition to, or in substitution for, an injunction' in any cases where the court has the 'jurisdiction to entertain an application for an injunction' and leaves no doubt that damages can be awarded in any case: there is no need for any injunction claim to succeed, merely for it to fall within the jurisdiction of the court.[18]

This then raises the question of the way in which these non-contractual damages will be awarded. An answer is provided by a return to the torrid world of stair carpet grip manufacture in *Seager v Copydex (No 2)*.[19] This hearing followed the first case in which it was held that damages should be paid for unconscious copying, since the parties could not agree on an appropriate measure. Lord Denning MR[20] drew an analogy with damages for conversion, where damages are paid reflecting the value of the goods stolen. Here too information has effectively been stolen and so the court has to place a value on it. This can be done in one of two alternative ways. If the information is ordinary confidential information which could be obtained by the use of the services of an expert consultant, then the measure of damages should be the cost of using such a consultant for that is in effect the cost of the information. If, however, the information has a special character and was so inventive or otherwise unusual that no consultant would be likely to be able to provide such information the value of it is what it would receive if sold on the open market between a willing seller and a willing buyer or, perhaps, based on what royalties may be gained by exploitation of the information, though this would have the side-effect of legitimising the acquisition of the information by the defendant.

This approach is not without its problems. Though claiming to be tortious in approach, the focus seems to be not so much on the plaintiff's loss, as is usual in tort, but on the defendant's gain, making the claim more quasi-contractual in character.[1] The *de jure* approval of the defendant's de facto acquisition of the information may also be harsh on a plaintiff who may still want to exploit the information himself. The fact that the Court of Appeal remitted the application of these principles back to the court of first instance is not helpful to understanding their precise operation.

---

17   [1957] RPC 207.
18   Megarry V-C in *Malone v Metropolitan Police Comr* [1979] Ch 344 at 360, [1979] 2 All ER 620 at 633.
19   [1969] 2 All ER 718, [1969] 1 WLR 809.
20   Ibid at 719 and 813.
1   See Jones 'Restitution of Benefits Obtained in Breach of Another's Confidence' (1970) 86 LQR 463.

■

A particular problem in assessing damages in breach of confidence actions arises in cases where it is not clear what proportion of the defendant's subsequent trade is due to the misuse of the information and what is due to other factors, such as his own efforts, contract, reputation, etc. This was the problem in *Universal Thermosensors Ltd v Hibben*.[2] The defendants left their employment with the plaintiffs to set up a rival business. They took customer information and other documents away with them. This was clearly in breach of their obligations of confidentiality, but since there was no contractual bar on their setting up a rival business and since they were not using any trade secrets and given that they were free to use contacts and other information within their own memories, the rest of their activity was legal. The plaintiffs argued, however, that all the business of the defendants was irrebuttably presumed to be due to the misuse of the confidential information. This was not accepted by Sir Donald Nicholls V-C. Each item of business was to be looked at separately to see whether the profits were gained by use of the information though. The use of common sense might suggest that it was more likely that contracts were made through use of a list of customers deliberately stolen for that purpose than through memory (why else steal the list?). Indeed, generally doubts would tend to be resolved in the plaintiff's favour. However, applying these principles to the facts, the judge found that only one minor contract was due to misuse of the secret information and the plaintiff's claim for over £36,000 in damages was reduced finally to £18,610 – scant reward for five weeks in court and a reflection of the fact that the plaintiff had to show both that the defendants had made contracts using the plaintiff's information *and* that they would not otherwise have gained the contracts themselves.[3]

Other equitable remedies

The equitable character of the breach of confidence action means that the range of equitable remedies is also available to the plaintiff. Most significant amongst these is the action for an account of profits, whereby the plaintiffs can simply demand that the profits made by the defendant after the acquisition of the confidential information are handed over. This is the essence of the claim in *Peter Pan Manufacturing Corp v Corsets Silhouette Ltd*.[4] Peter Pan licensed Silhouette to make on their behalf a then new design

---

2   [1992] 3 All ER 257, [1992] 1 WLR 840.

3   The defendants successfully counterclaimed for £20,000 for losses suffered by them due to the excessive breadth of the interlocutory injunction awarded to the plaintiffs and the consequent harm to their business.

4   [1963] 3 All ER 402, [1964] 1 WLR 96.

of women's brassieres. After a while Silhouette used diagrams and examples provided under the licensing agreement to make similar garments to their own account. The obvious problem is again to what extend did the breach of confidence contribute to the profits made by Silhouette. Pennycuick J accepted the principle that the account should only be of that proportion of the profits attributable to the breach of confidence but on the facts of the case he found that the manufacture of the garments by Silhouette would have been entirely impossible without the information, reflecting presumably the quantum leap forward that *Peter Pan* had taken with this new type of garment, and in the light of this the entire profits made on the products in question should be passed to Peter Pan.

In *Spycatcher*,[5] an account of profits was allowed by the House of Lords in favour of the Government as owner of the information against the *Sunday Times* who ran extracts from the offending book. However this award begs the kind of questions just raised. Fearing an injunction, no prior publicity was given to the fact that the extracts were to be published; indeed the first edition did not include them in case an injunction was promptly obtained. It is far from easy to calculate what proportion, if any at all, of the profits of that edition, which of course carried hundreds of articles and advertisements, was due to the unlawful publication of the confidential information.

It is worthwhile noting that other possible remedies that may be available include orders for delivery up and/or destruction of goods which have been made by virtue of unauthorised confidential information;[6] such orders were appropriately made in the *Peter Pan* case, but again this must hinge on the fact that no such manufacture could possibly have taken place, but for the misuse of the plaintiff's confidential information.[7]

INFORMATION - THE INTERNATIONAL DIMENSION

This whole area of confidential information has been regarded as very much the creation of the common law or, rather, of equity. But here too the internationalisation of the law of intellectual property is now having its impact. Two separate developments need to be noted. Firstly, the problems

---

5   *A-G v Guardian Newspapers (No 2)* [1990] 1 AC 109, [1988] 3 All ER 545.
6   *Ocular Sciences Ltd v Aspect Vision Care Ltd, Geoffrey Harrison Galley v Ocular Sciences Ltd* [1997] RPC 289 at 410.
7   Ibid. However, that case also illustrates the point that all legitimate interests of all parties will need to be balanced carefully before these remedies are awarded in all cases where the defendant's activity is not in every single detail based on misuse of the confidential information.

of patent licensing in EU law, discussed earlier, spill over to information which is not in itself patentable but which may be essential to the operation of the patented product or process or for the most economical manner for using a patented process. Examples might be the instructions for the best possible use of a patented machine. A block exemption on such know-how was created alongside the block exemption on patent licensing[8] and these have now been fused together into the technology transfer block exemption discussed previously.[9] It is important to note that know-how type information and the patented product or process are inherently distinct legal notions but, that said, the controls on their use and dissemination are now the same.

The second development that needs noting is that the TRIPs agreement also extends to cover trade secrets,[10] this phrase not equating to the same words in the domestic law, but rather, again, relating to the know-how type of information. Signatory states have to ensure that such information is given an appropriate level of legal protection.

Further problems arise due to the fact that confidential information is protected in different national ways in each country. No international level of protection exists. On the other hand the use of international communication networks such as the internet substantially facilitated and increased the international and cross-border flow of (confidential) information. Which court will have jurisdiction to deal with actions concerning breach of confidence or any equivalent action and which law will be applied by that court? These formidable questions of private international law remain to be answered and a solution is urgently needed.[11]

CONFIDENCE – AN OVERVIEW

Information is not property,[12] at least for the purposes of the criminal law. That said, the law of breach of confidence has, as it has developed, gone forward to construct a network of rights and duties which protect information and its owners. Once the information crosses the threshold of

---

8   Regulation 2349/84 on the application of Article 85(3) of the Treaty to certain categories of patent licensing agreements, (1984) OJ 219/15 as amended and Regulation 556/89 on the application of Article 85(3) of the Treaty to certain categories of know-how licensing agreements, (1989) OJ L61/1, as amended.
9   Commission Regulation (EEC) 240/96 on the application of Article 85(3) to certain categories of technology transfer agreements (1996) OJ L31/2.
10   See further JJ Fawcett and P Torremans *Intellectual Property and Private International Law* Clarendon Press (1998).
11   Part II, Section 7, Article 39 of the TRIPs Agreement [1994] 25 11C 209-237, at 224.
12   *Oxford v Moss* (1978) 68 Cr App Rep 183.

confidentiality and is transmitted on what we have described as an occasion of confidence that protection is attained. In defining what is confidential, the law is defining the boundaries of truth which is protected from revelation, and in drawing this line it is setting out the balance between the right of the individual or firm to keep a secret and the right of the public at large. Whether this balance is correctly drawn is ultimately a matter for the individual reader, but the existence and importance of the public interest defence is of significance on the side of the public's right to know, vital in an open and democratic society. If information does not fall within this exception, then it has almost tangible form in the range of rights and remedies open to its owner against those who abuse its confidential character.

The employment cases create variants on this information right. Trade secrets are the subject of strong protection and increasingly appear to be part of a company's property but cases such as *Hivac Ltd v Park Royal Scientific Instruments*[13] show a broader legal recognition and protection of a wider range of trading activity, while in non-trade secret cases, it seems that it is the employee who is allowed to transfer skills and knowledge from one job to the next as part of his repertoire, and he cannot be restrained by his former employer from so doing. So the employee too gains new intangible rights from the developing law of breach of confidence, and all these rights have the potential to grow into more tangible forms in years to come, if that is the way the law wishes to progress; legal history shows that such rights can develop slowly but inexorably if there is a perceived need for them so to do. As more and more information becomes available, through the evolution of time and the revolution of technology, it may be that such a need will be perceived: this is not a prediction so much as an awareness of future potential of what may lie at the end of the information superhighway down which we inexorably surf.

It may be that trade secret and confidentiality law will evolve into some form of 'right in information'.[14] It will be encouraged to do this while a common law action can arise without the need to resort to expensive, yet limited term, patent or trade mark protection but can protect the essential secrets underlying those property rights. It seems an obvious area for the potential development of a yet stronger new right in due course.

Meanwhile actions for breach of confidence can already be clearly seen as filling the gaps between longstanding rights. Copyright could not protect the idea for *Rock Follies* but confidence could. Patent law could not protect

---

13 [1946] Ch 169, [1946] 1 All ER 350.
14 See Reichman 'Legal Hybrids between the Patent and Copyright Paradigms' (1994) 94 Col LR 2432, and critiques thereof at ibid 2559 et seq.

Nichrotherm's hopeless pig-rearing machine, but confidence could. In these and many other cases it is at the difficult early stages of a project, where a formal intellectual property right is a target, but one that has yet to be achieved, that rights in confidential information may have their most valuable role to play.

Chapter 26

Computer technology and intellectual property

The relationship between computer technology and intellectual property is a complicated issue and a huge number of theoretical and practical problems arise in relation to it. It is not our intention to go into much detail here.[1] Our analysis will focus on the headlines and we will accordingly discuss five issues:

– the availability of patent protection for computer hardware and for computer software (computer programs),
– copyright in computer software,
– databases and the sui generis right,
– the internet, and
– semiconductor chip protection.

It should be emphasised that the protection for databases also involves copyright. That aspect was already referred to in the chapters on copyright and not all the details will be restated here. Most databases are nowadays in electronic form, hence our decision to discuss them in the computer technology chapter. However, the regime of protection for databases also extends to non-electronic databases (eg those based on paper supports).

PATENT PROTECTION FOR COMPUTER TECHNOLOGY

Hardware

It is obvious, but nevertheless important to note, that the normal requirements of patent law will apply in this area. In other words, any piece

---

1   We refer the reader to the specialised works on computer law and information technology law.

of computer equipment has to be new, involve an inventive step and has to be capable of industrial application if it is to attract patent protection. This does not create specific problems, although the number of patents granted is in relative terms rather low because most developments in computer hardware are constant minor improvements of existing technology and though they are new they do not involve an inventive step and are obvious.

Software[2]

More difficulties arise when one attempts to determine whether a computer program can attract patent protection. The starting point seems rather easy as s 1(2)(c) of the Patents Act 1977 explicitly excludes computer programs. It is not entirely correct to conclude though that a computer program will never be patentable as the exclusion is restricted to a computer program as such. This means that patents cannot be granted for the computer program alone and this rule applies irrespective of the content of the program. For patentability purposes the invention must comprise something else apart from the computer program. It must be a computer-related invention.

Various attempts were made to patent software incorporated in a ROM chip[3], as a piece of hardware, or recorded on any other carrier, such as a floppy disk as a software carrier. They were all unsuccessful on the grounds that the applications involved nothing else than the computer program as such.

'The disc or ROM is no more than an established type of artefact in which the instructions are physically embedded. It is merely the vehicle used for carrying them.'[4]

It would indeed make no sense at all to exclude a computer program from the scope of patent law and allow it back in in the form of a floppy disc containing the very same program.[5] The same conclusion is normally reached when a computer program is loaded into a computer as it would deprive the computer software exclusion of any practical sense if a non-patentable program whose only conceivable use it is to run on a computer would become patentable if the claims made reference to conventional hardware elements.[6]

2   For a detailed analysis see I Lloyd *Information Technology Law* Butterworths (2nd edn, 1997) Ch 18 and Dworkin 'The patentability of computer software' in C Reed (ed) *Computer Law* Blackstone (2nd edn, 1993) Ch 5.
3   *Gale's Application* [1991] RPC 305.
4   *Gale's Application* [1991] RPC 305 at 325, per Nicholls LJ.
5   See *Genentech Inc's Patent* [1989] RPC 147, per Dillon LJ.
6   See *IBM/Documents abstracting and retrieving* (T22/85) [1990] EPOR 98 and *IBM/ Text processing* (T65/86) [1990] EPOR 181.

Computer-related inventions are not excluded from the scope of patentability though. This category is extremely wide in scope, as more and more new inventions involve the use of some software, which is incorporated in the device. For example, production line robots are instructed through the use of a computer program and all kinds of engines, from the one in your car to the ones that move the lens and the film in your camera, are controlled by computer software. As long as a technical effect is produced and a technical problem is solved the exclusion of a computer program as such no longer applies and the invention might be patentable. An example of this approach is found in the *Vicom* case[7] where the patent application was concerned with a method and apparatus for improving the quality of pictures and speeding up their processing. All this was guided by a computer program, but the technical invention produced a technical effect on the pictures and was thus patentable. One should look at the invention as a whole[8] in assessing whether a technical effect occurs and it is the question whether the whole invention as a combination between a computer program and all other elements is patentable which is at issue. It is also not relevant when the technical effect occurs and there is no need to balance the technical features of the invention against the non-technical features of it. If these requirements are met a software-related invention may be patentable if it meets the other standard requirements for patentability.[9] The focus of all attention is therefore placed on what the claimed invention achieves rather than on the manner in which it achieves it.

It must be emphasised though that the courts seem to apply the exclusion test twice. The exclusion does also apply if a technical effect is produced, but only if that effect or result is itself caught by the exclusion. This means that what is produced is a prohibited item under s 1(2). A clear illustration is found in Merrill Lynch's application for a patent for a business system and specifically for an improved data processing system for implementing an automated trading market for securities. It was said that

'[…] whatever the technical advance may be, is simply the production of a trading system. It is a data processing system for doing a specific business, that is to say making a trading market in securities. The end result, therefore, is simply "a method […] of doing business", and is excluded by section 1(2)(c) […] A data processing system operating to produce a novel technical result would normally be patentable. But it cannot, it seems to me, be patentable if the result itself is a prohibited item under s 1(2). In the present case it is such a prohibited item.'[10]

7   *Vicom Systems Inc's Application* (T–208/84) [1987] 2 EPOR 74.
8   *Koch & Sterzel/X-ray apparatus* (T–26/86) [1988] EPOR 72 and *Merrill Lynch's Application* [1988] RPC 1.
9   See Kolle 'Patentability of Software-Related Inventions' (1991) 22 IIC 660.
10 *Merrill Lynch's Application* [1989] RPC 561 at 569.

Merill Lynch's application failed on the second application of the test, even though there was a technical effect.

The position on the issue of patents for software was subsequently summarised neatly in the case of *Fujitsu's application*.[11] The patent application concerned crystal structures that could be depicted and manipulated on a computer screen by chemists through the use of virtual reality, replacing the use of three-dimensional lattices. The application was turned down for lack of a technical effect. Laddie J summarised the general position as follows at first instance:

'1. The types of subject-matter referred to in s 1(2) are excluded from patentability as a matter of policy. This is so whether the matter is technical or not.

2. The exclusion from patentability is a matter of substance, not form. Therefore the exclusion under section 1(2) extends to any form of passive carrier or recording of excluded subject matter. Thus, merely because a piece of paper is in principle patentable (safe to the extent that it lacks novelty), it is not permissible, for example, to record a literary work (s 1(2)(b)) or a computer program (s 1(2)(C)) on a piece of paper and then seek patent monopoly for the paper bearing the recorded work. Similarly, it is not permissible, without more, to seek protection for a computer program when it is stored on a magnetic medium or when merely loaded into a computer.

3. Prima facie a computer running under the control of one program is a different piece of apparatus from the same computer when running under the control of another program. It follows that a claim to a computer when controlled by a program or to a method of controlling a computer by a program or to a method of carrying out a process by use of a computer so controlled can be the subject of patent protection. However, because the court is concerned with substance, not form, it is not enough for the designer of a new program to seek protection for his creation merely by framing it in one of these terms. The court or patent office has to direct its intention not to the fact that the program is controlling the computer, but to what the computer, so controlled, is doing.

4. Therefore, a data processing system operating to produce a novel result would not be deprived of protection on the ground that it was a program as such. On the other hand, even if the effect of the program is to make the computer perform in a novel way, it is still necessary to look at precisely what a computer is doing, ie at the nature of the process being carried out. If all that is being done, as a matter of substance, is the

11   [1996] RPC 511 (High Court) and (1997) Times, 14 March.

performance of one of the activities defined under s 1(2) as unprotectable, then it is still unprotectable.'

COPYRIGHT PROTECTION FOR COMPUTER SOFTWARE

Preliminary issues

The drafters of the Copyright, Designs and Patents Act 1988 included computer programs in the category of literary works.[12] We outlined the provisions of the 1988 Act that apply to literary works in Chapter 9 and we do not intend to repeat them here. These normal copyright rules simply apply to computer programs. We will only highlight specific provisions and the troublesome application of some copyright provisions in relation to computer programs.

The 1988 Act does not define computer programs. This allows for the necessary amount of flexibility in a fast developing area, where technological evolutions outdate definitions rapidly. In general terms it can be said that a computer program is a series of coded instructions which are intended to bring about a particular result when used in a computer.[13] Most computer programs are first written in high level programming languages, such as COBOL, which bear a fair amount of similarity with normal languages, before they are compiled into machine code in order to allow the computer to run them. This machine code is in binary form – the well known collection of 0s and 1s.

The 1988 Act protects computer programs. It does not protect as such individual files or parts of a program, just as it protects for instance a novel as a literary work rather than each individual chapter of the novel. It is submitted that the distinction is vital in infringement cases in order to determine whether or not substantial copying has taken place. The program must be taken as a whole when analysing whether infringement has taken place. This seems logical in relation to a novel where the test is whether there has been substantial copying of the novel, rather than of a chapter or sentence. This applies *mutatis mutandis* also to computer programs. Separate programs can of course afterwards be combined in one program, which would in copyright terms be treated as a compilation.[14]

A number of authors and practitioners have in this area relied heavily on US case law. We do not intend to follow that approach because there is

12   CDPA 1988, ss 1(1)(a) and 3(1)(b); preparatory design materials for a computer program is also protected as literary work, CDPA 1988, s 3(1)(c).
13   See I Lloyd *Information Technology Law* Butterworths (2nd ed, 1997) Ch 20.
14   It is not clear from the report in FSR whether this distinction was really made in *Ibcos Computers Ltd v Barclays Mercantile Highland Finance Ltd* [1994] FSR 275.

an important difference between US copyright law and our copyright law in that the US courts have systematically excluded functional works from the scope of copyright. This has had a profound influence on the case law in relation to computer programs and we will therefore not take this case law as the starting point of our analysis. Although we may have to come back to some of the American cases we agree with Jacob J that the provisions of the 1988 Act must be the starting point of the analysis.[15]

Computer programs as literary works in copyright

Originality

Only original literary works attract copyright protection and a computer program must thus be original if it is to attract copyright. The 1988 Act does not define originality. We have traditionally in the UK always used the minimalist definition of originality that required only that the work was not copied and that a sufficient amount of skill, judgment and labour had been invested in it. In the copyright chapters we drew the reader's attention to the marginally higher threshold in the European copyright Directives. And as computer programs is one of the areas where the provisions inserted in the 1988 Act find their origin and raison d'être in the Computer Software Directive[16] it is crucial to interpret the originality requirement for computer programs in a European sense which requires the program to be the author's own intellectual creation. The lack of a definition of the concept of originality in the 1988 Act enables us to adopt the European approach for computer programs and we are bound to accept it because otherwise we would be in breach of our duty to implement the Directive.

Idea and expression

Copyright only protects expression and does not protect ideas. This statement, which was qualified in the copyright chapter, must now be applied to computer programs. What is an idea? Clearly the starting point and the reason for which a computer program is written come within this category. In the famous American *Whelan* case[17] a program was written to manage a dentistry laboratory. This was clearly part of the idea, as was the list of functions the program should be able to perform and the targets it should meet. How all this was to be achieved in practice forms part of the

15   *Ibcos Computers Ltd v Barclays Mercantile Highland Finance Ltd* [1994] FSR 275 at 302.
16   EC Council Directive on the legal protection of computer programs (1991) OJ L122/42; the modifications were introduced in the CDPA 1988 by the Copyright (Computer Programs) Regulations 1992, SI 1992/3233.
17   *Whelan Associates Inc v Jaslow Dental Laboratory Inc* [1987] FSR 1.

expression of that idea. This not only includes the code lines of the program, but also its structure. The latter refers to the way in which the various parts and files are organised.[18] The precise borderline between idea and expression cannot be drawn in theory. As Judge Learned Hand said already more than half a century ago: 'Nobody has ever been able to fix that boundary and nobody ever can'.[19] It has to be fixed in each individual case on the basis of the facts of that case.

Fixation

The obvious way that comes to mind of recording a computer program is the written draft version of the source code of a program. It is indeed reasonable to expect that many software developers would write the source code down and develop flow-charts and other similar things when developing a new computer program. In this scenario the machine code version of the program could be seen as an adaptation of the work. But it is possible that the program never existed in such form and this does not deny it copyright protection. Section 3(2) of the 1988 Act allows the work to be recorded 'in writing or otherwise' and what is really required is a fixation of the work with a certain degree of permanency. Fixation on the hard disk or on a floppy disk clearly meets this requirement. A program can also be permanently hard-wired in a microprocessor in the form of 'microcode' or 'microprograms'.[20] The RAM memory of a computer constitutes a difficult problem. A program that exists only in the RAM memory of the computer exists only in the form of electrical currency and when the power supply is interrupted the program disappears. At first sight this does not involve the required degree of permanency, but the conclusion may be different if such a program lives in the RAM or a similar memory of a computer network[1] and if it is quite unreasonable to expect the network to be shut down in the foreseeable future.[2] The example of software made available via the various bulletin boards of the internet comes to mind.

---

18   Jacob J rejects the idea-expression dichotomy in *Ibcos Computers Ltd v Barclays Mercantile Highland Finance Ltd* [1994] FSR 275 at 291 but reintroduces it as the general-detailed idea dichotomy. It is submitted that there is no difference on substance between his concept and ours.
19   *Nichols v Universal Pictures Corpn* 45 F 2d 119 (1930).
20   Programs stored in the ROM (read only memory) of the computer are still literary works in the copyright sense as the mode of storage does not affect the nature of the program. See the US case *NEC Corpn v Intel Corpn* 645 F Supp 1485 (D Minn 1985).
1   See *TriadSystems Corp v Southeastern Express Co* US District Court for the Northern District of California 31 USPQ 2D 1239 and *Mai Systems Corporation v Peak Computer Inc, Vincent Chiechi and Eric Francis* US Court of Appeals for the ninth Circuit 991 F 2d 511, 26 USPQ 2D 1458.
2   Especially as other electro-magnetic ways of storing works, such as audio cassettes, will also only last for a number of years.

So what is really protected?

In a computer program the expression is protected. We held this to include the code lines and the structure of the program. But this expression is only protected in so far as it meets the originality requirement. It must be the author's own intellectual creation. This implies that there is more than one way to express the idea, otherwise the one possible way of doing so cannot be the author's own intellectual creation or his or her particular way of expressing the idea. This leads us to the conclusion that the parts of the computer program which can only be expressed in one way if a certain result is to be achieved and where this is due to technical restrictions are not original and do not attract copyright.[3] These parts of the program can be copied freely. To hold otherwise would bring the development of new software and the whole software industry to a standstill.

It can be seen here why the European interpretation of the originality requirement is vital in this context. It fulfils an essential role in the system set up by the Directive and implemented in our law. It also allows us to avoid the need to rely on the American case law[4] and its principle that functional works do not attract protection for which there is no legal basis at all in our copyright law.

Infringement

Infringement can take various forms, but the most obvious one is copying. It is important to keep in mind that in relation to copying a three stage test has to be applied. First, does the work attract copyright protection? Secondly, has there been copying of the elements protected by copyright? And thirdly, was the copying substantial?[5] If copying took place, the next issue to consider is whether a defence was available, but let us now first turn to infringement and more specifically to the various forms of copying.

Literal copying

This aspect of copying of a computer program where parts of code lines are copied and both programs are written in the same programming language was discussed at length by Jacob J in *Ibcos Computers v Barclays Mercantile Highland Finance*.[6] Having established that copyright existed in the program

3   Compare *Total Information Processing Systems v Daman* [1992] FSR 171.
4   *Whelan Associates Inc v Jaslow Dental Laboratory Inc* [1987] FSR 1 uses the phrase that the task dictates the form while *Computer Associates v Altai* 982 F 2d 693 (1992) (2nd Cir) refers to elements dictated by efficiency.
5   Compare *Ibcos Computers Ltd v Barclays Mercantile Highland Finance Ltd* [1994] FSR 275.
6   *Ibcos Computers Ltd v Barclays Mercantile Highland Finance Ltd* [1994] FSR 275.

that was allegedly copied the judge turned his attention to the question of whether there had been copying. He stated that

'For infringement there must be copying. Whether there was or not is a question of fact. To prove copying the plaintiff can normally do no more than point to bits of his work and the defendant's work which are the same and prove an opportunity of access to his work. If the resemblance is sufficiently great then the court will draw an inference of copying. It may then be possible for the defendant to rebut the inference – to explain the similarities in some other way. For instance he may be able to show both parties derived similar bits from some third party or material in the public domain. Or he may be able to show that the similarities arise out of a functional necessity – that anyone doing this particular job would be likely to come up with similar bits.'[7]

and went on to clarify that

'... at this stage ... both the important and the unimportant bits of the works being compared count.'[8]

In the case before him Jacob J found that there was plenty of evidence of copying. There were common spelling mistakes, similar headings, redundant and unexplained bits of code which appeared in both programs and the allegedly infringing program contained a part of the original program in its source code while it did not use this part.[9] All these items are good examples of the kind of evidence that the plaintiff is looking for and with which the defendant will have great difficulties if he or she is to explain the similarities away.

The next issue is whether that copying amounts to the copying of a substantial part of the copyright protected work. It should be remembered that a purely quantitative approach is not appropriate here and that qualitative issues are predominant. Jacob J suggested that it comes down to

'... a question of degree where a good guide is the notion of overborrowing of the skill, labour and judgment which went into the copyright work. ... In the end the matter must be left to the value judgment of the court.'[10]

7   Ibid at 296–297.
8   Ibid at 297.
9   Ibid at 297–301.
10   Ibid at 302.

He agreed with the statement of Ferris J in the *John Richardson* case that

'Consideration is not restricted to the text of the code ...'[11]

while adding that

'That must be right: most literary copyright works involve both literal matter (the exact words of a novel or computer program) and varying levels of abstraction (plot, more or less detailed of a novel, general structure of a computer program). I therefore think it right to have regard in this case not only to ... "literal similarities" but also to ... "program features" and "design features".'[12]

In the *Ibcos Computers* case substantial copying had clearly taken place. Reference was in this respect made to the program structure, to an extremely long list of individual parts of the program and to the file transfer programs.[13]

Non-literal copying

It flows from our discussion of what is the expression that is protected by copyright in the context of computer programs that non-literal copying can infringe the copyright in a computer program too. Examples are the copying of the structure of the program and the copying of parts of the program, while translating it in another programming language. The test we described in the previous section applies also to cases of indirect copying, but it will in practice be more difficult to determine what exactly has been copied and whether that copying is substantial. Ferris J was confronted with a case of indirect copying in the *John Richardson* case.[14] In this case the original program was written in BASIC (for use on a Tandy computer) and aimed to assist pharmacists in controlling their stock and in producing labels for prescriptions. The allegedly infringing version was produced by a former employee and it was written in QuickBasic for use on an IBM personal computer.

Due to the use of different programming languages the judge found no literal copying, but when looking at the structure and the sequence of the programs, the input and output routines, the formats, the menus, the options and facilities of the programs he found 17 objective similarities which could not readily be justified by the defendant. Ferris J then

---

11 *John Richardson Computers Ltd v Flanders* [1993] FSR 497 at 526.
12 *Ibcos Computers Ltd v Barclays Mercantile Highland Finance Ltd* [1994] FSR 275 at 302, per Jacob J.
13 Ibid at 304–314.
14 *John Richardson Computers Ltd v Flanders* [1993] FSR 497.

considered and applied the test in the American *Computer Associates v Altai* case.[15] He stated that

'In the test propounded in *Computer Associates* the discovery of a program's abstraction is the first step. The second step is to filter these abstractions in order to discover a "core of protectable material". In the process of filtration there are to be excluded from consideration (a) elements dictated by efficiency; (b) elements dictated by external factors and (c) elements taken from the public domain.'[16]

We agree with Jacob J's comment in *Ibcos Computers* that this approach is not appropriate or helpful.[17] Ferris J found it in any case difficult to apply the test to the facts of the case he had in front of him and his application was criticised for not carrying out the second stage of the test. We submit that a proper application of the originality criterion, as explained above, will result in the elements the *Computer Associates* test sets out to eliminate to arrive at the core of protectable elements not being protected by copyright in the first place. At the infringement stage it is then only necessary to consider those parts that are protected by copyright, determine which of them have been copied and whether that copying is substantial. This is also the core of the approach taken by Jacob J in *Ibcos Computers*. Although that was a case involving literal copying, he seemed to suggest that his approach was also valid in non-literal copying cases.[18]

Adaptations

Copyright can also be infringed by making an adaptation of a protected work. This also applies to computer programs.[19] In this context an adaptation of a computer program is made whenever the source code which is written in a high level programming language is compiled into machine code (also referred to as object code) in binary code. An adaptation is also made when the binary machine code is disassembled into a low level assembly language. This process is used to reveal the ideas and the techniques which are contained in the program and which are not identifiable in an endless binary sequence. The reverse process is called assembling and involves obviously also an adaptation of the program.

---

15   *American Computer Associates v Altai* 23 USPQ 2d 1241 (1992).
16   Ibid at 526.
17   *Ibcos Computers Ltd v Barclays Mercantile Highland Finance Ltd* [1994] FSR 275 at 302.
18   Ibid and see Jacobs 'Demystifying Copyright Infringement of Computer Software: *Ibcos Computers v Barclays Mercantile*' [1994] 5 EIPR 206 at 208–209.
19   See CDPA 1988, s 21(3) and (4).

Defences

Copyright contains a long list of defences against alleged copyright infringement. We will only refer here to defences that are only available in relation to computer programs.

Reverse engineering

In the software industry it is a common practice to reverse engineer a computer program. This means that the object code version of the program is converted into a more readily understandable version, such as the source code. This allows the programmer to discover how the program works and this knowledge will then be used to develop a new program. This new program can eventually be a competing program although in most cases the main objective of the process of reverse engineering is to discover the interfaces of the program which are to be copied in the new program if it is to be compatible with the existing program. The latter technique is known as decompilation for interoperability purposes and the European Software Directive[20] has introduced it into copyright as a defence against copying which forms necessarily part of the technique. It has to be emphasised that copyright only allows the reverse engineering decompilation technique to be used for the purposes of achieving interoperability.

The decompilation right makes it lawful to convert a computer program which is expressed in a low-level language into a version in a higher level language[1] and to copy the program incidentally in the course of converting it.[2] A number of conditions apply to this decompilation right. First, it must be necessary to decompile the program to obtain the information necessary to create an independent program which can be operated with the program decompiled or with another program.[3] Secondly, the information which is obtained is not to be used for any purpose other than the objective which is outlined in the first condition.[4] The decompilation right does not exist if the potential decompiler has ready access to the information he or she needs to obtain interoperability.[5] This will obviously be the case if for example the interfaces are described in the user manual or are available from the producer of the program upon simple request. The right also no longer exempts any infringement if the information obtained is communicated to third persons when this is not necessary to achieve interoperability,[6] or when

20   (1991) OJ L122/42, Article 6.
1   CDPA 1988, s 50B(1)(a).
2   CDPA 1988, s 50B(1)(b).
3   CDPA 1988, s 50B(2)(a).
4   CDPA 1988, s 50B(2)(b).
5   CDPA 1988, s 50B(3)(a).
6   CDPA 1988, s 50B(3)(c).

the information obtained is used to create a program that is similar in its expression.[7] Other acts that are restricted by copyright cannot be defended by invoking the decompilation defence, which means that the decompiler's activity is restricted to those acts that are necessary to get access to the information concerning the interfaces.[8]

The defence will make it possible to gain access to the technical details of, for example, an operating program such as Microsoft Windows, should Microsoft not make that information available themselves. As it is vital for independent producers of application software that their program can be run under Windows, which is the world's most popular operating program, in order to make their potential market as large as possible, they need to know these interfaces and incorporate them into their program. The defence thus plays an important role in the software industry and enhances competition, while not permitting the outright copying of other parts of a computer program. To make sure that it fulfils this role adequately, it cannot be restricted or prohibited by contract.[9]

An important restrictive condition which applies to the decompilation right as well as to any of the other computer software specific defences which we will discuss in the next two sections is that the defences can only be invoked by a person described in the 1988 Act as a lawful user.[10] This is a person who has the right to use the computer program and who has obtained this right under a licence or otherwise. Licensees and persons who act for them, such as their employees are clearly lawful users, but it is submitted that the category also includes independent consultants and agents working for the licensee and all persons who need to use and eventually copy the program if they are to exercise their legal duties, such as receivers, auditors or solicitors executing an Anton Piller order.[11] It also includes persons who obtained a copy of the program through rental or loan.

Back-up copies, adapting a program and error correction

The lawful user of a computer program is allowed to make a back-up copy of the computer program if he or she needs to have such a copy for the lawful use of the program[12] and this right cannot be restricted or prohibited by contract.[13]

The lawful user can also adapt the program or copy it if this is necessary for the lawful use of the program, for instance to adapt the standard program

---

7   CDPA 1988, s 50B(3)(d).
8   CDPA 1988, s 50B(3)(b).
9   CDPA 1988, s 50B(4).
10   CDPA 1988, s 50A(2).
11   See chapter 29 on remedies for more details.
12   CDPA 1988, s 50A(1).
13   CDPA 1988, s 50A(3).

slightly to meet the specific needs of the lawful user, but this facility can be prohibited by the terms of the contract under which the lawful user is using the computer program.[14] But the lawful user always has the right to correct errors in the program.[15] To hold otherwise would deprive the lawful user of the full use of the program and of some of his or her contractual rights, because it must be an implied term of each contract by which a computer program and the lawful right to use it is acquired that the program is supplied for error free use.

DATABASES

The UK has now implemented the EU Database Directive.[16] The discussion which follows is therefore primarily based on the Copyright and Rights in Databases Regulations 1997.[17] The new regime[18] came into force on 1 January 1998.

A database

The term 'database' has been defined as a collection of independent works, data or other materials which are arranged in a systematic or methodical way, and are individually accessible by electronic or other means.[19] First of all, a database has to be a collection of independent material. In practice this means that separate items that do not interact with each other are stored in a database. The non-interaction rule excludes items such as film in which the script, music, etc interact to form the final work. Secondly, the works in a database can be works that are protected by copyright, as well as non-copyrightable data or any other materials. Copyright protection for these items as such is not required, and a database can contain a mixture of different items, eg a combination of copyright works and other data. Thirdly, the items in a database must be accessible on an individual basis. One must be able to retrieve them individually. This excludes numerous multimedia works in which the user necessarily gets access to a combination

14   CDPA 1988, s 50C(1).
15   CDPA 1988, s 50C(2).
16   Directive of the European Parliament and of the Council on the protection of databases [1996] OJ L77/20.
17   SI 1997 No 3032.
18   See Adams ' "Small Earthquake in Venezuela": The Database Regulations 1997' [1998] EIPR 129; Stamatoudi 'The EU Database Directive: Reconceptualising copyright and tracing the future of the sui generis right' (1997) Revue Hellénique de Droit International 436 and see also Smith 'Legal Protection of Factual Compilations and Databases in England – How Will the Database Directive Change the Law in this Area?' [1997] IPQ 450.

of works in different media at any one time during the use of the work. Fourthly, both electronic and non-electronic collections or databases are included in the scope of the definition. And finally, the independent works etc must be arranged in a systematic or methodical way. Putting random information and items in a box will therefore not create a database. But, on the other hand, it can be argued that a newspaper is a database, since the articles in it (independent and individually accessible works) are arranged in a systematical way (home news pages, overseas news pages, etc). This final requirement creates specific problems in relation to electronic databases. Often the information is fed into the system in a random way, while the software of the database[20] organises the information afterwards. The physical storage of the information in the memory of the computer (or floppy disk, CD-Rom etc) is not even necessarily in the same or another systematic way. It is submitted that these collections nevertheless meet the arrangement criterion. A systematic or methodical arrangement exists and it is provided by an element of the database itself. The technical way in which this is achieved is irrelevant in this context. The conclusion must be different when the arrangement is provided by an element outside the database itself. A clear example is the internet, which forms a collection of independent and individually accessible materials. A systematic arrangement is missing, though, and the presence of search engines[1] cannot change that. These search engines are external to the collection of materials and so is the arrangement of the materials which they provide. A collection such as the internet is therefore not a database.

Copyright protection for a database

A database is a complex product or work. Copyright can be involved at many stages. A first distinction needs to be drawn between the computer program[2] which allows the database to be set up and which organises the data, provides the search facilities etc and the contents of the database. The special regime of protection for database does not affect either of them. The computer program will potentially be protected by copyright as a computer program, under the provisions that implement the Software Directive, if it meets the standard requirements for computer programs. Those items that are included in a database and which were works protected by copyright will continue to benefit from the protection afforded to them by copyright. The rights of the owner of the copyright in these works will not change and

19   CDPA 1988, s 3A(1).
20   Which forms part of the database as a product and is sold or made available as an integral part of it.
1   These pieces of software can be protected by copyright as computer programs.
2   See Article 1(3) of the Directive.

neither will the ownership of that copyright. Unprotected works, data and other materials will not attract copyright through their inclusion in a database.

Secondly, the contents and the computer programs and the copyright in them need to be distinguished from the database and any potential copyright in the database. Any copyright in a database will have to be independent from the rights in the contents etc and will come on top of the existing rights. It may also be awarded to different owners. What is left apart from the contents etc resembles a compilation. Prior to the implementation of the Database Directive many databases could indeed be protected and the new regime makes it clear that the category of compilations now excludes any work that is a database.[3]

Copyright in a database is thus confined to the selection and arrangement or structure of the materials that are contained in it. As a work a database has been categorised as a form of a literary work.[4] The originality criterion that applies to databases is the slightly higher originality criterion that is found in all European Directives. This means that '[...] a literary work consisting of a database is original if, and only if, by reason of the selection or arrangement of the contents of the database the database constitutes the author's own intellectual creation'.[5] This 'author's own intellectual creation' criterion has now been copied *expressis verbis* into our legislation in relation to databases. In as far as this implies that it only applies to databases, the UK is flagrantly in breach of the Sofware Directive because, as we saw above, the slightly higher criterion should apply there too. The new originality criterion means that some intellectual judgment which is the author's own must have gone into the selection of the materials or into the method of their arrangement.[6] This approach will deny copyright protection to most modern databases, for example because they aim at a complete coverage of a certain topic, rather than at selecting material or because they arrange their materials in an alphabetical or other standard way, rather than in an original way. This approach must be applauded, because the alternative would have involved the grant of multiple copyrights in standard and commonplace structures. Such a multitude of exclusive rights could have stifled competition in this area.

As a form of literary work a database is subject to the normal copyright regime. For example, copying the selection of the materials or the structure of the database or a substantial part of them will be an infringement of the copyright in the database. A few special provisions exist though. Making

3 CDPA 1988, s 3(1).
4 Ibid.
5 CDPA 1988, s 3A(2).
6 Compare the US approach in *Feist Publications v Rural Telephone* 499 US 330 (1991), US Supreme Court. In the domestic case *Waterlow Directories Ltd v Reed Information Services Ltd* ([1992] FSR 409) the opportunity to address this issue was missed.

an adaptation or doing a restricted act in relation to an adaptation of a database will still be an infringement of the copyright in the database, but the term adaptation has been redefined to mean an 'arrangement or altered version of the database or a translation of it' in relation to a database and a database has been excluded from the list of works to which the normal definition of an adaptation applies.[7] The fair dealing for the purposes of research and private study defence does not apply to databases in its normal form either. The special rule stipulates that 'fair dealing with a database for the purposes of research or private study does not infringe any copyright in the database provided that the source is indicated' and it has been added that 'doing anything [...] for the purposes of research for a commercial purpose is not fair dealing with the database'.[8] And a legitimate user of a database is allowed to do anything which is necessary for the purposes of gaining access to the database and for the use of the contents of the database. That latter right cannot be restricted by agreement.[9]

The database right

A new sui generis right to protect databases has been created and that right operates irrespective of whether the database, or any of its contents, attract copyright protection.[10] The creation of this right was necessary because copyright was not the appropriate instrument to protect non-original databases, which are nevertheless valuable and have required a substantial investment. Electronic databases especially are in such a situation extremely vulnerable and it was felt that some form of protection was needed to protect the valuable investment in these databases.

The new database right has been defined as a property right and it is granted 'if there has been a substantial investment in obtaining, verifying or presenting the contents of the database'[11]. Once again this right does not interfere with any of the existing materials and the rights in them. As a right in the database it comes on top of any existing rights and its existence rewards, and is conditional on, a substantial or sizeable investment either in collecting, in verifying or in presenting the contents of the database. For example, the substantial investment requirement will not be met by simply putting different works together on a single support. Such a collection will not be protected by the database right.

---

7   CDPA 1988, s 21(3).
8   CDPA 1988, s 29(1A) and (5).
9   CDPA 1988, s 50D.
10   Copyright and Rights in Databases Regulations 1997, reg 13(2).
11   Ibid, reg 13(1).

The first owner of the database right has been identified as the maker of the database.[12] The maker of the database is in turn 'the person who takes the initiative in obtaining, verifying or presenting the contents of the database and assumes the risk of investing in that obtaining, verification or presentation'.[13] Making a database may involve more than one person. If several people act together in relation to the activities that have to be undertaken by the maker, they will be the joint makers of the database and the joint first owners of the right.[14] A database made by an employee in the course of his employment will be considered to have been made by the employer of the employee, subject to any agreement to the contrary.[15]

The database right exists for a 15-year term. That term starts running from the end of the calendar year in which the database was completed, but that rule is displaced if the database is made available to the public before the end of that period. In that case the right expires 15 years from the end of the calendar year in which the database was first made available to the public.[16] A substantial change to the contents of the database that can be considered to be a substantial new investment will lead to the grant of a new 15-year term of protection. Such a change may be the result of the 'accumulation of successive additions, deletions or alterations' to the database.[17] Any sustained effort and investment to keep the database up to date will therefore automatically lead to permanent protection through the ever renewed database right in the latest version of the database.

The owner of the database right is granted the right to object to the extraction or re-utilisation of all or a substantial part of the contents of the database. The right in the investment clearly covers the use of the contents of the database. The right will be infringed by the unauthorised extraction or re-utilisation of all or a substantial part of the contents of the database.[18] The threshold of a substantial part of the contents of the database can be passed through the repeated and systematic extraction or re-utilisation of insubstantial parts of these contents.[19] A typical example of an infringement would consist of the taking out of a substantial part of the contents of the database and their re-arrangement by computer into a different organisation and a prima facie different database.[20]

The exceptions to the database right are not numerous and they are also narrower in scope than their copyright counterparts. Some form of fair

12   Ibid, reg 15.
13   Ibid, reg 14(1).
14   Ibid, reg 14(5).
15   Ibid, reg 14(2), provisions on Crown rights are contained in reg 14(3) and (4).
16   Ibid, reg 17(1) and (2).
17   Ibid, reg 17(3).
18   Ibid, reg 16(1).
19   Ibid, reg 16(2).
20   Such a case could have been problematical under a 100% copyright system.

dealing exception exists, but not for the purpose of criticism, review or news reporting and the library exceptions are missing too. Regulation 20 contains the narrow exception that:

> '(1) Database right in a database which has been made available to the public in any manner is not infringed by fair dealing with a substantial part of its content if –
> (a) that part is extracted from the database by a person who is apart from this paragraph a lawful user of the database,
> (b) it is extracted for the purpose of illustration for teaching or research and not for any commercial purpose, and
> (c) the source is indicated.
> (2) The provisions of Schedule 1 specify other acts which may be done in relation to a database notwithstanding the existence of database right.'[1]

There is also a qualification requirement that has to be met before the database right can be granted. The main principle here is that an attempt has been made to require reciprocity in the sense that non-European Economic Area persons will only be granted the right if their country offers a similar level of protection to European makers of databases. Qualification is made dependent on the fact that at least one of the makers of the database was at the material time when the database was made:

> '(a) an individual who was a national of an EEA state or habitually resident within the EEA,
> (b) a body which was incorporated under the law of an EEA state and which, at that time, satisfied one of the conditions in paragraph (2), or
> (c) a partnership or other unincorporated body which was formed under the law of an EEA state and which, at that time, satisfied the condition in paragraph (2)(a).'[2]

These conditions are:

> '(a) that the body has its central administration or principal place of business within the EEA, or
> (b) that the body has its registered office within the EEA and the body's operations are linked on an ongoing basis with the economy of an EEA state'[3].

1   Ibid, reg 20.
2   Ibid, reg 18(1).
3   Ibid, reg 18(2).

■

These rather vague provisions will undoubtedly give rise to a whole series of disputes before the courts.

The database right presents the inherent danger that it will grant a monopoly right over major sources of (statistical or other) information and that that right will be owned by a single rightholder (either the producer of the information or the holder of the sources). Any abuse of the database right will be restrained through the use of Article 86. There are no special provisions available to counter this threat, apart from the *Magill* style action against the abuse of a dominant position.

THE INTERNET

It would lead too far to discuss all intellectual property related aspects of the internet in this chapter. We will restrict our comments to some copyright related issues.[4] Three major questions will be addressed. Is material found on the internet protected by copyright, and if so how? What amounts to copyright infringement in an internet context? How do the defences to copyright infringement apply to alleged infringement on the internet?

Two preliminary points need to be addressed as well. The first of these is that the internet and the use of works on it does not change copyright. Works that are protected as such do not loose this status when they appear on the internet. The situation here is identical to the one we described in relation to copyright in databases. And copyright applies also to internet-related issues. Up to now there has been no change to the provisions of copyright. We simply need to apply the existing rules to the internet. Our comment will highlight some of the problems that arise through that application. The second preliminary point flows naturally from the borderless and international nature of the internet. Works cross borders on the internet as a way of life. The contrast with the national nature of our copyright legislation gives rise to numerous issues of private international law. Examples are in plentiful supply, but the most obvious one is the copying of a work. Where does the copying take place? Does it take place on the server where the work is stored, on the foreign terminal on which the user views the work and where he prints a copy of it, or in any of the countries through which the work passes on its way from the server to the user's computer? Which national court will have jurisdiction to decide the issue? And under which law will the issue be decided? These issues come on top of the discussion that follows and which will describe the UK's substantial provisions. The private international law issues are highly complex and we refer the reader to J Fawcett and P Torremans *Intellectual*

---

4   See MacQueen 'Copyright and the Internet' in C Waelde and L Evans *Law and the Internet: Regulating Cyberspace* Hart Publications (1997) at 67.

Property and Private International Law (Clarendon Press, Oxford, 1998) for further details.

Existence of copyright and classification

A lot of websites contain text, music and artistic works such as photographs and drawings. These works will be protected as literary, musical or artistic works as long as they meet the normal copyright requirements. Copyright in the works that are specifically created by the creator of the website for that purpose will be owned by that creator, subject to the employer-employee rule. Collaborative efforts may give rise to joint authorship and joint ownership. Sound recordings, films, broadcast and cable programmes also maintain their copyright status when the are put on the internet. Can a website as such be classified as a work that attracts copyright protection though?

The arrangement of a website can be protected through the copyright in a typographical arrangement. This conclusion is reached through the interpretation of the concept of publication. The website is published, because copies are made available to the public by means of an electronic retrieval system.[5] The internet fits in with that requirement. This means that the author of the arrangement of a website has a typographical arrangement copyright in that arrangement.

The Scottish *Shetland Times* case[6] suggests that a website is a cable programme service or a cable programme. A cable programme is any item that is included in a cable programme service under the 1988 Act. Such a service is defined as 'a service which consists wholly or mainly in sending visual images, sounds or other information by means of a telecommunication system, otherwise than by wireless telegraphy, for reception at two or more places [whether or not simultaneously ...], or for presentation to members of the public'[7]. Two-way or interactive communication systems are excluded.[8] Lord Hamilton came to the conclusion that a website came within this definition by rejecting the argument that the public accessed information rather than being sent information and the argument that a website was an interactive system. One could indeed argue that the information is sent by the owner of the website when the request of the user arrives or at least that the Act allows for the word sending to include the concept of enabling the information to be sent. The interactivity exists because the user can send e-mail messages to the operator of the website

5 CDPA 1988, s 175(1).
6 *Shetland Times v Wills* 1997 SLT 669, 1997 SCLR 160. See also *British Telecommunications plc v One in a Million* (1998) Independent, 31 July.
7 CDPA 1988, s 7(1).
8 CDPA 1988, s 7(2).

and is even invited to do so. However, for the exclusion to apply the interactivity, or the potential for interactivity, must be an essential feature of the service. The definition that is given to the word essential is clearly the crucial point. Sites that are mainly there to provide information in a passive way, such as the websites of a newspaper, may well escape the exclusion, but it is hard to see how a website that is accessed for the purposes of interactivity, such as the catalogues of mail order shops or the internet ticket reservation sites of airlines, can escape the exclusion. Clearly, the *Shetland Times* case has not provided the definitive answer, it has merely got the discussion started.

Infringement issues

Browsing the internet involves storing material in the RAM memory of the computer. Does this amount to copying? Copying is defined as 'reproducing the work in any material form' in as far as literary, dramatic, musical and artistic works are concerned. Such a reproduction may be made through the storage of the work in any medium by electronic means.[9] Transient or incidental copies are also included.[10] Loading software or the contents of a page of a website into the RAM memory of a computer must thus involve an act of copying. When material is downloaded, things become even clearer. Printouts and copies on the hard disk or on floppy disk are clearly copies. The typographical arrangement copyright in the site is also copied on each occasion and if a website is held to be a cable programme the acts named above will also involve copying through the making of a photograph of the whole or a substantial part of any image that forms part of the cable programme.[11] As with software, there may also be case of non-literal copying when (only) the design and the structure of the website are copied.[12]

The copyright in literary, dramatic or musical works can also be infringed through their public performance, showing or playing.[13] That might easily be done by displaying them on a computer screen or by playing them over the computer's audio system. The only problematical point is the fact that the performance etc need to take place in public. The latter concept no longer requires that there be a group of paying people forming an audience for which the work is performed. Neither is there a need for a gathering of people in one place. In public rather seems to mean that there must be an audience, an audience from which the author is entitled to expect a

9   CDPA 1988, s 17(2).
10   CDPA 1988, s 17(6).
11   CDPA 1988, s 17(4) and (5).
12   See MacQueen 'Copyright and the Internet' in C Waelde and L Evans *Law and the Internet: Regulating Cyberspace* Hart Publications (1997) at 81.
13   CDPA 1988, s 19.

remuneration for the enjoyment of his work. Recent foreign decisions have shown that such an audience exists in cases where several people listen at different times to recorded music when their call is put on hold when they use their mobile phones[14] or when several people watch non-simultaneous TV and video broadcasts in individual hotel rooms[15]. The incorporation of copyright works, without owning the rights in them or without authorisation, into a website for it to be accessed by internet users clearly amounts to a very similar activity, which will infringe the copyright in these works. The individual user will not normally be affected and even the site-owner seems to benefit from a statutory defence under s 19(4). That section exonerates the person who sent the works if electronic means are involved. Computer equipment must qualify as such. But in an internet context such activity will involve the making of infringing copies. The uploader of works will therefore still infringe the copyright in the works.

Hypertext links to other websites create a special problem if websites are seen as cable programmes. Does such a link amount to copyright infringement through the inclusion of a cable programme in another cable programme service?[16] Arguably, most hypertext links are more akin to endnotes, bibliographies or to hints for further reading. They refer to the other sites, but they do not include them in the site of the alleged infringer. However, it is submitted that that conclusion is no longer valid if the alleged infringer organises the links in such a way that the other sites will be shown inside the frame of the alleged infringer's site. Such a link is stronger and should be seen as inclusion, especially as the alleged infringer sets out to derive an economic benefit from the contents of the other site.[17]

Copyright infringement by authorising someone else to commit certain acts[18] is less of a problem in relation to the internet. It is true that those who provide end users with access to the internet, for example universities or cybercafes that make networked terminals available, provide these users with the means to copy etc. All that equipment can also be used for the lawful use of the internet and that is sufficient to counter the threat of infringement liability.[19] Service providers that participate in the infringing activities of the users, for example by providing road maps to items that can be downloaded, may not escape liability though.

14 *Australasian Performing Right Association Ltd v Telstra Corp Ltd* [1997] IIC 136 (Federal Court of Australia, 23 August 1995).
15 *SGAE v Hotel Blanco Don J SA* [1997] 1 EIPR D-21 Supreme Court of Spain, 11 March 1996).
16 CDPA 1988, s 20.
17 Compare MacQueen 'Copyright and the Internet' in C Waelde and L Evans *Law and the Internet: Regulating Cyberspace* Hart Publications (1997) at 84.
18 CDPA 1988, s 16(2).
19 See *CBS Inc v Ames Records and Tapes Ltd* [1982] Ch 91 and *CBS Songs Ltd v Amstrad Consumer Electronics plc* [1988] AC 1013.

Defences that may come to the rescue

There are no doubt a whole host of reasons that motivate people to set up there own website and homepages and to make material available on them. One of these reasons must be that other users may access their material and that they feel they have something to say or to offer to these other users. The whole concept of an internet or any other network is that a connection will be made with other people, with whom content will be shared.

From a legal point of view this must mean that whoever makes material available on the internet does consent to the fact that that material will be accessed by others. There must be some kind of implied licence to do certain acts which are necessary to access the material. Such a licence must be non-exclusive in nature, because it is given on equal terms to all potential accessors of the material. Copyright law finds no problem with such a non-exclusive implied licence, because there is no ban on them and no written instrument is required for this type of licence. The licence can be implied from the way in which the dealings between the parties have been set up. Here the whole set-up of the internet points towards the conclusion that an implied licence must exist.[20]

The remaining problem is that it is not necessarily clear what can be done under such an implied licence. The starting point seems uncontroversial. It must be a licence for any internet user to access the material on the site and to perform all acts of copying that are necessary to gain access. Any intermediary provider of services must be allowed to transmit the material and to make transient copies in as far as this is required from a technical point of view. It is less clear whether the user can download the accessed material onto any hard disk, CD, etc, whether he can print it and whether he can make any further use of the material. It is submitted that this depends on the type of material that is accessed and the type of site on which it is found. The starting point must be that the internet medium does not change the basic rules of copyright. Any material that qualifies for copyright protection will still be protected when it is made available on the internet. Users are licenced to access the site on which the material is contained in the same way as they are licensed to read a book or to play a CD or a videotape. Copying or any other restricted act requires a further licence. That further licence can only be implied if it is clear from the type material or from the type of site that further use is intended or at least authorised. That can be derived from the fact that the material on the site has no use through access only and that further potentially infringing acts are required to use the material. For example, pieces of software are clearly not intended to be read on a computer screen and must therefore come with an implied

20   Compare MacQueen 'Copyright and the Internet' in C Waelde and L Evans *Law and the Internet: Regulating Cyberspace* Hart Publications (1997) at 89–90.

licence to download and to use, while poetry or other texts can be read on the screen and need not be downloaded before proper access to them can be gained. Sites that are labelled shareware clearly come with an implied licence to copy the material on them and to make further use of the material. The only limitation on such further use may be that the product can only be used as such and in its entirety under the implied licence. Maybe it is only a licence to share the original product with other interested users, even if that sharing can be undertaken on a commercial basis.[1]

It is submitted that notices on sites can obviously change the pattern. The siteowner can licence any other users to make use of the material in a particular way and that may even take the form of a blanket licence to do anything with the material. Obviously, a site owner can only waive rights through such a licence in as far as he possesses these rights himself. For example, he cannot waive copyright in material on his site in which he does not own the copyright himself, unless he is authorised by the rightowner to do so. Alternatively, certain or all types of use may explicitly be prohibited or made subject to a further authorisation. A clear notice that certain materials or certain rights in them are for sale or the presentation of the site as a commercial trade catalogue must be seen as an example of the latter reservation of rights. Certainly, the use of notices on sites would provide a far greater degree of transparity and clarity than is currently available on the net.

The copying of site addresses and the use of search engines raises further issues. Sites are created in order for access to them to be gained. This must mean that an implied licence is given to any user to copy the address of the site onto the hard disk of his computer, in order to gain easy access to that site on a future occasion. Copying undertaken by search engines must also be allowed under an implied licence in as far as it is necessary to facilitate access to the site. The access aim of the creator of the site can only be realised through the use of search engines due to the un-transparent technical structure of the internet. Hypertext links to other sites are covered by the implied licence for the same reason that any facilitation of access needs to have been intended. Obviously, this only covers the pure signposting function. All that is covered is the provision of access to the other site as such. The implied licence does not allow any site owner to put in place a system that allows access to other sites, while the frames of the first site are retained. It must be access to the other site as it is and in its complete and original form. All the aspects of the implied licence that have been described in this paragraph apply only to addresses and titles in as far as the latter are protected by copyright in the first place for obvious reasons.[2]

1   See the Australian case *Trumpet Software Pty Ltd v OzEmail Pty Ltd* [1996] 12 EIPR 69.

2   See eg *Exxon Corp v Exxon Insurance Consultants International* [1982] Ch 119; [1982] RPC 81.

∎

The fair dealing defence to copyright infringement[3] may also be used in an internet context. It may be fair dealing for the purposes of research and private study to make hard or electronic copies of a certain part of the material that the user accesses on the internet. The constraints of the defence apply here as in any other copyright context though. It must for example be the user's own research and private study that is facilitated and it may be difficult to justify the copying of whole works. Copying materials from other websites to put them on your own site is clearly something that is not exempted by this defence. Fair dealing for the purposes of review and criticism can also be used as a defence, but here a fair level of review and criticism is required. The amount of copying must be justifiable in comparison with the amount of commentary.

The 1988 Act also allows cable material to be viewed at a time which is more convenient to the viewer.[4] This time shifting exception could be pleaded by the users of a website that copied the contents of the site, if the site is considered to be a cable programme service. It must be questionable though whether this defence can justify copying in a technical context where the same cable programme/site can be accessed at any convenient time anyway. Copying is arguably not required to achieve the timeshifting aim of the defence. In that sense the defence is not required to achieve that aim and websites are different from the traditional broadcast or cable programme for which the defence was intended.[5]

New initiatives

Recently various attempts have been made to update copyright and to make it more suitable for use in relation to the information society and the problems that it creates. The most significant of these initiatives are the WIPO Copyright Treaty that was signed on 20 December 1996 and the draft EU Parliament and Council Directive on the harmonisation of certain aspects of copyright and related rights in the Information Society.[6]

The WIPO Treaty is linked to the Berne Convention and it contains various provisions to update the minimum substantive provisions that are contained in the Berne Convention. It adds to the protection for computer programs and databases and it introduces a right of distribution, a right of rental and a right of communication to the public, among other changes and additions. The Treaty currently awaits ratification and it is expected to come into force in the near future.

3   CDPA 1988, ss 29 and 30.
4   CDPA 1988, s 70.
5   Compare MacQueen 'Copyright and the Internet' in C Waelde and L Evans *Law and the Internet: Regulating Cyberspace* Hart Publications (1997) at 88–89.
6   COM(97) 628 final, dated 10 December 1997.

The EU draft Directive sets out to deal with the information society linked aspects of copyright and in doing so it will implement most of the provisions of the WIPO Copyright Treaty. Most importantly the draft Directive contains a reproduction right that covers also indirect and temporary reproduction[7], a right of communication to the public that includes 'the making available to the public of their works in such a way that members of the public may access them from a place and at a time individually chosen by them'[8] and a distribution right[9]. This element can be of particular importance to guarantee adequate levels of protection for works and performances in the context of the internet and other elements of the information society. It will no doubt be another few years before the process of the adoption of the Directive and its implementation by the member states will be completed.

SEMICONDUCTOR CHIP PROTECTION

Introduction

Semiconductor chips are integrated circuits, which are usually made out of layers of materials that are conductive to a different extent. Mostly some layers are not conductive at all while other layers are made out of semi-conductive materials such as silicon. The production of these chips involves an etching process whereby photographically made masks are used. These masks determine the final wiring of the chip. It was not immediately clear which intellectual property right should be used for the protection of semiconductor chips and what exactly would be the subject of protection. The latter issue was solved when it was decided to protect the topography of the integrated circuit rather than the chip itself. Because they were dissatisfied with the protection offered by the conventional intellectual property rights and after intense lobbying by the chip industry, the US became the first country to enact a statute which provides a sui generis intellectual property right which covers semiconductor chips.[10] The European Community followed suit and a Directive[11] obliged the member states to introduce protection for topographies of integrated circuits. Most member states created a sui generis right, while the UK decided to offer protection via the design right.

---

7   Article 2 of the Directive.
8   Article 3 of the Directive, see Article 8 of the Treaty.
9   Article 4 of the Directive, see Article 6 of the Treaty.
10 Semiconductor Chip Protection Act of 1984, Pub L No 98–620, title III, Stat 3347 (codified at 17 USC 901–914, Supp II 1984).
11 EC Council Directive on the legal protection of topographies of semiconductor products (1987) OJ L24/36.

The Design Right (Semiconductor Regulations) 1989[12]

These regulations rely upon the provisions in the 1988 Act for the design right and add a number of special provisions to them to protect semiconductor topographies. A design is further defined as:

> '(a) the pattern fixed, or intended to be fixed, in or upon –
>   (i) a layer of a semiconductor product, or
>   (ii) a layer of material in the course of and for the purpose of the manufacture of a semiconductor product, or
> (b) the arrangement of the patterns fixed, or intended to be fixed, in or upon the layers of a semiconductor product in relation to one another.'[13.]

A semiconductor product is in turn defined as:

> 'an article the purpose, or one of the purposes, of which is the performance of an electronic function and which consists of two or more layers, at least one of which is composed of semiconducting material and in or upon one or more of which is fixed a pattern appertaining to that or another function.'[14]

A semiconductor topography which forms such a design is only protected if it is original and, as is usual for designs, it will not be original if it is commonplace in the relevant design field at the time of its creation. There is also a qualification requirement.[15] Its only noticeable difference with the one for designs is that any sale or hire or any offer or exposure for sale or hire which is subject to an obligation of confidence[16] is to be taken into account when qualification through first marketing is examined. A semiconductor topography design which satisfies these requirements is owned in the same way as any other design right, apart from the fact that commissioners and employers do not have to be qualifying persons.[17] The term of protection expires normally 10 years after the end of the year in which the design was first commercially exploited anywhere in the world. Exceptionally the design right expires 15 years from the time the topography was first recorded in a design document or from the time when an article was made to the design, whichever is the earliest. This rule will apply in

12   The Design Right (Semiconductor Regulations) 1989, SI 1989/1100.
13   Regulation 2(1).
14   Ibid.
15   Regulation 4.
16   Regulation 7.
17   Regulations 4 and 5.

case the design is not exploited within 15 years of the creation of the topography.[18]

In general the provisions on primary and secondary infringement are similar to those which generally apply to design rights. The Regulations introduce some particular provisions however. Anyone can freely reproduce the design privately for non-commercial purposes[19] and:

> 'the reproduction of a design for the purpose of analysing or evaluating the design or analysing, evaluating or teaching the concepts, processes, systems or techniques embodied in it.'[20]

will not infringe the design right in the topography. But the most interesting departure from the traditional design rules is the introduction of a provision, which allows for the reverse engineering of a semiconductor design right. Regulation 8(4) states that it is not an infringement of the semiconductor design right to create another original topography on the basis of the outcome of the reverse analysis and evaluation of an existing semiconductor design. This exception even includes the making of a copy of that existing semiconductor design.[1] This exception is narrow in scope though, as it will only apply if the new design meets the originality requirement.

Two minor provisions should also be mentioned here. The exhaustion doctrine is applicable in relation to semiconductor designs[2] and licences of right, which are normally available during the last five years of the term of design protection, are not available in relation to semiconductor designs.[3]

INTELLECTUAL PROPERTY RIGHTS IN COMPUTER TECHNOLOGY – AN OVERVIEW

The presence of several pages dealing with the issue of how computer technology can be brought under the intellectual property umbrella can be explained in two ways. The easy solution is that computer technology is not easy to understand and that it is appropriate to give more details as to how it fits in with intellectual property. A difficult example simply needs more explanation. The second explanation is that computer technology does not fit in any of the existing intellectual property rights and that all attempts to make it fit distort the existing intellectual property rules. From this point of view sui generis regimes need to be created for the various aspects of

18 Regulation 6.
19 Regulation 8(1).
20 Ibid.
1   Regulation 8(4).
2   Regulation 8(2).
3   Regulation 9.

computer technology if the long term effectiveness and viability of intellectual property is not to be undermined.

The relatively smooth interaction between copyright and software seems to support the first explanation, while the sui generis approach taken in relation to databases and semiconductor chips seems to support the second explanation. It is indeed not possible to regard the semiconductor design right as a 100% normal design right. It is submitted that it is at present not possible to choose between both explanations. But it is clear that computer technology raises a series of complex and challenging questions in relation to intellectual property.

Chapter 27

Character merchandising

This is a topic of great commercial significance but as yet only limited legal recognition in the UK.[1] We are concerned with rights in character, another vague concept which the law has to struggle to turn into something tangible.[2] A right to character can take two forms. It could be seen as the private right of an individual to develop and protect his own character; this is really an issue that falls within the ambit of any tortious protection of privacy, a topic on which tort lawyers wail endlessly and, so far, fruitlessly. This falls outside the ambit of a work such as this, unlike the other forms of character right, which relate to the commercial exploitation of a character and its attributes.

The commercial exploitation of character is the antithesis of privacy. Far from wishing to keep quiet about one's character, the character merchandising industry is devoted to at times ruthless exposure of it. No self-respecting rock star would nowadays dream of giving a concert without ensuring the supply at the venue of T-shirts and other souvenirs; a celebrity can command fees for showing his home to the excited readers of *Hello* magazine or for telling amusing tales of past antics to Michael Aspel. The entire Disney industry shows the value of successful character merchandising activity.

As a broad generalisation it may be argued that the whole development of intellectual property law has been as a response to commercially important activity which has merited legal protection. Thus patent law grew as a response to growing industrialisation while copyright's expansion has reflected the growing importance of, and differing forms of, mass media.

---

1   See Frazer 'Appropriation of Personality – a new Tort?' (1983) 99 LQR 281, Holyoak 'UK Character Rights and Merchandising Rights Today' [1993] JBL 444, Carty 'Character Merchandising and the Limits of Passing-Off' [1993] LS 289.
2   See J Adams *Character Merchandising* Butterworths (2nd edn, 1996).

However, as yet, character merchandising does not have much in the way of specific recognition in UK law in spite of the eloquent arguments of Frazer[3] that there should be a statutory tort giving a right to protection to a victim of the unlawful appropriation for commercial purposes of aspects of character such as name, image or voice. Indeed, the recent review of the law on trade marks, faced with the opportunity to create a form of character right, declined so to do, claiming that so to do would create 'legal or administrative difficulties disproportionate to any problems that it would obviate'.[4]

Faced with this refusal to address their concerns directly, the character merchandising industry, for such it is, has to seek legal protection in the form of the adaptation of other intellectual property rights and their application to the merchandising field. It may be that statutory protection would be a simpler approach, but equally it will be seen that, taken overall, a fair range of protection is provided and we are now at a stage where the number of worthy cases that will slip between the gaps between the various intellectual property rights that may be relevant to a character merchandising situation will be few indeed.

In assessing the way in which copyright, trade mark law and various torts combine to confer legal protection on character merchandising it is important at the outset to point to an important distinction between two types of character. Merchandising may take place in relation to either a real character or characters – Madonna or Take That – or in relation to a fictitious character such as Noddy or Superman, but the key distinction is that copyright is only relevant to the latter category. It is thus sensible to look at ways in which the law can protect any type of character merchandising before returning to the specific issue of fictitious characters.

TRADE MARK LAW

Clearly many characters will be associated with an image and this, if distinctive, may very well form part of the character merchandising activity. If de facto distinctive then of course it will be able to attract the protection of registration as a trade mark under the 1994 Act. Pictures of celebrities, their real names or nicknames, caricatures of them or representations of objects associated with them, such as Dame Edna Everage's spectacles could all be protected in this way.

However in the past relatively little use has been made of trade marks in this way. The likely reason for this was the prohibition, by s 28(6) of the Trade Marks Act 1938, of trafficking in trade marks by disallowing

3 (1983) 99 LQR 281.
4 Cm 1203, para 4.43.

registration of any mark used for trafficking. This was considered by the House of Lords in *Re Hollie Hobby Trade Mark*[5] where the image of a winsome small girl, originally in use on greeting cards, was the subject of considerable licensing activity with other traders so that goods such as toys and toiletries could be made featuring the girl's image. Unfortunately this perfectly legitimate commercial activity could not be protected by trade mark law. The House of Lords was clear that, to its regret, this was trafficking, described by Lord Brightman[6] as:

'dealing in a trade mark primarily as a commodity in its own right and not primarily for the purpose of identifying or promoting merchandise in which the proprietor of the mark is interested.'

Most characters do not want to get their hands dirty in making the merchandise themselves and it is normal and sensible for the exploitation to be carried out by others under licence. The *Hollie Hobby* case denied the protection of trade mark registration to this typical example of valuable commercial activity. This was unacceptable, so the White Paper on Trade Mark Reform that presaged the 1994 Act recommended that s 28(6) should be repealed and the 1994 Act contains no reference to the problem of trafficking and a simplified licensing system now applies to trade marks.[7]

The future of the trade mark approach to character merchandising thus looks promising, at least from the viewpoint of the celebrity who is actively engaging in merchandising activity. The emphasis in the 1994 Act on distinctiveness accords with the desire of the marketing expert to accentuate the distinctive. It seems likely that many other celebrities will follow, for example Paul 'Gazza' Gascoigne may obtain trade mark registration, in that case for his nickname, to help with lucrative merchandising activity. Others who may seek to register the character as a mark will be likely to fall foul of the provisions in s 3(3) and (6) preventing deceptive marks and marks sought in bad faith from being registered. On the other hand such non-authorised use may prevent the character himself from registering a descriptive type of mark as being not distinctive enough for the purposes of the proviso to s 3(1)(c) of the 1994 Act, if personal origin is regarded as within that subsection. Geographical origin is seen as descriptive as are 'other characteristics' and it must at least be arguable that personal origin is a factor belonging in this subsection. This could mean that earlier unauthorised use could prevent the registration of a trade mark in legitimate character merchandising activity.

5   [1984] RPC 329.
6   Ibid at 356.
7   Trade Marks Act 1994, ss 28-31.

The requirement of distinctiveness could prove to be the major hurdle. This was already clear in the *Elvis Presley* case,[8] even though that case was still decided under the 1938 Act. Laddie J emphasised that distinctiveness means that the trade mark must enable the consumer to distinguish the goods of one trader from the similar goods of another trader. In his view the use of the names 'Elvis' and 'Elvis Presley' did not provide the consumer with an indication concerning the origin of the product. The name of the celebrity was rather the subject matter of the goods. Laddie J did not accept that the consumer would expect that a product bearing either of the marks originated from Elvis Presley Enterprises Inc, the company that had applied to register the marks. Most people would buy the product because it had the name of the celebrity on it and would not bother about the origin of the product. That conclusion was reinforced by the fact that other manufacturers did *de facto* manufacture and sell Elvis Presley memorabilia, without there being any indication that the consumer believed that these products originated from Elvis Presley Enterprises. The judgment indicates that similar problems would arise in relation to the registration of the Elvis Presley signature as a trade mark. It is also clear from the emphasis on distinctiveness that the approach taken in this case will also apply under the 1994 Act.

The judgment in the *Elvis Presley* case can be criticised for its refusal to accept that the public is aware of these merchandising activities. One could indeed argue that the public may in certain circumstances believe that a product that is labelled with the name of a celebrity originates from a producer that has been approved by the celebrity.[9] The celebrity's name could then distinguish these products from similar products (without the name on them) made by other traders. In those cases the application to register the celebrity's name as a trade mark may be able to pass the distinctiveness hurdle, but the facts of the *Elvis Presley* case make it clear that the situation was quite different in that case. And Laddie J did accept that someone might be able to build up a reputation and goodwill in a celebrity name in the course of trade.

DESIGN LAW

In some cases the two design rights may be appropriately used to protect character merchandising. Under the Registered Designs Act 1949 a design could be registered for the shape of an industrially manufactured object if not functional. The production of a coffee mug shaped so as to depict the facial feature of a well-known personality would fit easily within this

8   *Re Elvis Presley Trade Mark* [1997] RPC 543.
9   See indirectly *Re Anne Frank Trade Mark* [1998] RPC 379 (a Trade Mark Registry case).

definition. Similarly such an object could fall within the newer unregistered design right created by s 213 of the Copyright, Designs and Patents Act 1988. However, this expressly excluded surface decoration so a mug bearing a picture of a celebrity would not qualify for this right, though would appear to be within the registered design right. However a mug shaped in the form of the face of a celebrity could be the subject of an unregistered design right. In each case it is an article or features thereof that are the subject of the right, and this obviously limits the use of these rights to a small proportion of merchandising activities.

TORT

Passing-off

Prior to the passage of the new trade marks legislation, it was this tort that was doing most to protect the commercial exploitation of character by merchandising. It seems likely that the tort will continue to function in this area though in the future will be overshadowed more by trade mark law. However it is only recently that the tort of passing-off has come to play a role in this field, having been held back for some time.

The problem was that it was generally thought that for liability to exist the parties must be working in a common field of activity. So an action would be between two rival clothing manufacturers, but not between a celebrity and a clothing manufacturer, even if the celebrity wanted to engage in merchandising activity involving clothing. This was used to prevent a claim from succeeding in respect of authorised character merchandising as long ago as 1947. In *McCulloch v Lewis A May (Produce Distributors)*[10] the plaintiff was a well-known broadcaster to children known as Uncle Mac. As a BBC employee at that time, involvement with anything so sordid as commerce was out of the question so he was doubly appalled when the defendant began selling 'Uncle Mac's Puffed Wheat' without permission. The breakfast cereal was advertised in such a way as to associate closely product and celebrity. Wynn-Parry J found against the plaintiff. He was a broadcaster, not a cereal manufacturer, and there was thus no common field of activity and no passing-off claim.

This approach was resolutely adhered to by the UK courts. In *Lyngstad v Anabas Products*[11] an attempt to prevent the sale of unauthorised Abba merchandise was unsuccessful on this ground, in spite of the fact that Abba had developed a sizeable merchandising trade alongside their musical

10 [1947] 2 All ER 845.
11 [1977] FSR 62.

activities. Similarly in *Tavenor Rutledge Ltd v Trexapalm Ltd*[12] the supposed lack of common field of activity was enough to defeat an attempt to prevent the sale of 'Kojakpops' lollipops designed to evoke the image of Kojak, a popular television and lollipop-sucking detective. This was especially ironic because by being first in the field the unauthorised trader was able to prevent a properly licensed manufacturer from putting 'Kojak lollies' on the market. Law and commercial reality were not working hand in hand at this stage of the law's development.

Already the Australian courts were showing the way forward. In *Henderson v Radio Corpn Pty Ltd*[13] the High Court of New South Wales rejected the *McCulloch* approach and allowed two well-known dancers to prevent the unauthorised use of their picture on the cover of a record of dance music. Particularly instructive is *Children's Television Workshop Inc v Woolworths (NSW) Ltd.*[14] Here the plaintiffs had rights in the characters from the Muppet Show and they were able to prevent the sale by the defendants of unauthorised Muppet memorabilia by demonstrating that they had their own merchandising operation and although it was conducted on a licensed basis, they continued to exercise close quality control over it. It was also relevant that the public were aware of the merchandising link and, in particular, of the existence of quality control.

Slowly, however, the UK courts have come to grips with the phenomenon of character merchandising. An important first stage was recognition of the practice and, with it, recognition that the public were aware of it. This came in *IPC Magazines Ltd v Black and White Music Corpn Ltd*[15] where the proprietors of a magazine featuring the exploits of Judge Dredd sought protection against the release of pop record featuring the fabled jurist. Although no injunction was awarded (damages at full trial being thought to be an adequate remedy) Goulding J was prepared to recognise that the public would assume that the plaintiffs had in some way authorised the record. In other words, once it is realised that character merchandising does go on and that the public have realised that, say, not every Abba sweatshirt was personally knitted by one or other of the Swedish superstars but that Abba are nevertheless trading in sweatshirts as well as songs, the celebrity has goodwill which the tort of passing-off can protect in not only songs and records but also sweatshirts. This reflects the modern reality that many films, shows or articles are nowadays launched as a package in which the revenue from merchandising activity is as important as that derived from the entertainment on performances. There is no point launching, for example, a new pop group into the world to great acclaim if

12   [1977] RPC 275.
13   [1969] RPC 218.
14   [1981] RPC 187.
15   [1983] FSR 348.

you have no souvenirs to sell to their excited fans and in practice these will be already in the warehouse, waiting.

The recognition of broader ideas of goodwill in these claims and the more general renewed emphasis on goodwill in the *Jif Lemon* case[16] all help the use of the tort of passing-off in character merchandising situations, but formal recognition of its role at last transpired in *Mirage Studios v Counter Feat Clothing Co*[17] where the use of images of the Teenage Mutant Ninja Turtles on clothing was at issue. The launch of the Turtles was a classic example of the development of an overall product where sales of merchandise were as significant as sale of the television programmes. It was thus clear that the plaintiffs enjoyed goodwill in the clothing trade as well as the entertainment business. The knowledge of the buying public that properly licensed merchandising activity is common meant that there was a misrepresentation in the form of the unauthorised sales and obvious damage could be envisaged to the trade of the plaintiffs. Thus the elements of passing-off were satisfied and an injunction granted. The earlier Australian cases were approved and the earlier English cases distinguished as being inappropriate where the plaintiff has copyright in the character and is already in the business of merchandising. In reality it is unlikely that the 'no common field of activity' argument has any life in it.

Meanwhile the Federal Court of Australia has gone yet further in the protection of character merchandising in *Pacific Dunlop Ltd v Hogan*.[18] The actor and comedian Paul Hogan, star of 'Crocodile Dundee', successfully brought an action against an advert for shoes which mimicked one particular scene in the film; the Hogan character in the advert wore similar clothes to those worn by Hogan in the film. It was held that Hogan, who himself appeared in many adverts and always in the role of 'a good-natured larrikin'[19] had a right to be protected against the unauthorised use of his character because it would harm his own marketing opportunities. Hogan was trading not just an actor and comedian but as a general all-round celebrity and thus any activity deriving from his fame would be protected by the tort of passing-off.

One further development in passing-off is also relevant, and perhaps accords with the *Hogan* case. As we have seen in an earlier chapter, the case of *Lego System Aktieselkab v Lego M Lemelstrich Ltd*[20] allowed Lego to use the tort of passing-off against another but totally unrelated user of the Lego name on the basis that the fame of Lego is such that anyone seeing the name would automatically assume, whatever the context, that it was the name of

---

16 *Reckitt & Colman Products Ltd v Border Inc* [1990] 1 All ER 873, [1990] 1 WLR 491.
17 [1991] FSR 145.
18 (1989) 14 IPR 398.
19 Ibid at 400.
20 [1983] FSR 62.

the renowned Danish toy brick manufacturer, and any defects would be assumed to be their fault, thus risking harm to their reputation. This fits well into the character merchandising field. For example, an unauthorised dealer sells a Peter Mandelson pen which often leaks. The public know of the practice of character merchandising and thus blame Peter Mandelson for the leaks. This would harm his current merchandising activity, if there were any, but after *Lego* the possible harm to any future merchandising activity will also be enough to sustain an action in passing-off.

We have argued earlier that this is a tort bursting with vigour in recent years. Its application to character merchandising shows this well if, perhaps, belatedly. The flexibility and adaptability of the common law afforded protection comparable to that which legislation might be expected to provide.

Recently fresh doubt was cast over the fact that the public is now aware of the practice of character merchandising. But at the same time Laddie J seemed to recognise in the *Elvis Presley trade mark* case[1] that it must be possible to use the name of a celebrity to market a product and to build up a reputation and goodwill in that name in the course of trade. This point receives additional support from the judgment in the *Alan Clark* case[2]. It was readily accepted in the latter case that Mr Clark had goodwill in his name and that the passing-off of the spoof diaries in the *Evening Standard* newspaper through the false attribution of authorship could lead to substantial damage to his reputation (and earnings) as a columnist and diarist. However, Mr Clark had the advantage that he had a reputation as a writer and not just as a celebrity. It is no doubt still easier to succeed in an action in passing-off if the goodwill relates specifically to the merchandising activity or to any other commercial activity, rather than to the general reputation and goodwill, which one acquires as a celebrity.

Defamation

We have elsewhere in this book noted the decision in *Tolley v J S Fry Ltd*[3] that an amateur golfer could sue in defamation for the unauthorised use of his character in an advert which carried the implication that he had compromised his amateur status. This is clearly applicable to protect character merchandising activity, but its use is limited to those cases where reputation is lowered. So it would be defamatory to create a false quote from the Dean of the Law Faculty seemingly endorsing a pornographic magazine, but it was not appropriate for David Frost to use defamation law against a

1   *Re Elvis Presley Trade Marks* [1997] RPC 543.
2   *Clark* v *Associated Newspapers Ltd* [1998] 1 All ER 959.
3   [1931] AC 333.

hotel which falsely[4] claimed his endorsement since no harm was done to his reputation thereby.

Malicious falsehood

If character merchandising activity is already under way it is easy to see how the unauthorised merchandising of poor quality goods could be seen by customers as being an attack on that activity by implication, and, if false and denigratory, thus actionable in the tort of malicious falsehood. However, the use of this tort has been considerably enhanced in the context of character merchandising by the notable decision in *Kaye v Robertson*[5] where an injured actor was able to use the tort to prevent the publication of a true story about his condition in hospital after a serious accident. The basis of the decision was that publication would imply that the actor had consented; the tawdry context of the publication would be harmful to his image as a celebrity but, more particularly, it would harm his own right to sell his story on his own terms for his own gain on his recovery. This loss then forms the necessary damage to complete the grounds for a claim.

The easier availability of injunctive relief was a key to Kaye's success in malicious falsehood rather than defamation. Another reason for preferring to use malicious falsehood is that, unlike in defamation, it is possible to obtain legal aid for it, a point highlighted in *Joyce v Sengupta*.[6] A newspaper claimed that the plaintiff, Princess Anne's maid, had stolen embarrassing royal correspondence, but this was false. She was allowed to frame her claim in malicious falsehood in view of the obvious harm to her trade as royal servant caused by the inaccurate story.

These two cases show that malicious falsehood can be used against any falsity that may have the effect of harming the victim's trade and that, after *Kaye*, if the victim is a celebrity, it will be assumed that they are trading not just as, in that case, an actor but also as a celebrity. This notion neatly parallels that in the *Crocodile Dundee* case. Still, however, there are limits on the use of this tort. A celebrity who does not trade as such may have difficulty establishing that there is damage and the exception to this requirement by section 3 of the Defamation Act 1952 in cases of words calculated to cause pecuniary damage is also of no assistance to a plaintiff who is not using his celebrity status as the base of merchandising activity.

More seriously, there is a need to prove malice and this may be difficult if a trader honestly but without authorisation puts good quality character

4   Example cited in Wacks *The Protection of Privacy* Butterworths (1980) p 167.
5   [1991] FSR 62.
6   [1993] 1 All ER 897, [1993] 1 WLR 337.

■

merchandise on the market. In *Kaye*, however, it was asserted by Glidewell LJ[7] that:

> 'malice will be inferred if it be proved that the words were calculated to cause damage and that the defendant knew when he published the words that they were false or were reckless as to whether they were false or not'.

False words may be equated to the act of merchandising goods falsely attributing them as being authorised by the character in question and, on this basis, it would seem that malice will be found to be present at least if the plaintiff is himself engaged in merchandising activity.

COPYRIGHT

If we now confine our attention to fictitious characters it is evident that copyright protection for artistic or literary works will be available. An unauthorised drawing of Donald Duck on a T-shirt will soon be met with a writ from the Disney organisation, while the creation of a character in the words of a book is the result of much literary effort, whether in putting together the stunts and wit that are Ian Fleming's James Bond or the more refined characteristics that make up Agatha Christie's Miss Marple. The principal authority in this field is the decision of the House of Lords in *King Features Syndicate Inc v Kleeman*[8] where unauthorised merchandise was being sold exploiting the popular newspaper cartoon figure of Popeye the Sailorman. This merchandise was held to infringe the copyright in the Popeye character.

The case is particularly significant in so far as the drawings of Popeye were made by the defendant and were not direct copies of any of the plaintiffs' drawings. Of course they used the distinctive features of Popeye to ensure the necessary recognition essential for sales. The problems of using copyright in cases of imprecise copying were referred to in *Mirage Studios v Counter Feat Clothing Ltd*[9] where the drawings of humanoid turtles were again not directly copied by the defendants. Although an interlocutory injunction was granted it was by no means clear that at trial there would be no problem in saying that drawings of the concept of a humanoid turtle infringed copyright in the plaintiff's specific drawings. This is a classic example of the problems posed by the way copyright law will protect the expression of ideas, but not the ideas themselves.

---

7   [1991] FSR 62 at 67. Cf *Gatley on Libel and Slander* Sweet & Maxwell, paras 303, 323.
8   [1941] AC 417.
9   [1991] FSR 145.

Further problems arise where a fictitious name is used. Copyright is only granted to those who have exercised some degree of creative energy. Thus in *Exxon Corpn v Exxon Insurance Consultants International Ltd*[10] the invented name Exxon was not capable of copyright protection as being a highly artificial word that was not the product of creative endeavour, but it was conceded by Graham J at first instance[11] that a title could be registered for copyright if it has qualities or characteristics in itself. Lewis Carroll's 'Jabberwocky' is cited as an example where the name, coupled with the literary work in which it appears and the images evoked by it is enough to justify the grant of copyright protection. However in *Mirage Studios* the name 'Ninja Turtles' alone was held not to be capable of copyright protection so doubt remains as to the precise boundary of copyright protection of names. The general rule remains that there will be no copyright in a name as such, or in a signature.[12]

The image of a celebrity is also probably not capable of protection by copyright. The pop star Adam Ant used to wear distinctive face make-up but this was not regarded as an artistic work for copyright purposes in *Merchandising Corpn of America Inc v Harpbond*.[13] Maybe a more permanent form of decoration would provide a different decision and, it is clear in general that copyright provides a useful protection against the unauthorised merchandising of fictitious characters, particularly given the length of protection afforded.

The moral right to object to the false attribution of authorship[14] may also assist celebrities, albeit in a defensive way. It can be used to stop the unauthorised use of the celebrity's name to suggest that he or she is the author of work with which no such link exists in reality. The successful use of this right by Alan Clark to stop the attribution to him (or at least that belief in the eyes of a substantial number of readers) of the spoof diaries that appeared without his authorisation in the London *Evening Standard* newspaper demonstrates this point clearly.[15] However, the right cannot be used positively to protect any form of merchandising activity.

10   [1982] Ch 119, [1981] 3 All ER 241.
11   [1982] Ch 119 at 131, [1981] 2 All ER 495 at 504. The decision was upheld by the Court of Appeal, and nothing said there contradicts the approach of Graham J at first instance.
12   *Re Anne Frank Trade Mark* [1998] RPC 379 (a Trade Mark Registry case), see also *Re Elvis Presley Trade Marks* [1997] RPC 543.
13   [1983] FSR 32.
14   CDPA 1988, s 84.
15   *Clark v Associated Newspapers Ltd* [1998] 1 All ER 959.

CHARACTER MERCHANDISING – AN OVERVIEW

Although no specific character protection right has been developed in the UK this does not of itself dent the initial suggestion in this chapter that intellectual property rights develop in response to the need to protect commercially significant activity. As recently as when Frazer argued[16] that a new character right was needed such an argument had more force than it does now. Since then, the law of trade marks has been amended to remove a key block to character merchandising activity's protection in law, while passing-off has learnt to recognise the existence and importance of such activity in the *IPC* and *Mirage Studios* cases, which when coupled with the broad sweep of the *Lego* decision too, give a far broader degree of protection than seemed likely a decade or so ago. Meanwhile the recognition that one can trade as a celebrity, in *Kaye*, gives further protection to the famous.

It may be argued that this patchwork of remedies is fine for the famous but does not protect ordinary citizens from exploitation. The answer to this once again is the law's reflection of commercially important activity, and the fact that there is no such commercial need for legal intervention. There is no need to protect Holyoak and Torremans from the unauthorised use of their names on T-shirts since such a use has no commercial value (yet). There may be reasons related to personal privacy to extend protection, but these we leave to civil libertarians to debate. From our commercial standpoint, however, we would assert the need to take care in the formulation of any new law. It would be absurd if, say, everyone on board a crowded paddle steamer had any right to prevent the sale, or demand a royalty from, a postcard showing the vessel heading into port.

It may be that a simple statutory move to create a character right would be beneficial in terms of simplicity and legal elegance. However the developments of the last decade show that the law has become seized of the legal and commercial importance of character merchandising activity and has moved to protect it in an entirely adequate manner.

---

16   (1983) 99 LQR 281. See n 1 p 523.

Chapter 28

Franchising and intellectual property

THE CONCEPT OF FRANCHISING

Franchising is typically a business situation where a franchisee pays a franchisor for the use of the latter's name, reputation and get-up, the exploitation of which will normally remain under the franchisor's control and supervision. 'Normally' is an important word here; there is no specific legal definition of a franchise. Rather, it is up to the (presumably) freely contracting parties to define the nature and extent of their relationship.

In the most common situation a common business format is developed by the franchisor. A series of intellectual property rights may substantially increase the value of this format: trade marks, know-how, copyrights and sometimes even patents. This results in a package of rights which is licensed by the franchisor who wishes to establish a franchise network in which the franchisees trade under a common name in order to obtain an optimal return from the business format he developed. Apart from paying a fee for the use of the common business format and the associated intellectual property rights, the franchisee undertakes to maintain and preserve the character of the franchise.

This system presents a major advantage to undertakings that lack the capital and/or the skills to undertake the eventually world-wide exploitation themselves. They become franchisors and their franchisees undertake the exploitation. But from the franchisee's point of view the franchise system presents the advantage that it becomes possible to enter the market without having to invest in the creation of a business format and a name. The existing package and the business reputation of the franchise network reduce the risks for the franchisee. If the system operates properly the market sees the beneficial arrival of new independent operators, who run in a sense their own business, and the control system put in place by the franchisor allows the consumer to get the same product with a standard quality level from each of these operators.[1]

Recognition of trade names and a quality level guarantee are surely advantageous for the consumer, which means that a properly operated franchise system can be beneficial to all parties involved.

No one can deny the importance of franchising today. Pre-recession estimates suggested[2] that by 1994 turnover of franchised businesses in the UK would approach £10 bn, with 10% of all retail sales in the EC being made in franchises. While recession may always affect such estimates and predictions, it may well be that this is one area of business activity that is relatively immune from the effects of economic depression. Cynically, the source of many investments into new franchises by franchisees may be redundancy pay-offs. It is also likely that the sharing of capital burdens between the two sides of the agreement and the motivation of the often newly self-employed franchisee will combine to give the business a fighting chance in stormy economic times.

An enormous range of businesses are operated on a franchise basis. These may be large business ventures necessitating considerable investments: the Holiday Inn chain of international hotels is a franchise operation, as are the hundred or more Clarks Shoes shops around the UK. Many smaller operations such as various domestic cleaning firms are also run in this way. The provisions of the Business Names Act 1985[3] enable readers who wish to become franchise-spotters to track down their prey by insisting, inter alia, that premises operated by a business under a different name from that of the actual owner must identify the actual owner 'in a prominent position'. Thus if I become the franchisee of a national fast-food chain, marketing my goods with reference to their name, I would need to identify my name, or that of my company, on the premises so used.

Franchising is a little-investigated area of the law.[4] This may in part be due to the relatively recent growth in its importance but may also be due to the fact that the relevant legal rules emanate from a range of different sources. As already indicated, contract law is of direct relevance to the creation and content of a franchising agreement and particular care must be taken to avoid an agreement becoming void as being in restraint of trade. Similarly the perils of the laws, both domestic and European, that exist to promote free competition, must be borne in mind since the interests of the parties to a franchising agreement will often lie in creating a monopoly. Last but not least, the use of images, logos and other marketing material as part of the franchisor/franchisee relationship gives rise to significant difficulties

---

1   See Whish *Competition Law* Butterworths (3rd edn, 1993) p 544.
2   Abell *The Franchise Option* Waterlow (1989) p 5.
3   Section 4(1)(b).
4   Though it is served well by Adams and Prichard-Jones' thorough *Franchising* Butterworths (3rd edn, 1990) and Abell's *The Franchise Option* Waterlow (1989).

in intellectual property law, and it is with these issues, rather than those in other areas of law in so far as they can be treated separately, that we are concerned in this chapter.

FRANCHISES AND TRADE MARK LAW

How do the basic provisions of trade mark law, as outlined in Chapter 23 above, help or hinder the franchisor and franchisee? The law in this area is equally applicable to services, since the entry into force of the Trade Marks (Amendment) Act 1984. The first problem is the difficult question of who is the proprietor of the mark given that the franchisor has created the trade marks which characterise his business – the logos of Colonel Sanders that haunt the shops of the Kentucky Fried Chicken chain worldwide are a good example to consider – while the franchisee, not the franchisor, is the person actually responsible for delivering the product and service. The mark is defined[5] as 'any sign capable of being represented graphically which is capable of distinguishing goods or services of one undertaking from those of other undertakings'. The goods or services which are distinguished from those of other undertakings are the goods and services of the franchise chain, not those of the individual franchisee. Therefore the franchisor should apply for trade mark registration and become the proprietor of the trade mark.

The simplest way forward is to assign the mark to the franchisee and this is perfectly permissible.[6] The problem here is clear, however; the franchisor who has fully assigned the mark has assigned all the rights associated with it, and thus loses any rights in connection with it.[7] Under the Trade Marks Act 1938 the proprietor who did not use the mark himself could find that he was the victim of an action to strike out the mark on the grounds of non-use,[8] though in the absence of any direct authority on the point in terms of franchising law it seemed strongly arguable that use in the sense of being the basis of a franchising operation is still 'use in relation to goods' (albeit an indirect use) and therefore not attackable by these provisions. Successful non-use cases were typically where there was no current intention to trade[9] or to trade commercially.[10] The new Trade Marks Act 1994 removes all doubt. Revocation of the trade mark is not possible if the trade mark has been used genuinely by the proprietor of the mark or with his consent.[11] The latter provision clearly applies to a franchising operation.

5   Trade Marks Act 1994, s 1(1).
6   Trade Marks Act 1994, s 24.
7   All kinds of partial assignments are possible though, Trade Marks Act 1994, s 24(2).
8   Trade Mark Acts 1938, s 26.
9   Eg *Pussy Galore Trade Mark* [1967] RPC 265.
10   Eg *Imperial Group Ltd v Philip Morris* [1982] FSR 72.
11   Trade Marks Act 1994, s 46(1).

Trade mark legislation, however, offers a more specific method of protecting franchise operations. By ss 28 and 29 of the 1994 Act, it is possible to grant a licence, including an exclusive licence, to use a trade mark. This does not involve a transfer of the ownership of the trade mark, but it does normally result in use of the trade mark with the consent of the proprietor and thus steers clear of the sanction of s 46. Such a transaction can be registered[12] and a licensee registered as such in the register will obtain certain rights. The complicated provisions of s 30 can be summarised as allowing the registered user to require the proprietor to act in relation to any infringement of the mark and he can in default institute an action himself. Exclusive licensees get the rights of an assignee and can therefore independently bring an infringement action.[13]

One hazard that need no longer be considered here is the issue of trafficking. Whereas the use of a trade mark purely as an item in its own right was not permissible under the provisions of the 1938 Act, the Trade Marks Act 1994 has repealed that provision and no longer refers to the issue.

In summary it can be seen that the most appropriate way forward to protect a franchise agreement is to grant a licence to use the trade mark to the franchisee and to register that transaction, thus enabling the franchisee-licensee to share the protection already enjoyed by the franchisor against the outside world. The franchisee is not by this method protected against the activities of the franchisor, and will have to look at the terms of the contract agreed between the parties for assistance there. An exclusive license clearly offers more protection here, as it excludes also the use by the licensor-franchisor of the trade mark in the manner authorised by the licence.[14] In exceptional cases, it may be that a franchise operation will fall within the category of certification trade marks,[15] but this would not be common given the infrequency with which this type of mark is used in any situation, let alone a franchising situation.

It must be emphasised that failure by the franchisor to use either the assignment or licensing routes will leave the franchisee unprotected since his use of the mark with the consent of the franchisor justifies the award of the mark to the franchisor[16] and not to the franchisee. A franchisee who has to face competition from a third party and who fails to gain the support of the franchisor to take action against that third party is unprotected by trade mark law and will only find a remedy at common law.

12   Trade Marks Act 1994, s 25.
13   Trade Marks Act 1994, s 31.
14   Trade Marks Act 1994, s 29(1).
15   Trade Marks Act 1994, s 50.
16   Trade Marks Act 1994, s 32(3).

FRANCHISING AND PASSING-OFF

At the heart of any franchise relationship lies the concept of goodwill. The franchisee wishes to attract some of the goodwill created by the franchisor; likewise the franchisor will wish to see his goodwill extended, and certainly not harmed, by the activities of the franchisee. Where goodwill is mentioned, inevitably the tort of passing-off, whose function it is to protect goodwill, will become involved. The key question is whose goodwill is at stake?

The creator of the franchise is the most obvious candidate to be the owner of the goodwill and thus the plaintiff in a passing-off action. That this is so is confirmed by the decision of the Privy Council in *JH Coles Pty Ltd v Need*,[17] an appeal from Australia. Coles were a chain of stores, one of which was operated on a franchise basis by Need. The business relationship failed to endure and eventually Coles went into liquidation while Need, now without authority, continued trading under the Coles banner. In his speech, Lord Wright identified the ability of Need to use the Coles trading name as being a revocable licence to use the name so long as the business arrangement continued.[18] Given that the relevant licence had been revoked unequivocally by Coles, it was therefore clear that Need was now unlawfully passing himself off as being authorised to use the Coles name, and that this deception would prejudice Coles' reputation and goodwill. In passing, it is by no means obvious that Coles, being in liquidation, still enjoyed such reputation and goodwill, but the decision can be explained by reference to the fact that Coles' initial complaint was made prior to the sad demise of the business.

If the franchisor's goodwill is protected against the franchisee, it seems to follow inexorably that he will also be protected against outsiders. Protection by the tort of passing-off is valuable to a franchisor, given the currently vigorous and expansionist nature of the action which as we have seen[19] is capable of extending its net to capture similar advertising campaigns and 'get-up' of goods by rival traders, and also will cover future trading areas by well-known names. All these points may be of particular relevance in a franchise environment.

A more problematic question is whether all these benefits of a passing-off action can also be enjoyed by the franchisee. Consider a far from implausible scenario; the Kentucky Fried Chicken fast food store outlet in Leicester suddenly finds its business in serious decline because a rival operation has started trading selling similar products and using logos and other promotional material sufficiently similar to that of the Kentucky firm that an action in passing-off appears viable. We have just seen that the

17 [1934] AC 82.
18 Ibid, at 87.
19 Above in Ch 24.

franchisor is protected, but the loss is more likely to fall on the franchisee, whose immediate income will be reduced but who may, depending on the precise terms of the franchise agreement, still have to pay fixed sums, perhaps based on pre-agreed turnover calculations for the franchise. In an ideal world, the contract between the parties may incorporate an appropriate term forcing the franchisor to act and providing for the franchisee to benefit from the fruits of that action. However, such clauses do not appear to be in regular use.

Authority on the specific issue of franchisees' rights of action in passing-off appears non-existent. The problem comes in the way that the public recognises and responds to the goodwill and reputation of the franchisor, from which the (to the public) unknown franchisee then indirectly benefits. However, it is clear that there is no reason for an action in passing-off to hinge on the identity of the victim of the tort. In *Birmingham Vinegar Brewery Co v Powell*,[20] a dispute concerning two rival versions of a sauce called 'Yorkshire Relish', it was asserted that the failure of the defendant to identify himself as the manufacturer of the sauce was no bar to a successful action even though 'the customer does not know or care who the manufacturer is, but it is a particular manufacture that he desires'.[1] It seems sensible to adopt a similar approach where the source of the plaintiff's goods or services is similarly confused, between franchisor and franchisee. It also seems compatible with the general approach of the courts that permits a passing-off action by someone with only an indirect or partial involvement with the goods or services in question,[2] and the solution suggested also appears to accord with good policy given the difficulties the franchisee may otherwise face, as outlined in the previous paragraph.

In summary, that passing-off protects the franchisor is undoubted. For the franchisee, the tort, in its currently vigorous form, appears capable of providing the necessary protection and it is clear that to protect the financial and personal commitment of the franchisee it should do so.

FRANCHISING AND OTHER AREAS OF INTELLECTUAL PROPERTY LAW

A franchising operation will often give rise to many of a wide range of intellectual property issues. The purpose of this section is to do little more than identify those areas since, unlike in the previous sections of this chapter, we feel that there are no unique features which arise only in franchising situations. Most obviously, the creation of the identity of the franchise will often give rise to the possibility of copyright protection for the original work

---

20   [1897] AC 710.
1   Ibid, per Lord Halsbury LC at 713.
2   See Cornish *Intellectual Property* Sweet & Maxwell (3rd edn, 1996) pp 551-554.

of the franchisor. This may cover logos, as artistic works, or advertisement copy, as a literary work, or promotional photographs or drawings. Of course, there would be no problem within a properly established franchise, since authorised use of copyright material by a licensed user does not amount to infringement.[3] Clearly, however, unauthorised use, even by a franchisee acting beyond his remit, would be an infringement. The various provisions protecting designs, as discussed in Chapters 20 and 21, are also potentially relevant on a similar basis.

Patent law may also provide an essential element in a franchising operation. I may invent a wonderful new type of dishwasher which can be taken from door to door to clean up after wild parties, but I may not have the energy or ability to set up a business to exploit properly this new wonder. I may well wish to set up a franchise operation so to do, which would be based at its heart on the franchisees being granted licences to operate the patented invention.

Finally, and briefly, much know-how and trade information will inevitably pass between franchisor and franchisee and, subject to any specific contractual provision, obligations of confidentiality are inevitably likely to arise as between them.

FRANCHISING AND COMPETITION LAW

It is inevitable that franchisees will seek some form of monopoly. There is no point in spending time and effort developing the franchise business if the franchisor has also contracted with your next door neighbour, or another resident of the same town, region or even country, depending upon the scale and type of business in question. Likewise, a franchisor will be keen to ensure that the franchisee will loyally devote himself to selling the franchisor's goods and services and will not dilute the value of the franchise by also selling the goods and services of commercial rivals of the franchisor. Terms to cover these sorts of problems are common in franchise agreements but are immediately confronted by UK and EC competition law which seeks to limit anti-competitive monopolies.

In UK competition law the relevant provisions for franchise agreements are found in the Restrictive Trade Practices Act 1976. They result in the submission for registration of a number of franchise agreements although most franchise agreements are not accompanied by competition problems which are envisaged by UK competition law. If they are caught, this is normally only due to the formalistic nature of the system put in place by this piece of legislation. The most common attitude of the Director General is to seek a section 21(2) direction, but very often this does not imply any modification of the franchise agreement. Such directions discharge the

3   CDPA 1988, ss 16(2) and 90.

Director General from taking further action on the basis that the restrictions contained in the franchise agreement are not of such significance as to call for further investigation.[4] The Competition Bill which was pending in Parliament at the time of writing and which is expected to have been enacted by the time the second edition of the book reaches the bookshops sets out to abolish the Restrictive Trade Practices Act 1976 altogether (see s 1(b)). The new system is modelled on Article 85 of the Treaty of Rome and it is to this provision that we now turn.

In the EC context it is obvious that Article 85 of the Treaty of Rome is relevant, because a franchise agreement can be an agreement which may affect trade between member states and has as its object or effect the prevention, restriction or distortion of competition within the European Union.

The provisions of Article 85 were first applied to a franchise agreement by the Court of Justice in *Pronuptia de Paris v Schillgalis*.[5] As is so often the case, Article 85 was invoked as a defence in contractual proceedings. Pronuptia de Paris, the franchisor, sued Mrs Schillgalis, the franchisee for Hamburg, Oldenburg and Hanover in Germany, on the basis that her royalty payments were insufficient as compared to the royalty provisions of the franchise agreement. Mrs Schillgalis argued that Pronuptia could not rely on the franchise agreement because that agreement was void as it contravened Article 85.

First, the Court analysed the specific nature of a franchise agreement. In the Court's analysis the transfer of intellectual property rights from the franchisor to the franchisee is not only relevant to distinguish a franchise agreement from more conventional distribution systems, but it is a vital element if a franchise agreement is to realise its main aim which is to allow the franchisee to operate as an independent business which is using the franchisor's name and know-how. This implies that certain restrictions need to be imposed regarding the maintenance of the common standards of the franchise and regarding the protection of the intellectual property rights involved. The franchisor should indeed be able to impose common standards on all franchisees if the franchise system is to work effectively and to benefit from its main asset, the common business format which is recognisable by the consumers and attracts them because they are entitled to expect the same quality standards from each outlet. The protection of the intellectual property rights involved is equally essential, which requires the franchisor to impose certain restrictions upon the franchisee on top of the fee which is already paid by the franchisee for the use of the franchisor's know-how, trade mark, design, logo and other intellectual property rights.

---

4   See Howe 'Franchising and Restrictive Practices Law: the Office of Fair Trading View' (1989) 9 ECLR 439.

5   Case 161/84 [1986] ECR 353 and [1986] 1 CMLR 414, see Venit 'Pronuptia: Ancillary Restraints or Unholy Alliances' (1986) 11 ELRev 213.

As a result of its analysis the Court reached the conclusion that these restrictions which are imposed to maintain common standards and to protect intellectual property rights did not fall within the scope of Article 85(1). The Court indicated that these essential elements of a franchise agreement did not restrict competition at all.

In a second part of the judgment, the Court made it clear that only the essential elements described above fall outside the scope of Article 85(1). Restrictions which are able to partition the Common Market on a territorial basis are caught by Article 85(1). Eventually they may be granted exemption under Article 85(3). Such an exemption is not available for restrictions imposing resale price maintenance. The latter restrictions are caught by Article 85(1) and will not be granted an exemption on the basis of Article 85(3).

We think this fairly favourable treatment of franchise agreements by the Court of Justice can be explained by the high degree of integration which characterises franchise agreements. Indeed, the commercial policy of the franchise network is essentially determined by the franchisor, as if it were one single business, although all franchisees run an independent business from a legal point of view. The Court had clearly in mind that one cannot compare a franchise network with its restrictions on competition to a series of independent businesses in free competition without taking into account that the alternative to the franchise network would probably be one single business with a whole series of outlets. Independent franchisees would then simply be replaced by employees of the producer-franchisor and there would be no competition at all.

It is worth mentioning a number of individual decisions published by the Commission of the European Communities in which the Commission brought the main principles of the Court's ruling in the *Pronuptia* case into practice.[6] These decisions deal with territorial restrictions. The type of franchise agreements under which the franchisor manufactures or selects the goods that are sold by the franchisee was at the heart of the *Pronuptia*[7] and *Yves Rocher*[8] cases. In *Computerland*[9] the Commission applied the principles laid down by the Court to a franchise agreement which provided only a distribution method and left the franchisee free to buy microcomputers wherever it wished. The Commission was confronted for the first time with a service franchise in the *ServiceMaster* case.[10] Such franchises provide a common business format for the provision of services rather than for the distribution of goods. In this case services provided by the franchisee to commercial and domestic customers were related to housekeeping, cleaning and maintenance. The Commission indicated that the same principles could be applied to this slightly different type of

6   See Whish *Competition Law* Butterworths (3rd edn, 1993) p 598.
7   OJ (1987) L13/39, [1989] 4 CMLR 355.
8   OJ (1987) L8/49, [1988] 4 CMLR 592.
9   OJ (1987) L222/12, [1989] 4 CMLR 259.
10 OJ (1988) L332/38, [1989] 4 CMLR 581.

franchising agreement and granted an individual exemption. Based on these individual decisions the Commission drafted a block exemption for certain types of franchise agreement,[11] which we will now discuss.

THE FRANCHISE BLOCK EXEMPTION

Only certain types of franchise agreement fall within the scope of Regulation 4087/88.[12] It provides block exemption for distribution and service franchises. The Regulation does not deal with industrial franchises and wholesale franchises.[13] In an industrial franchise the franchisor authorises the franchisees to produce goods within a common business format. A number of these industrial franchises involve a patent and most of them involve know-how. That means that they are covered by the transfer of technology block exemption.[14] The reason for the exclusion of wholesale franchises is simply the lack of experience of the Commission with this type of franchise agreement. This is indeed a different type of franchise agreement. Service and distribution franchises are located at the end of the economic chain linking the producer with the consumer, but the wholesale franchise is located one level upwards and presents no direct link with the ultimate consumer. The Regulation does on the other hand not only cover direct distribution and service franchises, but also applies to master franchises. The latter system implies that the franchisor permits a master franchisee to conclude franchise agreements with other potential franchisees.[15] This includes the case in which a Japanese franchisor simply deals with one British firm. That British firm becomes the master franchisee for the UK and will try to attract other potential franchisees in this country. There is no involvement of the Japanese firm in the latter stage, it only deals with its master franchisee, just as the potential franchisees will not deal with the Japanese firm, but only with the master franchisee.

We think these restrictions on the scope of the Regulation are sound. A block exemption should cover the common cases. It makes no sense to ask the Commission to grant an individual exemption for each franchise agreement if they are all almost identical. The block exemption solution is also much more convenient for the parties to the franchise agreement as they no longer have to apply for an individual exemption. But wholesale franchises are relatively rare and moreover they are a different type of franchise agreement. Here the most suitable solution is an individual

---

11   Regulation 4087/88 OJ (1988) L359/46, [1988] 4 CMLR 387 (with annotations by
     Valentine Korah).
12   This Regulation will expire at the end of the century.
13   See recitals 4 and 5.
14   Regulation 96/240 [1996] OJ L31/2.
15   Regulation 4087/88, Article 1(2).

exemption. It permits the Commission to examine the special provisions of the agreement and it allows the parties to go ahead with the franchise if competition is not restricted too much. The same solution and comments apply to the few industrial franchises which are not covered by the patent licence or the know-how block exemption. All other industrial franchises are already covered by a block exemption and efficiency requirements indicate that it would not be desirable to cover them in yet another block exemption as well.

Now that we have identified the scope of the Regulation, we shall examine its various provisions. Article 1 deals with the basic exemptions, as could logically be expected. Distribution and service franchises are exempted in Article 1(1) and Article 1(2) does the same for master franchises. Article 1(3) defines all the terms used in the Regulation:

> 'A package of industrial or intellectual property rights relating to trade marks, trade names, shop signs, utility models, designs, copyrights, know-how or patents, to be exploited for the resale of goods or the provision of services'

is what forms a franchise for the purposes of the Regulation. This definition makes it clear that the Regulation is only concerned with franchise agreements in which intellectual property rights are prominently present. As we have seen in the discussion of the provisions on the free movement of goods and services and the provisions on competition law in the EC Treaty and intellectual property rights, intellectual property rights are indeed very often the tool used to restrict competition as they legitimise some form of monopoly. So, this special concern of the Commission is absolutely reasonable and fully justified. A franchise agreement, a master franchise agreement, the franchisor's goods and the contract premises are also defined, but as it is the most valuable element in a majority of franchises, the definition of know-how is extremely important. Know-how is defined as:

> 'a package of non-patented practical information, resulting from experience and testing by the franchisor, which is secret, substantial and identified'.

Briefly,

> '"secret" means that the know-how, as a body or in the precise configuration and assembly of components, is not generally known or accessible'.

The substantiality requirement implies that the information included in the know-how is of importance for the sale of goods or the provision of services and improves the competitive position of the franchisee and the need for identification of the know-how is satisfied if it is described in a comprehensive way, which makes it possible to verify whether the criteria of secrecy and substantiality are met.

So the precise recipe for a particular fried poultry dish may be secret, being withheld from competitors. It may equally be substantial, if the relevant ingredients add to the value and popularity of the dish. The relevant information must be described fully and clearly so that it enables the franchisee to apply this know-how in the exploitation of the franchise agreement he or she concluded with the franchisor.

A list of the various restrictions which are exempted is found in Article 2. Three types of restrictions are included:

- restrictions on the franchisor;
- restrictions on the master franchisee; and
- restrictions on the franchisee.

A franchise agreement may contain a clause that stipulates that the franchisor is not allowed to exploit the franchise itself in the franchisee's territory. Clauses which prohibit the grant by the franchisor of further franchises which cover that territory to third parties and the supply by the franchisor of its goods to third parties are also exempted. A master franchisee can be restricted from concluding franchise agreements with potential franchisees outside its territory. But the longest list of possible restrictions only contains restrictions which are imposed on the franchisee. This list includes an obligation to exploit the franchise only from the contract premises, a prohibition to seek actively customers outside the territory for which the franchise has been awarded and another prohibition to manufacture, sell or even use in the course of the provision of services goods which are in competition with the franchisor's goods which are relevant for the franchise agreement. The latter prohibition may nevertheless not cover spare parts or accessories. Although it may seem that these restrictions can put a heavy burden on the franchisee, the fact that the law exempts them should be seen together with the view that to a certain extent the whole network is run by the franchisor. Here the favourable treatment of franchise agreements by the EEC, which we mentioned while analysing the *Pronuptia* case, is brought into practice.

Article 3(1) sees the return of the ideas of the protection of the relevant intellectual property rights and the preservation of the common identity and reputation of the franchise network which were so prominently present in the Court's ruling in the *Pronuptia* case. A series of obligations, which are permitted if they are necessary for the realisation of these aims, are listed. This means that the obligations contained in this list are within the scope of Article 85(1) and are not exempt under the block exemption whenever they are not necessary for the realisation of these two aims.[16] These obligations are listed as:

- the obligation to sell or use goods matching minimum objective quality specifications laid down by the franchisor;
- the obligation to sell or use goods which are manufactured only by the franchisor or by third parties designated by it where it is impractical owing to the nature of the goods which are the subject matter of the franchise to apply quality specifications;
- the obligation not to engage directly or indirectly in any similar competing business;
- the obligation not to acquire financial interests in a competitor which would enable the franchisee to influence the latter's conduct;
- the obligation to sell the franchise goods only to end users, to other franchisees and to resellers within other channels of distribution supplied by the manufacturer of these goods or with its consent;
- the obligation to use best endeavours to sell the goods or provide the services that are the subject of the franchise and to offer minimum ranges of goods, achieve minimum turnover, keep minimum stocks and provide customer and guarantee services;
- the obligation to pay to the franchisor a specified proportion of revenue for advertising and itself to carry out advertising for the nature of which it shall obtain the franchisor's approval.

Thus, let us take two random examples from this list. The franchisee of a shoe shop can be made only to sell shoes which meet the minimum quality standards of the franchisor. But this restriction is only exempted if it is necessary to uphold the quality reputation of the franchise network. Equally the approval of the franchisor for the advertisements in which the franchisee uses the trade mark of the franchise network is only exempted if the sole reason for which the franchisor can refuse its approval is the improper use or variation of the trade mark.

A separate list of obligations which may, due to particular circumstances, fall within the scope of Article 85(1) but may nevertheless be imposed and are exempted if necessary,[17] is contained in Article 3(2). Obligations:

- not to disclose the franchisor's know-how to third parties;
- to inform the franchisor of any experience gained in exploiting the franchise (this may eventually lead to the grant of a non-exclusive know-how licence to the franchisor) and of any infringement of the franchisor's intellectual property rights;

16   See Whish *Competition Law* Butterworths (3rd edn, 1993) p 600.
17   See Regulation 4087/88, Article 1(2).

- to attend or have its staff attend training courses arranged by the franchisor;
- to apply the commercial methods devised by the franchisor; and
- to comply with the franchisor's standards for the equipment and presentation of the contract premises and/or means of transport

figure among others in this list, as do the obligations not to change the location of the contract premises without the franchisor's consent and not to assign the rights and obligations under the franchise agreement. Few of these are out of line with ordinary and reasonable commercial agreements.

As with most block exemption Regulations, the Commission equally has a blacklist of clauses. The presence of these clauses will prohibit the block exemption from applying. But before addressing this issue, the Regulation contains in its Article 4 some positive requirements which need to be satisfied if the block exemption is to apply. The franchisee must remain free to obtain the franchise goods from other franchisees. Any guarantee which the franchisee is obliged to honour should apply to franchise goods supplied by any member of the franchise network and the franchisee must be obliged to indicate that it is an independent undertaking.

The next step is the negative or blacklisted clauses. As a result of Article 5 the block exemption will not apply if:

- former competitors become parties to a franchise agreement;
- subject to Articles 2 and 3 as discussed above, the franchisee may not obtain supplies of goods of an equivalent quality to the quality offered by the franchisor;
- without objective justification the franchisor refuses to accept suppliers proposed by the franchisee and obliges the franchisee to sell goods manufactured by the franchisor or by someone designated by the franchisor;
- when the know-how has by then fallen into the public domain, the franchisee is prevented from using the know-how which was licensed to it during the franchise agreement after the termination of that agreement;
- any attempt is made by the franchisor to fix resale prices;
- the franchisee may not challenge the validity of the franchisor's intellectual property rights;
- franchisees are obliged not to supply within the Common Market the goods or services which are the subject of the franchise to end users because of their place of residence.

A franchise agreement which does not contain any blacklisted clauses but nevertheless contains restrictive clauses which are not explicitly exempted by the Regulation can be submitted to the Commission under the opposition procedure.[18] If the Commission does not oppose the exemption of such a franchise agreement within six months, the agreement is treated as an exempted agreement.

As is the case with the benefit of each of the block exemptions, the benefit of this block exemption can be withdrawn[19] if a franchise agreement would unduly restrict competition, although it met the requirements of the block exemption.

It is clear that franchise agreements can restrict competition and that competition law interferes with this type of agreement. Nevertheless, even if the EC attitude towards franchising agreements is less lenient than the UK attitude, one can say that franchising is generally seen as a beneficial commercial system and that competition law only tries to stop the undue restrictions to competition which are not the rule, but clearly the exception. Trade marks are clearly at the heart of many franchising agreements. The Trade Marks Act 1994 facilitates the use of trade marks in this context and the law of passing-off may still provide valuable assistance. Intellectual property law now offers adequate protection to what are often the most valuable assets of a franchising operation, its mark and the reputation linked to it.

---

18   Regulation 4087/88, Article 6.
19   Regulation 4087/88, Article 8. Experience teaches that this is merely a theoretical option.

Chapter 29

Remedies in intellectual property litigation

Throughout this book we have been pointing out the way in which the various legal remedies can be used in relation to the various different intellectual property rights. In this chapter we will give a relatively brief overview of the enforcement procedures that are used in relation to intellectual property rights, of the civil remedies that apply and of some issues that arise in relation to the gathering of evidence in intellectual property cases.

Intellectual property rights are often applied for in many countries. In such cases many of these rights may be involved in a single infringement action or similar infringing acts may have been committed in the various jurisdictions. Intellectual property rights are also increasingly exploited internationally. That exploitation may also give rise to transnational litigation. The interaction between intellectual property and private international law gives rise to complex issues, both at the jurisdiction level (which court will decide the case) and at the choice of law level (which law will that court apply). A full discussion of these issues would lead too far and we refer the reader to the full discussion of these issues that can be found in J Fawcett and P Torremans *Intellectual Property and Private International Law* Clarendon Press (Oxford, 1998).

ENFORCEMENT ISSUES

Intellectual property rights can be enforced in four ways. Most commonly civil actions are used. Criminal proceedings, administrative proceedings and measures of self help complete the picture.

Civil actions

Despite a slight reservation for breach of confidence, most intellectual property rights can be characterised as property rights. And the way in which that property right is affected in cases of infringement can be described as tortious in nature. Essentially what we are dealing with are torts committed against property. On top of that come the actions between assignors and assignees and between licensors and licensees, some of which are contractual in nature, because their claim is not based on the infringement of the intellectual property right involved, but on a breach of the contractual provisions that had been agreed. This can lead to actions for breach of contract.

Infringing acts may also give reason for concern to licensees of intellectual property. However, while it is obvious that the owner of the right is entitled to bring an action against the alleged infringer, the same cannot be said about the licensee. The starting point is that a licensee cannot sue for infringement and must rely on the owner of the intellectual property right to bring the action. Exceptionally, an exclusive licensee can bring the action. This possibility is subject to a number of restrictions. First, it has only been made possible in relation to exclusive patent,[1] trade mark,[2] copyright[3] and unregistered design[4] licences. Registered design licences, know-how licences etc are not covered by it. Secondly, the exclusive licence must be fully exclusive in the sense that even the licensor cannot exploit the right in the area that has been allocated to the licensee.[5] Thirdly, the licensor has to be joined as a party to the proceedings, normally as a plaintiff, or alternatively as a defendant.[6]

On the defendant's side one finds obviously the alleged infringer. This is normally the person who performed the restricted act. Anyone who collaborates with that person in common design can be sued as joint tortfeasor.[7] An employer, but not someone who commissions a work, is vicariously liable for the infringement of intellectual property that an employee committed in the course of his employment, just as this is the case for any other tort.

---

1 Patents Act 1977, s 67.
2 Trade Marks Act 1994, s 31.
3 CDPA 1988, s 101.
4 CDPA 1988, s 234.
5 And it must exist when the writ is issued. *Procter & Gamble v Peaudouce* [1989] FSR 180.
6 See eg CDPA 1988, ss 102 and 235.
7 See *Mölnlycke AB v Procter & Gamble Ltd* [1992] RPC 21 at 29 and *Unilever plc v Gillette (UK) Ltd* [1989] RPC 583 at 608

All these civil actions are normally brought before the Chancery Division of the High Court of England and Wales[8] or before the Outer House of the Court of Session in Scotland. Actions that involve lower amounts of money can also be brought in the County Court and there is now in London also a specialised Patents County Court.

Criminal proceedings

Criminal proceedings do not play an important role in the area of intellectual property. However, some offences exist and this type of proceedings is specifically concerned with cases of infringement that are seen as particularly serious from a public policy point of view. Obvious examples are actions against copyright or trademark pirates.

The commission of the kind of acts that amount to secondary infringement of copyright now also leads to criminal liability in the circumstances that are described in s 107 of the Copyright, Designs and Patents Act 1988.

In those case, where both criminal and civil proceedings can be brought the court cannot express a preference or make a choice. The rightowner makes his choice when bringing the case either via civil or via criminal proceedings.[9] These offences can in serious instances be prosecuted summarily or on indictment.[10]

Counterfeiting of registered trade marks can also give rise to criminal liability. This will for example be the case if the trade mark or a similar and confusing mark are applied to goods or their packaging, if such goods are sold or offered for sale, or if such a sign is applied to packaging or labelling material.[11] The goods to which the mark is applied can obviously be goods within the class for which the mark has been registered, but other goods are also covered in cases of improper dilution.[12]

Other offences exist in relation to intellectual property registers. It is an offence to make or cause to be made false entries in the trade mark register.[13] Another offence covers the act of falsely representing a trade mark as registered.[14] Both these types of offences exist also in relation to patents[15] and registered designs.[16]

8   Within the Chancery Division of the High Court the Patents Court deals with patent matters.
9   *Thames & Hudson Ltd v Designs and Artists Copyright Society Ltd* [1995] FSR 153.
10   CDPA 1988, ss 107-110.
11   Trade Marks Act 1994, ss 92 and 93.
12   Trade Marks Act 1994, s 92(4).
13   Trade Marks Act 1994, s 94.
14   Trade Marks Act 1994, s 95.
15   Patents Act 1977, ss 109 and 110. See also s 111.
16   Registered Designs Act 1949, ss 34 and 35.

In more general terms the crime of conspiracy to defraud can also be committed in relation to intellectual property. This could for example be the case if those agreeing together try to bribe cinema employees into handing over copies of films that would subsequently be copied and released on video in an unauthorised way, because the conspirers seek to obtain a pecuniary advantage and they try to make others act contrary to their duties.[17] The crime also applies where the conspirers are proposing to acquire property, which could include intellectual property, dishonestly. The outcome of the attempt to obtain an advantage, or to make others act against their duties, or to acquire property is not particularly relevant, since it is the conspiracy element that counts, and neither is the fact that the infringement of the right amounts to an offence as such.

These criminal offences are hard to prove. The defendant must be shown to be guilty beyond reasonable doubt, rather than on the balance of probabilities as is the case in most civil cases, and the type of mens rea in the defendant must be that he knew, or had reason to believe, that he was committing an infringing act or another offence.

Administrative procedures

Customs officers, trading standards authorities, advertising standards authorities, the Radio Authority and the Independent Television Commission play an ancillary role in the enforcement of intellectual property rights. Only the role played by customs officers is really of great significance in relation to the main intellectual property rights. At the request of the rightholder they may arrest infringing imports at their point of entry. These infringing imports must either be infringing copies of literary, dramatic or musical works, of sound recordings or of films[18] or, in the case of trade marks, goods in relation to which the use of the trade mark would amount to an infringement.[19] These measures operate together with an EU Regulation to stop the release into free circulation of counterfeit goods.[20] All these procedures are based on an application by the owner of the right (tip-off, including a description of the goods)[1] and involve indemnification provisions. The EU Regulation gives the right holder 10

17 See *Scott v Metropolitan Police Commissioner* [1975] AC 819.
18 CDPA 1988, ss 111 and 112.
19 Trade Marks Act 1994, ss 89 to 91.
20 Council Regulation 3295/94 laying down measures to prohibit the release for free circulation, export, re-export or entry for a suspensive procedure of counterfeit and pirated goods [1994] OJ L341/8.
1 See eg Article 3 of the Regulation.

days from notification of seizure to start full-scale infringement proceedings[2] and counterfeit goods are normally destroyed.[3]

Self-help

The Copyright, Designs and Patents Act 1988 gives the copyright owner an additional right which can be used as a self-help remedy. This is the only example of self-help in the intellectual property area and no equivalent to the general right of recaption for those that are entitled to the possession of chattels (tangible property) exists.

Section 100 of the 1988 Act enables the copyright owner or his agent to seize and detain infringing copies. A series of restraints quite rightly applies to this far-reaching right. First of all the infringing copy must be exposed or otherwise immediately available for sale or hire.[4] No force may be used and advance notice of the time and place of the proposed seizure must be given to a local police station.[5] Anyway, nothing may be seized from what appears to be a regular place of business and only premises to which the public[6] has access may be entered in the exercise of this right. While it may be clear that stalls outside pop concerts are not regular places of business, it will depend on the circumstances whether market stalls are permanent or at least regular places of business.[7] It should also be emphasised that the term premises is given a wide definition and includes vehicles, vessels, aircraft and hovercraft apart from land, buildings and moveable structures.[8] A notice in a form prescribed by the Copyright and Rights in Performances (Notice of Seizure) Order[9] must be left behind when anything is seized. This notice should mention the grounds on which the seizure took place and the identity of the copyright owner.[10] The seizure is normally followed by an application for an order for forfeiture or destruction of the infringing goods.[11]

The remainder of this chapter will be concerned with civil actions and the remedies and evidence issues that relate to them.

---

2   Article 7 of the Regulation.
3   Article 8 of the Regulation.
4   CDPA 1988, s 100(1).
5   CDPA 1988, s 100(2) and (3).
6   CDPA 1988, s 100(3).
7   See J Phillips, R Durie and I Karet *Whale on Copyright* Sweet & Maxwell (4th edn, 1993) at p 89.
8   CDPA 1988, s 100(5).
9   Copyright and Rights in Performances (Notice of Seizure) Order 1989, SI 1989/1006.
10   CDPA 1988, s 100(4).
11   CDPA 1988, s 114.

CIVIL REMEDIES[12]

Injunctions

The rightholder's first concern in cases of infringement is that the infringement of his right stops. The sooner this happens the easier it will be to limit the damages to his trade, rights and reputation. As an order of the court that directs a party, here the alleged infringer, to do an act or to refrain from doing an act, the injunction is an excellent tool and remedy for that purpose, hence its frequent use in intellectual property cases. The injunction will almost necessarily be prohibitory and will either stop the threatened commission[13] of infringing acts or the continuation of infringing activities. The order is normally highly effective, in part because its wilful disobeyance will amount to contempt of court and contempt is punishable by fine, imprisonment or sequestration of assets.[14]

Interlocutory injunctions

If you discover that a rival trader is seeking to attack your market share by flooding the shops with counterfeit clothing, bootleg records or stair carpet grips made in breach of confidence, there is no time to waste. Allowing this trade to develop will obviously be harmful to you, yet the losses will be difficult to calculate precisely in a competitive capitalist society. So immediate action is necessary and the obvious legal route to take is to seek an injunction to prevent the allegedly illegal trade that is about to develop. Here, too, the usual delays of the civil justice system are not helpful and it is therefore necessary to expedite matters with the use of an interlocutory injunction in a quest to freeze the situation before damage can start to occur, pending a subsequent trial on the merits. Of course the reality in many cases is that proceedings are subsequently abandoned or settled and thus the interlocutory stage is the only formal litigation that is ever recorded. This means that the basis of such proceedings must be examined closely.

In order to obtain any injunction two basic points need to be established. First it must be clear that damages must not be an adequate remedy,[15] though this, as just explained, should not be too frequent a problem in an intellectual property case. Secondly it is important to remember that an

---

12 Note that the action for breach of confidence forms a special case. The comments underneath apply in general terms to all other intellectual property rights.

13 The *quia timet* injunction.

14 See *A-G v Newspaper Publishing plc* [1987] 3 All ER 276 and *Director General of Fair Trading v Smith's Concrete* [1991] 4 All ER 150.

15 *London & Blackwall Rly v Cross* (1886) 31 Ch D 354 at 369, per Lindley LJ.

injunction is an equitable right and is thus subject to equity's ever-present requirement of conscionability.[16]

The leading case on interlocutory injunctions remains the decision of the House of Lords in *American Cyanamid Co v Ethicon Ltd.*[17] Here the plaintiffs were the holders of a patent for absorbable surgical sutures and they were displeased to discover that the defendants were proposing to put on to the market a similar and allegedly infringing product. The House of Lords agreed with the judgment of the court of first instance and allowed the plaintiffs an interlocutory injunction preventing Ethicon from proceeding with their plans.

The House of Lords, in the sole speech of Lord Diplock, took the opportunity to clarify the general approach to interlocutory injunctions.[18] Lord Diplock pointed out that the general practice was to require the plaintiff to undertake to compensate the defendants for any losses incurred by them if the plaintiff failed to prove the case at full trial.[19] This appeared to justify a generous approach to the award of interlocutory injunctions. It was necessary merely to show that there was a 'serious question to be tried'[20] and that the balance of convenience as between the parties, having regard to the utility or otherwise of an award of damages to the plaintiff or an indemnity by the plaintiff, should then be considered.[1] Both these factors were found to be favourable to the plaintiffs.

It should be noted therefore that there is not really in most cases an enquiry into the merits of a dispute, but rather simply a finding that there is a genuine issue at stake. This therefore carries a vitally important implication which has been alluded to frequently but needs to be spelt out clearly at this juncture. The decision to award an interlocutory injunction in, say, a case of alleged passing-off does not mean that a right has been infringed but merely that one might have been – there is a serious issue to be tried, in theory, at a future date. So the court is saying 'maybe' rather than 'yes' to the question as to whether a right exists. On the other hand a refusal to award an interlocutory injunction is really rather damning. Not only is an injunction refused but the basis of the plaintiff's entire argument is regarded as quite unsustainable.

However it is more appropriate to examine the merits of the claims more closely where, as in a typical passing-off or trade mark infringement case, the interlocutory stage is likely in fact to be the only stage of the proceedings.

---

16 See eg *Leather Cloth Co Ltd v American Leather Cloth Co Ltd* (1863) 4 De G J & Sm 137, affirmed 11 HLC 523.
17 [1975] AC 396, [1975] 1 All ER 504.
18 Recently this approach was again confirmed by the Court of Appeal in *Dyrlund A/S v Turberville Smit Ltd* (6 April 1998, unreported).
19 Ibid at 406 and 509.
20 Ibid at 407 and 510.
1   Ibid at 408 and 511.

The evident strength of the plaintiff's claim may assist in gaining injunctive relief,[2] and this is a justifiable consideration where it is the only stage in the proceedings; the courts are prepared to make a preliminary assessment of the evidence in deciding whether the grant of an injunction is justified or not.[3]

Plenty of examples can be found of courts endeavouring to apply these general principles. In *BBC v Precord Ltd*[4] the defendants proposed to make a rap record featuring illicitly obtained extracts from an unbroadcast interview in which the then Opposition leader had famously lost his temper. This was an appropriate case for interlocutory relief. Although a delay to the record might harm its sales at the peak Christmas season and there were arguable defences the key point was that a clear property right had been infringed and this was the fundamental issue that merited protection. On the other hand the complete lack of likely confusion meant that no interlocutory relief was permitted in the passing-off claim in *Mothercare UK Ltd v Penguin Books Ltd*[5] where the defendants were allowed to continue publishing a serious sociological study entitled 'Mother Care/Other Care'. Likewise the small and quantifiable harm to an established plaintiff as compared with the very disruptive effects of an interlocutory injunction on a new magazine with a similar title just in the process of being launched meant that no injunction was awarded in *Emap Pursuit Publishing v Clive (t/a Matchday)*.[6]

The courts do seem prepared to look very carefully at where the balance of convenience lies and should 'take whichever course appears to carry the lower risk of injustice if it should turn out to have been "wrong" '.[7] Thus in *Neutrogena Corpn & Neutrogena (UK) Ltd v Golden Ltd and L'Oréal (UK) Ltd*,[8] a dispute concerning possible passing-off of the plaintiffs' product Neutrogena by the defendants' new Neutralia, Ferris J considered that an injunction would cause loss to the defendant through loss of sales, wasted preliminary expenditure, loss through having to compensate others, loss of opportunity to enter the market and general disruption and, in the light of these factors, refused interlocutory relief. This case and the *Emap* case both show that the time of the actual launch of a rival product may well be too late to gain injunctive relief, given the commitments entered into by the defendant and the resultant shift in the balance of convenience.

2   *Quaker Oats Co v Alltrades Distributors Ltd* [1981] FSR 9.
3   See eg *Rizla Ltd v Bryant & May Ltd* [1986] RPC 389.
4   [1992] 3 EIPR D-52.
5   [1988] RPC 113. Cf *Games Workshop Ltd v Transworld Publishers Ltd* [1993] 9 EIPR D-221.
6   [1993] 2 EIPR D-40.
7   Per Hoffmann J in *Films Rover International Ltd v Cannon Film Sales Ltd* [1986] 3 All ER 772, [1987] 1 WLR 670 at 781 and 680. See also *Dalgety Spillers Foods Ltd v Food Brokers Ltd* [1994] FSR 504.
8   [1994] 6 EIPR D-157.

■   ■

Overall the post-*Cyanamid* approach to the award of interlocutory injunctions shows the courts able to invoke a range of potentially contradictory factors in a generally sensible way. The more cautious approach to their use in cases where they may well be the final solution rather than a mere preliminary[9], which will be the case in many intellectual property examples, in any event goes some way to cushion the impact of *Cyanamid* in this particular area. They will thus remain a significant way of resolving intellectual property disputes.

Final injunctions

A final injunction can be granted as a remedy after a trial in which the infringement of the plaintiff's right was established. The injunction is at that stage granted to protect the proprietary right or interest of the plaintiff, but the court retains its discretion. An injunction is readily[10] granted against the proven infringement of patents, designs, trade marks and copyright. Otherwise the plaintiff would be unable to stop the continuation of the infringement and would be compelled to grant a *de facto* licence.

Delivery up

An injunction may stop any further infringement, but the defendant may be left with a supply of infringing goods. The pile of illegally copied tapes or the T-shirts illegally labelled with a famous trade mark may still be sitting in a warehouse. An order for delivery up of all infringing articles is the ideal tool to solve this problem. The defendant is ordered to hand over all infringing articles or documents and these will normally be destroyed. Exceptionally the defendant can also be authorised to destroy them under oath or the erasure of the trade mark can be ordered. All these measures will effectively remove the infringing goods or documents, or at least their infringing element, from circulation.[11] In relation to trade marks this power for the court to make an order for delivery up has now been incorporated in the Trade Marks Act 1994.[12] The Copyright, Designs and Patents Act 1988 adds to this general power of the courts through special provisions in

---

9   Eg an injunction cannot be used as protection against irrecoverable losses, or to avoid
     damages which would be too remote, if suffered. See *Peaudouce SA v Kimberly-Clark
     Ltd* [1996] FSR 680.
10   Unless the plaintiff comes with unclean hands or if any repetition of the infringement is
     not likely. Other special circumstances may also change the situation and the plaintiff
     can obviously decline to seek an injunction.
11   See eg *Peter Pan Manufacturing Corpn v Corsets Silhouette Ltd* [1963] 3 All ER 402.
12   Trade Marks Act 1994, ss 15-19.

relation to copyright and (unregistered) designs. Orders for delivery up for destruction are still possible under these special provisions, but the infringing copies, article and apparatus may at the discretion of the court be forfeited to the rightholder in order to compensate him for the loss suffered as a result of the infringement.[13]

Damages

Damages are awarded with the aim to undo the effects of a breach of contract or the commission of a tort by the defendant. The plaintiff is compensated for the harm that is caused by the tort or the breach of contract. Losses that are unforeseeably remote are excluded though. Exemplary damages that exceed the amount needed for the compensation of the harm suffered may only be awarded in exceptional cases where the defendant's conduct was calculated to make a profit that would exceed the damages that would have to be paid to the plaintiff.[14]

There is no standard rule for the assessment of damages in intellectual property cases. In a first scenario the plaintiff and the defendant may be competitors. If the plaintiff would have been willing to grant a licence if only the defendant had applied for one, the amount of damages will normally be calculated on the basis of the royalties and other costs that would have been payable under the licence.[15] If the plaintiff would not have been willing to grant a licence, the amount of damages is normally calculated on the basis of the losses suffered by the plaintiff through the defendant's competition. Lost profits, lost opportunities and competitive position acquired by the defendant may all be taken into account.[16] In a second scenario the parties do not find themselves in a competitive relationship. Damages are then calculated on the basis of a reasonable royalty for a licence for non-competing use.

Damages are also payable for the innocent infringement of a trade mark.[17] However, the same rule does not apply to copyright, registered designs, designs and patents. In these cases Parliament felt that it would have been rather harsh to oblige an innocent infringer to pay damages. The concept of innocence is defined in a narrow way and the alleged infringer must show that he made reasonable enquiries to check whether his activities would infringe any existing rights. The defendant will only be innocent if he did

---

13   CDPA 1988, ss 99 and 230.
14   See *Rookes v Barnard* [1964] AC 1129 at 1220-1231.
15   *General Tire and Rubber Co v Firestone Tyre and Rubber Co* [1976] RPC 197 at 212.
16   See *Gerber Garment Technology Inc v Lectra Systems Ltd* [1995] RPC 383.
17   *Gillette (UK) Ltd v Edenwest Ltd* [1994] RPC 279.

not know and had no reason to believe that the rights that he infringed existed.[18]

The Copyright, Designs and Patents Act 1988 introduced the concept of additional damages for the infringement of copyright and (unregistered) design rights. These additional damages come on top of the normal damages[19] and are awarded in flagrant cases of infringement. The court will determine the amount on the basis that justice must be done in each case and will take the flagrancy of the infringement and the benefit accruing to the defendant by reason of the infringement into account when deciding whether or not to award additional damages.[20]

Account of profits

The plaintiff is entitled to reclaim the amount earned by the defendant by way of unjust enrichment through the infringement of the plaintiff's intellectual property right. To achieve this the plaintiff can use the remedy of an account of profits, which is restitutionary in nature. Rather than be compensated by damages the plaintiff may opt to investigate the actual accounts of the defendant and to require that any profit that was made as a result of the infringement of his rights be handed over to him.[1] That profit may be the profit on each article that is sold and in which the protected subject-matter is included[2] or the increase in the defendant's profit made through the use, other than by inclusion in the defendant's products, of the protected subject-matter.[3] This remedy is not used often, because it involves a lot of work and an expensive accounting procedure. The decision by the House of Lords that additional damages cannot be awarded in copyright or unregistered design cases in which the plaintiff opted for an account of profits is bound to make it an even less popular remedy.[4] Nevertheless, the plaintiff could be well advised to consider the use of this remedy in those cases where he could never have made the profits that were made by the defendant, since it may enable him to obtain a higher amount by way of compensation.

18   Registered Designs Act 1949, s 9(1); Patents Act 1977, s 62(1); CDPA 1988, ss 97(1) and 233.
19   They can only be awarded if damages are the other remedy that is awarded. *Redrow Homes Ltd v Bett Brothers plc* [1998] 1 All ER 385, [1998] 2 WLR 198, overruling *Cala Homes (South) Ltd v Alfred McAlpine Houses East Ltd (No 2)* [1996] FSR 36.
20   CDPA 1988, ss 97(2) and 229(3).
1   See Patents Act 1977, s 61(2); CDPA 1988, s 96(2).
2   *Peter Pan Manufacturing Corpn v Corsets Silhouette Ltd* [1963] 3 All ER 402.
3   *United Horse Shoe v Stewart* (1888) 13 App.Cas. 401, 3 RPC 139 at 266-267.
4   *Redrow Homes Ltd v Bett Brothers plc and Nail Co* [1998] 1 All ER 385, [1998] 2 WLR 198, overruling *Cala Homes (South) Ltd v Alfred McAlpine Houses East Ltd (No 2)* [1996] FSR 36.

THE GATHERING OF EVIDENCE

The gathering of evidence is often a crucial issue in intellectual property cases. In this part of the chapter we will highlight the instruments that are used more often. An overview of all the relevant aspects of the law of civil procedure is not envisaged.

Anton Piller orders

The origin of the order

The success of infringement actions and the effectiveness of remedies depend on the availability at the trial stage of evidence concerning the alleged infringement. It is vital that the plaintiff is given the opportunity to discover this evidence. It is relatively easy for a *mala fide* defendant to alter or to destroy incriminating documents, to move goods or to hide machinery and raw materials once he or she has been served with a writ. The production of infringing copies of audio cassettes provides a good example. All that is needed is a number of cassette players and tapes plus some labels. All this can be moved within a few hours and it can be hidden in any spare room or shed. What is required is a tool that would allow the plaintiff to discover the evidence without any advance warning being given to the defendant. This tool would involve an ex parte application to the court which would then authorise the plaintiff and his or her solicitors to enter the defendant's premises so as to discover the evidence. It would be a kind of civil search warrant.

Such a tool was introduced by the Court of Appeal[5] in *Anton Piller KG v Manufacturing Processes Ltd*[6] and is therefore known as the Anton Piller order. Lord Denning MR described the order as follows:

'Let me say at once that no court in this land has any power to issue a search warrant to enter a man's house so as to see if there are papers or documents there which are of an incriminating nature. But the order sought in this case is not a search warrant. It does not authorise the plaintiff's solicitors or anyone else to enter the defendants' premises against their will. It only authorises entry and inspection by the permission of the defendants. It does more, it actually orders them to give permission – with, I suppose, the result that if they do not give permission they are guilty of contempt of court.'[7]

5 On the basis of a limited previous practice in the Chancery Division, see *EMI v Pandit* [1975] 1 All ER 418, [1975] 1 WLR 302.
6 *Anton Piller KG v Manufacturing Processes Ltd* [1976] Ch 55, [1976] 1 All ER 779.
7 *Anton Piller KG v Manufacturing Processes Ltd* [1976] Ch 55 at 58.

The order and its expansion

The essential prerequisites for making such an order were set out by Ormerod LJ. He required that:

> 'First, there must be an extremely strong prima facie case. Second, the damage, potential or actual, must be very serious for the applicant. Third, there must be clear evidence that the defendants have in their possession incriminating documents or things, and that there is a real possibility that they may destroy such material before any application inter partes can be made.'[8]

The plaintiff's solicitor will be authorised to carry out the order as an officer of the court and the defendant is obliged to permit the inspection, otherwise he or she will face proceedings for contempt of court.[9] This does not however deprive the defendant completely of the possibility to refuse to permit the inspection, but this option becomes very risky and needs to be combined with a swift application for discharge of the order. The applicant has a duty of full and frank disclosure of all relevant elements to the court and the granting of the order is subject to the applicant making a cross-undertaking in damages.

It is the basis of the Anton Piller order to preserve evidence that may otherwise be destroyed by the defendant. The real need meant that the order became an instant success rather than the exceptional measure it was supposed to be. One of the first cases to extend the order slightly was *EMI Ltd v Sarwar and Haidar* where the defendants were also ordered:

> 'to disclose to the person serving the order, the names and addresses of the persons or companies responsible for supplying the defendants and to place into custody all invoices, books of sale, order books, and all other documents in their possession, power, custody or control relating to the acquisition, disposal or distribution of the infringing tape recordings'.

This will enable the defendant to obtain full evidence regarding anyone involved in an infringement network on the basis of a single Anton Piller order and increases the value of the order substantially. It also became possible to obtain an order against a represented class of persons if there is a sufficient amount of identity of interest among the members of such a class. This extension allowed EMI Records to act against all persons dealing in a certain type of pirated audio cassettes with one Anton Piller order, as they

---

8   *Anton Piller KG v Manufacturing Processes Ltd* [1976] Ch 55 at 62; see also *Thermax Ltd v Schott Industrial Glass Ltd* [1981] FSR 289 and *Columbia Picture Industries v Robinson* [1987] Ch 38, [1986] 3 All ER 338, [1986] 3 WLR 542.
9   On the issue of failure to comply see *Wardle Fabrics v Myristis* [1984] FSR 263.

all had an interest in preventing EMI from tracing the source of these pirated cassettes.

The expansion of the Anton Piller orders and their growing effectiveness came under threat when the House of Lords decided that orders which required the defendant to make disclosure which could be self-incriminating were contrary to the principle of privilege against self-incrimination.[10] The possibility for the defendant to withhold information on the basis that he or she would otherwise be incriminating themselves reduces the potential and value of the order substantially. This conclusion reached by a reluctant House of Lords was reversed by s 72 of the Supreme Court Act 1981 as the legislature stepped in to preserve the order. The self-incrimination defence will now no longer be available against the implementation of an Anton Piller order,[11] although the statements or admissions made at that stage will not be admissible as evidence in relation to any related offence.

Abuse of the order and its redress

ABUSE

Not only did Anton Piller orders become a frequently used tool, they also gave rise to abuses.[12] Two forms of abuse can be identified. The courts became too flexible in granting the order[13] and it became fashionable to use them to go on a fishing expedition. An order was in such cases granted on the basis of a mere suspicion of infringement rather than on the basis of a very strong prima facie case and was used to find out whether the infringement took place.[14] Often very valuable commercial information on a competitor was also obtained by the applicant. Secondly, the execution of the order was not always impeccable. The limits and restrictions imposed in the order were often exceeded, documents disappeared[15] etc. And the orders were also used to harass the defendant and drive him or her out of business.[16] Orders were executed at impossible times[17] or with a great deal

---

10   *Rank Film Distributors Ltd v Video Information Centre* [1982] AC 380, [1981] 2 All ER 76, [1981] 2 WLR 668.

11   See *Universal City Studios Inc v Hubbard* [1994] Ch 225, [1984] 1 All ER 661.

12   See eg *TRP v Thorley* [1993] Court of Appeal, unreported, Lexis transcript available and *Lock International Plc v Beswick* [1989] 3 All ER 373, [1989] 1 WLR 1268 per Hoffmann J.

13   See the remarks in this sense by Whitford J in *Systematica Ltd v London Computer Centre Ltd* [1983] FSR 313.

14   *Systematica Ltd v London Computer Centre Ltd* [1983] FSR 313.

15   *Universal Thermosensors v Hibben* [1992] FSR 361, [1992] 3 All ER 257, [1992] 1 WLR 840.

16   *Columbia Picture Industries v Robinson* [1987] Ch 38, [1986] 3 All ER 338, [1986] 3 WLR 542.

17   *Universal Thermosensors v Hibben* [1992] FSR 361, [1992] 3 All ER 257, [1992] 1 WLR 840.

of publicity. So much material was taken that the defendant could no longer operate properly and meet his or her contractual obligations[18] or improper publicity surrounding the order scared customers away from further dealings with the defendant.[19]

TOWARDS A SOLUTION

The urgent need to weed out these abuses, while at the same time preserving the Anton Piller order as an extremely useful tool in certain circumstances became clear and Sir Donald Nicholls V-C suggested a way to achieve this double goal in *Universal Thermosensors v Hibben*.[20] Most points of his advice have now been incorporated in a new Practice Direction.[1] From now on Anton Piller orders should only be executed on working days in office hours and not during weekends or early in the morning or late at night.[2] This implies that the defendant should be in a position to use effectively his or her right to consult a solicitor and obtain legal advice at the very moment he or she is presented with an order before complying with it and without running the risk of being in contempt of court by delaying the execution of the order.[3] A woman should also be present when the order is to be executed by a male solicitor at premises which are likely to be occupied by an unaccompanied woman.[4] And when the nature of the items which are removed makes this necessary, the applicant should insure them.[5] The Practice Direction contains a further range of provisions and also allows the judge more time to consider the application more in depth,[6] but by far the most important change is that an Anton Piller order should now no longer be executed by the plaintiff's solicitor. The role of the plaintiff's solicitor is reduced to securing the grant of the order and afterwards the execution is entrusted to a solicitor who does not act for the applicant.[7] This

18   *Columbia Picture Industries v Robinson* [1987] Ch 38, [1986] 3 All ER 338, [1986] 3 WLR 542.
19   *BUPA v First Choice Health Care* [1993] 4 EIPR 87.
20   *Universal Thermosensors Ltd v Hibben* [1992] 1 WLR 840 at 860–861.
1   Practice Direction [1994] 4 All ER 52, [1994] RPC 617.
2   Practice Direction [1994] 4 All ER 52 at 54, Annex 1 and *Universal Thermosensors Ltd v Hibben* [1992] 1 WLR 840 at 860 per Sir Donald Nicholls V-C.
3   *Universal Thermosensors Ltd v Hibben* [1992] 1 WLR 840 at 860 per Sir Donald Nicholls V-C.
4   Practice Direction [1994] 4 All ER 52 at 53; CDPA 1988, s 3B(2) and *Universal Thermosensors Ltd v Hibben* [1992] 1 WLR 840 at 860, per Sir Donald Nicholls V-C.
5   Practice Direction [1994] 4 All ER 52 at 53; CDPA 1988, s 3B(3).
6   Practice Direction [1994] 4 All ER 52 at 53, CDPA 1988, s 3A(1) and 3B(5).
7   See also *Universal Thermosensors Ltd v Hibben* [1992] 1 WLR 840 at 861, per Sir Donald Nicholls V-C.

'supervising solicitor should be an experienced solicitor, having some familiarity with the operation of Anton Piller orders, who is not a member or employee of the firm acting for the applicant.'[8]

In the old situation the plaintiff's solicitor was torn between the interests of his or her client who was also footing the bill and his or her neutral role as an officer of the court. This will now no longer be the case although the risk of bias remains at the application stage due to the ex parte nature of the proceedings.[9] The Practice Direction is also unsuccessful in solving the difficult problem who may consent to entry to the premises, the searching of these premises and to seizure. In the absence of the obvious defendant the Practice Direction gives this power to 'a responsible employee of the defendant' as well as to the more established category of 'person(s) appearing to be in charge of the premises'.[10] The precise definition of these categories is bound to cause confusion which may lead to incidents when an Anton Piller order is executed under these circumstances.[11]

It is nevertheless submitted that the Practice Direction will be successful in eliminating the abuse and in securing the survival of the Anton Piller order. In the new system plaintiffs who:

'... wish to take advantage of this truly draconian type of order ... must be prepared to pay for the safeguards experience has shown are necessary if the interests of defendants are fairly to be protected.'[12]

Anton Piller and Mareva

A Mareva injunction[13] is often called a freezing injunction because this ex parte injunction freezes the assets of a party by restraining that party from removing them from the jurisdiction. Lord Denning MR laid down the following guidelines in *Third Chandris Shipping Corpn v Unimarine SA*.[14] First, the plaintiff must make full and frank disclosure of all relevant information and materials. Secondly, he must set out his claim and the grounds for it as well as the arguments raised against this claim by the

---

8   Practice Direction [1994] 4 All ER 52 at 53, CDPA 1988, s 3B(1)(a).
9   Davies 'Anton Pillers after the Practice Direction' [1996] 15 CJQ 17.
10   Practice Direction [1994] 4 All ER 52 at 54–55, Annex 1.
11   Davies 'Anton Pillers after the Practice Direction' [1996] 15 CJQ 17.
12   *Universal Thermosensors Ltd v Hibben* [1992] 1 WLR 840 at 861, per Sir Donald Nicholls V-C.
13   The name of the injunction is derived from the name of one of the parties in the oldest case in this area: *Mareva Cia Naviera SA v International Bulk Carriers SA* [1980] 1 All ER 213 n, [1975] 2 Lloyd's Law Reports 509.
14   *Third Chandris Shipping Corpn v Unimarine SA* [1979] QB 645, [1979] 2 All ER 972.

defendant. He must also give indications that the defendant has assets within the jurisdiction and that there is a risk that the assets will be removed from the jurisdiction. Finally, he must give an undertaking in damages. These guidelines were later supplemented by two other ones. The plaintiff must show his or her case has a certain strength and that strength needs to be balanced against all other relevant factors before the judge uses the discretion to grant a Mareva injunction.[15]

Banks and other third parties can be bound by a Mareva injunction[16] which therefore becomes another useful tool in the war against untrustworthy defendants in intellectual property infringement cases. Quite often an Anton Piller order is combined with a Mareva injunction[17] and while this offers a great deal of relief to the plaintiff, it must be clear that this can also be used quite effectively to put a defendant out of business.[18] This risk is especially present in cases brought by commercially powerful plaintiffs against small innovative competitors as the latter may go out of business before the case is fully argued in court. It can even be said that on certain occasions that was the purpose as it was quite clear on these occasions that no infringement would eventually be found and an application for an Anton Piller order and a Mareva injunction was nevertheless brought.

The Norwich Pharmacal action

Infringement action often starts when the owner of an intellectual property right finds an infringing product at the end of the distribution chain; or the goods may be in transit. It is vital for the rightowner that he is able to trace the source of the infringing product in order to be able to stop the infringement at its roots. The person in whose hands the product is found may not even know that the product is a copy or an infringing product and may not be infringing himself. He may also be unaware of the fact that others must have infringed any intellectual property right. The only way for the rightowner to proceed successfully in such a case is to get hold of the names and addresses of any consignors or consignees and to track the infringing product all the way up to its manufacturers.

The Norwich Pharmacal action has the same aim and such an order obliges the party against whom it is made to reveal these names and addresses. In the original case *Norwich Pharmacal v Comr of Customs and*

---

15 *Ninemia Maritime Corpn v Trane Schiffarhtsgesellschaft mbH und Co KG (The Niedersachsen)* [1984] 1 All ER 398.
16 See *Z Ltd v A–Z and AA–LL* [1982] QB 558, [1982] 1 All ER 556.
17 See eg *McDonald v Graham* [1994] RPC 407.
18 See *CBS United Kingdom Ltd v Lambert* [1983] Ch 37, [1982] 3 All ER 237, [1982] 3 WLR 746.

Excise,[19] from which the name of the order is derived, the Commissioner of Customs and Excise was obliged to reveal the names of the importers of a patented drug. The order is discretionary in nature and will normally only be granted if it is the only way for the plaintiff to get hold of the information and if it is demonstrated that the person against whom it is made is (unwittingly) facilitating the infringement or any other wrongful act. The order may be extended to cover also a prohibition to remove the infringing goods.

REMEDIES – AN OVERVIEW

Three elements are really important in the relationship between intellectual property rights and remedies. First, there are the traditional remedies headed by damages which are normally granted at the trial and which we discussed in the various chapters concerned with each of the substantive intellectual property rights. Second, intellectual property infringement often requires immediate action or a pre-emptive strike. This is where interlocutory injunctions play an important role. Finally, gathering evidence which is vital for the full trial is not always easy, but it would not be just to let infringers get away with it because the rightowner did not have the means to discover the evidence needed in an infringement case. Anton Piller orders address this problem.

---

19 [1974] AC 133, [1974] RPC 101; see also *British Steel Corpn v Granada Television Ltd* [1981] AC 1096, a case that shows the potential of the order in a wider context.

Postscript

Though each of the three main proprietary intellectual property rights has been with us for a long time it is significant that all three, patents, copyright and trade marks, have needed to be completely rewritten by Parliament within the space of the last two decades. This is no surprise, reflecting as it does simultaneously the growth of European and international obligations, which are so important when the law of intellectual property has to try and operate on a global basis, and also the growth of new technologies. While these forces of change continue to exert their influence it is a safe prediction that the law of intellectual property will continue to be reformed to reflect the changing conditions.

Some hundreds of pages ago we began by considering the range of potential intellectual property rights that might arise from a great operatic performance. Had this scenario been devised twenty years earlier, it would have been far shorter. Even at what seems a date in modern history the reader would have had no notion of compact disc players, satellite television and much of contemporary computer technology. Intellectual property law is forced to keep pace with the pace of technological development and a legitimate method of critique of the law is to ask whether it has always succeeded in protecting the full range of commercially valuable activity that has continued to constantly evolve. Equally if we look forward twenty years it may be confidently predicted that the position will have dramatically changed yet again. Opera fans may access the performance along their fibre optic cables along with thousands of other choices of entertainments; biotechnology may have produced a new race of Italian super-tenors. In whatever event, the law will be requested to adapt and evolve to meet the evolution of technological achievement.

Equally the law has had to take on new responsibilities for the protection of other intangible but commercially important interests and has had to add to the range of protected interests, goodwill, information and character, for example. It may be that these areas will benefit from a codification in future years, especially if the inherent vagaries of the common law are thought to be inappropriate in addressing rights which, like their older counterparts, inevitably operate on a global basis. Information, in particular, seems a potential candidate for reform; literary copyright and common law or equitable rules of confidentiality hardly seem the best approaches to the protection of the ever growing flood of electronic data encircling the world. Likewise the law's lack of quality control – for instance copyright protection is afforded equally to grand opera and radio jingles – will have to be addressed at some stage.

It seems likely therefore that the law that we have set out to illuminate will continue its evolutionary, and occasionally revolutionary, path into the future. At present, though, we express the hope that we have helped in some way to bring to wider attention issues we believe to be of great legal and national interest and importance and which have in the past been confined to the somewhat closed world of the specialist lawyers and law reports. In doing so that should result in a larger audience for wherever we are taken by the next steps in the evolution of intellectual property.

Index

■

■

■

■

■

Literary work—*contd*
 co-existing, 153
 compilations, 150, 151, 152
 computer program, 151, 414, *see also*
  COMPUTER PROGRAM
 de minimis rule, 151, 152
 definition, 150-1
 directories, 151
 duration, 16
 educational use, 211, 212
 examples
  protected works, 151, 152
  unprotected works, 151-2
 infringement, 200, 202, *see also*
  COPYRIGHT INFRINGEMENT
 licence, 226, 228, *see also* LICENCE OF
  COPYRIGHT
 moral rights, 184, 187, 190
 non-patentability, 70, 72-3
 originality, 149-50, 151
  Europe, in, 150, 153
 protection, general, 149-50
 public performance, and infringement,
  201, 212
 quality, 151
 selections, 153, 199
 skill and labour requirement, 149, 152-
  3
 song lyric. *See* Lyric
 term of protection, 171-2
 timetables, 151, 152
 trade marks and titles, 152
 translations, 152
 typographical arrangement, 165
Local authority
 libel action, availability for, 373
Logo, *see* TRADE MARK
Lyric, 151, 155, 160
 paternity right in, 184, 185

Madrid Agreement Concerning the
  International registration of
  Marks, 26
Madrid Agreement Protocol, 26, 295,
  327, 329
Malicious falsehood, 372, 373-7
 character merchandising as, 375, 434-5
 damage, 377
 damages, quantum, 377
 derogatory statement, 374-6
 elements, 374-7
 extent of tort, 373-4
 falsity, 374

Malicious falsehood—*contd*
 flexibility of, 376
 injunction, obtaining, 376
 legal aid, 435
 malice, 376-7, 435
  definition, 376
Mareva injunction, 460
 disclosure duty on plaintiff, 460
 ex parte, 460
Mark, 300-1, *see also* TRADE MARK
Market mechanism, and, 15, 16
Mathematical model
 non-patentability, 46, 70, 72
Medical product, 45, 54-5, 68-9, *see also*
  PHARMACEUTICAL PRODUCT
Medical treatment
 method of, 68
 patentability, 54-5, 68-9, 70
 substance used in, 54-5, 68
Medicine
 preparation of, and patent
  infringement, 122
Merchandising. *See* CHARACTER
  MERCHANDISING
Microbiological process, 75, 76
Mime, 217, *see also* DRAMATIC WORK,
  PERFORMANCE
Monopoly, patent licensing, and, 85,
  90, *see also* COMPETITION LAW IN
  EUROPE, FREE MOVEMENT OF GOODS
Moral rights. *See* COPYRIGHT (GENERAL)
Music as trade mark, 303
Musical work
 copyright, 148-50, 155
  arrangements and transcriptions,
   155
  broadcast of, 202
  composer as 'author', 175, 184
  derogatory treatment, objection to,
   187, 189
  educational use, and, 212
  history of, 10
  identification as author, right to,
   184, 185-7
  infringement, 200, 202, *see also*
   COPYRIGHT INFRINGEMENT
  length of piece, 155
  moral rights, 184, 187, 190
  originality, 149
  performance, rights in, 217, *see also*
   PERFORMANCE
  public performance, and
   infringement, 201, 212

■